Essentials of American Democracy

Robert K. Carr
Oberlin College

Marver H. Bernstein
Princeton University

Walter F. Murphy
Princeton University

Essentials of American Democracy

FIFTH EDITION

Holt
Rinehart
and
Winston
Inc.

New York   Chicago
San Francisco   Atlanta
Dallas   Montreal
Toronto   London

To our students
who will help to determine
the future of American Democracy

Preface

This book, first published in 1951, has appeared in three different versions and in numerous editions. When we have decided to prepare a new edition, we usually have sworn great oaths to ourselves and our wives that this time we would only update material, clarify a few passages, and perhaps revive a public official or two we may have erroneously listed as dead.

Once again, however, we have succumbed to the temptation to rewrite, revise, and generally reshape the text. Our excuse to our wives is contained in the next paragraph; we hope it will suffice for our colleagues. While similarities with one or more earlier editions remain, this book is very different in focus, in emphasis, and even in length from its predecessor of sixteen years ago.

In an era of massive welfare programs, civil rights laws and race riots, of sit-ins and teach-ins, of cooing hawks and screaming doves, of brush-fire wars and threats of hydrogen happenings, of aggressively strident calls to love and to be different just like everybody else, politics is even more exciting—and important—than ever. With the discipline of political science undergoing a series of upheavals at least comparable in scope to those in the world of the practicing politician, revising a book about politics in the United States presents many and varied challenges. In prudent fashion we have tried to ignore some of these challenges. We also believe, perhaps immodestly, that in many instances what we have said in earlier editions offers an analytical framework adequate to provide an understanding of recent events. On the other hand, we felt a need to grapple with many of these new challenges by thoroughly reworking rather than merely repeating or even refurbishing our older volumes.

We have made changes in format as well as in substance. In previous years we had three rather different books. The National, State, and Local edition differed from the National one only in the obvious fact of including chapters on state and local politics. The Essentials volume was written and later revised at different times from the other two and so covered similar materials as the bigger books, but in a modified and abbreviated fashion. We now have only two versions, written at the same time and, if our lives are spared and our families permit, they will be revised together. The two differ only in that the Essentials version omits two chapters on the role of government in economic life and in promoting human welfare and two chapters on state and local governmental systems.

We have tried to shorten as well as to revise by cutting, for example, old material while adding new sections on the programs of the Great Society and on foreign policy. Our aim has been to provide a pair of books that are sufficiently detailed to be used alone as basic texts and still sufficiently short and inexpensive to serve as core reading in a course that also makes use of the many specialized paperbacked volumes that are now available.

Each new edition lengthens the list of those to whom we are indebted, and it has now grown too long to permit individual acknowledgements here. Our greatest debt, as usual, remains with the students and faculty who have used—and criticized—this book, and to our wives, who have, though for different reasons, been even more sharply critical. We, of course, assume full responsibility for errors of commission and omission.

Robert K. Carr

Marver H. Bernstein

Walter F. Murphy

October, 1967

Contents

We hold these truths to be self-evident, that all men are created equal, that they are endowed by their Creator with certain unalienable Rights, that among these are Life, Liberty and the pursuit of Happiness. That to secure these rights, Governments are instituted among Men, deriving their just powers from the consent of the governed. That whenever any Form of Government becomes destructive to these ends, it is the Right of the People to alter or abolish it, and to institute new Government, laying its foundation on such principles and organizing its powers in such form, as to them shall seem most likely to effect their safety and Happiness. Prudence, indeed, will dictate that Governments long established should not be changed for light and transient causes; and accordingly all experience hath shown, that mankind are more disposed to suffer, while evils are sufferable, than to right themselves by abolishing the forms to which they are accustomed. But when a long train of abuses and usurpations, pursuing invariably the same Object evinces a design to reduce them under absolute Despotism, it is their right, it is their duty, to throw off such Government, and to provide new Guards for their future security.   **July 4, 1776**

We the People of the United States, in Order to form a more perfect Union, establish Justice, insure domestic Tranquility, provide for the common defence, promote the general Welfare, and secure the Blessings of Liberty to ourselves and our Posterity, do ordain and establish this Constitution for the United States of America.
March 4, 1789

Must a government of necessity be too strong for the liberties of its own people, or too weak to maintain its own existence?
Abraham Lincoln, July 4, 1861

1

Introduction

GOVERNMENT BY THE PEOPLE

"Democracy" is a vague, value-laden term. In a very broad and general sense, it means what Lincoln called "government of the people, by the people." There are two essential elements here: people and government. The people, as citizens, are the source of political authority, but they are also the objects of political authority. They may participate in government directly or indirectly, but are at the same time subject to regulation by government.

Although this definition of democracy is useful in pointing up the dual role of the citizen, it leaves many questions unanswered, even unasked. It says nothing about what kind of government the people will have, or how that government will be organized. It does not tell us whether the government will exercise limited authority or whether it will be all-powerful and totalitarian—for it is at least logically possible for democratic authority to be either. Will government consist of the citizens meeting together in person to direct their common affairs or will

1

governmental activity be conducted by elected representatives of some sort? And who are "the people"? Are all men citizens, or some? What criteria will be used to separate them?

Representative, Limited Government

Democracy in the United States means, however, a specific, and to some extent a peculiar, kind of political system. It means, first of all, representative government. The popular will is expressed, usually delayed, and often distorted through elected and appointed officials. By frequent elections the voters choose the principal legislative and executive officers of government and, in some states, many judicial officers as well. A citizen's formal role in the governmental process is normally limited to participating in the selection of representatives, although he can influence in many other ways the decisions his representatives will make.

Several states use a number of instruments of direct democracy whereby governmental decisions are immediately made by the people as a whole rather than by their representatives. Most notable are the initiative and the referendum. The initiative is a means by which a specified number of citizens may

To cast a ballot a prospective voter is required by law to appear before election officials, indicate his ability to meet legal requirements, and have his name placed on the voting list. Registration makes the enforcement of voting qualifications more orderly and helps prevent fraudulent ballot casting. This photograph shows a board of elections in operation during a recent presidential election. (Capa from Magnum)

propose a statute or constitutional amendment and compel a popular vote on its adoption. Similarly, the referendum is a practice of referring measures proposed by a state legislature to the vote of the electorate for approval or disapproval. Neither of these instruments can be used by the federal government without a constitutional amendment, and only the referendum appears to have been effectively utilized in state politics.

Democracy in America also means limited government. The United States has a "constitutional government," what Edmund Burke referred to as a "free government," blending restraint and liberty.[1] The citizen has a voice in ruling himself, but his power is limited because he shares it with a vast number of his fellow-citizens, because his views on policy issues are usually expressed through representatives rather than directly, and because he is bound by the resulting decision. In addition, both the constitutional rules of his government and

"In a Democracy, It Would Be Nothing But Choice, Choice, Choice All the Time"

Drawing by Mahood. © 1959 the New Yorker Magazine, Inc.

the less formal—but not necessarily less important—"rules of the game" by which American politics operate foreclose certain kinds of governmental decisions. While this kind of restriction limits a citizen's power to get what he wants through government, it also protects him from possible oppression by government.

Embedded in the Constitution and in American political culture are the twin and sometimes competing doctrines of majority rule and minority rights. According to the doctrine of majority rule, candidates with a majority vote and proposals endorsed by a majority of representatives should become binding on society. On the other hand, according to the doctrine of minority rights, government, no matter how large its majority at the polls or in the legislature, should respect certain rights of minorities, most especially the right to try to win the next election and the right to secure repeal or enactment of a controversial measure.

Public officials in the United States, usually with strong popular support, have occasionally interfered with the right of minorities to speak and vote freely. More often, government officials have prevented minorities from obtaining full benefits of public services such as education. But despite these inequities, the American record toward minority groups has on the whole been good compared with that of other nations. Even racial discrimination, at least by public officials,

---

[1] See especially Alpheus T. Mason, *The Supreme Court: Palladium of Freedom* (Ann Arbor, Mich.: University of Michigan Press, 1962), Chapter 1.

appears to have drastically declined in recent years, and instances of interferences with the right to speak, assemble, and vote are becoming more infrequent.

This relative success in protecting the political rights of minorities has been made easier because most Americans view the stakes of politics as low and also because, while the great majority of adults think of themselves as Democrats or Republicans, partisan cleavages do not cut deeply into the flesh of society. For example, a poll conducted by Professors Gabriel Almond and Sidney Verba showed that in 1960 only 41 percent of a sample of Americans over eighteen felt that the activities of the federal government had a great impact on their lives, and 11 percent said they felt no impact at all from the federal government. Only 27 percent of this sample claimed that they followed political affairs on a regular basis. As would be expected under these circumstances, only about one out of every three persons interviewed could name four or more cabinet-level departments of the federal government.[2]

War, of course, can make a major difference in the perceived impact of governmental activity. The University of Michigan's Survey Research Center found in late 1966 that, with Vietnam casuality lists lengthening and draft calls

Qualities Attributed to Republican and Democratic Supporters
by Republican and Democratic Voters
(in percents)

Qualities	Repub. views of Repubs.	Repub. views of Dems.	Dem. views of Repubs.	Dem. views of Dems.
Positive				
Interested in defense and independence	63	49	44	52
Intelligent people	35	25	27	31
Interested in humanity	46	41	27	49
Negative				
Selfish people	3	14	23	4
Betrayers of freedom and welfare	1	4	4	2
Ignorant and misguided	0	8	6	1
Fascists, imperialists, etc.	0	1	2	0
Atheists	0	1	0	0
Neutral				
Religious people	11	6	8	13
All sorts	13	15	15	13
Other	0	0	4	2
Total percent[a]	172	164	160	167
Total number of cases	309	309	464	464

[a] Percentages exceed 100 because of multiple responses. "Don't know" respondents omitted.

SOURCE: Gabriel Almond and Sidney Verba, The Civic Culture (Princeton, N.J.: Princeton University Press, 1963), p. 125.

[2] Gabriel Almond and Sidney Verba, The Civic Culture: Political Attitudes and Democracy in Five Nations (Princeton, N.J.: Princeton University Press, 1963), pp. 80, 89, 96.

increasing, almost two out of every three adult Americans said that the policies of the federal government were making a good deal of difference in their lives. Interest in politics, however, increased by a considerably smaller margin and knowledge of public affairs hardly at all.

Moreover, the images of each other that Democrats and Republicans have are not in the majority of cases radically different (see table). Each tends to look on members of his own party as more intelligent, patriotic, and humane, but few see the majority of opposing partisans as stupid, disloyal, or cruel. Another important indication of the seriousness of political cleavage is how a partisan would react to the suggestion that his son or daughter might marry a member of the other party. In this sample, 93 percent of Republicans said they did not care if their children married Democrats, and 92 percent of Democrats said that they did not care if their children married Republicans.[3]

Who Are "The People?"

"The people" in American democracy has been a changing concept. In 1787 "We, the People" meant, at most, white, male adults; and it often meant only white, male adults who owned taxable property. As Chapter 8 will point out, the franchise has been extended over the years, so that "the people" now includes all adults, male or female, white or colored, rich or poor, although practice in many places still lags behind the principle of "one man, one vote."

AMERICAN POLITICAL CULTURE

Since most of this book focuses on the institutions and processes of government in the United States, it is worthwhile to examine briefly the American political culture, that is, the general climate of opinion and values in which Americans learn about politics and in which their government operates. Both the broadest ideals of American culture and the failure to realize them fully are well known and amply documented, but some politically relevant particulars may be less obvious.

The Declaration of Independence proclaims the equality of man and his possessions of certain inalienable rights. No less than ministers, priests, and rabbis, civics textbooks, and public officials extol human brotherhood, the integrity of the individual, and the sacredness of human life. As a whole Americans endorse these ideals; more and more of them also accept the practical consequence that diversity is inevitable, even if it creates a complex society in which each citizen cannot always satisfy his individual needs.

At the same time as Americans have come to expect honesty, and even generosity, in personal dealings, their political culture acknowledges the imperfect nature of man, with the consequent need for the restraining force of government, and for checks on government officials, lest they too succumb to human weaknesses. The prevailing attitude, however, is closer to skepticism than to cynicism.

---

[3] Almond and Verba, p. 135.

Social Trust and Distrust
(in percents)

Percent who agree that	U.S.	Great Britain	West Germany	Italy	Mexico
Statements of distrust					
"No one is going to care much what happens to you, when you get right down to it."	38	45	72	61	78
"If you don't watch yourself people will take advantage of you."	68	75	81	73	94
Statements of trust					
"Most people can be trusted."	55	49	19	7	30
"Most people are more inclined to help others than to think of themselves first."	31	28	15	5	15
"Human nature is fundamentally cooperative."	80	84	58	55	82
Total number of cases	970	963	955	995	1007

SOURCE: Gabriel Almond and Sidney Verba, *The Civic Culture* (Princeton, N.J.: Princeton University Press, 1963), p. 267.

The poll conducted by Almond and Verba strikingly brought out this combination of trust and caution. Eighty percent of American respondents agreed with the statement, "Human nature is fundamentally cooperative"; but 68 percent of that same sample also agreed that others were ready to take advantage of them. On balance, 55 percent thought that most people could be trusted. The table on social trust and distrust gives a breakdown of responses to these and similar questions in five countries. The results indicate that Americans are somewhat more trusting than the British and far more so than the West Germans, Italians, and Mexicans.

Despite their apparent indifference to politics, Americans take great pride in their system of government. In reply to the question, "Speaking generally, what are the things about this country that you are the most proud of?" 85 percent of the American sample mentioned their political institutions. In contrast, only 3 percent of the Italians and 7 percent of the West Germans gave this kind of answer. The question was open-ended; that is, respondents were not offered a set list of choices but had to make up their own.[4]

Coupled with, or perhaps because of, pride in their political system, is the expectation shared by more than four out of five Americans who were interviewed that they will receive the same treatment as anyone else from police and other governmental officials. There is also a widespread feeling of personal political effectiveness. Three quarters of those interviewed said that they believed they could do something to repeal a state or national regulation that they felt was unjust.[5]

---

[4] Almond and Verba, p. 102.
[5] Almond and Verba, pp. 184–85.

One would not anticipate that this general optimism, at least about equal treatment, would be widely shared among Negroes. In 1960 Almond and Verba found that only 49 percent of Negroes thought they would get such treatment. In 1966, however, a Survey Research Center poll showed that three out of four adult Negroes expected equal treatment from public officials, a marked improvement that, because of the careful way in which the two surveys were administered and the size of the differences in responses, cannot be attributed to sampling error.

Relevant to the American political culture are public attitudes toward debate of government policies and candidates for government office. The Almond-Verba poll found that less than one in every four American adults admitted that he never discussed politics; the remainder said they talked about it "regularly," or at least "sometimes." Only 29 percent, however, said that they felt free to talk about politics with anyone. While this proportion may seem small, it was about the same as that in Great Britain and considerably higher than that in West Germany, Italy, and Mexico.[6]

Closely related are public attitudes toward the proper political role of an ordinary citizen. Only 51 percent of American respondents felt he should be active in his local community, while 27 percent thought he should participate only passively. Again, it is instructive to compare these figures with responses from other countries. The proportion of people who feel that an average citizen should play an active political role is significantly higher in the United States than in many other democracies (see table).

These figures are interesting in a more general respect. There probably is

How Active Should the Ordinary Man Be in His Local Community
(in percents)

An ordinary man should[a]	U.S.	Great Britain	West Germany	Italy	Mexico
Be active in his community	51	39	22	10	26
Only participate passively [a]	27	31	38	22	33
Only participate in church affairs[a]	5	2	1		
Only be upright in personal life[a]	1	1	11	15	2
Do nothing in local community	3	6	7	11	2
Don't know	11	17	21	35	30
Other	2	5	1	7	7
Total percent	100	101[b]	101[b]	100	100
Total number of cases	970	963	955	995	1007

[a] Multiple answers were possible but were eliminated from this table.
[b] More than 100 percent because of rounding off of figures.

SOURCE: Gabriel Almond and Sidney Verba, *The Civic Culture* (Princéton, N.J.: Princeton University Press, 1963), p. 169.

[6] Almond and Verba, p. 120.

a point below which political participation could not fall without incurring a serious danger of a constitutional democracy's turning into an elective despotism or into an oligarchy. On the other hand, there is also probably a point beyond which active partisan participation could not go without a serious danger of tearing society apart. Unfortunately, neither public officials nor political scientists have any precise knowledge about the location of these two points; but one can extrapolate from the statistics obtained in Great Britain and the United States and at least intelligently begin an analysis of how much participation can be tolerated and how much is required for the maintenance of democratic institutions.

General Culture and Political Behavior

The capacity of a democracy to remain democratic, some scholars have argued,[7] is enhanced if patterns of authority in other spheres of its social life are similar to those within the political sphere. They believe that it would be difficult to maintain any kind of stable government, much less a democracy, in a totally permissive society, in which parents refused to discipline their children, teachers did not use any coercion in the learning process, and all economic arrangements were conducted on a plane of absolute freedom and equality. In such a social system governmental restraints would probably appear as alien and terrible forces and would likely be resisted or, at best, ignored. At the other extreme, it would also be difficult to maintain a democratic government on anything like the British or American model in a society in which fathers ruled their families with an iron discipline that tolerated neither discussion nor dissent, teachers rigidly enforced conformity and learning by rote, and employers demanded and got absolute, unquestioning obedience from their workers. Some people would be able to switch from playing passive or authoritarian, or completely irresponsible and unfettered, roles in most phases of their lives to being both responsible participants in and reasonably willing subjects of the governmental process; but it is questionable how many people could make such shifts with any facility.

According to the Almond-Verba survey, three out of four American adults remembered having, as children, some influence in family decisions; over half felt free to protest family decisions to which they were opposed; and about two out of three recalled actually having made such protests. This survey also supports the thesis that the American family has been growing more "democratic" over the years. If the memory of older persons is to be trusted, there is far more discussion and tolerance of dissent within the family today than in the past, a development that parallels increasingly broader participation in the political processes.[8]

Similar patterns can be found in school training. A majority of respondents remembered being able to take part in debates and discussions in school, and

---

[7] See especially Harry Eckstein, *Division and Cohesion in Democracy: A Study of Norway* (Princeton, N.J.: Princeton University Press, 1966).

[8] See Almond and Verba, Chapter 12, for an analysis of the findings reported here and in the following paragraphs.

45 percent said that they could recall feeling free to talk about possible unfair treatment with their teachers. Again, the breakdown by age indicates a progressively increasing trend toward greater freedom of discussion. Of those in the eighteen to twenty-five age bracket, 68 percent could recollect participating in school debates; the percentage decreases as age increases to a low of 15 percent for those sixty-one and older.

Work patterns also indicate a society of consultation, if not of active participation. More than three out of four of those interviewed in this study reported that they were sometimes or often consulted about decisions at their place of employment; and more than four out of five said they felt free to protest business decisions with which they disagreed. Predictably, managerial personnel reported the greatest frequency of consultation about job decisions and unskilled workers the lowest.

Analysis of the responses to this survey strengthens the logical link between general culture and political outlooks. Those who had felt free to discuss family decisions were more likely than those who did not to take active political roles in their communities. Almond and Verba made the same finding when they asked about school and work discussions. Moreover, the effects of nonpolitical participation were cumulative. That is, those who participated in both school and job decisions[9] were more likely to feel politically competent than those who merely took part in school discussions.

CHANGING ROLE OF GOVERNMENT

The Constitution has not been altered much since 1787, but the role of government along with American society itself have changed. It is difficult now to imagine that when the Constitution was adopted the United States was a backward, underdeveloped nation that had just won its independence and had done so only with the help of foreign aid—troops, warships, money, and supplies from France, moral support from Spain, and technical assistance from Polish and German professional soldiers. Through much of its first century as a nation American development was heavily supported by foreign investment. One hundred and eighty years later the United States has become the richest nation in the world, with the highest levels of education and general standards of living. Only the Soviet Union can come close to matching its military power, and American wealth spills out into foreign-aid programs that are assisting, or have recently assisted, almost every other nation.

In this very different society, citizens make very different demands on public

---

[9] Education apparently has some moderating effect here. Among the better educated, participation in family or school discussions made little difference in feelings about political competence. Participation in decisions at work, however, did go along with increased feelings of political competence across all educational levels.

It is interesting that when the information about school participation is analyzed, the group with the lowest percentage of feelings of political competence is not comprised of those who had no opportunity to participate but of those who had such opportunities and did not take advantage of them.

officials. The independent frontiersman is supposed to have wanted government to leave him alone, except perhaps when Indians were on the warpath, outlaws were about, or produce had to be moved to market. Today, a chain reaction of technological revolutions, population explosions, and mass migrations have necessitated detailed divisions of labor that make most people almost completely dependent on one another for survival. City dwellers cannot grow food; farmers need manufactured fertilizers and chemicals to enrich their soil, keep down insects, and prevent crop diseases. Farmers also depend on the cities for the machinery that enables a few men to tend profitably several thousand acres. The farms themselves, once largely self-sufficient islands of civilization in a sparsely populated land, now produce for particular markets. Even giant industrial concerns typically buy rather than mine their raw materials and also subcontract to other firms the manufacture of many parts of their finished products.

Such mutual dependence obviously brings many great advantages, but it also brings risks of serious social disadvantages. A new industrial plant may pollute a stream on which an entire city depends for its water or the air that hundreds of thousands of people must breathe. Slum conditions may breed crime that will fester and infect other parts of the city. A labor dispute in the steel industry; an electric power failure; increases in interest rates on loans, transportation fares, medical services and supplies, prices farmers get for their crops; or changes in the terms under which one may buy and sell stocks and bonds—all intimately and often vitally affect millions of people, not just the parties to any particular agreement or disagreement.

In these circumstances citizens have turned more and more to government, and increasingly to the federal government, as the only agency with the resources and authority to cope with current problems. As a result, government has become a planner and promoter as well as a regulator. Many public officials are still concerned with traditional functions of maintaining law and order, enforcing contracts, and defending the country's interests in foreign affairs; but increasingly public officials are concerned with wars against poverty or crusades against racial discrimination or with promoting foreign trade and economic prosperity or with aiding educational institutions to train doctors, scientists, and teachers.

These changes in governmental roles are continuing, but they have not come about quickly or easily nor have they yet been fully accepted. "I am not a friend to a very energetic government," Thomas Jefferson wrote in 1787, and many Americans still feel the same way, though most have accepted as inevitable, however undesirable, the enlarged scope of public functions. More than three quarters of those interviewed in the Almond-Verba survey said they believed that the effects of governmental action were beneficial.[10] Yet the nagging fear lingers on that big government, however necessary and however staffed by men of good will, poses a threat of big despotism. One of the central problems facing the United States in the closing part of the twentieth century is precisely the one that James Madison described at the time of the Constitutional Convention: how to make

---

[10] Almond and Verba, p. 82.

government strong enough to allow it to govern, and yet also keep government officials from oppressing the people or from working for special interests.

Much of this book is taken up with the general problem of providing strong yet limited government. Part 1 offers a brief historical description of the framing of the Constitution, the fundamental principles of that Constitution, and a discussion of some general aspects of federalism. Part 2 consists of five chapters explaining the less formal phases of the American political system—who can and does vote, the reasons underlying actual voting behavior, and the processes by which political parties, public officials, candidates for public office, and interest-group leaders interact to influence elections and public policy.

Parts 3 and 4 focus on the powers of Congress and the President to govern. These chapters examine actual practice as well as constitutional prescriptions. Here, too, however, there will be some discussion of how governmental power is limited, for the authority of Congress and that of the President overlap, with institutional jealousy often playing a significant role in the decision-making processes of the federal government, just as it does in relations between state and federal officials. Part 5 examines the operations of the judiciary and its functions of administering justice between individuals and of both limiting and validating exercises of political power. Part 6 is devoted to the analysis of those civil rights that the Constitution purports to protect.

Part 7 deals with problems of foreign affairs and national defense. In the longer version of this book we have also included two additional parts. The first analyzes domestic policies that vitally affect economics and welfare. The second takes up in general outline the organization of governmental institutions at the state and local level.

Time and again in all of these chapters we shall refer to certain problems facing the American government as massive, immense, intricate, or complex and to possible solutions, whether to substantive problems of policy or to the more general problem of controlling public officials, as also infinitely complex. We dislike using the same adjectives over and over, but we have preferred accuracy to stylistic elegance, for the first step in understanding any phase of American politics is acceptance of a pair of basic facts. First, the most serious problems confronting the country are truly immense and at the same time invulnerable to simple solutions. Second, beliefs currently prevalent in the political culture notwithstanding, the welfare and even the survival of all of us are closely bound up with the daily actions of public officials trying to cope with—and sometimes trying to ignore—those problems.

Selected Bibliography

Bryce, Lord James, *The American Commonwealth* (2 vols.; New York: Crowell-Collier and Macmillan Company, Inc., 1888). A comprehensive description of the workings of the political system; a classic study of government.

Cassinelli, C. W., *The Politics of Freedom* (Seattle, Wash.: University of Washington Press, 1961). An interesting analysis of the modern democratic state.

Clark, John Maurice, *Alternative to Serfdom* (New York: Alfred A. Knopf, 1948). A vigorous defense of the use of government to promote human welfare.

Dahl, Robert A., *A Preface to Democratic Theory* (Chicago: University of Chicago Press, 1956). An analysis of American democracy that rejects Madisonian and populistic models as inadequate.

Hallowell, John M., *The Moral Foundation of Democracy* (Chicago: University of Chicago Press, 1954). The moral and religious basis of modern democracy.

Hayek, Friedrich A., *The Road to Serfdom* (Chicago: University of Chicago Press, 1955). Argument that there is a fundamental conflict between a planned society and the democratic tradition; excoriates government regulation as antidemocratic.

Lipset, Seymour Martin, *Political Man* (New York: Doubleday & Company, Inc., 1960). Original essay by a political sociologist evaluating the conditions making for stable democracy; demolishes the myth, among others, that the "working class" is the special carrier of "liberal" virtues.

Mill, John Stuart, *Considerations on Representative Government* (New York: Harper & Row, publishers, 1862). Probably the most notable and influential nineteenth-century statement articulating and defending a theory of democracy.

Tocqueville, Alexis de, *Democracy in America* (Phillips Bradley, ed.; 2 vols.; New York: Alfred A. Knopf, 1945). Remains one of the most perceptive and rewarding analyses of American democracy, a classic interpretation of American politics.

Part 1 The Living Constitution

THE RAW MATERIAL OF POLITICS

by Felix Frankfurter

PERHAPS the dominant feeling about government today is distrust. The tone of most comment, whether casual or deliberate, implies that ineptitude and inadequacy are the chief characteristics of government. . . . But the fact is that we ask more from government than any society has ever asked. At one and the same time, we expect little from government and progessively rely on it more. We feel that the essential forces of life are no longer in the channels of politics, and yet we constantly turn to those channels for the direction of forces outside them. . . . The paradox of both distrusting and burdening government reveals the lack of a conscious philosophy of politics. It betrays some unresolved inner conflict about the interaction of government and society. I suspect that it implies an uncritical continuance of past assumptions about government and about society. We have not adjusted our thinking about government to the overwhelming facts of modern life, and so carry over old mental habits, traditional schoolbook platitudes, and campaign slogans as to the role, the purposes, and the methods of government. Perhaps such confusion is part of the process of travail toward a more conscious attitude. Certainly there is a great deal of speculative writing about the state. . . . Certainly theory and practice interact. Political societies represent dominant contemporary forces, dominant practical demands made upon government by society. But theories, intellectual systems, notions about what is desirable and what is undersirable, may themselves create demands or determine their direction. Ideas and books have played their share in the drama of government. . . . It is not without significance that the most profound contribution to political thought in America, namely, *The Federalist,* was not the work of doctrinaire thinkers but of men of affairs. *The Federalist* was a lawyer's brief by the framers of the Constitution in support of their handiwork.

. . . let me ask you to bring into sharp focus what it is that a modern state like our own government is actually called upon to do. Before we can consider the aptness of political ideas or the adequacy of political machinery, the relevance of past experience or the promise of new proposals, we must be fully alive to what might be called the raw material of politics—the nature and extent of the demands made upon government and the environment in which it moves.

* * * * *

"The real difficulty appears to be . . . that the new conditions incident to the extraordinary industrial development of the last half-century are continuously and progressively demanding the readjustment of the relations between great bodies of men and the establishment of new legal rights and obligations not contemplated when existing laws were passed or existing limitations on the powers of government were prescribed in our Constitution. In place of the old individual independence of life in which every intelligent and healthy citizen was competent to take care of himself and his family we have come to a high degree of interdependence in which the greater part of our people have to rely for all the necessities of life upon the systematized cooperation of a vast number of other men working through complicated industrial and commercial machinery. Instead of the completeness of individual effort working out its own results in obtaining food and clothing and shelter, we have specialization and division of labor which leaves every individual unable to apply his industry and intelligence except in co-operation with a great number of others whose activity conjoined to his is necessary to produce any useful result. Instead of the give and take of free individual contract, the tremendous power of organization has combined great aggregations of capital in enormous industrial establishments working through vast agencies of commerce and employing great masses of men in movements of production and transportation and trade, so great in the mass that each individual concerned in them is quite helpless by himself. . . . And in many directions the intervention of that organized control which we call government seems necessary to produce the same result of justice and right conduct which obtained through the attrition of individuals before the new conditions arose."

Political man has on the whole merely the limited resources of the past. In native intelligence we can hardly be said to excel Aristotle, and in the field of political ideas man's inventive powers have been pitiably meager. Not only have the burdens cast upon politics immeasurably increased; the environment within which politics operates immensely increases the difficulties.

From Felix Frankfurter, *The Public and Its Government* (New Haven, Conn.: Yale University Press, 1930) Chapter 1. The long quotation in this passage is from Elihu Root's *Addresses on Government and Citizenship* (Cambridge, Mass.: Harvard University Press, 1916) pp. 448–449.

2

The formation
of a more
perfect union

THE UNITED STATES:

THE FIRST "EMERGING NATION"

The United States of America, which declared its independence in 1776 and worked out its present form of government eleven years later, was in a very real sense the first "emerging nation" of modern times—the first "underdeveloped area" to throw off its colonial status and become an independent country. It is not surprising, then, that the Constitutional Convention of 1787 has always been of great interest to historians and to students of political institutions. This has never been truer than in the years since World War II, a period in which dozens of new nations have declared their independence and—always the more difficult task—have become "countries" in the sense of achieving substantial social cohesion and establishing a stable and effective plan of self-government.

Thus there has been a steady flow of new books[1] dealing with the American

---

[1] Carl Van Doren, *The Great Rehearsal* (New York: The Viking Press, Inc., 1948); Clinton Rossiter, *1787: The Grand Convention* (New York: Crowell-Collier and Macmillan Company, Inc., 1966); Catherine Drinker Bowen, *Miracle at Philadelphia* (Boston: Little, Brown & Company, 1966).

Constitutional Convention of 1787. Their very titles—*The Great Rehearsal; 1787: The Grand Convention; Miracle at Philadelphia*—underscore the relevance for the modern world of a venture in constitution-making that took place nearly two centuries ago. Or, to use Jefferson's[2] words, America's "example of changing a constitution by assembling the wise men of the state, instead of assembling armies" still remains a relevant challenge to today's emerging nations.

The Declaration of Independence of 1776 required a seven-year Revolutionary War to give it meaning by establishing a United States of America. Many men paid with their lives for the freedom that was finally won in 1783. Those who survived faced an unfinished task—a need to demonstrate to themselves and the world that thirteen "sovereign states" could voluntarily join together as one country capable of governing itself. The fifty-five men who met in Philadelphia during the hot summer months of 1787 to write a new constitution thus truly determined the fate of a nation. Through the fortunes of war and much trial and error politics, a good deal of practical experience had been gained during the eleven years between 1776 and 1787. It remained, however, an open question whether that experience could be put to good use in establishing a stable political system. John Dickinson, a delegate from Delaware, advised the Philadelphia convention: "Experience must be our only guide. Reason may mislead us." Thus, the pragmatism that is still a strong element in American politics was manifest even in 1787. But several of the Founding Fathers were careful students of political philosophy, and in spite of Dickinson's advice, they did not hesitate to draw heavily upon their academic knowledge as well as upon their practical experience. They believed the science of politics includes a concept of *constitutional* government, and they were consciously trying to set down on paper a series of written rules that would commit their nation to this concept.

The Meaning of Constitutional Government

Constitutional government may be said to be the means by which the people of a nation organize for collective action through government, while reserving to themselves an area of freedom upon which government is forbidden to encroach. The most important single factor in the meaning of constitutionalism is this concept of *limited government*. Indeed, a good brief definition of a constitution is that it is the means whereby authority and liberty are balanced in a state. Germany under Hitler had a political system, a very specific and carefully organized one, but because the power of the Nazi regime was unchecked by real as opposed to merely paper limitations it was able to exert almost total control over its subjects.

In the history of government few actual constitutions have ever been very successful or lasted very long. It is always a difficult undertaking to find a balance

---

[2] Letter to David Humphreys, March 18, 1789. *The Papers of Jefferson*, Julian P. Boyd, ed. (Princeton, N.J.: Princeton University Press, 1950), 14:678.

between liberty and authority that will work. In particular, it is difficult to set down in writing in a single document the terms of a constitutional settlement. If the document is too long or precise it may force the settlement into such a rigid mold that it will rapidly prove unsatisfactory in a changing world. If it is too short and vague it may fail to limit the power of government sufficiently.

Government under the Articles of Confederation

It is important to remember that the Constitution of 1787 was *constitution number 2* in the political history of the United States of America as a sovereign, independent nation. The first constitution was known as the Articles of Confederation and was in formal effect from 1781 to 1789, at the end of which period the present constitutional system went into operation. Between 1776 and 1781 the national government was a provisional one, consisting of the Continental Congress, which governed without benefit of any constitutional charter.

During the decade from 1776 to 1787 the American people also had a good deal of experience with state constitutions, for the Declaration of Independence made states out of thirteen colonies, and the people of these states had to replace their colonial charters with a new legal foundation befitting their status as sovereign entities. However, it will be sufficient here to examine the experience under the Articles of Confederation and the effect of that experience upon the Convention of 1787.

Article II of the Articles of Confederation provided, "Each state retains its sovereignty, freedom and independence, and every power, jurisdiction and right, which is not by this confederation expressly delegated to the United States, in Congress assembled." This provision strikingly indicates two significant characteristics of the government under the Articles. First, the "perpetual union" created by the Articles was that of "a firm league of friendship" of independent states rather than a federal union in which sovereignty rested in the national state. Second, the only constitutional agency of the central government was a unicameral Congress. The Articles did not set up an executive branch, although they did authorize Congress to establish such "committees and civil officers as may be necessary for managing the general affairs of the United States under their direction." There were also no national courts except those that Congress was authorized to establish for the limited purposes of trying piracy and prize cases or settling disputes among the states. Congress itself was not so much a national legislative assembly as it was a conference of state ambassadors. Each state was authorized to send from two to seven delegates, but, regardless of its population, was to have but one vote in Congress. Important public laws required the approval of nine states.

Congress under the Articles could coin money, issue paper currency, borrow money, establish a postal system, fix standards of weights and measures, regulate Indian affairs, and appropriate funds to meet governmental costs. In foreign affairs its powers were relatively extensive. It could negotiate treaties, send and receive ambassadors, raise and equip an army and a navy, appoint officers in these armed services, and declare war.

The Weaknesses of the Articles of Confederation

The Articles were seriously defective as an adequate constitutional basis for a system of national government in the United States in several ways. First, the silence of the Articles about an executive branch meant that the new government could legislate, that is, prescribe policy, but could not carry it out. In 1781, Congress did establish four executive departments; this administrative machinery, however, was largely ineffectual, because since the Articles did not provide for a chief executive, there was no central unity or guidance. Second, it is even an exaggeration to say that Congress could "legislate"; the laws it passed were merely directives to the states and did not bear directly on the people. Congress could "resolve and recommend but could not command and coerce." [3] Insofar as there was any "law of the land" that the people had to obey, it was the law of the individual states. Third, the powers actually granted to Congress were inadequate for the needs of a truly national government. Most serious was the absence of Congressional power to tax and regulate commerce. Without the taxing power, Congress had to depend for its revenues upon state contributions to the national treasury. And with no Congressional power to regulate commerce among the states, each state was free to establish barriers against the trade of neighboring states if it so wished. This made the establishment of a uniform national commercial policy impossible. Fourth, the Articles did not draw a line between the powers and functions of the national and state governments. Congress was authorized to supervise the settlement of disputes between states, but there was no way to settle conflicts between the national government and the states. Finally, the Articles were extremely difficult to amend; the legislatures in all thirteen states had to ratify changes proposed to them by Congress.

Although the Articles had been in effect only six years when the Philadelphia convention met, their constitutional inadequacies were all too apparent. [4] The financial status of the central government was exceedingly precarious. During the Revolutionary War the army had gone chronically unpaid and, by 1780, $40 million in paper currency had been issued. Under the Articles little was done to reverse this trend toward national bankruptcy, largely because of the failure of the states to meet the fiscal levies assigned to them by Congress. In 1786 the entire income of the national government would have paid less than one third of the interest on the new nation's already acquired debt. The Northwest Ordinance of 1787 was a last-minute effort to establish a national policy for the development of the western lands, but Congress had failed strikingly up to that time to protect

---

[3] Rossiter, p. 52. Professor Rossiter's study has been a useful source of information in revising this chapter.
[4] See A. H. Kelly and W. A. Harbison, *The American Constitution,* 3rd ed. (New York: W. W. Norton & Company, Inc., 1963), pp. 100–110, from which much of the information in this paragraph has been drawn.

settlers against the Indians or to force England and Spain to respect American rights in the west. Perhaps the most serious failure of the government under the Articles was that the nation was allowed to drift near commercial chaos by 1787. Congress had found it difficult to negotiate favorable commercial agreements with foreign nations, in part because other nations were aware that Congress had no means of compelling its states to honor such agreements. And at home the trade wars of the states were threatening to injure domestic commerce severely, if not bring it to a complete halt. These commercial difficulties were particularly acute because political independence had divorced the new nation from the English trade system. The favorable three-way trade of pre-Revolutionary days among England, the thirteen colonies, and the West Indies was now a thing of the past. Finally, the 1780s were for Europe a period of general economic depression, the impact of which was keenly felt by both agricultural and commercial interests in this country.

Just when "the sharp social struggles within the states appeared to presage general civil war," however, the nation found a way to save itself. Virginia and Maryland set in motion a chain of events that led to the Philadelphia convention and to a new constitution when they undertook to come to an agreement concerning commerce on the Potomac River. Pleased with their progress, they decided to broaden negotiations and invite other states to participate. As a result, a convention was held at Annapolis in 1786. It accomplished little, largely because only five states sent delegates, but before it adjourned it issued a call for a second meeting to be held in Philadelphia the following year. Moreover, it proposed that at this second meeting something more than the commercial problem be considered. It recommended that this new convention

take into consideration the situation of the United States, to devise such further provisions as shall appear to them necessary to render the constitution of the federal government adequate to the exigencies of the Union, and to report such an Act for that purpose to the United States in Congress assembled, as when "agreed to by them and afterwards confirmed by the legislatures of every state" will effectually provide for the same.

Congress was reluctant to issue a call for such a convention, but the fears created by Shays' Rebellion in Massachusetts late in 1786 and the fact that seven states had already appointed delegates led Congress to vote its approval in February of 1787.

WHY THE PHILADELPHIA CONVENTION SUCCEEDED

There were many reasons why the Philadelphia convention might have failed to draft a constitution that would have provided a firm basis for a lasting national government in the United States. While the thirteen states shared a common language and, as the former colonies of a single nation, also shared "common legal and political institutions, common culture, common enemies, and common memories of a successful drive toward independence," they had, in a century and a half, developed diverse social and economic interests and were as ready to quarrel among themselves as independent political states always have been.[5] They were contiguous geographically, but the distance from Massachusetts to Georgia was great, not only in miles but in eighteenth-century means of communication and transportation and also in ways of thinking about goals so vague as *national* purpose and *national* opportunity.

Yet the Founding Fathers managed to draft a Constitution that has since been regarded by all students of political history as a brilliant achievement in statecraft. More important, they sensed the needs of a particular emerging nation and correctly estimated the mind and mood of a people who were ready for a bold step toward a single country with a strong national government operated by means of republican principles. Above all, they were willing to compromise on details, and even occasionally on principles, in order to achieve fundamental purposes and goals.

In addition to a decade of experience, the delegates were meeting at a propitious moment in history. By 1787 certain historical forces were beginning to operate in the world that were conducive to the building of a powerful new nation. The philosophy of the Age of Reason had reached its full development and was at the peak of its influence. Even so short a time as a generation earlier it probably would have been impossible to undertake a national political experiment characterized by the faith in reason, the belief in progress, and the confidence in the importance of the individual that were so prevalent at Philadelphia.

ORGANIZATION AND PROCEDURES
OF THE CONVENTION

In seeking an explanation of the highly successful outcome of the American constitutional assembly, the procedures of the convention should be noted, for many an assembly of able men, meeting under generally favorable circumstances, has failed to accomplish its mission because of faulty organization and ways of going about its business.

The convention was in session from the end of May to the middle of September in 1787. In all, fifty-five delegates attended, but many of these were late in arriving; only forty-two stayed until the end, and only thirty-nine signed the finished Constitution. Twelve states were represented, Rhode Island refusing to send any representatives. The delegates were generally appointed by the state legislatures; in no instance was a delegate elected by the voters. The states sent varying numbers of representatives, but, although the large states favored a weighted system of voting based on population, a decision was made early in the convention that each state should cast one vote. Thus there was a maximum of twelve votes on any question. A simple majority was sufficient to carry any proposal.

The convention met five hours a day, six days a week. The usual hours of the meetings were from ten in the morning until three in the afternoon. The cobblestones in the streets outside the State House were covered with earth to deaden the sound of passing vehicles and provide a more favorable environment for a

---

[5] Rossiter, p. 38.

Docr. Franklin. It is too soon to pledge ourselves before Congress and our Constituents shall have approved the plan.

Mr. Ingersol did not consider the signing, either as a mere attestation of the fact, or as pledging the signers to support the Constitution at all events; but as a recommendation, of what, all things considered, was the most eligible.

On the motion of Docr. Franklin
N. H. ay. Mas. ay. Ct. ay. N. J. ay. Pa. ay. Del. ay. Md. ay. Va. ay. N.C. ay. S.C. div. Geo. ay. Mr. Genl. Pinkney & Mr. Butler disliked the equivocal form of the signing, and on that account voted in the negative.

Mr. King suggested that the Journals of the Convention should be either destroyed, or deposited in the custody of the President. He thought if suffered to be made public, a bad use would be made of them by those who would wish to prevent the adoption of the Constitution.

Mr. Wilson preferred the second expedient. he had at one time liked the first best; but as false suggestions may be propagated it should not be made impossible to contradict them.

A question was then put on depositing the Journals and other papers of the Convention in the hands of the President. on which,
N. H. ay. Mas. ay. Ct. ay. N. J. ay. Pen. ay. Del. ay. Md. no. Va. ay. N.C. ay. S.C. ay. Geo.
The negative of Maryland was occasioned by the language of the instructions to the deputies of that State, which required them to report to the State, the proceedings of the Convention.

The President, having asked what the Convention meant should be done with the Journals &c. whether copies were to be allowed to the members of applied for. Resolved nem: con: "that he retain the Journal and other papers

James Madison appointed himself unofficial secretary to the Constitutional Convention and kept a record of its activities. His lengthy résumés of remarks and speeches are recorded in his diary, Notes on the Federal Convention. *On this page of the journal, Madison discusses several proposals regarding the safekeeping of the papers of the Convention—whether they should be thrown out or deposited with the President.* (Library of Congress) successful undertaking. The convention was, accordingly, a small, uncomplicated assembly. The way was open for a relatively easy establishment of rapport among the delegates and for essentially simple, indeed informal, ways of doing business. Debate was not limited in any way; discussions were frequently lengthy and vigorous.

There is no official or formal record of the proceedings of the convention. The meeting appointed William Jackson to serve as its secretary, but he kept very sparse and inadequate minutes of the sessions. Apparently, the significance to a democracy of preserving a careful record of such an important event as a constitutional assembly had not yet been formally recognized. Fortunately, other delegates also kept notes and recorded them in personal papers, diaries, and memoranda. The most valuable source of information is a diary kept by James Madison, in which he reported the story of the convention, including lengthy résumés of the remarks and speeches made by the delegates on the floor of the assembly.

Meeting as it did nearly two centuries ago, the convention was able to do a number of things that undoubtedly helped it to succeed but that almost certainly could not be done by such a body meeting today. The first of these was a conscious and deliberate adoption of a secrecy rule by which "nothing spoken in the house [was] to be printed, or otherwise published or communicated without leave." This rule was consistently adhered to throughout the convention's sessions. There were no "leaks" by delegates; what is more, the press seems to have been content to respect the confidental nature of the proceedings, for there were no clever attempts to penetrate the barrier against news releases.

It is clear that in those troubled times, with strong disagreement throughout the country over the propriety and wisdom of thoroughgoing constitutional reform, the work of the Philadelphia convention was greatly simplified because it took place behind closed doors. Had its progress been reported from day to day, it is quite likely that strong popular opposition would have developed to many of the specific principles and proposals that found favor within the convention. Madison himself wrote that "no Constitution would ever have been adopted by the Convention if the debates had been public."

The work of the convention over its four-month span was undoubtedly facilitated by a basic plan of proceeding that, while formal and regular, was largely free from the complicated parliamentary devices that are considered essential to the functioning of most contemporary assemblies. Early in the convention a detailed substantive proposal for what was, in effect, a new constitution was laid before the convention by certain of its members. About two weeks later a second, quite different, proposal was submitted by other delegates. Sitting as a "committee of the whole" [6] through this period, the convention considered these proposals,

---

[6] The "committee of the whole" is a parliamentary device that has long been used by all kinds of assemblies that are attempting to do business under formal rules of procedure. As a "committee" made up of all the members of an assembly, it temporarily escapes from these rules and is thereby enabled to consider business informally and take votes and arrive at decisions that are tentative only, for, as a committee, it always reports back to the assembly itself as the official body. The assembly then usually ratifies the decision reached in the committee of the whole, although it need not do so if "second sober thought" suggests the wisdom of another outcome.

rather quickly preferring one over the other and thereafter examining the favored plan in detail. All decisions were taken by simple votes on resolutions identifying the specific issues that required action by the delegates. As the summer went by, the convention adjourned twice, once for ten days and once for two days, to permit two special committees to take stock of the convention's progress and, in the light of its decisions, to prepare new drafts of a constitution for its further consideration. The convention went over the report of the first of these agencies, known as the committee of detail, with great care for five weeks, debating the committee's proposed constitution section by section and attempting to make final decisions on each point. The second committee was appointed early in September "to revise the style of and arrange the articles which had been agreed to by the house." In many significant ways the exact language of the finished Constitution was determined by this "committee of style." The convention then spent three days scrutinizing the committee's draft, a few last-minute changes were made, and the Constitution was ready to be signed.

At one point, midway in the convention, when the disputed issue of representation of the states in the two houses of a proposed Congress threatened to wreck the convention, a special committee, consisting of one delegate from each state, was appointed. This committee was able to make a recommendation that was accepted by the convention.

At no point was any attempt made to write a constitution on the floor of the convention. Nor was any use made of so-called standing committees to which business was referred in specific substantive areas on a continuing basis. Instead, all crucial problems were examined in the committee of the whole, with such use of special committees as the convention found helpful.

THE PERSONNEL OF THE CONVENTION

The fifty-five delegates who went to Philadelphia in 1787 were a remarkable array. Without doubt, the presence of these particular men had a profound influence upon the character of the Constitution that emerged from the Philadelphia meeting. Twenty-six of the delegates had had college educations. Two college presidents and three professors were present. More than thirty had had training in the law. The Fathers also had much practical experience in politics. Forty-two or the fifty-five delegates had been members of Congress; twenty had served in state constitutional conventions; seven had been state governors; thirty were serving in state legislatures at the time the Philadelphia convention met.

The Founding Fathers provide a splendid example of men of widely differing ages working together to solve a common problem. The oldest, the most experienced, and the wisest in the ways of men, Benjamin Franklin, was a venerable eighty-one. The youngest delegate, Jonathan Dayton of New Jersey, was only twenty-six. Four delegates were in their twenties, fifteen in their thirties, twenty-two in their forties, seven, including Washington, in their fifties, and seven were sixty or older. The average age was just over forty-three.

George Washington was easily the most eminent and respected member of the convention. As presiding officer, he spoke formally only once, but his opinions were frequently strongly held and generally known. Unquestionably, his great personal dignity and prestige, and the fairness with which he presided, were important assets to the convention. James Madison, like Washington a Virginia delegate, has been called "the Father of the Constitution." Although he was only thirty-six years old, as a co-author of the Virginia Plan, as an active participant in the convention's deliberations, as its real if not official secretary, and as a member of the final committee of style, his influence was great.

Benjamin Franklin was not one of the leaders of the convention, but, as "a spectacle of transcendent benevolence," he was unfailingly optimistic and good humored. He helped soothe injured feelings, encouraged compromise, and helped give the gathering dignity and prestige. Two other Pennsylvania delegates played important roles. James Wilson's contribution was second only to that of Madison, whose able assistant he was. Gouverneur Morris was one of the five members of the committee of style and gave the Constitution some of its most important language.

Alexander Hamilton was only thirty years old at the time of the convention. His contribution to the drafting of the Constitution was not a substantial one. His own personal ideas were far too reactionary and undemocratic even for his conservative colleagues. Moreover, he was frequently outvoted by the other two delegates representing New York. In fact, his influence was so slight that he spent little time in attendance at the convention's sessions, although he was present to sign the finished document. Hamilton's great service came later, when he helped to secure New York's ratification of the Constitution.

Max Farrand[7] mentions fifteen other men who stood out above their colleagues and made important contributions to the work of the convention. Among this group were Charles Pinckney of South Carolina; George Mason of Virginia; Oliver Ellsworth, William Johnson, and Roger Sherman of Connecticut; and Rufus King and Elbridge Gerry of Massachusetts. Clinton Rossiter also mentions all of these men but adds to his list of "the influentials" John Rutledge and Charles Cotesworth Pinckney of South Carolina, Nathaniel Gorham of Massachusetts, and Edmund Randolph of Virginia.

Thomas Jefferson, from his diplomatic post in Paris, wrote John Adams in London that the convention was "an assembly of demigods." In slightly more restrained fashion, a modern scholar has written,[8] "No gathering of the leaders of a newly independent nation at any time in history has had more cumulative political experience than the convention of 1787." Most significantly, there was a high degree of cohesion and unity among the fifty-five men responsible for the Constitution. Almost all of the delegates came from seaboard towns or tidewater

---

[7] *The Framing of the Constitution of the United States* (New Haven, Conn.: Yale University Press, 1926), pp. 14–41. This excellent book has been helpful in the preparation of this chapter. Professor Farrand also collected all of the documents relating to the work of the convention, such as Madison's Diary, in a monumental four-volume work, *The Records of the Federal Convention* (New Haven, Conn.: Yale University Press, 1911, 1937).

[8] Rossiter, p. 144.

plantations. Few came from the back-country areas of the twelve states that sent delegates to Philadelphia. The delegates were, by and large, the important people of the day—holders of government securities, owners of plantations and large areas of western lands, creditors, slaveowners, and men with mercantile and trading interests. "Not one member represented in his immediate personal economic interests the small farming or mechanic classes." [9] But likewise only three had interests in manufacturing. "The sway of agriculture went as yet unchallenged." [10]

Many of the men who had played important roles during the Revolutionary years were missing. John Adams and Thomas Jefferson were abroad serving their country as diplomats. Samuel Adams was at home in Massachusetts, growing old. John Hancock also stayed in Massachusetts, where he was governor of the state. Patrick Henry declined to serve. His laconic explanation for this conduct was, "I smelt a rat!" Thomas Paine was in Europe. Among others who, for one reason or another, were missing were George Clinton and John Jay of New York and John Marshall of Virginia. Only eight of the fifty-six men who had signed the Declaration of Independence eleven years earlier were numbered among the fifty-five delegates to the Philadelphia convention.

The Motives of the Framers

During the eighteen decades since the Philadelphia convention there has been widespread controversy about the motives of the framers. The traditional view has always been that they were men of great wisdom and integrity who were guided in their labors by high ideals and much practical experience. In 1913 Charles A. Beard published his controversial book, *An Economic Interpretation of the Constitution of the United States,* in which he argued that the framers had been influenced by much more personal considerations than had previously been recognized. Beard asserted that the Founding Fathers were troubled by the lack of a positive governmental program for the protection of property, for the encouragement of economic enterprise, and for the preservation of law and order. As Beard saw it, the security holders among the delegates were concerned about the inability or unwillingness of both state and national governments to meet the interest and principal payments on the public debt. The western landowners wanted roads into the west and protection against Indians. Creditors were worried about the increasing tendency of debtors to seek legislation from their state governments freeing them from part or all of their obligations. Merchants and manufacturers were handicapped by the lack of a uniform national currency and were suffering because of the disruption of America's foreign trade and the growing stagnation in interstate trade. In short, these men all had strong personal reasons for desiring a strong, central government in the United States that would protect and promote their own economic interests.

In the more than half century since its appearance, Beard's book has set the

---

[9] See Charles A. Beard, *An Economic Interpretation of the Constitution of the United States* (New York: Crowell-Collier and Macmillan Company, Inc., 1913), p. 149.
[10] Rossiter, p. 52.

pattern for a widely accepted view of the framers and their work. Beard's theories, however, have also repeatedly been questioned. In recent years Robert E. Brown and Forrest McDonald have sharply criticized Beard's historical methodology and, in particular, his selection of evidence as biased and uncritical. The conduct of most of the delegates, McDonald contends, rather than reflecting personal economic and political considerations, "was to a much greater extent a reflection of the interests and outlooks of the states and local areas they represented." [11]

The views of both Beard and his critics about the Founding Fathers' motives undoubtedly express some part of the truth. As patriots and statesmen, the delegates were devoted to their country, were anxious for its success as an independent nation, and were determined to build as carefully as they knew how. But they were also practical men of affairs who saw only too clearly that the failure of the new nation and the failure of their own personal interests were inextricably related. George Washington[12] spoke both as a patriot and as a hard-headed businessman when he wrote: "I do not conceive we can exist long as a nation without having lodged somewhere a power, which will pervade the whole Union in as energetic a manner as the authority of the State governments extends over the several States."

Professor Arthur Schlesinger,[13] who, like Charles Beard, stressed the economic motivation in the writing of the Constitution, pointed out:

No discriminating reader need feel that such a presentation carries with it the imputation of ignoble or unworthy motives to the Fathers of the Constitution; rather, it forms an illuminating commentary on the fact that intelligent self-interest, whether conscious or instinctive, is one of the motive forces of human progress.

Beard[14] himself observed in an earlier book: "never in the history of assemblies has there been a convention of men richer in political experience and in practical knowledge, or endowed with a profounder insight into the springs of human action and the intimate essense of government."

THE CONVENTION'S ALTERNATIVES:
THE VIRGINIA AND NEW JERSEY PLANS

Two days after enough representatives had arrived at Philadelphia to permit the convention to begin its formal sessions, a group of delegates submitted the famous Virginia Plan, providing for a bicameral congress in both of whose houses the states would have representation based on population. This congress was to have all of the powers of its predecessor under the Articles of Confederation, and in addition, the authority "to legislate in all

---

[11] Robert E. Brown, *Charles Beard and the Constitution: A Critical Analysis of "An Economic Interpretation of the Constitution"* (Princeton, N.J.: Princeton University Press, 1956); Forrest McDonald, *We the People: The Economic Origins of the Constitution* (Chicago: University of Chicago Press, 1958), p. 416.

[12] George Washington, *Writings,* W. D. Ford, ed. (New York: G. P. Putnam's Sons, 1891), 11:53–54.

[13] *New Viewpoints in American History* (New York: Crowell-Collier and Macmillan Company, Inc., 1925), p. 189.

[14] *The Supreme Court and the Constitution* (New York: Crowell-Collier and Macmillan Company, Inc., 1912), p. 86.

cases in which the separate states are incompetent, or in which the harmony of the United States may be interrupted by the exercise of individual legislation." It could also veto all state laws that in its opinion violated the Constitution and thus would have power to draw the line between national and state authority and to determine the limits of its own powers. Congress was to choose a "national executive" and provision was made for a "national judiciary." The executive and judiciary would constitute a "council of revision" with a veto power over the congress; the vetoes, however, could be overruled by a subsequent vote of both houses.

As we have seen, the convention proceeded to consider this radical and far-reaching plan for some two weeks in a committee of the whole. At the end of that period, those delegates who advocated a more modest increase in the powers of the central government presented the New Jersey Plan, which retained a uni-cameral congress in which the states would have equal representation. To the existing powers of this congress were to be added the authority to tax and to regulate interstate commerce. Congress was also to be given power to elect a "federal executive," and provision was made for a "federal judiciary." Perhaps the most striking proposal in the New Jersey Plan was that federal laws and treaties were to be "the supreme law of the respective states" and that state courts were bound to enforce these federal enactments. Kelly and Harbison[15] say, "This was in reality the key to the solution of federalism, but at the time it escaped notice, for momentarily the Convention was altogether preoccupied with the legislature."

When the committee of the whole chose between the Virginia and New Jersey plans, the vote was seven to three for accepting the former as a basis for further deliberations. It seems clear that the presentation of a scheme for drastic constitutional reform at the very beginning of the convention was significant because it accustomed the delegates to the thought of radical revision of the constitutional system. It is possible that, had the two plans been presented simultaneously, the New Jersey Plan would have been preferred as being more in line with the modest revision of the Articles of Confederation for which the convention had been called.[16]

COMPROMISE IN THE CONVENTION

Since most of the fifty-five men who attended the Philadelphia meeting were members of the upper classes—socially, economically, and intellectually—they found it quite easy to agree on many of the basic issues of the day. Particularly, there was general accord on such propositions as (1) the need for a stronger government to cope with the nation's economic and social problems, (2) the wisdom of providing such increased power in the central government rather than in the states, and (3) the desirability of incorporating the principles of separation of powers and checks and balances

---

[15] Kelly and Harbison, pp. 127–128.
[16] Farrand, *The Framing of the Constitution,* p. 89.

into the new governmental system to prevent abuse of these increased political powers. More specifically, such crucial issues as giving more powers to the national legislature, providing for much-needed executive and judicial branches in the central government, and placing certain specific prohibitions upon the central and state governments were settled with little debate and a minimum of dissension.

Nonetheless, there were important differences of opinion among the delegates, and writing a constitution that all could agree upon was a far from easy task. The delegates did, after all, come from twelve different states, many of which were widely separated geographically and economically, and their views reflected their varying state interests. Here, in the Philadelphia convention, an issue appeared that has troubled the nation throughout its entire history. Granted the wisdom of joining many states together in one great federal union, how can each state be assured that its own economic and social interests will receive satisfactory consideration from the national government?

Compromise between the Large and the Small States

One of the most serious conflicts in the Philadelphia convention was that between the large and the small states. The dividing line was not a precise one, but in general there was a large-state group, led by Virginia, Pennsylvania, and Massachusetts, that supported the Virginia Plan. This group was opposed by a small-state faction, including New Jersey, Delaware, and Maryland, that backed the New Jersey Plan. Because the large states expected to dominate the new national government, they favored increasing its power. The smaller states, afraid that they might be outvoted in the councils of the new government, were inclined to balk at the proposed increase of power. John Dickinson, a small-state delegate, told Madison:[17]

Some of the members from the small States wish for two branches in the General Legislature, *and are friends to a good National Government;* but we would sooner submit to a foreign power, than submit to be deprived of an equality of suffrage, in both branches of the legislature, and thereby be thrown under the domination of the large States.

As Dickinson's comment indicates, the crux of the problem was not so much a conflict in principle between centralized power and states' rights as it was a question of representation in the new Congress. We have seen that the large states (large in the sense of more people rather than greater area) supported the Virginia Plan, which called for a bicameral legislature in which representation in both houses would be based on population. The less populous states favored the New Jersey Plan for a unicameral legislature in which all states would be equally represented. The more populous states had a majority, and the convention voted that in the lower house representation would be based on population. But the vote on the upper house resulted in a tie. Debate had become acrimonious, and it was apparent that the convention was on the verge of breaking up.

---

[17] James Madison, *The Debates in the Federal Convention of 1787 Which Framed the Constitution of the United States of America,* G. Hunt and J. B. Scott, eds. (New York: Oxford University Press, 1920), p. 102. Italics added.

The delegates then appointed a special committee of one representative from each state to recommend a solution. In retrospect, the committee's compromise of representation by population in the House of Representatives and equal representation of states in the Senate seems obvious; but the convention approved it only after considerable soul searching. This agreement is called the Great Compromise, or the Connecticut Compromise, because of the supposedly leading role played by delegates from that state in formulating the proposal.

Compromise over the Election of the President

Another perplexing problem with which the convention had to deal concerned the election of the President. At least six methods for choosing the President were proposed. These included election by the people, by the state governors, by Congress, and by an electoral college. In general, those who favored election by Congress wanted the legislative to be stronger than the executive—this is known as the doctrine of legislative supremacy. Those who favored popular election of the President wanted a strong, independent executive. The convention twice gave its approval to election by Congress. Each time, those who favored a strong executive vigorously, and successfully, opposed this decision, arguing that election by Congress would make the President ineffectual and subservient. Election of the President by the people never commanded much support in the convention, although a few delegates strongly favored it. Finally, toward the close of the convention, the electoral college system was approved. However, instead of providing for the selection of electors by state legislatures, as had been earlier proposed, the convention decided that they should be chosen by each state "in such a manner as its legislature may direct." This left the door open for election of the electors by the people.

The plan for the election of the President also involved a further compromise between the large and the small states. In the electoral college the large states would enjoy an advantage, since the electoral vote of each state was to be equal to its representation in both houses of Congress. But it was provided that if no candidate received a majority of the electoral vote, the House of Representatives, *voting by states,* should proceed to elect a President from among the five highest candidates. Thus, in the event of a selection of the President by the House of Representatives, the small states would enjoy another advantage, because each state would have one vote. Moreover, since the two-party system was not yet in existence in 1787, it was expected that the electoral college vote would frequently be widely distributed among several candidates, thus making election of a President by the House a fairly common occurrence.

Compromise on the Issue of Democracy

There was a further split between those delegates who favored following the democratic principle in the new political system and those who were less enthusiastic about democracy. The conflict never became acute because the great majority of the delegates adhered to the latter position. When George Mason asserted that permitting the people to elect the

President would be as "unnatural" as "to refer a trial of colors to a blind man," he expressed a sentiment that most of the delegates approved. As we have seen, however, there were a few delegates, led by James Wilson, who argued for the election of the President and of the members of both houses of Congress by the people.

The compromise between these opposing factions was largely implicit. Those who were opposed to participation of the people in governmental affairs certainly carried the day, for only the House of Representatives was made directly responsible to the voters; the Senate, the Presidency, and the federal judiciary were all placed at least one step beyond their immediate control. But revealingly, these initial undemocratic features of the document were not made irrevocable or inflexible. Subsequently it proved possible, for example, to make the election of the President quite democratic without changing a single word of the written Constitution. The direct election of senators did require alteration of the Constitution, but in the amending clause of the Constitution its framers invited formal change. The convention also left it to the states to determine the extent of the suffrage. Thus, through changes in state requirements, it proved possible to establish the universal right of all white men to vote without altering a word of the national Constitution. Formal amendments were utilized, however, to extend the suffrage to Negroes and to women.

Compromise on New States

Many delegates were apprehensive about the new states that might be carved out of the western wilderness. They felt that these states might reflect the radical interests of the debtor and small-farmer classes that they had learned to distrust during the Confederation period. Accordingly, they favored language in the Constitution restricting the admission of new states and providing for their membership in the Union on an inferior basis. As it turned out, there were enough delegates favoring free development of the west to insist upon compromise. It proved impossible to put into the Constitution a clause guaranteeing the right of new states to come into the Union "on the same terms with the original States," but neither was any express language adopted condemning new states to an inferior position. Instead, the power to decide finally the terms upon which new states might be accepted was delegated to Congress, which ultimately accepted fully the doctrine of complete equality.

Compromise between North and South

A more intense geographical conflict separated the northern and southern states. The northern states had important interests in commerce and shipping and were ready for their first steps toward a manufacturing economy that the next half century would bring. In the South, a large-scale plantation system of agriculture was emerging. That section was producing increasingly large surpluses and was eager to exchange them in outside markets for the finished goods that were unavailable in its own economy. The slave-labor system of operating such plantations was already well developed;

the invention of the cotton gin in 1792 was to accentuate these developments, bringing about a one-crop agricultural economy that would dominate the South for a century.

Accordingly, each section was apprehensive lest the increased power of the new central government be used to advance the economic interests of the other section at its own expense. To deal with these apprehensions the delegates agreed that there should be an absolute prohibition upon export taxes. In this way the fear of the South that Congress might try to tax both the flow of the agricultural surplus out of and the flow of finished goods into its territory was quieted.

A second compromise between North and South concerned the ratification of treaties. The South was fearful that the new government would enter into commercial agreements with foreign nations detrimental to its interests, such as a treaty with Spain that might sacrifice American interests in the Gulf of Mexico and Mississippi River areas. Thus, the requirement of a two-thirds majority in the Senate for the ratification of treaties assured the South of a veto power over agreements with foreign nations.

A number of conflicts concerned the slaves. A compromise was arranged on the issue of counting the slaves as population in determining the representatives to which a state would be entitled in the lower house. Some southerners were inclined to demand that representation be based upon all the slaves. Northern extremists among the delegates, on the other hand, argued that none of the slaves should be counted. The compromise spirit prevailing, it was agreed that three fifths of the slaves would be counted in determining a state's quota of seats in the House of Representatives and also its quota whenever a direct tax was levied by the central government.

Although the convention did not debate the institution of slavery, it had to arrange a compromise on the question of the slave trade. Delegates from the Deep South were anxious to see the importation of slaves from Africa continue without restraint. The middle states, particularly Virginia, which bred their own slaves and had a surplus for sale, were willing to see the importation of slaves brought to an end, as were some of the northern delegates for moral reasons. A compromise decision finally allowed the slave trade to continue until 1808, when Congress might forbid further importation—which it promptly did when that year arrived. In the meantime, imported slaves were not to be taxed by the national government at a figure in excess of ten dollars a head.

THE ISSUE OF SLAVERY IN THE CONVENTION

It has been said that the most fateful decision *not* taken at Philadelphia in 1787 "was to do something imaginative about Negro slavery." [18] The institution of slavery and its impact upon the formation of "a more perfect union" should have been very much in the minds of the Founding Fathers. As we have seen, they found it necessary to deal with slavery in order

---

[18] Rossiter, p. 266. Rossiter qualifies this judgment by adding "or so it appears to men of the 1960s and must have appeared to men of the 1860s."

to compromise between North and South at several points.[19] Moreover, slavery was widely viewed as inconsistent with the ideas and principles of free government, at least half of the states having made slavery unlawful.

Since it took one of the bloodiest wars in history to end slavery and the United States is still striving to establish full racial justice and equality, one wonders whether the Founding Fathers might not somehow, whatever the price, have managed in their new Constitution to make express provision for the ultimate, if not the immediate, emancipation of slaves by peaceful means. This is, of course, one of the great "if onlys" of American history. The best judgment of scholars is that the basic issue of slavery itself could not have been dealt with by compromise—and certainly not by a frontal attack—at Philadelphia in 1787. All of the arguments against slavery were known and could have been voiced systematically on the floor of the convention. The issue could easily have been made the subject of a resolution that, in a showdown, would probably have been approved by a majority of the states. But it is even clearer that such a step would have been utterly unacceptable in 1787 to the five states south of Delaware. John Rutledge was undoubtedly correct when he told the convention that the question of what to do about slavery was in effect the question of "whether the southern states shall or shall not be parties to the Union." As Clinton Rossiter[20] puts it, "The climate of American opinion in 1787 . . . smiled guardedly upon would-be builders of a nation and frowned coldly upon would-be emancipators of slaves."

There is little or no evidence that any of the Founding Fathers were abolitionists in the sense of believing that theirs was the time when the national government should eliminate, or even regulate, slavery. Conceivably, a union in which slavery would have been forbidden that was acceptable to the eight states from New Hampshire to Delaware might have been established in 1787. Conceivably, the other five states would have joined together in a different confederation tolerating slavery. Conceivably, economic, social, and political pressures would at some later date have brought these two unions to a peaceful merger on a nonslavery basis. And conceivably, the Civil War and the racial tensions of the twentieth century could have been avoided had the convention of 1787 somehow brought greater wisdom to bear on the issue of slavery. All of this, however, is extremely doubtful. If one may point to the critical moment when provision might have been made by the national government for the emancipation of slaves and the ultimate avoidance of racial tensions in American society, it would be the 1850s rather than the 1780s.

RATIFICATION OF THE CONSTITUTION

The Extralegal Character of Ratification

The ingenuity of the framers and the spirit of compromise that pervaded the convention's sessions had made possible the fashioning of a document that thirty-nine of the forty-two delegates who were

---

[19] See Article I, sections 2 and 9, Article IV, section 2, and Article V of the Constitution.
[20] Rossiter, p. 269.

present at the end were able to sign.[21] But there was good reason to fear that the Constitution might not be ratified by the states. Although most of the delegates to the convention viewed the years under the Articles of Confederation as a "critical period," their opinions were not shared by all persons. The farmers in the rural areas and many of the mechanics, traders, and shopkeepers in the towns were reasonably well satisfied with the existing political system even though they had their social and economic grievances. Certainly there was no overwhelming public demand for the new constitution, or, as Charles Beard put it, there is no evidence that "the entire country was seized with a poignant sense of impending calamity."

The Fathers were well aware that drastic action was called for. By the terms of the Articles' amending clause, revision of the fundamental law could take place only by a vote of Congress and the approval of the *legislatures* in all *thirteen* states. The Fathers were not willing to run the risk of complying with these rigid requirements. Approval by the old Congress was highly uncertain. Some of the state legislatures were likely to be antagonistic to the document. It was unthinkable that all thirteen states, including Rhode Island, which had refused even to send delegates to the Philadelphia convention, would ratify. Accordingly, in wording the section of the Constitution that prescribed the manner in which it was to be ratified, the Fathers did not hesitate to depart from the stipulations of the Articles in three specific ways. They proposed to Congress that it send the Constitution to the several states without giving the document its own consideration or approval; second, they recommended that consideration in the states be by special conventions; and third, they provided that approval by nine states should be sufficient to put the new Constitution into operation in those states. Faced with the virtual impossibility of securing a new constitution by established methods, therefore, the Fathers resorted to extralegal action. Their decision to require the approval of only nine states was certainly consistent with democratic principles, for democracy does not mean that constitutional reform shall be had only by unanimous vote. In voting to submit the Constitution to state conventions rather than to state legislatures, the delegates probably reasoned that the document would get more favorable treatment this way. Nonetheless, several delegates argued that the new method was more democratic, in that approval by delegates to state conventions chosen by the voters for that one purpose would more nearly approximate popular ratification of the Constitution than would approval by the state legislatures.

The exceedingly close margin by which the Constitution was ratified demonstrated that the fears of the Fathers about its fate were not unfounded. Such small states as Delaware, New Jersey, Georgia, and Connecticut quickly ratified the Constitution—the first three by unanimous votes. In all, seven of the states ratified the Constitution by a margin of two to one or better. But in several states the ratifying vote was very close: In Massachusetts, 187 to 168; in Virginia, 89 to 79; and in New York, 30 to 27. It is true that all of the states finally ratified the Con-

---

[21] The three who refused to sign were Edmund Randolph and George Mason of Virginia and Elbridge Gerry of Massachusetts. However, Randolph later changed his mind and supported the Constitution in the Virginia ratifying convention.

stitution, but it seems clear that North Carolina and Rhode Island did so only because they realized that the new system was going into operation and they did not want to stay out of the Union. Had their consent been necessary before the Constitution could take effect, there is reason to believe they would not have approved the change.

Some scholars, including the Beards, have estimated that either because of restrictions upon suffrage that prevailed in many of the states or because of disinterest or disaffection, not more than one fourth of the adult white males participated in the elections in which the delegates to the state ratifying conventions were chosen, and that the actual voters favoring the Constitution did not exceed 100,000 in a population of 4 million.[22] This estimate has been challenged by other historians who believe that the idea of a severely restricted suffrage in the 1780s is an exaggerated one.[23] In any event, it is difficult, if not impossible, to speak with any accuracy of a popular vote "for" and "against" the Constitution, since in many districts the delegates to the state ratifying conventions were elected on an "uninstructed" basis, that is, they were elected without being told how to vote.

The statesmanship of the delegates did not stop with their extralegal action easing the requirements for the Constitution's ratification. There remained the task of securing a favorable vote in nine state conventions—a difficult one, as the close vote that actually occurred in several of these conventions shows. Opposition to the new Constitution period was extensive and vociferous. Many small farmers, debtors, poorer people in the towns, and state politicians were opposed to ratification. Moreover, the opposition was strongly entrenched in many of the state conventions. The following comment by a rural member of the Massachusetts convention reveals the strong feeling of these opponents[24]:

These lawyers, and men of learning, and moneyed men, that talk so finely, and gloss over matters so smoothly, to make us poor illiterate people swallow down the pill, expect to get into Congress themselves; they expect to be the managers of this Constitution, and get all the power and all the money into their own hands, and then they will swallow up all us little folks, like the great *Leviathan,* Mr. President; yes, just as the whale swallowed up Jonah.

To meet these views, many of the framers served in the state conventions, working long and hard for favorable action, and they were active on the hustings and in the press in shaping a positive public opinion in support of the Constitution. The most best-known effort on behalf of the Constitution during the ratification struggle was made in New York. There, Alexander Hamilton, James Madison,

[22] Charles and Mary Beard, *The Rise of American Civilization* rev. & enlarged ed. (New York: Crowell-Collier and Macmillan Company, Inc., 1947), 1:332.

[23] Robert E. Brown, for example, has estimated that property qualifications in the original states in most cases excluded as little as 5 to 10 percent of the voters and in no case more than 25 percent. Brown attributes the low vote in the election of delegates to the state ratifying conventions to "indifference" and not to "disfranchisement."—Robert E. Brown, pp. 197–199. See also Chilton Williamson, *American Suffrage from Property to Democracy* (Princeton, N.J.: Princeton University Press, 1960); Martin Diamond, "Democracy and the Federalist: A Reconsideration of the Framers' Intent," *The American Political Science Review,* 53 (March 1959), 52–69.

[24] Jonathan Elliot, *The Debates in the Several State Conventions on the Adoption of the Federal Constitution* (Philadelphia: J. B. Lippincott Company, 1888), 2:102.

This drawing, done about 1850, shows one of the floats used in the Federalist Procession of July 23, 1788. The parade celebrated the ratification of the Constitution after many months of debate and uncertainty. (Brown Brothers)

and John Jay joined forces to write a series of letters analyzing the Constitution and extolling its merits. These letters, widely printed in the newspapers of the day, have been preserved under the title *The Federalist*. It is significant that America's greatest single contribution to the literature of political thought was called forth by the practical necessity of winning support for the proposed Constitution.

To the last the Fathers showed their willingness to compromise. As the struggle over ratification proceeded, it became evident that a decision of the Philadelphia convention to omit a bill of rights from the Constitution had been a mistake. To win for the Constitution the support of those numerous people who were vigorous in their demands for the inclusion of such a bill, a promise was given that the first Congress under the new Constitution would draw up a series of amendments that would provide a fundamental guarantee of a free people's traditional liberties.

Selected Bibliography

Beard, Charles A., *An Economic Interpretation of the Constitution* (New York: Crowell-Collier and Macmillan Company, Inc., 1913). Argues that the Founding Fathers were influenced chiefly by economic motives in the drafting of the Constitution.

Elliot, Jonathan, *The Debates in the Several State Conventions on the Adoption of the Federal Constitution* (Philadelphia: J. B. Lippincott Company, 1888). The standard source for the debates in state conventions that ratified the federal Constitution.

Farrand, Max, *The Framing of the Constitution* (New Haven, Conn.: Yale University Press, 1926). An authoritative account of the work of the Philadelphia convention, designed for the general reader.

————, *The Records of the Federal Convention of 1787* (4 vols.; New Haven, Conn.: Yale University Press, 1911). A compilation of documentary sources bearing on the work of the Philadelphia convention.

The Federalist, the title given to the collection of letters written by Hamilton, Madison, and Jay in support of the proposed constitution during the ratification period. See editions By R. H. Gabriel (New York: Liberal Arts Press, 1954); H. S. Commager, *Selections from the Federalist,* (New York: Appleton-Century-Crofts, 1949): and Max Beloff (New York: Crowell-Collier and Macmillan Company, Inc., 1950).

Jensen, Merrill, *The Articles of Confederation* (Madison, Wisc.: University of Wisconsin Press, 1940). The story of the formation and drafting of the Articles.

Kelly, Alfred H., and Winfred A. Harbison, *The American Constitution: Its Origins and Development,* 3d ed. (New York: W. W. Norton & Company, Inc., 1963). One of a number of excellent histories of constitutional development from colonial beginnings.

McDonald, Forrest, *We the People: The Economic Origins of the Constitution* (Chicago: University of Chicago Press, 1958). A balanced and fruitful reinterpretation of Beard's thesis of the economic motivations of the framers of the Constitution.

Rossiter, Clinton L., *Seedtime of the Republic* (New York: Harcourt, Brace & World, Inc., 1953). An excellent analysis of the intellectual ferment and political ideas current during the Colonial and Revolutionary periods.

3

A constitution intended to endure for ages to come

When the Founding Fathers drafted a constitution, they created a system of government based on existing institutions. In 1787 all Americans with any knowledge of politics were already familiar with courts, legislatures, executive officers, and popular elections, since each of these had existed in the colonies. What was novel in the new Constitution was its allocation of authority among various agencies of government and its ordering of power between government and private citizen.

The values and concepts of government the framers put forth were also familiar, even though some doctrines—national supremacy, for example—had controversial aspects. General propositions in the Constitution itself and the Bill of Rights regarding the importance of individual liberty and of restraints on government were as little challenged then as now, though practice lagged far behind ideals. The commands of the Constitution, moreover, were often worded so broadly that even those who had adamantly opposed its ratification soon discovered the document could be interpreted to support their convictions.

37

Perhaps because it was more than simply compatible with American values, the new Constitution soon became a symbol of political virtue. Political rhetoric, widespread prosperity, national expansion, and accompanying heavy bursts of patriotism all contributed to a well-nigh universal[1] feeling that the Constitution was as close to being a divinely inspired document as was possible during an age in which miracles had gone out of fashion. "Constitution worship," as Max Lerner[2] calls it, became a persistent and significant element in American political culture, more prevalent and important today than in the last century. It often seems that "Is a proposal constitutional?" is asked far more frequently in political debate than "Is it good?" or "Is it wise?"

It would be useful to know exactly how this spirit of constitutionalism has become such an integral part of American political culture, for reverence for constitutions, even moderately successful ones, is hardly universal. For instance, Ireland has enjoyed political stability, democratic government, civil liberty, and a generally rising degree of economic prosperity during the thirty years under its present constitution, but the recent remark in private of a high public official, "The Constitution is a bloody nuisance!" is often echoed, though in more restrained tones, in legislative debates.

The framers of the American Constitution wanted a strong national government, able to cope with all serious economic and political problems, but they were apprehensive about abuses of power. As James Madison saw it, the core of the problem was to establish a government that would be able "to controul one part of the society from invading the rights of another, and at the same time sufficiently controuled itself, from setting up an interest adverse to that of the whole society."[3] This problem, of course, is as old as society itself, and the solution of the framers was to establish an intricate means of distributing political power. As Madison[4] explained:

Ambition must be made to counteract ambition. The interest of the man must be connected with the constitutional rights of the place. It may be a reflection on human nature, that such devices should be necessary to control the abuses of government. But what is government itself, but the greatest of all reflections on human nature? If men were angels, no government would be necessary. If angels were to govern men, neither external nor internal controls on government would be necessary. . . . A dependence on the people is, no doubt, the primary control on the government; but experience has taught mankind the necessity of auxiliary precautions.

Many lawyers, judges, and textbook writers speak of a separation of powers in the Constitution, and it is possible and often convenient to talk in such terms. Even some of the framers themselves found it expedient to use this phrase. In

---

[1] As exceptions to this rule, many abolitionists, especially from the 1840s to the Civil War, attacked the Constitution as a "covenant with hell," because it recognized slavery as a legitimate institution.

[2] Max Lerner, *Ideas for the Ice-Age* (New York: The Viking Press, Inc., 1941), p. 238.

[3] James Madison, *Vices of the Political System in the United States* (1787); reprinted in Alpheus T. Mason, *Free Government in the Making*, 2d ed. (New York: Oxford University Press, 1956), p. 172.

[4] James Madison, *The Federalist* (New York: Random House, Inc., 1937), Modern Library ed. No. 51, p. 337.

fact, however, it is more precise to say that as much as separating power the Constitution provides for a sharing of different kinds of authority among public officials. The Constitution also expressly prohibits all state and federal officials from exercising certain powers. This combination of separating, sharing, and prohibiting powers can most fruitfully be analyzed under the headings of federalism, distribution of powers within the national government, and limited government.

FEDERALISM

We may define federalism as a political system that divides power between a central government, having authority over the entire country, and a series of local governments, collectively covering the entire territory. In a true federal system, each of these two levels of government must be more or less independent of the other.

Federalism may be contrasted with unitary or centralized government, such as that found in Britain. In that country there are local units of government in addition to the central government in London, but these local divisions are created by and subject to the control of the central government. They can be changed or abolished at the will of Parliament. Federalism may also be contrasted with the political arrangement in a confederation, which is a league of independent states. Under the Articles of Confederation, for instance, the American national government did not govern the people directly, but operated only through state governments.

The Constitution of the United States established a federal system. The national government has authority to govern the people directly in regard to many matters of domestic as well as foreign policy, and the authority of the national government comes from "the people" of the United States, not from the individual states as separate political entities. On the other hand, the states, while no longer sovereign as they were under the Articles of Confederation, are not mere subdivisions of the central government. As the Supreme Court noted after the Civil War, the Constitution "looks to an indestructible Union, composed of indestructible States." [5]

Three sections of the Constitution have established the legal framework within which American federalism has developed. The most important of these is paragraph 2 of Article VI, which makes explicit the doctrine of national supremacy:

This Constitution, and the laws of the United States which shall be made in pursuance thereof; and all treaties made, or which shall be made, under the authority of the United States, shall be the supreme law of the land; and the judges in every State shall be bound thereby, any thing in the Constitution or laws of any State to the contrary notwithstanding.

Clearly, this clause renders illegal any effort by a state to contravene the Constitu-

---

[5] *Texas v. White,* 7 Wallace 700, 725 (1869).

tion or valid federal laws or treaties. Moreover, this clause provides for national supremacy in those many areas—control of commerce, for example—in which both federal and state governments may legitimately act. In addition, the Supreme Court has on several occasions ruled that state authority must give way before that of the federal government where, on such vital matters as national security, Congress has enacted a pervasive scheme of regulation, even if conflict between state and federal authority is only a potential danger.[6]

A second constitutional provision for federalism is the doctrine of "reserved powers," or "states' rights," in the Tenth Amendment:

> The powers not delegated to the United States by the Constitution, nor prohibited by it to the States, are reserved to the States respectively, or to the people.

A hasty reading of this amendment might lead to the view that there are two watertight compartments of authority: the legitimate powers of the federal government as enumerated in the Constitution and a vast residue of state power. Unhappily for those who like simple political solutions, no such clear-cut division of power exists. The Tenth Amendment does serve as a constitutional reassurance that the states are not mere creatures of the national government, but it does not restrict national authority to those functions specifically listed in the Constitution. The amendment does not say that the powers not *expressly* delegated are reserved, only those "not delegated." Several times during the debate in Congress on this amendment, proponents of states' rights tried to insert the word "expressly," but each time they were voted down.

These matters are closely related to the provision of Article I, section 8, the so-called sweeping clause, with its doctrine of implied federal power:

> The Congress shall have power . . . to make all laws which shall be necessary and proper for carrying into execution the foregoing powers, and all other powers vested by this Constitution in the government of the United States, or in any department or officer thereof.

By the terms of this clause, Congress has authority that goes far beyond any listing of specific powers. It also has been delegated whatever powers are "necessary and proper" to carry out its general and particular responsibilities.

In 1819, in *McCulloch v. Maryland,* the Supreme Court spelled out the implications of the doctrine of implied powers. In question was the constitutionality of the Bank of the United States, a quasigovernmental institution that Congress had established. No clause of the Constitution mentioned congressional authority to charter banks or other corporations. But, speaking for a unanimous Court, Chief Justice John Marshall held that, when coupled with the sweeping clause, the expressly delegated powers of Congress to borrow and coin money, to collect taxes, to regulate commerce, to raise armies, and to wage war implied that Congress had authority to create institutions that would enable it to carry out its work. Marshall[7] carefully rejected placing close limits on congressional power to choose means that legislators thought most convenient:

---

[6] See, for example, *Pennsylvania v. Nelson,* 350 U.S. 497 (1956).
[7] 4 Wheaton 316, 421 (1819).

Let the end be legitimate, let it be within the scope of the constitution, and all means which are appropriate, which are plainly adapted to that end, which are not prohibited, but consistent with the letter and spirit of the constitution, are constitutional.

The concept of implied powers in the federal government is not easy to reconcile with a doctrine of reserved state powers. Once it is conceded that the national government has implied as well as expressed powers, the exact limits of national authority become difficult to fix. How far can implied power be stretched? What laws can Congress pass on this basis without invading the realm of reserved state powers? Such questions have no clear-cut answers. Some answers have been given by federal judges appointed for all practical purposes for life, some by locally elected congressmen, and some by administrators, including the President, who must often work through state and city officials even though he is responsible to a national constituency.

DISTRIBUTION OF POWERS

Federalism requires a geographic distribution of power among state and national officials. The distribution of power among federal officials is more on the basis of function. Following the scheme of the French political theorist Montesquieu, the framers established three separate departments within the national government. To an independent Congress, they gave primary authority to legislate, to make the laws. "All legislative power herein granted," Article I reads, "shall be vested in a Congress of the United States. . . ." To an independent President they gave basic authority to administer, to carry out, and to enforce the commands of the laws. "The executive power," Article II says, "shall be vested in a President of the United States of America." To an independent judiciary the framers gave fundamental authority to adjudicate, to apply laws and executive orders to specific legal proceedings. "The judicial power of the United States," Article III provides, "shall be vested in one Supreme Court and in such inferior courts as the Congress shall from time to time ordain and establish."

The framers, however, provided then that these distinct and legally equal departments should share many powers. The President can participate in the legislative process through his authority to call special sessions of Congress, to propose legislation, to veto bills, and to influence members of Congress in informal but perhaps effective ways. Legislators can participate in administration through their authority to create the basic rules under which federal executive agencies function as well as through their authority to appropriate money for every operation of each federal office. Senators can further influence administrative action through their authority to advise and consent to the appointment of important executive officers. Federal judges participate in the legislative and administrative processes by deciding exactly what the words of a federal statute or executive order really mean. The President can participate in the judicial process through his authority to nominate judges and to pardon all persons convicted in federal courts. And, in case of impeachment, the Senate sits as a trial court; there is no appeal from its decision.

In providing for a system of shared powers among three branches of government, the Constitution in essence requires a consensus among public officials if a particular policy is to become effective. Thus the power of any single official or group of officials is restricted. In addition, the Constitution provides each of these three agencies with direct checks on the power of the other two. For example, judges can declare acts of Congress or the President unconstitutional, but the President can refuse to enforce judicial decisions, and the House can impeach and the Senate convict and remove a federal judge or any other federal official, including the President. Furthermore, Congress, by the express terms of Article III, has wide discretion in determining the kinds of cases that federal courts can hear and decide. The President, if balked in Congress, can appeal over the heads of legislators to the voters and ask them to send new men to Washington. Similarly, members of Congress can campaign against a President or even refuse to appropriate money to carry out his programs. A mere one third plus one of the Senate can reject a treaty negotiated by the President.

Just as there are many uncertainties about the application of implied powers, national supremacy, and federalism, so too there are many serious problems concerning the distribution of power among federal officials. How far may Congress properly go in altering the jurisdiction of federal courts or in increasing the size of the Supreme Court? How far may the President properly go in trying to persuade congressmen to vote for particular proposals? How readily may judges substitute their judgment for the judgment of Congress as to whether a statute is constitutional? The process of checking, like the process of implying, has no precise limits. Both leave much room for flexibility in the joints of the political system.

LIMITED GOVERNMENT

Like the other concepts we have been discussing, the term "limited government" permeates the Constitution, although it is not explicitly set forth there. First, sections of the original Constitution and, of course, of the Bill of Rights expressly forbid government officials to perform certain kinds of acts. Second, whatever the effect of the doctrine of implied powers, the fact that the national government is based upon delegated power has become a part of American political culture and may often act as a significant psychological check on public officials. Reinforcing this limitation is the statement of the Tenth Amendment that some powers are reserved "to the people" and the explicit reminder of the Ninth Amendment that "enumeration in the Constitution, of certain rights, shall not be construed to deny or disparage others retained by the people."

Also of great importance is the establishment of popular elections, which Madison called the primary check against the arrogance of officials, and which enable the people to remove at least some potential oppressors from public office and to keep others out of office.

This limiting concept is offset at many points. The doctrine of implied powers competes as much with the notion of limited government as it does with state autonomy in a federal system. Furthermore, many Supreme Court decisions have held that most of the Constitution's prohibitions against governmental action are relative. The First Amendment, for instance, explicitly says that Congress "shall make no law" abridging freedom of speech or press; but in times of national emergency, Congress has enacted, the President has signed, and the Supreme Court has approved the constitutionality of statutes restricting what American citizens may speak or write. In sustaining convictions under a 1917 sedition law, Justice Oliver Wendell Holmes[8] said for a unanimous Court:

We admit that in many places and in ordinary times the defendants in saying all that was said in the circular [opposing the draft during World War I] would have been within their constitutional rights. But the character of every act depends on the circumstances in which it was done. . . . The question in every case is whether the words used are used in such circumstances and are of such a nature as to create a clear and present danger that they will bring about the substantive evils that Congress has a right to prevent.

Later justices, most notably Hugo L. Black, have challenged the soundness of this relativistic attitude. To date, however, these justices, while winning specific cases, have not yet been able to persuade a majority of their colleagues to hold that as a matter of constitutional law some rights, even those of the First Amendment, are absolute.

FLEXIBILITY

The framers wished to give their new government sufficient authority to cope with national problems while minimizing the chances that officials would abuse that authority. In addition, the framers were aware of their own limitations; they realized that they could envision only a small portion of the problems that a new nation would encounter. Thus they deliberately refused to draw a detailed blueprint outlining specific political actions and instead tried to sketch a flexible governmental system that could cope with unforeseen crises. As Edmund Randolph, an influential member of the convention's committee on detail, wrote[9]:

In the draught of a fundamental constitution, two things deserve attention:
1. To insert essential principles only lest the operations of government should be clogged by rendering those provisions permanent and unalterable, which ought to be accommodated to times and events; and
2. To use simple and precise language, and general propositions, according to the examples of the several constitutions of the several states; for the construction of a constitution necessarily differs from that of law.

Three decades later, in the great case of *McCulloch v. Maryland*, Chief Justice John Marshall expressed much the same thought when he said: "we must never

---

[8] *Schenck v. United States*, 249 U.S. 47, 52 (1919).
[9] Max Farrand, ed., *The Records of the Federal Constitution of 1787*, 4 vols. (New Haven, Conn.: Yale University Press, 1911, 1937), 2:137.

forget that it is a constitution we are expounding." To make clear what he meant by a "constitution," the chief justice stated:

A constitution, to contain an accurate detail of all the subdivisions of which its great powers will admit, and of all the means by which they may be carried into execution, would partake of the prolixity of a legal code, and could scarcely be embraced by the human mind. It would probably never be understood by the public. Its nature, therefore, requires that only its great outlines should be marked, its important objects designated, and the minor ingredients which compose those objects be deduced from the nature of the objects themselves.

Then Marshall[10] spoke of the American Constitution in particular, as

a constitution intended to endure for ages to come, and consequently, to be adapted to the various crises of human affairs. To have prescribed the means by which government should, in all future time, execute its powers, would have been to change, entirely, the character of the instrument, and give it the properties of a legal code. It would have been an unwise attempt to provide, by immutable rules, for exigencies which, if foreseen at all, must have been seen dimly, and which can best be provided for as they occur.

The brevity, generality, and, on some issues, silence of the Constitution have in fact functioned as the framers foresaw. Many of the most important aspects of the American political system have developed without having been explicitly described in the Constitution. For example, there is not a single word about how candidates for the Presidency, for Congress, or for any other government post will be chosen. Instead, the way has been left open for the development of nomination procedures either by custom or by statute. As it has turned out, nomination of presidential candidates is largely a matter of custom, while selection of congressional candidates is regulated by many state and a few federal statutes.

The Cabinet system is an example of a development by executive action. Although the Constitution authorizes the President to require opinions in writing from heads of administrative departments, it says nothing that requires an advisory council. It has been by presidential choice that the heads of executive departments meet together in council.

Many aspects of the American political system are not described in the Constitution, but can be derived from these clauses only by subtle interpretation. A good example is judicial review. The Constitution did not expressly provide that the Supreme Court should have the power to declare acts of Congress null and void. Yet, in the case of *Marbury v. Madison,*[11] when the Supreme Court in 1803 ruled that the courts possessed such a power, it did so by constitutional interpretation. The justices read the idea of judicial review into such clauses of the Constitution as that requiring judges to take an oath to support the Constitution, reasoning that in taking such an oath a judge is in effect promising to refuse to enforce a statute that, in his opinion, conflicts with the Constitution.

Constitutional development by interpretation has not been the exclusive work of the courts. At times, Congress, the President, and even lesser public officers have taken part in this process. For example, the question of when the

---

[10] *McCulloch v. Maryland,* 4 Wheaton 316, 407, 415 (1819).
[11] *Marbury v. Madison,* 1 Cranch 137 (1803).

We the People of the United States, in order to form a more perfect Union, establish Justice, insure domestic Tranquility, provide for the common defence, promote the general Welfare, and secure the Blessings of Liberty to ourselves and our Posterity, do ordain and establish this Constitution for the United States of America.

Article. I.

Section. 1. All legislative Powers herein granted shall be vested in a Congress of the United States, which shall consist of a Senate and House of Representatives.

Section. 2. The House of Representatives shall be composed of Members chosen every second Year by the People of the several States, and the Electors in each State shall have the Qualifications requisite for Electors of the most numerous Branch of the State Legislature.

No Person shall be a Representative who shall not have attained to the Age of twenty five Years, and been seven Years a Citizen of the United States, and who shall not, when elected, be an Inhabitant of that State in which he shall be chosen.

Representatives and direct Taxes shall be apportioned among the several States which may be included within this Union, according to their respective Numbers, which shall be determined by adding to the whole Number of free Persons, including those bound to Service for a Term of Years, and excluding Indians not taxed, three fifths of all other Persons. The actual Enumeration shall be made within three Years after the first Meeting of the Congress of the United States, and within every subsequent Term of ten Years, in such Manner as they shall by Law direct. The Number of Representatives shall not exceed one for every thirty Thousand, but each State shall have at Least one Representative; and until such enumeration shall be made, the State of New Hampshire shall be entitled to chuse three, Massachusetts eight, Rhode Island and Providence Plantations one, Connecticut five, New York six, New Jersey four, Pennsylvania eight, Delaware one, Maryland six, Virginia ten, North Carolina five, South Carolina five, and Georgia three.

When vacancies happen in the Representation from any State, the Executive Authority thereof shall issue Writs of Election to fill such Vacancies.

The House of Representatives shall chuse their Speaker and other Officers; and shall have the sole Power of Impeachment.

Section. 3. The Senate of the United States shall be composed of two Senators from each State, chosen by the Legislature thereof, for six Years; and each Senator shall have one Vote.

Immediately after they shall be assembled in Consequence of the first Election, they shall be divided as equally as may be into three Classes. The Seats of the Senators of the first Class shall be vacated at the Expiration of the second Year, of the second Class at the Expiration of the fourth Year, and of the third Class at the Expiration of the sixth Year, so that one third may be chosen every second Year; and if Vacancies happen by Resignation, or otherwise, during the Recess of the Legislature of any State, the Executive thereof may make temporary Appointments until the next Meeting of the Legislature, which shall then fill such Vacancies.

No Person shall be a Senator who shall not have attained to the Age of thirty Years, and been nine Years a Citizen of the United States, and who shall not, when elected, be an Inhabitant of that State for which he shall be chosen.

The Vice President of the United States shall be President of the Senate, but shall have no Vote, unless they be equally divided.

The Senate shall chuse their other Officers, and also a President pro tempore, in the Absence of the Vice President, or when he shall exercise the Office of President of the United States.

The Senate shall have the sole Power to try all Impeachments. When sitting for that Purpose, they shall be on Oath or Affirmation. When the President of the United States is tried, the Chief Justice shall preside: And no Person shall be convicted without the Concurrence of two thirds of the Members present.

Judgment in Cases of Impeachment shall not extend further than to removal from Office, and disqualification to hold and enjoy any Office of honor, Trust or Profit under the United States: but the Party convicted shall nevertheless be liable and subject to Indictment, Trial, Judgment and Punishment, according to Law.

Section. 4. The Times, Places and Manner of holding Elections for Senators and Representatives, shall be prescribed in each State by the Legislature thereof; but the Congress may at any time by Law make or alter such Regulations, except as to the Places of chusing Senators.

The Congress shall assemble at least once in every Year, and such Meeting shall be on the first Monday in December, unless they shall by Law appoint a different Day.

Section. 5. Each House shall be the Judge of the Elections, Returns and Qualifications of its own Members, and a Majority of each shall constitute a Quorum to do Business; but a smaller Number may adjourn from day to day, and may be authorized to compel the Attendance of absent Members, in such Manner, and under such Penalties as each House may provide.

Each House may determine the Rules of its Proceedings, punish its Members for disorderly Behaviour, and, with the Concurrence of two thirds, expel a Member.

Each House shall keep a Journal of its Proceedings, and from time to time publish the same, excepting such Parts as may in their Judgment require Secrecy; and the Yeas and Nays of the Members of either House on any question shall, at the Desire of one fifth of those Present, be entered on the Journal.

Neither House, during the Session of Congress, shall, without the Consent of the other, adjourn for more than three days, nor to any other Place than that in which the two Houses shall be sitting.

Section. 6. The Senators and Representatives shall receive a Compensation for their Services, to be ascertained by Law, and paid out of the Treasury of the United States. They shall in all Cases, except Treason, Felony and Breach of the Peace, be privileged from Arrest during their Attendance at the Session of their respective Houses, and in going to and returning from the same; and for any Speech or Debate in either House, they shall not be questioned in any other Place.

No Senator or Representative shall, during the Time for which he was elected, be appointed to any civil Office under the Authority of the United States, which shall have been created, or the Emoluments whereof shall have been encreased during such time; and no Person holding any Office under the United States, shall be a Member of either House during his Continuance in Office.

Section. 7. All Bills for raising Revenue shall originate in the House of Representatives; but the Senate may propose or concur with Amendments as on other Bills.

Every Bill which shall have passed the House of Representatives and the Senate, shall, before it become a Law, be presented to the President of the

Page one of the final draft of the Constitution. (The Granger Collection)

President must consult with senators to secure their advice and consent to treaties or to appointments to high federal office has been answered in various ways by different executive and legislative officials.

Although formal change in the Constitution is difficult and so has been accomplished relatively infrequently, amendment is possible and it is one important means of providing for a flexible governmental system. Lest this be thought too obvious even to mention, it should be recalled that the British North America Act, which serves as the Constitution of Canada, has no provision for amendment, so that, to change their own Constitution, Canadians must petition the Parliament in England.

In the United States to become a part of the Constitution, an amendment must first be proposed and then ratified. An amendment may be proposed by a two-thirds vote of both houses of Congress or by a national convention called by Congress in response to an application by two thirds of the states. In practice, only Congress has ever proposed an amendment. Although various state legislatures have from time to time petitioned Congress to call a convention, such a petition has not yet come from two thirds of the states with respect to the same issue at the same time. To be ratified, an amendment must be approved by three quarters of the states. The Constitution provides that one of two methods may be used: either the state legislatures or special conventions chosen for this purpose may vote on an amendment.

In proposing an amendment, Congress specifies which method shall be used and has, in all but one instance, that involving the Twenty-first Amendment repealing prohibition, required state legislatures to make the choice.

There are many technical questions concerning the amending procedure that the Constitution does not answer. May the President veto a proposed amendment? How long a time may be allowed to secure ratification by three fourths of the states? May a state, having ratified or rejected an amendment, change its mind? The Supreme Court has answered some of these questions, although in its latest decision the Court has indicated that Congress is the proper agency to give the final answer to such questions.[12] Actually, all these questions have been answered by one means or another. The President does not pass upon an amendment, having authority neither to approve nor to veto it. Congress may fix a time limit within which the necessary number of states must ratify an amendment if it is to go into effect. If Congress fails to do so, the Supreme Court has said that Congress itself must determine whether an amendment ratified over a long period of years should be put into effect. A state that has approved an amendment may not reconsider its action, but a rejection is not regarded as final action and may be reversed.

The Bill of Rights, or the first ten amendments, may be regarded as part of the original Constitution. If so regarded, the Constitution has been formally amended only fifteen times between 1791 and 1967. Moreover, two of the fifteen amendments cancel each other. The Eighteenth Amendment gave Congress the

---

[12] See *Hawke v. Smith,* 253 U.S. 221 (1920); *Dillon v. Gloss,* 256 U.S. 368 (1921); and, in particular, *Coleman v. Miller,* 307 U.S. 433 (1939).

power to prohibit the sale of liquor and the Twenty-first Amendment withdrew that power.

Of the other thirteen amendments, three make relatively minor changes in the mechanics of government: The Twelfth corrected the manner in which members of the electoral college cast votes for a President and a Vice President; the Twentieth changed the calendar of the government so as to eliminate lame-duck sessions of Congress and provide for inauguration of the President in January rather than in March; and the Twenty-third gave residents of the District of Columbia the right to vote in presidential elections. One amendment, the Eleventh, withdrew part of the jurisdiction originally granted the federal courts in Article III by forbidding them to hear cases in which a state is sued by a citizen of another state. Three amendments, the Thirteenth, Fourteenth, and Fifteenth, defined United States citizenship and forbade the states to encroach upon certain civil rights; and the Fifteenth outlawed all governmental efforts to interfere with the right to vote, if they were based upon race, color, or previous condition of servitude. The Sixteenth Amendment granted Congress authority to levy income taxes without apportioning them among the states on the basis of population. The Seventeenth Amendment provided for popular election of United States senators. Under the original provision, they were chosen by the state legislatures and only members of the House were directly elected. The Nineteenth Amendment conferred suffrage on women. The Twenty-second Amendment prohibited Presidents from serving for three or more full terms. The Twenty-fourth Amendment forbade both the United States and the states to deny the right to vote in federal elections because of failure to pay any poll tax or other tax. The Twenty-fifth Amendment makes detailed provisions for what is to happen if a President becomes disabled.

A number of these amendments have been far reaching in their consequences; yet it is very clear that the amendments added since 1791 hardly even begin to reveal the tremendous changes that have taken place in the American system of government in the century and three quarters since that date.

STRUGGLES FOR POLITICAL SUPREMACY

By establishing a government based upon shared powers, the framers achieved what Alpheus T. Mason has called "institutionalized tension,"[13] that is, Presidents, congressmen, and even Supreme Court justices compete to attain a dominant political position. Shortly before his death, Alexander Hamilton wrote that the resulting "vibrations of power are the genius of our government."[14] Tensions and vibrations connote a dynamic rather than a static system, precisely the kinds of terms one would expect to be descriptive of a flexible constitutional arrangement.

At times, in the nineteenth century, there seemed to be a real likelihood that power would be so concentrated in Congress that the United States would come

---

[13] Alpheus T. Mason, *The Supreme Court: Palladium of Freedom* (Ann Arbor, Mich.: University of Michigan Press, 1962), p. 8.

[14] Quoted in Mason, *The Supreme Court,* p. 8.

close to having a parliamentary system of government. At the beginning of that century two developments threatened to make the President a mere servant of the legislature. One was the congressional caucus, by which congressmen selected nominees for the Presidency. The other was the power of the House of Representatives to elect a President in case of a tie vote or in the absence of a majority vote in the electoral college. This power was exercised in 1800 and again in 1824.

By the age of Jackson, however, the congressional caucus had given way to the national nominating convention in which congressmen had to share power with other party leaders, and 1824 proved to be the last election in which the House made the final selection of a President. Moreover, Andrew Jackson gave new vigor to the office of the President, leaving a series of precedents for his successors to utilize if and when they wished to exercise national leadership. On the other hand, the impeachment and near conviction of President Johnson in 1868 once again threatened to subordinate the executive to the legislature. Had Johnson been convicted, Congress might thereafter have used the threat of impeachment to curb initiative and independence in the judicial as well as the executive branch of government.

At other times in American history, there have been indications that power and prestige were being centered in the Presidency. In the last century, Jefferson, Jackson, and Lincoln all challenged Congress on various issues and, in winning their way, asserted the superiority of executive over legislature. In the present century, Wilson and the two Roosevelts brought the Presidency to a new high level. In fact, the movement toward executive supremacy, if not domination, is perhaps proving to be the more persistent tendency. The growing number and complexity of the problems, both domestic and foreign, that all nations face and the speed with which many of these problems must be met have tended to compel legislatures to confine lawmaking to broad declarations of policy and to confer wide discretionary power on executive officers.

The Supreme Court has at many points in history enjoyed great prestige and has wielded much influence in the conduct of public affairs in America.[15] As early as 1803, the justices asserted authority to invalidate acts of Congress, and during the Marshall period the Court rendered decisions that were profoundly important in shaping the fundamental character of American government as well as in laying down specific public policies. In particular, Marshall and his Court helped to establish for all time the principle that the national government possesses broad and flexible authority under the Constitution, authority sufficient to enable it to safeguard and promote the interests and needs of a developing nation in a changing world.

On the eve of the Civil War, when the executive and legislative branches were trying to solve the slavery problem, the Court attempted, in the ill-fated *Dred Scott* decision,[16] to prescribe its own solution. Again, at the end of the last

---

[15] See, for example, Charles G. Haines, *The American Doctrine of Judicial Supremacy,* 2d ed. (Berkeley, Calif.: University of California Press, 1932); and Robert G. McCloskey, *The American Supreme Court* (Chicago: University of Chicago Press, 1960).

[16] *Dred Scott v. Sandford,* 19 Howard 393 (1857).

century, the Court in a long series of decisions challenged the policies of the executive and legislative branches. In the present century, the Court's frontal attack upon New Deal policies in the mid-1930s provided a notable example of the justices' power to protect at least temporarily the status quo in the face of executive and legislative efforts at reform. In the 1950s and 1960s the Court displayed its power to bring about social change by reading into the Constitution: (1) prohibitions against all forms of state action establishing distinctions or discrimination based on race; (2) requirements that the U.S. House of Representatives and both houses of every state legislature be elected in substantial accordance with the principle of "one man, one vote"; and (3) extensions of the restrictions of the Bill of Rights to the states as well as the national government. Perhaps more than ever before in its history, the Supreme Court in recent years has been making fundamental public policy. Cases concerning segregation in the schools, rulings about "one man, one vote," and sharp limitations of police efforts to obtain confessions from suspected criminals have produced bitter criticism of the Court, some of it taking the form of efforts to amend the Constitution so as to undo the Court's work. The fact that most of these efforts have so far failed only emphasizes the extent to which the Court has shaped public policy in these areas.

CONTRACTING AND EXPANDING
GOVERNMENTAL ACTIVITY

Vibrations of power within the political system have also had significant effects on the general scope of governmental activity. One of the most protracted conflicts in American history between governmental power and constitutional restraint of that power involved the police power and due process of law. The police power enables government to foster and protect the health, safety, morals, and welfare of its citizens. Although the police power is usually exercised by state governments, the national government possesses a similar authority. The clauses concerning due process of law in the Fifth and Fourteenth amendments forbid all government officials—national, state, and local alike—to deprive persons of their life, liberty, or property "without due process of law."

In the face of social problems created by rapid urbanization and industrialization in the decades following the Civil War, state governments began passing numerous police-power measures, establishing safety and health standards, providing special protection to women and children, fixing minimum-wage and maximum-hour standards for labor, and generally extending government regulation of private enterprise as a means of promoting the public welfare. At about the turn of the century, the national government also undertook a somewhat similar but less extensive program of social legislation, which, inevitably, curbed the freedom of certain persons and business organizations at the same time that it promoted the interests of others. Accordingly, the contention was soon heard from those restricted that these interferences amounted to deprivations of liberty and property without due process of law and were thus contrary to the Constitution. The Supreme Court at first rejected this argument, but in the 1890s it began using the due process clauses to invalidate both federal and state statutes. For forty years conservative judges interpreted the Constitution so as to curb much federal police-power activity.[17] In 1936, in one of the last decisions of this type, the Court, by a five to four vote, invalidated a statute of the state of New York prescribing minimum wages for women and children.[18] In the very next year, however, in a decision upholding a minimum-wage law of the state of Washington, the Supreme Court not only reversed its decision of the year before but also generally repudiated the doctrine that the due process clauses of the Constitution forbade legislation to promote social welfare.[19]

As this long period in American constitutional development was drawing to a close, another began which has not yet run its course. In this new period the Court has made extensive use of the due process clause of the Fourteenth Amendment to invalidate a wide variety of state laws on the ground that they interfere with the civil rights of individual citizens. Many of these cases are examined in the later chapters of this book dealing with civil rights, but it may be observed here that most of these invalidated statutes, unlike social welfare laws, were designed to protect the social and/or political status quo.

PROTECTING THE CONSTITUTION

The Constitution, in one of its great silences, fails to say who has primary responsibility to protect it. Often private citizens, elected and appointed officials, and judges themselves think of the judiciary as its chief guardian. To the extent that legislative and executive officers are content to dodge constitutional issues and pass them on to judges, this opinion is accurate; but judges have no legitimate monopoly of the task. All public officials, legislative, executive, and judicial, take an oath to support and defend the Constitution, and many presidential and congressional acts, especially those concerned with foreign affairs, can never be challenged in the courts. The President and members of Congress must frequently interpret their own powers and duties under the Constitution as Jefferson did when he agreed to the Louisiana Purchase, as Lincoln did when he determined to use force to save the Union, and as Franklin Roosevelt, Harry Truman, and Lyndon Johnson did when they decided to use American military power without a formal declaration of war.

Selected Bibliography

Corwin, Edward S., *The Constitution and What It Means Today,* 12th rev. ed. (New York: Atheneum Publishers, 1964; paperback). An extremely useful and authoritative analysis of the Constitution section by section and clause by clause, done briefly and concisely.

---

[17] See, for example, *Chicago, Milwaukee and St. Paul Ry. v. Minnesota,* 134 U.S. 418 (1890); *Lochner v. New York,* 198 U.S. 45 (1905); *Adair v. United States,* 208 U.S. 161 (1908); *Adkins v. Children's Hospital,* 261 U.S. 525 (1923); *Tyson v. Banton,* 273 U.S. 418 (1927); and *Railroad Retirement Board v. Alton R. Co.,* 295 U.S. 330 (1936).

[18] *Morehead v. Tipaldo,* 298 U.S. 587 (1936).

[19] *West Coast Hotel v. Parrish,* 300 U.S. 379 (1937).

Friedrich, Carl J., *Constitutional Government and Democracy* (Boston: Ginn & Company, 1946). A systematic analysis of present-day democratic constitutional institutions.

Grodzins, Morton, *The American System* (Daniel J. Elazar, ed.) (Chicago: Rand McNally & Company, 1966). A fresh look at the way federalism influences and is influenced by politics in the United States.

Holcombe, Arthur N., *Our More Perfect Union* (Cambridge, Mass.: Harvard University Press, 1950). An account and defense of the constitutional system created by the Founding Fathers.

Mitchell, William C., *The American Polity* (New York: The Free Press, 1962). An effort to analyze American politics as an integral part of a social system.

Small, Norman J., ed., *The Constitution of the United States of America: Analysis and Interpretation,* revised and annotated (Washington, D.C.: United States Congress, Sen. Doc. No. 39, 88th Congr., 1st sess., 1964). The most complete and authoritative treatment of the interpretation of the federal Constitution; the 1964 edition relies heavily on an earlier edition by Edward S. Corwin.

4

The nation
and the states

In the long run of history there has been a recurring trend toward larger states and stronger governments. In some countries, federalism has seemed to provide a means of avoiding an extreme concentration of power in a central government. For example, two or more lands that have previously enjoyed some political independence but now want to join forces have often united in a federal state combining central government with independent local governments. But political history has also proved that a federal compromise is very difficult to arrange. Few experiments with federalism have ever enjoyed any large measure of success or permanency. Referring to the task that faced the Founding Fathers, one American historian has observed[1]:

That was a question that might well have confused the clearest brain of the time; no more delicate and intricate problem in practical politics and statecraft ever confronted a thinking people. If a system could be found which did not involve the destruction of the states, which

---

[1]A. C. McLaughlin, *The Confederation and the Constitution* (New York: Harper & Row, Publishers, 1905), pp. 176–177.

preserved an equitable distribution of authority between the centre and the parts, the great problem of imperial organization had found a solution. If this could be done, America would make one of the greatest contributions ever made by a nation to the theory and practice of government.

GROWTH OF THE AMERICAN FEDERATION

The Founding Fathers were aware of their country's vast potential for further growth, and they did not want to cut off the possibility of physical expansion. Thus, in Article IV of the Constitution they granted Congress virtually unrestricted power to admit new states to the Union. Vermont and Kentucky were admitted as the fourteenth and fifteenth states in 1791 and 1792. Alaska and Hawaii became the forty-ninth and fiftieth states in 1958 and 1959. Of the thirty-seven states admitted to the Union, two (Vermont and Texas) made the transition from the status of independent nation, one (California) was acquired from Mexico at the end of the Mexican War and passed directly to statehood, three (Kentucky, Maine, and West Virginia) were separated from existing states, and the remaining thirty-one first served periods of apprenticeship as territories.

Admitting New States

Congress is under no legal obligation to admit a new state in any given situation. It can be arbitrary in refusing statehood to a territory, or it can make the process as easy as it wishes. Nonetheless, congressional practice over the years has set minimum requirements for statehood. These were explained in 1953 in a report of the Senate Interior and Insular Affairs Committee in these terms:

1. The inhabitants of the proposed new state are imbued with and are sympathetic toward the principles of democracy as exemplified in the American form of government.
2. A majority of the electorate wish statehood.
3. The proposed new state has sufficient population and resources to support state government and . . . carry its share of the cost of Federal Government.

Few territories, however, ever acquired statehood merely by meeting these conditions. This is well illustrated by the case of the last two states to enter the Union.

Many arguments long weighed against the admission of Alaska and Hawaii in spite of their having met the traditional requirements. Some of these were explicit and serious objections; others were implicit and partisan. In the first category was the argument that since both territories were noncontiguous to the existing states, a dangerous precedent would be established in granting them statehood and thereby breaking the geographical solidarity of the American Union. In the second category was the objection of Republicans to Alaskan statehood based on the fear that Alaska would send Democratic members to Congress, and the objection of Democrats to Hawaii for the opposite reason. Even less explicit was the objection of southern Democrats, who opposed the admission of both ter-

This July 4th ceremony in Honolulu celebrates the first raising of the new 50-star American flag. (UPI)

ritories in the belief that their representatives in Congress would support civil rights bills and other liberal legislative proposals, and the objection of conservative Republicans, who opposed statehood for the two areas because they distrusted further expansion of the American Union as carrying dangerous "internationalist" implications.

In 1958 the "pro" arguments in Alaska's favor prevailed, and both houses of Congress voted by substantial majorities to give it statehood. Whereas in the past, objections to other grants of statehood had been overcome by bringing territories into the Union in pairs, this time the key to action was found in separating the Alaskan and Hawaiian petitions and voting on Alaskan statehood alone. With Alaska's admission, it proved easy to enact a Hawaiian statehood bill one year later.

In 1796, in admitting Tennessee to the Union, Congress set a precedent by declaring the new state to be "one of the United States of America," "on an equal footing with the original states in all respects whatsoever." Did this mean that once in the Union a new state could throw off special conditions imposed upon it by Congress at the time of admission? New states have generally assumed they had such power, and special conditions have frequently been repudiated. In 1911, in the case of *Coyle v. Smith,* the Supreme Court ruled that Oklahoma, which had entered the Union in 1907, might change its capital from Guthrie to Oklahoma City, in spite of the fact that the congressional enabling act specifically forbade such a move before 1913. The Court stated[2]:

> The power of Congress is to admit "new states into *this* Union." "This Union" was and is a union of states, equal in power, dignity, and authority, each competent to exert that residuum of sovereignty, not delegated to the United States by the Constitution itself.

For three quarters of a century following the adoption of the Constitution there was much argument as to whether states might withdraw from the Union. This issue was settled on the battlefields of the Civil War, and in 1869 the Supreme Court gave legal approval to what had been already determined by force of arms when it declared that the "Constitution, in all of its provisions, looks to an indestructible union, composed of indestructible states."[3]

INTERGOVERNMENTAL RELATIONS

The Place of Local Governmental Units

The Constitution makes no specific reference to local units of government, such as counties, cities, school districts, and townships. From the constitutional point of view, these units are all subdivisions of the states, created by the states and responsible to them. As such, they are subject to all of the same restrictions and prohibitions that the Constitution places on the states. Their purposes, powers, and status, however, are determined by the states, except, of course, that a state cannot grant authority or functions to a subdivision that it does not itself possess.

What the Constitution establishes as a two-way governmental relationship between the nation and the states has today in many ways become a three-way federal plan, in which nation, states, and local units interact in exceedingly varied and complex ways. Under the so-called home rule provisions of certain state constitutions, cities, in particular, have gained significant measures of independence that enable them, among other things, to deal directly with the national government. On the other hand, no American city has ever been wholly free from state control. This has been strikingly illustrated in recent years by the case of the nation's largest city. New York City has had to turn continuously to its parent state for permission to attack its problems and also for financial support in meeting the staggering costs of doing so.

For the most part, no further reference will be made in this chapter to state-local or federal-local unit relations. Wherever the word "state" is used, it will be assumed that the reference encompasses the state's subdivisions. Some attention will be given to cities at the very end of this chapter and in the next chapter.

---

[2] 221 U.S. 559 (1911).

[3] *Texas v. White,* 7 Wallace 700 (1869).

Federal-State Relations

The Constitution prescribes certain intergovernmental obligations, one set concerning federal-state relations, one set, state-state relations. The federal government is directed: (1) to guarantee the states a republican form of government; (2) to protect the states against invasion and, upon application of the legislature or executive of a state, against domestic violence; (3) to refrain from changing the boundaries of a state without its consent; and (4) to maintain equality of state representation in the Senate. Upon the states, in turn, is placed the duty of conducting elections for federal offices.

The clause of Article IV of the Constitution providing that "the United States shall guarantee to every state in this Union a republican form of government" limits the states with respect to their political systems in the sense that they must not establish any unrepublican governmental machinery. The Supreme Court has generally refused to decide any cases brought to secure enforcement of this clause, taking the position that the enforcement of the guarantee is the function of the "political" branches of the national government.[4] Instances of congressional or presidential intervention have been so few in number that no body of precedent exists to define the line between a state government that is republican in form and one that is not.

The second federal obligation has been the subject of much controversy. In general, the President, who has been authorized by Congress to intervene federally in a state whenever a need arises, has waited for a request from state authorities before he has acted. But upon occasion, the President has gone ahead without such a request and has defended his action by asserting that the enforcement of federal laws required the presence of federal troops within a state. For example, against the wishes of Governor John P. Altgeld of Illinois, President Grover Cleveland sent an army regiment to Chicago in 1894 during a railroad strike, claiming that this was necessary in order to keep the mails moving and to assure free movement of interstate commerce.[5]

Presidents Eisenhower, Kennedy, and Johnson all used federal force, against the wishes of officials of the states in question, to guarantee federally secured civil rights. For example, in 1962 President Kennedy ordered federal marshals and troops to go to Oxford, Mississippi, to ensure that federal court orders directing the University of Mississippi to enroll a Negro, James F. Meredith, as a student would be carried out and that he would be safe on the university campus. These court orders had been flouted by the governor of Mississippi, Ross R. Barnett, and university officials.

The only real controversy that has ever taken shape under the third obligation occurred in 1862 in the instance of the admission of West Virginia into the

---

[4] See, for example, *Luther v. Borden,* 7 Howard 1 (1849) and *Pacific Telephone Co. v. Oregon,* 223 U.S. 118 (1912).

[5] See the decision of the Supreme Court in *In re Debs,* 158 U.S. 564 (1895), a case that grew out of this same episode.

This photograph was taken in Montgomery, Alabama on May 24, 1963 during a freedom ride. Outside the bus is the National Guard called up by the President over the protests of state and local officials. (Davidson from Magnum)

Union. This event occurred during the Civil War and resulted from the unwillingness of the loyal western counties of Virginia to follow that state into the Confederacy. A pretense of obeying the requirement of the Constitution was made by obtaining from an allegedly Unionist or "restored" government of Virginia permission for a change in the state's boundaries. But in fact Virginia quite clearly did not give its consent.[6]

No issues have ever arisen under the fourth obligation.

State-State Relations

In their relations with each other, the states are directed by the Constitution (1) to give full faith and credit to each other's official acts; (2) to extend the same privileges and immunities to citizens from other states that they extend to their own citizens; and (3) to deliver up fugitives from justice at the demand of the executive authority of the states in which the crimes occurred. The first of these has had many applications and has been much interpreted by the courts. For example, the clause is held to require each state to give effect to private contracts made under the laws of other states. Thus, a contract for the sale of land made in Ohio can be enforced in the courts of Texas. Similarly, marriages performed or granted under the laws of one state

---

[6] In 1820, with the consent of the Massachusetts legislature, Maine was detached from Massachusetts and admitted to the Union, as part of the Missouri Compromise.

are valid in all other states; divorce, however, raises more complicated problems[7] that may make it possible for a state to refuse to recognize a divorce granted by another state.

The privileges and immunities guarantee means generally that a state must extend to citizens from other states the rights to acquire and hold property, to make contracts, to engage in business, and to sue and be sued, on the same basis as these rights are enjoyed by its own citizens. But a state need not follow the literal meaning of the guarantee in all respects. It may, for example, deny to citizens of other states the "privilege" granted its own citizens to attend its university or to enjoy many other services that it renders. On the other hand, a state cannot deny citizens of other states such a privilege as use of its highways. Usage and common sense have had a good deal to do with drawing the line between privileges that must be granted and those that can be denied altogether or granted on a restricted basis. The same thing is true of the extradition of criminals. Although the obligation is prescribed in the Constitution in binding language, in practice state officials have occasionally refused to surrender fugitives at the request of other states. Federal courts have consistently refused to order state authorities to meet this obligation imposed by the Constitution. From time to time such a refusal by a state governor receives nation-wide publicity, but in the main this obligation is being quietly met all the time.

CENTRALIZATION VERSUS STATES' RIGHTS

American federalism has shown a remarkable capacity to endure. Much of the success can be traced to the flexibility of the American Constitution concerning the boundaries of power between the national government and the state and local governments. The Constitution has permitted experimentation and adjustments in federal-state relations. There have been numerous stresses and strains in all periods, and the relation has been a decidedly dynamic one, but the Union itself has remained unchanged in its basic outline through eighteen decades.

How Political Parties Stand on States' Rights

Advocates of national power and states' rights have shown little adherence to principle for principle's sake. Social and economic considerations have always been important motivating forces in determining the attitudes of people toward centralized or decentralized government. In making up his mind a practicing politician has usually asked himself: For what purpose is national or state power being used at the moment? Who is likely to benefit and who to lose if the balance shifts from state activity toward national activity, or vice versa? How will these shifts affect me?

The vacillating stands that America's political parties have taken on the

---

[7] See the two cases entitled *Williams v. North Carolina,* 317 U.S. 287 (1942) and 325 U.S. 226 (1945), which involved the obligation of North Carolina to recognize a Nevada divorce.

issue of national power versus states' rights reflect such practical considerations. In the first years of the new government, the lines were drawn between the two parties somewhat as follows: On the one side, Federalists supported the new Constitution and favored a strong central government. On the other, Antifederalists accepted the Constitution, but worked for a system in which state power would be dominant. The triumph of the Antifederalists in the election of 1800 drove the Federalists from power permanently and enhanced the position and power of the states in the Union. But it by no means resulted in a drastic reduction in national power. Under such Presidents as Thomas Jefferson and Andrew Jackson, groups that had distrusted and opposed centralized government made vigorous use of the national government to further ends that they supported.

Few statesmen have ever turned exclusively to the Constitution to determine the stand they have taken on states' rights or national power. For example, no man in American history ever worked out a more careful and systematic set of political principles, nor in the end held more firmly to the states' rights position, than did John C. Calhoun. Yet his biographer in the *Encyclopaedia of the Social Sciences* says of him[8]:

Calhoun's political career was closely tied up with the economic interests of his state, South Carolina, and of the entire South; his principal significance in American history lies in the cogency with which he framed syllogisms of political theory which rationalized these interests.

The arguments of the Federalists and Antifederalists were taken up by the Republican and Democratic parties that succeeded them. The Republican party, born to fight for the cause of the Union, usually favored enhancement of national power as a superior means of protecting property, stimulating commerce and business enterprise, and serving conservative interests generally. State power, on the other hand, was often distrusted by the Republicans because of its greater usefulness to local interests having "radical" aims.

In contrast, the Democratic party tended to distrust national power because of the traditional use of this power to serve business interests. It viewed state power much more favorably because the interests the party represented had on the whole much more influence at the state than at the national level.

Whatever its position in principle, each party has tended to deplore the national power when its rival is in office, only to make extensive use of this power when in office itself. The Democratic party was in power nationally during the two great wars of this century. That experience itself was sufficient to compel the party to pursue more highly centralized programs of governmental activity than its rival had ever dreamed of undertaking. But the change of heart was not the result of international developments alone. Under Woodrow Wilson, and later under Franklin Roosevelt, Harry Truman, John Kennedy, and Lyndon Johnson, the Democratic party abandoned its historic battle cry of states' rights and deliberately chose to make vigorous use of national power to put into effect great reform programs in domestic policy. In one of the basic shifts in American politics,

---

[8] William S. Carpenter, "John Caldwell Calhoun," *Encyclopaedia of the Social Sciences,* 3:144.

the states' rights party of the nineteenth century became the agency through which a national "welfare state" was established in the United States.

The Republican party did not view with equanimity these attempts to use national power. Federal legislation providing for social security, public works, full employment, collective bargaining, wage and hour control, reciprocal trade agreements, rural electrification, rehabilitation of tenant farmers, governmental utilization of atomic energy for peacetime purposes, urban rehabilitation, and ultimately aiming at the elimination of poverty itself was regarded by the Republican party as endangering the interests of property and business. Republicans denounced centralization of governmental activity in Washington and argued for a return of political power to state capitals "where it belongs." Under Dwight Eisenhower, the New Deal drive toward centralization was slowed down, but little was done to satisfy the demands of "Old Guard" Republicans for a sharp reduction in federal programs. In 1964, the Republicans nominated a presidential candidate who sincerely and vigorously advocated a drastic curtailment of federal power and programs. He thereupon encountered one of the most decisive electoral defeats in American history, a defeat that was obviously contributed to by many persons who normally voted Republican. That these forces did not abandon their aims, however, was shown by the election of one of them to the governorship of California in 1966, with overtones of presidential aspirations.

SHIFTS TOWARD CENTRALIZATION

The enormous growth in the activities of the national government frequently obscures the expansion that has also taken place at state and local levels. Today, state and local governments are spending more money, employing more people, and engaging in more functions than ever before. They have expanded their activities primarily in such fields as public highway construction and public health. Although all of these activities are to some degree controversial, they have not matched the newer activities of the national government in terms of cost or political interest and conflict. Until recently, state and local governmental expansion has tended to be somewhat more gradual and regular, and therefore somewhat less noticeable.

Ideally, governmental activity in a democracy increases only in response to demands that citizens make. However, demands for governmental action rarely attain majority political support until the need for national action is demonstrated by some great crisis. Accordingly, much of the expansion in national activity has been associated with war, economic depression, social injustices and inequities in certain sections, or revelations of corruption in state and city government or in business. Thus, the reform laws of the Progressive period in American politics (1900–1917) were in large part a moral reaction to disclosures of corrupt party politics and fraudulent business practices. Similarly the New Deal and Fair Deal programs (1933–1952) drew their major support from Americans who had suffered much during the Great Depression of the 1930s. In recent years the need to put civil rights on a firmer basis, economic as well as legal, has led to a more vigorous use of national power.

The industrial development of the country and the growth of cities have also focused demands for governmental aid on the national government. As business activity became more truly national in scope, and all sections of the country were linked by modern modes of transportation, many problems requiring governmental action could no longer be handled satisfactorily at state and local levels but would require federal-city programs.

The growth of government has had significant effects upon the distribution of political power between national and state governments. Despite increases in activities of state and local governments, the national government has grown relatively larger and more powerful. As the balance of political power has shifted, the issue of national power versus states' rights has become more controversial. But the vehemence of public debate has tended to obscure the central point that all agencies of government in a democracy are engaged in providing essential services. Too often, identity of objectives among governmental levels is minimized, and antagonisms and rivalries are emphasized. Most governmental problems can no longer be solved by one level of government acting alone.

The history of federal-state relations indicates that the distribution of power in a federal system of government cannot be permanently fixed. As the first Hoover Commission said, "Emphasis shifts from generation to generation as the American people fashion their government to meet the needs of changing times and changing conditions." [9] In terms of constitutional interpretation, attitudes of political parties, and public response to industrial and social developments, American federalism has been characterized by flexibility and adaptability. In the process of adjusting its federal system, the country has debated the advantages and disadvantages of centralization and decentralization and has explored a number of devices to bring the national government and the states into closer cooperation and to serve as alternatives to a continuous expansion of national power.

THE CASE FOR CENTRALIZATION

One of the principal advantages of centralized government is its capacity to deal effectively with nation-wide problems, particularly in the face of emergency conditions. State governments can deal with serious national economic, military, and social problems only in piecemeal fashion. A central government can treat problems comprehensively and utilize its planning facilities more effectively and on a wider scale. For example, in a period of widespread unemployment, a central government can analyze the causes and centers of unemployment, without regard to the political boundaries of the states. It can plan national policies with a view toward maintaining a minimum standard of welfare deemed basic for decent living and can attempt to eliminate gross differ-

---

[9] Commission on Organization of the Executive Branch of the Government, *Overseas Administration, Federal-State Relations, Federal Research* (Washington, D.C.: Government Printing Office, 1949), p. 25. During the Truman Administration a Commission on Organization of the Executive Branch of Government was created by act of Congress to conduct broad studies of governmental organization and activity. This and a successor agency created in 1953 were chaired by Herbert Hoover, and were known as the first and second Hoover Commissions. Frequent references are made hereafter to the findings and recommendations of these two agencies.

Text of Summary of 18-Month Study Made by A Special Presidential Commission

SPECIAL TO THE NEW YORK TIMES

WASHINGTON, Feb. 18— Following is the text of the summary of the report on crime by the President's Commission on Law Enforcement and Administration of Justice:

In the process of developing the findings and recommendations of the report the commission called three national conferences, conducted five national surveys, held hundreds of meetings, and interviewed tens of thousands of persons.

The report makes more than 200 specific recommendations—concrete steps the commission believes can lead to a safer and more just society. These recommendations call for a greatly increased effort on the part of the Federal Government, the states, the counties, the cities, civic organizations, religious institutions, business groups, and individual citizens.

They call for basic changes in the operations of police, schools, prosecutors, employment agencies, defenders, social workers, prisons, housing authorities, and probation and parole officers.

But the recommendations are more than just a list of new procedures, new tactics, and new techniques. They are a call for revolution in the way America thinks about crime.

Many Americans take comfort in the view that crime is the vice of a handful of people. This view is inaccurate. In the United States today, one boy in six is referred to the juvenile court.

An independent survey of 1,700 persons found that 91 per cent of the sample admitted they had committed acts for which they might have received jail or prison sentences.

Many Americans also think of crime as a very narrow range of behavior. It is not. An enormous variety of acts make up the "crime problem."

Many Americans think controlling crime is solely the task of the police, the courts, and correction agencies. In fact, as the commission's report makes clear, crime cannot be controlled without the interest and participation of schools, business, social agencies, private groups, and individual citizens.

What, then, is America's experience with crime and how has this experience shaped the nation's way of living? A new insight into these two questions is furnished by the commission's national survey of criminal victims.

In this survey, the first of its kind conducted on such a scope, 10,000 representative American households were asked about their experiences with crime, whether they reported those experiences to the police, and how those experiences affected their lives.

An important finding of the survey is that for the nation as a whole there is far more crime than ever is reported.

The existence of crime, the talk about crime, the reports of crime, and the fear of crime have eroded the basic quality of life of many Americans.

Young people commit a disproportionate share of crime and the number of young people in our society is growing at a much faster rate than the total population. Although the 15- to 17-year-old age group represents only 5.4 per cent of the population, it accounts for 12.8 per cent of all arrests. Fifteen- and 16-year-olds have the highest arrest rate in the United States. The problem in the years ahead is dramatically foretold by the fact that 23 per cent of the population is 10 or under.

Despite the seriousness of the problem today and the increasing challenge in the years ahead, the central conclusion of the commission is that a significant reduction in crime is possible if the following objectives are vigorously pursued:

First, society must seek to prevent crime before it happens by assuring all Americans a stake in the benefits and responsibilities of American life, by strengthening law enforcement, and by reducing criminal opportunities.

Second, society's aim of reducing crime would be better served if the system of criminal justice developed a far broader range of techniques with which to deal with individual offenders.

Third, the system of criminal justice must eliminate existing injustices if it is to achieve its ideals and win the respect and cooperation of all citizens.

Fourth, the system of criminal justice must attract more people and better people— police, prosecutors, judges, defense attorneys, probation and parole officers, and corrections officials with more knowledge, expertise, initiative, and integrity.

Fifth, there must be much more operational and basic research into the problems of crime and criminal administration, by those both within and without the system of criminal justice.

Sixth, the police, courts, and correctional agencies must be given substantially greater amounts of money if they are to improve their ability to control crime.

Seventh, individual citizens, civic and business organizations, religious institutions, and all levels of government must take responsibility for planning and implementing the changes that must be made in the criminal justice system if crime is to be reduced.

ences among the states with regard to health, welfare, income levels, and economic development. Again, it can insist that there are certain essential standards of individual freedom, civil rights, and racial equality that must be accepted and maintained on a uniform basis throughout the entire nation. Finally, a central government has the further advantage of vastly superior financial resources. If a problem is national in scope, in all likelihood only a central government can raise the money required to eliminate social distress or to finance expensive remedial programs.

Throughout much of American history, malapportionment in state legislatures has given the majority of citizens in many states something less than a majority of votes and has sometimes had the effect of delaying, if not obstructing, adoption of policies and programs demanded by urban sections of the population. It has therefore been argued that majority rule is defeated unless the national government takes action. Beginning in 1962, the Supreme Court ruled in a series of cases that unrepresentative districting of a state legislature violates the equal protection clause of the federal Constitution. In 1964, the Court directed that both houses of a state legislature must be apportioned substantially on a population basis.[10] These rulings have set in motion a corrective policy that may lead to a much more equitable representation of urban and rural interests in state government. If this happens here the argument for centralization presented may lose some of its force.

A final argument for centralization is that state and local governments seldom measure up to the national government in terms of efficient administration. Twenty states lack genuine merit systems for selecting governmental personnel, and only a handful of states pay salaries large enough to attract competent professional employees. Many state and local units still clutter their ballots and befuddle the electorate with long lists of nominees for such positions as judge, secretary of state, attorney general, and treasurer, not to mention many lesser posts, such as coroner and dog catcher. In addition, most states carry on the business of lawmaking without such aids as legislative reference services, bill-drafting services, libraries, and adequate office space and clerical help for legislators. Salaries for legislators are so low in many states that they encourage poor legislation and at times even venality. Given the financial, political, and administrative weaknesses of local units, a citizen who wants government to "do something" turns, more often than not, to the national government for action.

THE CASE FOR DECENTRALIZATION

It is often said that the greatest value of decentralization is protection against dictatorship and regimentation. So long as political power is divided among many states and local units, it is extremely difficult to usurp governmental power and exercise dictatorial control. It is also claimed that decentralization prevents dictatorship by strengthening and encour-

---

[10] See *Baker v. Carr,* 364 U.S. 339 (1960) and the following cases decided on June 16, 1964: *Reynolds v. Sims, WMCA v. Lomenzo, Maryland Committee v. Tawes, Davis v. Mann, Roman v. Sinock,* and *Lucas v. Colorado General Assembly.* These cases are discussed in detail in Chapter 8.

aging local self-reliance. Under this "grass roots" doctrine, local officials are pictured as being closer to and more responsive to the electorate than are national government officials. There have undoubtedly been countless examples in our history of the grass roots doctrine's working out in practice. But it must be recognized that the most serious trends toward one-party government, and, even occasionally, dictatorship, have taken shape in individual states rather than in the nation at large.

Lord Bryce, an eminent British commentator on the American political system in the late nineteenth century, was one of the first to argue for the experimental value of the states. He said:[11]

Federalism enables a people to try experiments in legislation and administration which could not be safely tried in a large centralized country. A comparatively small commonwealth like an American State easily makes and unmakes its laws; mistakes are not serious, for they are soon corrected; other States profit by the experience of a law or a method which has worked well or ill in the State that has tried it.

It is possible to earmark several areas of policy and governmental machinery in which state experimentation has been helpful. Wisconsin's experience with unemployment compensation was of great value to the drafters of the federal Social Security Act in 1935. After the failure of the Prohibition Amendment, many states tried a variety of methods to control the sale of alcoholic beverages, including the establishment of governmental monopolies through state liquor stores. And states have experimented at length with various devices of direct democracy, including the initiative and referendum, the recall of elected officials, and direct primaries to nominate party candidates. But, in the main, the record of the states since Bryce's day has hardly been such as to qualify them as testing grounds for public policies.

An argument may, however, be made that in a federation the most progressive states will both aspire to and manage to achieve higher (and perhaps more expensive) goals than the entire nation can or will. Thus, a rich and populous state like California could at one time choose to establish a complex and exceedingly costly system of higher education; a state like New York, with a varied population in which many racial and religious minorities are represented, can protect civil rights to the fullest possible degree. Of course, the other side of this argument is that the least enterprising and poorest states are likely to have inadequate state universities and weak civil rights laws. In this respect, the choice may lie between a decentralized nation in which state standards range from the very highest to the very lowest and a centralized country seeking reasonably high standards for all of its citizens.

Decentralization permits adaptation of governmental programs to local needs. In view of the great size of the United States and the widely differing problems of different sections, depending upon such factors as climate, rainfall, industrial development, growth of cities and suburbs, and concentration of minority groups, it is argued that national policies applied uniformly throughout the country

---

[11] James Bryce, *The American Commonwealth,* new ed. (New York: Crowell-Collier and Macmillan Company, Inc., 1914), 1:353.

may be inappropriate in some areas and inapplicable in others. Diversity of needs must be matched by policies and programs that are adapted to fit local needs.

Conversely, a decentralized political system may make it possible to localize undesirable policies and practices. Discrimination against minority groups may perhaps be confined to a state or region without necessarily spreading to other states. By localizing prejudice and by insulating harmful political experiments, such as the Huey Long Movement in Louisiana, federalism may make it possible for the nation to tolerate undesirable political practices in a state temporarily.

Decentralization also makes it possible to separate state issues from national political issues. Because of demands now made upon voters, a democratic system that makes the citizen's task more manageable has much to commend it. In a decentralized system, it is possible to vote for one party's candidates for national office without making a commitment to the same party's candidates for state offices. And it is perhaps possible to give more adequate attention to state issues when they are separated from national issues.

Although state and local units have not been as successful as the national government in developing administrative efficiency, the higher administrative capacity of the national government may be offset by the increased difficulty of managing an establishment of several score of departments and agencies and hundreds of thousands of government employees. Despite administrative in- adequacies, the states, some observers believe, do not suffer in comparison with the national government in view of the inefficiency of the latter's huge overhead staff, the difficulties of coordinating so many agencies, and the red tape that inevitably develops in a complex administrative mechanism.

STRIKING A BALANCE

It is difficult to weigh the cases for and against centralization. Some advantages claimed for a system of decentralized government are very appealing, but, in practice, state governments have not always fulfilled their promise as vigorous units of local self-government. Similarly, the national government has at many points in American history failed to measure up to expectations of its people. As time has gone by, however, the exigencies of war and depression have increasingly focused attention on the national govern- ment's superior ability to solve nation-wide problems. The question thus has become how to preserve the vitality and competence of state governments and, at the same time, improve the nation's capacity to deal with national problems. In response to President Eisenhower's request, Congress in 1953 established a Commission on Intergovernmental Relations to conduct an intensive study of national-state-local relations. Its final report, published in 1955, declared that most Americans prefer the existing balance between centralized and local govern- ment. The commission found that the American federal system

is still an asset and not a liability. To be sure, it is not a neat system, and not an easy one to operate. It makes large demands on our sense of responsibility, our patience, our self- restraint. It requires toleration of diversity with respect to taxes, roads, schools, law enforcement, and many other important matters. . . . Nevertheless, the federal principle, along with the principle of checks and balances, remains one of the great institutional embodiments of our traditional distrust of too much concentrated authority in government.[12]

Perhaps the most significant contribution of the commission was its insistence upon renewing the vitality of state governments. "Power will not long rest with any government that cannot or will not make proper use of it. . . . Our system of federal government can be in proper balance, therefore, only when each level is effective and responsible." [13]

CHANGING FEDERALISM

Significant attempts have been made in recent decades to adapt the federal system to the needs of the twentieth century in such a way as to preserve the advantages of both centralization and decentralization. These efforts include federal grants-in-aid to states, federal-state administrative cooperation, and various forms of interstate cooperation. Observers who hold that the states can no longer be effective units of American federalism look hopefully to such alternative forms of decentralized government as regionalism and federal administration of regional projects.

Federal Grants

Increasing use is being made of federal grants to states to make the superior resources of the national government available for financing services administered by state governments. A grant-in-aid is a sum of money derived from a tax levied and collected by a higher level of government for expenditure and administration by a lower level of government in accordance with certain standards or requirements. Although the present system of federal grants to states developed very largely in the present century, its beginnings go back to 1785 when Congress, under the Articles of Confederation, set aside a section of every township in the Northwest Territory for the maintenance of local schools. During the nineteenth century Congress aided the states in a variety of ways, including the distribution of surplus federal funds to states, the allocation of grants of land for schools and colleges, and the development of agricultural experiment stations in connection with state agricultural colleges. Since 1900 the federal grant-in-aid has been used to help finance construction of highways and airports, development of forests, vocational education and rehabilitation, public health and social security programs, and lunches for school children. In 1968 federal aid for elementary education was approximately $3.7 billion; total federal aid to education at all levels ran to about twice that figure. Some federal grants require states to meet only minimal conditions. Others require compliance with detailed administrative standards. Federal grants are almost

---

[12] The Commission on Intergovernmental Relations, *A Report to the President for Transmittal to Congress* (Washington, D.C.: Government Printing Office, 1955), pp. 2–3.
[13] *A Report to the President,* p. 4.

always conditioned on the willingness of the states to match federal contributions in accordance with some prescribed ratio.

There are two basic arguments in favor of federal grants to states. First, money collected by the national government under personal income and corporate income tax programs in prosperous industrial areas can be redistributed in the form of grants to less prosperous states. Thus, high standards of governmental service and performance can be set, and implemented financially, for the country as a whole—rich and poor sections alike.

The second argument favoring federal grants-in-aid is that the program enhances the role of state governments in the federal system and enables the nation to resist what otherwise might be an inexorable trend toward complete centralization. Federal grants can stimulate state activity in such fields as agricultural research, welfare and public health services, vocational education, and construction of secondary roads. Because of the requirement that states meet certain federal

FEDERAL AID TO STATE AND LOCAL GOVERNMENTS
(Budget and Trust Fund Expenditures)

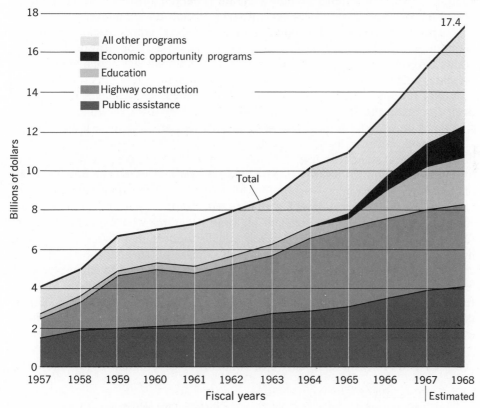

SOURCE: The Budget of the United States Government, 1968 (Washington, D.C.: Government Printing Office, 1967).

A National Teachers Corps intern instructs 3d graders in Macy, Nebraska, which is located in the Omaha Indian Reservation. (Paul Conklin, PIX, Inc.)

administrative and technical standards, grant programs tend to increase the level of competence and professional skill of state officials and employees.

There are also two basic arguments against federal grants to states. Its critics maintain, first, that the haphazard and uncoordinated development of the federal grants covering a large number of services and functions has actually weakened the states financially. As the first Hoover Commission reported: "In order to secure necessary revenues, the national tax base is expanded, which makes it more difficult for State and local governments to secure their own revenue, and hence stimulates pressure from more and more groups for more and more grants." [14]

Second, because many of the basic conditions of administration are laid down by federal standards, it is said that much of the initiative and independence of state governments is destroyed. Moreover, the basic decisions on how to spend limited funds are made in Washington. Unable to resist federal grants, the states end up using their own funds on a matching basis for these purposes. For example, some states have developed excellent highway programs with the help of federal funds, but have then failed to develop equally important programs for which limited or no federal aid was available, such as basic public education or medical care for poor people under sixty-five. Federal grants also tend to encourage state legislatures to earmark state revenues for specific expenditures. Federal highway funds, for example, have probably served to rigidify state budgets by making it difficult to use state revenues for purposes other than highway construction, however essential other programs may be.

In spite of these arguments against federal grants, they have been widely accepted as a "fully matured device of cooperative government." [15] As the Com-

---

[14] Commission on Organization of the Executive Branch of the Government, *Overseas Administration, Federal-State Relations, Federal Research* (Washington, D.C.: Government Printing Office, 1949), pp. 31–32.

[15] *A Report to the President,* p. 120.

mission on Intergovernmental Relations concluded, where federal aid is necessary to achieve an important national objective, federal

grants represent a basically sound technique, despite their piece-meal development and hodge-podge appearance. It is the only technique that is in any sense self-limiting, both as to objectives and amounts of expenditure and as to the extent and nature of National control.[16]

Federal-State Cooperation

Some governmental programs require a very high degree of unity of action. Others, however, may be administered more effectively if identical action is not followed in every state. For example, protection against forest fires can be adapted effectively to the needs of particular regions. But the grading of cotton or wheat would be unfair unless it were uniform in all parts of the nation. The national government and the states are now cooperating in a number of administrative areas. The National Guard, for instance, is composed of the organized militias of the states. The national government finances members' training and provides most of their equipment. During peacetime, they are under the command of the state governors, who commission the officers and supervise their training subject to minimum national standards. In time of military emergency, guard units become an integral part of the national military establishment.

Similarly, a number of national and state agencies find it mutually advantageous to keep each other informed about their activities and problems and to profit by one another's experience. Perhaps the most common form of informal federal-state relations is cooperation in police matters. The Federal Bureau of Investigation assists in training state and local police officers, and its fingerprint files and other facilities are developed with the aid of, and are available to, local police officials. In the same way, the Alcoholic Tax Unit in the Department of the Treasury works cooperatively with state officials charged with enforcement of state liquor control laws.

World War II stimulated other cooperative governmental efforts. The Selective Service System and the wartime price and rationing boards of the Office of Price Administration depended heavily upon the assistance of the states and local communities in furnishing office space, encouraging citizens to volunteer their services, and in providing police protection.

Decentralized Federal Activity

The fact that the national government has its headquarters in Washington tends to obscure the fact that the great bulk of federal activities is administered in local communities by local people. The great majority of the employees of the largest federal agencies, including the Department of Defense, the Veterans Administration, and the Departments of Agriculture, the Treasury, and the Interior are scattered throughout the country

[16] *A Report to the President*, p. 122.

in every state. These employees staff veterans hospitals, maintain dams and flood control projects of the national government, keep the voluminous records of the old-age insurance program in working order, help track down persons suspected of committing federal crimes, and operate military installations. They share with their neighbors a concern for the safety and peaceful development of their neighborhoods, their communities, and their states. They bring to their jobs not the outlook of faraway government officials intent on imposing discipline on a supine citizenry but the same range of values and attitudes that characterize Americans in each state and community throughout the country.

The success of the Tennessee Valley Authority illustrates the way in which the national government can exercise broad authority and responsibility for the development of a region of the country without concentrating additional power in Washington. By creating a separate agency, the valley authority, with a broad grant of power to develop the natural and material resources of a region, to encourage its economic development, and to provide for comprehensive utilization of water resources for flood control, hydroelectric power, irrigation, and recreational purposes, Congress was able to provide initiative and leadership at the top without undermining the capacity of state and local units for self-government.

Interstate Cooperation

Federal-state cooperation and the localization of federal functions have helped avoid the extreme of a highly centralized, overpowering government. In addition, the states have met certain needs for uniform governmental activities and services without any federal assistance or activity. They have accomplished this through interstate compacts, uniform state laws, and interstate consultation.

Interstate compacts are agreements between two or more states that are approved by Congress. These compacts make it possible for states to solve their interstate problems without waiting for the national government to act. Between 1/89 and 1920, only thirty-five compacts between states were completed, all of which were used to settle boundary or jurisdictional disputes between two states. None created a permanent administrative agency. Between 1921 and 1967, however, over 100 compacts were concluded. Interstate compacts today fall into three groups. First is a group of compacts creating technical commissions to handle problems of allocating water supplies from interstate rivers. A second group includes several commissions created to investigate a particular problem and make recommendations to the states involved. A third group establishes continuing interstate enterprises such as parks, bridges, river basins, ports, and educational programs.

Perhaps the best-known example of an interstate agency created by compact is the Port of New York Authority. Established in 1921 by joint action of New York and New Jersey, the Port Authority deals with common problems of transportation affecting New York City and nearby communities in New Jersey. These units of local government were unable, acting individually, to take care of the complex transportation needs of the metropolitan area and to finance construction of adequate bridges, tunnels, highways, airports, and terminals. Among the Port Authority's famous projects are the La Guardia, Kennedy, and Newark airports, the Holland and Lincoln tunnels, and the George Washington Bridge.

Groups of states in different parts of the country have entered into compacts to pool their resources and thereby improve the facilities for higher education available to students who live in the regions in question. For example, thirteen western states, reaching all the way from New Mexico to Alaska, have established the Western Interstate Commission for Higher Education (known as WICHE), with headquarters at Boulder, Colorado.

In spite of these encouraging illustrations, the interstate compacts have not been as extensive as expected. In the 1920s a number of political analysts predicted that the interstate compact would be widely used and would eventually create a new layer of government between the federal government and the states, capable of solving regional problems. Compacts were hailed as the appropriate alternative to more federal centralization. Today it is clear that these predictions are not being borne out, although interstate compacts had proved to be useful in certain limited areas.

On certain issues, the need for identical treatment by individual states has also led to an increasing demand for uniform state laws. The plight of the trucker who carries freight from one state to another illustrates the obstacles that confront a businessman when different states apply different rules to a single business transaction. One state may allow a trucker to carry a load of ten tons, whereas a neighboring state to which the trucker is going allows only eight tons for the same type of truck. Similarly, a businessman may want to transfer property to a buyer from another state, or he may want to sign a contract to close a business deal. Unless he can be certain that all the states involved in the transaction will enforce the contract in their courts with reasonable uniformity, he will be discouraged from entering into the agreement.

Since the organization of the National Conference of Commissioners on Uniform State Laws in 1892, the enactment of identical statutes by the states has been held out as a desirable alternative to federal legislation. As of 1966, the National Conference had prepared seventy-one acts that were recommended for adoption by all states on a uniform basis, eighteen acts recommended only as models because complete uniformity among the states was not deemed essential, and twenty-five acts that had not been widely adopted but that the Conference still chose to recommend for consideration by the states. Among the recommended acts that have been most widely enacted are a criminal extradition act, a gifts to minors act, a partnership act, a narcotic drug act, and a simultaneous death act. Recommended laws enacted by a very few states include an adoption act, a marriage license application act, a paternity act, and a uniform rules of evidence act. Since state courts do not necessarily interpret identical laws in the same way, there is no guarantee that uniformity of administration will prevail.

A considerable amount of machinery has been established to promote interstate cooperation through consultation. The Council of State Governments was created in 1933 to promote interstate cooperation through a program of research and publication. The council maintains headquarters in Chicago and comprises nine affiliated organizations, including the annual governor's conference. It publishes a periodical, *State Government,* as well as a *Book of the States,* the major storehouse of data on state developments. It also lobbies for the states' point of view in Washington and actively promotes uniform state legislation and improved state administrative organization.

Although several experiments in interstate cooperation have succeeded, the total progress made by the states has been disappointing. Either the great issues of the day have thus far not lent themselves to state action on a cooperative basis or the states have not shown sufficient initiative to overcome the obstacles to the adoption of cooperative schemes. The failure of state officials to make wider use of interstate cooperation raises a serious question as to whether the American people really want to avoid a further concentration of power and responsibility in the national government.

Impact of Federal Activity on Cities

As the nation's population has become more and more concentrated in and around large cities, the impact of federal programs and functions on metropolitan areas has been intensified. Apart from general influences of federal action on the nation at large, American cities have been directly affected by the federal government's major programs in urban areas —housing and urban renewal, water resource and pollution control activities, airport construction, military installations and defense industries, civil defense, and highways, not to mention all the phases of the war on poverty. The course of growing federal involvement in urban affairs in the past quarter-century suggests that this role of the federal government will increase in the future. In his 1967 State of the Union Message, for example, President Johnson said he would ask the Congress for full authorization for his "demonstration cities" program. As a recent study of the problem concludes, "metropolitan problems cannot be solved without federal leadership. Inevitably, the needs of two-thirds of the American people will make the case for federal action even stronger in the future." [17]

Housing development illustrates well the trend toward greater federal interest in urban affairs. The initial step was taken by the federal government during World War I to meet emergency needs. The program lapsed after the war but the depression of the thirties dramatized the plight of millions of low-income families. Under the Housing Act of 1937, the federal government provided financial aid to local public agencies established under state law for constructing and operating low-rent public housing projects. An emergency military program during World War II and the needs of returning veterans led to an expansion of the housing program into a network of loans, grants, mortgage insurance and guarantees, and finally urban renewal.

---

[17] Robert H. Connery and Richard H. Leach, *The Federal Government and Metropolitan Areas* (Cambridge, Mass.: Harvard University Press, 1960), p. 8.

Federal-urban ties have been strengthened in part through the expansion of grants-in-aid. For example, under the Federal Airport Act, the states have been by-passed by the allocation of federal grants directly to cities. Grants cover up to 25 percent of the cost of acquiring land for airports and half of all other costs. In the first ten years of the grant program, over 1100 airports were built or improved with federal funds, but the federal government provided little or nothing in the way of planning, guidance, or supervision and has not pressed for metropolitan planning of airport facilities.

Perhaps more important to cities than federal grants has been the impact of federally administered activities. In locating and developing military installations and defense plants; in sponsoring research on problems of air-pollution control; in carrying out programs of irrigation, flood control, electric power development, recreation, and soil conservation; and in attempting to prevent water pollution, a host of federal agencies directly influences the character and quality of life in the cities of the nation.

New Patterns of Partnership

With the emergence of the Great Society programs in the congressional legislation of 1965 and 1966, rapid change has become the dominant characteristic of the American federal system. And the principal direction of this change is toward a great variety of forms of partnership. The federal government is taking shape not only as a partner of state governments and cities in carrying out national programs financed through federal grants-in-aid, but also as a partner of nongovernmental groups, professional associations, and private businesses in administering important phases of public programs. In the war against poverty, for example, federal funds have become available to support programs administered by community action programs, which usually are established outside of regular governmental channels and administered by private boards of directors. In the medicare program, the federal government has in effect contracted with private insurance companies to handle claims of persons over sixty-five and with professional associations to determine the eligibility of hospitals and nursing homes for participation in medicare. Similarly, other federal partnership arrangements have developed in new programs in community development, urban transportation, air and water pollution, and manpower for state and local governments. As President Johnson noted in conference with governors in March 1967, state and local governments should look forward in years ahead to a vast increase in federal grants, perhaps four- or fivefold. If, as seems likely, this prediction is validated, we can count on the development of still more variations on the federal theme in American public life.

Selected Bibliography

Anderson, William, *The Nation and the States: Rivals or Partners?* (Minneapolis, Minn.: University of Minnesota Press, 1955). Probably the best general treatment of the American federal system.

Connery, Robert H., and Richard H. Leach, *The Federal Government and Metropolitan Areas* (Cambridge, Mass.: Harvard University Press, 1960). Historical description of the growing involvement of the federal government in urban affairs since the 1930s, noting new trends and problems.

Goldwin, Robert A., ed., *A Nation of States: Essays on the American Federal System* (Chicago: Rand McNally & Company, 1963). A series of provocative essays on federalism by a group of leading scholars.

Macmahon, Arthur W., ed., *Federalism: Mature and Emergent* (New York: Doubleday & Company, Inc., 1955). A large collection of essays on various aspects of federalism in American politics.

Mason, Alpheus T., *The States Rights Debate: Antifederalism and the Constitution* (Englewood Cliffs, N.J.: Prentice-Hall, Inc., 1964). An analysis of the historical origins of the current and recurrent debate about national power and states rights.

Wheare, K. C., *Federal Government,* 4th ed. (London: Oxford University Press, 1964). A useful general treatment of federalism in a number of political systems.

5

The nation
and the metropolis

At the time of the first census in 1790, about 200,000 people lived in towns and cities of over 2500 and were classified as urban population. Every census since that time has revealed a steady urban trend, although as late as the turn of the present century 60 percent of the population was still classified as rural. Not until 1920 were more than half of the people living in urban communities. Thereafter, economic depression, the mechanization of farms, and wartime prosperity in industry and business speeded the flight of people from the countryside to the town and city. By 1960, seven out of every ten Americans were classified by the Census Bureau as urban dwellers. By 1980, perhaps 90 percent will be living in cities.

Even more important, the 1960 census showed that nearly two thirds of the nation's citizens—or 113 million people—were residing in 212 standard metropolitan statistical areas covering only 7 percent of the nation's land area.[1] Of this

---

[1] The Census Bureau defines a "standard metropolitan statistical area" as a county or two or more adjacent counties that contain at least one city of 50,000. Other counties than the one or ones in which such a city is located are included in such a standard metropolitan area if they are essentially metropolitan in character and socially and economically integrated with the central city. There were 168 metropolitan areas in 1950, 184 in 1958, and 212 in 1960, not including 3 in Puerto Rico.

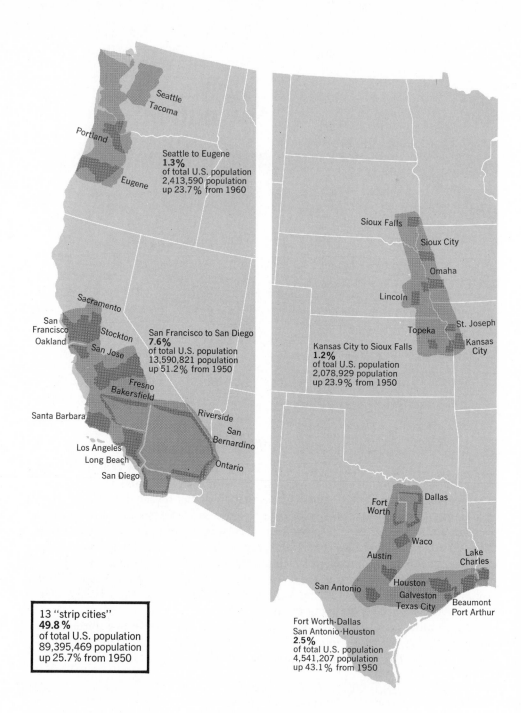

Seattle
Tacoma

Portland

Eugene

Seattle to Eugene
1.3%
of total U.S. population
2,413,590 population
up 23.7% from 1960

Sacramento

San
Francisco
Oakland

Stockton

San Jose

Fresno
Bakersfield

Santa Barbara

Riverside

San
Bernardino

Los Angeles
Long Beach

Ontario

San Diego

San Francisco to San Diego
7.6%
of total U.S. population
13,590,821 population
up 51.2% from 1950

Sioux Falls

Sioux City

Omaha

Lincoln

Topeka

St. Joseph

Kansas
City

Kansas City to Sioux Falls
1.2%
of toal U.S. population
2,078,929 population
up 23.9% from 1950

Fort
Worth

Dallas

Waco

Austin

Lake
Charles

San Antonio

Houston
Galveston
Texas City

Beaumont
Port Arthur

Fort Worth·Dallas
San Antonio·Houston
2.5%
of total U.S. population
4,541,207 population
up 43.1% from 1950

13 "strip cities"
49.8%
of total U.S. population
89,395,469 population
up 25.7% from 1950

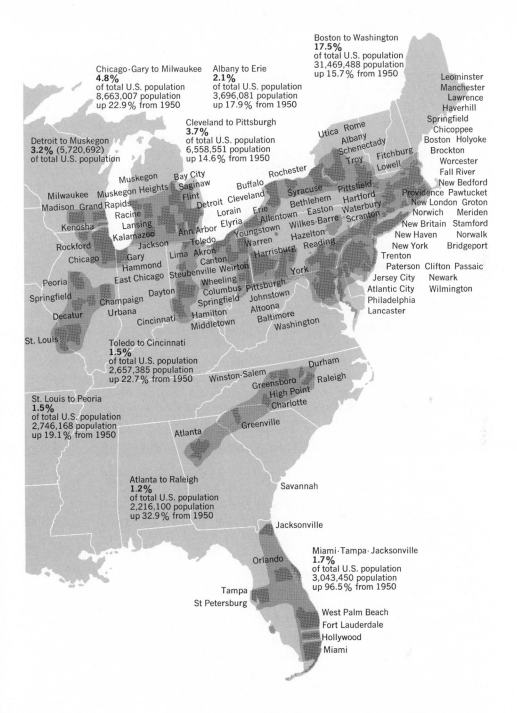

Boston to Washington
17.5%
of total U.S. population
31,469,488 population
up 15.7% from 1950

Chicago·Gary to Milwaukee
4.8%
of total U.S. population
8,663,007 population
up 22.9% from 1950

Albany to Erie
2.1%
of total U.S. population
3,696,081 population
up 17.9% from 1950

Leominster
Manchester
Lawrence
Haverhill
Springfield
Chicoppee
Boston Holyoke
Brockton
Worcester
Fall River
New Bedford

Cleveland to Pittsburgh
3.7%
of total U.S. population
6,558,551 population
up 14.6% from 1950

Detroit to Muskegon
3.2% (5,720,692)
of total U.S. population

Utica Rome
Albany
Schenectady
Troy Fitchburg
Lowell

Muskegon   Bay City
Muskegon Heights Saginaw
Milwaukee   Flint
Madison Grand Rapids
Racine
Kenosha Lansing
Kalamazoo
Rockford Jackson
Chicago   Gary
Hammond
East Chicago
Peoria
Springfield
Decatur   Champaign
Urbana
St. Louis

Buffalo Rochester
Detroit Cleveland
Lorain Erie
Ann Arbor Elyria
Toledo Youngstown
Lima Akron Warren
Canton
Steubenville Weirton
Wheeling
Columbus Pittsburgh
Dayton Springfield Johnstown
Cincinnati Hamilton Altoona
Middletown Baltimore
Washington

Syracuse Pittsfield Hartford
Bethlehem Easton Waterbury
Allentown Wilkes-Barre Scranton
Hazelton
Harrisburg Reading
York

Providence Pawtucket
New London Groton
Norwich Meriden
New Britain Stamford
New Haven Norwalk
New York Bridgeport
Trenton
Paterson Clifton Passaic
Jersey City Newark
Atlantic City Wilmington
Philadelphia
Lancaster

Toledo to Cincinnati
1.5%
of total U.S. population
2,657,385 population
up 22.7% from 1950

St. Louis to Peoria
1.5%
of total U.S. population
2,746,168 population
up 19.1% from 1950

Winston-Salem
Greensboro Durham
High Point Raleigh
Charlotte
Greenville

Atlanta

Atlanta to Raleigh
1.2%
of total U.S. population
2,216,100 population
up 32.9% from 1950

Savannah

Jacksonville

Orlando

Miami·Tampa·Jacksonville
1.7%
of total U.S. population
3,043,450 population
up 96.5% from 1950

Tampa
St Petersburg

West Palm Beach
Fort Lauderdale
Hollywood
Miami

SOURCE: U.S. Bureau of the Census, 1960 census data.

metropolitan population, 51 percent, or 56.6 million persons, were living in central cities, and the remaining 55 million in adjacent suburban areas. Two thirds of the population increase from 1950 to 1960 came in the suburbs.

This urban trend has split into two parts in recent decades. First, there is the original aspect, which shows no signs of slackening: People are still leaving farms and small towns of less than 2500 for life in urban communities. Second, within the typical urban area an "explosion" is taking place in the sense that people are moving away from the central city to the outer edges of the metropolitan community. A few central cities still show gains or are at least holding their own. But everywhere spectacular increases are occurring in the outlying areas. During the decade from 1950 to 1960, the population of St. Louis declined 12.5 percent while its suburbs showed a 52 percent increase. Chicago declined 2 percent while its suburbs were gaining 71.5 percent in population. The population of New Orleans increased by 10 percent, but its suburbs showed a 110 percent gain.

The most dramatic change emerging in the urban distribution of population is the crowding of millions of people into vast urban "belts" that form continuous cities, some hundreds of miles long. The terms "interurbia" and "megalopolis" have been used to identify the new "strip city." The currently largest of these strip cities stretches along the Atlantic seaboard from Boston to Washington, D.C., and curves along the Potomac River to Norfolk, Virginia, while the potentially largest is taking shape in California, sprawling from the San Francisco Bay area to Los Angeles, and some say, eventually, to San Diego. Half of all Americans now live within thirteen strip city areas. Moreover, these islands of dense population account for 60 percent of all factory workers, 62 percent of all manufacturing activity, and 55 percent of the country's retail trade. Population experts predict that by 1975 strip cities will contain 60 percent of the total U.S. population.

PROBLEMS OF THE CENTRAL CITY

The exploding metropolis has created serious problems for both central cities and suburban municipalities. It would be difficult to decide which face the greater difficulties, for both are the victims of a fragmenting process that is weakening the personnel and resources of entire urban communities. Both lack the ability to plan comprehensive solutions to community-wide problems.

The Loss of Leadership Potential

Basic to the plight of the central city is its continuing loss of leadership potential as "better citizens" move to the suburbs. The shortage of leaders may not yet be acute in the political field. Indeed, many great cities, such as New York, Philadelphia, Pittsburgh, Detroit, and San Francisco, have been well governed of late, in some instances better than ever before. The loss of potential leaders in the social field is more serious. In many cities, charitable, cultural, and civic organizations are finding it increasingly difficult to recruit personnel, both at leadership and field-worker levels. Many of the community's natural leaders hasten "homeward" to the suburbs at the close of the day. They may be vaguely aware of the city's problems. But in the main they do not really identify themselves with the city, or, frequently, in any very meaningful way with their suburban municipalities, particularly if they do not have children of school age. One wit has noted that the commuter to the central city is at home a weekend gardener with sex privileges.

The Influx of Inexperienced Citizens

As the central city is losing its leaders, it is simultaneously experiencing an influx of "new citizens" who for the moment lack both the will and the capacity to serve the city's political and social needs. Indeed, the poverty and cultural handicaps of these people frequently magnify the city's political problems at the very time that its ability to meet these problems is declining. In the 1950s, New York City's white population declined almost 7 percent, while its nonwhite population increased nearly 50 percent. In Chicago, the white population dropped 13 percent as the nonwhite population increased 64 percent. Between 1950 and 1960, the twelve largest cities lost over 2 million white residents and gained nearly 2 million Negro residents. The urban problem today is in large measure a Negro problem.

One of the traditional and most civilizing functions of the American city

As new immigrants arrive in the cities, they contribute to the nation's customs and economy. (Miriam Bernstein)

has been the creation of stable, cultivated citizens out of immigrants and other new settlers.

For the American city during the past hundred and fifty years, the raw material was the stream of immigrants pouring in from Britain, Ireland, Germany, Norway, Russia, Italy, and a dozen other lands. The city needed these immigrants to build its streets and offices, to man its factories, service its houses and hotels and restaurants, and do all the dirty and menial jobs that older residents disdained. But the city did more than use its newcomers: it equipped them to take their place as fully participating members of U.S. society. Doing this—bringing people from society's back waters into the mainstream of American life—has always been the principal business, and the principal glory, of the American city.[2]

Much of the crisis now facing the large cities arises from the fact that this function is no longer viable, that the city

isn't dealing successfully with its newcomers. They are still pouring in—not from County Cork, or Bavaria, or Sicily, or Galicia, but from Jackson, Mississippi, and Memphis, Tennessee, and a host of towns and hamlets with names like Sunflower, Rolling Fork, and Dyersburg. The new immigrants are distinguished from the older residents not by religion or national origin, but by color.[3]

Urban-Suburban Conflict

The sharpening contrast between the residents of central city and suburb is resulting in increasing resentment and conflict, particularly as the problems of the metropolitan community grow more acute. In part, this antagonism reflects differences in social attitudes and wants. But it also reflects the resentment of city residents, who feel that the suburbanite is "free-loading," that he has pulled up stakes and moved away from the core of the metropolitan area while he goes on earning his living there and, without any financial contribution, enjoys the benefits of services financed by the city dweller. Mayor Lindsay in New York has tried to remedy this situation by imposing a city income tax on commuters as well as residents. Whatever its causes and attempted remedies, this antagonism poses a formidable obstacle to regional unity and the attainment of consensus at the governmental level. In addition, the suburbanite, in point of fact, is neglecting his own interests. For regardless of the magnitude of the suburban trend, it is improbable that the welfare of a metropolitan area and the personal interests of all its residents will ever be unaffected by what happens to the central city. Almost of necessity it will remain the major source of goods and services, as well as of economic opportunities and cultural advantages.

Inability to Meet Demands for Improved Services

Many a central city in this country is now contained within rigid political boundaries within which it is entirely built up. Thus, its potential for further population growth or economic development is severely restricted. This condition of geographic and economic stability is not,

---

[2] Charles E. Silberman, "The City and the 'Negro,'" *Fortune,* March 1962, pp. 88–89.
[3] Silberman, pp. 88–89.

however, accompanied by a leveling off of municipal services and costs. Instead, the demand for increased expenditures is stronger than ever. Outmoded streets leading to the suburban areas must be replaced with costly freeways. Traffic congestion in the downtown business section necessitates the development of off-street parking areas, often at city expense. School costs mount as teachers' salaries are improved and the number of backward students requiring remedial training increases. Social and economic decline in slum areas is reflected in increased crime and juvenile delinquency, which lead in turn to increased law-enforcement costs.

Under these pressures for broader public services in the central city, the costs of municipal government increase steadily. Meeting them tries the ingenuity and patience of even the most able city officials. At best, the tax resources of the central city are likely to be static; at worst, they may be declining substantially. Housing and urban-renewal programs may result in small increases in the property tax base. A city sales or income tax may supply a new revenue source. But these gains are being offset in many metropolitan areas by the opening up of major shopping areas outside the limits of the central city, with an accompanying decline of business in the heart of the city. Similarly, new industries, both light and heavy, are showing a marked preference for suburban locations along throughways that provide easy access for a motorized labor force. At times, it almost seems as though all of the changes in the suburbs are for the good; all those in the central city for the bad. Citizen and official alike in the central city often despair of the future. The wonder is that they have managed to achieve any progress at all in recent years.

PROBLEMS OF SUBURBAN CITIES

Growing Pains

One of the ironies of the metropolitan problem is that life in the suburbs is not the unrelieved round of sylvan pleasures that the discouraged inhabitant of the central city sometimes fancies. Rapid change is the order of the day in the suburbs. But this does not always bring peace and satisfaction.

The exploding metropolis is steadily encompassing the pastoral, rural areas that used to surround the compactly settled American city. Wooded ravines and hillside meadows are leveled into monotonous plains by bulldozers and earth-movers. Potato farms and truck gardens give way to Levittowns. The resident of the central city seeking the quiet and beauty of the countryside on a Sunday afternoon drives fifteen or twenty miles through a nightmare of traffic lights, hot dog stands, filling stations, and real estate developments before he can vaguely sense that he is reaching rural America. The suburban communities—the Happy Acres, the University Heights, the Spring Lakes, the Glen Hills, the Valley Views, the Rivertons—slip endlessly by as he doggedly tries to escape the haunts of men, cars, homes, and stores. More often than not, belying their picturesque names, these suburban towns seem very much alike—equally new, equally booming,

UPPER-INCOME FLIGHT TO SUBURBS

LOW-INCOME MIGRATION TO CITIES

TAX SQUEEZE

SHORTAGE OF RECREATION AREAS

EXODUS OF HIGH-WAGE INDUSTRIES

CRIME RISE

RISE IN JUVENILE AND AGED GROUPS

POLLUTION

CITIES

TRANSPORTATION JAMS

OVERCROWDED SCHOOLS

HOUSING GHETTOS

©1966 HERBLOCK
THE WASHINGTON POST

"Help!"

Herblock in the *Washington Post.*

equally marked by growing pains and architectural mediocrity. But just below the surface are subtle differences and gradations. The range is great. At one extreme is the town that is wholly the creation of real estate speculators—a square mile into which are tightly packed some ten thousand homes, their boxlike character only slightly concealed by picture windows and offset garages. Streets wind slightly but the layout is essentially the age-old gridiron. Trees have been planted but shade is a generation away; lots are small; schools, churches, and stores are badly located, if indeed any provision has been made for such service facilities at all.

At the other extreme, the century-old country village is preserving its charm and character, even though it is being invaded by the suburban horde, through the rigid enforcement of strict zoning regulations. These, plus high taxes and minimum house costs, are keeping a few towns as havens for the fortunate members of the lower-upper classes or the upper-middle classes who want true bucolic charm combined with a high level of community services, and are able and willing to pay for this somewhat unlikely combination.

Another way of emphasizing the differences between suburbs is to note the varying functions that they serve. Some have been described as dormitory suburbs, places where people whose occupational and even social interests are identified with the central city spend the night. If such a town does not acquire other qualities and values, its residents feel little sense of identification with it, and this inadequacy is soon reflected in the town's political life. Other single-function suburbs are primarily industrial, such as the Chicago suburb of Gary, Indiana, or the Detroit suburb of Dearborn, or recreational, such as Coney Island, near New York City, or Revere Beach, near Boston. As suburban cities grow in size, however, they tend to lose their one-dimensional character and become typical cities with business districts, residential areas, and even industrial sections. Many of the nation's metropolitan areas now contain one or more sizable secondary cities with 50,000 or even 100,000 people. When this point is reached, the range of the suburban city's governmental problems is often virtually as wide and serious as is that of the central city.

Shortcomings of Suburban Governmental Machinery

In the metropolitan areas of the United States there are perhaps 20,000 separate units of local government. This fantastic duplication of political machinery is not entirely without merit. It does provide the inhabitants of many different communities with an almost unlimited opportunity for public service. Moreover, it allows them potentially to tailor the landscape, public services, and taxes to their community needs and desires. The urban trend of the last century pretty effectively destroyed the small-town life that is such a cherished aspect of the American tradition. The creation in our own day of thousands of suburban communities, each possessed of some measure of independence and individuality, however slight, may be a means by which the spirit and value of "community" can be preserved.

Organizing and servicing thousands of governmental units in metropolitan areas, however, is on its face almost a hopeless undertaking. Roughly speaking, this is nothing less than an effort to create and maintain one hundred times as many units of local government as common sense and sound political principles suggest are needed. It means that the organization of local governments in the metropolitan areas of the country ranges from something approaching a single unified area government to an anarchic arrangement that defies logical analysis or correction. Suburban growth is taking place at the point at which the American political system has always been weakest—rural government. Whether village, town, township, or county, this has long been the backwater of American political life, a stagnant area in which what was good enough for our forefathers is deemed good enough for us, an area marked by extreme conservatism, minimal services, and inefficient if not corrupt personnel. Yet overnight some of these units have been called upon to provide a foundation for the political programs of the most enterprising and demanding populations of contemporary America.

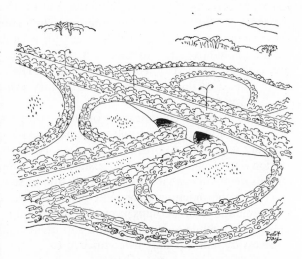

"They're Starting to Move! I Told *You We Should Have Been In the Other Lane!"*

Drawing by Robt. Day; © 1959 the *New Yorker* Magazine, Inc.

Services, Poor; Taxes, High

When the city dweller moves to his suburb, he is quick to demand the full range of public services to which he has been accustomed. Good schools are often his first interest, but he also makes known his desire for good roads, snow removal in the winter, an ample water supply, regular garbage and trash collection, efficient fire and police protection, not to mention a generous program of public utility services and parks and other recreational facilities. Even were the local governmental machinery efficient, the cost of supplying these many services in rapidly developing rural areas would be high. Given inadequate machinery, the effect of the mushrooming program of suburban services on the local tax rate can be catastrophic. Moreover, the tax base in many suburban communities is extremely narrow. Some communities are fortunate in having business and industrial enterprises within their boundaries, but the typical new residential suburb is often wholly dependent on the taxation of homes for its local revenues. Sooner or later, the dilemma in suburbia becomes clear: either services must be held to a modest level or property owners must be prepared to assume a heavy tax burden. Whichever alternative is elected in a particular community, life on the fringes of the metropolis can become something less than idyllic.

Failure To Plan

If the central city in the metropolitan area finds its program of public services hampered by a need to try to correlate its efforts in such areas as highway construction and maintenance, police protection, and water supply with the similar programs of dozens of satellite cities, the latter are even more seriously handicapped by the relative absence of the means for sensible planning and coordination. The central city may well have been at the business of supplying such services for a century or more. It has more than a little know-how and experience; it has a going government machine; it enjoys access to established varied revenue sources. The result is that it can, if necessary, go it alone and do a reasonably satisfactory job of meeting the demands of its citizens for services.

The suburban community is often in a desperate position. Its political boundaries are wholly irrational and often not even known to its residents. It cannot possibly undertake to provide a satisfactory water supply or efficient police protection—to single out just two examples—by itself. Only through joint efforts with its neighbors can it hope to embark upon a sensible program of public services. Yet when the machinery for joint planning and administration of such services is fragmentary, or perhaps even wholly lacking, the community may have no choice, for a while at least, but to try to make a go of things by itself. Where this is necessary, citizens may be compelled to accept a lower level of public services.

Urban sprawl is not solely the result of population growth, human mobility, and technological change. It is also a consequence of inadequate planning. The development of the nation's great metropolitan centers has been almost wholly haphazard, at least so far as conscious human design is concerned. It seems clear that the metropolitan problem would be much less severe today if a few decades ago hardheaded men in the nation's communities had understood the need to "plan" a way out of the growing dilemma. Moreover, it is safe to assume that metropolitan areas will be in even worse shape tomorrow unless the planning of today is better than it was yesterday.

The appearance of water-supply shortages in areas of the East that enjoy an abundant rainfall provides a graphic illustration of the price society pays for its failure to use planning to meet a predictable and measurable urban need. It is true that new forms of industrial production and domestic living have increased the demand for water, but the extent of current water needs was largely predictable, and some greater measure of foresight and action was possible. Many of the urban areas now experiencing severe water shortages would today have water to spare if in the past more rainfall had been captured and stored instead of being permitted to run out to sea. In many instances, some action to contain this water could have been taken as recently as the 1950s with relative ease and at reasonable cost. Today, the problem for many a community is frightening in its fiscal and engineering aspects. For example, as population and industry have expanded rapidly and spread into all areas of the country, the number of stream valleys providing low-cost reservoir sites has steadily been reduced. This need to take immediate and drastic remedial action, rather than the moderate, preventive action that might have sufficed in the past, characterizes the metropolitan problem. And solution by a single community is rarely feasible.

FINDING SOLUTIONS

No other social-political problem now confronting the American people seems more difficult to solve. For many years, experts in metropolitan problems in planning councils, civic associations, and the universities were almost unanimous in believing that the root of most urban deficiencies as well as the principal obstacle to their solution was the decentralized political system of metropolitan areas. Without respect for political boundaries, the problems of the metropolis could not be resolved, it was argued, by the fragmented political system of local governmental units.[4]

In the pages of the local government textbooks, the metropolitan surveys, and the planning and civic bulletins, areawide government was steadfastly promoted as the sure cure for the many ills of the metropolis.

As Danielson notes:

Since their origins during the heyday of the boss and the machine, the forces of good government have sought to overcome the corruption, inefficiency, and excessive partisanship of city government through structural overhaul.

---

[4] Michael N. Danielson, ed., *Metropolitan Politics: A Reader* (Boston: Little, Brown & Company, 1966), p. 116.

Today the views of structural reformers are regarded with skepticism. Some analysts suggest that the size and complexity of the modern urban community rule out a single area-wide government. They believe that only modest improvements will derive from a restructuring of government in most metroplitan regions. Other observers contend that every public function tends to have its own ideal service area. The ideal areas to provide water and drainage, secondary education, or police and fire protection may not necessarily be identical or even similar.

Whatever matters the experts may designate as area-wide rather than local, it is argued, the only true metropolitan problems are those that are so perceived by voters and public officials. The number of such services or programs tends to be small because recognition of a service or problem as area-wide appears to be conceived as threatening the political independence and fiscal integrity of a local community. Hence, this line of analysis concludes, reforms should concentrate not on massive structural reorganization along area-wide lines but rather on piecemeal accommodations within the existing decentralized network of local governments. Various efforts at both structural revolution and piecemeal accommodation are surveyed in the following section. Given these rough choices, most metropolitan areas have opted for change within the decentralized local political systems.

Annexation

Traditionally, American cities have grown by annexing surrounding territory, thereby bringing new areas and new people under a common municipal government. By this method Chicago grew from a community of 10.5 to 190 square miles. Boston increased from 4.5 to 38.5 square miles and Minneapolis from 8 to 53 square miles. The present area of Los Angeles is four and one half times greater than it was in 1910. The largest single annexation of territory by an American city, took place in 1898, when Brooklyn, part of Queens County, and Staten Island, totaling 255.5 square miles, were added to New York City.

In spite of these impressive statistics, annexation does not appear to be a promising means of solving the typical urban community's metropolitan problem. In most states the law does not favor easy annexation. It may require, for example, that the people in each separate political unit give their approval in referendum elections before annexation can take place. A few states permit action on a more arbitrary basis. Today, moreover, it is a rare suburban town that actively favors annexation to the central city. Real and imaginary advantages in status, services, and tax rates persuade the typical suburbanite that he has more to lose than gain by the annexation of the town in which he lives to the city in which he works. Since resistance to annexation is strongest in incorporated municipalities, central cities might still grow through the addition of unincorporated areas, but most central cities are now completely surrounded by a circle of suburban cities and thus permanently cut off from more distant unsettled areas.

In Los Angeles the process of annexation has occurred so rapidly and completely that it has become difficult to distinguish the city itself from its adjacent suburbs. (Litton Industries—Aero Service Division)

The County As An Area-wide Government

Some form of city-county consolidation is often favored as a solution to the metropolitan problem. Ideally, the combined city-county would become the all-inclusive unit of government within the metropolitan area, and those functions that are common to all parts of the community would become the responsibility of this master government. Unfortunately, there are basic difficulties to this solution. The county is not always coterminous with a metropolitan area, although in about two thirds of the metropolitan areas of the country the entire urban community is contained within a single county. More important, county government is, more often than not, obsolete and inefficient. In the constitutional scheme, the county is a subdivision of the state and has few or none of the powers of self-government that most states have granted to "municipalities."

More success has been achieved recently in developing agreements between cities and counties for the consolidation of specific municipal and county services and functions. The most common occur in public health, prisoner care, election services, and planning assistance. Others include library service, assessment and collection of taxes, police and fire protection, water supply, sewage, street maintenance, and recreation. These agreements do not alter the formal constitutional and legal status of the cooperating units and therefore encounter less opposition than do general consolidation schemes.

Vigorous campaigns for transforming counties into area-wide governments for metropolitan regions have been waged in recent years in such places as Miami (Dade County), Nashville (Davidson County), Cleveland (Cuyahoga County), and St. Louis. But only two metropolitan governments have emerged from these battles —in Miami and Nashville. Major opposition comes from existing office holders, from suburbia, and from organized groups that fear the subordination of interests in area-wide government.

Organized in 1957, the Miami Metro government may be described as a kind of local supergovernment superimposed on the individual municipal and unincorporated areas within the county. The main objective of Metro is to provide essential urban services more efficiently and at less cost than can its twenty-seven little governments operating separately. Its central problem has been how to deal with some of the smaller governments that have balked at having their operations and powers taken over by Metro. While municipalities retain control over strictly local affairs, Metro has broad powers to overrule town authorities in such areas as major road construction, transport regulation, zoning, traffic control, and urban renewal. At first Metro had little success in installing efficient county-wide services to replace a multitude of separate municipal services. It limited itself generally to those functions previously administered by the county government. But some accomplishments can be noted: a uniform traffic code, a metropolitan traffic court, a county-wide planning board, an integrated county-wide bus system, expansion of hospital facilities, and garbage collection in unincorporated areas.

Since Miami Metro is in these ways a rare example of a successful metropolitan creation, it has been widely studied.[5] Several key factors emerge. Differences between the central city and the suburbs in Dade County were not as great as in other metropolitan areas. Most residents had few emotional ties to the area, which resembled one big suburbia. The county commission commanded high respect and strong support, while the Miami city council was widely condemned. The city's businessmen were anxious to shift the financial burden of some of the city's area-wide functions (municipal hospital and port authority) to the county. Other favorable factors included the lack of a strong labor movement with vested interests in the central city, the relative absence of strong racial or religious minorities, the rapidity of population growth with a high degree of turnover, and the absence of the traditional two-party system. All of these factors tended to minimize commitments to the status quo and to favor change. Finally, the Metro campaign was led very effectively and had strong support from newspapers, business groups, civic organizations, and state legislators.

Special Districts

A common method for relieving some of the most pressing aspects of the metropolitan problem is the creation of special districts, of either a single or a multipurpose character and superimposed on all

_____

[5] See especially Edward Sofen, *The Miami Metropolitan Experiment* (Bloomington, Ind.: Indiana University Press, 1963).

Life in Harlem: View From the Back Street

"For the past two weeks, we have heard from America's officialdom, Cabinet officials and mayors of some of our major cities. . . . We learned a lot. But we saw the view from the highest level as to the enormity of the problem. Today and this week, we hope to view that problem from the back street of the ghetto itself."

Thus did Senator Abraham Ribicoff, Democrat of Connecticut and chairman of a Senate subcommittee looking into "the crisis of the cities," preface two full days of testimony last week from those who know the ghettos best—American Negroes. Among the witnesses were Claude Brown, Harlem-born author of "Manchild In The Promised Land," his friend Arthur Dunmeyer, who at the age of 30 has spent half his life in prison, and Ralph Ellison, author of "The Invisible Man" and other works of fiction. The following are excerpts from their testimony:

SENATOR RIBICOFF. Go ahead. Tell us how old you are and what you do and what you have by way of family and some of your experiences.

MR. DUNMEYER. I am married, I am 30 years old. I have eight kids by various different women. The same problems that existed when I was a kid are existing now. It is just that I know how to handle them a little better now. . . . I would like to clarify something, Senator. I might go back to jail again because this is a way of life. A lot of people don't realize this. We have those who do go and those who don't. I have never been ashamed of it. . . .

SENATOR RIBICOFF. How old were you when you first came in contact with the law and received a sentence or were placed in some state institution?

MR. DUNMEYER. I was between eight and ten. Being a kid, I got in trouble and I had to go to Juvenile Courts. This was the record. . . .

MR. BROWN. Our society is always condemning the high rate of illegitimacy in Negro ghettos, and it always seems so ridiculous to me to give any group of people so little means with which to cope with the dictates, the moral dictates of the society and expect them to live up to them. So sex and the Negro society and the views that the white society has on it are so completely diverse that the two will almost never get together.

SENATOR RIBICOFF. What is the impact on the Negro who comes from the South, the rural South, to come up to the slums of New York?

MR. BROWN. Once they get there and become disillusioned, they can see the streets aren't paved with gold, and there exists no great economic opportunities for them, they become pressured, you know. . . . How can you support a family of five kids on $65 a week? So he just leaves. He just ups one day and leaves, maybe becoming an alcoholic.

The wives, they will say, well, they lose respect for their husband. They can't really support their family.

SENATOR RIBICOFF. How old were you when you started selling drugs?

MR. BROWN. I was selling drugs at 13.

The TV's were saying, yes, get this, you know, have a car. Everybody should have a car. Even color TV. How are you going to get it? You can get it selling drugs. You can get it taking numbers. You know, you can get it playing the Murphy. You can get it if you ran around taking off people, sticking up people, this sort of thing. And so it is like if you—as long as you were making it, as long as you were a success and you had to do it, that is why you know in Harlem people respect the guy who is always clean.

MR. DUNMEYER. You are in jail in the hole or out of the hole. You are in jail in the street or behind bars. It is the same thing, a matter of existing, and this thing of feeling like a person regardless of if it is illegal or not.

(Mr. Ellison, who took a more sanguine view of Harlem, testified separately on the following day. Extracts from his testimony follow.)

SENATOR RIBICOFF. Do the people who live in Harlem want to get out of Harlem?

MR. ELLISON. I doubt that very seriously. . . . People want Harlem improved, not torn down. . . . I think it is just that simple . . . these places are precious to them. These places are where they have dreamed, where they have lived, where they have loved, where they have worked out life as they could.

SENATOR RIBICOFF. Do you have any thoughts of what should be done with the American city, so people can live in it and live with it and people can use it, and the city can reach what it should be in a concept of society—the best of society instead of the worst of society.

MR. ELLISON. Well, I think that one of the things that we can do about the city is to look at it, to try to see it, not merely as an instrumentality for making money, but a place for allowing the individual to achieve his highest promise. . . . You would teach, if at all possible, the immigrants who come, whether they are black or white or brown, that there is certain knowledge which one must have in order to live in the city without adding too much discomfort to his neighbors. . . . I must remain optimistic because fortunately, if we reach crises in the cities of the North, there has been an expansion of freedom for Negroes in the South. And as the next generations, the next two generations say of college people and others leave and they come here, or they find places within the South—this is very important—as they function, as they start functioning within the governments of the South, the Negro in the slum is going to feel much more optimistic about this. This is where he is going to have to look, as the nation is going to have to look there.

existing units of government, to take care of certain service needs on a community-wide basis. Among such needs have been water supply and other public utility services, sewage disposal, law enforcement, the operation of a comprehensive park system, and development of a community airport. The largest districts are the Port of New York Authority and the Metropolitan Water District of Southern California.

The best-known type of special district is the "public authority," more or less independent of state and local governments and created to finance and operate such facilities as toll roads, bridges, ports, and parking lots. More than 3000 such authorities are in operation. Their number increased substantially after World War II because of the assumed advantage stemming from their one common characteristic: they finance their operations with bonds secured by anticipated revenues from specific charges for the services they render, and thus they serve to hold down local indebtedness of the traditional type.

Objections to special districts are numerous. They add to, rather than relieve, the confusion of overlapping local units of government in a community; they seldom facilitate comprehensive planning of the entire local governmental program in either fiscal or service terms; and they are frequently undemocratic in organization and operation and insulated from the local political process. Nonetheless, special districts do have the pragmatic advantage of seeming "to work," at least for the short run. They undoubtedly often permit sensible action toward the solution of such a broad community need as development of a comprehensive water supply system, a need that simply cannot be met efficiently and economically by independent municipalities. One factor that helps to account for the increasing use of special districts to ease the metropolitan problem is their acceptability to the plural interests in the local governmental system. They do appear to threaten local community control. They do not raise taxes directly but tend to be financed by user fees. They can be tailored to fit the unique problems of a particular function in a particular area. They are usually free from the sort of restraints imposed by states on the tax and debt-incurring authority of local governments. And they appeal to citizens who tend to distrust politicians and normal processes of local government.

Federated Forms of Metropolitan Government

One of the most intriguing solutions to the metropolitan problem is federalism. The proposal is that the presently independent political units of a metropolitan area join forces in establishing a meaningful system of centralized government to take care of common community needs, while preserving their own individuality and continuing to meet those public needs that lend themselves to service through the "town" or "neighborhood." In view of successful experimentation with a federation at the national level, it is surprising that such a plan has not more often been tried at the community level. New York City does use a plan that vaguely resembles federalism. It is divided into five boroughs, each of which has certain public officers of its own and a limited responsibility for administering services. But for all practical purposes, New York City government is unitary in form and practice. Moreover, its mild form of federalism has seemingly lost its power of expansion and is not today providing a basis upon which additional suburban areas can be brought within an over-all scheme of metropolitan organization. On the other hand, it seems clear that at the time the five boroughs were joined together in a single city this arrangement did help to overcome the opposition of Brooklyn and other fringe areas to out-right annexation.

Perhaps the best example of a municipal federation in the western world is found in the government of metropolitan London. Twenty-eight boroughs plus the ancient City of London have been joined together in a federal scheme. Most of the community-wide services of government are supplied by the London County Council, whereas the boroughs are responsible for a number of local services. However, not all areas of present-day London have been brought within this arrangement, and certain functions, such as police and transport, are cared for by independent agencies. On this continent a somewhat similar federal plan oper-ates in metropolitan Toronto. The central government of the area is responsible for such services as water supply, sewage disposal, highways, public transportation, and administration of justice, while local governments in thirteen localities take care of such services as police and fire protection, libraries, and public relief.

Central-City Services for the Entire Community

Another solution to the metropolitan problem that has enjoyed a certain measure of pragmatic success is the supplying of various governmental services to the people in outlying areas by the central city. Sometimes these services are brought to the suburban towns, as where the central city extends its water supply, fire protection, or transportation systems into these areas; sometimes they are available only in the central city, as where schools, libraries, parks, and commuter highways are made available to sub-urbanites. Since this arrangement has the great advantage that "it works," it, too, is likely to be a continuing means of relieving some of the most unendurable aspects of metropolitan disorganization. But the disadvantages of the method are numerous. Frequently it is difficult to allocate charges for these services so that both the central-city taxpayer and the suburban customer bear equitable shares of their cost. And the arrangement is inconsistent with the principle of democratic local government because it is seldom possible to give the suburban users of these services a voice in their planning or administration.

Interlocal Cooperation

The stresses of the metropolitan problem in many urban areas would long since have become intolerable if local units had not made cooperative efforts to cope with certain of the most pressing and common aspects of the problem. Central cities have in many instances come to the rescue of suburban towns by offering them such services as water supply and public transportation on a pay-as-you-go basis. Similarly, the police and fire departments of separate municipalities frequently have understandings, formal and informal, by which they come to each other's assistance in time of acute need. Individual planning agencies charged with the development of fiscal and governmental programs of separate municipalities have exchanged information and ideas informally and have upon occasion attempted to correlate their planning activities so that something vaguely resembling a master plan for the entire area may take shape.

Interlocal cooperation has taken many forms. Philadelphia, the fourth largest metropolitan area in the country, has more than 700 interlocal agreements ranging from informal to contractual agreements. An agreement usually relates to a single function and is more likely to develop between communities that are similar in social and economic terms.

Extension of State and Federal Services

The line between state and local public services is breaking down in certain areas. Highway construction and maintenance, police protection, social welfare services, public health measures, and the operation of institutions of higher learning are increasingly the responsibilities of government at both state and local levels. In the fields of public housing, urban renewal, airport construction, education, and antipoverty, the federal government is playing an important role at the local as well as state level. And the states themselves deal in the same way with various problems of their local governments. It is possible that a hidden solution to the metropolitan problem is taking place in the form of increases in such federal and state activities to compensate for the failure of local governments in metropolitan areas to meet the needs of urban citizens for such services.

Where they work in close cooperation with the established units of local government, the nation and the states can make major contributions to the solution of metropolitan problems without endangering local self-government. But if local governments in metropolitan areas demonstrate through inaction that they are either unable or unwilling to move toward the solution of the problems of these areas, citizens will look to higher levels of government for direct action.

The Metropolis and the Federal Government

Faced with inadequate legal authority, hampering constitutional restraints, insufficient tax resources, and lack of trained man power, metropolitan areas similarly continue to look to the federal government for increasing assistance. The Commission on Intergovernmental Relations, set up by Congress in 1959 to study intergovernmental problems, has stressed the importance of mounting a new attack on excessive costs, inadequate services, and chaos and confusion in metropolitan development.

Federal grants and technical assistance are now available to state and local governments for general urban planning. The aid, administered by the Department of Housing and Urban Development, is intended to help solve planning problems resulting from increasing concentration in urban areas and smaller communities. The preparation of comprehensive urban transportation surveys and plans to aid in solving traffic congestion are assisted by federal grants. Separate grants are available for urban renewal and slum clearance projects and for demonstration city projects. To finance surveys and plan projects advances may be obtained before federal loans or grants are arranged. Short-term loans are available to initiate financing of renewal projects. Capital grants may be authorized to cover up to two thirds of the direct costs of a renewal project. Grants are also arranged for relocation payments to families and businesses displaced from renewal areas by a project for which a federal capital grant has been approved. In addition, the department may provide technical and professional assistance, special mortgage insurance for local public improvements, and grants covering up to two thirds of demonstration projects for developing methods for preventing and eliminating slums and blight.

The transformation, in 1965, of the Housing and Home Finance Agency into the Department of Housing and Urban Development (HUD) with Cabinet rank symbolized the growth of the federal commitment to the amelioration or solution of metropolitan problems. While the increasing importance of federal policy in urban affairs is one of the major political developments in recent years, the federal role remains limited in scope and effectiveness. The President tends to be more responsive to urban needs than Congress is, and congressional support for urban development comes hard, though reapportionment will undoubtedly change this situation in the long run. Meanwhile, the President's pressing responsibility for national security and international affairs means that he can be only a part-time exponent of urban interests at best. A further complication is the scattering of urban responsibilities—for community development, urban transit, poverty, education, and health—within the executive branch and within congressional committees. In urban affairs, as in all other policy fields, the federal government is one of diffused responsibilities and shared powers.

Selected Bibliography

Banfield, Edward C., *Big City Politics* (New York: Random House, Inc., 1965). A compact study of the political systems of nine large cities.

Connery, Robert, and Richard Leach, *The Federal Government and the Metropolitan Areas* (Cambridge, Mass.: Harvard University Press, 1960). Discusses the range of federal activities and responsibilities in urban areas, advocating an active federal leadership in solving metropolitan problems.

Danielson, Michael N., *Federal-Metropolitan Politics and the Commuter Crisis* (New York: Columbia University Press, 1965). A study of transportation problems that emphasizes the interaction of the several governmental authorities acting within any metropolitan area.

Editors of *Fortune, The Exploding Metropolis* (New York: Doubleday & Company, Inc., 1958). A lively and still-relevant examination of the nature, scope, and possible solutions for metropolitan problems.

Martin, Roscoe C., *The Cities and the Federal System* (New York: Atherton Press, 1965). A thorough analysis of direct federal-city relationships established to administer programs dealing with metropolitan problems.

Sanford, Terry, *Storm over the States* (New York: McGraw-Hill Book Company, 1967). An imaginative reappraisal of federal-state-metropolitan relations by a former governor of North Carolina.

Sayre, Wallace S., and Herbert Kaufman, *Governing New York City* (New York: Russell Sage Foundation, 1960). An extensive study of the political system governing the nation's largest city and the dynamics of its political process.

Part 2 The Politics of Democracy

Byrd's Victory Was
Machine's Doom

By Robert E. Baker

WASHINGTON POST STAFF WRITER

Time and change caught up with the once invincible Byrd organization in Virginia last Tuesday. It was a case of the cities, and not the land, prevailing in the Old Dominion.

No longer could the rural courthouses deliver the vote that had stoked the organization to a successful 40-year run in Virginia.

Down to defeat in the Democratic primary went Sen. A Willis Robertson, 79, at the hands of William B. Spong, 45. Knocked out of Congress after 36 years of impregnability was Rep. Howard W. Smith, 83, by a Fredericksburg lawyer, George C. Rawlings, 44.

Yet Byrd machine stalwarts could roll with these defeats. After all, Robertson was never an organization leader; he was merely a frequent follower, often a loner. Indeed, organization men had sensed Spong's strength and had tried to dump Robertson, but he stubbornly refused to bow out.

As for Judge Smith, the Byrd men knew trouble was brewing. Smith, with wisdom, had technically moved his home from Alexandria to rural Broad Run in 1952, when the Tenth Congressional District was formed, to escape the hostility of the growing suburbs. But urban growth forced a redistricting that pushed a part of suburban Fairfax County into Smith's Eighth District and Byrd men feared, correctly, that this might do him in.

But it was not the defeat of Smith and Robertson that shocked the Byrd machine. It was the slim victory of Sen. Harry F. Byrd Jr.

Here was the heir apparent, the magic name, the son of Sen. Harry F. Byrd Sr. of Berryville, who had built the machine and controlled it for so many years.

But last Tuesday, the son won over Armistead L. Boothe, a long-time Byrd battler, with less than 51 per cent of the vote compared to the mammoth majorities his father customarily got: 63 per cent in the 1946 primary, 72 per cent in the 1952 primary, for example, and 70 per cent in the 1958 and 1964 general elections.

To the Byrd machine, this was the political disaster of last Tuesday. The elder Byrd, the giant of the past, lay critically ill; the younger Byrd barely got the nomination to finish the four years of his father's term. It was the end of an era. How did it happen? What lies ahead?

It was more evolution than revolution, which, after all, is the Virginia way of doing things. In the old days, the senior Byrd was the leader of the dominant wing of the Democratic Party and almost all of the Republican Party. In times of challenge, the Byrd organization often called on the Republicans for help. Its control stemmed from the courthouses and office holders of a predominantly rural state.

The urban areas began to grow steadily after World War II, and in the 1960 census, urban people equaled rural people in numbers. Redistricting, the end of the poll tax, the increasing activity of Negro voters gave the urban areas more power.

These people were different. They approved higher taxes for schools, mental health and welfare. They didn't look upon a Federal program as an ogre about to devour them. "Pay as you go," the cornerstone of the Byrd organization's conservative philosophy, was all right only as long as you were going somewhere.

The machine, as it had before, adjusted from time to time to the new challenge. But with the senior Byrd still the titular head, it didn't adjust enough. It was forced into hypocrisy. In the 1960 State Democratic Convention, the senior Byrd and his organization stiff-armed protesting delegates into endorsing Sen. Lyndon B. Johnson for President. In 1964, he led a fight to repudiate President Johnson—by this time loyalist Democrats had had enough and beat him.

Here again was urban influence. The big urban complexes of the Washington suburbs and the Norfolk area, combined with the mountainous . . . Southwest which never had been reliable Byrd territory, combined to administer the 1964 defeat.

The map of political power in Virginia today no longer focuses on the vast rural areas of the Shenandoah Valley, the Southside or the Northern Neck. A map drawn to show where the voters are today would present the urban areas in massive size. People, not land, are guiding the political destiny of Virginia today.

Harry F. Byrd Jr. . . . can read the election results as well as any man and, again barring an upset in November, has four years to adjust.

This would require a move toward Federal aid to education; perhaps a new look at "pay as you go,"; a more conciliatory attitude toward Federal Government and state cooperation, reflecting the progressive attitudes of the urban areas; a new look at welfare and unions, and steadfast party loyalty.

If that comes about, then the Byrd machine might be welded together again with Harry Byrd Jr. in the driver's seat, holding high the banner of liberal conservatism or conservative liberalism: in short, contemporary moderation. . . .

6

The American
party system

Part 1 dealt mainly with the background
of the Constitution and the structure of the American federal system. We tried,
even when discussing constitutional history, to point out that the structure of
government is never static; today, in the urban revolution, we have the most recent
upheaval changing the nature of federalism. The five chapters in Part 2 analyze
processes and behavior rather than history and structure. The first four chapters
concentrate on the means that public officials, candidates for public office, and
private citizens use to influence each other in trying to achieve their various goals.
The last chapter in this section will examine closely the factors that have actually
affected voting behavior in national elections.

NATURE AND FUNCTION OF PARTY

A political party is an organization that
attempts to acquire and maintain control of a government. A party differs from
an interest group in the inclusiveness of its purposes and in the basic means it uses

to attain them. An interest group tries to influence a single policy or a set of public policies. To do so, it may or may not enter into electoral campaigns. In contrast, a party has as its goal not only influencing a wide range of public policies but also directing those policies through its own personnel. Thus, to democratically oriented parties, winning elections is vital in accomplishing these ends.

Ideally, political parties perform certain functions in a democracy. From the point of view of aspirants for public office, the party mobilizes electoral support, organizes a government if successful at the polls, and helps recruit new personnel to carry out these tasks. From the point of view of the citizens, the party helps inform the public about the nature of existing political problems, clarifies and simplifies the alternatives, and offers the electorate a choice among solutions. In addition, the party serves as a continuing body on whom responsibility for achievements and failures may be placed and on whose future candidates rewards and punishments may be dispensed at the next election.

It takes only a passing acquaintance with the American political scene to realize that political parties in the United States have not always performed each of these functions in a creditable manner. Nevertheless, as Lord Bryce observed, "the spirit and force of party has in America been as essential to the action of the machinery of government as steam is to a locomotive engine." [1]

The question of whether or not the American party system can continue to provide the motive force for effective democratic government in the second half of the twentieth century is better postponed until after we have thoroughly examined the three distinct characteristics of that system. First, America has a two-party system at the national level. Since the 1790s, there have almost always been two, and only two, serious contestants for control of the national government. Second, the parties appear to agree on many fundamentals of political philosophy and do not present radically different programs to the voters. Third, each of the two national parties is decentralized. Party policy is more apt to be the result of bargaining among leaders at many levels than of decisions made at the top of a formal hierarchy.

THE AMERICAN TWO-PARTY SYSTEM

The Attitude of the Framers toward Parties

The Constitution is entirely silent about political parties and about such all-important matters as presidential nominating conventions, direct primaries, caucuses, party committees and officers, and other details of party machinery and procedure. Since political parties (though not in the fully modern sense) were known in 1787, this decision of the framers was probably a conscious one. There is no record of debate on party government in the Constitutional Convention, but George Washington apparently expressed the attitude of many of the Founding Fathers when in his Farewell Address at the

---

[1] James Bryce, *The American Commonwealth,* rev. ed. (New York: Crowell-Collier and Macmillan Company, Inc., 1914), 2:3.

end of his Presidency he warned against the "baneful effects of the spirit of party." Most of the framers must have thought it would be somehow possible to elect the President and the members of Congress and to run the government without the controlling or integrating force of parties.

It is possible that some members of the Philadelphia convention realized that the development of political parties in American government was inevitable. James Madison seemed to sense this in Number 10 of *The Federalist,* which was originally published in November 1787. He wrote:

A landed interest, a manufacturing interest, a mercantile interest, a monied interest, with many lesser interests, grow up of necessity in civilized nations, and divide them into different classes, actuated by different sentiments and views. The regulation of these various and interfering interests forms the principal task of modern legislation, and involves the spirit of party and faction in the necessary and ordinary operations of government.

Be that as it may, by the beginning of Washington's second administration there were already two political parties operating. Washington had gradually come under the influence of Alexander Hamilton and consistently sided with him against Thomas Jefferson in controversies over public policy. What may have remained a simple factional squabble within a ruling clique grew into the makings of a party battle when Thomas Jefferson and James Madison worked with members of Congress and local political leaders in southern and middle Atlantic states to create a coalition of small property owners and yeoman farmers to oppose Hamilton's policies. In 1793, Jefferson resigned from Washington's Cabinet, and in a few years the Republicans—or the Democracy or Mobocracy, as Hamilton's followers preferred to call the Jeffersonians—were a full-fledged political party, challenging the Administration's pro-British foreign policy and domestic economic policy.

The Federalists, as the followers of Washington and Hamilton styled themselves, were men of wealth and station and lacked the willingness or foresight to form local party organizations that could mount an effective counterappeal to the growing electorate. Out of touch with the newly enfranchised groups and lacking the machinery to mobilize the conservative vote, the Federalists were routed in the election of 1800 and by 1816 had ceased to exist as a party. The lesson of their disaster was not lost, however. Leaders of all succeeding parties have realized that to win office one must win votes; and to win votes one must have an effective organization at every electoral level.

After the demise of the Federalists the nation experienced a short period of one-party rule. Still, while the old Jeffersonian party tried to encompass all points of political view, it could not accommodate every political, economic, and social interest. By the mid-1820s there were two warring factions within the party, the Democratic Republicans and the National Republicans. The split grew until by 1840 the two factions, now called Democrats and Whigs, had become coalitions of economic and geographic interests and had taken on the character of national parties.

Through the mid-1850s the two parties fought on almost even terms, but with the death of old Whig leaders such as Henry Clay and Daniel Webster and

This cartoon by Thomas Nast, which appeared in November 1864, is notable for the first use of the elephant as the Republican party symbol. The collected animals—representing various issues, states, and newspapers—are frightened by the donkey's cry for "Caesarism," a term referring to a move to re-elect President Ulysses S. Grant for a third term in 1876. The donkey as a symbol of the Democratic party had already been introduced; here, however, Nast uses the fox to represent the Democrats. (Brown Brothers)

the worsening of the crisis over slavery, the Whig coalition between eastern capital and southern planters disintegrated. A number of third parties were agitating for national status, but many of the Whig rank and file as well as a large contingent of liberal Democrats found the new Republican party most attractive. In 1856, the Republicans rallied behind General John C. Fremont and made a respectable showing in the presidential campaign. In 1860, their candidate Abraham Lincoln carried only a minority of the popular vote but won a solid majority in the electoral college. Not since that election has a third party even come close to capturing the White House; and only in 1912, when the progressive wing of the Republican party broke from the regulars to nominate Theodore Roosevelt as the Bull Moose candidate, has a third party polled as many votes as the loser of the major parties. Yet third parties have continued to have a voice in American politics. In the late 1960s, former Alabama Governor George Wallace spoke vehemently of offering himself as a third-party choice in 1968, and militant Negro leaders hinted as strongly that neither of the two existing parties provided an answer for them.

Why Two Parties?

One of the questions that has most puzzled foreign observers of American politics is why the United States has a two-party rather than a multiparty system. After all, most modern democracies, France, Italy, Belgium, Holland, and Switzerland, for example, have a multiparty system, and even England and Canada have at times in this century had a three-party system. V. O. Key, certainly one of the most astute students of American parties, concluded that there is no fully satisfactory answer.[2] The best explanation that can be offered is that a number of factors have operated together to encourage a two-party system.

First, there have been historical factors. The colonists brought a two-party tradition with them. It is easy to exaggerate this influence, since England in the eighteenth century did not have a party system in the modern sense, yet the factional divisions between Whigs and Tories probably did have some effect on colonial ideas of party politics. After independence, there was the division between Federalists and Antifederalists over the adoption of the Constitution; then a few years later came the split between the Federalists in power and the Jeffersonians out of power. This latter division occurred at a time when the electorate was small and the social and economic structure of the country relatively uncomplex. The basic appeals to two different sets of social groups, by the Federalists to the mercantile class, men of means and substance, and by the Jeffersonians first to yeoman farmers and small property holders and later also to the small but rapidly growing working classes in the cities, set a pattern that, except for the period 1801–1824, has to a large extent been continued to the present day.

Institutional factors have also played a role. First was the Founding Fathers' choice of a presidential rather than a parliamentary form of democratic government. It is easier for a majority of multiparty representatives in a legislature to compromise their differences and pick a prime minister than it is for the masses of voters, owing allegiance to three or more parties, to select a President. Moreover, the specific language of the American Constitution requiring majority agreement, whether the President is chosen by the electoral college or by the House of Representatives, has provided a further force limiting the number of presidential candidates— and thus national political parties. The election of single chief executive at state and local levels of government has further served to encourage would-be factions to unite behind a single candidate and aim for that magic target, a majority vote.

Another institutional arrangement that has operated to foster a two-party system is the use of single-member districts for the election of members of Congress. In a single-member district only one party can win an election, and under such circumstances third parties are discouraged unless they can achieve a voting

---

[2] V. O. Key, *Politics, Parties, and Pressure Groups* 5th ed. (New York: Thomas Y. Crowell Company, 1964), p. 207.

strength comparable to that of the established major parties. The Constitution does not require the election of members of the House of Representatives from single-member districts. But throughout most of American history Congress has by law required the use of the district system. Moreover, the election of senators is in effect a single-member district undertaking. Many state legislatures, on the other hand, utilize multimember districts.[3]

Social factors have also been important in the maintenance of a two-party system. Where a society is beset by cleavages that follow geographic, socio-economic, ethnic, or religious lines, conditions are ripe for a multiparty system. Where there is relatively little class consciousness, general agreement exists over fundamental political and economic arrangements, and political divisions cut across religious, ethnic, geographical, and socioeconomic lines, a two-party system has a far better chance of taking firm root. In such a situation, "the stakes of politics are smaller, and the kinds of tolerance, compromise, and concession necessary for a two-party system's majoritarian parties can prevail." [4]

It must be kept in mind in discussing class consciousness and other societal divisions that we are speaking only in relative terms. There is some class consciousness in the United States, and there are societal divisions along economic, ethnic, geographic, and religious lines. Each of the two major parties does tend to focus its appeals in considerable part on certain groups; and as Chapter 10 will indicate, these groups often respond positively to these appeals. The point to be stressed, however, is that when compared to many countries, France and Italy, for example, class and other social lines in the United States are relatively indistinct and do not cut deeply into the vitals of society. Whether this situation will continue to be true in the face of the ongoing Negro "revolution" depends on whether the parties offer Negroes real alternatives. Because of their conscious or subconscious appreciation of this situation, leaders of both parties try to aim their appeals at a wide spectrum of interests and groups. Each party may gather its basic support from different groups, but each usually tries to muster some support from all groups. It is a rare party platform that does not offer something to everybody.

Consequences of the Two-party System

Because there are only two major parties, it is probable that in a national election one or the other will win not only the Presidency but also a majority of both houses of Congress. The peculiarities of the American electoral system make it possible, of course, for one party to gain the White House at the same time that the other wins a majority of seats in Congress. This, however, has happened only once since 1848. It is far more likely

---

[3] See the interesting article by Maurice Klain, "A New Look at the Constituencies: The Need for a Recount and a Reappraisal," *American Political Science Review,* 49 (December 1955), pp. 1105–1119, in which it is shown that multimember state legislative districts are far more common in the United States than has generally been recognized.

[4] Frank J. Sorauf, *Political Parties in the American System* (Boston: Little, Brown & Company, 1964), p. 30.

Two 'Freshmen' Representatives

Show Contrast in the G.O.P.

By Nan Robertson

SPECIAL TO THE NEW YORK TIMES

WASHINGTON, Feb. 3— A dozen years is a long time between Congressional classes.

In this, the 90th Congress, a freshman who is really not a freshman and a freshman who really is, both Republicans, are classic examples of contrast and change.

William C. Wampler of Virginia, now the "bald eagle of the Cumberland" to his constituents, was, at the age of 26, the youngest member of the House of Representatives in the 1953-54 session.

He was swept into office during the Eisenhower landslide as his district's first Republican Representative in a generation. He ran again twice, was twice defeated, and now is back in office after an absence of 12 years.

Faces Are Unfamiliar

In the interim, Mr. Wampler has lost most of his hair, gained 25 pounds, acquired two children and seen his Congressional salary double from $15,000 to $30,000, his workload increase enormously and his staff rise from two to five. He was one of six Southern Republicans in the 83d Congress. Now he is one of 20.

Mr. Wampler was astonished to see so many unfamiliar faces in this House— half its members have served six years or less. Among them was a real freshman, 28-year-old Donald W. Riegle Jr. of Michigan, only four months older than the youngest member of Congress, Representative William J. Green of Pennsylvania, also 28.

Both men are tall, handsome, vigorous and eloquent. They belong to the same party and they scored unexpected victories over their incumbent opponents, Virginia's W. Pat Jennings and Michigan's John C. Mackie. At this point the differences begin to emerge.

Mr. Wampler's district, wedged into the Cumberland Mountain counties of Virginia's southwestern tip, has an economy founded on farming and coal mining. Its Protestant people are mostly of Scottish-Irish descent antislavery Whigs who turned to the Republican party during the Civil War and remained faithful until the black Depression years. The Negro population is 7 per cent.

Political observers in Virginia say Mr. Wampler is considered locally to be a moderate but would be rated nationally as a conservative. He is all-out for increasing the war effort in Vietnam.

Mr. Wampler calls most poverty programs "a waste and an extravagance," and thinks it deplorable that any President, specifically Lyndon B. Johnson, "makes the assumption that we must have a deficit budget." He wants to see a "rekindling" of the traditional alliance between Republicans and conservative Democrats in Congress.

Donald Riegle's district is light-years away from Mr. Wampler's homogenous rural constituency. It includes the highly unionized, industrialized city of Flint, Mich., and the surrounding area, inhabited by Poles, Czechs, Rumanians, Greeks, Italians, Lebanese and "a little bit of everything else," according to its Representative in Congress. The Negro population of the city stands at 20 per cent and Catholics are almost as numerous.

Campaign Differences

Unlike Mr. Wampler, Mr. Riegle was an unknown political novice, returning home to campaign last spring from Harvard University.

He looks and acts a good deal like Mayor Lindsay of New York, with an earnest, gee-whiz manner that contrasts with Mr. Wampler's smooth Southern charm. He conducted, he says, a "Lindsay-style" campaign in his district, one considered absolutely safe for the Democrats (two years ago, Mr. Mackie won by a margin of 50,000 votes). "The word 'Republican' did not appear on our campaign literature," Mr. Riegle said.

While Mr. Wampler was out working the hills and hollows and attending get-togethers of hard-shell, free-will Baptists, Mr. Riegle was haunting the Buick factory gates, bowling alleys and movie queues. He crashed Democratic rallies and won the first endorsement ever given a Republican candidate by the Negro Community Civic League. He swamped the Democratic incumbent by 11,000 votes.

Although only 12 years apart—Mr. Wampler is now 40—the gap between the two men at times seems at least a generation. For one thing, the Virginian served 27 months in the Navy during World War II. Mr. Riegle was a baby of 3 at the time of Pearl Harbor. He was 12 when the Korean War broke out, and has never been called to service.

Mr. Riegle views the Vietnam war as "a constantly enlarging stalemate with no satisfactory solution now or in five years." He thinks additional American troops and weapons will never win the war. He believes the best hope lies in fostering social, political and economic growth in South Vietnam.

Mr. Riegle is worried about inflation and wants to reduce Government spending, but he is not entirely opposed to the antipoverty campaign. He thinks some programs such as Head Start are sound, and others are inefficient.

that the minority party will obtain control of both houses of Congress in an off-year election than in a presidential election, as has in fact occurred in nine of the twenty-one off-year elections since 1884. Nevertheless, during 105 of the 178 years from 1789 to 1967, the same party has controlled the Presidency and both houses of Congress.

In facilitating control of the government by one party, the two-party system thereby places almost irresistible pressure on party leaders to achieve that goal. To do so they must win a majority or close to a majority of the popular vote. This means that a party cannot concentrate on one interest to the exclusion of all others, nor can it depend solely on one segment of the country for victory. Thus, the two-party system encourages party leaders to form coalitions. Typically, the Republican party in this century has brought together the financial interests of the Northeast, the farmers and small-town residents of the Midwest, and white collar workers and many professional men throughout the nation. The Democrats, on the other hand, have historically united—at least for purposes of electing a President—the South, blue collar workers in urban areas across the country, small farmers in the Midwest and Far West, northern liberals, and a portion of white collar workers.

Exceptions to the Two-party System

Although the national party system in the United States is basically one of two parties, two reservations must be made. First, for long intervals many states have had one-party systems. The South since the Civil War is the most obvious example of a regional one-party system, though at one time New England was an equally striking case. After analyzing electoral behavior in presidential, senatorial, and gubernatorial campaigns from 1914 to 1954, Austin Ranney and Willmoore Kendall[5] found that in only twenty-six of the then forty-eight states during this forty-year period did the minority party win 25 percent or more of these contests. Similarly, Duane Lockard[6] classifies, on the basis of elections from 1944 to 1960, only twenty-seven states as having truly competitive two-party systems, though he qualifies this conclusion with a statement that an additional nine states have a party system in which the minority party is likely to capture at least 40 to 45 percent of the popular vote.

Thus when we say the United States has a two-party system, we must be careful not to imply that the two parties compete effectively in each state. Indeed, as Chapter 8 will indicate, one-party domination of congressional districts, either because of deliberate rigging of district lines or because of the voting habits of the local population, is such that in less than half of the 435 districts can the election of congressmen be called serious two-party contests. Nevertheless, at least until recently, the trend in American politics has seemed to be away from one-party monopoly in national elections and, though less markedly, in state and local

---

[5] *Democracy and the American Party System* (New York: Harcourt, Brace & World, Inc., 1956), pp. 161–164.

[6] *The Politics of State and Local Government* (New York: Crowell-Collier, Macmillan, Inc., 1963), pp. 183–185.

campaigns as well. As the 1964 election showed, it would be the height of folly for a Democratic presidential candidate to assume that the South was solidly behind him or a Republican to act as though northern New England or the Midwest was in his camp.

The second reservation that must be made about the two-party system is that third parties have been a constant part of the American political scene. Free-soilers, Greenbackers, Populists, Farmer-Laborites, Prohibitionists, Bull Moosers, Socialists, Dixiecrats, Progressives, and even Communists have been frequent contestants for state and national office. As we have already seen, however, no third party, with the possible exception of Theodore Roosevelt's Bull Moose group in 1912, has even come close to winning the Presidency since the Republicans did it in 1860. On the other hand, third parties, such as the Progressives in Wisconsin and the Non-Partisan League in the Dakotas, have often been influential in state politics and have sent representatives and occasionally senators to Washington.

Despite their short lifespans and the restriction of their tangible political power to single states or small geographic areas, third parties have often made important contributions to public policy. Many third parties have won enough support among the voters to threaten the major parties with the possibility that they might gain a balance of power on the political scene. This situation has forced the major parties to pay constant attention to the pressures exerted by third parties. Often the third party has taken a more decisive, and generally more progressive, stand on issues than has either of the major parties. But whenever it has appeared that any large number of voters were being attracted to such a party, sooner or later one (or both) of the major parties has been sufficiently impressed by its gains to take over at least a part of the third party's program, thus cutting the ground from beneath it. For example, in 1932, when it appeared that the Socialist party, under Norman Thomas' leadership, might well make considerable headway because of the economic depression, the Democratic party itself turned to the left, and the resulting New Deal program under Roosevelt quickly brought to an end Socialist party growth. The unexpectedly small vote polled by Henry A. Wallace's Progressive party in 1948 is in part explained by the extent to which the Democratic party under President Truman moved to the left on such issues as civil rights and labor-management relations to meet the threat offered by the new third party. Thus it has been the chief function of the third party to make American politics more dynamic and progressive.

AMERICAN PARTIES AND IDEOLOGY

A second characteristic of the American party system is that the two major parties usually appear to differ slightly if at all in their basic ideology and in their general programs, when, indeed, a coherent program can be discerned in party platforms. American parties offer the voters a choice between politicians, but rarely offer a clear-cut choice between specific political programs.

Two preliminary remarks must be made here. It is easy to exaggerate the ideological divisions among European parties, at least among those that have a chance of playing a major role in running the government. In England, for instance, the Labour party is something more than a vehicle for the labor unions and something less than a true Socialist party; and the Conservative party is a good deal more than a party of business or of laissez-faire capitalism. Many contemporary issues provoke little or no disagreement between them. A Conservative member of the House of Commons has described the situation in the House as one in which "about 5 percent of our chaps on the extreme Right and about 10 percent of theirs [Labour's] on the extreme Left are firing away at each other while the remainder are pretty well agreed on what must be done, although they differ to some extent on methods." [7]

Second, the two parties in the United States do differ in their general policy orientations, though, of course, these differences cannot be compared to those between Fascists and Communists. The popular impression of the Democrats as the more liberal and the Republicans as the more conservative party is essentially accurate, although there are liberals and conservatives in each party. A study of the attitude of delegates to the two national conventions—a group that includes senators, congressmen, governors, state and county chairmen, and petty party officials, as well as private citizens—showed that these leaders displayed marked differences in their respective attitudes toward a whole series of political problems in the fields of civil rights, governmental regulation of the economy, taxation, public ownership of natural resources, and foreign policy. As a group, the Democrats favored more government activity to protect the civil rights of minority groups, more government regulation of business, less government regulation of labor, more public ownership of natural resources, higher taxes on business and upper income groups, and more of an internationalist orientation toward foreign policy than did Republican leaders.[8]

The difference in approach between the two parties in America can also be gauged by comparing the concepts of the office of the Presidency held by Democratic Presidents Wilson, Franklin Roosevelt, Truman, Kennedy, and Johnson, with those of nearly all the Republican incumbents of this century. The Republican exception, Theodore Roosevelt, took a grand view of his office, as did each of the Democrats. For these men, the Presidency was a position of dynamic power, a post to control the executive bureaucracy, to push social and economic legislation through Congress, and to mold public opinion to accept, even to demand, such governmental action. For Taft, Harding, Coolidge, Hoover, and Eisenhower, the Presidency was more a place for repose than for energetic action. They were content to reign and seldom tried to rule.

Another indication that there is a meaningful difference between the two parties is in their voting records in Congress. Party affiliation, Key concluded,[9] "appears to be the strongest and most persistent factor associated with the actions

---

[7] The *New York Times,* January 21, 1954. From a dispatch by the *Times'* London correspondent.

[8] Herbert McClosky, Paul Hoffman, and Rosemary O'Hara, "Issue Conflict and Consensus among Party Leaders and Followers," *American Political Science Review,* 54 (June 1960), pp. 406–427.

[9] P. 678.

Party Unity* Scoreboard

	Total roll calls	Party unity roll calls	Percent of total
	1966		
Both chambers	428	198	46
Senate	235	118	50
House	193	80	41
	1965		
Both chambers	459	213	46
Senate	258	108	42
House	201	105	52
	1964		
Both chambers	418	171	41
Senate	305	109	36
House	113	62	55
	1963		
Both chambers	348	166	48
Senate	229	108	47
House	119	58	49
	1962		
Both chambers	348	149	43
Senate	224	92	41
House	124	57	46
	1961		
Both chambers	320	185	58
Senate	204	127	62
House	116	58	50
	1960		
Both chambers	300	125	42
Senate	207	76	37
House	93	49	53
	1959		
Both chambers	302	151	50
Senate	215	103	48
House	87	48	55

* Note: "Party Unity" role calls are those on which a majority of voting Democrats oppose a majority of voting Republicans. It should be noted that this is only one of many possible indexes of party cohesiveness in Congress.

SOURCE: *Congressional Quarterly Weekly Report,* April 3, 1964, p. 650 and December 9, 1966, p. 2990.

of Senators and Representatives." Roll call votes indicate that party unanimity in Congress is rare, but that party cohesion is not.

When these observations are made, it is apparent that the image that the two major parties present to the voters is more apt to differ in matters of style and policy detail than on fundamental issues of political philosophy. As already noted, both parties appeal to citizens of all social classes and geographical areas. Both accept the basic, though vague, principles of democratic government as embodied in the American Constitution. Both reject socialism and endorse a free enterprise system, though one modified by a degree of government regulation.

Why Few Ideological Differences?

Part of the explanation of the lack of fundamental differences between the major parties can be traced to America's having a written Constitution that broadly defines the goals and restricts the legitimate means that political parties may advocate, and to its being revered as a sacred document. From time to time there have been extremist groups of abolitionists or segregationists, of radicals from the right or from the left who have attacked the Constitution, but these groups have been well outside the mainstream of American politics.[10]

Moreover, the United States has lacked a class consciousness of the sort that has divided many European nations. Without such class antagonism, development of ideological parties becomes very difficult. An appeal in this country pitched only to blue collar workers might well fall on uncomprehending if not deaf ears. Whether this relative lack of a class struggle can be traced to the absence of a feudal tradition in American history, the comparative prosperity of the American economy, the existence of a frontier to absorb dissident elements, frontier ideals of egalitarianism, or to some combination of these and other factors, the prevalent political standards of American society have been those of the middle class. In fact, most Americans think of themselves as belonging to the middle class. No party can wander very far from these standards without risking disastrous defeat.

Furthermore, the two-party system encourages formation of coalitions. As we have seen, to control the national government party leaders must make a broad appeal to voters that cuts across social, economic, ethnic, and geographical lines. Given the diversity of background, outlooks, aspirations, and loyalties of the American people, it is virtually impossible, except in times of severe crisis, to organize a majority coalition behind a lucid, specific, and all-encompassing party program. A more promising alternative for national party leaders is a vaguely worded statement of ultimate goals—glowing allusions to "The Great Society," for example—with much hedging on specific proposals to achieve this noble purpose. Even the New Deal, which was the closest thing to a comprehensive governmental program the United States has ever had, was a crazy-quilt pattern of uncoordinated and at times conflicting individual policies, some of which were geared as much to satisfying each of the diverse groups in Roosevelt's grand coalition as to overcoming the depression through coherent, systematic governmental action.

An additional factor militating against ideological and programmatic parties is the indifference of many Americans to politics. In 1953, when debate in Con-

---

[10] See Chapter 3.

gress and in the press over Senator John Bricker's proposed constitutional amendment to limit the President's treaty-making power was at its height, the Gallup poll reported that 81 percent of the persons interviewed disclaimed knowing anything about the proposal. Furthermore, public opinion may be so inchoate as to defy prediction of how it will respond to a given policy. During the 1952 presidential campaign, when repeal or modification of the Taft-Hartley law was being heavily pressed by the Democrats, the Survey Research Center at the University of Michigan found the following distribution of opinion in the national sample of the population its pollsters interviewed:[11]

	Percent
Should be repealed	10
Changed quite a bit to favor labor	1
Changed a little in favor of labor	2
Left as it is	13
Changed a little in favor of business	1
Changed (but direction or amount not indicated)	16
Don't know what ought to be done	25
Haven't heard of	30
Not ascertained	2
	100

Finally, opinion where it does exist may be internally contradictory. The same people who disapprove of big government in Washington and want to cut federal spending may favor a larger defense budget, extended federal loyalty-security programs, increased aid to veterans, and a local airport built for them.

Since available evidence, though not conclusive, indicates that the bulk of American voters tend to cluster just to the right or left of the political center, the magic goal of winning 50.1 percent of the electorate has pulled party leaders into aiming for many of the same voters and then into making similar appeals. Reports from public opinion polls in the summer of 1964 moved Senator Barry Goldwater to moderate somewhat the original right-wing orientation of his presidential campaign, but this shift came too late to save him from resounding defeat. In 1968 Richard Nixon and Hubert Humphrey tried to crowd each other out of the middle of the road, leaving to George Wallace the task of gathering votes from the fringes.

DECENTRALIZATION
OF AMERICAN POLITICAL PARTIES

The third salient characteristic of the American party system is the decentralized organization of both major parties. Schattschneider[12] goes so far as to label decentralization as "the most important

---

[11] V. O. Key, *Public Opinion and American Democracy* (New York: Alfred A. Knopf, 1961), p. 83.

[12] E. E. Schattschneider, *Party Government* (New York: Holt, Rinehart and Winston, Inc., 1942), p. 129.

single characteristic" of the party system in the United States. Conventional wisdom often pictures the parties as having a pyramidal structure, with the membership at the base and the President or opposition leader at the apex and a chain of command running from top to bottom. This analogy is convenient but very misleading. First, it is difficult to speak of membership in either American political party. In Europe a citizen is typically admitted to party membership only after subscribing to certain specific political doctrines and after paying dues. In the United States party membership is far more casual, usually involving no more than voting at a general election or occasionally at a primary. In most states a citizen who votes in the primary of one party is barred from voting in the primary of another for a period of several months or years; but nothing can prevent that citizen from voting for the other party's candidates at the general election. In another group of states the primaries are "open." A citizen is legally free to change party allegiance and to vote in either primary. In fact, in the state of Washington it is possible for citizens to vote in both party primaries. And while both parties constantly solicit money from likely donors, neither even remotely hints that non-contributors are not welcome in the bosom of the party.

Second, party organization is complex and disorderly, with agencies of overlapping and conflicting jurisdiction. In addition, formal organization is frequently supplemented by an informal organization that wields the actual power within that segment of the party. For example, presidential candidates have, typically, put together personal staffs that usurp many of the campaigning functions of their respective national committees. As we shall see in a few pages, federalism, in providing independent bases of political power, also plays an important role in decentralizing American parties. First, however, it would be useful to take a closer look at the actual organization of the two major parties.

Party Machinery for Winning Elections

Generally speaking, party machinery, formal and informal, can be divided according to the two functions of winning elections and running the government. The basic unit in the American party corresponds to the basic unit of electoral administration, the precinct. Here the party organization may consist of one man, called a precinct captain or executive, or he may have a small staff of assistants, usually part-time volunteers. Historically, it was at this level that most of the personal contact between party officials and party constituencies occurred, though this is far less true today. Above the precinct in urban areas is the ward organization, again perhaps consisting of only a few people. In small towns and rural areas the unit above the precinct is the county committee. Its committeemen are usually the precinct captains, and its chairman, as Key[13] says, "may be a local political potentate of considerable significance." The 3000 or more county chairmen wield real power within each party organization.

---

[13] *Politics, Parties, and Pressure Groups*, p. 327.

Local precinct volunteers man precinct headquarters, canvass for voters, transport voters from their homes to voting places, and help the voters at the polls. (Shelton from Monkmeyer Press Photo)

One step above the county committee, at least on paper, is the state committee. Depending on local laws and customs, its members may be elected or hold their offices by virtue of their position in county organizations. The functions that state committees are supposed to perform vary widely from state to state, but they frequently include coordinating the campaign work of county committees, calling state party conventions to nominate candidates for office, and arranging the administrative details for primaries.

Much of the organization and operation of party machinery at the local and state level is prescribed by state law, while at the national level party machinery is strictly a matter of custom. The two parties, however, have established very similar patterns of organization. There are four main agencies—or agents—heading the national parties: the national convention, the national committee, the national chairman, and the national committee secretariat.

The national convention consists of some 1300 to 3000 delegates[14] from the fifty states and the federal territories who meet every four years to select the party's candidates for President and Vice President and to determine party policy through a platform in which a stand, forthright or evasive, is taken on the issues of the day. Apart from these functions, the national convention has little authority. It has nothing whatever to do with the nomination of the party's candidates for

---

[14] There is a difference between "delegates" and "votes" in a national convention. Some delegates may have only a half-vote.

Congress, nor can it compel congressional candidates to pledge support to the party's platform.

National conventions have no authority of a continuous nature. During the four-year period between conventions a party is supposedly run by the national chairman and the national committee. The latter consists, in the case of the Democratic party, of 108 members—one man and one woman from each state and territory. Beginning in 1952, the Republican party added a third member from each state—the chairman of the state Republican committee—provided the state gives its electoral vote to the Republican candidate for the Presidency and has a Republican governor or a Republican majority in its congressional delegation. Ordinarily, a national committee meets only on call by the chairman, and such calls are infrequent. Apart from offering advice and help during the campaign and meeting early in presidential years to determine the date and place of the national convention, a national committee more often than not exercises no further authority. If a party is passing through a trying period and there is rivalry among prominent figures in the party for its control, resolving such a conflict may become its responsibility. But the committee never actually runs the party, and it seldom determines party policy except in the sense of ratifying proposals laid before it by the chairman or party members holding public office. Individual members, known as national committeemen, however, frequently wield considerable power in their own states and within the federal government.

The national chairman is chosen by the national committee every four years following the nomination of the presidential and vice-presidential candidates. In practice the chairman is the personal choice of the presidential nominee and the committee merely ratifies the name suggested. The first task confronting the new chairman is to organize and conduct the party's campaign for the Presidency, and in the long run this is his most important function. He is also active in the biennial congressional campaigns occurring between presidential elections, but here he and the national committee share power and responsibility with the Senate and House campaign committees organized by the party groups in Congress. The national chairman's day-to-day duties are of a varying character, but are almost never concerned with the actual operation of the government itself unless he also holds a government post, such as the office of Postmaster General. He keeps in close touch with state and local party organizations, makes many speeches, and is engaged in an almost continuous effort to raise party funds. Seldom, if ever, does a national chairman become a "boss" in the sense that state and local chairmen sometimes do. During the last two decades the post has been declined in importance. James A. Farley, who served as Democratic national chairman during the first eight years of the Roosevelt Administration, was the last man to bring great prestige and authority to this position.

The vitality and effectiveness of the national party organization is in large measure affected by the caliber of the salaried secretariat that serves the national committee and the national chairman. In the main, this secretariat attracts little attention and its organization varies from time to time and party to party. Its functions are to write speeches for use by important party members, to supply re-

Democratic National Convention, 1964. (NBC)

search assistance, to help raise money, to keep track of political trends, to prepare publicity releases, to handle correspondence with state and local party agencies, and to engage in a great many housekeeping tasks whose successful performance may have much to do with party unity and strength in the next campaign.

Party Machinery for Running the Government

Party machinery for winning elections has little to do formally with running the government, although county chairmen and other party officials may offer advice, often unsolicited, on the distribution of patronage and frequently convey to office-holders constituents' requests for favors that may affect the formation or administration of important public policies. More formally, party influence makes itself felt in the day-to-day operation of the government through party units that parallel governmental machinery. Thus, each party has units inside Congress, such as a caucus, a steering (or policy) committee, and a floor leader, through which party influence is brought to bear on federal policy-making. The national chairman and the national committee have very little to do with the activity of party members in Congress. Any attempt by these agencies to exert party pressure on congressmen is apt to be vigorously resisted. These agencies are supposed to be in close touch with the executive branch if the party controls the Presidency. But, even here, the President's Cabinet, his White House secretariat, or his informal advisers and "trouble shooters" are more often than not the agencies through which party control of the administrative aspects of government is exercised.

The President, of course, is the chief of his party and in staffing his administration has responsibility not only to run the government efficiently but also to keep the party organization together by rewarding friends and punishing enemies. Although, as we shall discuss later, the President's control over party machinery is not necessarily as tight as one might think, his immediate access to mass media of communication, the enormous prestige of his office, and his power over patronage do secure for him a position of party leadership, if he cares to use it. Like it or not, other party leaders have to live with the fact that the public at large usually identifies the President with his party, and the party's fate at the next election is heavily dependent on the public image of the President.

On the other hand, the opposition party has no powerful, national leader around whom to rally. The titular leader of the minority party is the defeated presidential nominee, but his actual power position is ambiguous. The fact that he was rejected by the voters to some extent counterbalances the fact that he was chosen by the party for the country's highest office. As Adlai Stevenson,[15] twice titular leader of his party, commented:

The titular leader has no clear and defined authority within his party. He has no party office, no staff, no funds, nor is there any system of consultation whereby he may be advised of party policy and through which he may help to shape that policy. There are no devices such as the British have developed through which he can communicate directly and responsibly with the leaders of the party in power.

Adding to the difficulties of the titular leader are the facts that the party leaders of the minority party who opposed his nomination are rarely persuaded of the error of their ways by having the electorate confirm their views, and new presidential hopefuls seldom see any point in helping to increase the prestige and power of a prominent rival for the next nomination.

If this were all there was to the story, then the titular leader's position would be unambiguously impotent. Most important, as Stevenson himself admitted, the titular leader is generally looked on by press and public as the spokesman of his party, whether or not he deserves the accolade. This is true in great measure because there is rarely any other person who can legitimately claim the right to speak for the party, if the titular leader asserts himself. Senators, congressmen, and governors represent interests that are too parochial. New candidates have not yet received the mantle of nomination from a national convention.

---

[15] *What I Think* (New York: Harper & Row, Publishers, 1956), pp. ix–x.

"Despite its ambiguity, perhaps even because of it," three close students of the American party system have concluded, "the titular leadership has become a post that offers many opportunities for initiative, at least for a first time incumbent."[16] The prime example of imaginative use of this position was given by Stevenson himself. In the period 1953–1956 he moved vigorously to rebuild Democratic morale—and finances—after the crushing defeat of 1952. Traveling abroad he built up an international reputation as a statesman that gave added weight at home to his policy pronouncements. Together with his careful fence-mending operations with state organizations, this national and international reputation assured him of renomination in 1956.

Federalism and Party Decentralization

The most important point about the decentralization of the American party system is that power within each party is diffused. There is little in the way of a chain of command from the top to the bottom of the party hierarchy, only many avenues of persuasion, of requests, demands, threats, and bargaining. Each of these is a two-way street, and often the demand and threat traffic is heavier going up than down.

Federalism in the formal governmental structure of the nation increases the decentralization of power within the party system. There are approximately 91,000 units of government in the United States that are empowered to levy taxes and upwards of three quarters of a million elective political offices. An independent source of revenue or an elective office means that an independent power base may exist from which a party satrap may operate. The President cannot fire a mayor who refuses to support an urban renewal program on which the President's prestige depends. Nor can he dismiss a senator or representative who consistently votes against administration bills in Congress. Each of these officials is elected by a local constituency and is legally responsible for his tenure in office only to that constituency. If he is sure of electoral support, he can thumb his nose at his colleagues, at the nation at large, or at any other governmental official or set of officials.

National supremacy and the increased activity of the federal government in providing money for such diverse measures as public housing, highways, farm surpluses, urban renewal, mental health, school lunches, and university research might seem to indicate that local government officials, and therefore local party officials, are coming more and more under domination, potential if not actual, by Washington. Three factors, however, act to offset this expected trend.

First, in committing the federal government to these vast undertakings, congressmen—locally elected, locally responsible, and wary of centralizing party or governmental power in the White House—usually make sure that all levels of government share in spending the money. Very often the money appropriated by Congress out of the federal treasury is ultimately spent by a state official or by

---

[16] Paul T. David, Ralph Goldman, and Richard Bain, *The Politics of National Party Conventions* (Washington, D.C.: The Brookings Institution, 1960), p. 84.

a man elected by a local group to administer part of a program. Frequently the administrator is a political hybrid. Using a striking but not untypical example, Morton Grodzins[17] described a local health officer:

[He] is appointed by the state under merit standards established by the federal government. His base salary comes jointly from state and federal funds, the county provides him with an office and office amenities and pays a portion of his expenses, and the largest city in the county also contributes to his salary and office by virtue of his appointment as a city plumbing inspector. It is impossible from moment to moment to tell under which government [he] operates. His work of inspecting the purity of food is carried out under federal standards; but he is enforcing state laws when inspecting commodities that have not been in interstate commerce; and somewhat perversely he also acts under state authority when inspecting milk coming into the county from across the state border. He is a federal officer when impounding impure drugs shipped from a neighboring state; a federal-state officer when distributing typhoid immunization serum; a state officer when enforcing standards of industrial hygiene; a state-local officer when inspecting a city's water supply; and (to complete the circle) a local officer when insisting that the city butchers adopt more hygienic methods of handling their garbage.

Second, congressional participation in administering federal programs operates against centralization. A considerable part of a congressman's time, and even more of the time of his staff, is taken up talking to administrators about problems his constituents are experiencing. In 1944, for instance, the Office of Price Administration received an average of 1397 congressional "contacts" each week. These contacts consisted of letters, telephone calls, and personal visits. More formal, but no less effective, is the kind of reception that congressmen may give agency heads during annual appropriations hearings or at special investigations. A federal bureaucrat who, even with the cooperation of the President, tries to use his authority to build up a national party to compete with a congressman's local group is likely to find himself in very troubled waters when dealing, as he must, with Congress.

The third factor is the tendency—at times the necessity—for federal administrators to play a partisan political role. Because the President often cannot control congressmen when their interests run counter to his policy aims, he cannot always control his bureaucracy. Administrators constantly need appropriations to carry out their programs, and they frequently need new legislation to make their work more effective. To get money and new laws, they must have the active cooperation of congressmen. To obtain that cooperation, administrators frequently rely on the President, but when they cannot, they have to have a reservoir of good will with congressmen or with interest groups who in turn can influence congressmen. Directly or indirectly, the bureaucrat "must find support from legislators tied closely to state and local constituents and state and local governments. The political activity of the administrator, like the administrative activity of the legislator, must often be turned to representing state and local interests in national programs."[18]

---

[17] "The Federal System," in the Report of the President's Commission on National Goals, *Goals for Americans* (Englewood Cliffs, N.J.: Prentice-Hall, Inc., 1960), pp. 265–266.

[18] Morton Grodzins, "American Political Parties and the American System," *Western Political Quarterly*, 13 (December 1960), p. 991.

Party Discipline: The Local Machine

Decentralization, like two-party competition, may stop at the state and local level. There discipline may sometimes be strict and real power centered in the hands of one man or a small group of men. The literature and folklore on colorful, and not always honest, city and county bosses is as enormous as it is fascinating. The fragmented power structure of the national parties actually assists these people in running their machines. Decentralization of governmental and party power means local control and, as Lockard says, "plays into the hands of the boss: he is at the bottom of the pyramid, he has contact with all the elements of the party system, but he usually is beyond the authority of any higher echelon of the party. He has and uses the weapons of discipline to keep control over his organization, but he is usually free of effective control or discipline from above." [19]

Many eulogies have been recited at the supposed graveside of the local boss and his machine, but both of them seem able to survive the funeral and to enjoy the obituaries. Yet it is also true that increased prosperity, the spread of civil service, and wider assumption by government agencies of the social welfare functions that the bosses once exercised to keep the poor immigrants loyal have cut into the number and efficiency of party bosses. Political machines, however, are still with us—now generally headed by "leaders" rather than bosses—and may, as the Byrd organization in Virginia did for so many years, bring all agencies of a state government under its taut discipline.

REFORM OF THE PARTY SYSTEM

At the turn of the century the American party system was the principal target for political reformers. Their goal was then to curb the power of the party politician. To accomplish this, they fought, in some localities, for nonpartisan elections in which the party affiliation of candidates would not be labeled on the ballot. In other areas they fought for primary elections to take the power of nominating candidates away from party leaders. The party system is still the target of political reformers, but ironically the goal is now to strengthen party leadership, to centralize power with the parties, and to shore up party discipline. The over-all objective of this new reform movement is to make the parties more responsive to the popular will and more responsible for the behavior of their elected candidates.

Critics of the Present System

The decentralized, compromise character of the national parties has been much criticized on the ground that such parties fail to fulfill two of the primary functions in a democracy. First, they do not present the voters with a clear choice on the really important public issues. Indeed, they

---

[19] P. 223.

often do not even discuss the really important issues. There is, James M. Burns[20] charges, "a vast boredom" in America with party politics. "Because it has failed to engage itself with the problems that dog us during our working days and haunt our dreams at night, politics has not engaged the best of us, or at least the best in us."

The second criticism of the American party system is that its diffusion of power causes a diffusion of responsibility. Because no one man or one committee or one convention can set party policy, no man or committee or convention can be held responsible. Some of these critics argue that we now have a four-party rather than a two-party system, with the Democrats and Republicans each having a congressional party and a presidential party. Thus the parties are not able to effect consistent governmental policies and the voters are unable to hold either party as a party responsible for the action or inaction of its members while in office.

This criticism was brought to a head in 1950 by a Committee on Political Parties set up by the American Political Science Association. In its report, "Toward a More Responsible Two-Party System," the committee stated its dissatisfaction with the present party system:[21]

Historical and other factors have caused the American two-party system to operate as two loose associations of state and local organizations, with very little national machinery and very little national cohesion. As a result, either major party, when in power, is ill-equipped to organize its members in the legislative and the executive branches into a government held together and guided by the party program. Party responsibility at the polls thus tends to vanish. This is a very serious matter, for it affects the very heartbeat of American democracy. It also poses grave problems of domestic and foreign policy in an era when it is no longer safe for the nation to deal piecemeal with issues that can be disposed of only on the basis of coherent programs.

The committee made a large number of recommendations looking toward (1) an increased measure of efficiency, centralization, and internal democracy in party machinery, (2) the formulation of more meaningful party programs, and (3) more vigorous and responsible efforts by public officers to carry out the program of the party winning an election. The committee's specific proposals can only be sampled here. To meet the first objective, one of the committee's recommendations was that each party should have a national *party council* of fifty members so selected as to constitute a representative cross section of the party's leaders in federal and state public office and also of the rank-and-file party members. The council would have power to "consider and settle the larger problems of party management," including preparation of a preliminary draft of the party platform for submission to the national convention, interpretation of the platform between elections, suggestion of suitable congressional candidates to the states and districts, and preliminary screening of presidential candidates before the national convention meets.

To meet the second objective, the committee proposed that national party platforms should be formulated every two years (rather than the present four),

---

[20] *The Deadlock of Democracy,* rev. ed. (Englewood Cliffs, N.J.: Prentice-Hall, Inc., 1963), p. 1.
[21] *American Political Science Review,* Supplement, 44 (September 1950), p. v. Also published separately under the same title (New York: Holt, Rinehart and Winston, Inc., 1950).

and that they should state national principles and policies to which all party candidates for public office at any level of government would be expected to adhere.

To meet the third objective, the committee laid particular stress upon the need for improved party responsibility in Congress. This could be achieved, in the committee's opinion, through the consolidation of the existing numerous leadership groups in Congress into a "truly effective and responsible leadership committee for each party"; through the abandonment of the seniority rule which discourages party regularity by automatically giving committee chairmanships to senior party members; and by holding more frequent party caucuses at which congressmen would be pledged to support bills designed to carry out the party's platform.

Defenders of the Present System

A strong argument has been advanced in support of our present party system by many political scientists. For example, Pendleton Herring has developed the thesis that a democratic society can survive only where there is a constant reconciliation of conflicting economic and social interests. Herring argues that politicians perform an essential social role by acting as mediators, and he also defends the political party because of the way in which it appeals to a wide variety of groups and wins their support by offering something to each. "The accomplishment of party government," Herring[22] says, "lies in its demonstrated ability for reducing warring interests and conflicting classes to cooperative terms." This also means that when parties write their platforms, however inconsistent and evasive, they make it possible for people who have clashing interests to live together in peace. In other words, opposing groups that are contending for power must keep their quarrels within narrow limits. Once the lines of conflict are too clearly drawn, once the stakes in politics are set too high, there is danger that the defeated faction in an election will refuse to accept the result in a peaceful manner. It may conclude that too much has been lost and that it is better to oppose the result with force and violence than to permit the government to pursue policies antagonistic to its interests.

Government by Majority or by Consensus?

One can speak of a kind of democracy that stresses the right of a well-defined majority to control the government and to put its program into effect and of a somewhat different kind of democracy under which sharply defined party programs are avoided, "everybody" gets "something," and government seeks to rule by consensus rather than by majority. In a very large measure, the present American party system, defended by Herring and others, is based, consciously or unconsciously, on a belief that policy-making by consensus is possible in a society as complex as America's. Critics of the present system, however, believe, explicitly or implicitly, that it is impossible to transfer the

---

[22] *The Politics of Democracy* (New York: Holt, Rinehart and Winston, Inc., 1940), p. 132.

consensus achieved in the committee room to decision-making in a society made up of more than 200 million individuals. They argue that the only real alternative to allowing the majority to call the tune is government by a small group of powerful and largely irresponsible office holders.

THE PATTERN OF THE PARTY SYSTEM

The term "party system" was deliberately chosen for this chapter, because "to speak of a party *system* is to imply a patterned relationship among elements of a larger whole."[23] And what we have described and analyzed here is a pattern of relationships, although that pattern is dynamic rather than static. The three main characteristics we have been discussing are all parts of a larger pattern. They are so interrelated that it is difficult to say which are causes and which are effects of the others, or how the consequences of each shape the consequences of the others.

A two-party system encourages efforts to form majorities and thereby coalitions. The relative absence of deep and antagonistic class cleavages discourages strong ideological or programmatic stands as does a written Constitution which the public mind touches with divinity. These factors also can encourage coalitions, which in turn facilitate a two-party rather than a multiparty system. A presidential form of government and a winner-take-all electoral arrangement for congressional seats also encourage two parties and coalitions and move parties to stress social unity rather than divisiveness. At the same time, such political arrangements are feasible only in the absence of class consciousness. A pluralistic society spread over half a continent makes federalism an attractive political arrangement. Federalism, in turn, creates independent bases of power for local politicians and works against disciplined parties. If parties are not disciplined, they are not apt to be able to unite on specific matters of ideology and comprehensive program. A federal arrangement, in the absence of a presidential system, might work in favor of regional parties; but the electoral institutions counterbalance any such tendency, and when combined with federalism again encourage coalitions rather than splinter parties. The dangling bait of a majority vote and the apparent middle-of-the-road and rather indifferent political attitude of large portions of the electorate move the parties to make similar appeals to similar groups of voters; at the same time the similarity of these appeals may tend to make large blocs of voters somewhat lukewarm in their attention to politics and, after being educated in an environment of political moderation, to adhere to the middle of the political road.

To say all of this is not to claim that the party system has never changed or can never change. Surely in some respects it has changed over the years, and inevitably will change in the future. The attempt in 1964 by elements within the Republican party to swing that party away from the center would have, if continued for any length of time, brought about sweeping changes in the nature of the party system. The stinging defeat of Goldwater in the presidential election

---

[23] Key, *Politics, Parties, and Pressure Groups,* p. 206.

of that year convinced many Republican leaders to try to halt popular abandonment of their party by uniting behind Richard Nixon, a more moderate conservative than Goldwater. Another possible change is a spread of genuine two-party competition. In 1968, despite George Wallace's appeals to racism and states rights, Nixon was able to carry Florida, Kentucky, South Carolina, Tennessee, and Virginia. Outside the South, many Republican candidates for congressional and state offices have recently won support from Catholics—as did Eisenhower and Nixon—as well as from Jews and Negroes.

Nor does the description of the patterns of party behavior as a system imply that positive steps should not be taken to reform that system. What the concept of a party system does indicate is that reform is a more difficult process than merely changing the mechanics of party organization and also that successful reform of the party system may have widespread effects throughout the entire governmental and social system in the United States. If power within the parties is in fact centralized and they are converted into disciplined, programmatic bodies, we should, for example, expect equally fundamental changes in the relationship between the states and national government and possibly even in the degree of political agreement in the country. These may or may not be desirable side effects of party reform, but we should be fully aware that they are very likely to occur.

Selected Bibliography

Agar, Herbert, *The Price of Union* (Boston: Houghton Mifflin Company, 1945). Stresses the role that political parties have played in American history in furthering compromise and building consensus.

Binkley, Wilfred E., *American Political Parties,* 4th ed. (New York: Alfred A. Knopf, 1963). Provides historical background for the present-day party system.

Cotter, Cornelius P., *Politics Without Power* (New York: Atherton Press, 1964). An analysis of the national committees of the two major parties.

Duverger, Maurice, *Political Parties: Their Organization and Activity in the Modern State* (New York: John Wiley & Sons, Inc., 1954). The leading comparative study of party systems in several countries.

Key, V. O., *Politics, Parties, and Pressure Groups,* 5th ed. (New York: Thomas Y. Crowell Company, 1964). The most recent edition of the standard—and, in many ways, the classic—textbook on American political parties.

——, *Southern Politics in State and Nation* (New York: Alfred A. Knopf, 1949). A brilliant analysis of the politics of one section of the United States.

McKean, Dayton, *The Boss* (Boston: Houghton Mifflin Company, 1940). A detailed study of the late Mayor Hague of Jersey City and his political machine.

Michels, Robert, *Political Parties* (New York: Dover Publications, Inc., 1959). A sociological study of the emergence of leadership, the psychology of power, and the oligarchic tendencies of organization, first published in English in 1915.

Schattschneider, E. E., *The Struggle for Party Government* (College Park, Md.: University of Maryland Press, 1948). In contrast to volumes by Agar, Herring, Brogan, and others, this pamphlet presents a plea for stronger and more highly disciplined parties.

7

Interest groups and public opinion

No aspect of the American political system has been the subject of more heated and persistent controversy than interest groups. To some political observers such organizations may seem less than legitimate, but their impact on government cannot be denied.

An interest group is a formal organization of people who share one or more common objectives or concerns and who try to influence the course of public policy to protect and promote these aims. Such organizations differ widely: they are large or small, permanent or temporary, rich or poor, powerful or weak. Their exact number is impossible to calculate. Members and allies prefer the term "interest groups" to describe their organizations; enemies prefer the pejorative implication of "pressure groups." Since they are typically organized to protect an interest by exerting political pressure, each term is rather accurate, and we shall use them both with no moral judgment implied.

One way to understand an interest group is to note how it differs from a political party. Although a party and an interest group overlap in many ways, the two do have certain obvious differences. As elaborated in Chapter 6, the Democratic and Republican parties are large agencies that seek to win the active support of 40 million or more voters. Consequently appeals must be broad and programs must deal with many problems. An interest group is seldom actively supported by more than a tiny minority of people. Consequently, an interest group's appeal is narrow and its program limited. In general, a party is primarily interested in winning control of and operating the government; an interest group is primarily interested in shaping a particular public policy. On the other hand, having won control of the government, a party can hardly avoid the responsibility of shaping many public policies, whereas to influence public policy an interest group may find it necessary to elect its supporters to public office.

THE SPECTRUM OF PRESSURE POLITICS

The spectrum of pressure politics is very broad indeed. Business, labor, agriculture, the professions such as law, medicine, and education, regional, racial, religious, and nationality groups, war veterans— almost every type of group allegiance known to man seems to be represented in the list of well-known organizations. The range of interest groups is suggested by some of the names of the organizations that annually spend $50,000 or more for lobbying activities in Washington. Each year's list will usually include the American Medical Association, the AFL-CIO, the American Farm Bureau Federation, the U.S. Savings and Loan League, the National Association of Electric

15 Top Spenders

The 15 top spenders of the 304 organizations filing lobby spending reports in Washington for 1965, with comparative figures for 1964.

Organization	1965	1964
American Medical Assn.	$1,155,935.30	$ 45,514.87
United Federation of Postal Clerks (AFL–CIO)	175,365.09	131,912.89
AFL–CIO (national headquarters)	148,343.61	153,541.69
American Legion	139,537.74	123,913.60
Committee for Automobile Excise Tax Repeal	116,394.46	
American Farm Bureau Federation	115,846.00	123,645.00
U.S. Savings and Loan League	105,840.20	98,233.10
International Assn. of Machinists, District Lodge #44 (AFL–CIO)	104,766.96	123,568.59
National Housing Conference Inc.	95,534.40	88,224.37
National Farmers Union	87,351.78	80,946.01
Brotherhood of Locomotive Firemen and Enginemen, Grand Lodge (AFL–CIO)	86,945.40	8,622.70
International Brotherhood of Teamsters	86,428.79	73,196.21
National Federation of Independent Business, Inc.	80,747.36	67,143.05
National Education Assn., Division of Federal Relations	79,213.73	60,008.69
Council for a Livable World	76,983.16	123,981.73

SOURCE: *Congressional Quarterly Weekly Report*, Aug. 19, 1966, p. 1790.

Companies, the International Brotherhood of Teamsters, the National Association of Letter Carriers, and the National Education Association.

It is probably safe to say that every American is identified with and represented by at least one vigorous interest group. But not every interest is so represented. A striking and continuing phenomenon of pressure politics in the United States is the relative lack of organization by consumer groups. Every person is a consumer and complaints about high prices are perennial, yet consumers have not organized for effective political action. Americans have been keenly aware of the importance of the economic factor in modern life, but with few exceptions they have chosen to emphasize their interests as *producers* rather than as *consumers* in their pressure group activity. The success consumer interest groups might have was demonstrated in 1966 when groups of marching housewives in various locations throughout the country succeeded in getting food prices lowered.

Economic Interest Groups

Historically, the most effective pressure groups have been those based on the simple economic interests in earning a living and in acquiring, holding, and profitably using property. The associations that have most influenced government in the United States over the years have been those representing the three basic occupational groupings in our economy: business, labor, and agriculture. The recent activity of racial organizations may seem to mark a new trend, but even there economic factors are closely tied to problems of social justice.

It is commonly but erroneously believed that producer interest groups in a particular area are solidly united and always stand shoulder to shoulder in fighting this government measure or supporting that one. In fact, there are often serious divisions within business, labor, and agriculture groups. Labor is torn between the rival aims of craft and industrial unions and of skilled and unskilled workers. The dairy farmer of Wisconsin finds himself pitted against the cotton farmer of Texas over the issue of oleomargarine taxation. Similarly, the manufacturer and independent retail merchant find themselves locked in a bitter struggle with chain-store operators and discount houses. The former want the support of government through "fair trade" laws fixing minimum retail prices; the latter want economic freedom to sell products at whatever prices they choose to charge. Moreover, segments of organized labor identified with certain businesses or industries tend to reflect the industry position on many political issues. In other words, on many issues certain businessmen and workers may be much more closely identified with each other in their interest group activities than with other people entirely within the business or labor categories.

Noneconomic Interest Groups

When we move away from the economic area, the organizational loyalties of the American people become so numerous that it is impossible to present an inclusive analysis of the resulting interest groups. Moreover, some associations that appear to be primarily noneconomic in character often show a very strong interest in economic issues. Some idea of the nature and complexity of these groups can be gained by noting their number and activity under such headings as race, religion, the professions, women, and the military.

Many strong organizations represent the interests of racial and religious groups on the national scene. For example, two, the National Association for the Advancement of Colored People (NAACP) and the National Urban League, keep a constant watch over government policy as it affects the interests of Negroes. Perhaps even more powerful today are the Student Non-Violent Coordinating Committee (SNCC) and the Congress of Racial Equality (CORE), though both depend on methods of mass protest rather than conventional lobbying to pressure public officials. Protestants frequently seek to influence government through the National Council of Churches, Catholics through the National Catholic Welfare Council, and Jews through the American Jewish Committee, the American Jewish Congress, and the Anti-Defamation League.

Most professions have strong organizations which are active from time to time in pressure politics in promoting noneconomic as well as economic interests. This is particularly true of doctors and lawyers, who through the American Medical Association and the American Bar Association have sought to influence many aspects of governmental programs ranging all the way from court organization and public health to administration of antitrust laws. In general, the interest groups of the professions are exceedingly conservative, and while claiming to be anxious about maintaining high professional standards or serving the public good often seem mainly concerned to protect the vested interests of their members or clients.

Organizations representing war veterans find an immediate and powerful incentive for political activity in such issues as pensions for veterans and their dependents and relief and rehabilitation for the disabled. But their interest has also encompassed such issues as national defense and foreign policy. By all odds the largest veterans' organization today is the American Legion. Smaller organizations are the Veterans of Foreign Wars and the American Veterans of World War II (AMVETS). Like the Daughters of the American Revolution (DAR), the American Legion is controlled and administered by a group of very conservative leaders. Both of these organizations illustrate the enormous power often wielded, in interest groups of all kinds, by the professional secretariats at group headquarters. It is doubtful whether the average member of the DAR or the American Legion shares the ultraconservative view of the paid workers who run these particular organizations. This is one reason why public officers do not pay more attention to lobbyists. They know that on many issues professional lobbyists simply do not speak for any large number of rank-and-file members.

TECHNIQUES OF INTEREST POLITICS

An interest group can use three basic techniques in trying to secure its purpose. First, it can try to place in public office those persons most favorably disposed toward the interests it seeks to promote. This technique may be labeled *electioneering*. Second, an interest group can try to persuade public officers, whether they are initially favorably disposed toward it or not, to adopt and enforce the policies that it thinks will prove most beneficial to its interests. This technique may be labeled *lobbying*. Third, it can try to influence the making and expression of public opinion and thereby gain an indirect influence over government, since government in a democracy is ultimately affected by public opinion. This technique may be labeled *propagandizing*.

Electioneering

Although interest groups and political parties are distinct and separate agencies, they are sometimes closely associated in their activities. In particular, an interest group often seeks to work within a party, since it is there that government is organized and public policy is controlled. This means that an interest group must frequently be active at election time. Now and then an organization, such as the League of Women Voters, does succeed in maintaining neutrality between parties and candidates, even though it may be intensely interested in influencing public policy decisions. But such organizational neutrality is the exception rather than the rule. Many interest groups campaign actively for particular candidates and vigorously support a particular party.

A typical interest group first undertakes to influence the nomination of congressmen, by trying to win promises of support from candidates in both parties and then by backing those candidates giving such a promise. It may even send a representative to the national party conventions to argue for inclusion in party platforms of a plank calling for enactment of the desired law. The association will thereafter take stock of its gains and losses, noting with pleasure the nomination of friendly candidates, marking for defeat unfriendly candidates, and perhaps sizing up the party situation with an eye toward supporting either the Republican or the Democratic party as such if either appears to be more strongly committed to the proposed law.

Having made these assessments, association leaders will then undertake to raise money in support of approved candidates, supplying them with favorable publicity and getting out votes for them on election day. Of course, the organization must watch its step very closely at this stage. Discretion may suggest some appearance of neutrality or even financial support for both sides, particularly in those areas in which both candidates are committed to support a bill, or where both are equally undecided about the proposal. For the real struggle lies still ahead—securing the enactment of the bill when the newly elected Congress meets —and it is almost as important not to antagonize doubtful congressmen as it is to secure the election of fully committed congressmen.

It may be asked why an interest group, particularly if it is a large and important one, does not run candidates of its own for public office and seek direct control of government, thereby becoming a political party. If its purpose is to bring about the enactment of laws favorable to its cause and to kill those that it views as unfavorable, how can it better achieve this purpose than by electing its own men to office? As a matter of fact, many interest groups are subject to a strong temptation to do just that. Now and then a group succumbs to this temptation. The Prohibition party, a one-issue party that sought the outlawing of intoxicating beverages in the years before the adoption of the Eighteenth Amendment, is a good example. But much more often the temptation is resisted. No interest group, least of all a specific organization, has the support of more than a minority of the voters. Consequently, a direct attempt to take control of the government could not ordinarily hope to enjoy more than a very limited success. On the other hand, if a well-organized minority sells its support as dearly as it can to one of the major parties in an election, or remains neutral and then brings its pressure to bear upon the victorious party, threatening opposition in the next election, it has an excellent chance of influencing the course of government.

The experience of labor illustrates why even a large and well-organized minority sometimes prefers to use pressure politics rather than party politics to secure its ends. In foreign countries, such as England, and in a few American states labor has organized its own parties. These attempts have met with some success, for labor in a highly industrialized area is a sufficiently numerous group to have a chance of winning an election. But at best that chance is less than even, unless a labor party is able and willing to broaden its appeal to include farmers, consumers, professional men, trades people, or other groups. In fact, to become one of Britian's two major parties the Labor party has had to pursue such a policy, and in so doing it has ceased to be a pure labor party. In the United States, the labor movement, following the lead set by an early AFL president, Samuel Gompers, has steadfastly refused to organize a party and has instead tried to follow a policy of "rewarding its friends and punishing its enemies" without regard to party affiliations.

Lobbying

The legislative process is, of course, the target of vigorous and conflicting activity by interest groups, which bring pressure to bear directly upon public officers in an effort to shape governmental decisions. This is a vital arena of lobbying activity. But the influence of government upon individual interests depends upon a great deal more than the words of statutes. The final impact of a statute subjecting labor-management relations to government control inevitably depends upon the vigor with which it is enforced and also upon the interpretation it receives through administrative rulings and court decisions. Accordingly, business and labor associations cannot limit their lobbying activity to legislators when they know that important decisions affecting government policy remain to be made in the executive and judicial arenas. Lobbying methods vary greatly. An approach that may prove effective with congressmen is almost certain to give way to other methods in dealing with an agency head or a member of a regulatory commission.

In the Legislative Branch

Lobbyists—or Washington representatives, as they usually prefer to be called—have sometimes found congressmen susceptible to influence through the "wining and dining" approach. This fact was demonstrated a few years ago when

The Teachers' Union, lobbying here in a New York City hotel, seeks to influence legislators and the public through such means as brochures, exhibits, and discussions. The Teachers' Union is one of the nation's largest and most powerful lobbying groups. (Mildred Grossman)

a New England textile manufacturer testified before a congressional investigating committee concerning the free hotel visits and other favors he had showered on legislators and White House staff officers. But the lobbyist has learned that he must also use technical data and logical argument to persuade a congressman that the course of action he favors is sound and, better yet, that it will promote the interests of the congressman's constituents and win him their gratitude and support. The extent to which lobbyists work closely with congressmen in drafting bills, testifying at committee hearings, helping write committee reports, supplying data for speeches to be made in Congress and elsewhere, and lining up votes in the House and Senate is not fully appreciated. The close relationship that may exist between a congressman and a lobbyist is better understood when it is recognized that the congressman himself is frequently a lobbyist in the sense that he has been sent to Washington by a particular constituency to represent the economic and social interests of that area. A senator from Kansas has little difficulty cooperating with the lobbyists of the farm organizations, a senator from Texas readily accepts the help of the petroleum industry in working out the details of an oil bill, and a representative from Akron or Pittsburgh is likely to be predisposed to support organized labor's position on a "full-employment" bill.

Of course, many congressmen represent states or districts with varied backgrounds and are not so heavily committed to the support of any one interest. Others manage to temper their sense of obligation to a particular interest group with a strong concern for the general welfare. The task of a lobbyist who wishes to win the support of these congressmen is more difficult. Similarly, the lobbyist who represents a small, poor, or underprivileged group cannot usually assume the existence of an initial bond of sympathy with congressmen.

It is generally true in all areas of government that the lobbyist who seeks to persuade public officers to act *positively* by adopting or enforcing a particular policy has a more difficult task before him than the lobbyist whose purpose is a negative one of persuading government not to act, or to leave the status quo undisturbed. There is a tremendous force of inertia to overcome in persuading government to embark upon any new policy. This reluctance to take positive action is particularly pronounced in Congress, where the enactment of a bill usually requires successfully surmounting half a dozen major hurdles. To put it the other way round, the lobbyist whose task is to kill a bill can effect his purpose at any one of these hurdles. He can lose out at five points, win at the sixth, and carry the day.

In the Executive Branch

There is a great deal more lobbying in the executive branch of the government than is commonly realized. It begins with the opportunity that interest groups have of influencing the appointment of administrative personnel to important posts and continues with the maintenance of close and friendly working relations on a day-to-day basis between many administrators and lobbyists. That corporations should be in close touch with the Antitrust Division of the Department of Justice, unions with the National Labor Relations Board, or farm groups with the Department of Agriculture is not surprising. Neither is it surprising that men on both sides of these relationships should get to know and learn to work with one another. Many of these relationships attract little or no public attention, and the possibility that the lobbyist may succeed in influencing administrative officers beyond the limits of propriety is an ever-present one. In the end, more than one administrative agency has been "captured" by the very group that it was supposed to regulate in the public interest.

In the Judicial Branch

In the sense that the term is used in the legislative process, there is little if any room for "lobbying" in the courts. Indeed, such lobbying is usually unethical and frequently criminal. Yet, in a broader sense, interest groups regularly lobby in the judicial process. Such lobbying is inevitable, since court decisions play a crucial role in molding public policy. The interest of the National Association of Manufacturers, for instance, in favorable judicial interpretation of a statute is hardly less salient than its interest in getting the law passed in the first place.

"Judicial lobbying" takes several forms. First, interest group leaders can use their influence in the executive or legislative process to help select judges whose general philosophy of government may be favorable to the group's aims. Second, interest groups can carry on lawsuits themselves or can help others in court actions challenging or defending the legality of governmental or private action. This sort of aid is more important than it might at first appear. Because the American legal process is typically slow and costly, it often takes a large amount of money to pay for lawyers, research expenses, and court fees. The cost merely of printing the briefs and records for a case brought to the Supreme Court can easily run into thousands of dollars. Third, if it can meet certain technical requirements, an association can enter a legal dispute already in progress as *amicus curiae,* a friend of the court, and offer its views as to the proper decision.

These kinds of interest group activities come as a surprise to many people, and there is some conflict with the naïve view that courts and judges are remote from struggles over public policy-making. But the U.S. Supreme Court has held that the First Amendment's protection of freedom of speech, association, and petition gives organizations a right to use the courts to further their policy aims.[1]

Lobbying with the Home Organization

Lobbying is not a one-way street. A Washington representative has to devote much of his time to channeling information and advice back to his home organization. After years of dealing with various government agencies, a lobbyist often develops personal sources of information about public policies planned for the future as well as a keen sense of likely official reactions to suggestions for changes in existing policies. This sort of intelligence can be of great use to his organization in responding to proposed legislative or administrative action, and if it is a business group, in designing products intended to be sold to the government.

Curiously, a lobbyist is often more perplexed about his relations with his employers than with public officials. To facilitate his work, a Washington representative would prefer that he be considered as an ambassador from his organization to the federal government, not only transmitting specific information and performing set tasks but also advising and being consulted on broad policy issues. At least among business firms, however, the tendency has been for the home office to take a more limited view of the lobbyist's functions.[2]

Propagandizing

An interest group seldom limits its campaign for favored governmental treatment to lobbying alone. Success in this direction is unlikely unless its demands appear to have broad public support. Occasionally in an area of policy-making in which the public is disinterested or in which the issues are exceedingly technical, an organization will concentrate all its energies in a frontal attack at the point at which policy is to be made. But more often than not a group mounts simultaneous assaults upon government agencies and the public mind. Many illustrations can be given. The American Medical Association unsuccessfully spent millions of dollars to arouse public opinion against Medicare and other public health proposals, which it condemned as "socialized medicine." In the months preceding the enactment of the Taft-

---

[1] *National Association for the Advancement of Colored People v. Button,* 371 U.S. 415 (1963).
[2] For an interesting analysis of the problems of the Washington representative of the large business firm, see Paul W. Cherington and Ralph L. Gillen, *The Business Representative in Washington* (Washington, D.C.: The Brookings Institution, 1962).

City and State Lobbyists
Are Newest Washington Breed

They Vie for $15-Billion a Year

By Douglas W. Cray

SPECIAL TO THE NEW YORK TIMES

WASHINGTON, Nov. 12— Post-election assessments, mutterings and head shakings replaced even the fortunes of the Redskins football team last week as the No. 1 diversion of this city's legions of pundits. The voters' decisions will provide grist for the pundits' mills for many months to come.

But when the new Congress convenes in January, some old faces will be missing in the House and Senate, and some new faces will be taking their place, thus temporarily complicating the task of this city's legions of lobbyists.

The business and economic consequences of this semiannual changeover remain, as always, to be seen. To some degree at least, each of the 50 states and the citizens and businesses within them will all be affected by the changing of the guard in the elected representatives in the nation's capital.

In the case of at least 12 states and several cities, however, this particular changeover should have little or no enduring effect on the operations of their lobbyists, who are appointed rather than elected.

They vie, in a sense, for the close to $15-billion in U.S. funds that are annually pumped into the fifty states in the form of grants, contracts and other financial aid. Their objectives range from such things as a proposed atom smasher, at a site still to be picked, to far more modest funds for research and development grants and so on from assorted Federal agencies.

These men about town vary widely in experience and sophistication. They are variously used, some concentrating on little more than chamber-of-commerce-type promotion. Others, however, including those from Illinois and New York, have much larger horizons than limning the beauties of their state's foliage.

At last count, the states and the cities with a "man in Washington" include Illinois, New York, California, West Virginia, Maryland, Pennsylvania, Ohio, Indiana, Oklahoma, Virginia, Massachusetts and Texas.

Others have been on hand long enough to have fully staffed offices. These include men such as Daniel F. Ruge, a lawyer who is director of the New York State Department of Commerce's Washington office; Kyran McGrath, chief of the Washington office of the Department of Business and Economic Development, State of Illinois, and his colleague, Thomas G. Fitzsimmons, the deputy administrator of the Washington office.

He is, indeed, all on that, as far as his native soil and roots are concerned. But he moves with an easy gait and the wide-open eyes and ears of a seasoned pro through the padded-shoulder commercial and government circle that gathers daily at such popular watering sites as Duke Zeibert's, the Black Steer and others.

Their Illinois bosses, Gene Graves, director of the department, and Gov. Otto Kerner, who signed legislation establishing the whole undertaking in July of last year, do not, of course, have either of them in this city simply to quench thirst at Duke's, where, amid the din, much of interest may certainly be heard.

This pair, and New York's urbane Dan Ruge, move with equal ease and genuine welcome through the corridors of the Executive Office Building, where the Bureau of the Budget dwells, and the newer corridors elsewhere in town where such money-allocating agencies as Health, Education and Welfare, Housing and Urban Development and the Atomic Energy Commission are housed.

They do not, of course, simply stop by and pick up anything like a regular weekly, monthly, semiannual or yearly allotment of feed and seed funds for their states. Nothing anywhere, especially here, is ever that simple. But they do make a full-time attempt to keep track of what's going on, what's available and what's coming up.

Though only a handful of states so far have formally taken this comparatively new step in Federal-state relationships, it has, as a way of life in the science called politics, already achieved at least academic credentials.

The fact, is there is nothing wholly academic about the still comparatively modest collection of lobbyists—their jobs are too varied and too tentative. Massachusetts, for example, is represented by a public relations concern.

After all, this national capital that stretches so attractively along the banks of the murky Potomac, has long since counted among its fixtures the often sumptuous and always active foreign embassies. The latter have become an integral part of the endless, seasonally adjusted tourist attractions. . . .

Foreign governments and nations long ago saw fit to maintain missions here. It is not surprising that some of the more alert of the 50 states have, considering the stakes involved, rather belatedly borrowed a leaf from abroad and augmented their elected representation in Washington with some hand-picked, business-oriented representation.

It makes, as one of Duke's genial bartenders might say, "dollars and sense."

Hartley Act by the Eightieth Congress in 1947, both industry and labor spent vast sums of money in efforts to swing public support to one side or the other of the issue. In newspaper and radio advertisements and in countless leaflets and mailing pieces businessmen told the public that the iniquitous Wagner Act must be amended if the specter of a "labor dictatorship" was to be destroyed, whereas the unions argued that the proposed law would establish "slave labor" in the United States.

Although much has been written about propaganda and its use, the term remains a vague and inexact one. Propaganda may be good or bad. It may be factually true or false and distorted. It may be designed to further the general welfare or have a narrow, selfish motivation. It may be aimed at reason or play upon emotion. It may try to persuade through fact and logical argument or through an appeal to prejudice. But in any case propaganda has an end in view; it seeks to influence the public mind with respect to certain issues, specific or general, short-term or long-term. Further attention will be given to propaganda and its effect on public opinion in the concluding section of this chapter.

REGULATION OF INTEREST GROUPS

Whether or not interest groups are healthy and desirable aspects of a democratic society continues to be much debated. But whether one views them as an asset or a liability to a democratic society, it is hard to avoid the conclusion that they are prone to abuse their power. There is general agreement that this is one aspect of private institutional arrangement in America that should be subjected to a measure of legal control in the interest of the general good. Over three quarters of the states, as well as the national government, have enacted laws for the regulation of lobbying. Many of these laws make use of the two devices of *registration* and *disclosure*. Organizations, as well as their agents, that seek to influence government policy and practices are compelled to register with some public agency and to disclose certain information about themselves. The hope behind such regulation is that if vital information concerning lobbies is a matter of public knowledge, the electorate will be able to evaluate the propriety of the pressures interest groups bring to bear upon government officers and that legislators will thereby be able to resist pressure to which they submitted in the past out of fear that public opinion would not support resistance.[3]

The Federal Regulation of Lobbying Act

In 1946, Congress undertook for the first time to control interest groups in the Regulation of Lobbying Act.[4] Actually, the law is poorly named, since it provides for little actual *regulation*. Any person or

---

[3] These state regulations are analyzed in Edgar Lane, *Lobbying and the Law: State Regulation of Lobbying* (Berkeley, Calif.: University of California Press, 1964).

[4] 60 *Stat.* 839. The act is a "Title" of the Legislative Reorganization Act.

organization soliciting or receiving money to be used "principally to aid," or any person or organization whose "principal purpose" is to aid, the passage or defeat of legislation before Congress is required to register with the clerk of the House of Representatives and to file quarterly reports showing all money actually received and expended, including the names and addresses of all persons contributing $500 or more, or to whom $10 or more has been paid. Each lobbyist is required to disclose

the name and address of the person by whom he is employed, and in whose interest he appears or works, the duration of such employment, how much he is paid and is to receive, by whom he is paid or is to be paid, how much he is to be paid for expenses, and what expenses are to be included.

The law further requires that the reported data shall be published at quarterly intervals in the *Congressional Record*. Severe penalties for those convicted under the act are prescribed, ranging up to a $10,000 fine and a five-year prison term, and including a three-year ban against further lobbying.

The 1946 act has been much criticized. Its most serious defect is its vague and confusing language, which has encouraged a good deal of noncompliance.[5] The absence of any enforcement agency has the same effect. The public has shown little interest in the data voluntarily reported under the act, which are printed at regular intervals in the *Congressional Record*. It is doubtful whether the pattern of lobbying has been affected very much by the law. Several large organizations, well known for their active interest in governmental affairs, either have been slow to register or have failed to register at all, asserting that they are not lobbies as defined by the act. Moreover, the information filed is often exceedingly scanty and fails to reveal the extent and significance of an organization's or a lobbyist's political activity.

CONSTITUTIONALITY
OF INTEREST GROUP REGULATION

The power to regulate interest groups is subject to a potentially severe constitutional restriction. The First Amendment, which forbids Congress to make any law abridging the right of the people to assemble and to petition the government for a redress of grievances, protects the basic right of lobbying against any outright federal prohibition. And the extension of the right of petition into the area of state government through the due process of law clause of the Fourteenth Amendment similarly bars state or local governments from such action.

In spite of the fact that the Regulation of Lobbying Act of 1946 provides for only a very weak measure of lobby control, some serious constitutional objections have been raised against it. For example, the three-year ban against further lobbying by anyone convicted under the law might in effect deprive such persons

[5] See Belle Zeller, "The Federal Regulation of Lobbying Act," *American Political Science Review,* 42 (April 1948), pp. 239, 245.

of their right of petition. Similarly, it has been argued that the act is so vague and indefinite that it fails to provide an ascertainable standard of guilt and thus violates an essential requirement of due process of law. In 1954, the Supreme Court upheld the validity of the act, stating that Congress was not "constitutionally forbidden to require the disclosure of lobbying activities. To do so would be to deny Congress in large measure the power of self-protection." [6] The Court, however, avoided some of the more difficult constitutional questions by giving the statute the narrowest possible interpretation. According to the majority opinion, the act applies only to lobbyists who enter into direct communication with members of Congress with respect to pending or proposed federal legislation and does not extend to lobbyists who seek to influence the legislative process indirectly by working through public opinion.

After the Supreme Court's decisions in the *School Segregation* cases, a number of southern states attempted to curb or outlaw the activities of the NAACP within their borders. The unconstitutionality of these campaigns was made clear in 1958 when the Court temporarily checked efforts by the attorney general of Alabama to enjoin the NAACP from further activities and to oust it from the state. In particular, the Court ruled that the state could not compel the association to disclose the names of its members. Speaking for a unanimous Court, Justice John Harlan observed:

It is beyond debate that freedom to engage in association for the advancement of beliefs and ideas is an inseparable aspect of the "liberty" assured by the Due Process Clause of the Fourteenth Amendment.

And he added:

it is immaterial whether the beliefs sought to be advanced by association pertain to political, economic, religious or cultural matters, and state action which may have the effect of curtailing the freedom to associate is subject to the closest scrutiny.[7]

PUBLIC OPINION

Ideally, democratic government is based on an intelligent, informed, and politically active citizenry. Supposedly, contro-

---

[6] *United States v. Harris,* 347 U.S. 612, 625 (1954).

[7] *National Association for the Advancement of Colored People v. Alabama,* 357 U.S. 449, 460–461 (1958). After this decision the Alabama supreme court refused to reverse its decision sustaining the injunction against the NAACP because, the judges claimed, the U.S. Supreme Court had misunderstood the case. A second U.S. Supreme Court decision, 360 U.S. 240 (1959), affirmed that Court's 1958 decision. The Alabama courts, however, refused to take any action until a third U.S. Supreme Court decision, 368 U.S. 16 (1961), ordered a federal district court to hear the case if state courts did not act promptly. It was not until December 1961, more than five years after the "temporary" injunction had gone into effect, that the NAACP had its first full hearing in an Alabama court. The trial court made the injunction permanent, and the state supreme court affirmed. In its fourth decision in the case, the U.S. Supreme Court again reversed the Alabama courts and sharply rebuked them for their violation of the NAACP's constitutional rights. The Court then said that if the Alabama supreme court did not quickly dissolve the injunction, the justices in Washington would do that themselves. 377 U.S. 288 (1964). The Alabama judges complied several months later.

versial public problems will be discussed by an educated population, differing solutions will be carefully weighed, and public judgments will be transmitted to government officials, whose policy decisions will reflect the collective wisdom of the people. Democratic practice quite obviously only rarely measures up to this ideal. Public opinion is often nonexistent on many issues with which public officers must deal or, where it does exist, these officers may choose to ignore it and find that they can safely do so. In other situations public opinion does not rest upon a careful grasp of the facts of a problem but is charged with emotion or represents a crass concern for local or individual interests.

Forces Influencing Public Opinion

The concept of an informed public opinion as the basis of democracy remains valid insofar as broad issues of public policy are concerned, though not necessarily for detailed, technical aspects of particular bills or administrative proposals. On the other hand, it must be remembered that emotions do compete with intelligence in the making of public opinion. Thus a nation's experience under democracy may well be good or bad depending on the extent to which its people are influenced by rational forces in their thinking about public affairs. As V. O. Key[8] has commented, "The operation of a democratic order, the linking of public and government, requires an enormous amount of ingenuity and dedication at leadership levels in the explanation and translation of the specifics and technicalities into terms that will capture the attention and understanding of many people." A medley of forces, rational and irrational—some of the individual's own making, others beyond his control—influence the formation of public opinion.

The first force influencing public opinion may be labeled ideology. Most persons in a democracy have a general point of view, a scheme of life, or a set of values or morals. Many belong to a formal church which prescribes a set of religious dogmas for them to accept. Many belong to a political party and accept certain political principles and traditions, vague though they may be. All have ancestral and nationality allegiances. These and other influences produce in each person an ideological outlook against which he tests his thinking concerning political issues and problems. The testing is sometimes conscious, sometimes unconscious, and the ideological influence with respect to a particular issue may be weak or strong. But an individual's general ideology commonly plays a significant part in influencing his stand on many issues.

Second, public opinion is influenced by economic or material considerations. In a capitalist society almost everyone is interested in making his way ahead so far as the acquisition or enjoyment of material goods and wealth is concerned. Accordingly, an individual usually becomes identified with an economic group. He typically regards himself as a businessman, as a worker, as a farmer or, as has already been noted, as a producer rather than a consumer, and thereby ac-

---

[8] *Public Opinion and American Democracy* (New York: Alfred A. Knopf, 1961), p. 91.

quires specific interests and loyalties. Similarly, he lives in a certain section of the country and recognizes that he is identified with the very real material interests of that section. In these and other ways he comes to feel that he is a member of a competitive system. His bread seems to him to be buttered on one side rather than the other and he is very likely to take this point of view into account in taking his stand on the issues of the day.

Third, public opinion is affected by a psychological factor. More than either the ideological or the economic factor, this factor is apt to be unconscious and in some measure irrational. Each individual has a personality that is the result of a variety of complex drives and forces. The person who is relatively well adjusted and happy is likely to react differently to social problems than will an embittered and unhappy person. Interest groups are frequently clever in the way in which they exploit human frustrations and inhibitions. The calculated and repetitious use of words with a "good" connotation, such as "home," "country," "patriot," "the American way of doing things," to describe one's own position, and the labeling of the opposition with words that carry a "bad" connotation, such as "un-American," "regimented," "socialist," "bureaucratic," and "monopolistic," are well-known devices in pressure politics. The use of the scapegoat and of the half-truth, or of the lie that is repeated until it seems to become the truth, are also well-known weapons in the arsenal of the individual or group that consciously seeks to advance its interests by exploiting human weaknesses. The leaders of totalitarian movements have been particularly adept at employing psychological knowledge concerning man's sensitivity to irrational forces and arguments to win support.

Even in democracies such as the United States there has been a growing tendency for both office seekers and public officials to obtain manipulative assistance from professional public relations firms. These experts can frequently be of great help in advising on popular reactions, but a number of firms specializing in political campaigning go further and insist that, if hired, they must control the entire campaign. They claim to be able to merchandise a candidate or a policy issue as effectively as they create a demand for detergents or deodorants.[9]

The prevalence of Madison Avenue political techniques indicates the extent to which public opinion leaders in all walks of life are already committed to the use of psychological techniques in their efforts to control the public mind and social habits. This is not to question the validity or usefulness of the increased knowledge that we now possess about the unconscious and irrational forces that influence men. The basic issue here is whether this new information about man's psychic complexity is to be used to enable individuals and groups of individuals to understand and discipline the irrational forces to which they are subject so that they may become informed and useful members of a free society or to exploit and control people in order to advance the interests of a particular group.

A fourth factor influencing public opinion is technological. The technically advanced character of American civilization makes it possible through mass-

---

[9] For a perceptive analysis of the operations of public relations experts, see Stanley Kelley, Jr., *Professional Public Relations and Political Power* (Baltimore, Md.: The Johns Hopkins Press, 1956).

circulation newspapers and magazines and through radio and television to bring essential information about social problems to every citizen and thereby to encourage the formation of intelligent public opinion. At the same time, technology makes the problems themselves so complex that even highly educated citizens find it difficult to think about these problems intelligently and rationally. For example, two of the greatest issues of our time—finding satisfactory systems to control atomic energy and space weapons and satellites—are made enormously difficult to comprehend because of the secrecy seemingly required by national security. When it is impossible to inform even the members of Congress on such a vital point as the number of atomic bombs that have been stockpiled by the United States, the American people cannot engage in the intelligent deliberation necessary if social control of atomic energy is to be democratic in character.

Mass Media and Public Opinion

In a modern democracy the means of communicating ideas are numerous and varied. The roles played by newspapers, magazines, books, radio and television, motion pictures, literature in the mails, lectures, forums, schools, and churches in making available factual information and in suggesting points of view have long been obvious, if imperfectly understood. Recently a good deal of stress has been laid upon the faults of our communications system, and it must be admitted that there is reason to be discouraged.

The press has become a "big business" enterprise largely inclined to look with favor upon the conservative side of issues. The number of newspapers has been declining steadily and those that remain have become increasingly wealthy and Republican. In the 1964 campaign most papers opposed Senator Goldwater; but traditional party allegiance reasserted itself in 1968, and a majority of papers that took a stand endorsed Richard Nixon. The cost of starting a newspaper has grown so greatly that only rarely does such a paper make an appearance and even more rarely does it survive for any length of time. The day is past when every important political, social, and economic faction had its own journal or easy access to one, and the "one-newspaper town" is common. Radio, television, and movies often oversimplify their material and emphasize the sentimental and romantic, the cheap and the vulgar. Even the mails are loaded with slick "hard sell" propaganda. The public lecture and forum have lost most of the vitality they enjoyed seventy-five years ago. Now the problems of the space age and racial crises are bringing a searching look at the public schools. A few years ago critics were concentrating on alleged inadequacies of training offered in mathematics and science. More recently instruction in the social sciences and the humanities has come in for criticism. If defects of the educational system are threatening to reduce the supply of scientists, similar defects may also be failing to prepare a citizenry—black and white—to cope with difficult social and political problems.

Still, it is easy to paint too dark a picture. There is much evidence that no

President Lyndon B. Johnson conducts an informal White House press conference. (Magnum)

society has ever been able to come closer to an approximation of the democratic idea of an informed and intelligent citizenry than has America. Even the evils of excessive propaganda and inadequate communication, for example, seem to be lessened by competition—in propaganda and among the agencies of communication. Private interest groups may offset each other in their efforts to influence the public mind. Moreover, government agencies themselves have become increasingly interested in disseminating information about public issues and problems. Radio, television, and motion pictures, increased publication of books and the paperback revolution; and expansion of education do, in part at least, compensate for ground lost with the decline in number of newspapers and influence of debates. In the new media of expression, particularly, there are some encouraging trends. Not all motion pictures or radio or television programs are bad, by any means. Sometimes these media do come to grips with serious problems in the area of public affairs and treat them in a responsible manner. In broadcasting the national party conventions or such unusual events as the 1954 McCarthy-Army congressional hearings and the Kennedy-Nixon debates of 1960 or the Fulbright hearings on Vietnam in 1966, radio and television put the citizen in touch with the realities of the political process in a new and exciting way. Moreover, faulty though American schools may be, they form an impressive and comprehensive educational system offering every person free education through high school. There is, of course, the perennial danger that all these competing agencies will merely confuse the public mind rather than promote the formation of enlightened public opinion.

Dissemination of information by government officials raises the issue whether public officers in a democracy should try to influence public opinion or should only be influenced by it. They must show a high sensitivity to public opinion, but it is also clear that they must often provide strong leadership as public opinion takes shape on a difficult issue. For example, where the President possesses expert information concerning such matters as the international situation or economic trends within the country, that in his judgment seems to require particular policies, he must do his best to shape favorable public support of these policies.

How Public Opinion Is Measured

How does public opinion influence the political process? How do public officers find out what the public wants? These questions point to one of the most crucial aspects of the democratic process—the means by which government is made responsive to the people. Some public opinion is bound to exist on most major issues, and it is desirable that public officers should know what that opinion is, by how many people and how intensely it is held. But there is no magic mirror in which public opinion is automatically reflected, only a series of ways by which it may be gauged, often in rather imprecise ways.

Elections

The traditional instrument by which public opinion has been measured in a democracy is the ballot box. In selecting public officers voters, it is hoped, pass judgment upon differing platforms and give a mandate to the victorious candidates and parties to carry out their campaign promises. In practice there has been much argument about the kind and extent of mandate that the American people give in a national election. For example, it is very difficult to prove what kind of mandate the voters gave John F. Kennedy in 1960. His campaign had centered around the theme that new forms of government activity were necessary to restore the growth of the American economy. Yet his margin of victory was slight, and the Eighty-seventh Congress, chosen at the same election, systematically rejected much of the President's program for the domestic economy. On the other hand, the Eighty-eighth Congress gave President Lyndon Johnson, before he had been elected President in his own right, most of the legislation he requested. In any case, whatever the deficiencies of elections as a means of measuring public opinion, there are long intervals between our national elections during which new problems arise and public opinion takes shape concerning them.

Interest Groups

Public officers learn much about public opinion between elections through interest groups, which convey information by a variety of methods—through barrages of letters and telegrams, testimony before congressional committees and other public agencies, and direct personal contact with lobbyists and ordinary citizens who visit these officers to communicate their views. In his dealings with interest groups, however, the public officer is always confronted with the difficult business of deciding how many people the lobbyist or the visitor is speaking for and how intensely or wisely these people hold the opinions attributed to them. Thus, he may want to check public opinion by other means.

Direct Citizen-Contact

Legislators and administrators from time to time go directly to the people to sound out public opinion. The President or Cabinet members make various tours to tell the people about some aspect of the Administration's program and to gauge public sentiment concerning it. Congressmen go back home and talk on Main Street with the voters. Indeed, it was the intention of the Legislative Reorganization Act of 1946 that Congress should adjourn its regular session not later than July of each year so that legislators might spend five months of each year at home and thereby keep in touch with their constituents. Unfortunately, there have been few years since the law was passed in which this has happened.

Initiative, Referendum, and Recall

The initiative, referendum, and recall are devices designed to allow public opinion to be registered directly upon the policy-making process in the interim between regular elections. The *initiative* is a formal means whereby the voters themselves legislate. A proposed statute or constitutional amendment is placed upon the ballot by securing the signatures of a required number of voters and, if it is approved by the voters, goes into effect. The *referendum* is a means whereby a bill or constitutional amendment that has been voted by the legislature is submitted to the electorate for its approval before going into effect. Finally, the *recall* is a means whereby the voters may remove a public officer before his regular term is up, presumably because of disapproval of his policies. All three of these devices have been used by American state and local governments. But there is no provision for their use by the federal government, and it would take constitutional amendments to make them part of federal procedure.

In a sense the initiative, referendum, and recall represent an attempt to return to *direct* democracy. Any such attempt is almost certainly doomed to failure, for the complexity of modern life and the technical difficulty of most policy decisions inevitably commit the United States to *indirect* or *representative* democracy.

Public Opinion Polls

Taking "straw votes" is an ancient pastime, and since the 1930s renewed efforts have been made to measure public opinion by scientific polling techniques. Early polls strove for accuracy by questioning large numbers of persons. In the 1936 campaign the *Literary Digest* mailed out ballots to some 10 million persons, more than 2 million of which were marked and returned. In spite of the size of this sample, the faulty character of the method was exposed when a count of the ballots indicated a victory for Alfred Landon in an election that was actually a landslide for Franklin D. Roosevelt.

This 1936 fiasco destroyed confidence in unscientific "mass" polling of the electorate. Since then, attention has shifted to commercial polls and to university centers for the study of public opinion, all of which claim to achieve a scientific result by controlling their samples for quality rather than by striving for mere quantity. Pollsters try to reach an accurate cross section of the population with respect to such variables as place of residence, age, sex, religion, professional interests, and economic status, or by selecting a "random sample" of the population with infinite care. By such means experts assert that it is possible to secure a highly accurate indication of public opinion through the polling of a remarkably small but carefully chosen group of people. For example, the

"*Nixon? He's Wonderful Too. They're* All *Wonderful—Wonderful, Warm People and Great Americans*"

Drawing by Stevenson. © 1967 the *New Yorker Magazine*, Inc.

Survey Research Center at the University of Michigan has made strikingly accurate studies of public opinion in recent presidential elections on the basis of random samples that are sometimes as small as 1450 people.

The modern poll is used not only to predict the results of elections but to measure opinion on controversial public issues, and poll results have affected government policy. There is evidence, for instance, that polls on international issues encouraged both the President and Congress in the months before the attack on Pearl Harbor to break sharply with the American tradition of isolationism and to give the Allied Powers every aid short of war. It is also claimed that a Gallup poll that showed less than 4 percent of the people supporting the Townsend Plan had much to do with cutting the ground from under the powerful old-age pension movement of the late 1930s.[10] It is possible that more systematic use of scientific polling will often show public officials that the groups making the most noise or spending the most money do not speak for a majority of the country, and that these officials will thereby be encouraged to show a greater concern for the larger interests of all the people.

Public opinion pollsters have not solved all their technical problems. The preparation of accurate and representative samples is still troublesome. Likewise, in polling people on complex issues rather than on candidates there are difficulties about the wording of questions to achieve strict impartiality and avoid prejudicing a person's answer. For example, a question couched in "Do you think taxes ought to be reduced?" terms is likely to be answered affirmatively by many people, who would also give a "yes" answer to such questions as, "Do you think we should

---

[10] See G. H. Gallup and S. F. Rae, *The Pulse of Democracy* (New York: Simon and Schuster, Inc., 1940), pp. 145–147.

spend more money on national defense?" or "Do you want better schools and roads?"

Similarly, there is a danger that at the moment a person is polled concerning a political issue he may not feel very strongly about it or may not yet really have made up his mind concerning it. He may nonetheless be quite willing to give an offhand answer to the pollster that he may later reject when the chips are down and a public policy is being hammered out in Congress or some other governmental arena.

Much the same objection has been made against public opinion polls as against the initiative, referendum, and recall, namely, that they represent an unwise attempt to move toward direct democracy in an age when the solution of complex issues requires the flexibility of a representative democracy. A vigorous critic of polling writes:[11]

What questions could be put to an electorate? In an age when 531 representatives and senators who are paid so well for their time that they do not have to have other means of livelihood, and who are staffed for the investigation of the merits of proposed legislation, have to throw up their hands and say there are many details on which they cannot pass and which they must leave to administrative determination, it is absurd to suggest that counting the public pulse can give any light or leading save on the simplest kind of a proposition.

Admittedly, on many issues opinion is at best superficial. For legislators to follow it blindly would destroy the deliberative and compromise aspects of policy-making. Admittedly, there is also the danger that polling of public opinion will encourage public officers to try to find out what the "average voter" wants rather than try to provide responsible leadership. On the other hand, in a democracy there are many major issues on which it is important to determine dominant public opinion. There is also reason to suppose that a courageous public official, who understands that in a democracy he must lead as well as follow, will find the facts supplied by polls highly useful in undertaking the task of overcoming an unfriendly public opinion.

Dr. George Gallup[12] has put the case for the polling of public opinion on issues in these modest terms:

To the extent that a political leader does take public opinion into account in making his decisions, he should have an accurate and objective measure of that opinion rather than mere guesswork. What polls endeavor to supply is a more systematic and more objective measure of opinions.

Selected Bibliography

Bentley, Arthur F., *The Process of Government* (Bloomington, Ind.: The Principia Press, 1949). A theory of the role of interest groups in politics.

---

[11] Lindsay Rogers, *The Pollsters* (New York: Alfred A. Knopf, 1949), p. 78.

[12] The Case for the Public Opinion Polls," *New York Times Magazine,* February 27, 1949, pp. 11, 55.

Blaisdell, Donald C., *American Democracy under Pressure* (New York: The Ronald Press Company, 1957). A vigorous account of the operations of several interest groups, and a theoretical statement of their role and status.

Childs, Harwood L., *Public Opinion: Nature, Function, and Role* (Princeton, N.J.: D. Van Nostrand Company, Inc., 1965). A comprehensive text by one of the pioneers in the study of public opinion.

Herring, E. Pendleton, *Public Administration and the Public Interest* (New York: McGraw-Hill, Inc., 1936). A study of the impact of interest groups on day-to-day administration of federal regulatory programs.

Key, V. O., *Public Opinion and American Democracy* (New York: Alfred A. Knopf, 1961). A thoughtful attempt to place sociological knowledge about public opinion into a meaningful political context.

Odegard, Peter H., *Pressure Politics: The Story of the Anti-Saloon League* (New York: Columbia University Press, 1928). A standard account of the efforts of one group to control the legislative process.

Truman, David, *The Governmental Process* (New York: Alfred A. Knopf, 1951). A contemporary and significant statement and analysis of the group basis of politics, with a comprehensive analysis of the operation of the American political system.

Zeller, Belle, *Pressure Politics in New York* (Englewood Cliffs, N.J.: Prentice-Hall, Inc., 1937). An excellent study of regional pressure politics and interest groups.

8

Electing the policy-makers

SUFFRAGE AND DEMOCRACY

Certainly a minimum requirement of democratic government is that officers who make public policy should be elected by and responsible to the people. To the question: Who are "the people"? we answered in Chapter 1 that ideally, each mature and sane member of society should have one vote, equal in weight and effect to the vote cast by every other person. American government has not yet achieved this ideal, but the political system is moving toward that goal.

Constitutional Provisions on Voting

The original Constitution provides in Article I, section 2, that "the electors in each state [voting for members of the House of Representatives] shall have the qualifications requisite for electors of the most numerous branch of the State legislature," and that the members of the electoral college who are to elect the President should be selected in each state "in such manner as the legislature thereof may direct." Six amendments to the Constitution

144

also have a bearing on the right to vote. The Seventeenth Amendment, in providing for the direct popular election of U.S. senators, repeats the language of Article I, that the qualifications for voting shall be the same as those used in each state in the election of the most numerous branch of the state legislature. The Fifteenth and Nineteenth Amendments provide that no citizen shall be denied the right to vote *in a national or state election* on account of race, color, previous condition of servitude, or sex. The Twenty-third Amendment, adopted in 1961, gives residents of the District of Columbia a voice in presidential elections by awarding the District three votes in the electoral college. No provision is made, however, for local self-government or representation in Congress, which acts as the District's municipal legislature. The Twenty-fourth Amendment, ratified in 1964, commands that an American citizen's right to vote for federal officials not be abridged because of failure to pay a poll tax or any other levy.

The Fourteenth Amendment, in forbidding the states to deny to persons the equal protection of the laws, prohibits unreasonable classifications or discriminations affecting the right to vote. The Fourteenth Amendment also contains a so-called penalty clause, which was designed to give Congress a weapon to use against states abridging the right to vote. It authorizes Congress to reduce the representation in the lower house of Congress of those states that deny male citizens, twenty-one years old or more, the right to vote, with the reduction proportional to the percentage of citizens prevented from voing; but this clause has never been invoked.

Except for these constitutional provisions, none of which establishes a right to vote in positive terms, the states are today free to fix the qualifications for voting in both national and state elections as they see fit.

GROWTH OF THE SUFFRAGE

From 1789 on, the history of American suffrage is one of more or less continuous extension of this right. The story divides itself into three parts: (1) gaining universal, white, manhood suffrage; (2) extension of the right to vote to male Negroes; (3) extension of the suffrage to women.

Gaining Universal, White, Manhood Suffrage

Universal suffrage for all white men depended upon abolition of property-holding and taxpaying qualifications. The first real acceptance of the ideal of suffrage for all white men regardless of economic status occurred in the new states west of the Appalachian barrier which were admitted to the Union at the beginning of the nineteenth century. On the frontier all men were social equals, and it was taken for granted that all should have an equal voice in the operation and control of government. But as this egalitarian ideal slowly filtered back into the seaboard states, strong conservative opposition had to be overcome. The Age of Jackson in the 1830s saw great gains toward universal suffrage in the older states, and by the time of the Civil War the victory was largely complete.

Extension of the Right to Vote to Male Negroes

In terms of constitutional law, Negro males gained the suffrage in 1870 with the adoption of the Fifteenth Amendment, which, as has been seen, forbids all governmental interference, based on race or color, with the right to vote in state or federal elections. In practice, the fight to implement the amendment has been bitter and difficult and is not yet won.

The history of Negro disfranchisement has been marked by the use of an almost endless series of devices to circumvent the Fifteenth Amendment. These devices fall into two categories: those that have had a presumed basis in law and those frankly beyond the law. It is probable that intimidation, force, and even violence—and the *threat* of these—have been most influential in keeping the Negro from the polls. But continuous efforts have also been made to find a regular, or lawful, method of getting around the Constitution. As one method has been held unconstitutional, another has taken its place; and, until the last few years, the ingenuity of officials in the dozen or so states in which the Negro has been generally disfranchised enabled them to keep pace with adverse Supreme Court decisions. Among the principal "legal" methods historically used to prevent the Negro from voting are (1) literacy tests, (2) the "grandfather clause," (3) the "white primary," and (4) the poll tax.

Of these, one of the earliest was the literacy test. For example, a provision in the constitution of Mississippi that became effective in 1892 required a voter to be able to read any section of the constitution, or to understand and give a

Voter registration in Selma, Alabama. (Vernon Merritt from Black Star)

reasonable interpretation of a section read to him. There seemed to be no dis-crimination against the Negro in this provision, but it was relatively easy to administer these tests in such a way as to pass whites and reject Negroes. In 1898, in *Williams v. Mississippi,* the Supreme Court refused to declare this kind of test unconstitutional, holding that it had not been proved that administration of the program was discriminatory, but only that discrimination was possible.[1]

More recently, however, both congressmen and judges have looked closely at the actual operation of voting tests.[2] The 1964 Civil Rights Act requires that all literacy tests be administered in writing unless the Attorney General of the United States gives special permission to state officials to conduct the test orally. This statute also makes a sixth-grade education a presumption of literacy.[3] The 1965 Voting Rights Act goes further and authorizes the Attorney General of the United States to suspend, under certain circumstances, the operation of any state literacy test that he believes has been administered in a racially discriminatory fashion in the last five years.[4] The state of South Carolina promptly challenged the constitutionality of this legislation, but the Supreme Court, after a candid review of the history of Negro disfranchisement, found this restriction on state power to be a reasonable exercise of federal authority.[5]

The "grandfather clause" was often used in conjunction with literacy tests. This clause provided that persons could qualify to vote either by showing that they or their ancestors had been eligible to vote prior to the adoption of the Fif-teenth Amendment or by passing a literacy test. In general, whites could qualify under the first alternative and avoid the perhaps embarrasing need to take the literacy test, whereas the only course open to Negroes was to submit to the test. In 1915, the Supreme Court declared unconstitutional Oklahoma's grandfather clause,[6] but Oklahoma reenacted the provision in a more subtle form and con-tinued to use it against Negroes until 1939, when the Supreme Court again held it invalid.[7] However, during the years when the clause was in effect in Oklahoma and other states, it served its purpose by enabling whites to get their names on permanent registration lists. Negroes still had to pass literacy tests, nondiscrimi-natory at best.

For many years, the white primary was the most effective "legal" device for disfranchising Negroes. Its object was to prevent Negroes from participating in the primary election of the Democratic party, where the real choice of public officers was made in the one-party South. After a good deal of vacillation, the Supreme Court finally outlawed the white primary in 1944 in *Smith v. Allwright.*

---

[1] 170 U.S. 213 (1898). As late as 1959, the Supreme Court took a similar view of a North Carolina literacy test. *Lassiter v. Northampton,* 360 U.S. 45 (1959).

[2] See, for example, *Schnell v. Davis,* 336 U.S. 933 (1949), striking down an Alabama requirement that a prospective voter be able to satisfy a registrar that he "understood" any clause of the Constitu-tion; and *Louisiana v. United States,* 380 U.S. 145 (1965), invalidating a similar Louisiana provision.

[3] 78 *Stat.* 241.

[4] 79 *Stat.* 437.

[5] *South Carolina v. Katzenbach,* 383 U.S. 301 (1966).

[6] *Guinn v. United States,* 238 U.S. 347 (1915).

[7] *Lane v. Wilson,* 307 U.S. 268 (1939).

In this case the Court held that even though the Texas white primary rested upon a party resolution rather than a state law, the Democratic party acted as the agent of the state in conducting the primary; thus party exclusion of Negroes was *state* action falling within the ban of the Fifteenth Amendment. The Court said:[8] "when, as here, [the] privilege [of membership in a party] is . . . the essential qualification for voting in a primary to select nominees for a general election, the State makes the action of the party the action of the State."

Several southern states tried to evade the effect of the *Allwright* decision by repealing all statutes regulating primaries and allowing these elections to be conducted by local "private clubs" or by having "preprimary" contests. Federal courts, however, struck down all of these crude efforts.[9]

In the past, many states required the payment of a poll, or a head tax, as a prerequisite to voting. In some states the tax was cumulative, and the taxpayer who fell behind had to pay more than one year's tax in order to vote. The poll tax effectively disfranchised large numbers of whites as well as blacks, but because of the poor economic status of the average Negro in the South, the tax, even where administered without discrimination, was an important factor in keeping Negroes from voting. By the early 1960s, only Alabama, Arkansas, Mississippi, Texas, and Virginia had not abolished the poll tax. And in contrast to the protracted filibusters of earlier years, there was little opposition on Capitol Hill in 1962 when Congress proposed the Twenty-fourth Amendment, forbidding abridgment of the right to vote for federal officials because of failure to pay a poll or other tax. Within two years the amendment was ratified by the states.

Before adoption of the Twenty-fourth Amendment, the Supreme Court twice declared the poll tax constitutional as a prerequisite to voting in a state or a federal election.[10] In 1966, however, a majority of the justices reversed themselves and held the tax unconstitutional even as a requirement for voting in a state election. For the Court, Justice Douglas[11] wrote: "a State violates the Equal Protection Clause of the Fourteenth Amendment whenever it makes the affluence of the voter or payment of any fee an electoral standard. Voter qualifications have no relation to wealth nor to paying or not paying this or any other tax."

The Future of Negro Suffrage

After the *School Segregation Cases* of 1954, a number of southern states stepped up their activities against Negro voting. New legislation was frequently enacted, but the key element in this "legal" campaign has been discrimination in the administration of regulations rather than passage of laws that are openly unfair. To overcome these obstacles, Negro and white civil rights supporters have persuaded Congress to pass a series of statutes.

---

[8] 321 U.S. 649, 664–665 (1944); see also *Nixon v. Herndon*, 273 U.S. 536 (1927); *Nixon v. Condon*, 286 U.S. 73 (1932); *Grovey v. Townsend*, 295 U.S. 45 (1935).

[9] *Rice v. Elmore*, 165 F. 2d 387 (1947); *Baskin v. Brown*, 174 F. 2d 391 (1949); *Terry v. Adams*, 345 U.S. 461 (1953).

[10] *Breedlove v. Suttles*, 302 U.S. 277 (1937); *Butler v. Thompson*, 341 U.S. 937 (1951).

[11] *Harper v. Virginia*, 383 U.S. 663, 666 (1966).

The federal Civil Rights Act of 1957[12] authorizes the Attorney General not only to prosecute local officials for discriminating against Negro voters but also to institute suits for injunctions forbidding interference with voting rights. Equally important is the act's establishment of the U.S. Commission on Civil Rights, a group of distinguished citizens appointed by the President to investigate alleged denials of equal protection of the law. The 1959 report[13] of the Commission was one of the chief factors behind the passage of the Civil Rights Act of 1960,[14] though the nearness of a presidential election and the strategic significance to both parties of the northern Negro vote undoubtedly constituted more effective persuasion.

The act of 1960 sets up a cumbersome system whereby a federal judge who finds, in a case before him, convincing evidence of a pattern of racial discrimination in voting may appoint a "referee" to determine whether applicants have met the requirements of valid state laws. If the referee determines that they have, he or the judge may then issue certificates identifying the holders as qualified to vote in any election in which federal officers are chosen.

Despite efforts at energetic enforcement, the awkward machinery—requiring a court suit before referees may act—did little to help the cause of Negro voting. In 1961, the Commission on Civil Rights reported that the most prevalent form of discrimination consisted in arbitrary registration procedures. Evidence showed close cooperation between White Citizens Council leaders and state officials—in some instances White Citizens Council leaders *were* state officials—to purge already registered Negroes from the voting lists. Negroes attempting to register for the first time were confronted with a battery of dilatory and evasive maneuvers. Some registrars held office hours at irregular times and were seldom available when Negroes showed up. At other times, registrars refused to accept from Negroes such standard identification as drivers' licenses and required that a prospective Negro voter bring in two already registered voters (that is, whites) to identify him. There were also cases in which registrars rejected Negro applicants for such minor errors as underlining rather than circling "Mr." on the application form.

To meet this kind of situation, the 1964 Civil Rights Act,[15] in addition to its literacy test provisions, forbids unequal administration of registration requirements and makes it illegal for state officials to refuse to allow a prospective voter the franchise because of immaterial errors or omissions on registration forms. The act also strengthens earlier statutes permitting the Attorney General to intervene in voting cases, and directs the Bureau of the Census to gather registration and voting statistics based on race, color, and national origin.

Although less awkward than its predecessors, the 1964 act proved to be an ineffective answer to discrimination against voting rights. In 1965, Congress passed a new statute,[16] one even more complex than any previous civil rights law, but

---

[12] 71 *Stat.* 634.

[13] *Report of the United States Commission on Civil Rights 1959* (Washington, D.C.: Government Printing Office, 1959).

[14] 74 *Stat.* 90 (1960).

[15] 78 *Stat.* 241.

[16] 79 *Stat.* 437.

Negro Vote Can Be Potent, If—

By Tom Wicker
SPECIAL TO THE NEW YORK TIMES

WASHINGTON, May 14— In Newark, N.J., this week, in the Democratic primary, Mayor Hugh Addonizio failed to win a majority. The Mayor faces a runoff against his principal opponent, Leo P. Carlin, primarily because a third candidate, Kenneth A. Gibson, polled just under 20 per cent of the total vote.

Mr. Gibson is a 33-year-old Negro, and he was running in a city where Negroes make up almost 50 per cent of the population. In a larger field, and polling a few more votes than Mr. Gibson, another Negro, Calvin West, won election as a city councilman-at-large.

These results did not attract as much national attention as the Alabama Democratic primaries last week, and Newark is not really analogous to the South because the city's Negro community is a higher proportion of its total population than Negroes ever will achieve in any Southern state.

'Poor' Majority

But some political analysts here believe that, as more and more Negroes vote and reach political sophistication in the South, the Southern political order will develop somewhat like Newark's. They were influenced by the following realities of Southern politics:

(1) In the South, the dominant majority in the region as a whole and in every state is white—and the Negro proportion of the population is generally declining.

(2) Another majority exists in the South that is not, so far, dominant. It is the majority of the less advantaged, of whatever race—of those from the middle income groups ranging down to the poverty-stricken.

(3) For nearly a century, the white majority of the South has dominated the "poor" majority because the issue of race has been used to unite white men of whatever economic class—all too often for the benefit of the Bourbons.

The smashing victory of Mrs. Lurleen Wallace, running as a stand-in for her husband, Gov. George Wallace of Alabama, disclosed these underlying realities once again.

Resistance

There now are, in Alabama, 235,572 registered Negroes—and about 115,000 of these have been put on the polling books since the passage of the Voting Rights Act of 1965. Yet, the total is only 16 per cent of Alabama's registered voters, and in the period since the voting act was passed, so many whites were also registered that Negroes succeeded in "closing the gap" between their vote and the white vote by a net of only 12,000.

Moreover, the whites of Alabama were sufficiently united—no matter what their other interests—by two factors. Governor Wallace had made himself a symbol of white resistance to Federally imposed Negro gains. His wife's principal opponent, Attorney General Richmond Flowers, openly campaigned for the Negro vote. The race issue, however soft pedaled in speeches, was central to the election.

Mr. Flowers got an estimated 90 per cent of the Negro vote—suggesting that only about 150,000 Negroes voted in the gubernatorial race—but even with eight other candidates in the field, Mrs. Wallace won a majority of about 52 per cent and avoided a runoff. She is estimated to have received more than 60 per cent of the white vote.

Political Realities

Negroes did win Democratic nominations for some local offices, in electorates where their numbers were in higher proportion. In the Texas primary in the same week, three Negroes won nominations for the State Legislature.

All this suggests that astute Negro political leadership in the South will grasp two overriding facts: that the Negro in that region is a political minority and will remain so, and that when the issue of race is raised either by white bigots or by obvious Negro bloc voting, the white majority will unite at the ballot box, at least in the foreseeable future.

That is why the Newark results become relevant to the South. Newark showed that Negroes can influence important elections without trying to dominate them; that they need no longer be ignored or ridden over by white leaders. It showed that factors other than race—for instance, Mayor Addonizio's City Hall organization and powers—can influence the Negro as well as any other voter. It showed that important local offices can be won by Negroes—not only improving their present political power but building up experienced politicians (not merely Negro politicians) for the future.

New Order

Such an approach in the South appears numerically necessary, because of the Negro's permanent minority position. And it is the only route that offers any real hope anytime soon of uniting that other majority in the South—the vast body of whites and Negroes whose economic interests are identical.

Wherever the issue of race is openly raised, by whites or by Negroes, that majority is likely to be split, as it always has been before; where the race issue can be kept in the background, a new political order might be built in the South.

complex in the sense of having interlocking rows of sharp teeth rather than loose layers of verbiage. The heart of the statute is a series of specific, practical remedies. As indicated, the Attorney General of the United States may suspend operation of any state, county, or parish voting test of literacy, education, or character that he believes has been used to discriminate in the last five years if less than half the residents of voting age in that governmental unit were not registered to vote in November 1964 or did not vote in the 1964 presidential election.

Second, the Attorney General may also suspend the operation of any change in state or local electoral law or practice made after November 1964 if he believes it likely to be discriminatory in effect. Third, the Attorney General may certify that federal supervision in an area is necessary to ensure fair voting procedures; the U.S. Civil Service Commission must then assign examiners to determine who are qualified voters. State officials must then register anyone certified by a federal examiner as a qualified voter. If requested by the Attorney General, the Commission must also assign federal officers as poll watchers to make certain that qualified voters are allowed to cast their ballots.

State officials may obtain judicial review of decisions of the Attorney General under this act only through the U.S. District Court for the District of Columbia, not through state or local federal judges. Attempts to interfere with the administration of this statute or to intimidate anyone trying to vote or trying to persuade others to vote are felonies, punishable by prison terms of up to five years.

The provisions of the 1965 act apply to all elections, general or primary, whether of state, local, or federal government officials, political party officers, or popular determinations of public policy issues. Moreover, where a voting case is brought before a federal district court in the regular course of litigation, that judge may, in addition to his usual authority, exercise powers substantially similar to those of the Attorney General.

Initial enforcement of the 1965 Voting Rights Act was hampered by a lack of trained personnel who could investigate complaints or serve as examiners. On the other hand, this show of force by the federal government encouraged civil rights organizations such as the NAACP and CORE to intensify their voter registration drives in the South—and in the North as well. Negro registration figures have climbed dramatically in the last few years, as the table for 1966 indicates. Even in states of the Deep South like Alabama and Georgia, Negro voters had become by that year an important political force.

How effective a political voice Negroes will have will depend on several factors other than voting laws. The 1961 Report of the Commission on Civil Rights[17] pointed out that in twenty-one "black belt" counties (counties in which Negroes outnumber whites), the local economic situation appeared to be a crucial factor in the Negro's use of the ballot.

It seems no mere accident that in three of the four [Black Belt] counties where Negroes are registered and vote in significant numbers, the economies are active and diverse, and Negroes

---

[17] *Report of the United States Commission on Civil Rights 1961* (Washington, D.C.: Government Printing Office, 1961), Book I, pp. 190–191.

are for the most part independent of local white economic control. . . . Where Negroes do not vote, they are for the most part subservient to crop, land, and landlord. Agriculture dominates the economies of 15 of the 17 nonvoting counties and the domination is of a special kind. Two-thirds of the 15,257 Negroes who till the soil in the 15 are tenants or croppers; some of the remainder are share croppers. Moreover the agricultural changes that are taking place have reduced the need for Negro tenants and farm labor. Hence the possibility of economic reprisal offered most frequently as a reason why Negroes do not register in significant numbers, becomes more real. It is easier to retaliate against someone for whom there is declining need, and more difficult to prove that the reprisal was in fact racially motivated.

The Commission also concluded that throughout the South apathy and lack of education among Negroes played a part in their not voting. Undoubtedly much of the future of Negro suffrage lies in the hands of the Negro minority: it depends on how vigorously they take advantage of their new opportunities to vote and how wisely they actually do vote.

Extension of the Suffrage to Women

The adoption of the Nineteenth Amendment in 1920 culminated nearly a century of agitation to outlaw suffrage restrictions based upon sex. As early as 1838, Kentucky established a limited right of women to vote in school elections. Wyoming, while still a territory in 1869, became the first unit to grant women a right to participate in all elections. A few states followed this lead, but the movement as a whole made slow progress. In the second decade of the present century a well-organized and effective organi-

Negro-White Voter Registration in the South
Summer 1966

State	White voting-age pop.	Negro voting-age pop.	White reg.	Negro reg.	Percent White reg.	Percent Negro reg.
Alabama[1]	1,353,058	481,320	1,192,075	246,396	88.1	51.2
Arkansas	850,643	192,626	598,000	115,000	70.3	59.7
Florida[2]	2,617,438	470,261	2,093,274	286,446	80.0	60.9
Georgia[3]	1,797,062	612,910	1,378,005	289,545	76.7	47.2
Louisiana	1,289,216	514,589	1,071,573	242,130	83.1	47.1
Mississippi[2]	748,266	422,256	481,000	163,000	64.3	38.6
North Carolina	2,005,955	550,929	1,653,796	281,134	82.4	51.0
South Carolina	895,147	371,104	718,061	190,609	80.2	51.4
Tennessee	1,779,018	313,873	1,375,000	225,000	77.3	71.7
Texas	4,884,765	649,512	2,600,000	400,000	53.3	61.6
Virginia	1,876,167	436,720	1,159,000	205,000	61.8	46.9
Totals	20,096,735	5,016,100	14,309,704	2,620,359	70.2	52.2

[1] 10,000 voters not registered by race.
[2] Florida and Mississippi figures on Negro registration are estimates.
[3] 14,000 voters not registered by race.
SOURCE: Southern Regional Council Voter Education Project (1966).

zation attempted to secure the adoption of an amendment to the federal Constitution. After a sometimes bitter campaign, marked by repeated picketing of the White House and hunger strikes by "suffragettes" arrested and jailed for "obstructing traffic," the Constitution was amended in time to permit women to participate in the 1920 presidential election. In contrast with state efforts to circumvent the Fifteenth Amendment, there have been no subsequent attempts to interfere with the right of women to vote.

PRESENT-DAY VOTING REQUIREMENTS

Voters are required to meet five general conditions today. These have to do with citizenship, residence, age, registration, and still occasionally literacy.

There is nothing in the Constitution that requires the states to limit voting to citizens, and in the past many states granted suffrage to aliens. Citizenship is now, however, an absolute requirement for voting in every state. Each state also has a residence requirement, although the specific length of time required by law varies from six months to two years. Some sort of minimum requirement is certainly defensible as a means of compelling persons to prove their good faith as residents of particular states, and to prevent persons from voting more than once. But in view of the increasing mobility of the population, a requirement that goes beyond the minimum needs of the situation—say, six months—may well disfranchise in an unfair manner otherwise highly qualified voters.

Twenty-one years has long been the minimum voting age in state law, and indeed this figure is given negative recognition in the "penalty" clause of the Fourteenth Amendment. In 1944, however, Georgia reduced the requirement to eighteen years, accepting as valid the argument that a person who is old enough to fight in defense of his country is old enough to vote. In 1955, Kentucky followed Georgia's lead. When they became states, Alaska and Hawaii set the minimum voting age at nineteen and twenty years, respectively. In his State of the Union message in 1954 President Eisenhower proposed that the Constitution be amended to fix the minimum voting age at eighteen years for all the states, but Congress took no action on his suggestion. From time to time this question is again raised, most recently with the war in Vietnam, and it is quite possible that some day the voting age will be lowered.

Qualifications for voting are almost everywhere administered through a registration system. Persons desiring to became voters are required by state law to appear before election officials, indicate their ability to meet legal requirements, and have their names placed on the voting list. Some states maintain permanent registration lists; others employ periodic registration systems by which voters are required to register anew at regular intervals. Periodic registration perhaps holds down the possibilities of fraud by ensuring the elimination of inactive names at regular intervals, but it has the disadvantage of discouraging voting because of the annoyance of new registration. As discussed in the section on Negro suffrage, before passage of the Voting Act of 1965 about a third of the states employed a literacy test of one kind or another as a prerequisite to voting. Since passage of that statute, many states have suspended such tests—or have had them suspended by the federal government. Another relevant portion of the 1965 act stipulates that if a prospective voter has completed the sixth grade in an accredited school in Puerto Rico or in any American state or territory in which English is not the predominant classroom language, he does not have to demonstrate literacy in English.[18] This guarantees that a Spanish-speaking person will not be prohibited from voting.

Disqualification by Gerrymandering

Unfair apportionment of population for election purposes, or gerrymandering, may be accomplished by positive legislative action in which lines of electoral districts are deliberately drawn so as to give one party or set of interest groups advantages over another. Gerrymandering may also be achieved by default, by legislative inaction in the face of major population shifts. The latter method has been widely "used" in this century and, with the mass exodus from farms to cities, has been effective in overweighting rural representation in state legislatures as well as in Congress. As late as 1964 it was not unusual to find urban and suburban congressional districts with populations three or four times the size of rural districts in the same state, and there was an even more pronounced pattern of imbalance in most state legislatures.

In a series of decisions over the years, the Supreme Court had refused to hear lawsuits asking judges to command reapportionment. The justices were often divided in their reasoning, but most observers interpreted these refusals as based on the doctrine that reapportionment was not a justiciable but a political question; that is, a problem that the Constitution left to be resolved by the political branches of government. In 1962, however, the Court in *Baker v. Carr*[19] ruled that gerrymandering by default was a violation of the Constitution that courts could remedy. The *Baker* case, however, involved only the lower house of a state legislature, and it was not until *Wesberry v. Sanders*[20] in 1964 that the Court ruled that such malapportionment of congressional districts was also an infringement of the right to vote that courts could order corrected.

Later in 1964 a majority of the justices held in *Reynolds v. Sims* that even the seats in the upper house of a state legislature had to be apportioned on the basis of population. The Court rejected the analogy to the U.S. Senate in favor of a ruling that the democratic ideal of "one man, one vote" was a constitutional command subject only to the specific exceptions of the Senate and the electoral

---

[18] The act says: "except that in States in which State law provides that a different level of education is presumptive of literacy, [a prospective voter] shall demonstrate that he has successfully completed an equivalent level of education" in an accredited school in which the predominant classroom language was not English.

[19] 369 U.S. 186 (1962).

[20] 376 U.S. 1 (1964).

college. "Legislators," Chief Justice Warren said for the Court, "represent people, not trees or acres. Legislators are elected by voters, not farms or cities or economic interests. As long as ours is a representative form of government . . . the right to elect legislators in a free and unimpaired fashion is a bedrock of our political system."[21]

These decisions have stirred what may turn into a peaceful revolution in American politics, strengthening the political power of the cities and even more so of the suburbs, since it was the most recently developed areas that suffered most from gerrymandering by default. Since 1962, virtually every state legislature in the country has, voluntarily, as a result of a court order, or because of a threat of such an order, undergone some reapportionment. By 1966, the editors of the *Congressional Quarterly*[22] estimated that in forty-six states electoral districts were approaching equality of population. Moreover, as a result of *Wesberry v. Sanders,* twenty-seven states had by 1966 redrawn their congressional district lines to provide greater equality of representation.

These political results were not easily achieved. In each state groups that were faced with loss of influence fought doggedly to retain as much of the status quo as possible, and in many instances succeeded in delaying reapportionment and in minimizing their losses through clever drawing of district lines. The reapportionment decisions, especially *Reynolds v. Sims,* also ran into heavy congressional opposition. Led by Senate Minority Leader Everett Dirksen, the foes of the "one man, one vote" doctrine mounted several legislative counterattacks that came close to pushing through Congress a proposed constitutional amendment to modify the effect of the Court's decisions. Indeed, on two occasions Dirksen's proposal to allow states to apportion one house of the legislature on grounds other than population received, in the Senate, 57 to 39 and 55 to 38 majorities that fell just short of the two thirds vote needed to propose a constitutional amendment.

The end of the reapportionment struggle is not yet in sight. New legislative and court battles will be waged as political parties and interest groups vie for advantage. Moreover, the 1970 census will undoubtedly reveal fresh discrepancies in district populations and touch off another round of maneuvering. It is probably not possible to draw electoral lines without conferring some partisan advantages and disadvantages. Positive gerrymandering of electoral districts of substantially equal population but such geographical configurations as to benefit one party or set of interest groups remains a practical if not a legal possibility.

In 1961, a full year before *Baker v. Carr,* the Supreme Court held unconstitutional Alabama's gerrymandering of the town of Tuskegee.[23] But there were special circumstances present in that situation. Alabama's gerrymandering had been a crude, crass effort to disfranchise Negro citizens, and the Court specifically declared that this sort of gerrymandering violated the Fifteenth Amendment's

---

[21] 377 U.S. 533, 562 (1964).
[22] *Congressional Quarterly Weekly Report,* June 17, 1966, p. 1285.
[23] *Gomillion v. Lightfoot,* 364 U.S. 339 (1961).

prohibition against racial discrimination in voting. Whether the Supreme Court will—or can—prevent gerrymandering where nonracial factors are dominant remains to be seen.[24]

Even if each state eventually makes all of its congressional districts substantially equal in population, the federal nature of American government will still cause some areas to be overrepresented in Washington. First, unequal representation in the Senate necessarily results from each state's electing two senators regardless of its population. In 1967, the number of people represented by two senators ranged from more than 19 million in California to a little over 250,000 in Alaska. Any alteration of this arrangement would require a constitutional amendment that might have to be ratified by all fifty states, since the Constitution provides that no state shall be deprived of its equal representation in the Senate without its consent. Thus any suggestion that the system might be changed is purely academic.

A second difficulty is found in the unequal representation in the House of Representatives. The apportionment following the 1960 census of 435 seats in the House among the fifty states provided a reasonably close approximation of representation based on population. Under the Constitution each state must be given one seat. This resulted in three states obtaining a seat even though their populations were less than the average-size district, which was about 410,000. Then the remaining 385 seats were assigned. In effect a state got an additional seat for each additional 410,000 people. But no fractional seats could be assigned, so some states got a final seat for less than 410,000 people, whereas others failed to get such a seat because the remainder after their populations had been divided by 410,000 was not large enough to justify another seat. For example, the 1960 apportionment gave Kentucky one less congressman than Maryland, even though Kentucky's population was only 62,000 less than Maryland's.

WHICH OFFICES SHOULD BE ELECTIVE?

After determining who should vote, a second fundamental question in establishing a democratic electoral system is which offices should be elective. Certainly the major policy-makers should be elected by the people. On the other hand, officers who merely carry out policy may properly be appointed. No such clear line, however, can be drawn. It is easy enough to place *legislators* in the first category, but not so easy to put *administrators* in the second, for some of the latter do, in fact, make as well as carry out policy. One might also ask—without expecting a definite answer—in which category judges should be placed.

One reason for limiting the number of elective offices is the burden on voters who must choose among candidates for a great many offices about whom they may not have adequate information. Experience shows that in electing officers a point is quickly reached at which the voters find it increasingly difficult to exercise

[24] See, for example, the Court's dodging of this issue in *Wright v. Rockefeller,* 376 U.S. 52 (1964).

the franchise wisely and efficiently. The terms "short ballot" and "long ballot" have come to be used to describe the alternatives available to the people of a democracy in this respect. The former describes an electoral system in which elective offices are kept to a minimum, including as a rule only the seats in the legislature and the post of chief executive. The latter describes a system in which many additional officers, such as heads of executive departments and judges, are elective.

The Federal Ballot

The federal ballot is a short one, for in national elections each voter helps choose not more than four or five officers— a President, a Vice President, a senator (in two out of each sequence of three elections), a representative from the voter's district, and occasionally a representative from the state at large. Moreover, with one "X" the voter expresses his preference for both a presidential and vice-presidential candidate. There is a sharp contrast between this federal short ballot and the long or "jungle" ballot that is widely used by state and local governments in the United States. State and local ballots vary considerably, but the typical state or city elects not only its chief executive and the members of its legislature but also a variety of subordinate executive officers and a number of judges.

On the other hand, the federal ballot is not short at all compared with the ballot in a British national election. There the voter helps select just one officer directly, the member of the House of Commons from his home district. The prime minister is not directly elected by British voters. Instead, the party that wins a majority of the seats in the House of Commons chooses one of its leaders to serve as prime minister and he is appointed to that post by the queen. This is the short ballot reduced to its absolute minimum, and a case can be made that this British electoral system more nearly expresses the democratic ideal than does that of the United States.

TWO STAGES IN ELECTING PUBLIC OFFICERS

The election of public officers in the United States by the voters is a twofold process consisting of the nomination and the election. These two stages are quite distinct from each other, and each has been institutionalized in elaborate, highly formalized procedures. The nomination of national officers is nowhere referred to in the federal Constitution. In a two-party system the formal nomination of candidates for public offices by the parties is of great significance, for it limits the choice of the voters to just two possibilities —a very substantial restriction.

The development of a separate, formalized nomination stage in the electoral system of a democracy is not inevitable. In Britain the nomination of public officers has remained relatively uncomplicated. Any properly qualified person can declare his candidacy for a seat in the House of Commons by obtaining the signatures of ten voters and posting a deposit of £150 which he forfeits if he fails to poll one eighth of the total vote in his district on election day. In fact, however, most candidates running for the House of Commons are chosen by the party organizations in a quite informal way.

A party nomination in the American political system is, more often than not, much sought after. And this pressure at the nomination stage has resulted in the development of relatively complicated mechanisms to determine party candidates. V. O. Key[25] mentions three other reasons why "nominating processes in the United States are much more elaborate than in any other democratic regime." One is the long list of elective offices in federal, state, and local government which gives the nominating process great significance. Second is the existence of numerous one-party areas in the United States in which the nomination is equivalent to election and is thus certain to be vigorously sought after. And third is the similarity of the two major parties which tends to blur voters' choices *between* parties and thereby accentuates the importance of choice *within* a party.

ELECTING CONGRESSMEN

Provisions of the Constitution

Every two years the entire membership of the House of Representatives and one third of the members of the Senate are chosen by the voters of the states in a November election. The Constitution provides that representatives shall be apportioned among the states on the basis of population. Although it does not say so, the implication is that Congress shall make a new apportionment every ten years following the taking of the census. The Constitution does not fix the number of seats in the House, leaving that to be determined by Congress itself, and Congress has set the number at 435. The Constitution does fix the terms and minimum qualification of senators and representatives. Senators must be thirty years of age and citizens of the United States for nine years; they serve for six years. Representatives must be twenty-five years of age and citizens for seven years; they serve for two years. Both senators and representatives are required to be inhabitants of their states at the time of their election, but as shown by the election in 1964 of Robert Kennedy as senator from New York, the term "resident" may sometimes be liberally construed. Representatives are not required by law or the Constitution to be residents of the districts they serve; however, by practice this is almost invariably the case.

The most important provision in the federal Constitution concerning the conduct of congressional elections is the paragraph in Article I, section 4, which states: "The times, places and manner of holding elections for Senators and Representatives, shall be prescribed in each State by the legislature thereof; but the Congress may at any time by law make or alter such regulations. . . ." It is this pro-

---

[25] *Politics, Parties, and Pressure Groups,* 3rd ed. (New York: Thomas Y. Crowell Company, 1953), p. 399.

A congressman delivering a speech in western Texas. In addition to his responsibilities in Washington, a congressman must keep in touch with his constituents by attending social and political gatherings and by making it convenient for individuals and groups to speak with him personally. (Meisel from Monkmeyer Press Photo)

vision that has served as the basis for the conduct of congressional elections by the states. Congress might, however, if it wished, under this paragraph take the control of congressional elections completely out of the hands of the states and provide for their direct operation by the national government itself.

Whether or not the "times, places and manner" clause gives Congress power to regulate the nomination of congressmen is a question that gave the Supreme Court considerable difficulty. In 1921 the justices were unanimous in reversing the conviction of Truman Newberry for spending too much money in a campaign for a senatorial nomination. This decision was widely interpreted as denying Congress authority to regulate nominations, since the opinion which was labeled that of the Court explicitly stated this limitation. In separate opinions, however, five justices—a majority of the Court—either said this limitation did not exist or declared it was not necessary to pass on the issue to decide the specific case before them. In 1941, the Court finally cleared up the confusion by expressly ruling that Congress might regulate congressional primaries if it so wished.[26]

In Article I, section 5, the Constitution states: "Each House shall be the judge of the elections, returns and qualifications of its own members." Under this provision the two houses possess exclusive power to determine whether newly elected members have been properly chosen or have the qualifications set forth in the Constitution. In 1900, the House refused to seat a polygamist, and in 1919 it

---

[26] *Newberry v. United States,* 256 U.S. 232 (1921); *United States v. Classic,* 313 U.S. 299 (1941).

barred a Socialist who had been convicted under the sedition laws. In 1926, the Senate refused to seat senators from Pennsylvania and Illinois because they had made excessive campaign expenditures. In 1967 the House refused to seat Adam Clayton Powell of Harlem, Chairman of the Committee on Education and Labor. A special committee charged that he had abused his congressional immunity by defying court judgments against him for libel and had "wrongfully and willfully" misspent government funds. Powell's case was complicated because he was a Negro and because, as a similar situation in the Senate at the same time, involving Thomas Dodd of Connecticut, indicated, Powell was not alone in his financial irregularities.

Thus each House has in effect established qualifications for membership beyond those in the Constitution. But because Congress is the exclusive judge of the qualifications of its members, no argument concerning the constitutionality of such action can be carried beyond Congress itself. A constituency can, of course, reelect the unseated candidate, but Congress can again refuse to admit him.

Statutory Control of Congressional Elections

Although Congress has not exercised its constitutional power to "nationalize" congressional elections, it has enacted several statutes establishing a limited measure of federal supervision of these election. An act of 1842 provided that representatives should be chosen in each state by districts rather than at large, and an act of 1872 provided that each state should hold its election of federal officers on the first Tuesday after the first Monday in November. For a period Congress required that the districts from which representatives are chosen be so arranged by the states as to be compact, contiguous, and equal in population, but this requirement was dropped from federal law in 1929, as was, indeed, the 1842 requirement that representatives be chosen by districts. As we have already noted, Congress has also enacted legislation protecting qualified voters in all elections against interference by violence, intimidation, or racial discrimination, and it has provided penalties against fraud and dishonesty in presidential and congressional elections. Finally, it has enacted so-called corrupt practices legislation which limits campaign expenditures by candidates for federal office.

The Nomination of Congressmen

Today the party primary is widely used to nominate both senators and representatives. Only Delaware uses the convention system for the nomination of both. In Connecticut senators and representatives are nominated by party conventions, but any unsuccessful candidate who receives at least 20 percent of the convention vote may, if he can obtain 750 to 5000 signatures on a petition—the number varies with the office being sought—run against the convention's nominee in a primary election. New York and Indiana nominate their senatorial candidates by convention and their representatives by primaries.

All other states use the primary system. There are, however, wide differences in types of state primaries.

In a majority of states congressional primaries are of the so-called closed type. Voting in such a primary is limited to party members. Voters must declare their party affiliation either at registration or at the primary election. Some provision is ordinarily made for voters to change party affiliations from time to time, but this must usually be done in advance of a primary election. A few states use the open primary, which allows voters to make up their minds on the day of the primary election in which party primary they will participate. Actually the distinction between these two types is not always a sharp one; in some states the closed primary is so loosely organized or administered that it allows almost the same freedom of action possible in the open system.

Eleven southern states use a runoff primary system. Here, if the leading candidate in the first primary fails to poll a majority of the vote, a second, or runoff, primary is held in which the choice is narrowed to the two highest candidates in the first primary. In one-party states this system has the advantage of guaranteeing that the person who wins the nomination—and thereby the election—has the support of something more than the small plurality that is often enough to win in a race in which three or more strong candidates are seeking nomination. Few of these states, however, can count on being one-party any longer. It remains to be seen what effects this will have on primary systems.

A further variation is found in the timing of primary elections. Some states nominate their congressional candidates as early as April in election years, whereas others do not do so until September. This staggering of congressional primaries has a pronounced decentralizing effect upon the selection of national legislators. Because of the long primary season, it is extremely difficult to focus the attention of voters upon national issues. National party organizations and leaders are ordinarily unable to exert much influence upon the selection of their congressional candidates in the several states. Instead, local organizations and leaders play a dominant role, and voters are very much inclined to make their selections on the basis of local personalities and issues.

The primary election is usually viewed as a means of nominating candidates for Congress, but in fact it serves very widely as the means by which congressmen are elected. A study made by Cortez Ewing[27] of elections to the House of Representatives showed that 53.5 percent of victorious candidates between 1896 and 1946 won by at least a 60 to 40 margin. This suggests that the outcome of the final election in these instances was never much in doubt and that the real decision was made by the voters in the primary election of the dominant party. In the 1956 congressional election, Democratic candidates received more than 60 percent of the vote in 151 districts and Republican candidates won by a similar margin in 104 districts. In 1960, Democratic candidates received 60 percent or more of the popular vote in 173 districts and Republicans in 58. In 1964, unofficial returns put

---

[27] "Primaries as Real Elections," *Southwestern Social Science Quarterly,* 29 (March 1949), pp. 293–298.

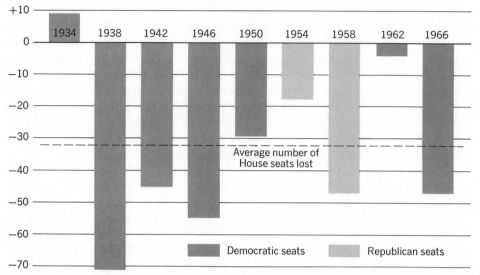

THE HOUSE

Party in power has lost House seats in every off-year election since 1936.

SOURCE: *The New York Times,* November 6, 1966 and *Congressional Quarterly Weekly Report,* November 11, 1966.

at 209 the number of Democrats winning by 60 percent or more of the votes, with 44 Republican congressional candidates obtaining a similar majority. In 1968, the corresponding figures were 163 for the Democrats and 118 for the Republicans. Thus one can see that in more districts than not, nomination was almost equivalent to election.

Moreover, usually only a rather small percentage of congressional seats shift from one party to another in a single election. In 1956 twenty seats in the House changed party hands. Democrats won eleven from Republicans, Republicans nine from Democrats. In 1960, thirty-six seats changed. Republicans won twenty-eight from Democrats and Democrats eight from Republicans. 1964 was a disastrous year for Republican presidential hopes, yet party control of only 58 of 435 House seats changed. The Democrats won 48 from Republicans and Republicans captured 10 from Democrats. 1968 saw a shift of only 14 seats. Republicans took nine from Democrats but lost five of their own.

Ballot Forms Used in Congressional Elections

The ballot forms used in American elections vary widely. The Australian, or secret, ballot is a comparatively recent development, having been adopted by the first state as late as 1880. There are two principal ballot forms in use today: the party-column ballot and the office-block ballot. Most states use the former, in which a party's candidates for all offices are grouped together in a vertical column, with the highest offices at the top and the ones of lesser importance at the bottom. A substantial minority of states use the office-block type, in which all the candidates for the same office are grouped together, with the party designation usually following the name of each candidate. It is possible to vote a straight party ticket on either type of ballot, but the party-column ballot more easily lends itself to this procedure.

The office-block ballot is often favored on the grounds that it discourages straight party voting and thus encourages the voter to think in terms of the best candidate for each office rather than of the best party for all offices. On the other hand, those who favor stronger and more responsible parties often regard straight party voting as desirable.

ELECTING THE PRESIDENT

The Original Method

The democratic character of a present-day presidential election seems all the more remarkable when compared with the method provided for in the Constitution in 1787. The plan finally approved by the Convention for the selection of a chief executive was an ingenious one, and it is clear that the Fathers expected it to work along very different lines from those that ultimately prevailed. Article II of the Constitution provided that the President and the Vice President were to be chosen by the members of an *electoral college*. This college was to be a small body in which each state would have as many members as it had senators and representatives. Members of the college were to be chosen every four years in each state in such a manner as the legislature thereof might direct, and were to meet in their respective states at a time designated by Congress and vote by ballot for two persons. These ballots were then to be forwarded to Congress to be opened and counted in the presence of the two houses. The person having the greatest number of votes, provided such number was a majority of the whole number of electors, was to be President, and the person standing second Vice President. If no person had a majority, the House of Representatives was to choose one of the five highest on the list to serve as President, with the representatives from each state having one collective vote and a majority of all the states required for election.

A need for constitutional change was shown by the election of 1800, the first to be dominated by political parties. All of the electors pledged to the Republican party cast their two votes for Thomas Jefferson and Aaron Burr, intending the first to be President and the latter Vice President. But since both men had the same number of electoral votes there was no legal way of carrying out the intention of the electors, and it was necessary for the House of Representatives to break the tie. It was clear that the same result would prevail in subsequent elections if political parties continued to be active. Accordingly, the Twelfth Amendment was added to the Constitution in 1804, directing the electors to cast one of their votes specifically for President and one for Vice President.

Not a word appears in the Constitution about the nomination of presidential candidates. It was regarded as a foregone conclusion that George Washington would be the first President. But thereafter the Convention apparently expected that in each election the members of the electoral college would have a free hand in canvassing a wide list of possible candidates and that there would be no "nominees" in any formal sense. Since the electors were never to meet in any one place as a single unit, this was almost certain to mean that the electoral vote would be widely distributed. It seems likely that the Convention viewed the electoral college as an agency that would *nominate* up to five candidates for the Presidency, and the House of Representatives as the agency that would frequently have to *elect* the President. At any rate the system rapidly began to operate along quite different lines. During the first third of the nineteenth century it remained in a state of flux, but in the Jackson era the method of electing the President, as we know it today, became more or less crystallized.

The Present-day System:
Nominating Presidential Candidates

Political parties have made an all-important contribution to the American electoral system, for it is not too much to say that the means by which the choice of the voters is narrowed to two candidates are almost completely controlled by the parties. Not only is the Constitution utterly silent concerning the nomination of presidential candidates by party conventions; there is little statutory control over this phase of the election system. A small body of state law deals with some of the details of convention organization and procedure, such as the method of selecting the delegates and the manner in which some of the state delegates cast their votes in the convention, but neither the states nor the federal government have attempted to control the larger aspects of the convention system—the total number of delegates, the time and place of the meeting, the vote required for nomination. Instead, the organization and the control of a national convention are largely the responsibility of the party and are determined for the most part by custom.

In recent decades the Democratic and the Republican national conventions have had from 1200 to 3000 delegates (many with only a one-half vote), with each state having a number of votes roughly equal to twice the size of its congressional delegation. Actually, both parties now use modified formulas by which states giving a party substantial election support enjoy increased voting power in that party's convention. In order to reduce the power of delegations from states with weak party organizations, the Republicans in 1924 adopted a system of granting bonus votes to delegations from states carried by Republican candidates for various national offices in recent elections. The bonus system was adopted by the Democrats in 1944 and has been expanded since. Democrats have tended more than Republicans to use fractional votes and oversized delegations. In the 1964 conventions, the Democrats had 2316 votes, and the Republicans 1308. Despite these changes, "the apportionment rules tend to over represent the small states and under represent the large. They also over represent the areas of low voter turnout and under represent those of higher voter turnout. In states where one party is much stronger than the other, the rules tend to over represent the weaker party and under represent the stronger." [28]

Both parties leave it to the individual states to determine how their delegates will be selected. Two methods are widely used—the convention system and the primary system. Throughout the nineteenth century delegates were chosen by state and local conventions or caucuses. Early in the present century a desire to make the presidential election system more democratic led to the presidential primary, in which the rank and file of party members in a state were not only allowed to choose the state's delegates to the national convention but were often given an opportunity to express their preferences for a presidential candidate. At first it appeared that the primary would soon entirely replace the state convention as a means of choosing delegates, but after 1916 a reaction set in. By 1964 only seventeen states held presidential primaries. Moreover, in many of the states where a primary is authorized, it has become a formality. In the last few presidential election years the number of significant state presidential primaries has not exceeded five or six.

Procedure in the Convention: Adopting a Platform

When a national convention meets there are two important items of business to be transacted: drafting and adopting the party platform and nominating the candidates for President and Vice President. The platform is drafted by a committee on resolutions consisting of one man and one woman from each state and territory selected by their own delegations. This committee usually holds public hearings at which representatives of interest groups are given a chance to present their views. Much of the platform, however, is often prepared in advance by a small group of party leaders or, in the case of the party in power, by the President and his advisers. The platform is submitted to the delegates on the floor of the convention on the second or third day and is usually approved with a minimum of debate or controversy. Occasionally an effort is made to amend the platform from the floor, and once in a while such a move succeeds.

It is easy enough to ridicule the average platform, for as V. O. Key[29] says, it "speaks with boldness and forthrightness on issues that are already well settled; it is likely to be ambiguous on contentious questions." But such criticism frequently overlooks the importance of compromise in politics. The evasive platform is one of the forces that makes it possible for parties to hold together at least long enough to elect every four years a President who has the backing of 40 million or more voters. This is an achievement whose importance should not be minimized.

---

[28] Paul T. David, Ralph M. Goldman, and Richard C. Bain, *The Politics of National Party Conventions,* paperback edition, Kathleen Sproul, ed. (Washington, D.C.: The Brookings Institution, 1960), p. 108.

[29] Pp. 462–463.

At the same time, the price paid for it is sometimes a heavy one in terms of the confusing of issues that ought to be brought out in the open and intelligently discussed.

Procedure in the Convention: Nominating Candidates

Both major party conventions now employ much the same method of nominating candidates. First the roll of the states is called so that the candidates for the presidential nomination may be placed before the convention in formal nominating speeches. Then the balloting begins, each state casting its votes orally as the roll is called from Alabama to Wyoming. The District of Columbia and the territories and dependencies also cast a small number of votes. A majority of all votes cast is necessary for nomination, and successive ballots are taken until a majority is obtained by one of the candidates. The first ballot frequently proves effective; in fact, from 1900 until 1968, fifteen Republican and twelve Democratic candidates were chosen on the first ballot.

Following the presidential nomination, the convention quickly names a vice-presidential candidate. The presidential nominee's advice is sought and usually accepted. The vice-presidential candidate may be some one who could not have been nominated and elected President, but whose qualities offset and complement those of the presidential nominee. The heart attacks of Eisenhower and the assassination of Kennedy have increased awareness of the possibility of the Vice President's becoming the Chief Executive and thus focused attention on the abilities of vice-presidential candidates. It is probable that this concern narrowed Nixon's margin of victory in 1968.

The Dynamics of the Presidential Nominating Process

Unless it is clear that a party is committed to the renomination of a President in office, anywhere from two or three to a dozen or more candidates for the nomination may be expected to be active in the preconvention campaign. Most of these men have well-known records in politics. Only rarely does a businessman or military figure step directly into the role of a party's standard bearer with little or no previous experience in politics, as did Wendell Willkie in 1940 or Dwight Eisenhower in 1952.

State politics has historically been a very important training ground for presidential candidates. Eleven of the twenty men nominated by the two major parties for the Presidency between 1900 and 1956 were state governors or former governors. With the increased importance of foreign policy, the Senate is becoming a fertile spawning ground for leading presidential hopefuls. Each of the presidential candidates in 1960, 1964, and 1968, Barry Goldwater, Lyndon B. Johnson, John F. Kennedy, Hubert H. Humphrey, and Richard M. Nixon, had been senators, as had several of their major rivals for the nomination.

Despite such exceptions as Al Smith in 1928 and John F. Kennedy in 1960, most leading candidates for a major party nomination have been Protestant in religion. Geography is also an important factor in determining the availability of presidential candidates. A candidate from a state with a large electoral vote that is also a "doubtful" state politically, such as California, New York, Ohio, or Illinois, will seem much more attractive to the party than one from a small state that is sure to be in one party column or the other. Beyond that, if an aspirant has a large and attractive family, a pleasing appearance and personality, and, above all, a knack for campaign oratory, he will have no difficulty about qualifying as an available candidate. Whether lightning will finally strike him depends upon a further complex of forces and circumstances that defies any systematic analysis and in which luck is by no means the least important factor.

The notion that a few party leaders get together in a smoke-filled room and agree upon a candidate, who is then meekly accepted by the delegates, is not a valid one. Two forces operate in the present-day national convention to bring about the nomination of a candidate who has strong backing among the rank-and-file party members. One is the influence of the public opinion poll, which unquestionably carries great weight with both convention leaders and delegates. In fact, in the presidential elections since polling has come to occupy such a prominent place on the American scene, both parties have almost always nominated the candidate who stood at or very near the top of the polls. The Republicans in 1964 violated this practice and paid a high price at the ballot box.

Second, the presidential primary, for all of its shortcomings, continues to have some value as an indicator of public opinion. For example, in 1952 the first state primary, in New Hampshire, substantially affected the chances of candidates in both parties. In the Republican primary Eisenhower won a decisive victory over Taft, a victory that gave a great impetus to the Eisenhower movement at a time when the General was seemingly not sure whether he wanted to run for the Presidency. Truman's poor showing was undoubtedly a factor in his decision not to seek reelection. In 1960, Kennedy's triumphs in Wisconsin and West Virginia made him the front-runner. Similarly, in 1964 Barry Goldwater's victory in California made him the candidate whom no other Republican hopeful could reach. Primaries in 1968 did not play quite so critical a role, but they did emphasize Nixon's strength as well as the general disunity of the Democrats.

The Present-day System:
The Final Election of a President

In presidential elections over 70 million voters go to the polls to select the members of the electoral college. Before election day each of the parties selects a full slate of candidates for the seats to which a state is entitled in the electoral college. The identity of these candidates and the manner of their selection are of little consequence, provided there is no question of a revolt on the part of a state's electors against their party's candidate for the Presidency. Indeed, in most states the names of the candidates for the

An election night dinner in New York City during the 1960 presidential election. (Cornell Capa from Magnum)

electoral college no longer appear upon the ballot. Instead, the ballots in these states carry only the names of the party candidates for President and Vice President, and a phrase for each party column indicating that the proper number of candidates for the electoral college is pledged to vote for the party's nominees. This is known as the Presidential short ballot.

In all the states the electors are chosen at large, which means that the entire slate of the party receiving the most votes in the state-wide election is elected and the electoral vote of the state is thereafter cast as a unit. There is nothing in the Constitution to prevent a state legislature from providing for the choosing of electors by single-member districts, an arrangement that would make possible a divided state electoral vote. No state has followed such a plan since 1891 (and few before that date) because the dominant party in each state naturally opposes any plan that would give the minority party a chance to win any electoral votes. Moreover, state legislators have reasoned that the possibility of a divided electoral vote would lessen their state's influence and prestige in national politics.

By midnight of election day it is usually possible to determine which party has the majority of the votes in the electoral college and thus to know who will be the next President. But technically the voting for President and Vice President occurs in December when, on a day fixed by federal law, the victorious electors meet in their respective state capitals and formally cast their ballots. The outcome is not officially recognized until the new Congress assembles in January, counts the ballots of the electors in a joint House-Senate session, and proclaims the result. It is at this point that the House of Representatives would proceed to elect a President in case of a tie vote or in case no candidate had a clear majority of electoral votes, the Senate electing a Vice President under similar conditions. Since the Twentieth Amendment fixes January 20 as Inauguration Day, Congress would have to act promptly were the electoral vote to prove ineffective.

HOW THE STATES VOTED IN PRESIDENTIAL ELECTIONS, 1936–1964

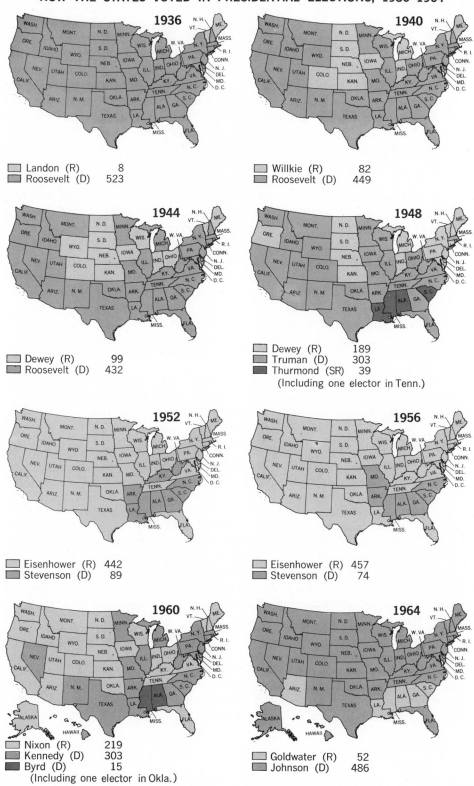

1936
- Landon (R)   8
- Roosevelt (D)   523

1940
- Willkie (R)   82
- Roosevelt (D)   449

1944
- Dewey (R)   99
- Roosevelt (D)   432

1948
- Dewey (R)   189
- Truman (D)   303
- Thurmond (SR)   39
(Including one elector in Tenn.)

1952
- Eisenhower (R)   442
- Stevenson (D)   89

1956
- Eisenhower (R)   457
- Stevenson (D)   74

1960
- Nixon (R)   219
- Kennedy (D)   303
- Byrd (D)   15
(Including one elector in Okla.)

1964
- Goldwater (R)   52
- Johnson (D)   486

SOURCE: Adapted from *The New York Times* and *Congressional Quarterly Weekly Report*, March 26, 1965.

Defects of the Electoral College System

The electoral college has functioned reasonably well through the years. Actually the system has three weaknesses, each of which offers a threat to the democratic character of presidential elections. In the first place, there is no provision in the federal Constitution or federal law to prevent an elector from voting for someone other than his party's candidates. Only a couple of states expressly compel electors to fulfill their pledges, although several others have laws that make an incidental recognition of this obligation.

The second weakness is the ever-present possibility that the popular vote and the electoral vote will get out of line and that the victor in the electoral vote will actually receive fewer popular votes than his opponent. This possibility results primarily from the fact that in each state the winning candidate receives the state's entire electoral vote regardless of the popular vote won by the losing candidate. This condition has prevailed in two elections since the Civil War, as follows:

Year	Candidates	Popular Vote	Electoral Vote
1876	Hayes (Rep.)	4,033,768	185
	Tilden (Dem.)	4,285,992	184
1888	Harrison (Rep.)	5,439,853	233
	Cleveland (Dem.)	5,540,329	168

Moreover, the same result could have prevailed in many other elections had small blocs of popular votes been cast the other way in certain states.

The third weakness is the possibility that the electoral college may fail to give a majority to any candidate and the election will be thrown into the House of Representatives. This has happened only twice in American history and only once since the adoption of the Twelfth Amendment: in 1824 four presidential candidates divided the electoral vote in such a way that no one of them had a majority. But there have been other elections in which strong third-party candidates threatened to win enough electoral votes to throw the election into the House. The 1968 election provides a good example. The third party candidate, George Wallace, won in five states and received 45 electoral votes. Had Humphrey rather than Nixon carried Alaska, Delaware, Missouri, and New Jersey (Nixon's combined margin of victory in these four states was less than 80,000), Nixon's electoral vote would have been 267 and Humphrey's 224. Both would have been short of a majority—270—and the House would have been called upon to choose among Humphrey, Nixon, and Wallace.

It may be asked why there should be any misfortune about having a presidential election thrown into the House of Representatives. Two difficulties should be mentioned. In the first place, the voting in the House for President is by states and not by members. It is entirely possible mathematically for the minority party in the House to have control of a majority of the state delegations and thereby to be in a position to elect its candidate to the Presidency even though he stood second in both the popular and the electoral votes. A second difficulty results from the constitutional requirement that the winning candidate must receive the support of a majority of all the states. It is possible for the party control of state delegations to be so scrambled that the House would be unable to elect a President. In that case, the Vice President, chosen by the Senate from the two candidates with the highest electoral votes, would serve until the end of a four year term or until the House could break its deadlock. If the Senate were unable to elect a Vice President—51 votes are needed and enough senators might abstain from voting to keep either candidate from obtaining that number—the Speaker of the House of Representatives would serve as President.

Selected Bibliography

David, Paul T., Ralph M. Goldman, and Richard C. Bain, *The Politics of National Party Conventions,* paperback edition, K. Sproul, ed. (Washington, D.C.: The Brookings Institution, 1960). Brings together a wealth of information on and interpretations of the operations of national party nominating conventions.

David, Paul T., Malcolm Moos, and Ralph M. Goldman, *Presidential Nominating Politics* (Baltimore, Md.: The Johns Hopkins Press, 1954), 5 vols. A monumental study of the Eisenhower and Stevenson nominations of 1952.

Downs, Anthony, *An Economic Theory of Democracy* (New York: Harper & Row, Publishers, 1957). A challenging investigation of the rational bases of political behavior.

Lubell, Samuel, *The Future of American Politics* (New York: Harper & Row, Publishers, 1952). Lubell's future has long come to pass, but this is still an interesting analysis of the American political system.

Wilmerding, Lucius, Jr., *The Electoral College* (New Brunswick, N.J.: Rutgers University Press, 1958). A thorough discussion of the machinery of the electoral college for electing a President.

9

Political campaigning

America has stamped its own character on political campaigning. On the local level housewives cannot go to the supermarket or city subway riders to work without shaking the hand of seemingly indefatigable candidates. To win state office candidates feel they must be seen eating the favorite food of every nationality their voters represent, must shake every hand and kiss every baby. And for national campaigns, trains, planes, and every media are marshaled to cover all corners of the land.

PRESIDENTIAL CAMPAIGNS

For some eight weeks before election day the country is treated to one of its most colorful and exhausting political spectacles. The candidates for the Presidency are the major players in the most intensive and prolonged effort to win high office that takes place in any modern democracy. In contrast, a British national campaign is traditionally limited to a seventeen-day period between the dissolving of Parliament and election day.

172

Traveling in elaborately manned and equipped campaign trains and planes, American candidates follow each other across the land, making a series of carefully planned addresses in key cities, as well as scores of more informal talks to the thousands who come to see them. Radio and television reach millions of listeners who find presidential sweepstakes almost as exciting as the Super Bowl. Party machinery is oiled, tens of thousands of campaign workers toil endlessly to win votes, millions of pieces of campaign literature are distributed, debates are held, promises are made, names are called, the air is full of prophecies of peace, prosperity, war, and depression. Millions of dollars are spent to persuade the lowly voter that the fate of the nation depends upon how he makes up his mind.

Do Campaigns Make a Difference?

Does all this make a difference on election day? There is much disagreement about the answer. Such diverse authorities as Jim Farley and polltakers George Gallup and Elmo Roper have all asserted at one time or another that campaigning has a limited value, since most voters have made up their minds before the campaign starts. But the unexpected victory of President Harry S. Truman in the 1948 election brought a change in viewpoint, for it seems clear that the particular kinds of campaign waged by Thomas E. Dewey and Harry S. Truman in 1948 profoundly affected the outcome of the election— Dewey lost votes by the generalizing that marked his "high-level" campaign speeches, and Truman won votes by carrying his down-to-earth message to all who heard him. Television debates were widely credited as an important factor in John F. Kennedy's 1960 victory.

Some light was thrown upon the effects of campaigning by the study of the impact of the 1940 presidential race upon a single county.[1] It was discovered that roughly half the voters in Erie County, Ohio, knew in May how they would vote in November and never deviated from their stands. Another 25 percent made up their minds immediately following the national party conventions in 1940 and also stayed firm. Thus only one voter in four had much sensitivity to the appeals of the two candidates during the campaign. Of course, this undecided minority would hold the balance of power in any presidential election and was, therefore, important enough to justify intensive campaigning by both parties. Moreover, the Erie County study showed that even for the "regulars" campaigning had the value of reinforcing their stands.

A somewhat similar study of the 1948 presidential election in Elmira, New York, found that most voters remained constant throughout the campaign.[2] In Elmira, 71 percent maintained the same party preference throughout the campaign, while 29 percent wavered between the parties or between their normal party affiliation and neutrality. The data on when voters made up their minds

---

[1] P. Lazarsfeld, B. Berelson, and H. Gaudet, *The People's Choice: How the Voter Makes Up His Mind in a Presidential Campaign* (New York: Duell, Sloan and Pearce, Inc., 1944).

[2] B. Berelson, P. Lazarsfeld, and W. McPhee, *Voting* (Chicago: University of Chicago Press, 1954).

as to how they would vote are even more striking than those in the Erie County study. Sixty-four percent, or nearly two thirds, had decided by June; another 15 percent came to a final conclusion in August; and only 11 percent in October and 10 percent as late as early November.

A more recent study concludes that 65 to 75 percent of those who vote make up their minds by the end of the national convention and before the campaign starts. Another 10 to 20 percent make their decisions in the period between the start of the campaign and two weeks before the election. One out of ten remains undecided until the last two weeks before the election.[3]

Campaign Strategy

In "safe" congressional districts or in one-party states campaigning may be little more than a ritual; but in two-party states and even in some presidential elections, such as those of 1948 and 1960, a shift of a relatively small segment of voters can be decisive. Thus political campaigns, as Stanley Kelley, Jr.,[4] has noted, "are waged to make marginal changes in political alignments." And to maximize the size of those potentially crucial "marginal changes," candidates and their advisers must make numerous decisions about campaign strategy. The following list suggests some of the issues that have to be faced.

1. Shall primary dependence for organization effort be placed upon the party machine or shall the formation of "independent committees" be encouraged? Most seasoned politicians distrust the latter and are inclined to rely upon traditional party machinery. Yet the independent Citizens for Eisenhower organization seemingly contributed substantially to the Republican victory in 1952, and various "nonpartisan" committees for Johnson helped swell his huge majority. One value of such independent organizations is the way in which they can appeal to dissatisfied members of the opposition party. A disgruntled Democrat who might find it hard to listen to the siren song of the Republican organization can much more readily be persuaded to become an enthusiastic member of an "independent citizens' committee."

2. Shall the candidate depend primarily upon a "mass appeal" for votes, using radio and television and huge rallies to reach and influence large numbers of voters? Or shall he bring his campaign down to a personal level by trying to reach as many voters as possible on a hand-shaking basis? The latter approach is more feasible in a congressional race, where the scope of the campaign and the number of voters are limited. But even presidential candidates sometimes feel the need to reach and talk with large numbers of voters on a direct basis. In

---

[3] Angus Campbell, Philip E. Converse, Warren E. Miller, and Donald E. Stokes, *The American Voter* (New York: John Wiley & Sons, Inc., 1960), Chap. 4.

[4] "The Presidential Campaign," in Paul T. David, ed., *The Presidential Election and Transition 1960–1961* (Washington, D.C.: The Brookings Institution, 1961), p. 57.

Time of Voting Decision in the Presidential Elections
(voters only)

QUESTION: "How long before the election did you decide that you were going to vote the way you did?"

	Percentage				
	1948	1952	1956	1960	1964
Knew all along	37	30	44	24	13
Before the conventions, when knew candidates would run	a	4	14	6	17
At the time of the conventions	28	31	18	30	19
During the campaign	14	20	12	25	16
In the last two weeks	12	11	8	11	10
Don't remember, not ascertained	9	4	4	4	25
	100	100	100	100	100

[a] Data not available.
SOURCE: University of Michigan Survey Research Center.

1960 each of the four television debates gave the two major candidates an audience in 27 to 30 million homes. The number of people who watched the first debate was close to 75 million, and it has been estimated that 120 million people saw one or more of the debates.[5] Yet, even with this unprecedented access to public attention, both candidates felt it necessary to spend much of their time on whistle-stop and jet-stop tours, making brief talks and shaking countless thousands of hands. In 1964, with no televised debates, both candidates spent most of their time touring the country.

3. How shall a winning majority of 40 million or more votes be pieced together? Shall a candidate pitch his campaign at party regulars or deliberately woo independent and disaffected members of the opposition? Since the New Deal, registration statistics have pretty well dictated each party's rational choice in this regard. Because Democrats have usually heavily outnumbered Republicans in the last thirty years, the Republicans to win must, as Vice President Nixon tried to do in 1960, play down party labels and try to convince wavering Democrats as well as Independents. The Democrats, on the other hand, can win if only they can hold their party members together and swing some Independents. The magnitude of Goldwater's defeat in 1964 was in part due to his refusal to appeal, outside the South, to Democratic and Independent voters. In contrast Richard Nixon's 1968 campaign carefully and deliberately courted dissident Democrats and Independents along with Republican stalwarts.

Group and geographic appeals are also problems in welding together a coali-

[5] Theodore H. White, *The Making of the President 1960* (New York: Atheneum Publishers, 1961), p. 296.

In order to get maximum political coverage, national candidates often travel by airplane as well as whistle stopping from town to town by train. (Cornell Capa from Magnum)

tion. Shall the candidate concentrate on certain interest groups such as labor, business, or farmers even if it means alienating other groups? Or shall he speak in generalities and hope to alienate no large group? Much the same problem must be faced in geographic terms. In recent years the issue of Negro civil rights has caused the most serious regional differences. The Negro vote in the big northern cities can mean capturing states like New York, Pennsylvania, Michigan, or Illinois. Yet southern states have an impressive share of votes in the electoral college. Again, the candidate must choose between a specific and a general appeal. John Kennedy came up with an interesting solution in 1960. With Senator Lyndon Johnson of Texas as his running mate, each man assumed primary responsibility for quieting the regional fears in his own area.

4. Shall the candidate take the offensive (as did Truman in 1948) or play everything safe (as did Johnson in 1964)? Shall he attack his opponent and try to answer charges against him and his party (as did Roosevelt's opponents in 1936 and 1940) or shall he ignore his opponent and charges against him (as did Roosevelt in the same years)?

5. Shall issues be emphasized or shall the campaign be waged on the basis of personality? Here as elsewhere, of course, no candidate ever has a completely free choice, nor is the choice an either-or affair. An Eisenhower who goes into a campaign with a name and personality already famous is likely to minimize

issues. But a John Kennedy or a Barry Goldwater faced with an uphill fight to win the Presidency must hammer away at issues.

6. Finally, there are all-important decisions of timing. The campaign must be started neither too early nor too late and must be brought to a crescendo at the proper moment to influence the largest number of voters.

There are so many crucial choices and so many possibilities of errors in judgment and action that a candidate might well despair of ever bringing a campaign to a successful conclusion. A sense of discouragement results also from the famous stories that are told of campaign "blunders"—for example, of how Charles Evans Hughes lost the Presidency in 1916 by failing to shake hands with Hiram Johnson on his visit to California during the campaign,[6] or how Vice President Nixon's poor make-up in his first television debate with Senator Kennedy may have lost him the few votes he needed to win in the electoral college. But most candidates soon throw off any sense of discouragement and early in the campaign do their best to create and maintain an illusion of victory. After all, each candidate runs much the same risks, and in the end it is unlikely that the Presidency will be won or lost on any one tactical error or even strategic mistake. And yet a campaign must be planned with care and shrewdness, since several errors coming together might cause disaster.

CONGRESSIONAL CAMPAIGNS

On a smaller scale the candidate for Congress has to face and make many of the same decisions that confront presidential candidates. But in other ways his problem is a different one.

If he is running for the House of Representatives from one of the 250 or more districts that are considered to be pretty safely in one party column or the other or for the Senate from a presumed "safe" state, his real campaigning must be done prior to the primary and be aimed at winning the nomination. His opponents will be members of his own party, which means that issues will probably affect the result less than will personalities and effective organization. Candidates within the same party can and do disagree upon issues, but the appeal to party voters is likely to be couched in terms of "I am an honest man who would greatly appreciate your personal support. I promise you that if I am nominated and elected I will serve the interests of this district to the best of my ability." There is no institutional arrangement that compels a candidate for Congress to seek the endorsement of a national party organization. If his local prestige is sufficient, he may even win the nomination in the face of active opposition by the national leaders of the party.

In presidential years congressional candidates usually try to ride on the coat tails of the presidential candidates. They tend to leave the discussion of issues to the national candidates and to concentrate upon winning friends among the voters and making certain that the local party machinery is in good running

---

[6] See the interesting article by F. M. Davenport, "Did Hughes Snub Johnson?—An Inside Story," *American Political Science Review,* 43 (April 1949), p. 321.

FACTOTUM—*In behalf of his candidate, the ideal campaign manager is expected to (1) brief campaign workers; (2) tread on other people's toes; (3) relieve his candidate of headaches; (4) enhance his public image; (5) muffle his personal attacks on opponents; (6) ride herd on volunteer organizations; (7) and (8) keep his candidate's eyes focused on the main target—votes; (9) hold petitioners at bay; (10) arrange TV schedules; (11) fit all the pieces of campaign strategy together, and finally (12) do the glad-handing his candidate hasn't the time for.*

condition. In midterm elections the national parties are relatively inactive; there is no party platform; the 1966 debate over Vietnam notwithstanding, issues generally recede into the background. The influence of the President is usually less strong than in a presidential year, voter interest wanes, and the size of the vote declines sharply. Under these circumstances campaigning is apt to be both decentralized and demoralized. Local interests, local personalities, and local party organizations influence the result even more than they do in presidential years. If the state or district is a "safe" one, the candidate of the dominant party can coast along, quite certain of election or reelection while his opponent goes through the forms of campaigning without creating even an illusion of victory. If the district is a marginal one, the candidate of the President's party will find himself at a disadvantage, for in every midterm congressional election since the Civil War, save that of 1934, the President's party has lost seats in Congress. Even in 1962, one of the most successful off-year elections for any administration, the Democrats lost several seats. And yet these are the districts that will be most bitterly contested, for the President's party must try to hold its midterm losses to a minimum and the opposition party must try to make its gains as broad as possible. Curiously, these midterm losses of the party in power do not necessarily foreshadow defeat in the next presidential election.

FINANCING CAMPAIGNS

Money and Politics

Political campaigns in the United States are costly undertakings. In 1956, national-level committees of the two major parties spent $17.2 million; in 1960, $25 million; and in 1964, almost $35 million.[7]

Summary of Political Spending at the National Level, 1964
(in thousands of dollars)

Committees	Gross Reported Disbursements	Known Debt	Total Campaign Costs	Transfers to Candidates and Committees	Direct Expenditures
18 Republican	$17,187	$	$17,187	$1,163	$16,026
32 Democratic	10,973	1,000	11,973	3,216	8,757
31 Labor	3,665		3,665	2,940	725
26 Miscellaneous	1,963		1,963	889	1,074
107 Total	$33,788	$1,000	$34,788	$8,208	$26,582

SOURCE: Herbert E. Alexander, *Financing the 1964 Election* (Princeton, N.J.: Citizens' Research Foundation, 1966), p. 8.

[7] Herbert E. Alexander, *Financing the 1964 Election* (Princeton, N.J.: Citizens' Research Foundation, 1966), p. 7.

POLITICAL CAMPAIGN EXPENDITURES 1952–1964

REPORTED VS. ESTIMATES OF ACTUAL SPENDING

- Reported Outlays in Presidential and Congressional Campaigns
- Estimates of Actual Nationwide Political Campaign Spending

1952 $23.1 MILLION $140

1956 $29.3 $155

1960 $32.9 $175

1964 $47.8 $200

GIFTS OF $500 OR MORE

WHAT PERCENTAGE OF TOTAL DOLLAR VALUE OF GIFTS THEY CONSTITUTED FOR EACH PARTY.

- Democratic
- Republican

1952   63%   68%

1956   44%   74%

1960   59%   58%

1964   69%   28%

PARTY SHARES OF NATIONAL-LEVEL POLITICAL EXPENDITURES 1952–1964

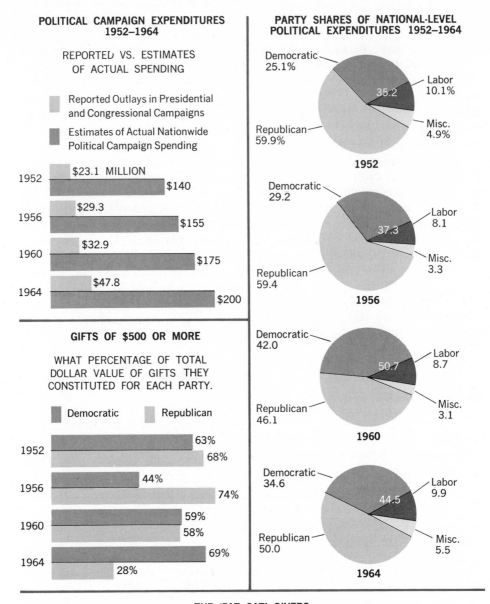

1952
Democratic 25.1%
Labor 10.1%
Misc. 4.9%
Republican 59.9%
35.2

1956
Democratic 29.2
Labor 8.1
Misc. 3.3
Republican 59.4
37.3

1960
Democratic 42.0
Labor 8.7
Misc. 3.1
Republican 46.1
50.7

1964
Democratic 34.6
Labor 9.9
Misc. 5.5
Republican 50.0
44.5

THE 'FAT CAT' GIVERS

PARTY RECEIPTS FROM DONORS OF $10,000 OR MORE

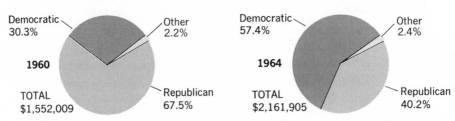

1960
Democratic 30.3%
Other 2.2%
TOTAL $1,552,009
Republican 67.5%

1964
Democratic 57.4%
Other 2.4%
TOTAL $2,161,905
Republican 40.2%

SOURCE: Congressional Quarterly Weekly Report, January 21, 1966.

Campaign Financing: 1954, 1958, 1962, and 1966

Reported campaign spending included in reports to the Clerk of the House for the mid-term campaigns since 1954. Numbers on the committee line indicate the number of groups reporting.

	COMMITTEE SPENDING REPORTED NATIONALLY			
	1954	1958	1962	1966*
Republican committees	27	14	11	21
Receipts	$ 5,380,994	$4,686,423	$ 4,674,570	$ 7,640,760
Expenditures	$ 5,509,649	$4,657,652	$ 4,637,586	$ 7,863,092
Percentage of total spending	53.5	53.7	39.4	41.5
Democratic committees	13	7	8	8
Receipts	$ 2,168,404	$1,733,626	$ 3,699,827	$ 4,055,310
Expenditures	$ 2,224,211	$1,702,605	$ 3,569,357	$ 4,282,007
Percentage of total spending	21.6	19.6	30.3	22.5
Labor committees	41	32	33	42
Receipts	$ 1,882,157	$1,854,635	$ 2,112,677	$ 4,262,077
Expenditures	$ 2,057,613	$1,828,778	$ 2,305,331	$ 4,289,055
Percentage of total spending	20.0	21.1	19.6	22.7
Miscellaneous committees	15	11	26	44
Receipts	$ 517,804	$ 492,710	$ 1,313,959	$ 2,123,868
Expenditures	$ 514,094	$ 486,430	$ 1,271,214	$ 2,545,080
Percentage of total spending	5.0	5.6	10.8	13.3
Totals				
Receipts	$ 9,949,359	$8,767,394	$11,801,033	$18,082,015
Expenditures	$10,305,567	$8,675,465	$11,783,488	$18,979,234

CONGRESSIONAL CAMPAIGN SPENDING REPORTED, 1950–1962

	1954	1956	1958	1960	1962	1966
Republicans	$ 1,596,031	$ 3,287,650	$ 1,670,933	$ 2,523,869	$ 3,475,847	$ 2,230,835
Percentage of spending	52.4	53.3	50.9	52.3	52.5	34.8
Democrats	$ 1,436,576	$ 2,856,978	$ 1,600,117	$ 2,249,719	$ 2,950,552	$ 4,081,685
Percentage of spending	47.2	46.3	48.7	46.7	44.9	63.6
Third party and independents	$ 13,333	$ 24,988	$ 12,605	$ 47,990	$ 172,622	$ 103,764
Percentage of spending	0.4	0.4	0.4	1.0	2.6	1.6
Total congressional spending	$ 3,045,940	$ 6,169,616	$ 3,283,655	$ 4,821,578	$ 6,620,627	$ 6,416,284
Total reported campaign costs	$13,351,507	$29,260,068	$11,959,120	$32,896,322	$18,404,115	$25,395,518

* The 1966 expenditure figures are "less transfers" that is, lateral fund transfers between national-level committees have been deducted.
SOURCE: *Congressional Quarterly Weekly Report,* August 11, 1967.

The cost of nominating and electing all federal, state, and local public officials was probably $140 million in 1952, $155 million in 1956, $175 million in 1960, and in the neighborhood of $200 million in 1964.[8] When one realizes that the cost of such a simple step in a national campaign as sending a single post card

---

[8] Alexander, p. 13.

to each eligible voter would be almost $4.5 million for postage alone, the wonder is that the total expenditures can be as low as the figure given.

The threat that certain candidates will "buy" their way into public office, or that certain interests will "buy" public policies favorable to their cause, is ever present. The result is one of the most difficult dilemmas of American politics: parties and candidates must be allowed to spend money in campaigns so that the voters may acquire necessary information; yet constant vigilance is necessary lest the democratic process be corrupted by the dollar sign.

How Money Is Spent

While it is not possible to compile an exhaustive list of the ways in which campaign money is used, we can suggest six purposes that illustrate the numerous ways in which a party organization can legitimately spend large sums of money during a campaign: (1) *general overhead* —for party headquarters at national, state, and local levels, including salaries, office rent, postage, and telephones; (2) *field activities*—the speaking trips of the candidates and campaign rallies and meetings; (3) *publicity*—telecasts and radio broadcasts, newspaper advertisements, campaign literature, public relations experts, and the like; (4) *grants to subsidiary committees*—transfers of funds from national organizations to state and local organizations and to special committees and groups; (5) *election day expenses*—transportation of voters to the polls and payments to party workers who try to bring out the vote and to watchers at the polls; (6) *public opinion polling* to gauge the effects of various campaign strategies.

In presidential campaigns a high proportion of campaign funds is spent for national television speeches and programs. But even in state-wide elections up to a third or more of all funds may be spent for television. A half hour on a nation-wide television hook-up will cost over $100,000—more than Abraham Lincoln spent on his entire campaign in 1860. Because of this high price both parties tend to rely more on spot announcements of from forty seconds to one minute than on long programs. In the 1960 presidential campaign the two parties at the national level spent approximately $4.7 million for television and radio time, and the networks donated $4 or $5 million in free time to the candidates. With no time donated by the networks in 1964 for debates, the cost to both parties was substantially higher, totaling, according to the Federal Communications Commission, $11 million.[9]

The Cost of Campaigning for the Senate

The cost of getting elected to the Senate, where a candidate has serious, organized opposition, ranges from about $100,000 to well over $1 million. While a senator cannot personally spend more than $25,000

---

[9] This figure includes only the money spent in the general election campaign for President and Vice President. The total television costs for all political candidates in both primary and general elections ran to almost $25 million, with the Republicans spending about $13 million and the Democrats $11 million. Radio time cost the parties another $10.8 million. See Alexander, pp. 52–53.

on his campaign, there is no limit to the number of committees that can be formed on his behalf by friends and supporters. In the largest states perhaps 25,000 to 30,000 persons may contribute to the campaign fund of a senatorial candidate.

Where the Money Comes From

Apart from the size of the sums raised to meet campaign expenses, the most striking thing about party finances is how few people give money to a party or a candidate. Historically, political leaders have had to rely on large contributors for party funds. During the 1950s about 90 percent of all money came from less than 1 percent of the population. The Gallup poll reported in 1954 that only one family in eighteen contributed to that year's election campaigns. Ten years later Gallup and the Survey Research Center of the University of Michigan estimated that this number had increased to 11 to 12 percent, still not of sufficient size to pay for waging campaigns on a national basis. As Dennis W. Brogan,[10] the leading British interpreter of American politics, has commented:

the American, normally so generous, normally so gullible, willing to subscribe to all funds, from community chests in very rich suburban communities to pensions for the widow of the unknown soldier, has proved curiously reluctant to contribute to his party. And the party has been forced to appeal to the hopes and fears of those with more to give than a few dollars.

The 1964 election presents an interesting paradox with regard to small contributors. The Democrats swept back into national office with a huge majority, yet their financial base of support was quite narrow. On the other hand, Barry Goldwater, although suffering one of the most stinging electoral defeats in American political history, received an unmatched degree of grass roots financial support. Not only did the total number of Republican donors greatly outnumber that of the Democrats, but more than 650,000 people made direct contributions to national-level Republican committees. While this may seem a small portion of the 12 million people who probably donated money to the campaign, it represents a substantially larger fraction of the electorate than those who contributed directly to President Johnson's funds. Yet the Republicans, like the Democrats, were forced to rely heavily on other sources of funds.

In addition to small contributions from ordinary citizens, there are five principal sources of campaign funds. Most important are the political angels, known inelegantly as "fat cats," wealthy people who are willing to give large sums. In the past the Republican party has benefited far more than the Democrats from such donations. In 1956, for example, of the contributions of $500 or more by officers and directors of the 225 largest corporations in the United States, $1.82 million went to the Republicans and only $103,725 to the Democrats. In 1964, however, there was an abrupt turnabout, with the Democrats raising more than $4.8 million and the Republicans less than $3.5 million from contributions of $500 or over.

---

[10] *Politics in America* (New York: Harper & Row, Publishers, 1954), p. 259.

A dinner in Washington's National Guard Armory held to raise funds for a recent Democratic congressional campaign. (Wide World Photo)

In part this change was due to the fact that Barry Goldwater's arch-conservatism and hard war talk frightened many business executives and in part to assiduous work by the Democrats to improve their relations with the business community. One example of this labor is the President's Club, begun under Kennedy but expanded under Johnson's administration. Admittance to the club—membership approached 4000 in 1964 but dropped to less than half that in 1965—is achieved through an annual gift of $1000 or more to the Democratic party. In return club members are invited to dinners and parties at which the President, Vice President, or other important officials may be present, and occasionally even to White House affairs.

Unions, the second major source of funds, have increased their political contributions in recent years. The bulk of their gifts go to the Democratic party. Since 1936, when John L. Lewis gave $469,000 to aid the reelection of Franklin D. Roosevelt, labor organizations have donated less spectacularly but more steadily. In 1960, labor organizations filed reports with the clerk of the House of Representatives stating that they had contributed $2.45 million to the campaign that year, a sum that is probably less than actual expenditures. Alexander estimates[11] that labor groups in 1964 spent over $3.6 million, with the AFL–CIO Political Action Committee putting out over a million dollars in voter-registration drives.

Government employees represent a third source of funds. While federal

_____
[11] Pp. 64, 96.

law prohibits government workers from soliciting funds from their co-workers, there is no law that forbids spontaneous giving by government employees. Many may be moved by conviction or expediency to make a contribution. A fourth and indeterminate source is the underworld, which is ready to pay off candidates by making campaign contributions in expectation of certain favors. Often the candidate himself may not know the underworld source of some of his funds. A fifth source of campaign funds is the large group of unorganized, voluntary contributors.

"*But, Pray, Spare the Holy Shrines!*"

Drawing by Haynie. Copyright Los Angeles Times.
Reprinted with permission.

In 1966 Congress created a potentially huge source of funds by authorizing each taxpayer to indicate on his income tax form if he desired one dollar of his taxes (two dollars for joint returns) to be placed in a fund to help finance the next presidential campaign. A rather complex formula controlled the way in which the money would be disbursed, but in general the two major parties would receive equal shares, not in excess of the amount spent in the last campaign. If a minor party candidate polled more than 5 million votes, for the next campaign his party would be entitled to one dollar for each vote over 5 million.

If every taxpayer contributed, the fund would receive over $100 million a year, enough to purchase a handsome set of campaign chests, even at current prices. In 1967, however, many congressmen had second thoughts about how party officials might spend the huge sums to which they would be entitled and passed a new law suspending operations of the 1966 act until Congress set guidelines for distribution of the money.

Even in years when there is no important election at stake the parties require considerable amounts of money to finance their activities. In 1965, expenditures by the Democrats at the national level came to almost $4 million, and Republican committees spent $4.5.[12] Although 1965 was an unusually expensive year for both parties, operating costs for a national political organization are always large. A staff must be maintained, debts paid off, research carried on, registration programs kept in operation, and capital accumulated for the next big campaign. Obviously, then, fund raising has to be a continuous process.

---

[12] *Congressional Quarterly Weekly Report,* January 14, 1966, p. 41.

Certain Contribution Sources Are Prohibited

As early as 1907 Congress forbade corporations chartered under federal law, such as national banks, to make contributions to *any* political campaign, federal or local, and forbade all corporations to make contributions in *national* campaigns. Labor unions were subjected to a similar ban in 1943. In the 1944 campaign the CIO refrained from making any contributions to the Roosevelt campaign fund, but it spent over $1 million on direct aid to the Roosevelt ticket through its own Political Action Committee. Accordingly, the Taft-Hartley Act of 1947 renewed the ban on labor union contributions and also extended it to cover direct expenditures by unions themselves as well as by business corporations on behalf of candidates for federal office. There is doubt about the constitutionality of such a ban on direct expenditures by labor unions and business corporations.[13] Since 1883 Congress has tried to protect government employees from requests for contributions to campaign funds. This protection extends, however, only to the solicitation of funds by one government employee from another and not to solicitation by private persons.

The Hatch Act of 1940 limits individual contributions to national party organizations to $5000 in a national campaign, and it also limits the total contributions that any one political committee may receive to $3 million.[14] The act also limits expenditures by a political committee to a maximum of $3 million in any one year. In 1925, Congress also placed limitations on the amounts that may be spent by candidates for Congress. These amounts were fixed at $10,000 for senatorial candidates and at $2500 for candidates for the House. However, recognizing that candidates in the populous states may legitimately incur greater expenses, Congress approved an alternative formula that allows a candidate to exceed these limits by spending three cents for every vote cast in the last general election, although in no event may the amount exceed $25,000 for senatorial candidates and $5000 for candidates for the House.

Since 1910 Congress has enacted laws requiring political committees and candidates for Congress to file statements at certain intervals with the clerk of the House of Representatives concerning contributions received and expenditures made. Among the required data are the name and address of each person contributing more than $100 and the names of persons to whom more than $10 is

---

[13] See *United States v. Congress of Industrial Organizations,* 335 U.S. 106 (1948), in which five justices held that the Taft-Hartley Act was not intended to prevent a labor organization from supporting a congressional candidate in a newspaper that it publishes. However, four justices felt that the act was intended to ban such activity and that, so construed, it was unconstitutional. *I. A. M. v. Street,* 367 U.S. 740 (1961), continued the debate in a different context; but once again a majority of the Court decided the case on statutory rather than constitutional grounds.

[14] A "political committee" is defined by the Federal Corrupt Practices Act as "any committee, association, or organization which accepts contributions or makes expenditures for the purpose of influencing the election of candidates . . . in two or more states. . . ." 2 U.S.C. § 241.

paid. Such information is then available for public inspection, and a certain amount of it is usually reported by the press in rather sketchy fashion.

In the end, most of the corrupt-practices legislation now in existence fails to achieve the specific purposes for which it was enacted. The limitation of $3 million on the total expenditure of a political committtee is meaningless because it does not prevent two or more separate "committees" from spending up to $3 million each in support of the same party ticket. There is no evidence that the Hatch Act has brought about a reduction in the total amount of money spent by the major parties in presidential elections. About all it has done is to encourage a decentralization of expenditures, a change of doubtful value to the public good, since such expenditures are much more difficult to keep track of.

The limitations on the expenditures of individual candidates for Congress are apt to be meaningless because of the impossibility of calculating the vast sums that may be and are spent directly by private persons on behalf of a candidate, without the candidate's receiving the money or even necessarily knowing that it is being used to aid him. Similarly, the $5000 limitation on the contributions of a single person is ineffectual because each member of a family can give such an amount. Inspection of the contribution lists filed with the House clerk reveals the presence of long lists of donors bearing the same family name, so that the total contribution of a family may run to many times $5000. Moreover, this limit applies only to the total contributions made by a person to national organizations. The same person can make as many additional $5000 gifts to state and local committees of the same party as he wishes.

Contributions of 12 Prominent Families, 1964

Name	Number of Members Contributing	Total Contributions	Republican	Democratic	Miscellaneous
duPont	21	$ 73,510	$ 71,010	$ —	$ 2,500
Field	2	16,500	1,000	15,000	500
Ford	2	45,100	4,100	41,000	—
Harriman	4	39,000	25,000	14,000	—
Lehman	6	40,000	2,000	37,000	1,000
Mellon	12	122,156	93,510	17,500	11,146
Olin	5	44,900	44,900		—
Pew	10	103,510	94,510	—	9,000
Reynolds	3	6,000	—	6,000	—
Rockefeller	14	65,500	65,500		—
Vanderbilt	2	2,750	750	2,000	—
Whitney	5	44,000	43,000	1,000	—
	86	$602,926	$445,280	$133,500	$24,146

SOURCE: Herbert E. Alexander, *Financing the 1964 Election* (Princeton, N.J.: Citizens' Research Foundation, 1966), p. 89.

By and large, the federal corrupt-practices laws do not regulate contributions and spending in congressional primaries or in the preconvention campaigns of persons seeking the presidential nominations. For a while there was doubt whether Congress had power under the Constitution to establish such federal controls at the nomination stage of the national elections, but the Supreme Court finally ruled that such power does exist.[15] Congress took a tentative step toward the establishment of such controls in the Taft-Hartley Act of 1947 by providing that the ban on contributions and expenditures by business and labor should cover the nomination of candidates as well as the election of public officers.

It would be a mistake to conclude that legislative efforts to curb the use of money in politics have had no value at all. It seems probable that such laws serve to remind parties, candidates, and voters alike that the proper use of money in campaigns is to provide the public with necessary information and not to "buy" public office. It is likely that these laws have restrained individuals and organizations from the bold and corrupt use of money that characterized certain earlier periods in American politics. Nonetheless, satisfactory control of money in American elections has not yet been achieved.

PROPOSALS TO IMPROVE CAMPAIGN FINANCING

To date, federal regulation of campaign financing has been negative in character, limiting the amount of money that may be given or expended. Even if these laws had no loopholes, serious problems would still exist. The costs of running a political campaign are enormous; the money must come from somewhere—from borrowing if not from contributions. As one analyst has pointed out: "Political parties that are beholden to a small number of large contributors constitute an unhealthy element in the body politic. Debt-ridden parties that exist from hand-to-mouth at the mercy of a few large creditors are in some respect even worse." [16] The two parties were able to finance the 1960 campaign only by going heavily into debt. The Republican National Committee ended up $993,000 in the red; the Democrats $3.82 million. The Republicans finished the 1964 campaign with a surplus of several hundred thousand dollars, but the Democrats ran into trouble again. Official figures have been a well-guarded secret, but estimates have ranged from $1 to $4 million.[17]

In 1907, President Theodore Roosevelt proposed to Congress that the federal government subsidize political campaigns, but it was not until 1961 that a President initiated and supported an attempt to reform the American system (or lack

---

[15] See *Newberry v. United States,* 256 U.S. 232 (1921), and *United States v. Classic,* 313 U.S. 299 (1941). The power of Congress to control the financing of congressional elections is clearly derived from the "times, places, and manner" clause of Article I of the Constitution. Its power to regulate the finances of presidential elections is less explicit but has been upheld by the Supreme Court on an implied-power basis. See *Burroughs v. United States,* 290 U.S. 534 (1934).

[16] Herbert E. Alexander, "Financing the Parties and Campaigns," in Paul T. David, ed., *The Presidential Election and Transition 1960-1961* (Washington, D.C.: The Brookings Institution, 1961), p. 148.

[17] *Congressional Quarterly Weekly Report,* May 27, 1966, p. 1078.

of system) of financing election campaigns. Within a year after taking office, President Kennedy appointed a distinguished bipartisan commission of political scientists and practicing politicians to recommend means of improving the collection and expenditure of money in presidential elections.

In 1962, the commission filed a concise report recommending a program of positive federal action.[18] The commission suggested that (1) Congress encourage individuals and private organizations to contribute to *bipartisan* political activities by making such contributions tax deductible; (2) Congress, for a trial period of two presidential campaigns, make partly tax deductible small contributions (under $1000) to the national committee of either party or to a state committee designated by a national committee; (3) Congress establish a more effective system of public disclosure of contributions and expenditures to be supervised by a Registry of Election Finance; (4) Congress abolish current "meaningless" ceilings on total expenditures and individual contributions; (5) the executive department strictly enforce existing statutes forbidding and restricting certain kinds of contributions and expenditures; (6) political parties make their fund-raising practices more efficient by utilizing recent research; (7) Congress appropriate money to pay "reasonable and necessary costs of preparing and installing in office new administrations during the 'transition' period between the election and inauguration of a new President";[19] (8) Congress temporarily amend the Federal Communications Act, as it did in 1960, to permit broadcasters to make free time available to the major party candidates without being legally obliged to make offers of equal time to minor party candidates; (9) the President call a nonpartisan White House Conference on Campaign Finance "to launch broad solicitation programs by all parties."

Finally, the commission recommended that if after a trial period further study showed that these measures had not appreciably improved campaign financing, the federal government should seriously consider direct subsidies to the two parties. The commission seemed most favorably impressed with the concept of "matching incentives." Under such a plan

contributions in amounts of, for example, $10 or less per person raised by designated political committees would be deposited by those committees with the U.S. Treasury, where the money would be matched by a like sum from appropriations. The combined total would be available to the committee to meet authorized types of costs, payments being made by Government check direct to sellers of goods and services.[20]

After receiving this report President Kennedy twice sent messages to Congress endorsing the commission's proposals. The President attached to his first message drafts of five bills designed to carry out the major portion of the com-

---

[18] *Financing Presidential Campaigns: Report of the President's Commission on Campaign Costs* (Washington, D.C.: Government Printing Office, 1962).

[19] Herbert Alexander estimated the 1960–1961 transition cost as high as $360,000. *Financing the 1960 Election* (Princeton, N.J.: Citizens' Research Foundation, 1962), p. 86.

[20] *Legislative Recommendations of the President's Commission on Campaign Costs,* Committee Print of the Senate Committee on Rules and Administration, 87th Cong., 2d Sess. (1962), pp. 31–32.

mission's recommendations as far as presidential campaigns were concerned and promised to carry out by executive action those parts of the report that would not require new legislation. In his 1966 State of the Union message President Johnson alluded to the need for reform along the lines of the commission's recommendations, but the Eighty-ninth Congress opted for a different and more limited tax checkoff plan, described earlier in this chapter. In 1967 Johnson sent Congress a message outlining a broad plan for federal subsidization of presidential campaigns. However, the first session of the Ninetieth Congress succeeded only in killing the 1966 tax checkoff, not in adopting new legislation.

Selected Bibliography

Bullitt, Stimson, *To Be a Politician* (New York: Doubleday & Company, Inc., 1959). An interesting and thoughtful description of what it is like to run for office.

Heard, Alexander, *The Costs of Democracy* (Chapel Hill, N.C.: University of North Carolina Press, 1960). A remarkable study of money in politics, with data on who contributes, why, in what amounts, and for what purposes.

Kelley, Stanley, Jr., *Political Campaigning: Problems in Creating an Informed Electorate* (Washington, D.C.: The Brookings Institution, 1960). The central concern here is how the discussion of policies and candidates in campaigns might make a greater contribution to electoral rationality.

———, *Professional Public Relations and Political Power* (Baltimore, Md.: The Johns Hopkins Press, 1956). A highly interesting account of the use of high-pressure public relations techniques on behalf of issues and candidates for office.

Lane, Robert E., *Political Life* (New York: The Free Press 1959). A study of "why people get involved in politics."

Shadegg, Stephen C., *How To Win an Election* (New York: Taplinger Publishing Company, 1964). A controversial account of political campaigning by an aide of Senator Barry M. Goldwater.

10

Voting behavior

VOTING STUDIES

It is far easier to describe in gross terms the behavior of American voters than to subject that behavior—or more properly those many kinds of behavior—to scientific analysis. There is little difficulty in obtaining complete and accurate statistics about the number and way in which votes were cast in an election. Furthermore, since these figures are usually available for subdivisions down to the precinct level, one can readily describe voting behavior along geographic lines. But official records have limited usefulness when one tries to find out how different segments of the electorate, such as men or women, whites or Negroes, Protestants or Catholics, have voted. Moreover, such records never reveal the "why" of election results.

Over a period of years students of political behavior have experimented with several techniques to minimize these difficulties. Commercial pollsters such as the Opinion Research Center have tended to rely on a "national sample." To obtain data about preferences and actions the polling agency interviews on a one-time basis a small number of people, usually about two thousand, who represent a cross section of the nation as a whole. The questions are often drawn up to be answered "yes" or "no," or "approve," "approve strongly," "disapprove," "disapprove strongly," or "no opinion," although many agencies are now relying more heavily on "open-ended" questions—such as "What do you think are the major differences between the two parties?"—to which the respondent replies in his own words.

"The panel method" is a somewhat different approach. By this technique a group of people, usually selected at random and often from one community, is interviewed not once but several times during a campaign to try to capture changes in individual reactions over time and correlate these changes with specific events. This method provides greater depth for opinion analysis, but there is no assurance that voters in one community will react like voters in another locality. The most promising—and expensive—kind of panel research is that in which the respondents are drawn from a national rather than a local sample.

Voting Choice

The research techniques of the various studies[1] have been very different, and analysts have not always drawn the same conclusions from the same evidence. In fact, on longer reflection some of the researchers have changed their minds about the meaning of the information they had earlier collected. Nevertheless, their findings are similar though not identical. This is encouraging in its indication that useful research methods are being developed, but the substance of the evidence is less heartening to those who hope to uncover a firm rational basis of the voter's choice at the polls. The conclusion of most experts has been that, for the overwhelming majority of people, an electoral decision has only a weak basis in an informed appraisal of issues and candidates or even in calculated self-interest. Rather, it is far more closely related to personal and group factors. It would, however, be premature to accept these interpretations uncritically. As Key and Munger[2] have commented in dissent against their colleagues' views:

In research the answer one gets depends in part on the kinds of questions he asks. If one inquires about social characteristics and political preference, he finds out about social characteristics and political preference. If one puts other sorts of questions into the research mill, he might well bring out other and more complex characteristics of the process of electoral decision.

[1] The most important of the voting studies are: Paul F. Lazarsfeld, Bernard B. Berelson, and Hazel Gaudet, *The People's Choice: How the Voter Makes Up His Mind in a Presidential Campaign* (New York: Duell, Sloan & Pearce–Meredith Press, 1944); Bernard B. Berelson, Paul F. Lazarsfeld, and William N. McPhee, *Voting: A Study of Opinion Formation in a Presidential Campaign* (Chicago: University of Chicago Press, 1954); Angus Campbell, Gerald Gurin, and Warren E. Miller, *The Voter Decides* (New York: Harper & Row, Publishers, 1954); Angus Campbell, Philip E. Converse, Warren E. Miller, and Donald Stokes, *The American Voter* (New York: John Wiley & Sons, Inc., 1960); and V. O. Key, Jr., *The Responsible Electorate* (Cambridge, Mass.: Harvard University Press, 1966).

[2] V. O. Key, Jr., and Frank Munger, "Social Determinism and Electoral Decision: The Case of Indiana," in Eugene Burdick and A. J. Brodbeck, eds., *American Voting Behavior* (New York: The Free Press, 1959), p. 299.

In recent presidential and congressional elections, candidates have depended increasingly on opinion polls to give an early indication of voters' attitudes and expectations. The last few national elections have also seen the widespread use of the computer for voting profiles on election day. (Tony Rollo from *Newsweek*)

Moreover, the elections studied by these intensive interview techniques have been too few in number to form the basis for final conclusions.

Presidential elections might be classified as (1) *maintaining,* in which the prevailing patterns of party loyalties persist; (2) *deviating,* in which basic partisan loyalties remain intact, but for some reason the majority party does not win; (3)

Party Identification in the United States, 1940–1966

QUESTION: *"In politics as of today, do you consider yourself to be a Republican, Democrat, or Independent?"*

Date	Percentage		
	Republican	Democrat	Independent
1966	26	48	26
1965	27	50	23
1964	25	53	22
1960	30	47	23
1950	33	45	22
1940	38	42	20

SOURCE: American Institute of Public Opinion, Press Release, June 30, 1966.

reinstating, in which the majority party regains control following a deviating election; and (4) *realigning,* in which old loyalties are disrupted to such an extent as to reshuffle majority and minority party statuses.[3] The elections of 1940, 1944, and 1948 were all fundamentally maintaining elections. Thus the close correlation between the 1940 and 1948 findings means only that in the same kinds of election situations people reacted in the same fashion.

The 1952 and 1956 presidential elections were deviating elections. Dwight D. Eisenhower won handily, but a large number of the voters who cast their ballots for him continued to think of themselves as Democrats and in 1954, 1956, and 1958 elected a Democratic majority to both houses of Congress. By a razor-thin margin the 1960 election would be classed as a reinstating election, and 1964 was probably another maintaining one. Although, as does not seem likely, if a large percentage of the Independents and Republicans who voted for Lyndon Johnson develop a relatively permanent allegiance to the Democratic party, the 1964 election would turn out to have been part of a realignment that could, for some time, eliminate the Republican party as a major contestant for the Presidency. It will not be until well after the 1968 presidential election, however, that one will be able to speak with any certainty about a possible long-range shift. Thus we still lack a study in depth of an election that can be classified as realigning, and this lack makes a full comparison impossible. Realigning elections, by the way, are relatively rare, those of 1896 and 1932 being the last ones up to 1964. The panic of 1893 was apparently the catalyst that raised Republicans to majority-party status. For various reasons 1912 and 1916 have been classified as deviating elections. The depression of 1929 started another cycle that restored the Democrats to majority status in 1932.

PARTISAN PREFERENCE

When comparative information of the same kind is available on each type of presidential election some conclusions about political behavior may become apparent that are very different from those we have now. There have already been some modifications of early conclusions. The first studies, limited to maintaining elections, agreed that a person's party preference was the best single determinant of his final vote. In the deviating elections of 1952 and 1956, however, large numbers of voters who continued to call themselves Democrats voted Republican, clearly swayed by the attractiveness of General Eisenhower as a candidate. Even in the reinstating election of 1960, a considerable number of Democrats again voted Republican. In 1964, vast numbers of Republicans voted Democratic. One cannot think, therefore, of parties as holding together "like a ball of sticky popcorn. Rather, no sooner has a popular majority been constructed than it begins to crumble."[4] Even a finding that the

---

[3] This classification has been developed and explained by Philip Converse *et al.,* "Stability and Change in 1960: A Reinstating Election," *American Political Science Review,* 55 (June 1961), p. 269; and V. O. Key, Jr., "A Theory of Critical Elections," *Journal of Politics,* 17 (February 1953), p. 3.

[4] Key, *The Responsible Electorate,* p. 30.

proportion of votes going to each party remains relatively constant would not necessarily mean that the same people are always voting the same way. New voters come of age or decide to participate in politics; old ones die or lose interest in government. Other voters may become disenchanted with the administration and support the opposition; still others may be won over to administration policies and, for this election at least, vote for the incumbents.

One further note of caution is in order. None of the voting studies claims to explain the political choices of all individual voters. Each explanation is hedged by such terms as "usually," "tend to," "generally," or "typically."

Group Influences

Even where a voter believes he is making a clear-cut choice between candidates based solely on policy considerations, innumerable factors in his background have helped form attitudes and outlooks that affect and perhaps even distort the image that candidates try to project. Students of voting behavior have reported significantly high correlations between electoral choice and such background characteristics as family, social class, religion, race, geography, and age.

An intensive study of Erie County, New York, in 1940 disclosed the cohesiveness of voting within the family, a striking factor that has been largely confirmed by subsequent investigations. Since husbands and wives tend to vote together, the children are normally raised in a one-sided political atmosphere. It is not unexpected, then, to find that when they come of age children are disposed to vote as their parents have. This, however, is only a general rule. Changes in social status, disagreements on important public policy questions, or an increasing age gap between the two generations may weaken "inherited" party allegiance. Still, probably three out of four voters who vote the first time vote for the same party their parents supported.

When the second generation marries, it is the wife who typically votes with her husband, assuming that the two partners come from different political backgrounds. The Erie County investigation showed that twenty-one out of twenty-two couples voted alike in 1940, and the Michigan Survey Center found a similar ratio of eleven out of twelve in the 1952 election. Looking over the evidence, an Elmira, New York,[5] study concluded in 1954: "In the end many American families vote *as a unit,* making joint decisions in voting as in spending parts of the common family incomes. Indeed, it would not be inappropriate to consider the family as the primary unit of voting analysis. . . ."

In most American communities there are no rigid class distinctions comparable to those of European society. Nevertheless, there is a kind of stratification that is sufficiently recognizable to delineate social classes in a rough way. Although these classes have never existed as formal, organized groups and their lines of demarcation are frequently only dimly perceived by their respective members,

---

[5] Berelson, Lazarsfeld, and McPhee, pp. 92–93.

social structure can affect individual motivation. Moreover, social structure does influence the availability of certain resources—money, leisure, and education, for example—needed to exploit fully the advantages of the political process.

One of the chief difficulties in evaluating the effect of social class on any aspect of behavior lies in establishing criteria to differentiate precisely one class from another. This is especially hard to do in America, and unfortunately no fine calibrators exist, but one can still speak in general terms with reasonable accuracy. If occupation, income, and education are used as three indexes of class (or socio-economic status, as some sociologists prefer), the results show that generally the higher his education and income and the more professional the nature of his work, the more likely a voter is to be a Republican. Conversely, the lower a voter's income and education and the more closely his occupation is related to manual, unskilled labor, the more likely he is to be a Democrat. There is, therefore, some evidence behind the old cliché that the rich tend to be Republicans and the poor to be Democrats, but the full truth is far more complex. Republican voting strength is largely based on a middle class of white collar workers and semiprofessionals, and the Democrats have often drawn their leaders from the ranks of the wealthy. It should also be noted that there is a significant exception to the tendency for the better educated to vote Republican. People who have had some college training do tend to be Republican, but American intellectuals, particularly social scientists, are overwhelmingly Democratic.

Despite trade union claims to the contrary, there is probably more political cohesiveness among businessmen than among workers. If this were not the case and the general lines of socioeconomic division were followed in every election, the Republicans would be hard put to win any offices above the ward level, or they would be forced into becoming a more liberal party. Perhaps one of the basic reasons for absence of political solidarity among working-class people is that American culture is predominantly that of the middle class.

Furthermore, as the authors of *The American Voter* have pointed out, the general relationship between social status and party loyalty is dynamic. At times the relationship has been marked, at other times almost trivial. Geographical influences also cut across class lines. In small cities outside the South, where the community is normally Republican, factory workers are less inclined to vote Democratic than are people who do the same work in large cities.

Religion, too, has been correlated with partisan political loyalty. White Protestants in northern states tend to vote Republican. Since the 1920s the Jewish vote has been heavily Democratic by about a four to one margin. Historically, Catholics have been much more likely to vote Democratic, even those in upper income brackets. Despite this traditional orientation, Catholic voters in 1952 and 1956 shifted their votes to the Republican column. Only slightly more than half supported Stevenson in 1952, and slightly more than half voted for Eisenhower in 1956. With Kennedy the candidate in 1960, however, four out of five Catholics voted Democratic, and analyses of the 1964 returns indicate that this Catholic support of the Democratic party continued.

Religion is a volatile issue when it comes out openly in a campaign, and

Voting Trends among Numerous Social Categories since 1948 (Presidential Vote, 1948–1964)

Percent Democratic of two-party vote for President

	1948	1952	1956	1960	1964
Female	49	40	37	46	68
Negro	68[a]	76[a]	63[a]	66[a]	98
Under 34	57	45	41	52	71
35–44	57	45	41	50	67
45–54	44	42	39	54	68
55–64	40[a]	34	32	43	68
65 or over	46[a]	36	43	37	53
Metropolitan areas	56	42	44	57	71
Cities over 50,000	c	51	33	50	66
Towns, 2500–50,000	c	37	36[b]	40	60
Rural	61	39	42	47	67
Protestant	43	36	35	36	61
Catholic	62	51	45	82	79
Jewish	b	71[a]	77[a]	89[a]	89[a]
Business and professional	19[a]	31	31	44	57
White collar	47[a]	35	39	48	63
Skilled and semiskilled	72	51	44	57	76
Unskilled	67	67	47	59	80
Farm operator	59[a]	37	46	33	63
Union member	76[a]	55	51	62	83
Grade school	63	48	41	54	78
High school	51	43	43	52	68
College	22[a]	26	31	35	53

[a] Fewer than 100 cases: sampling error may be sizable.
[b] Too few cases to compute a stable proportion.
[c] Data not available.
SOURCE: University of Michigan Survey Research Center.

most politicians are careful to avoid the subject. In 1928, religion was a major factor in Al Smith's defeat. Again in 1960, despite the efforts of both candidates, it played a significant role, though this time its ultimate effect is more difficult to assess because the number of Catholic voters had heavily increased in the intervening thirty-two years. On balance, however, it would appear that Kennedy's religion cost him more votes than it gained him. As V. O. Key, Jr.,[6] concluded: "Probably the best guess is that Kennedy won in spite of rather than because of the fact that he was a Catholic. It is thus premature to conclude that the election overruled once and for all the custom that excluded Catholics from eligibility to the Presidency." Some politicians, however, disagreed. The fact that William Miller was a Catholic was apparently an important consideration in his selection as Republican vice-presidential nominee in 1964.

---

[6] "Interpreting the Election Results," in Paul T. David, ed., *The Presidential Election and Transition 1960–1961* (Washington, D.C.: The Brookings Institution, 1961), p. 175.

Like religion, minority racial status can also be used as an indication of likely party choice. From Emancipation to New Deal, Negroes, at least those who voted, were strongly Republican; but Franklin D. Roosevelt won the Negro vote away from the party of Lincoln. Although the Republicans have made a number of serious attempts to woo back Negro support and Negro leaders have frequently urged their followers to vote more selectively, since 1932 Negroes have remained solidly Democratic. And in northern metropolitan areas, where Negroes do vote in relatively large numbers, their support can be crucial not only in presidential and senatorial elections but in congressional campaigns as well. As the Negro vote increases in size in the South it will be interesting to see if Republicans try to exploit the negative civil rights image of the southern wing of the Democratic party.

In their writings about politics Samuel Lubell and Louis Harris have speculated about the political implications of the movement of people away from central cities to the burgeoning suburbs. There has been an expectation that such movement normally involves moving as well from a lower-income bracket to a higher one, with a consequent change in political values and partisan preferences. Although evidence seems to indicate that Republicans are more likely than Democrats to move out of the cities to the suburbs, the Michigan survey finds little evidence of a Republican upsurge among former city dwellers. A picture of suburbia as a Republican political stronghold embracing large numbers of former urbanite Democrats seems exaggerated.

Voting studies have confirmed the long-suspected fact that farmers react to politics in a very different style than do city people. But one can speak of either a rural or an urban vote only in gross terms. Any remarks about voting behavior must be made with qualifications about income, race, religion, and a host of other factors, including geography. Northern farmers, for example, have a generally Republican tradition, southern farmers a Democratic one. Even outside the South, however, a considerable number of small farmers are quite likely to be Democrats; and, surprising as it may seem, in the Deep South there have traditionally been rural Republican enclaves.

Historically, farmers have a prolific source of radical third parties, parties that have received impressive local support in rural areas at one election only to vanish within an election or two. This tendency to support third parties may be dying out; but, according to the Michigan Survey Center, since 1948 the two-party division among farmers outside the South has shown the sharpest fluctuation of any major occupational grouping of voters.[7] Moreover, not only are farmers less disposed to carry over party loyalties from one election to another but they are also less likely than city dwellers to vote a straight party ticket in any one election. Finally, farmers' voting participation is erratic. They may turn out in mass for one election only to stay quietly at home for the next.

Many explanations have been offered for the lack of a coherent pattern in rural political behavior. Vulnerability to economic pressure is undoubtedly a

---

[7] Campbell *et al.,* p. 402.

Person-to-person contact continues to be an essential part of political campaigning. (Charles Harbutt from Magnum)

partial reason for farmers voting the way they do, or not voting. Another important aspect is the farmer's isolation—not only physical but to some extent cultural isolation from the rest of the nation. He tends to have less formal education. He is less exposed to the mass media of communications, even to radio and television. One could make similar observations about semiskilled factory workers, but there are differences. The farmer usually works pretty much alone. He is less likely to be approached by a party worker or to be reminded of his duty to vote "correctly" by a group official—despite lobbyists' claims, few farmers are active in farm organizations. The farmer is also less likely to have an opportunity to discuss politics. In short, many of the factors that operate in a city environment to stir up and maintain political interests and partisan loyalties operate far less efficiently or not at all in rural areas. Since he is unencumbered by party loyalty, the farmer is free of one of the principal emotional attachments that steady the vote of the urban worker. Without compunction the farmer can "vote the rascals out," whether they be Republicans, Democrats, or members of some agrarian party. This political style, of course, is not altogether different from that of the independent voter in the city, but the point is that the urban independent voter is greatly outnumbered by his committed neighbors. On the other hand, the independent farmer is apparently in the majority within his occupational grouping.

Age is a stabilizing factor in party preference. The Michigan Survey Center reported in 1960 that two thirds of its respondents who could recall their first vote still identified with the same party, and 56 percent claimed never to have crossed party lines in a presidential election. Typically, a young voter's loyalty to either party is not firm, but as he grows older this attachment apparently often hardens until it becomes very difficult for him to vote against his traditional party. Moreover, since the young voter's party loyalty is relatively weak, his party preference may shift, especially if his social status and income change. Indeed, the young citizens who vote for the same party their parents have are quite apt to call themselves independents. Available statistics indicate that it is far more likely that young Democrats will switch to the Republican party in middle age than that young Republicans will ever become Democrats, a difference usually accounted for on the grounds that one becomes more conservative as one grows older and also that in recent years it has been more likely that a voter's income increases as he grows older.

Longer life expectancy and its concomitant of greater medical-economic problems for the aged will make an interesting test of the ability of voters to respond rationally in terms of their self-interest in politics. At least through 1967, the Democratic party has been supporting more strongly than have Republicans increased federal aid for medical care for those whom politicians like to call senior citizens. Medicare, after all, was a key Democratic policy aim in the Truman and Kennedy administrations, though it became a reality only under Lyndon Johnson. It will be quite revealing to see whether the Democrats can attract elderly voters away from the Republican fold or whether the Republican party, in anticipation of such a shift, will begin to advocate an expanded medicare program or offer some alternative equally attractive to older people.

One of the most fascinating aspects of political behavior is the effect of individual personality traits on the voting decision. Since political choice is influenced by nonrational forces, electoral behavior cannot be explained fully without some comprehension of the way in which individual mental attitudes shape political opinions and selectively tune out some messages and tune in others. Some highly provocative studies in psychology and politics have been written,[8] but to date this research, for all its fascination, has not lent itself to clear-cut conclusions about specific aspects of political choice.

The Influence of Policy Views

Reacting strongly against what he conceived to be a deterministic thread running through many of the voting studies, Key asserted that great numbers of citizens do in fact vote according to their policy preferences. In his examination of Gallup studies ranging from 1936 to 1960 Key found a marked correlation between voters' views on public policy issues and their support of one party or the other. "From our analyses," he wrote,[9]

the voter emerges as a person who appraises the actions of government, who has policy preferences, and who relates his votes to those appraisals and preferences. One may have misgivings about the data and one can certainly concede that the data also indicate that some voters are governed by blind party loyalty and that some others respond automatically to the winds of the environment of the moment. Yet the obtrusive feature of the data is the large number of persons whose vote is instrumental to their policy preferences.

Key also stressed the dynamic character of party membership. Using responses to Gallup's questions concerning previous voting behavior, Key divided the voters in any given election into three categories: (1) "standpatters," who will vote in this election to support the same party as at the last election; (2) "switchers,"

---

[8] Among the first and most interesting analyses was that of Harold D. Lasswell, *Psychopathology and Politics* (Chicago: University of Chicago Press, 1930).

[9] *The Responsible Electorate*, pp. 58–59.

who will change their vote from one party to the other; (3) "new voters," both those who have just reached voting age and older citizens who did not vote in the previous election for one reason or another. Key estimated that in recent national political contests switchers constituted from one eighth to one fifth of the total electorate and new voters from 15 to 20 percent. While new voters tend to be less well informed and less politically interested than the others, Key found no material difference over the years in education, information, or interest between those who switched and those who stood pat. Furthermore, a voter was not necessarily frozen in any particular category. A standpatter in 1948 may have been a switcher in 1952; a switcher in 1956 may have been a standpatter in 1960. Key might have added that the Michigan Survey Center's finding that 56 percent of their respondents never crossed party lines in a presidential election also means that 44 percent—close to one out of every two voters—have been switchers in one election or another.

Given the nature of the American party system, there is no necessary contradiction between saying that there is a high correlation between policy preferences and voting and that there is a similar correlation between certain background characteristics as race, religion, or class and voting. As we have noted, most candidates try to appeal to a broad group spectrum, yet each party has also made special appeals to particular groups. Northern Democratic party leaders, for instance, have been quicker than most Republicans to try to attract new immigrants and to try to draw both blue collar workers and intellectuals to the party. While the Democrats outside the South have aimed their pleas at those most likely to be dissatisfied with the social and economic status quo, the Republicans have tended to concentrate on the middle class, Protestant community. Each party, then, has enjoyed a considerable degree of success in reaching its intended audience.

The Independents

Since membership in an American political party is very loose and informal, it is not easy to determine what portion of the electorate may properly be regarded as "independent." Many persons like to think of themselves as independents; yet studies show that they frequently support one party or the other at election time with a high degree of regularity. Current findings suggest that they number perhaps one fourth to one third of the total electorate.

There is a venerable body of middle-class opinion that asserts the moral and intellectual superiority of the independent voter. A study of Pittsfield, Massachusetts, found independents to be better educated than the average voter and to be more concerned with broad national and international issues.[10] On the other hand, research on a nation-wide sample conducted by the Michigan Survey Center led to the opposite conclusion. According to the authors of *The American Voter:*[11]

---

[10] Philip K. Hastings, "The Independent Voter in 1952: A Study of Pittsfield, Mass.," *American Political Science Review,* 47 (September 1953), p. 805.

[11] Campbell *et al.,* p. 143.

Far from being more attentive, interested, and informed, Independents tend as a group to be somewhat less involved in politics. They have somewhat poorer knowledge of the issues, their image of the candidate is fainter, their interest in the campaign is less, their concern over the outcome is relatively slight, and their choice between competing candidates, although it is indeed made later in the campaign, seems much less to spring from discoverable evaluations of the elements of national politics.

POLITICAL NONPARTICIPATION

So far we have been treating electoral behavior as if it involved only the basic question of which party or which candidate to support. In fact, there is a crucial question that must be answered first: whether to vote at all. As the most cursory glance at election and population statistics will show, nonvoting is a common phenomenon in American politics. Not since 1916 has more than two thirds of the potential electorate turned out for a presidential election, and on two occasions (1920 and 1924) less than half actually voted. But in recent presidential elections, about three out of every four of those registered actually voted. This figure, roughly equivalent to the turnout in Canada, England, and France, suggests that getting people registered may be the crucial step in getting out the vote in presidential elections. Statistics for congressional elections, however, manifest less citizen interest and more serious problems. In a presidential year up to 4 million persons who vote for President do not bother to vote for a congressman, and in a congressional election following two years after a presidential election the size of the national electorate falls off anywhere from 5 to 20 million votes.

Even though registration and voting involve inconveniences, they are relatively easy forms of political action. Writing letters to government officials, contributing money to a party or a candidate, ringing doorbells to encourage voter registration or to acquaint neighbors with a candidate, or actually running for office, all require considerably more effort and reflect far greater interest. The percentage of the population engaging in such activities is small indeed. A 1949 Gallup pool showed that political participation varied markedly with education. Thirty-nine percent of college graduates and 21 percent of high school graduates said they had written their representatives, but only 11 percent of those whose education had stopped at grade school had done so. Based on the evidence from surveys conducted in 1952, Robert E. Lane[12] concluded that only 2 percent of the population belonged to political clubs or organizations, and even these few people were largely concentrated in big cities.

Fatigue and competition from television entertainment may keep people from more strenuous forms of political activity, but they do not explain nonvoting. To be sure, some persons are ill or have recently moved and cannot meet local residence requirements or are traveling on election day or have religious scruples

[12] *Political Life: Why People Get Involved in Politics* (New York: The Free Press, 1959), p. 75.

against voting or are in the armed services and unable to secure absentee ballots or are in prison or are subject to deliberate disfranchisement. The total number of people in these categories may run as high as 20 million, but at least 20 million citizens stay away from the polls for other reasons.

Group Differences in Voting Turnout

On the basis of recent studies it is possible to state quite simply the basic facts about voting participation by various groups. More men than women vote, although the gap between the sexes has narrowed as women have gained more experience in voting since 1920. The proportion of people casting ballots varies directly with education; those with more education are more likely to vote than those with less. Similarly, people in upper income brackets are more likely to vote than those in lower income groups. Persons between the ages of thirty-five and fifty-five show greater interest in voting than do those in both younger and older age groups. Urban dwellers turn out in greater numbers than rural residents. Persons with strong attachments to a political party vote in relatively larger numbers than do those with weak party affiliations or political independents. Westerners have the highest rate of voting and southerners the lowest. Protestants are less likely to vote than Catholics and Jews.

As discussed in Chapter 8, legal and extralegal devices in southern communities discourage Negroes from voting, but, as the Civil Rights Commission has said, so do lethargy, lack of education, and simple despair at the efficacy of the political process. In the North Negroes are still less likely to vote than whites, but this statement conceals as much as it reveals. Negroes tend to come from the lower-income and lower-educated strata of society, in which nonvoting runs high among peoples of all races. Still, even where such economic and educational factors are held constant, Negroes in 1964 were less likely to be registered to vote than whites, even in northern cities.

Why People Stay Home

Tabulating group differences in voting participation still does not explain *why* some people do not go to the polls. Certain pressures placed on a voter may cancel out the effect of other pressures. Typical of the cross pressures that seem particularly onerous are having been reared in a home in which the mother and father were partisans of different parties or having recently changed one's socioeconomic status or having moved from a community predominantly of one party to one predominantly of the other. Voting studies have shown that many people respond to such electoral cross pressures by staying home on election day.

Nonvoting may also be the result of a rational decision. Registration and voting consume time and energy, involving what economists call "opportunity costs." A study published in 1967[13] has shown that, as one would guess, registration regulations have a very significant impact on voting. Length of required residence, however, is apparently less important than is the length of time in which citizens are allowed to register. There are similar convenience costs attendant to obtaining information needed to arrive at an intelligent choice between offered alternatives. These costs also explain in part why so many people find the party label a handy guide to decision-making. In addition, the effect one hopes to obtain through his vote must be discounted by the number of other voters. In any election above the ward or precinct level one vote more or less is unlikely to have any effect on the final outcome. And when one man stays away from the polls he is not apt to create a chain effect unless he announces his intention not to vote and tries to persuade others of the correctness of his choice. It was probably on the basis of such an analysis that the late Judge Learned Hand remarked that voting was "one of the most unimportant acts of my life."

What is known of the typical nonvoter, however, does not fit the picture of the shrewdly calculating man (or woman) employing his available time, energy, and money with meticulous economy. On the contrary, the nonvoter is usually relatively uneducated and unintelligent, and hardly disposed to tolerate coldly rational analysis or to indulge in it himself. Yet it is still possible that the nonvoter's decision to abstain is not altogether irrational. Registration takes time and effort, usually more so than does voting itself, and political participation may not have sufficient meaning for him to be worth the bother. Lacking the technical information and skills to utilize the other advantages of the political process, he has little reason to believe that casting a ballot will make much difference in his life.

If one puts aside for the moment the emotional appeals to citizens to exercise their "precious heritage" or to do their "civic duty," one might argue that the truly remarkable fact about American politics is that so many people do vote. Polls have indicated that, at least in peacetime, only a minority of adults think that the outcome of a presidential election would affect them personally. This widespread detachment may represent the price that must be paid for the existence of a broad consensus on political fundamentals and for a society in which so many people believe that they can achieve their social and economic goals through individual action. Or, it may be, as Schattschneider[14] has said, "The political system is now so preoccupied by *the cleavage within the* [voting population] that it has become insensitive to the interests of the largest minority in the world."

Nonvoters constitute a potentially volatile element in American politics. Pollsters have claimed that nonvoters divide in party preference pretty much along the same lines as do voters, though somewhat more in favor of the Democrats. Nevertheless, since these nonvoters generally have little attraction to either party,

---

[13] Stanley Kelley, Jr., Richard E. Ayres, and William G. Bowen, "Registration and Voting," *American Political Science Review,* 61 (June 1967), p. 359.

[14] Elmer E. Schattschneider, *The Semisovereign People: A Realist's View of Democracy in America* (New York: Holt, Rinehart and Winston, Inc., 1960), p. 108.

they might be rallied into a major force by an astute leader with a talent for skillful propaganda and efficient organization. If they were ever so stirred and organized they could decisively influence any national election.

WHY PEOPLE PARTICIPATE IN POLITICS

If there is a broad though vague consensus on political fundamentals, and if Americans are still basically oriented toward individual rather than governmental action to achieve their goals, it might well be asked why people participate in politics at all. We would hope that most people realize that intelligent public participation in government is one of the principal ways through which the consensus can be carried out in practice and individual liberty maintained. While few reliable statistics are available,[15] this sense of civic duty, drummed into children during their school years and into adults during every political campaign, is undoubtedly one of the more important reasons why 60 percent or more of the electorate actually vote in presidential elections.

In addition, politics fills a number of rather basic human needs, some conscious, others subconscious. Robert Lane[16] has offered a grammar of these needs. His categories are hardly mutually exclusive, but they do form a useful frame of analysis:

1. Men seek to advance their economic or material well-being, their income, their property, their economic security through political means.
2. Men seek to satisfy their needs for friendship, affection, and easy social relations through political means.
3. Men seek to understand the world, and the causes of the events which affect them, through observing and discussing politics.
4. Men seek to relieve intra-psychic tensions, chiefly those arising from aggressive and sexual impulses, through political expression.
5. Men seek power over others (to satisfy doubts about themselves) through political channels.
6. Men generally seek to defend and improve their self-esteem through political activity.

Economic Gain

There can be little doubt that for many men participation in politics is spurred by economic motives. Political activity may mean a government job or a contract; it may mean governmental policies of more generous tax exemptions, subsidies to business or farm groups, a closed or open shop for labor, or increased social security benefits and medical care for the aged. But economic gain is neither the sole nor perhaps the principal force behind political activity. If so few Americans believe that a national election will personally affect them, they are unlikely to perceive a great economic stake in voting or working for either candidate. Interestingly enough, the lowest income

---

[15] For one attempt to gather such statistics see Campbell, Gurin, and Miller, pp. 194–199.
[16] P. 102.

groups, with the most to gain from governmental welfare programs, are usually the most apathetic politically. Upper-income groups, with their stake more immediately visible, are far more likely to be political activists.

Social Drives

The stereotype of the back-slapping, fast-talking politician is usually a caricature, but it does contain enough truth to suggest that politics is an important avenue to social acceptance. Political meetings and conferences, doorbell ringing, and other forms of campaigning are all means of meeting people and making friends. Many extroverts prefer a life in which they are socializing during most of their waking hours; and politics, whether it be merely discussing current affairs or actually running for office, provides many such opportunities. Politics, however, is hardly the only outlet for such social drives; and, as the evidence offered earlier in this chapter indicates, it may not even be their major outlet in American society.

The Need To Understand

The need to understand the world in which we live is a motivation that can be readily grasped. Despite popular indifference, political decisions do vitally affect our everyday lives. Questions of war or peace, hydrogen-bomb testing or an atomic weapons moratorium, tariffs or free trade, school segregation or integration, government regulation of business or laissez faire, all are ultimately settled in the political process. It is normal that people want to know how such momentous decisions are made and perhaps even to have a voice in the final choice. Such people range from the "inside dopester" who merely wants to impress his friends with odd tidbits of information, to the serious student who tries to understand current happenings in terms of a broad philosophy, and to the practitioner who feels he must influence as well as comprehend his political environment.

Relief of Psychic Tensions

All human beings are beset by inner conflicts between opposing psychic drives or between drives and conscience. Some degree of aggression, frustration, guilt, and tension seem to be inevitable. Political participation is one of many means of letting off these pressures. The white man who actively supports school integration may be assuaging guilt feelings over personal or public unfairness toward Negroes. Another white man, brought up to believe racial intermarriage is wrong, may become an avid supporter of white supremacy as he recoils in guilt over being attracted to a Negro woman. The housewife who is dissatisfied with her home life may find political activity a welcome outlet for her pent-up emotions. So, too, a man who wishes to escape from some personal problem may immerse himself in politics (or in business) as a form of diversion or escape. The classic example is the Germans in the early 1930s who, still rankling over the humiliation of the Treaty of Versailles and bankrupted by the runaway inflation of the 1920s, had a ready means of release for their frustrations in the superemotional rituals of Nazism and its accompanying glorification of the Reich.

Voting, as one psychiatrist[17] has said, "is more than a political act. It is an expression of affirmation or protest and is therefore an emotive as well as an instrumental act. The act of voting or of non-voting [as well as other forms of political activity] fulfills covert and unconscious as well as overt and conscious needs and wishes." Thus for many Americans membership in the Communist party during the 1930s was not just a manifestation of economic despair. It was also an extreme form of protest against what these people saw as the rank injustices of the existing political and social system. In the 1960s participation by college students in civil rights movements demonstrated a similarly strong but far more mature and constructive reaction against what these young people also saw as raw injustice.

It should be pointed out here that there is no known correlation between neurosis and political activism. Although the evidence is inconclusive, it points the other way. What little research has been done indicates that the deeper an individual's inner conflict, the more apt he is to be politically apathetic. This does not mean that certain types of emotional problems are not more likely than others to move a man to political participation. Lane[18] reports that twenty case studies of political self-analysis have led him to believe that "persons who have a capacity for externalized aggression are more likely to become politically oriented than those for whom such external expression is inhibited."

The Quest for Power

Power motivation has always been recognized as a primary factor behind political activity. As Hobbes[19] noted over three centuries ago: "in the first place, I put for a general inclination of all mankind, a perpetual and restless desire of Power after power, that ceaseth only in death." Whether, or how much this is an exaggeration, the pursuit of power remains a fact of life confirmed by daily experience. And politics is an excellent way (though, again, by no means an exclusive one) of expressing the power urge, even if political activity is restricted to casting a ballot for a winning candidate. On the other hand, in a democracy, a person who is not able to control, or at least to conceal, a burning power drive will usually exclude himself from positions of leadership by alienating his colleagues (who usually also have power ambitions) and followers.[20]

---

[17] C. W. Wahl, "The Relation between Primary and Secondary Identifications," in Burdick and Brodbeck, p. 280.

[18] P. 119.

[19] Thomas Hobbes, *Leviathan,* Part I, Chap. 11.

[20] Harold D. Lasswell, "The Selective Effect of Personality on Political Participation," in R. Christie and M. Jahoda, eds., *Studies in the Scope and Method of "The Authoritarian Personality"* (New York: The Free Press, 1954).

The Need for Self-esteem

Gordon Allport[21] has pointed out that the individual's need for personal status "is apparently insatiable. Whether we say that he longs for *prestige,* for *self-respect, autonomy,* or *self-regard,* a dynamic factor of this order is apparently the strongest of his drives." Again, politics is one of many avenues to increased self-esteem. Seeing oneself or a member of one's family in the White House has historically been the apex of American ambition. At the other extreme, simply being informed about political affairs can be a source of prestige in a group. So, too, the act of voting, of participating in the choice of national leaders, is a status symbol.

Politicians are acutely aware of the local notoriety as well as self-esteem that comes to those who "know" a celebrity. This psychological knowledge explains in part the vast amount of handshaking in which candidates engage and the carefulness of most successful politicians to remember names and faces and to reward with some small personal attention all those who worked to elect them. No one who has watched the reaction of party workers who receive notes of thanks from the White House can doubt the effectiveness of appeals to self-esteem.

VOTING STUDIES AND DEMOCRATIC THEORY

The picture of the American citizen that the voting studies develop is not one that would overjoy ardent apologists for democracy; and it is a disquieting picture for those theorists who argue that stable democratic government must rest on a well-informed, highly active citizen body. Political participation is not attractive to a large minority in the country, and those who do vote are not always moved by strictly rational considerations. On the other hand, the picture is not completely that of a group of uninterested, uninformed, and irrational people. The fact that nonrational forces are significant influences on political behavior should come as no surprise to a society in which Freud is a household word. If nonrational factors are important, so too, to many citizens, are rational judgments about public problems. Indeed, no evidence has been offered that voting choices or political behavior in general are more influenced by nonrational factors than are other aspects of human life.

Selected Bibliography

Campbell, Angus, Philip E. Converse, Warren E. Miller, and Donald Stokes, *The American Voter* (New York: John Wiley & Sons, Inc., 1960). The most systematic analysis of voting behavior available, based on a twelve-year study by the Michigan Survey Research Center.

————, *Elections and the Political Order* (New York: John Wiley & Sons, Inc., 1966). The authors of *The American Voter* here continue their analysis, focusing on the impact of voting behavior on party structure.

---

[21] "The Psychology of Participation," *Psychological Review,* 52 (May 1945), p. 122.

Eulau, H., Samuel J. Eldersveld, and Morris Janowitz, eds., *Political Behavior* (New York: The Free Press, 1959). A collection of essays on the sociology of politics and political behavior.

Fuchs, Lawrence P., *The Political Behavior of American Jews* (New York: The Free Press, 1956). A specialized and informative account of the political behavior of one group of Americans.

Rogers, Lindsay, *The Pollsters* (New York: Alfred A. Knopf, Inc., 1949). A critical examination of the failure of the pollsters to predict the 1948 election results accurately.

Scammon, Richard M., *America Votes* (New York: Crowell-Collier & Macmillan, Inc., 1956, 1958, and 1960), 3 vols., 1945–1954, 1957, 1958. Extremely useful volumes of voting statistics.

Part 3 The Congress

It Costs to Be a Senator

By Ben A. Franklin

SPECIAL TO THE NEW YORK TIMES

WASHINGTON, June 11— "When private, unreported and mysterious funds sustain public officials, something is wrong with our system of government." So saying, a worried United States Senator quietly deplored in a recent interview the "flat calm" which greeted such facts as these about some of his Congressional colleagues.

Everett McKinley Dirksen, the Senate minority leader, has a special $10,000-a-year account for nonelection year radio and television broadcasts, maintained by friends who, Mr. Dirksen says, "give from the heart."

Friends of Representative Adam Clayton Powell, the Manhattan Democrat, gave him a "testimonial dinner" to help him pay a huge libel judgment.

Senator Edward M. Kennedy, Democrat of Massachusetts, filed campaign expenditure reports blandly asserting that not a penny was raised or spent by him in his two tough campaigns in 1962 and 1964.

And even Vice President Hubert H. Humphrey, as a campaigning Senator in 1960, has a perfectly balanced campaign fund intake and outgo of—would you believe it?—$650. Of this amount, Mr. Humphrey alleged that $100 covered his Minnesota filing fee and $500 was for "gas, oil, hotels and motels."

The vagaries, not to say absurdities, of present campaign expenditure and Congressional conflict-of-interest laws account for all these operations in two hardy dogmas of American politics: first, that Senators and Representatives are required by law to publicly disclose contributors, contributions and expenditures; and, second, that, unless they are greedy, they are paid enough to resist importunity by special benefactors between election years.

The triple whammy of Senator Thomas J. Dodd—the simultaneous investigation of the Connecticut Democrat's campaign fund handling and other activities by the Senate Ethics Committee, the Internal Revenue Service and the Federal Bureau of Investigation—has underlined two things.

One is that whatever Mr. Dodd may or may not have done to bring down upon him such misfortune, he is not alone. The Senate Ethics Committee is scheduled to begin hearings on Senator Dodd—significantly, in closed session at first—on June 20.

The other is that, as President Johnson put it in asking Congress for campaign fund reforms, the laws now on the books are "more loophole than law."

President Johnson's May 26 proposal for a new campaign expenditure law would end many of the unrealities of the 41-year-old Federal Corrupt Practices Act. It would require *full* campaign disclosures, allowing none of the demeaning concealment now practiced through a proliferation of "independent" campaign committees over which candidates nominally have no control and on which they therefore make no reports.

More important, it would establish for the first time as national policy the principle that many small contributions are better than a few big ones. Contributors could receive up to a $100 special income tax deduction for helping to finance what Mr. Johnson called "an unparalleled instrument of public education in the issues of the nation and of the community."

But the President's proposal would require no disclosure of investments or investment income. And if friends of members of Congress decided that their purchases of $100 tickets to testimonial dinners were actually "gifts," even though the total proceeds mounted to $100,000, neither the individual contributions nor the total nest egg might have to be reported.

But it is the off-election-year, non-campaign fund raising activities of Congressmen that probably will be most difficult to reach. The basic year-round question is this:

Can a member of Congress with a salary of $30,000, plus personal allowances of, at most, a few thousand dollars, and who is burdened with the cost of running for office (every two years for Representatives, every six for Senators) plus the inflating cost of simply doing his job, remain independent of special benefactors?

Paul H. Douglas, Democrat of Illinois, is one of the handful of Senators who attempts to deal with this question by making an annual, voluntary disclosure of all sources of income. His personal budget—reflecting modest comfort through prudent management—is both instructive and depressing.

Senator Douglas Reports

From Senate salary and allowances of $32,328 in 1965 —an average, non-election year for him—Mr. Douglas last week reported that his unreimbursed 1965 expenses were $3,212 for travel to and within Illinois, $3,000 for "political expenses" in Cook County (Chicago), $1,570 for radio and television time, $4,051 for entertainment, $635 for political contributions, and $748 for memberships, subscriptions, telephone and telegraph. Subtracting another $4,005 for income tax on his Senate salary, $2,250 for the Senate Retirement Plan, and $1,000 for property taxes in both Washington and Chicago, Senator Douglas reported, "my actual net income from my job was between $9,000 and $10,000." The average family income this year, after taxes, is about $7,000.

Stopping Congressional moonlighting, accordingly, will not be easy. "For those whose expenses here nearly equal the $30,000 salary," one Senate aide said this week, "it's a question of both financial and political survival and no Congressional pay raise that is in sight is going to change that."

11

The legislative process

POLICY-MAKING IS INEVITABLE

Every nation in the modern world confronts a long list of serious problems. Rivers regularly overflow their banks and cause great losses of life and property. Almost as regularly rivers dry up, and the land becomes parched and crops ruined. When factories are closed thousands of workers are unemployed and the economy suffers. When factories are operating at full production they pollute the air we breathe and the water we drink. Prosperity, if and when it does come, invariably leaves islands of poverty in its wake.

The number of problems caused by human and by natural forces is, for all practical purposes, endless; and each time a new problem arises or an old one worsens citizens are likely to demand that government "do something." In coping with these demands public officials immediately have a choice of whether to take or encourage positive action or to follow a course of prayerful drift. Either alternative inevitably makes policy, a decision to rely on unforeseen events to intervene benevolently constitutes a policy no less than, though of a very different character, a decision to meet a problem with an elaborate program.

For the last thirty-odd years America has been following the latter course in attacking the farm problem, motivated largely by the seeming fact that impersonal forces aggravate difficulties. The problem itself is inescapable. Agricultural and industrial production tend to get out of balance, with the result that the price the farmer receives for his products on a free market may not be sufficient to enable him to buy the industrial goods he would like. Moreover, faced with declining agricultural prices, the farmer is likely to increase his production in the hope that he may thereby enhance his income but in fact only causes his income to fall lower. In the long run he may give up farming and thereby unconsciously do his part toward bringing agricultural production into balance with the demand for farm goods. But often he sticks to his land. Consequently, the United States has governmentally planned goals and regulated farm production. Some people, however, still favor drastic curtailment of these controls and an increased dependence upon natural economic forces. Their course of action would not be any less a social policy than the present program.

A second choice government officials must make is between private and public action. Nongovernment groups, such as the family, the school, the church, the farmers' cooperative, the labor union, or the business corporation, can often effectively serve as agencies through which problems may be attacked, policies planned, and programs administered.

But as the most powerful and elaborately organized of man's social institutions, government is frequently in the best position to try to attack a social problem. Thus this choice arises in many areas of social activity. The American insurance system provides a case in point. The social problem here is one of providing the individual with a measure of protection against certain hazards of life over which he often has little or no control, such as unemployment, sickness, industrial accident, a dependent old age, or death. Long ago most Americans decided that the cost of such calamities could not be allowed to fall exclusively on the individual and that at least part of the cost should be assumed by society. In the future all citizens may even be required to have health insurance, as they now are required to carry automobile insurance. But this social obligation can be, and is being, met both by government and by private social institutions. Insurance companies, corporations, labor unions, fraternal associations, and other private agencies have worked out elaborate old-age pension plans and other social insurance programs. In addition, the federal government operates an extensive social security system. Such a "mixed" program of governmental and private activity exists in many areas—education is another good example.

Third, and by no means least important, if it is agreed that positive efforts must be made to evolve a satisfactory policy concerning a social problem, a choice must almost always also be made between alternative policies on a purely substantive basis. In a free society men are almost always certain to disagree profoundly as to what is a wise or feasible policy to attack a particular problem. Reference has already been made to the problem of floods, droughts, soil erosion, and of river valley development. Here there are almost as many policy proposals as there are river valleys. The Tennessee Valley Authority illustrates one approach to the problem, involving a highly integrated program of electric power production, improvement of navigation, irrigation of farm land, conservation of natural resources, and development of recreational facilities, all under federal supervision but with state and local cooperation. But the problem of no other river valley has yet been similarly attacked; in the Ohio, Mississippi, Missouri, and Columbia valleys many different policies have been proposed, debated, and sometimes adopted. For example, there is much argument as to whether it is feasible to combine such diverse purposes as flood control, improvement of navigation, and production of electric power in one program calling for "multipurpose" dams.

SCOPE OF THE POLICY-MAKING PROCESS

In general, policy-making and lawmaking are part of the same process and law is one evidence of policy. In order to examine American national policy and the process by which it gets made, one turns first to federal statutes. The Taft-Hartley Act, the Social Security Act, the Wages and Hours Act, the Selective Service Act, and the Atomic Energy Act state some of the most important public policies currently being pursued in the United States. But a statute is only the most highly formalized of policy statements; policy in its broader and all-encompassing aspects takes many other forms, such as customs, court decisions, executive orders, and administrative rulings. In fact, most of the rules that govern human conduct are found in these, and a policy expressed in a statute can always be traced back to a *prestatutory* phase and is certain to have an important *poststatutory* development. Often a rule of society begins as a custom that men observe more or less voluntarily. Somewhat later this custom may find expression in judicial decisions or administrative orders. In the absence of a pertinent statute a judge may find it necessary to make his own law in deciding a dispute between opposing parties.[1] Similarly, an administrator may find it necessary to evolve rules of his own to cover certain problems where there is no statute to guide him.[2] Thus when the time arrives for the legislature to enact a statute in a particular field there is almost certain to have been a good deal of earlier policy formation in this same field. Indeed, in most lawmaking situations the legislature does not initiate completely new policy but, instead, selects from or ratifies certain rules that have already taken shape.

A good illustration is the development of the American program of aid to the allies in World War II. This program was eventually formalized by Congress in the Lend-Lease Act of 1941, which authorized the President to aid those foreign nations whose defense was deemed vital to American defense. Actually, in September 1940, the President had already supplied England with fifty "over-age"

---

[1] On the participation of judges in the lawmaking process see Chapters 18 and 19.
[2] For a further discussion of the relationship between policy-making and the administrative process see Chapters 14–17.

destroyers and had accepted certain concessions in return, such as naval and air bases in Bermuda and Newfoundland. He took this step on the basis of his own constitutional power and certain vague congressional enactments authorizing him to dispose of governmental property. By this action he clearly gave shape to the main lines of the American policy that Congress later formally approved.

The process of policy formation by no means comes to an end when the legislature has acted. No matter what the character of a statute, a certain measure of policy refinement and extension is inevitable through the years as it is enforced. The complex problems of modern society compel legislatures to adopt statutes in more and more general terms. Many problems have become so technically complex and difficult that the legislature does not dare to attempt to deal with detail, but contents itself with indicating the broad lines of policy, leaving elaboration to other governmental agencies. This is an aspect of the governmental process that has always existed. Although the condition has become more striking in recent decades, the change is one of degree.

A good illustration is the parity-price aspect of the American farm program. In statutes Congress has set the ideal, that farmers ought to receive an income from the sale of their crops that will bring them into a position of parity with respect to the prices of the nonfarm goods that they must buy. But Congress has delegated to administrative officers a considerable measure of discretionary power to work out the details of this program. Thus the day-to-day meaning of the parity-price system is to be found very largely in administrative rulings.

Members of the National Farmers' Organization empty milk onto a dry wheat field as part of a protest against milk prices. (Wide World Photo)

Constitutionally, Congress retains the power at any time to veto or alter such rulings by enacting new amending laws, but Congress does not legislate easily. The national legislative process is exceedingly difficult and complex. Occasionally sufficient public opinion takes shape and congressional majorities can be organized to put through an important piece of legislation. But often once a statute is passed its moment is gone—public attention is diverted elsewhere, legislative coalitions dissolve, and new ones take their place. As a general rule congressmen have been unable, or unwilling, to follow up initial policy decisions with precise, periodic revisions. Congressmen cannot follow on a regular and intimate basis the work of the innumerable courts and administrative agencies to which they entrust the interpretation and enforcement of a wide variety of statutes; nor can they ratify or repudiate the more or less continuous legislative rulings of these bodies.

Policy-making without Statutes

The days when governmental policy was evolved in the complete absence of statutes are by no means gone. At many points in the governmental process policy is still formulated by agencies other than the legislature. This is particularly true of foreign policy. The Constitution gives such a large measure of power to the President in this field that he is capable of acting independently of Congress in a great many ways. The Monroe Doctrine is a famous example. One must be careful not to exaggerate the absence of congressional checks here, because, insofar as presidential foreign policy costs money to administer, Congress is ultimately bound to approve or disapprove a particular presidential action through its control of the purse strings. A wise President takes influential members of Congress into his confidence and tries to make the legislative branch a cooperative partner when he undertakes to shape some new bit of foreign policy. But this does not alter the fact that he can and does make foreign policy without any statutes. A good example of similar policy-making in the domestic field is seen in the loyalty program for employees of the federal government, originally announced by President Truman in 1947 by means of an executive order and continued in effect in revised form by Presidents Eisenhower, Kennedy, and Johnson. This controversial program has subjected federal employees, actual and prospective, to intensive loyalty and security checks. Congress might well have made the original provision for such a program through the enactment of a statute. But it chose to operate only on the margins of this problem, leaving it largely to the President, as Chief Executive, to decide just how the loyalty of federal employees should be judged.

This discussion of the scope of policy-making may be summed up by saying that the legislative, administrative, and judicial processes are in many ways inseparable. Policy decisions are made at many points, by many people. What we see functioning is a system of shared rather than separated powers. Formulation of policy by Congress is not isolated from questions of administration or judicial interpretation. The President advises Congress about pending legislation, as do the departments and agencies of the executive branch. This advice about policy matters is an outgrowth of administrative experience. Moreover, congressional committees advise and attempt to influence administrative officials about policy questions that arise in the course of law enforcement. This practice is so pervasive that some observers have concluded that in terms of actual supervision, executive departments and agencies receive more guidance from Congress and its committees than from the President. Advice from the courts is more formal, rendered through official opinions in specific cases; but it is not thereby less important in influencing policy development.

THE LEGISLATIVE STRUGGLE

The legislative process is often viewed as a continuous "struggle" on the part of opposing "groups" for power and control of public policy.[3] To bring about the enactment of a statute, groups form coalitions. It is usually much more difficult to forge a coalition majority for positive action than it is to organize a coalition strong enough to prevent action from being taken. This was demonstrated by Professor Stephen Bailey[4] in his study of the adoption by Congress of the Employment Act of 1946.

Put in its baldest form, the story of S. 380 adds up to the fact that majority sentiment expressed in popular elections for a particular economic policy can be, and frequently is, almost hopelessly splintered by the power struggles of competing political, administrative, and private interests, and is finally pieced together, if at all, only by the most laborious, complicated, and frequently covert coalition strategies.

Put in somewhat different terms, the legislative scene is frequently a confused one in which the individual legislators are subject to a wide variety of conflicting forces and influences. Many people regard the political party as dominating the action of congressmen. But pitted against the factor of party may be additional forces reflecting economic, sectional, and social considerations of much greater strength and importance.

Take, for example, the plight of a hypothetical congressman from an urban district in New England confronted with the necessity of making up his mind concerning a request by the President that the minimum-wage level be raised. If he belongs to the opposition party he will be inclined to oppose the measure; his own personal economic philosophy perhaps also tempts him to vote against it as a further instance of "government regulation"; the heavy labor vote in his urban district provides a tug on him to vote for the bill; and finally, the strong possibility that such a law may help New England stem the loss of its textile in-

---

[3] Bertram Gross, *The Legislative Struggle* (New York: McGraw-Hill, Inc., 1953).

[4] *Congress Makes a Law* (New York: Columbia University Press, 1950), p. 237. Bertram Gross was a member of the professional staff of one of the legislative committees that considered this same law. Thus the Bailey and Gross volumes reflect in part the same data and the same experience.

dustry to the South also inclines him toward support. His decision will almost certainly be the product of a combination of influences rather than of one isolated force.

This situation illustrates the way in which pressures that are brought to bear upon the policy-making process often tend to offset one another. This conflict of interests, or "legislative struggle," has both a good and a bad side. At times it brings about a balance or equilibrium in social forces which is highly desirable in a democratic, pluralistic society. It prevents any one group of forces from winning total power and compels all groups to accept bargaining and compromise as a price they must pay for partial victories. But the formulation of national policy on such a compromise basis also has its dangerous side. This is particularly true in foreign policy, where granting of concessions to particular groups may weaken policy and jeopardize national interests. Thus development of a sound program of economic and military aid to friendly nations may be weakened by the necessity of meeting the demands of shipping interests that a certain fixed percentage of goods sent to foreign nations be carried in American merchant vessels, or of farming interests that a fixed amount of the aid be farm produce, available in surplus supply in this country.

Moreover, under this "you scratch my back and I'll scratch yours" approach to policy-making, the conflicting forces present may offset one another to a point at which no action is possible. The various groups in a community may simply be unable to bridge the gaps between their interests. A striking example of such a failure occurred in the 1966 session of Congress when the Senate allowed the administration's civil rights bill to die. To begin with, there was a division over the bill's fundamental provisions, southern Democrats, of course, being bitterly opposed to any such proposal. Still, it seemed that there was a large majority for the bill, but soon its proponents began to splinter over the details of how far the federal government should go to guarantee "open housing" for people of all races. Complicating the situation were strident calls for "black power" from Negro leaders and destructive riots in several metropolitan areas. These events cooled the ardor of some civil rights supporters and made less committed senators waver. In the end the administration could not work out a compromise with potential Republican allies or muster enough votes to break a southern filibuster.

Whether the result of any particular legislative struggle turns out to be good or bad, it should be stressed that choices of an individual congressman are usually no more predetermined than those of Congress as a whole. In fact, except on one or two issues—say the race question for a Mississippi senator—a congressman typically enjoys considerable leeway. Rarely can he ignore the group struggle; neither can he always be deaf to pleas from party leaders or demands from his own constituents. But a shrewd legislator quickly becomes adept at playing interest groups off against one another, at bargaining with party leaders, and at taking advantage of public ignorance or apathy. He is seldom free to act completely as he pleases, but neither need he be a mere pawn who responds mechanically to external pressures.

Who Wants Action and Who Does Not

Since every group at some time desires positive legislative action and at other times opposes action, all groups must be experienced in the use of techniques both to facilitate and to frustrate the law-making process. Few groups are consistent over any long period of time in supporting or opposing "government regulation" or in defending or attacking legislative procedures that help or hinder positive action. The American farmer is often thought of as a conservative individual who is anxious to preserve his freedom to grow or not to grow crops, but he nonetheless comes to Congress again and again with demands for positive, remedial legislation. Similarly, conservative business groups frequently want action by the government. Manufacturers, for example, demand that state legislatures and Congress enact legislation permitting them to fix the retail prices at which their products may be sold and to compel retailers to observe these prices. On the other hand, labor, which is ordinarily thought of as "liberal" and thus desirous of much legislative action, is sometimes strongly opposed to the enactment of a particular law. In 1947, it vigorously opposed the Taft-Hartley bill, dealing with employee-employer relations, and was equally vehement in 1959 in trying to persuade Congress to shelve the Landrum-Griffin bill, which attempted to curb labor leaders' freedom to use union funds. Neither effort was successful.

Group attitudes toward particular legislative procedures are naturally also colored by the ways in which such procedures affect their interests. Among the legislative procedures that are frequently under attack by some group or other as "bad" are the Senate filibuster, the seniority rule for the selection of committee chairmen, and the power of the House Rules Committee to police the flow of bills to the floor of the House. A strong case can be made that each of these procedures is in some way undemocratic and that reform is necessary if the American legislative process is to be perfected. But there is almost no group that is unwilling to make use of these procedures if by so doing it can promote its own interests.

In 1964 and 1965, for instance, a number of liberal Senators who had repeatedly gone on record as favoring a change in Senate rules to curb filibustering used those very rules to "educate" their colleagues and the nation about the evils of efforts to thwart implementation of the Supreme Court decisions ordering legislative reapportionment. This educational process continued for a sufficient length of time to defeat all the objectionable bills and resolutions.

The observer who undertakes to predict whether a controversial bill will be passed or defeated in Congress must answer many questions. What groups are supporting the bill and what groups are opposing it? How strong numerically and how closely knit is each of these coalitions? Can the coalition that supports the bill muster the majority vote that is necessary at several crucial points along the way if the bill is to become law? On which side does time fight? Is there a deadline that one side or the other must meet if it is to control the result? Is public opinion moving noticeably toward support of one side, thereby compelling the other side to press for a quick decision if it is to win out? What is the procedural situation? What use may each coalition be expected to make of certain procedural opportunities and how effective is this use likely to be?

THE SHERMAN ANTITRUST ACT: A CASE STUDY

In 1890, Congress, coming to grips with a problem that was giving the nation serious concern, passed the Sherman Antitrust act, a statute that is still a key provision of national policy.

The Problem and the Choices

During a good part of the nineteenth century the nation had tried to build an economy based on the doctrine of free enterprise. It had placed its hopes in an unfettered market, in free competition, and in the law of supply and demand to provide a fair price structure and a satisfactory distribution of man's productive energies over the entire range of enterprise. But following the Civil War free enterprise was seriously threatened by the rapid growth of monopolies in certain of the nation's most basic industries, such as steel, oil, tobacco, farm machinery, and railway transportation. For example, the formation of the Standard Oil Company in 1882 represented a merging of some thirty-nine oil companies which had been doing business in every state of the Union. Where outright consolidation did not occur, competing business units frequently entered into agreements providing for price fixing, limitation of production, centralized selling, or quota systems of doing business. There thus took shape a clearly defined conflict between a national economic system that presupposed free competition and a practical development in the economic life of the nation that was tending to make free competition largely illusory.

What were the choices open to congressmen as the pressures to act took shape? First, and perhaps foremost, they had to decide whether the idea of a free market and competing business enterprises was still valid. Or was monopoly an inevitable and desirable economic condition that called for regulation and control rather than abolition? Perhaps a laissez-faire economy had been all right for the simple agrarian society of the late eighteenth and early nineteenth centuries, but had the time now come to recognize that the growth of cities and great industries meant that a new economic philosophy was in order?

Second, Congress had to decide whether the issue of competition versus monopoly should be resolved by private social agencies or whether government should intervene and try to influence the course of economic history. And if government should play a part, was this a proper area for action by the national government or should the problem be reserved for the state governments? And if this last issue were resolved in favor of national action, there was the further question of how far the Constitution allowed Congress to go in regulating the economic life of the nation.

If the Constitution made such a statute possible, many choices with respect to less basic issues remained. Should Congress enact a long and complex statute spelling out the details of an antitrust policy with considerable care or should it enact a brief statute and leave details to be worked out by those charged with the enforcement of the law, administrative officers and the courts? What kind of machinery should be set up for the enforcement of the new statute? Should the law be enforced by an existing agency, such as the Department of Justice, or should some new and special enforcement agency be created, as had been done three years before when the Interstate Commerce Act was passed? A closely related issue was that of a rigid versus a flexible policy. Should Congress make an all-out effort to protect free enterprise and competition or should it permit a limited and controlled measure of "big business?"

The Prestatutory Background

The monopoly problem had been taking shape for a considerable period of time before 1890, and there was already a good deal of public policy pertaining to the problem. The threat of monopolistic or unfair competitive practices to a system of free enterprise had been recognized in English and American common law for some time, and in deciding cases judges had established and followed rules that came to have the force of law. For example, it was early recognized that private persons might enter into a contractual relation with each other that would have the effect of restraining free trade and competition. A master craftsman might take on an apprentice and train him in his trade, but only on condition that he would agree never to set up business in competition with the master. Judge-made rules were laid down outlawing this and other similar private agreements as being counter to the public interest. In all, the common law came to outlaw six business practices, and a sixfold test as to what constituted a valid contract was subsequently applied.[5] The common law also developed rules as to conspiracy and illegal combinations which were employed to curb certain monopolistic business practices.

Common law rulings on monopoly had an element of flexibility. In general the common law regarded monopoly as illegal. But monopolies persisted in appearing, nonetheless, and eventually the argument was made that certain types of monopolies were the inevitable result of economic progress and were by no means opposed to the public interest. Ultimately there came into being the famous "rule of reason," which recognized that some monopolies, combinations, or agreements in restraint of trade might be reasonable and thus lawful. For example, a contract between an apprentice and his master craftsman might be reasonable if it applied only to a limited geographic area—say the confines of the town in which the employer had his business. Without this modification of the common law tradesmen and craftsmen might have refrained entirely from training apprentices for fear of the competition they would thereby encourage, and this would not have served the public interest.

---

[5] Milton Handler, "Restraint of Trade," *Encyclopaedia of the Social Sciences,* 13, p. 339.

In addition to this development of common law rules, a number of states enacted antitrust statutes during the decade before 1890. But these statutes differed widely and were irregularly enforced. Their chief influence upon the decisions of Congress was probably negative: the failure of the states to cope effectively with the threat of monopoly became a strong argument for federal action.

ENACTMENT

Congress decided that the problem should be subjected to positive statutory control, that there ought to be a single national policy rather than many state policies, and expressed faith in free enterprise and free competition by deciding that monopolies are basically evil and should be abolished. The guts of the statute were contained in the opening sentences of the first two sections:[6]

Every contract, combination in the form of trust or otherwise, or conspiracy, in restraint of trade or commerce among the several States or with foreign nations, is hereby declared to be illegal. . . . Every person who shall monopolize, or attempt to monopolize, or combine or conspire with any other person or persons, to monopolize any part of the trade or commerce among the several States, or with foreign nations, shall be deemed guilty of a misdemeanor. . . .

Thus, though it would not be historically accurate to say that Congress "made" an antitrust policy in 1890 in the sense of initiating an entirely new program, it did "declare" what the policy should be.

Demands for legislation against monopolies were widespread. The farmer's Granger movement of the 1870s and 1880s, which was a rebellion against the high rates charged by the railroads, grain elevators, and similar businesses supplying essential services, was joined by other groups including labor and small entrepreneurs. Pamphleteers, such as Henry George, Edward Bellamy, and Henry Demarest Lloyd, and the press took up the cause. Several minor party platforms in 1884 and both major parties in 1888 called for action against trusts, as did President Grover Cleveland in 1887 and 1888 and President Benjamin Harrison in 1889.

It is perhaps not surprising, therefore, that the Sherman Act was passed by Congress with a minimum of discussion and dissension. In the Senate it was debated for five days and passed by a vote of fifty-two to one. The House of Representatives debated the bill for a single afternoon and passed it without a dissenting vote. But the absence of a vigorous "legislative struggle" in Congress was deceiving, for beneath the surface there was much opposition to the bill. The powerful economic and political interests were able almost immediately to prevent enforcement of the bill through their influence with the executive and judicial branches. The Harrison Administration made almost no effort to enforce the law during the first three years after it was passed, nor did the succeeding Cleveland and McKinley adminstrations. Then, the Supreme Court in 1895, in the *E. C.*

---

[6] *26 Stat.* 209.

Knight Company[7] case in which the government was prosecuting a sugar trust that controlled over ninety percent of the sugar refining business, virtually interpreted the Sherman Act out of existence. It was not until the Theodore Roosevelt Administration and the beginning of the present century that the act came to have any real significance as a vital national policy.

Poststatutory Development

The Sherman Act, as passed by Congress, was vague and lacking in detail. Congress seemingly decided that trusts were basically evil and ought to be eliminated from the American economy. Beyond that it left an immense measure of discretion to other agencies of government to formulate a practical and detailed national antitrust policy. In part, this discretion was given to administrative officers. The enforcement of the act was the responsibility of the Department of Justice. This meant that the Attorney General, directed by the President, if the latter chose to concern himself with this matter, determined in the first instance what the antitrust policy should be. The Attorney General could, if he wished, ignore the law and bring no proceedings under it. Or he could pick and choose combinations or conspiracies to prosecute, perhaps ignoring a large industrial monopoly while taking action against some small labor union which by a strike or boycott was alleged to be restraining trade.

In part, discretionary power to develop the details of the antitrust policy rested with the courts, and with the Supreme Court in particular. Insofar as the Department of Justice did take steps to enforce the law, resulting cases were certain to raise difficult issues of interpretation and detail. Gradually there emerged a body of judge-made law that in the end largely determined what antitrust policy was to be. This process is still going on. There is perhaps no other federal statute that has come more frequently to the Supreme Court in recent years for interpretation than the Sherman Act. Thus, while this particular illustration of national policy making makes use of a statute originally passed over seventy-five years ago, it concerns a problem that is both timely and significant today.

Supreme Court Interpretation and Congressional Reaction

Three of the issues that have caused controversy over the years as the Sherman Act has been applied and interpreted are:

1. Does the act apply to monopolies in manufacturing?
2. Does it apply to "reasonable" as well as "unreasonable" monopolies?
3. Does it apply to labor as well as to business?

Many of these controversies reached the Supreme Court, where decisions were hammered out by trial and error. Today all forms of business enterprise come under antitrust laws. The Court often applies a modified version of the "rule of

---

[7] *United States v. E. C. Knight Co.,* 156 U.S. 1 (1895).

reason" to determine which monopolies are affected. At the present time the application of the laws to labor is somewhat restricted. But these decisions went different ways in years past.

Congress itself has reacted to these decisions by enacting new laws, notably the Clayton and Federal Trade Commission acts of 1914, the Norris-La Guardia Act of 1932, the Robinson-Patman Act of 1936, the Miller-Tydings Act of 1937, and the Anti-Merger Act of 1950. In the Clayton Act Congress undertook to supplement the Sherman Act by making an actual enumeration of forbidden practices which may cause restraint of trade. Among the practices listed were the making of price discriminations in favor of particular customers or localities, exclusive selling contracts, interlocking corporation directorates, and purchase of the stock of one corporation by another corporation. And in the Federal Trade Commission Act of the same year Congress created a new administrative agency, the FTC, and charged it to set a watch against "unfair methods of competition." It is significant, however, that, in amending the Sherman Act, Congress did not succeed in clearing up the three difficult problems of statutory interpretation listed here. In the Clayton Act[8] Congress did declare that "the labor of a human being is not a commodity or article of commerce" and that "nothing contained in the antitrust laws shall be construed to forbid the existence and operation of labor . . . organizations, . . . or to forbid or restrain individual members of such organizations from lawfully carrying out the legitimate objects thereof." This may have seemed to some people to be a clear enough indication of a congressional intention to exclude labor unions from the operation of the antitrust laws, but the Supreme Court did not agree. It read the language of the Clayton Act in its most literal sense and came to the conclusion that Congress meant only that the *lawful* activities of labor unions are not affected by the antitrust laws. A union that engages in an *unlawful* activity, such as a campaign to persuade the public to boycott a manufacturer's product, can be tried for violation of the antitrust laws. Since the 1940s, however, the Supreme Court has more narrowly construed the applicability of these statutes to labor unions.[9]

Thus, the antitrust law is far more detailed and elaborate than it was in 1890 when the Sherman Act was passed, and the executive and judicial branches of the government have helped in shaping policy in this area. Indeed, policy-making here, as in most critical fields, has been a continuing process.

LEGISLATIVE FUNCTIONS

Policy-making is often spoken of as the all-important function of the legislature and of statutes as the all-important product of legislative activity. But, as we have already seen, legislators are neither supreme as policy-makers nor is their work limited to enacting statutes. It is diffi-

---

[8] *38 Stat.* 730, 731.

[9] *Duplex Printing Co. v. Deering,* 254 U.S. 443 (1921); *Apex Hosiery Co. v. Leader,* 310 U.S. 469 (1940); *United States v. Hutcheson,* 312 U.S. 219 (1941).

cult to classify legislative functions, for they often overlap both in purpose and method. But it may be said that a legislature in a democratic political system has four functions to perform. These are: (1) determining, or "ratifying," policy; (2) controlling the purse strings; (3) supervising administrative agencies and the law-enforcement process; and (4) influencing public opinion. The first of these functions has already been examined. Controlling the purse strings is one of the oldest of legislative fuctions; for example, it had much to do with the emergence of Parliament as an important part of the British government in the thirteenth century. As one authority puts it:[10]

In the thirteenth century the kings called together on various occasions not only the chief magnates of the realm, a traditional practice, but also knights from the shires and burgesses from the towns. The purpose in assembling these enlarged councils was not the consideration and enactment of legislation in the modern sense but the obtaining of consent to new tax levies, since even in the thirteenth century it was a constitutional principle, sometimes honored in the breach, that the King could impose no new burden without the approval of the Great Council.

In the American Colonial period the rallying cry of "no taxation without representation" indicated how important the notion of legislative control of tax policy had become. The related notion that funds could be appropriated from the public treasury only by legislative action was only a little slower to take root. By 1787, it had become such a firmly established concept of Anglo-American political practice that the framers of the Constitution without hesitation prescribed that "no money shall be drawn from the treasury, but in consequence of appropriations made by law."

Supervising administrative agencies is also an ancient function. Administrative machinery existed in England before Parliament emerged. When it developed Parliament rapidly acquired an interest in overseeing the further development of governmental machinery, both judicial and administrative, and also in checking these other branches to see that public policy was enforced in a manner consistent with whatever directives had been laid down in acts. The American Constitution does not spell out this third legislative function in so many words. But in leaving it to Congress to create virtually all of the administrative and judicial machinery of the national government, the framers of the Constitution made the performance of this function inevitable.

The fourth function, influencing public opinion, is often overlooked. In a democracy government has a particular obligation to acquaint the people with the nature of social problems under consideration and with alternative courses of action that may be followed. Moreover, it is to the legislature as the chief agency *representing* the people and their interests that a considerable part of this educational responsibility falls. Much of the justification for legislative investigations is based on this function.

---

[10] Hiram M. Stout, *British Government* (New York: Oxford University Press, 1953), pp. 89–90.

This photograph of President Johnson and Senator J. W. Fulbright (Democrat, Arkansas) is in Fulbright's Washington office. Johnson's inscription, "I can see I haven't been very persuasive," indicates his frustration in dealing with one of the foremost critics of his foreign policy. (Wide World Photo)

STATUTE MAKING AND INVESTIGATING

A legislative body has at its command a variety of means for performing these functions. For example, a speech on the floor of the House or the Senate by a well-known member of Congress may influence both public opinion and administrative action. In January 1945, Senator Arthur Vandenberg of Michigan made a speech in which he repudiated his earlier isolationist leanings and announced that he would henceforth support an American foreign policy looking toward closer cooperation with the wartime allies. This address was important not only because it indicated the probable future course that an influential senator would follow, but also because it undoubtedly impressed many Americans who had hitherto hoped that their country "might go it alone," but who had learned to trust Senator Vandenberg's integrity and judgment. It also encouraged the Roosevelt Administration to adopt a bolder course of action.

Similarly, in 1965, 1966, and 1967, Senator William Fulbright's attacks on President Johnson's policies in Vietnam established an important rallying point for all groups who had doubts about the wisdom of American military participation in the Vietnamese war.

Such influential speeches are not made in Congress every day or even in every session. But from time to time the stage is set for an address that will profoundly affect the thinking of important segments of the American public. Such remarks need not even be spoken on the floors of Congress. So great is the attention paid by the press, radio, and television to certain congressmen that a few chance words uttered at a press conference or over the air may drastically alter the course of public thinking or of administrative policy. For instance, Senator Joseph McCarthy's speech at Wheeling, West Virginia, in 1950, in which he announced that he held in his hands the names of 205 persons "that were made known to the Secretary of State as being members of the Communist party and who nonetheless are still working and shaping policy in the State Department," marked the beginning of his strong influence on American public opinion. That he never succeeded in documenting his charge—and kept changing the number of alleged communists in the State Department from 205, to 57, to 81, to 10, to 116, to 121, and to 106—did not alter the effect of his speech. When a United States senator makes sensational charges, people listen and are impressed.

So, too, the power of the Senate to confirm or reject appointments made by the President can upon occasion be used to bring great pressure upon the administration to alter a course of action. Thus the action of the Senate in 1949 in refusing to confirm the reappointment of Leland Olds to the Federal Power Commission undoubtedly reflected opposition, both in the Senate and among businessmen, to a policy of vigorous regulation of the private public utility industry by the federal government. President Truman was forced to name a more conservative man to the post, and without any change in federal statutes, a substantial change in federal policy was soon effected.

Chief among the legislative tools of the American Congress are its statute-making and investigative powers. Each of these tools is capable of being used to perform any one of the four legislative functions. The statute-making power is frequently used to declare policy, as in the Medicare Act. This power is often used to control the purse, as is shown by the enactment of the annual appropriation acts and also by the more infrequent enactment of new tax laws. It is constantly used to create and revise judicial and administrative machinery, to prescribe the powers and duties of these agencies, and to indicate procedures for them to follow. It is used finally to influence public opinion, for the enactment of a law by the legislature often tends to crystallize public attitudes as well as to control individual conduct.

Similarly, congressmen can use the investigative power as a means of making policy, as has been well illustrated by the numerous committees that have been investigating subversive activity in recent years and have, in the process, helped shape substantial portions of national policy concerning such activity. It is also used to supervise the expenditure of public funds in accordance with congressional intent and is repeatedly used to bring pressure upon administrative agencies in connection with the latter's law-enforcement duties. With it congressmen time and again influence public opinion.[11]

Selected Bibliography

Berman, Daniel M., *In Congress Assembled* (New York: Crowell-Collier & Macmillan, Inc., 1964). A fine introduction to the national legislative process.

Galloway, George B., *The Legislative Process in Congress* (New York: Thomas Y. Crowell Company, 1953). A standard general treatment.

Griffith, Ernest S., *Congress: Its Contemporary Role* (New York: New York University Press, 1951). A defense of congressional pluralism and an argument against the need for more party discipline in Congress, by a former director of legislative reference in the Library of Congress.

Gross, Bertram, *The Legislative Struggle: A Study in Social Combat* (New York: McGraw-Hill, Inc., 1953). A lively portrayal of the legislative process in terms of intergroup conflict.

Woodrow Wilson, *Congressional Government: A Study in American Politics* (Boston: Houghton Mifflin Company, 1885). A classic study analyzing the way in which nineteenth-century Congresses predominated over the Presidency.

Young, Roland, *The American Congress* (New York: Harper & Row, Publishers, 1958). An attempt to develop a systematic framework for the analysis of legislative processes. Contains a useful research guide, including bibliography.

---

[11] Chapter 13 will consider further the statute-making and investigative powers of Congress.

12

Congress:
personnel
and organization

Who are the 535 members of Congress? Are they honest and able? Would Congress or its record be much changed if these people were suddenly replaced by 535 others? Or, to put the question differently, to what extent is the work of Congress affected by the people who operate it, and to what extent by the organization and procedures of Congress? Such questions are never easy to answer, for the record made by any government agency is almost always affected by both personal and institutional factors. Most experts are agreed, for example, that Congress today is handicapped in its work by faulty organization and outworn procedures.

Students of American government have also been concerned about the caliber of congressional personnel. A variety of criticisms comes from every direction: the congressman is called an ignoramus, a politician, a self-seeker; critics charge that he loafs on the job, puts persons on the public payroll who "kickback" their salaries to him (and he occasionally goes to jail as a result), votes himself a pension or an increase in salary, goes "junketing" to the far corners of the earth at the taxpayers' expense, criticizes administrators for accepting "gifts" or failure to break off their connections with private business while being guilty of the same offenses himself, holds blindly to outmoded, inefficient procedures, and has no interest in modernizing congressional organization.

It is easy to illustrate the validity of each of these criticisms by pointing to particular members of Congress, for stupid, selfish, dishonest, and even evil men do occasionally get elected to Congress. But such criticism is frequently overdone, for the personnel of Congress share good and bad qualities of people everywhere. It is significant that a committee set up by the American Political Science Association in 1945 to study Congress concluded that "our national legislature today is made up of substantial, conscientious, hard-working, well-educated men and women who are better qualified for their great tasks than is sometimes supposed."[1]

THE "AVERAGE" CONGRESSMAN

The "average" congressman is by no means ill prepared for the job he undertakes. He is a little over fifty, has served in Congress for a number of years, and has had previous political experience before coming to Congress, such as membership in his state legislature. He has a college degree, is a lawyer by profession, a war veteran, and, before coming to Congress, was a well-known and popular member of the community. He has been reasonably successful in business or the practice of law, although not so successful that he is sacrificing a huge income in giving up his private occupation for a public job.

Congress is clearly not an accurate cross section of the American people but neither is it a community of intellectuals and technicians. Although many— often a majority of—congressmen are lawyers, one can usually find a large number of senators and representatives who are former businessmen, journalists, farmers, professors, and even occasionally physicians, ministers, and labor leaders. This diversity is one of the strengths of Congress. Legislators should be able to grasp not only which of alternative public policies are most efficient or even most just, but they must also perceive what the people will see, or can be persuaded to see, as best or most just. This kind of perception calls far more for intelligence, hard work, and social sensitivity than it does for technical expertise.

In 1964, the salary of congressmen was raised from $22,500 to $30,000 a year. In addition, various other allowances and perquisites are available to congressmen. Each representative is allowed about $30,000 a year to employ an office staff, and senators are allowed an average of about $65,000 for this purpose. (The exact amount of this allowance depends on the population of a senator's state.) Every congressman is granted a travel allowance of twenty cents a mile for one round trip per session between Washington and his home. In addition, he is supplied with free office space in Washington and in his home state, free

---

[1] *The Reorganization of Congress,* A Report of the Committee on Congress of the American Political Science Association (Washington, D.C.: Public Affairs Press, 1945), p. 86.

use of the mails, and substantial allowances for air mail and special delivery stamps, stationery, and long-distance telephone calls and telegraph messages.

The 1964 increase in congressional salaries only momentarily ended the perennial complaint that national legislators are underpaid and that good men are deterred from running for Congress because of the fear that they will not be able to make ends meet on a congressman's salary. It is doubtful that the "money troubles" of congressmen will ever disappear.

ORGANIZATION AND PROCEDURE

The most obvious fact about the American Congress is its bicameral organization. It was by no means inevitable that Congress should be bicameral. Its parent legislative body, the Congress under the Articles of Confederation, consisted of a single house, as did all of the *national* assemblies of the American Colonial and Revolutionary periods. On the other hand, practically all of the assemblies in the thirteen American colonies and the legislatures set up in the American states after 1776 consisted of two houses. And the British Parliament, with which most Americans were familiar, was a bicameral body.

Faced as they were with definite precedents in either direction, why did the Fathers prefer a bicameral Congress? Of course, the Connecticut Compromise necessitated a bicameral arrangement. It seems likely, however, that the convention would have preferred this structure anyway, for bicameralism was consistent with the principle of checks and balances, one of the strongest forces that motivated the work of the convention. The story is told that when Thomas Jefferson returned from France after the Philadelphia convention he objected to the bicameral feature and asked Washington why the convention had taken such a step. The conversation occurred at breakfast, and Washington is said to have asked Jefferson, "Why did you pour that coffee into your saucer?" "To cool it," was Jefferson's reply. "Even so," answered Washington, "we pour legislation into the senatorial saucer to cool it."[2]

This original expectation has long ceased to be realized. Today it is not possible to say that one house is more conservative or liberal than the other. Certainly the Senate has long since ceased to function primarily as a "check" upon the House. Legislation, with very few exceptions, originates as readily in one house as in the other, and at any given moment either house may seem to be the more conservatively minded of the two. If the filibuster has proved to be a weapon that a conservative minority can use to prevent favorable action on a bill in the Senate, pigeonholing a bill in committee or refusal of the Rules Committee to give it the right of way on the floor are weapons that enable small groups of representatives to kill bills in the House.

Of course, there are differences between the two houses. Senators still repre-

---

[2] Max Farrand, *The Framing of the Constitution* (New Haven, Conn.: Yale University Press, 1926), p. 74.

sent states regardless of their population, whereas representatives are chosen from districts with an average population, according to the 1960 census, of about 410,000. Occasionally this distinction leads to important differences in the sensitivity of the two houses to the demands of interest groups. For example, the evidence suggests that the House has traditionally been more sensitive to the demands of farmers and the Senate to the demands of workers. Reapportionment as a result of recent Supreme Court decisions may modify these differences.

A New Congress Every Two Years

Congress operates on a two-year cycle. The Congress that convened early in January, 1967, was the Ninetieth Congress, there having been eighty-nine previous Congresses in one hundred and seventy-eight years. The Constitution does not clearly prescribe this two-year cycle, but it is the logical result of an election system whereby all the seats in the House of Representatives and one third of the seats in the Senate become vacant every two years. Accordingly, the Congress that meets in January of an odd-numbered year is a new body, many of its members having just been elected to their offices two months before. The meeting in the odd-numbered year is thus the "first" session, and, assuming that no special session is called, the meeting in the following even-numbered year is the "second" and final session of a Congress. Very early in a first session the two houses proceed to organize, and the resulting arrangements prevail for the two-year period. Any bill introduced in the first session of a Congress may be taken up without backtracking during the second session. But when the final session in the two-year cycle comes to an end all unfinished business automatically dies.

The opening days of a new Congress are marked by activity and excitement as the business of organizing is carried out. The presiding officers and other officials must be elected, members must be assigned to standing committees, a chairman selected for each committee, and parliamentary rules of procedure agreed upon. These tasks of organization give the House of Representatives a good deal more concern than they do the Senate, since only one third of the senators must run for reelection every two years. Of course, since there are likely to be a few elections to fill the unexpired terms of senators who have died, retired, or resigned, slightly more than one third of the Senate may be new members; but unless party control of the Senate is changing in a new Congress, the process of organizing is apt to be a mere formality. Moreover, the Senate has always regarded itself as a continuing body, and therefore has never reaffirmed its rules.

Party Influence in Organizing Congress

Although party lines often break down when Congress turns its attention to controversial legislative problems, in the work of organization they hold fast. The party groups in each house hold separate caucuses or "conferences" and agree upon their committee slates and upon their candidates for such congressional offices as Speaker of the House and President *pro tempore* of the Senate. Such party officers and agencies as floor leaders, whips, and policy committees are also selected at these caucus meetings. All party members are then expected to support the party position on these matters when the House or Senate votes.

In other respects the caucus is an agency of declining importance. At the height of its power it was a meeting of all members of a party in the House or the Senate called to determine party position on a controversial bill. Each congressman was expected to cast his vote on the floor of the house in accordance with a party decision made in the caucus. Today this binding character of the caucus decision has almost wholly disappeared, although party caucuses are still held from time to time during the session to discuss legislative strategy.

One of the most important tasks of organization in a new Congress is the selection of committee personnel. This is strictly a partisan affair. In both houses each party sets up its own committee on committees. These four committees, functioning independently, then proceed to give party members standing committee assignments. Before their work can begin, however, the majority party in each house must decide the ratio that is to prevail between Democrats and Republicans on each standing committee. There has long been a tradition accepted by both parties that the ratio must reflect fairly accurately the division between the two parties in the houses. The slates prepared by the party committees on committees are ratified by the party caucuses and the two houses, but this action is almost without exception a mere formality. Actually, in the House as well as in the Senate, the standing committees are reasonably continuous bodies, and the party task every two years is merely one of filling vacancies. This usually involves allowing some of the senior congressmen to move up to the vacancies on the more important committees and filling the vacancies at the bottom with the freshman members of Congress. The Democrats in the Senate are currently following a policy of trying to give each newly elected Democratic senator one appointment to a major committee and one to a minor committee. Most newly elected Republican senators must still be content with appointment to two minor committees and await their turn for appointment to major committees.

PRESIDING OFFICERS

The most important formal officers of Congress are those who preside over the two houses: in the House, the Speaker, who is chosen by the members on a strictly party basis; in the Senate, the Vice President, who holds the post of presiding officer by constitutional direction. Each house has a second presiding officer. In the Senate this is the President *pro tempore,* who is chosen by the members on a party basis and presides in the absence of the Vice President. (In fact the Vice President or the President *pro tempore* rarely presides; this dull duty is usually passed around among the most junior senators.) In the House it is the chairman of the Committee of the Whole. Technically speaking, the latter is not a House but a committee officer. Nonetheless, he is the officer who presides while the House is transacting much of its important business. He is not a permanent officer but is appointed from time to time by the Speaker as the House rises and goes into the Committee of the Whole.

Formal Powers of the Presiding Officers

It is not easy to give an accurate or meaningful description of the powers of the presiding officers of Congress. In part the authority and influence wielded by them depends upon their formal powers. But in large measure their importance is controlled by such intangible factors as their personalities, the respect they command from their colleagues, their party standing, the over-all strength and cohesion of the party groups, and the state of relations between Congress and the President. The Speaker of the House is almost always one of the two or three most respected and influential members of the majority party. The position of the Vice President is more uncertain. He may have little influence, as was true, for example, of Vice President Henry Wallace. Or he may be an ex-senator, as Lyndon Johnson was, and popular among his former colleagues. Accordingly, even though the Speaker and the Vice President have many of the same formal powers, their prestige and power may vary considerably. As a regular member of the House, the Speaker retains the right to vote and to speak on any proposal, whereas the Vice President has no regular right to participate in debate and may vote only to break a tie. Upon occasion the Speaker does leave the chair to enter the debate, and when he does he is apt to exert much influence.

No member of the House or Senate may address his colleagues or offer any motion without first being recognized by the presiding officer. In the House the Speaker may ask a representative who seeks recognition the question, "For what purpose does the gentleman rise?" If the Speaker is not satisfied with the reply, he may refuse to extend recognition. The Vice President must give the floor to senators without first ascertaining their business. Occasionally in moving from one piece of business to another the course of the legislative process may be profoundly affected by the recognition of a certain member at a particular moment, and the Speaker and Vice President sometimes deliberately give the floor to members with such considerations in mind. But in the course of debate on a particular measure the power of recognition is usually exercised on an impartial basis.

The presiding officer also has the authority to interpret and apply the rules when any question of proper procedure is raised. The routine use of this authority is rather unspectacular and noncontroversial, for mere reference to precedent[3] is often enough to indicate the proper interpretation. Every textbook cites the famous exercise of this power made by Speaker Thomas B. Reed in 1890 when

---

[3] See Asher C. Hinds, *Precedents of the House of Representatives* (Washington, D.C.: Government Printing Office, 1907), 8 vols.; Clarence Cannon, *Precedents of the House of Representatives* (Washington, D.C.: Government Printing Office, 1936–1941), 11 vols., (the first five of these volumes are a reprint of Hinds's *Precedents*); H. H. Gilfrey, *Precedents, Decisions on Points of Order with Phraseology, in the Senate* (Washington, D.C.: Government Printing Office, 1914); and C. L. Watkins and F. M. Riddick, *Senate Procedure: Precedents and Practices* (Washington, D.C.: Government Printing Office, 1958).

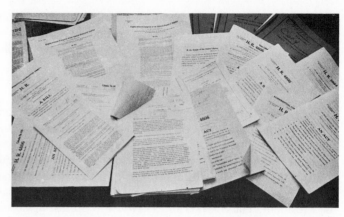

Of the 9684 bills and reso- lutions initiated in 1966, only 346 were eventually passed by both houses. (Cornell   Capa   from Magnum)

he changed the interpretation of the quorum rule so as to include in the quorum count those members present but not voting yea or nay on a bill and thereby frustrated the attempts of the Democratic minority to prevent the transaction of business by not voting either way. But the opportunity to make a new and signifi- cant interpretation of the rules is rare. In both houses any ruling of the presiding officer may be appealed to the floor and reversed by a majority of the members present, so that the power to determine the meaning of a rule ultimately rests with a simple majority of the members of the House or Senate.

In both houses the presiding officers refer the many bills introduced by the members to standing committees for consideration and action. As a rule it is clear which committee should have jurisdiction. Occasionally, however, a bill may be sent to any one of two or more committees, and the presiding officer may choose a friendly or unfriendly committee.

In addition, the presiding officers of the House and Senate are frequently called upon to name the members of special committees, such as special investi- gating committees and conference committees organized to work out differences between bills passed by the two houses in somewhat different forms. This action, however, is usually so controlled by tradition as to leave very little freedom of choice. For example, it is the almost unvarying practice in both houses to name the members of conference committees in order of seniority from the standing committees that originally considered a bill; if there is any question, the presiding officer usually defers to the chairman of the appropriate standing committee.

FLOOR LEADERS AND OTHER PARTY OFFICERS

Of first importance among the *party* offi- cers in Congress are the majority and minority floor leaders in each house. These men are chosen by the party caucuses, and, as their titles indicate, their main duty is to watch over and control business on the floor of the House or Senate from a strictly party point of view. A floor leader keeps in touch with party mem- bers, tries to persuade them to vote in accordance with the wishes of party leaders, supervises debate, directs the activity of the party whips, and is in general the party's chief strategist. The majority floor leader in each house also undertakes to plan and control the order of business, usually doing so on a weekly basis. This, however, is a power that he must share with other party agencies, such as the steering or policy committees, and in the House with the Rules Committee and with the Speaker.

Each party in each house chooses a whip. His function is supposedly to secure the attendance of the party rank and file at votes and to inform party members of the wishes of the leadership. Aiding the whip is an organization of perhaps fifteen to twenty deputies and assistants. All whips are, of course, members of Congress. Although they do notify party members of votes and convey the wishes of the leadership (often without visible effect on voting behavior), the whips also help inform the party leadership of the views of the rank and file.

The Legislative Reorganization Act of 1946 established in the Senate a Democratic and a Republican policy committee. Each of these groups has a small staff and an annual budget paid for out of federal funds. The Reorganization Act charges the two committees with "the formation of over-all legislative policy of the respective parties." Practice, however, has failed to conform to this mandate. While the two parties have used their committees in somewhat different fashions, some generalizations can be made. Hugh A. Bone, the closest student of their work, has concluded that the committees have been helpful in accommodating factionalism within each party, in collecting, analyzing, and disseminating data about public issues, and even sometimes in clearing legislation for floor action. But, Bone[4] has said, the committees "have never been 'policy' bodies in the sense of considering and investigating alternatives of public policy, and they have never put forth an over-all congressional party program."

In the House both parties use steering committees, though since 1949 the Republicans have called theirs the House Republican Policy Committee. It has been facetiously observed that the steering committees seldom meet and never steer. This is an overstatement, but it is clear that the committees are not in fact powerful or even very important agencies of party government in the House. This failure of the steering committees to function more actively illustrates the chief weakness of party organization in Congress: the absence of any centralized leadership. Within Congress the power to lead is diffused among a wide number of officers and agencies and at best is exercised on a collective basis. One of the few recent periods of aggressive and effective congressional leadership was from 1954 to 1960 when Lyndon B. Johnson was Senate majority leader; but, while Johnson's influence in the Senate was great, he had far less influence in the House, where he had to rely on his old friend from Texas, House Speaker Sam Rayburn. To grasp more fully the reasons usually behind decentralized leadership system, the important roles played by the many standing committees of Congress must be understood.

---

[4] *Party Committees and National Politics* (Seattle, Wash.: University of Washington Press, 1958), p. 186.

THE COMMITTEE SYSTEM

There is a strong tendency for all modern legislative bodies to employ some sort of committee system so that a division of labor can be made in dealing with numerous and difficult proposals for legislation. An alternative method is assigning to administrative agencies the task of preparing statutory proposals. The latter policy is followed under parliamentary government and is the chief reason why the British Parliament is able to function with a much more rudimentary committee system than the American Congress.

The House of Representatives has twenty, and the Senate sixteen, permanent committees, each of which watches over a particular segment of legislative business. While the number of committees in the two houses differs slightly, the division of legislative responsibility among committees is very similar in both houses. Both houses have committees on agriculture, appropriations, the armed services, banking and currency, civil service, the District of Columbia, government operations, public works, rules, labor, taxation, foreign relations, the judiciary, and interstate and foreign commerce. In general, each senator is assigned to two of these committees, and each representative to one. Many of these committees make extensive use of subcommittees, some of which are permanent and are subject to little control by the parent committee.

Many state legislatures make use of joint committees which bridge the gap between the two houses. In Congress the parallel committee structures of the House and Senate are conducive to joint committee hearings and deliberations, but such sessions are seldom held. Instead, the committees of each house jealously guard their separate prerogatives. Congress, however, does make some use of such committees. Most influential are the conference committees; but a conference committee stays in existence only until the particular bill it was created to facilitate has either been passed or rejected by Congress. The House and Senate have also established a few equivalents of standing committees. Among these are the joint committees on printing, the Library of Congress, atomic energy, internal revenue taxation, and the economic report; but on the whole these committees have not played important roles.

From time to time the House or Senate creates a special committee to conduct a temporary investigation. From 1938 to 1945 the House Un-American Activities Committee was such a committee. In 1945, however, the House voted to make it a standing committee. In recent years the number of special committees has declined, and investigations have been assigned instead to the relevant standing committees or subcommittees thereof.

All of the standing committees in both houses are bipartisan. Most Senate committees have fourteen to nineteen members, and House committees range from nine to fifty members. Because of its size and its bipartisan membership, a committee inevitably possesses a certain cross-sectional character, but it is a mistake to think of each committee as constituting a House or a Senate in miniature, at least so far as the interests and voting inclinations of the members are concerned.

A congressional committee at work. A final version of a bill, with the correct technical wording, is drawn up by specialists in the field with which the bill is concerned. (Cornell Capa from Magnum)

Each of the committees is apt to have a somewhat larger percentage of its membership with vital constituent interests in the committee's substantive work than is true of Congress as a whole. In the words of one observer:[5] "There is a tendency for committees to represent special interests, leaving the guardianship of the general welfare to the full house and the Executive. Ex-soldiers seek places on the committee dealing with veterans; members from the farm states control the committees on Agriculture. . . . Similarly, a large majority on [the] Finance . . . committee, represent industrial states of the North and East."

The Role of Committee Chairmen

It is almost impossible to overestimate the importance of the role played by committee chairmen in the legislative process. To a chairman belongs the power to arrange the meetings of his committee; to select much of its professional staff; to appoint the personnel of its subcommittees; to determine the order in which it considers bills; to decide whether public hearings shall be held on a bill; to arrange to have a bill, which the committee has

---

[5] O. R. Altman, "First Session of the Seventy-fifth Congress," *American Political Science Review,* 31 (December 1937), pp. 1071, 1076.

reported favorably, brought to the floor of the house; to manage the floor debate on the bill; to ward off unwanted amendments; and, should a conference on a particular bill be necessary, to serve as a member of this committee and sometimes to influence the choice of other conference members from his house. The manner in which a chairman exercises these powers is supposedly subject to review and even control by the committee as a whole, but it is a rare committee that ever undertakes to check or rebuke its chairman. The 1967 action of the House to remove the chairman of the Committee on Education and Labor, Adam Clayton Powell, is a notable as well as a highly unusual exception.

Chairmen exercise their powers largely independently of one another and, in very large measure, independently of the presiding officers, floor leaders, and other congressional and party officials. This is a crucial factor explaining the absence of centralized leadership in Congress. As Woodrow Wilson[6] said more than seventy years ago: "The chairmen of the Standing Committees do not constitute a cooperative body like a ministry. They do not consult and concur in the adoption of homogeneous and mutually helpful measures; there is no thought of acting in concert." After a finely detailed study of the voting patterns in the Eighty-first Congress (1949–1950), David Truman[7] wrote that "no reason exists for revising Wilson's conclusion that the seniority leaders do not function as a collegial body. If they consult, they do not concur."

Committee Chairmen and the Seniority Rule

In each house the committee on committees of the majority party formally designates committee chairmen. In practice, however, each assignment goes automatically to that member of the majority party who has the longest unbroken service on a committee. Exceptions to this "seniority rule" are virtually unknown. No aspect of congressional organization is more controversial than this rigid system of selecting committee chairmen.

The case against the seniority rule is a strong one. It ignores ability; it puts a premium upon mere continuous service; it discourages any attempt to achieve recognition and high office by hard work and demonstration of interest or skill; and it sentences junior congressmen to a long period of apprenticeship that deters able and mature men in public life from seeking election to Congress. It is further argued that the seniority rule is undemocratic in that it tends to place in office as committee chairmen men from "safe" congressional districts that are often politically stagnant. Because of the certainty of their election to Congress, these men may be insensitive to changing public opinion and represent a point of view current at the time of their original election to Congress. For example, the election of President Dwight D. Eisenhower in 1952 unquestionably represented a victory for the liberal faction of the Republican party, but it resulted in a large number of committee chairmanships going to conservative or "old guard" members of the

---

[6] Woodrow Wilson, *Congressional Government* (Boston: Houghton Mifflin Company, 1885), p. 61.

[7] *The Congressional Party: A Case Study* (New York: John Wiley & Sons, Inc., 1959), pp. 134, 237–238.

President's party. Similarly, Democratic congressional victories in 1956, 1958, 1960, 1962, 1964, and 1966 automatically placed in positions of great power as committee chairmen a score or more of southern Democrats who were frequently lukewarm toward the President's welfare programs and opposed to his civil rights proposals.

It is also claimed that the seniority rule makes it difficult to provide for effective and responsible party government in Congress. A committee chairman usually can safely ignore the legislative wishes of his party organization in or out of Congress; for, as long as he has the support of a majority of voters in his state or district, his seat in Congress is safe, and under the seniority rule, so too is his chairmanship of a committee (provided his party is in power). The House of Representatives supplied a blatant case in point in 1967 when it selected William Colmer of Mississippi as Chairman of its powerful Rules Committee. This selection came strictly on the basis of seniority. Colmer had twice, in 1948 and 1960, publicly supported third party candidates for the Presidency and had time and again spoken and voted against the liberal policy proposals of Presidents from his own party. Critics of the seniority rule argue that one of the most effective ways of providing for increased party discipline and regularity in Congress would be to assign committee chairmanships on the basis of service and loyalty to the party and to insist upon such continued service and loyalty as the price of retention of a chairmanship over a period of years.

The strongest argument in favor of the seniority rule, one that apparently carries great weight with Congress itself, is a negative one. Any attempt to get away from a purely automatic method of selecting party officers, through paying greater attention to the qualifications of individual congressmen for particular offices, would result in a high degree of intraparty bickering and intrigue. It is contended that congressmen seeking good committee

"It's a Hell Of a Way to Run a Railroad"

From *The Herblock Book* (Beacon Press, 1952).

assignments and committee chairmanships would be forced to engage in all sorts of wirepulling and logrolling with their fellow party members. Admittedly, this is possible. Intrigue is particularly strong in a decentralized party, where vigorous leadership and discipline are absent. But opponents of the seniority rule argue that putting the selection of congressional officers on a merit basis would itself provide a real impetus for the development of a stronger party organization with sufficient power to enable it to control the assignment of its members to posts on a merit basis without undue bickering and intrigue. Moreover, the intraparty arguing that might accompany the making of these assignments could hardly be more demoralizing to party organization than is the seniority rule itself, under which party members know that party regularity has absolutely nothing to do with receiving the important posts that the party has to bestow upon its members.

Another argument that is seldom voiced publicly but that carries weight with the supporters of the seniority rule is that the rule strengthens the hand of the conservative elements in both parties and serves to minimize the influence of liberals. The senior members of Congress, having first been elected a generation or more ago and often having held their seats through the years without facing any real opposition, are apt to reflect political attitudes and pressures of the past rather than the present.[8]

STAFFING CONGRESS

Over the years the volume of government business has forced congressmen to build up a bureaucracy of their own that employs more personnel than many federal agencies. These professional staff members, often with technical experience and expertise that exceeds that of the representatives and senators for whom they work, have come to play an important part in the legislative process.

Each member of Congress is given an allowance for the maintenance of a personal office staff. In the case of representatives, these funds enable him to employ an administrative assistant, a legislative assistant, a professional secretary, and several clerk-stenographers. A senator's allowance is more generous, and a senator from a populous state may have a dozen or more persons working for him in his office. It is difficult to generalize about the duties of these administrative assistants or of professional secretaries, for much depends upon the care with which they are selected and the work that is delegated to them. But a competent assistant can act as executive director of a congressman's office, answer much of his mail, deal with visitors to his office, keep in touch with the executive agencies of the government, run many of the errands to these agencies for constituents, and offer the congressman advice and assistance in studying bills, researching, writing speeches, and running for reelection. In short, an able, shrewd, and loyal professional man can serve his employer as a sort of "assistant congressman."

---

[8] In a report published in 1945, the Committee on Congress of the American Political Science Association, after carefully weighing the arguments for and against the seniority rule, recommended its abandonment.

Additionally, in 1966, the many committees of Congress, standing and special, enjoyed the services of well over 1100 staff employees. The Legislative Reorganization Act of 1946 authorized each committee to engage up to four professional experts and six clerks. While many appointments have been made on the basis of merit, party affiliation has often been an important factor in selection.

A number of staff services are also available to the two houses of Congress at large. Chief among these are the Legislative Reference Service and the Office of Legislative Counsel. The former was established in 1914 but has been greatly expanded since the 1946 statute. It is a general research agency in the Library of Congress, which supplies various services and materials—pamphlets, digests of bills, data for use in speeches, abstracts of current literature, and studies of special legislative problems—requested by individual congressmen or by committees. In 1966, it had a professional and clerical staff of over 200 persons and an annual budget of more than $2.1 million. The Office of Legislative Counsel was established in 1918 and has also grown rapidly since 1946. Its chief function is to draft bills at the request of congressmen or committees, making certain that their technical legal language accomplishes the purposes that their sponsors have in mind. A former official in the agency has testified,[9] "Our office has nothing to do with policy whatsoever. We try to find out what the committee wants to do and help them do it." This may be an accurate statement of the way in which the Legislative Reference Service and the Office of General Counsel operate; but the intricacies and complexities of public problems make such demands on the time and energy of most congressmen, that other staff members have considerable opportunity to exercise their own discretion and so to influence policy-making.

Selected Bibliography

Bailey, Stephen K., *Congress Makes a Law* (New York: Columbia University Press, 1950). A lively study of the enactment of the Employment Act of 1946.

De Grazia, Alfred, *Public and Republic: Political Representation in America* (New York: Alfred A. Knopf, Inc., 1951). A history of the practice of representation in legislatures.

Fenno, Richard F., Jr., *The Power of the Purse* (Boston: Little, Brown & Company, 1966). An exhaustive account of the political processes involved in congressional appropriations.

Matthews, Donald R., *U.S. Senators and Their World* (Chapel Hill, N.C.: University of North Carolina Press, 1960). A detailed and well-written analysis of the formal and informal ways of the Senate.

Steiner, Gilbert Y., *The Congressional Conference Committee* (Urbana, Ill.: University of Illinois Press, 1951). A case study of this committee's operations from the Seventieth to the Eightieth Congress.

Truman, David, *The Congressional Party* (New York: John Wiley & Sons, Inc., 1959). A case study of party leadership and cohesiveness in the 81st Congress.

White, William S., *Citadel: The Story of the U.S. Senate* (New York: Harper & Row, Publishers, 1958). An admiring account of the unique qualities of the Senate.

---

[9] Quoted in George B. Galloway, *The Legislative Process in Congress,* (New York: Thomas Y. Crowell Company, 1953), p. 409. For a recent study of the problems of securing adequate assistance for congressional operations, see Kenneth Kofmehl, *Professional Staffs of Congress* (West Lafayette, Ind.: Purdue University Studies, 1962).

13

Congress at work

A DISAPPOINTING SCENE:
CONGRESS IN SESSION

The visitor to the House or Senate galleries is often disillusioned. He has envisaged an impressive parliamentary panorama with traditional ceremony, dignified debate, and high drama in the clash of political personalities. Instead, more often than not he finds a dull and inactive scene. Of the 435 representatives, or 100 senators, perhaps 30 or 40 of the former or a dozen of the latter are present. A lone figure has the floor, and while he drones along in an unexciting monologue a few inattentive colleagues read newspapers, work at their desks, or sit talking in back rows.

Such a glimpse of the House or Senate in session is hardly a reliable guide to the nature and importance of the legislative process. "Like a vast picture thronged with figures of equal prominence and crowded with elaborate and obtrusive details," Woodrow Wilson[1] once said, "Congress is hard to see satisfactorily

---

[1] Woodrow Wilson, *Congressional Government: A Study in American Politics* (Boston: Houghton Mifflin Company, 1885), p. 58.

244

and appreciatively at a single view and from a single stand-point." While a visitor to the galleries today witnesses forms and procedures that are more than a century and a half old, changing times have placed a steadily greater burden upon government, and Congress has adapted those forms and procedures to new needs. Assuredly Congress is not perfectly equipped to perform its functions in mid-twentieth century. But Congress has changed, and it does go about its work today by means of a complex institutional system that has evolved slowly through the years, and only part of which can be understood by observing the House and Senate in formal session.

A CONGRESSMAN'S DAY

If a Congressman, then, does not put in a great deal of time on the floor of the House or Senate, how does he spend his day? Although it is obvious that there can be no "typical day, or "average" congressman, much can be learned about the complex responsibilities and functions of all congressmen by introducing Representative Malcomb Durbin, a hypothetical member of Congress from a mixed urban-suburban district, and following him through a day's work in Washington.

Office Activity

Congressman Durbin arrives at his office at nine o'clock, having already breakfasted with a lobbyist who works for one of the civil rights organizations. Durbin finds his desk piled high with business, old and new. His first attention goes to the newly arrived mail, for letters are one of his most valuable contacts with the people back home. If the session of Congress has reached a climactic point, his letters may number hundreds, or even thousands each day. Mail must be handled rapidly, yet given close attention. The long sessions of modern times that keep the congressman in Washington the better part of each year make it relatively difficult for him to keep in close personal touch with many of his constituents. Thus the wise congressman tries to make sure that a member of his staff acknowledges every letter that comes into his office from his home district.

By 9:20 A.M. Durbin is consulting with his office staff. A weekly newsletter for publication in the newspapers of his districts must be ready for the noon mail, and a final draft awaits polishing. The congressman's secretary has some information about witnesses who are scheduled to appear later that morning before the Committee on Education and Labor, of which he is a member, to testify on a bill in which he is interested. Another staff member has been in touch with the offices of several other congressmen and has a report on the status of a bill that Durbin has introduced to provide increased federal financial aid to cities trying to maintain racially integrated schools.

Soon a steady stream of visitors begins to flow through the legislator's office. A few will be constituents from back home who must be courteously received. Some will have business to transact; some merely "want to say hello." Other congressmen will drop in to discuss legislative issues, to exchange views, and to seek advice. A newspaperman comes in to talk about a speech Durbin is to give before his home town Lions Club, for rumor has it that he intends to criticize sharply administration of existing civil rights laws.

Running Errands for Constituents

Between chats with visitors Congressman Durbin is on the telephone, and before the morning is over he has been in communication with a dozen administrative agencies of the government. Some of these calls provide the congressman with information needed in his work, but many of them are made to help him meet the inquiries and requests of constituents. He checks with the Department of Agriculture concerning the availability of agricultural agents to assist suburban home owners to keep their lawns green during the summer drought. Then he calls the Defense Department to arrange an interview for a businessman who is coming to Washington from his district. Next he puts in a request to the Legislative Reference Service for data to be used in the Lions Club speech. Finally, he gets in touch with the Civil Service Commission to inquire about the rating of a constituent on an examination recently taken.

This so-called errand running is a very controversial aspect of a congressman's work. On the one hand, it is vigorously defended on the ground that it helps to humanize government. Intercession by the congressman frequently helps to soften the harsh, impersonal character of law enforcement. On the other hand, in running these errands a congressman risks seeming to interfere with the executive process of government and to seek special favors for a privileged few.

LEFT *Republican Congressman F. Bradford Morse of Massachusetts arrives at the congressional office building.* BELOW *The congressman's staff answers constituents' letters and conducts research.*

Meeting with Interest Groups

Throughout the day a considerable portion of Durbin's time is taken up by discussions with lobbyists or government officials about legislative matters. Much of this time may seem wasted; the requests of many persons seeking to influence legislation are unreasonable or cannot possibly be met; or the congressman finds it difficult to maintain his dignity and his honesty in resisting the pressures that are exerted upon him. Still, he cannot refuse to listen: legislative policies are about to be determined; it is the congressman's duty to give representation to his constituents, and so he must listen patiently to requests or demands that he support this bill or oppose that one. Moreover, Durbin has discovered by experience that lobbyists and administrative officials are often experts in the areas in which they operate. Even when he disagrees with them, they can help him learn about policy problems.

Attending Committee Meetings

At 10:30 A.M. Congressman Durbin leaves his office and walks down to the first floor of the office building to the room where the Committee on Education and Labor is scheduled to meet. For two weeks the committee has been holding hearings on a bill to provide stronger federal support for higher education, and it will soon go into executive, that is, secret, session to determine the final language of the bill. During this period Durbin has found it necessary to devote much time to the careful study of the transcripts of hearings, the wording of proposed amendments, and data supplied by the committee's staff. This morning the chief witness is the head of an important civil rights organization. Durbin does not see eye to eye with this witness, and he in-

BELOW *Congressman Morse meets with one of his constituents.* RIGHT *Congressman Morse confers with a research assistant.* (Pictures of Morse and his staff by Cornell Capa from Magnum)

tends to question him vigorously on several points. Indeed, he spent most of last evening studying several of the organization's reports in preparation for this questioning. His breakfast meeting with a representative of another civil rights organization was arranged so that he might check his plans with him.

Congressman Durbin has served on the Committee on Education and Labor for nine years, and he is now the third member of his party in seniority. Long ago he became aware that the most important work of Congress is done in committee. He has come to give an increasing amount of time and energy to his committee responsibilities, and through hard work he has made himself something of an expert on educational policy. While he was going to school and for the first few years he was in law practice his wife taught at a city high school, and he got to know her friends and their teaching problems. Moreover, he had taught on a part-time basis at the local university. As a congressman he has built up a considerable fund of knowledge about the way the federal government can and has tried to help educational institutions. He knows what he would do to meet current problems, and he does not hesitate to speak his mind or try to influence policy in the direction he favors. In other legislative areas he is inclined to go along with the wishes of his party leaders. Occasionally a respected colleague may persuade him to vote otherwise, or somewhat more often strong pressure from his district dictates how he should cast his vote. But he is known as a good party man even though his voting record shows that he breaks way from the party line in about one out of every five votes.

Attending Sessions of Congress

Promptly at noon the committee adjourns. The session has been a lively one, and Durbin pressed the witness hard with a series of searching questions. Now he travels by an underground tunnel from his office building to the Capitol and comes on to the floor of the House, which convened at noon. The "morning hour" is in effect. Petitions and memorials and messages from the President, heads of departments, and the other house are being presented, and bills and resolutions introduced. Durbin does not linger long and at 12:20 P.M. goes downstairs to the congressional dining room for lunch. During the afternoon he is on and off the House floor several times. Twice he is called off the floor to talk with visitors, one a constituent from his home town and the other an official of one of the large farm organizations, who talks with him at some length about a pending farm bill. Durbin is no expert on agricultural matters and the lobbyist knows it. What the lobbyist suggests—subtly and obliquely—is that if the congressman can persuade some of his friends to vote for the farm bill, he, the lobbyist, can swing his farm organization behind the congressman's education proposals. Durbin is not sure that this trade is entirely in his interest; but he needs all the votes he can get for his own bill, and he promises to talk to the lobbyist again in a few days.

At 3:30 P.M. Durbin gets word that there will probably be no voting until the next day, and he goes back to his office to resume his work there, knowing that he will be warned by a bell should a vote be reached and that he will have ample time to get back to the floor to answer his name when it is called. Next month, when the higher education bill is brought to the floor of the House, he plans to speak at some length. But, although he is a respected member of Congress, he is not known as an active participant in debate. Occasionally he asks another member a question or raises a point of order, but his formal speeches seldom exceed three or four a year.

Homework

The House recesses for the day at 5:30 P.M., but Durbin remains in his office for almost an hour more, reading and signing outgoing letters. When he leaves for home he takes with him a bulky brief case. It contains the *Congressional Record* for the previous day's session, which he has not yet found time to examine, the morning newspapers, which have had only a quick glance, the rough draft of a committee report on the education bill that the committee staff has been working on, some notes for his Lions Club speech, a long letter from a trusted political adviser in his home town, which will have to be answered tomorrow with some care, and a thick file of education statistics and data recently supplied him by the Department of Health, Education and Welfare. After dinner and a visit with his children he will settle down to a long evening with these materials and his problems. As he drives his car away from the Capitol his mind runs ahead to next year and the election it will bring. His friend writes that he may face a strong rival in the party primary who is prepared to attack him on the ground that his "catering to the Negroes" has cut into the civil rights of whites. Furthermore, yesterday he read in his local paper that two Negro leaders had asserted that "black power" was the only answer to discrimination and that Negroes should force Durbin's party to nominate a Negro candidate for Congress next year. Durbin asks himself for the thousandth time why he stays in politics.

THE MAKING OF A FEDERAL STATUTE

It is difficult to exaggerate the importance of an adequate system of rules to a modern legislative body, and these rules are bound to be the result of a slow, evolutionary development in which conflicting forces contribute to the final result. The business of legislating for a country like the United States is a tremendous responsibility, and technical procedures concerning order of business, length of debate, amending bills, methods of voting, and reconciliation of House and Senate differences must be carefully prescribed. Yet there is constant danger that procedure will become so detailed and circumscribed that business can be transacted only with difficulty. Both houses have in part solved this dilemma by creating two entirely different sets of rules: a formal set that recognizes each distinct problem of parliamentary procedure and provides an official mode of action to take care of it; and an informal and largely unwritten set that makes it possible for the legislative body to transact much of its business

in disregard of prescribed procedures. It has been said[2] that the Senate "has operated so long as a gentlemen's club that two sets of rules have developed, one
written and the other based on custom. Only after specific warning is it considered
fair to enforce the written rules."

One manifestation of informal procedure in both houses is the extensive
transaction of business by unanimous consent. Either house can violate its formal
rules at any time so long as no member objects. Even though members of Congress have widely varying interests and points of view, they often recognize the
necessity of preferring the informal to the formal rules in transacting much legislative business. Yet they know that the formal rules may be invoked when the
issues at stake are vital or when the conflict of interests is not being compromised.

Perhaps the clearest way to illustrate the importance of legislative rules and
to indicate something of their substance is to describe the process by which a bill
becomes a statute. Leaving aside for the moment the approval or rejection of bills
by the President, there are six major stages through which a major bill usually
passes before it becomes law. These are (1) drafting and introduction of the bill;
(2) consideration and approval by committee in the house in which the bill is
introduced; (3) consideration and approval by that house itself; (4) consideration
and approval by committee in the second house; (5) consideration and approval
by the second house; and (6) ironing out differences between the two houses in
conference.

Drafting and Introduction of Bills

With very few exceptions any member
of either house may introduce a bill or resolution dealing with any subject over
which Congress has power. The exceptions are quickly stated. The Constitution
requires that revenue bills be introduced in the House of Representatives, and
by custom appropriation bills are also considered there first. Resolutions proposing the impeachment of federal officers may also be introduced only in the
House. Consent to treaties, confirmation of appointments, and trial of impeachment cases are all restricted by the Constitution to the Senate, and accordingly
any motion or resolution bearing on these matters can be presented only by a
senator.

Bills and resolutions are designated as follows: A bill carries the prefix "HR"
in the House, "S" in the Senate, and a number that indicates the order of its
introduction. Joint resolutions are labeled "HJ Res" or "SJ Res." Bills enacted
into law are also numbered in sequence. The Voting Rights Act of 1965, for example, is Public Law (or P. L.) 89–110, the 110th public law adopted by the Eighty-
ninth Congress. The title "public law" is used to differentiate statutes of general
application from private laws, such as an act to admit a particular person to the
United States as an exception to current immigration rules.

Concurrent resolutions are labeled "H Con Res" or "S Con Res," and reso-

---

[2] O. R. Altman, "Second and Third Sessions of the Seventy-fifth Congress, 1937–38," *American Political Science Review,* 32 (December 1938), pp. 1099, 1116.

lutions, "H Res" or "S Res." While bills and joint resolutions, if enacted, have the force of law, neither concurrent resolutions nor resolutions have such authority. A resolution is a statement by one house and a concurrent resolution, a statement by both houses. For example, a change in the rules of either house is effected by a resolution; a special House-Senate investigating committee is established by a concurrent resolution.

A legislative idea in Congress may originate in many ways. Responsibility for legislative proposals is not concentrated at any one point in the American government, as it is in the British cabinet. Some bills have their origins primarily within Congress and may reflect the wishes and labors of the congressmen who introduced them. Or a bill may have its birth in the deliberations of a standing committee which has given much time and consideration to the need for new legislation in a particular field. Most new tax bills are so prepared by the House Ways and Means Committee. Other bills have their origins primarily outside of Congress. Some originate with interest groups. A large number of bills, possibly now a majority of the more important proposals actually enacted into law, originate in one of the executive departments or agencies. In the end, the language of a major statute is usually determined by many persons. Few congressional committees report bills in exactly the language that may originally have been suggested by executive agencies or interest groups; on the other hand, few bills of major importance are written within Congress without any outside help or advice.

Committee Action on Bills

With very few exceptions all bills are referred to standing committees for consideration. The committee stage is the most crucial in the life of a bill. Here the great majority of bills introduced in Congress are pigeonholed and never heard of again. Here the bills that do emerge for later floor action are carefully scrutinized and their final language often determined. There is a great deal of variation in committee procedure. Important public bills are often made the subject of public hearings, but such hearings are far from uniform. They may be impressive sessions at which committee members honestly seek the advice and assistance of informed persons interested in the proposed legislation. Or they may be carefully staged proceedings in which a committee chairman seeks to confirm and give publicity to his own prejudices. Because the two houses accept so many committee recommendations without change, interest groups are as active at committee hearings as they are at any other point in the entire governmental process.

Following these public hearings, a committee meets in executive session to determine a bill's fate. If it views the legislative proposal favorably, it usually proceeds to "mark up" (revise) the bill and to prepare a formal report on it. Often the committee is split, and both majority and minority reports are submitted to the House or Senate. These reports are printed and, together with copies of the final bill, are made available to all members of the House or Senate.

Floor Action on Bills

A bill that has been reported by a committee is placed on a calendar to await consideration by the House or Senate. Its position on the calendar, however, has little to do with the order in which it is actually considered. Instead, both houses have developed varying procedures for determining the order of business. Since the committees report their bills without regard for each other's actions, some system of priorities has to be established.

Under the Senate rules any senator is entitled to move that the Senate take up any bill that has been reported by committee. If the motion is adopted by a majority vote, the Senate turns to the bill in question. In practice such motions are usually offered by the majority floor leader, who acts after consultation with other party leaders, such as the majority policy committee and the committee chairmen who have bills awaiting consideration. A motion to call up a bill is debatable, which means that a minority of senators can try to prevent consideration of a bill by filibustering against this motion. Noncontroversial bills are taken up by the "call of the calendar." This call takes place at irregular intervals. Each senator is limited to five minutes of debate on bills called up in this way.

Because of the size of its membership, the House system of determining the order of business is much more complex. Very few bills can be called up by a simple motion from the floor, as in the Senate. A few committees may do so and are said to be "privileged" in this respect. The Ways and Means Committee can move to call up a tax bill whenever it wishes; the Appropriations Committee can do the same with appropriation bills; and the Rules Committee can move at any time to call up any rule that it has reported.

Important public bills are brought to the floor of the House by means of a special rule or order prepared by the Rules Committee and adopted by the House by majority vote. It is standard procedure for the chairman of the standing committee reporting a bill to go to the Rules Committee to ask for such a rule. Often the committee has refused a special rule to bills supported by standing committees and by the majority party leadership. If granted, the special rule usually fixes the time that consideration of a bill by the House shall begin, limits the period of general debate, and guarantees the bringing of the bill to a final vote. Most special rules are "open," but a few are "closed" or "gag" rules, which limit or forbid the offering of amendments to a bill from the floor. For example, the Ways and Means Committee usually elects to bring tax bills before the House by means of a closed rule, so that they will not be subject to amendment from the floor.

In 1961, liberal Democrats in the House, anticipating that the Rules Committee, dominated by a conservative Republican-southern Democrat coalition under the leadership of Howard Smith of Virginia, would refuse to report out much of the domestic legislation desired by the administration, put forth a number of proposals to curb the committee's power. But the administration did not have either a large or a cohesive majority in the House, and the most that could be obtained was an increase in the committee's size from twelve to fifteen members. This increase had little impact, and in early 1965, a more effective liberal coalition pushed through two major changes in House rules to cut the authority of the Rules Committee. The first change allowed the House, by a majority vote and without Rules Committee action, to send to a conference committee a bill passed by both houses in different form. The second change was short-lived. It allowed a member of a standing committee to bring before the House a bill favorably reported by his committee if that bill had been before the Rules Committee for twenty-one days. Two years later, in the opening days of the Nine-

"Come In—Come In"
From *The Herblock Book* (Beacon Press, 1952).

tieth Congress, a coalition of northern Republicans and southern Democrats succeeded in repealing the twenty-one day rule. This was a significant victory for conservative legislative forces, since the new Rules Committee chairman, William Colmer of Mississippi, who was seventy-seven when he took over the job, was as adamant in his opposition to any form of political liberalism as his predecessor, Howard Smith of Virginia, had ever been.

A bill may also be brought to the floor of the House by discharging a standing committee from further consideration of it. Discharging a committee requires that a majority of all House members sign a petition and that the House then approve the motion to discharge by a majority vote of those present. Such action takes a bill away from committee and brings it to the floor of the House. If the Rules Committee refuses to report a special order for a bill, the same discharge petition method can be used to force a House vote on the special order. This procedure is rarely successful, in part because of the influence of senior members of committees, who are able to take revenge against their opponents by pigeonholing their bills.

The House of Representatives transacts much of its most important business while sitting as the Committee of the Whole, on which all 435 members of the House serve. Traditionally, the Committee of the Whole was employed by a parliamentary body to permit preliminary and tentative action, with the possibility of changing its mind later when it gave final, official consideration to a matter. In practice, however, action taken by the House of Representatives while sitting as the Committee of the Whole tends to be decisive. Normally, no further debate or amendments are in order when the committee rises and reports its recommendations to the House for final action. The chief reason for the use of this arrangement is that it enables the House to escape from its own rules, some of which are prescribed by the Constitution, and to operate instead under a different set of rules designed to expedite business. For example, a quorum is fixed at 100 members in the Committee of the Whole, whereas the Constitution fixes the quorum for the House and Senate at a majority of all the members (51 in the Senate; 218 in the House).

The Limitation of Congressional Debate

It is important in a democracy that proposed public policies be carefully debated before they are adopted and also that such proposals be brought finally to a vote so that they may be accepted or rejected by decision of the majority. Thus both houses of Congress have adopted rules that make it possible to bring debate to a close. Before turning to these rules we again should note that both houses transact most of their business in routine fashion with great dispatch. In the House and Senate bills debated over a period of several days now number no more than a dozen or so a session. This indicates, first, that many legislative proposals are noncontroversial and, second, that controversial issues are often thrashed out elsewhere than on the floor of the House or the Senate—in other words, at the time a bill is being drafted or at the time of committee consideration.

Under the House rules each member is entitled to speak for one hour on the subject under consideration. But this right means little in practice. First, it is usually in order for the member who has the floor to move the previous question. This motion must be voted on immediately. If it is supported by a majority, debate ends at once, and the bill or proposal, whatever it may be, is brought to a final vote. Furthermore, the House debates virtually all important measures while sitting as the Committee of the Whole. Here debate is divided into two sections: a period of general debate on a bill and a period when the bill is read section by section for amendment. The length of the period of general debate is fixed in advance by the Rules Committee, and two members, one favoring and one opposing the bill, have control of the time. In the second period debate occurs under the so-called five-minute rule, by which five-minute speeches are in order for or against proposed amendments. Debate in the House is thus apt to be brief and lively. But a bill may nonetheless be before the House for a considerable period. In the case of important bills, it is not unusual to allow two or three days for the period of general debate. Further debate under the five-minute rule may on occasion lengthen House consideration of a bill to a period of a week or more.

Under Senate rules, it is never in order to move the previous question. Except when "the calendar" is being called, senators may speak as long as they please on the matter under consideration. It is this situation that makes possible the

Senate practice of filibustering, which usually means prolonged debate by a minority in an attempt to prevent the majority from passing a bill. From the point of view of the majority right to rule, logic is against the filibuster, for it enables a very small minority to frustrate the will of the majority. But the defenders of the Senate's unlimited debate argue that it protects the right of the minority to present its views and to prevent hasty action. As the pressure of legislative business has mounted in modern times, however, and the enormity of the power wielded by a small group of filibustering senators has been realized, the Senate has been forced to utilize certain means of limiting debate.

1. *The Two-Speech Rule*. No member may speak more than twice on a single subject on the same legislative day. By recessing, rather than adjourning, at the end of a day's session the Senate can prolong a "legislative day" indefinitely, and thereby limit the amount of speaking that can be done on a single item of business.

2. *The Cloture Rule*. The Senate adopted a specific cloture rule in 1917 prior to American entry into World War I, after a particularly unpopular filibuster against a proposal by President Wilson for arming American merchant ships. Under the original version of the rule, sixteen senators might petition the Senate to close debate upon a pending measure. If such a petition were approved by a two thirds vote of the members present, no senator could thereafter speak for more than one hour on the measure and amendments pending thereto. But in 1948, the cloture rule was weakened. In the course of a filibuster against an anti-poll tax bill, the President *pro tempore* of the Senate, Senator Arthur H. Vandenberg, ruled that cloture was not applicable to debate on a motion to call up a bill but could be invoked only during debate on a bill itself. This ruling meant that if a group of minority senators started a filibuster on a motion to call up a bill, the cloture rule was of no use against them. In 1949, the Senate amended its rule to make cloture applicable to debate on motions to call up measures as well as to debate on measures themselves. But the price of this reform was a further change requiring that two thirds of the entire membership must vote to support cloture.

Since 1957, at the beginning of each new Congress, liberal senators have waged hard campaigns to strengthen the cloture rule. Despite vague pledges in both party platforms, up to 1967, the most the liberals had been able to accomplish was a return to the older rule allowing debate to be limited by a vote of two-thirds of the senators actually present. In practice, cloture has been extremely difficult to invoke. Only thirty-six cloture petitions were brought to a vote between 1917 and 1966, and the victory of the liberals during the debate on the 1965 Voting Rights Act was only the seventh time that the necessary two thirds vote has been attained to limit debate.

3. *Curtailment of Debate by Unanimous Consent Agreements*. Debate on most major bills is now brought to a close in the Senate, surprisingly enough, by unanimous consent agreements that a final vote will be taken at a set hour. How is it possible to obtain such unanimous consent when the two thirds majority needed to invoke cloture can almost never be obtained? The explanation is that attempts are made to invoke the cloture rule only in the face of an extensive filibuster against a highly controversial bill, whereas debate is closed by unanimous

consent as a matter of convenience where there is no real opposition to letting a bill come to a vote, particularly if the majority has allowed a reasonable time for debate.

Methods of Voting

Both House and Senate employ several methods of voting. The simplest and most common form is a voice vote, in which the members in turn call out the yeas and nays and the presiding officer judges which side has prevailed. Any member who doubts the result can ask for a rising, or division, vote in which the two groups rise alternately and are counted. In the House only, one fifth of a quorum may request a teller vote, by which the two groups leave their seats, pass between tellers, and are counted. Finally, in both houses, one fifth of the members present may demand a record vote, in which the roll is called and members are recorded by name as voting yea or nay.

Conference Committee Action on Bills

Many important public bills pass the two houses in differing versions. These differences must be compromised if any further progress in the enactment of a law is to take place. One house may vote to give way and accept the version approved by the other. Where the differences are slight or time is an important factor or the bill is an unimportant one, this often occurs. But if each house stands fast on its version of a bill, it is then necessary to make use of the conference committee as a means of effecting a compromise. The members of the conference committees are formally chosen by the Speaker and the Vice President. As discussed in the last chapter, however, the selection is usually made in bipartisan fashion from the standing committee in each house that originally considered the bill; if any question of selection arises, the standing committee chairman normally has the decisive word. Supposedly, a conference committee must produce a compromise version of a bill that falls somewhere between the House and Senate version. But conference committees sometimes find it necessary to introduce new ideas or provisions into bills, even though technically this is a violation of congressional rules. When the conference committee reports a compromise version, it must be accepted or rejected as it stands by both houses, and no amendments may be proposed on the floor of either house. Either house, however, may reject a conference report and send a bill back to conference a second time, making it clear that it desires a particular change before it will accept the bill.

PROPOSALS FOR CHANGING THE LEGISLATIVE PROCESS

The cards are stacked against action by Congress. It is usually far easier to kill a bill than to secure its adoption. This has led to assertions that the American legislative process is not only seriously defective in organizational and procedural efficiency but is undemocratic as well. It is argued that it ought to be easier for majority public opinion to take shape in the United States and to find positive expression in the adoption of national legislation.

A modest program for congressional reform was suggested in 1950 by the American Political Science Association's Committee on Political Parties.[3] These proposals are all within the ability of Congress itself to adopt, either by statute or by rule. According to the committee, the key to a more efficient and democratic Congress is a stronger and "more responsible" party system:

A general structure of congressional party organization already exists. It should be tightened up. . . . If such action were taken, it would not mean that every issue would become a party issue. It would not eliminate the need for or the possibility of nonpartisan and bipartisan policies. But it would result in a more responsible approach to party programs and a more orderly handling of *all* congressional activities.

The committee's recommendations are as follows:

1. "Leadership Committees" should be created by each party in House and Senate. Powers now scattered through such agencies as the steering or policy committees, the committees on committees, and the House Rules Committee would be concentrated in these new agencies. They would draw up the slates of committee assignments, issue calls for party caucuses, and, in the case of the majority party leadership committees, control the legislative schedule in the House and Senate.

2. The party caucus should be revived and strengthened as a means of allowing democratic discussion of the party program by all of a party's members in each house, and of providing for a *binding* decision on important legislative proposals that would force all party members to vote in accordance with the party's established principles and platforms.

3. Assignment of committee posts and distribution of patronage should deliberately be used to encourage congressmen's loyalty to the established party platform.

4. The seniority rule should be modified to permit the party leadership to name as committee chairmen senior members who are loyal to the party program.

5. Control of the legislative schedule in the House of Representatives should be transferred from the Rules Committee to the leadership committee of the majority party.

6. The Senate rule on freedom of debate should be modified to permit debate to be closed by a simple majority vote.

CONGRESSIONAL INVESTIGATIONS

While the visitor to the House or Senate gallery is frequently disappointed by the routine activity he sees, the visitor to a hearing of a congressional investigating committee seldom voices a similar complaint. If the committee is well known, and if the subject of investigation is important and controversial, the most ample room in the office buildings of the House or Senate will prove none too large for its meeting. Hundreds of people and dozens of press, radio, and television representatives will watch and listen as a much-ballyhooed witness testifies concerning an issue of great public interest—the flotation of worthless bonds by Wall Street bankers and brokers, the "truth" about

---

[3] "Toward a More Responsible Two-Party System," *American Political Science Review,* Supplement, 44 (September 1950), p. 57. Also published separately under the same title (New York: Holt, Rinehart and Winston, Inc., 1950).

Pearl Harbor, Cuba, or Vietnam, race track gambling, automobile safety, labor racketeering, allegations that a leading political official has used his public office for private gain, or charges that corporations have earned unconscionable profits in their contractual dealings with the government.

Types of Investigating Committees

A congressional investigation is to be contrasted with the normal, routine consideration of bills by the standing committees of Congress. An investigation is an inquiry into a *subject* or a *problem* rather than a specific legislative proposal. The most formal investigation occurs when Congress specifically authorizes an inquiry into a particular subject, designates a committee to make this study, votes an appropriation to cover the costs of the inquiry, and grants the committee power to subpoena witnesses. Most investigations are authorized by the House or Senate acting independently of one another, although on occasion the two houses take concurrent action and set up a joint investigating committee. Separate House and Senate investigations are today most often turned over to the relevant standing committees or subcommittees thereof. A joint committee is sometimes broadened to include members of the executive branch or even private citizens. But the many commissions of inquiry that are established by the President and which report to him are not properly regarded as *congressional* investigating committees.

Purposes of Congressional Investigations

The motives that lead congressmen to authorize an investigation are varied. First is the obvious need to obtain detailed and accurate information if Congress is to take intelligent action. A good illustration is the Wall Street investigation in 1933, in which Congress sought and obtained information about banking and stock exchange practices that led to the enactment of statutes establishing the Securities and Exchange Commission. A second purpose, only slightly less important, is the use of investigations by Congress to supervise or check the work of administrative agencies charged with enforcement of laws. Each house has a committee on government operations which frequently conducts such investigations. A third purpose of investigations is to influence public opinion by giving wide circulation to certain facts or ideas, as Senator William Fulbright tried to do through his committee's 1966 hearings on the war in Vietnam. As far back as 1885, Woodrow Wilson[4] called attention to "the instruction and guidance in political affairs which the people might receive from a body which kept all national concerns suffused in a broad daylight of discussion." And, he asserted, "The informing function of Congress should be preferred even to its legislative function."

These three purposes are often supplemented by others of a more personal and partisan character. Senator Joseph McCarthy was following a well-worn path

---

[4] Woodrow Wilson, pp. 297, 303.

in employing sensational investigatory techniques. More than one legislator has advanced his career—usually for a longer period than did McCarthy—through a reputation made as a hardheaded investigator. Hugo L. Black, who later became a Supreme Court justice, and Harry S. Truman, who spent some years in the White House, are cases in point. Accordingly, it is not surprising that hope for political advancement should strongly motivate congressmen to seek authorization for new investigations. Similarly, a political party often undertakes investigations to advance its own interests or to embarrass its adversary. In the 1920s and 1930s the Democratic party did its best to discredit the Republicans through investigations into the Harding Administration scandals and the misdeeds of bankers and businessmen. When the Republicans won control of Congress in the 1946 election, they facetiously announced that each day's session of the Eightieth Congress would "open with a prayer and close with a probe."

COMMITTEE VERSUS WITNESS: CONSTITUTIONAL ISSUES

Congressional investigating committees sometimes encounter witnesses who refuse to appear before a committee or to answer its questions. Out of such episodes have come congressional statutes and

Frank Costello, reputed underworld leader, testifies before the Kefauver Senate Crime Committee. The late Senator Estes Kefauver's (Democrat, Tennessee) investigations received considerable national attention in 1950–1951. (Acme News Pictures)

Supreme Court decisions concerning the relative status and rights of investigating committees and witnesses. In particular, answers have been sought to these questions:[5] What subjects may Congress properly investigate? On what grounds may a witness properly refuse to answer a committee's questions? To what extent may Congress provide for the punishment of uncooperative witnesses?

The Investigating Power of Congress

The Supreme Court[6] has held that the "power of the Congress to conduct investigations is inherent in the legislative process."

That power is broad. It encompasses inquiries concerning the administration of existing laws as well as proposed or possibly needed statutes. It includes surveys of defects in our social, economic or political system for the purpose of enabling the Congress to remedy them. It comprehends probes into departments of the Federal Government to expose corruption, inefficiency or waste.

In this same opinion the Court also pointed out:

It is unquestionably the duty of all citizens to cooperate with the Congress in its efforts to obtain the facts needed for intelligent legislative action. It is their unremitting obligation to respond to subpoenas, to respect the dignity of the Congress and its committees and to testify fully with respect to matters within the province of proper investigation.

As early as 1857, Congress enacted a statute[7] directing private persons to appear before investigating committees when subpoenaed and to answer pertinent questions or risk a criminal prosecution in the courts and imprisonment up to one year for failure to do so. The constitutionality of this statute has repeatedly been upheld by the Supreme Court.

The Rights of Witnesses

There are three standard situations in which a witness may properly refuse to cooperate with an investigating committee of Congress:

1. If the subject under examination lies outside the authority of the investigating committee, a witness is under no legal obligation to answer its questions. In 1953, for instance, the Supreme Court set aside the conviction of Edward Rumely, who had been prosecuted under the 1857 statute. Rumely, who was the secretary of a private organization known as the Committee for Constitutional

---

[5] Among the most important decisions of the Supreme Court bearing on the congressional power of investigation are: *Anderson v. Dunn,* 6 Wheaton 204 (1821); *Kilbourn v. Thompson,* 103 U.S. 168 (1881); *McGrain v. Daugherty,* 273 U.S. 135 (1927); *Sinclair v. United States,* 279 U.S. 263 (1929); *United States v. Rumely,* 345 U.S. 41 (1953); *Quinn v. United States,* 349 U.S. 155 (1955); *Watkins v. United States,* 354 U.S. 178 (1957); and *Barenblatt v. United States,* 360 U.S. 109 (1959).

[6] *Watkins v. United States,* 354 U.S. 178, 187–188 (1957).

[7] 11 *Stat.* 155, 2 U.S.C. § 192.

Government, had appeared as a witness before a House committee investigating lobbying. In the course of the hearing he refused to answer questions pertaining to cash gifts received by his organization to finance the distribution of books and pamphlets among private persons in order to influence public opinion. The Supreme Court[8] ruled that Rumely was within his rights in refusing to answer these questions because the resolution of the House of Representatives establishing the committee had authorized it only to investigate lobbying activities intended to influence Congress directly. Thus the committee had exceeded its authority in asking Rumely about the financing of his publications.

"*Is their most ominous threat yet, Comrade Commissar! Is subpoena from U.S. Congress Committee on UnAmerican Activities!*"

(GRIN AND BEAR IT by George Lichty, courtesy Publishers-Hall Syndicate)

2. If a committee asks a witness questions that are not pertinent to the subject under investigation, the law allows him to refuse to answer. Thus, in 1957, in the case of *Watkins v. United States,*[9] the Supreme Court set aside the conviction of a witness for contempt of Congress because the questions he had refused to answer had not been demonstrated to be pertinent to a proper line of inquiry.

3. If a witness's answers would provide evidence that might be used against him in a criminal proceeding, he can invoke the privilege of the Fifth Amendment against self-incrimination and refuse to reply to a committee's questions. The Court has made it clear that to invoke the privilege a witness need only believe that his answer *might tend* to incriminate him. Thus a silent witness is not necessarily guilty of the "offense" he refuses to discuss. Nonetheless, many of the witnesses who have lawfully invoked the privilege before congressional committees

---

[8] *United States v. Rumely,* 345 U.S. 41 (1953).
[9] 354 U.S. 178 (1957).

have been subjected to certain social sanctions.[10] Many such witnesses have been dismissed from their jobs, sometimes on the ground that they failed to meet a test of good citizenship by refusing to cooperate with a legislative committee, and sometimes on the ground that their silence created a presumption that they had been engaging in unlawful activity.

From time to time witnesses have tried to justify refusal to cooperate with congressional committees on other grounds, but generally speaking, the courts have refused to come to their rescue when they have been prosecuted for contempt of Congress. Judges have also consistently declined to look into the motives behind a congressional investigation. In 1961, for example, a five-justice majority of the Supreme Court sustained contempt of Congress convictions of two opponents of the House Un-American Activities Committee in cases in which it appeared that the real reason for calling the witnesses had been revenge for their sponsoring a petition urging abolition of the committee.[11]

Moreover, despite the statement in *Watkins v. United States* that "the Bill of Rights is applicable to investigations as to all forms of governmental activity," the Court held in 1959 in *Barenblatt v. United States* that a witness may not legitimately invoke the First Amendment to balk inquiries into his political beliefs and associations, at least if those beliefs and associations pertain to communism. Over bitter dissents from four of the six members of the *Watkins* majority, the Court ruled that the individual's right to silence about his political beliefs had to be "balanced" against congressional authority to protect national security. "In the last analysis," Justice Harlan[12] wrote for the new majority, the power to investigate communism "rests on the right of self-preservation."

For the minority, Justice Black[13] protested that the explicit wording of the First Amendment precluded "balancing." Even if balancing were the proper approach, Black continued, the majority had put the wrong weights on the scales. It was not Barenblatt's right to silence that should have been pitted against Congress' right to know, but "the interest of the people as a whole in being able to join organizations, advocate causes and make political 'mistakes' without later being subjected to governmental penalties for having dared to think for themselves."

IMPROVING CONGRESSIONAL INVESTIGATIONS

In a democratic state a citizen must be protected against arbitrary and unjust governmental procedures. Some of the practices of certain investigating committees have abused this right; moreover, they have tended to bring Congress itself into disrepute. Four lines of improvement have been suggested.

---

[10] See *Quinn v. United States,* 349 U.S. 155 (1955); and *Emspak v. United States,* 349 U.S. 190 (1955). See also *Slochower v. Board of Higher Education,* 350 U.S. 551 (1956); and *Beilan v. Board of Education of Philadelphia,* 357 U.S. 399, 409 (1958).

[11] *Braden v. United States,* 365 U.S. 431 (1961); *Wilkinson v. United States,* 365 U.S. 399 (1961).

[12] 360 U.S. 109, 127–128 (1959).

[13] 360 U.S. 109, 144 (1959).

Use of Substitutes

Some observers say that Congress should delegate the making of its investigations to administrative agencies and other bodies of experts who would report their findings and recommendations back to it. A precedent for this suggestion is the British Parliament's practice of having investigations made by so-called royal commissions, consisting of experts outside Parliament, usually in the administrative offices. When, however, investigations are undertaken by experts in the United States, it is sometimes difficult to obtain sufficient publicity for their findings or action upon their recommendations.

Perhaps the mixed commission, consisting of congressmen, administrators, and private citizens, provides a means of meeting both the objection that purely congressional committees are apt to be unfair or incompetent and the objection that purely administrative commissions have too little influence or publicity-getting power. The two Hoover Commissions on the Organization of the Executive Branch of the Government were good examples of a mixed commission. Both of these commissions conducted their inquiries in a generally careful and responsible way. Both received excellent publicity and their findings led to a number of important changes in federal administrative organization and practice.

Adoption of a Code of Fair Procedures

A good deal of attention has been given in recent years to the development of a code of fair procedures for congressional investigating committees. Certain specific committees have voluntarily adopted some of the recommended procedures, and in 1956, the House of Representatives prescribed a rudimentary code for all of its committees to follow. But neither house has yet been willing to put into effect a comprehensive set of procedural regulations with teeth in it. One difficulty lies in securing agreement among the experts as to which procedures should be prescribed, for most students of the subject agree that Congress must be careful not to go so far that it hamstrings its committees. There is, however, fairly general agreement on including the following procedures: hearings should be held only when authorized by a majority of a committee's members and only in the presence of two or more committee members representing both political parties; no committee reports or statements to be issued without the approval of a majority of committee members; witnesses should enjoy the assistance of counsel; persons attacked by witnesses should enjoy a reasonable right of reply; no radio or television broadcasts should be permitted without the approval of witnesses.

Increased Measure of Judicial Supervision

Many critics of congressional investigations have demanded a stricter measure of supervision by the courts. In particular, in cases in which witnesses are prosecuted for contempt, it is argued that the courts should carefully scrutinize committee authority and procedures for full compliance with the Constitution and statutes. As early as 1881, the Supreme Court checked the authority of a congressional investigating committee, but the Court has always been reluctant to impose any drastic restraints upon the legislative power of inquiry. The late Justice Jackson[14] once said, "I think it would be an unwarranted act of judicial usurpation to strip Congress of its investigatory power, or to assume for the courts the function of supervising congressional committees. I should . . . leave the responsibility for the behavior of its committees squarely on the shoulders of Congress."

In 1957, in the *Watkins* case, the Supreme Court indicated that it was prepared to exercise a tighter control over congressional inquiries. After a coalition of conservative Republicans and southern Democrats waged a narrowly unsuccessful fight to rebuke the justices for protecting the rights of witnesses, however, the Court executed a tactical withdrawal.[15] The Court has continued to reverse contempt of Congress convictions but has restricted itself to the most technical kinds of issues.[16]

More Responsible Use of the Investigating Power by Congress

In the final analysis, congressmen themselves must be persuaded to make a more responsible use of their investigating power. This means that both House and Senate must give greater attention to the authorization of specific investigations and refuse to approve those inquiries that seem primarily motivated by personal ambitions or by hopes for sensational hearings. Congressmen must also see to it that difficult investigations into complex, controversial subjects are made by colleagues who are respected for their integrity, their sense of fair play, their understanding of national needs, and their respect for the rights of individuals. And no code of fair procedures, however carefully drawn or complete, can excuse the House and Senate from the need to keep a close watch over all committees of inquiry and to employ a restraining hand at the first sign of abuse of the investigating power.

Selected Bibliography

Barber, James David, *The Lawmakers: Recruitment and Adaption to Legislative Life* (New Haven, Conn.: Yale University Press, 1965). An examination of the reasons why men go into and stay in legislative politics.

---

[14] Dissenting in *Eisler v. United States,* 338 U.S. 189, 196 (1949). Jackson's colleagues did not necessarily disagree with him on this point.

[15] Compare the *Watkins* and *Barenblatt* cases discussed in the preceding pages. For a full account of the congressional battle over the decisions of the Warren Court, see Walter F. Murphy, *Congress and the Court: A Case Study in the American Political Process* (Chicago: The University of Chicago Press, 1962).

[16] See, for example, *Deutch v. United States,* 367 U.S. 456 (1961); *Yellin v. United States,* 374 U.S. 109 (1964); and *Gojack v. United States,* 384 U.S. 702 (1966).

Carr, Robert K., *The House Un-American Activities Committee* (Ithaca, N.Y.: Cornell University Press, 1952). A thorough account of the role and activities of one of the most publicized congressional committees in decades.

Clark, Joseph S., *Congress: The Sapless Branch*, rev. ed. (New York: Harper & Row, Publishers, 1965). A liberal senator's biting critique of Congress and his passionate plea for reform.

Froman, Lewis A., Jr., *The Congressional Process: Strategies, Rules, and Procedures* (Boston: Little, Brown and Company, 1967). An analysis of the effects of congressional organization and rules of procedure on public policy formulation.

Haynes, George H., *The Senate of the United States* (New York: Russell & Russell, 1960), 2 vols. A reissue of a classic work on the Senate, originally published in 1938.

Kofmehl, Kenneth, *Professional Staffs of Congress* (West Lafayette, Ind.: Purdue University Studies, 1962). A useful analysis of the development since 1946 of professional staffs for congressional committees.

MacNeil, Neil, *The Forge of Democracy* (New York: David McKay Company, Inc., 1963). A detailed and well-written study of the House of Representatives.

Miller, Clem, *Member of the House* (New York: Charles Scribner's Sons, 1962), ed. by John Baker. A view of life in the House of Representatives as seen by a brilliant young congressman.

Taylor, Telford, *Grand Inquest* (New York: Simon and Schuster, Inc., 1955). Probably the best general account of congressional investigating committees, treated historically and critically.

Turner, Julius, *Party and Constituency: Pressures on Congress* (Baltimore, Md.: The Johns Hopkins Press, 1952). Seeks to measure the influence of party and constituency on congressmen over a twenty-five year period.

Part 4

The Presidency and the Executive Branch

PRESIDENTS LOOK AT THE PRESIDENCY

The Early Years

In all great and essential measures [the President] is bound by his honor and his conscience, by his oath to the Constitution, as well as his responsibility to the public opinion of the nation, to act on his own mature and unbiased judgment, though unfortunately, it may be in direct contradiction to the advice of all his ministers.—*JOHN ADAMS, in "Letters to a Boston Patriot,"* 1809.

In a government like ours, it is the duty of the Chief Magistrate . . . to endeavor, by all honorable means, to unite in himself the confidence of the whole people. This alone, in any case where the energy of the nation is required, can produce a union of the powers of the whole, and point them in a single direction, as if all constituted but one body and one mind; and this alone can render a weaker nation unconquerable by a stronger one.—*THOMAS JEFFERSON, in a letter to J. Garland Jefferson, Jan. 25,* 1810.

Republican Views

Was it possible to lose the nation and yet preserve the Constitution? By general law, life and limb must be protected, yet often a limb must be amputated to save a life. . . . I felt that measures, otherwise unconstitutional, might become lawful by becoming indispensable to the preservation of the Constitution through the preservation of the nation.—*ABRAHAM LINCOLN, in a letter to A. G. Hodges, April* 4, 1864.

The most important factor in getting the right spirit in my Administration . . . was my insistence upon the theory that the executive power was limited only by specific restrictions and prohibitions appearing in the Constitution or imposed by Congress under its constitutional powers. . . . I decline to adopt the view that what was imperatively necessary for the nation could not be done by the President unless he could find some specific authorization to do it.—*THEODORE ROOSEVELT, in "An Autobiography,"* 1913.

Any American who had a modicum of modesty would at times be overcome by the intensity and the importance of the problems that he would meet if he were called upon to serve in the chief official position of this country.—*DWIGHT D. EISENHOWER, in an address at Charlotte, N. C., May* 18, 1954.

Democratic Views

He [the President] is expected by the nation to be the leader of his party as well as the Chief Executive officer of the Government, and the country will take no excuses from him. . . . He must be prime minister, as much concerned with the guidance of legislation as with the just and orderly execution of law, and he is the spokesman of the nation in everything, even in the most momentous and most delicate dealings of the Government with foreign nations.—*WOODROW WILSON, in a letter to A. Mitchell Palmer, Feb.* 5, 1913.

The Presidency is not merely an administrative office. That is the least part of it. . . . It is preeminently a place of moral leadership. All our great Presidents were leaders of thought at times when certain historic ideas in the life of the nation had to be clarified. . . . Without leadership alert and sensitive to change, we are bogged up or lose our way.—*FRANKLIN D. ROOSEVELT, speech, Nov.* 12, 1932.

The President must know when to lead the Congress, when to consult it and when he should act alone . . . and he must be prepared to use all the resources of his office to ensure enactment of legislation.—*JOHN F. KENNEDY, January* 1960.

I have watched it [the Presidency] since Mr. Hoover's day and I realize[d] the responsibilities it carried and the obligations of leadership that were there, and the decisions that had to be made, and the awesome responsibilities it carried. . . . But I must say that when I started to make those decisions . . . the Presidency looked a little different . . . than it did . . . in the Congress.—*LYNDON B. JOHNSON, March* 14, 1964.

14

Presidential leadership

NATURE OF THE PRESIDENCY

The twentieth century has seen, in societies all over the world, a turning of people toward strong central executive power to solve their most troublesome problems. In its rawest, most extreme form, the result has been absolute dictatorship. Most Western democracies have tried to strengthen the resources and devices of executive leadership without abandoning the customary restraints that hold the executive within constitutional bounds.

The American Presidency has been deeply affected by these general trends. A summary view of presidential leadership shows a mixture of traditional duties and recently acquired responsibilities that would have seemed strange a few generations ago. Today a President of the United States is expected to symbolize the aspirations, grandeur, and unity of the American people; run the immense and complex machinery of the federal government; keep a firm hand on relations with foreign governments whose activities may affect the peace and prosperity of the United States; weld together America's allies in concerted action guided by common cause; command the armed forces of the United States; initiate and

269

actively promote, as spokesman of all the people, legislation that he believes will advance essential national interests; lead his political party so that it may continue in power; see that the federal government takes timely and sufficient measures to maintain economic prosperity and avoid disastrous inflations or depressions; maintain order if state and local authorities are unable to do so.

A Product of Many Forces

Over the years the Presidency has been a constantly evolving institution. The more important forces affecting it include the ideas of the framers of the Constitution, changing social and economic conditions, and the personalities of the Presidents.

Discussions of the nature of the executive occupied the members throughout the Constitutional convention. The problem was two-sided: to create an executive whose authority would energize the government and to surround him with sufficient safeguards to make dictatorship unlikely. One group of delegates shared the view of Roger Sherman,[1] who considered "the Executive magistracy as nothing more than an institution for carrying the will of the Legislature into effect" and thought that the executive "ought to be appointed by and accountable to the Legislature only, which was the depository of the supreme will of society." For a time this group was attracted to the idea of a plural executive, possibly three men, on the grounds that it would be less dangerous to liberty and would permit representation in the executive of the south and west as well as the eastern section of the country.[2] Finally, however, a majority of the convention came over to the view that the executive should be a single individual, with wide authority and independent of Congress. Because the minority view was based upon deep conviction, the framers compromised on the method of electing the President and on the choice of language to define his powers and duties. The compromise is embodied in Article II and related provisions of the Constitution.

"The executive power shall be vested in a President of the United States of America." This short opening statement is characteristic of the entire article, which goes on to declare: "the President shall be Commander-in-Chief of the Army and Navy"; "he shall nominate, and, by and with the advice and consent of the Senate, shall appoint ambassadors, other public ministers and consuls, judges of the Supreme Court, and all other officers of the United States whose appointments are not herein otherwise provided for, and which shall be established by law"; "he may require the opinion, in writing, of the principal officer in each of the executive departments"; "he shall receive ambassadors and other public ministers"; and "he shall from time to time give to the Congress information of the state of the Union, and recommend to their consideration such measures as he shall judge necessary and expedient."

This enumeration of powers is brief, and, if we look beyond the literal terms of the Constitution to the working Presidency, woefully incomplete. Yet Article II

---

[1] Max Farrand, *The Records of the Federal Convention* (New Haven, Conn.: Yale University Press, 1911), 1, 65.

[2] Leonard D. White, *The Federalists* (New York: Crowell-Collier & Macmillan, Inc., 1948), p. 14.

does provide the legal framework within which a President must operate. Each of the specific powers authorized by the article forms a nucleus around which cluster dozens of other powers brought into existence by legislation, judicial interpretation, custom, and, most of all, by varying presidential practices.

The demands created by changing social and economic conditions have also been a major shaping influence on the Presidency. To maintain the political support needed for survival, any government institution must to some extent be able to meet pressing demands, to satisfy existing needs, whether or not particular office holders wish to pay attention to such issues. Thus a President does not have a completely free hand in choosing what problems he wishes to devote his resources to solving—assuming, that is, that he wants to be reelected or to see his party's candidates win in the next election. Indeed, the matter may go deeper, even to the question of survival of a particular kind of government or of the nation itself. If the federal government had not been able to cope with—not necessarily immediately end—the depression of the 1930s, popular despair might have brought about a drastic change in the American form of government. So too marked inability of any administration to deal effectively with foreign policy problems since the end of America's nuclear monopoly might well result in the end of the United States as a nation.

All of this is not to say that a President is a mere prisoner of his times. Some problems may be thrust on him, but he still has a choice in deciding which other problems to confront. And he always has wide leeway in selecting the means he deems most appropriate to deal with any policy problem. There are times, of course, especially in domestic politics, when doing nothing, that is, leaving a problem to be worked out by nongovernmental processes, may be an attractive and effective way of handling an issue.

In choosing how to attack a problem, a third shaping influence on the Presidency is the personality of the Chief Executive. In the historical evolution of the Presidency there has been such a close relationship between office and personality that it is difficult to discuss the real power of the Presidency except in terms of specific men. The presidential powers under Lincoln were very different from those under Buchanan, just as Andrew Jackson's Presidency was hardly the same office that John Quincy Adams had held. The infinite subtlety of Franklin D. Roosevelt's leadership was far different from the bluntness of Harry Truman. Eisenhower's reliance on a staff to shield and inform him, his reluctance to immerse himself in politics, and his refusal to formulate a comprehensive legislative program stand in sharp contrast to the bubbling energy and curiosity of Presidents Kennedy and Johnson and their zest for political combat.

Strong and Weak Presidents

We might range all American Presidents along an action spectrum. At one extreme would be those whom Louis M. Koenig calls the "literalists."[3] Men like Rutherford Hayes, William Howard Taft, Warren

---

[3] *The Chief Executive* (New York: Harcourt, Brace & World, Inc., 1964), p. 13.

Harding, and Calvin Coolidge viewed the Presidency as a place of repose. They saw the President's main function as carrying out policy decisions made within Congress. Any positive presidential action had to be justified by a clear constitutional command. As Taft[4] phrased his philosophy:

The true view of the Executive functions is, as I conceive it, that the President can exercise no power which cannot be fairly and reasonably traced to some specific grant of power or justly implied and included within such express grant as proper and necessary to its exercise. Such specific grant must be either in the Federal Constitution or in an act of Congress passed in pursuance thereof. There is no undefined residuum of power which he can exercise because it seems to him to be in the public interest.

At the other end of the spectrum have been "strong" Presidents like Lincoln, both Roosevelts, Woodrow Wilson, and Lyndon Johnson. They have thought of the Presidency as the center of a tornado of activity, an ideal vantage point from which they could lead the nation. Theodore Roosevelt[5] summed up to the outlook of these men when he said:

My view was that . . . every executive officer in high position was a steward of the people bound actively and affirmatively to do all he could for the people, and not to content himself with the negative merit of keeping his talents undamaged in a napkin. I declined to adopt the view that what was imperatively necessary for the Nation could not be done by the President unless he could find some specific authorization to do it. My belief was that it was not only his right but his duty to do anything that the needs of the Nation demanded unless such action was forbidden by the Constitution or by the laws. . . . I did not usurp power, but I did greatly broaden the use of executive power. In other words, I acted for the public welfare, I acted for the common well-being of all our people, whenever and in whatever manner was necessary, unless prevented by direct constitutional or legislative prohibition.

Most Presidents do not fall so neatly at one extreme or the other but are rather somewhere in between. During their office many behave at some times more like literalists at others more like strong Presidents, but each incumbent has helped shape the office.

SOURCES OF PRESIDENTIAL POWER

The major work of the President, Harry Truman[6] liked to say, consists in "trying to persuade people to do the things they ought to have sense enough to do without my persuading them." There may be serious doubts whether the President's judgment is always correct, but Truman was certainly right in stressing that the power of the President, in both national and international politics, is based on persuasion rather than command. In domestic affairs both state and national legislators, as well as governors, mayors, and

---

[4] William Howard Taft, *Our Chief Magistrate and His Powers* (New York: Columbia University Press, 1916), p. 139.

[5] *Theodore Roosevelt: An Autobiography* (New York: Crowell-Collier & Macmillan, Inc., 1913), p. 389. Used with the permission of The Macmillan Company.

[6] Quoted in Richard E. Neustadt, *Presidential Power: The Politics of Leadership* (New York: John Wiley & Sons, Inc., 1960), pp. 9–10.

a host of other officials, have an independent electoral base, and federal judges have virtual life tenure. Thus there are few people outside the executive branch whom the President may command, and even there he may have problems. In dealing with foreign nations, of course, the need to rely on persuasion is obvious. Even use or threat of force, such as Kennedy's in dealing with Khrushchev's Cuban missile bases, are typically designed to compel an opponent to reason rather than to obliterate him.

The unique constitutional and political position of the President allows him to play many different roles, and in each role he may exercise different kinds of persuasion. On the other hand, in no role is he assured of exercising effective persuasion. Each facet of the Presidency presents the incumbent with an opportunity, not a guarantee. What must be kept in mind in any analysis of the Presidency is, as Neustadt[7] points out, the President "plays every 'role,' wears every 'hat' at once. Whatever he may do in one role is by definition done in all, and has effects in all. . . . He is one man, not many."

Party Leader

First and foremost the President is the leader of his party. When a candidate for the presidential office receives the nomination he becomes head of his party and continues to be head after election. He cannot be elected and cannot do his job without his party's support. As Chapter 6 pointed out, these parties are in reality loosely knit coalitions of state and local factions that cannot be directed easily from a central point—by the President or by anyone else. If he is a strong vote-getter, state and local leaders may feel indebted to him for helping them to stay in power. As often as not, however, these leaders boast of their achievement in electing a President who, they claim, would have failed without their support. If he is to be at all successful in getting his legislative program accepted, he must weld these factions into some reasonable facsimile of a party organization.

Chief of State

To Americans and to the rest of the world the President symbolizes the government of the United States. Like the British queen, he reigns; like the British prime minister and cabinet, he also governs. As the representative of the entire nation, the President can, when he thinks it necessary, rise above partisan politics and claim authority to lead in the name of America, gathering to himself all the emotions aroused by appeals to patriotism. It is most difficult for any American to ignore a President who says that the national interest requires a certain policy. A member of Congress or a private citizen may not necessarily be convinced by the President's logic, but it is very likely that he will listen attentively and respectfully.

---

[7] P. viii.

Chief Diplomat

The Constitution makes the President the principal officer in foreign affairs, though in some respects he shares authority with Congress. The President alone receives ambassadors and thus "recognizes" foreign governments. With "the advice and consent of the Senate" he appoints American ambassadors and top-level State Department officials. Only the President or his agents can communicate officially with other governments in the name of the United States. Only the President or his agents can negotiate treaties or other international agreements, though to be binding a treaty must be approved by a two thirds vote of the Senate. In addition, to become fully effective some treaties need to be supplemented by legislation, such as an appropriation, that must be passed by both houses of Congress.

Court decisions interpreting the Constitution have increased the importance of the President's position in foreign affairs. The authority of the federal government in international politics, the Supreme Court[8] has ruled, is not limited to those powers specifically listed or implied in the Constitution. "The powers to declare and wage war, to conclude peace, to make treaties, to maintain diplomatic relations with other sovereignties, if they had never been mentioned in the Constitution, would have vested in the Federal government as necessary concomitants of nationality." Moreover, the Court[9] has said that the power of the national government to deal with foreign affairs is also plenary in the sense that it is not limited by the powers reserved to the states. As Edward S. Corwin[10] once remarked, this power is inherent in the federal government in the sense that it "owes its existence to the fact that the American people are a sovereign entity at international law."

What the Constitution has allowed, political reality has demanded. The rapidity with which crises develop in foreign relations and the magnitude of their consequences require, if the nation is to survive, that federal authority not be shared with the states and that, at least for those issues demanding quick decisions, authority be centralized. Given the awesome potential of the American military establishment and the persistent recurrence of international crises, it is inevitable that the White House be a place from which a President can influence the course of world politics. His words and actions are taken seriously in Moscow, Peking, Hanoi, and Havana no less than in London, Paris, Bonn, or Ottawa.

Chief Legislator

As discussed in the preceding chapters, it is so difficult for effective leadership to develop within Congress that Presidents have taken over the role of chief legislator. While four or five Presidents of this

---

[8] *United States v. Curtiss-Wright Export Corp.,* 299 U.S. 304, 318 (1936).

[9] *Missouri v. Holland,* 252 U.S. 416 (1920).

[10] Edward S. Corwin, *The President: Office and Powers,* 4th ed. (New York: New York University Press, 1957), p. 172. (Italics omitted.)

century have dramatized their legislative role, it is hardly a recent innovation. Thomas Jefferson was one of the most effective Presidents in this respect. Over the years success in leading Congress has been one of the principal standards by which the caliber of a President's administration is gauged.

A President may not be able or may not choose to give Congress such leadership. The alternative of Congress' doing nothing is always open. Presidential leadership usually means positive action, and many congressmen prefer not to act and many prefer to act in ways other than those advocated by the White House.

Commander-in-Chief

Article II of the Constitution confers on the President the title of commander-in-chief of the armed forces of the United States. Thus, while only Congress can declare war, the President is responsible for the way a war is fought. Indeed, he can act as Thomas Jefferson did against the pirates of Tripoli, as Abraham Lincoln in the opening months of the Civil War, Franklin Roosevelt in the early stages of World War II, Harry Truman in the Korean conflict, and Lyndon Johnson in the Vietnamese war, that is, commit American military and naval personnel to combat without a declaration of war. A President can gain—or lose—considerable influence in international politics by his astuteness as commander-in-chief.

The way a President plays this role can also have a significant impact on domestic politics. A decision to fight an undeclared war can materially change a President's popularity at home and so impair or enhance his ability to get measures through Congress or to carry out programs already approved by the legislature. Lesser decisions such as hiring and firing professional soldiers can affect a President's standing with Congress or the electorate, as Lincoln found out as he shuffled generals during the Civil War and Truman when he dismissed General Douglas MacArthur during the Korean conflict.

As commander-in-chief the President may make a very different kind of

President Johnson, assisted by Secretary of Defense Robert McNamara, briefs members of the House of Representatives on the Vietnam War. (Wide World Photos)

impact on domestic affairs. Section 4 of Article IV of the Constitution[11] directs the national government to protect each state "on application of the legislature, or the executive (when the legislature cannot be convened), against domestic violence." Congress has authorized the President to use federal forces, including the National Guard and the state militia, in discharging this obligation. It was this authority that Lyndon Johnson utilized in the summer of 1967 when, at the request of Governor George Romney, he sent troops into Detroit to help put down race riots. Congress[12] also has provided for the use of troops when the enforcement of laws of the United States by ordinary judicial proceedings is, in the President's judgment, impracticable. Congress lists as obstacles to judicial enforcement "unlawful obstructions, combinations, or assemblages of persons, or rebellion." It was this latter authorization that President Eisenhower used in 1957 to dispatch troops to Little Rock, Arkansas, and President Kennedy in 1962 to send troops into Mississippi to enforce federal court decisions ordering desegregation of educational facilities. Before he can employ the armed forces under either of these two provisions the President must issue a proclamation commanding the "insurgents to disperse and retire peaceably to their respective abodes."[13] The issuance of this proclamation does not establish martial law. The military does not replace civilian agencies but merely assists them to maintain their authority and normal operations.

The President's responsibility to "take care that the laws be faithfully executed" also carries with it the right to use federal troops when federal property or activities are endangered. In its most drastic form use of military power within the United States means establishment of martial law and replacement of civil law and civilian courts by military law enforced by military tribunals. In Chapter 21 we discuss the implications of martial law on civil liberties.

Head of the Executive Branch

The Constitution charges the President "to take care that the laws be faithfully executed." The burden of executing or administering laws is increased by the generality and vague phrasing of many statutes. Choosing a general rather than a specific phrase is often used by congressmen as a means of compromise. Unable to agree on how to settle some policy issues, legislators may opt for a broad but not very clear provision, leaving final resolution of the problem to administrators, to judges, or perhaps to a future legislative decision. Furthermore, because of the great complexity of many problems with which the federal government deals, congressmen frequently find it expedient to lay down only general principles and guidelines and leave it to administrative agencies to formulate more precise regulations. During the 1930s a majority of the Supreme Court held that there were close limits to valid congressional delegation. Congress could not delegate legislative power; it had to lay

---

[11] 10 U.S.C. § 332.
[12] 10 U.S.C. § 333.
[13] 10 U.S.C. § 334.

down standards to guide administrative discretion.[14] Recently the justices have taken a more liberal view of congressional power in this regard and have approved as constitutional congressional instructions to agencies to formulate regulations that are "fair and equitable," "just and reasonable," or "in the public interest."[15]

The task of translating laws from statute books to real life requires a large administrative staff. Reacting against the evils of a spoils system whereby even low-level federal jobs changed hands with every major shift in party fortunes, Congress has established a civil service system that attempts to put on a merit basis the recruitment, retention, and advancement of the overwhelming majority of government employees. A President, however, may still nominate, for whatever reason he considers sufficient, a large number of officials, mostly at the top ranks of executive agencies or at the level of ambassador or federal judge.

The quality of a President's appointments sets the tone of his administration. Able subordinates who are devoted to his service rather than to self-advancement can relieve him of many of the cares of office and release energies for matters worthy of his attention. Dishonest, careless, or stupid assistants can disgrace their chief and do great damage to their country. Officials who feel they owe their primary loyalty to persons other than the President may sabotage his most cherished programs.

The Constitution states that except where Congress provides otherwise— and it often has—presidential appointments are to be made "by and with the advice and consent of the Senate." While senators have usually given the President a relatively free hand in choosing such national officials as members of his Cabinet, ambassadors, and, to a lesser degree, Supreme Court justices, a different practice has grown up for more locally oriented appointments—postmasters and district judges, for example. Since George Washington's day it has been customary for the President to consult, before making a nomination, with the senators in whose state the official will serve, if they are members of his own party. If the President fails to consult them, the senators may ask their colleagues to vote against confirmation. And under "senatorial courtesy" they will usually comply, thereby defeating the nomination. If the senators do not belong to his party, the President—more commonly, one of his subordinates—usually consults state or local leaders before making an appointment.

The framers of the Constitution expected that the Senate would use the confirmation power to scrutinize the qualifications of the President's appointments, but actual practice has been quite different. For one thing, usually only about 1 percent of the nominations sent to the Senate during a year involve high civilian officials. Joseph P. Harris,[16] after a searching inquiry into the practice of senatorial confirmation, concluded:

---

[14] *Panama Refining Co. v. Ryan,* 293 U.S. 388 (1934); see also *Schechter v. United States,* 295 U.S. 495 (1935).

[15] See especially *American Power & Light Co. v. SEC,* 329 U.S. 90 (1946); and *United States v. Sharpnack,* 355 U.S. 286 (1958).

[16] *The Advice and Consent of the Senate* (Berkeley, Calif.: University of California Press, 1953), p. 397.

The principal effect of senatorial confirmation of appointments has not been to subject the President's nominees to careful scrutiny of their qualifications, as the framers of the Constitution intended, but has served rather (1) to perpetuate patronage appointments to many offices and positions which should be placed in the career service, and (2) to afford the opposition party and insurgents within the ranks of the President's party an opportunity to attack his administration by contesting his nominations.

Whatever its defects, the constitutional provision of senatorial confirmation is not likely to be changed.

OBSTACLES TO PRESIDENTIAL INFLUENCE

As noted earlier, the various roles the President may play provide him with opportunities to influence and persuade others. A President who wants to have his policies accepted and put into operation must persuade large segments of the voting public, a working majority of Congress, executive officials, and, often, many state officers. He must also consider judicial opinions, for in very different ways federal judges may also block attainment of presidential goals.

The President and Public Opinion

In dealing with other public officials Richard Neustadt has pointed out,[17] a President's professional reputation for having both "the skill and the will" to exploit his position is crucial. So too is the President's prestige—what other government officials think the general public thinks about the President. Voters can defeat the President or his party only at election time, but their opinions, at least what officials perceive to be their opinions, can ignite or extinguish enthusiasm in Washington or a state capital for a President's plans. Many legislators are as reluctant to support an unpopular President's program as they are to oppose the proposals of a popular Chief Executive. Administrative officers too are often sensitive to fluctuations in both congressional and popular opinion.

Antagonisms between the President and Congress

Congress presents a second major obstacle to achievement of a President's program. Many Presidents have started out to lead Congress but have found the way long and hard. Whether the President is a Democrat or a Republican, to all senators and representatives he is to some extent a dangerous rival. The complexity of modern problems has more and more required Congress to restrict itself to establishing general policy goals leaving to administrators the equally important task of formulating specific policies. The constant broadening of the scope of federal operations has made it more difficult for congressmen to understand, much less carefully control, more than a small

---

[17] Chaps. 4–5.

portion of executive action. Increasing American involvement in world affairs, with the growth of personal rather than institutional diplomacy and the frequent necessity for quick decisions based on secret information, have combined to weaken congressional power. And in almost every instance, as the power of Congress has eroded, that of the President has grown.

Legislators may be displeased by this accretion of executive authority, yet they often need the President's help in influencing other congressmen, in signing legislation, in making appointments, or in campaigning for reelection. So, too, the President may often be frustrated by congressional action—or, more often, inaction—yet his power is also limited, and he needs the assistance of members of Congress if he is to govern efficiently and legitimately. The relationship between Congress and the President is thus complex. There is inevitable friction and conflict, but there must also be agreement and cooperation if either is to accomplish policy goals. In such situations, of course, the most likely tactics are negotiation and compromise. At times a strong President may dominate Congress, the extreme case being that of Franklin D. Roosevelt in 1933. Such periods of domination, however, have been short. Even Roosevelt was soon forced to make his share of compromises and occasionally to submit to serious defeats in the legislative process. More often there is the give and take of bargaining, sometimes expressed, sometimes tacit, with the President getting slightly the better of the final compromise.

The reasons for presidential-congressional friction are manifold. First, some conflict is built into a system of shared powers. The purpose of this constitutional device is to check the power of one group of officials by the power of another group so that no one person or faction can obtain a monopoly of political authority.

Second, the President and the members of Congress are chosen by very different constituencies and this influences each in quite different directions. The President is chosen in a national election and must receive the support of 40 million or more voters to win his post. He thus naturally tends to think and act in terms of grand strategy of national policy. A senator or representative, on the other hand, is chosen by a single state or district and must necessarily be sensitive to the demands of more local constituencies. There is no institutional reason that compels him to have a national point of view. These contrasting influences are bound to result in argument and conflict.

Moreover, the President is often led to recommend a positive attack upon social problems, whereas congressmen frequently prefer to take a let-well-enough-alone attitude. The causes of this condition are varied. For example, a congressman's sensitivity to the diverse and conflicting interest groups of his district often leads him to try to preserve the status quo. Further, the President has superior access to information. He may be a conservative person, disinclined to approve vigorous or broad exercise of the power of government. But when his advisers and subordinates in the executive branch brief him concerning the facts of a social problem, the case for positive action by government often becomes compelling. Congressmen, on the other hand, usually do not have such direct access to data, and such data as reaches them secondhand may not seem so compelling.

The President and the Bureaucracy

Officials of administrative agencies may present a third set of obstacles to achievement of presidential goals. One might think that as Chief Executive the President would be able to command his subordinates in much the same way as a general commands an army. In practice, however, such is often not the case. "Bureaucracy," Dahl and Lindblom[18] have written, "more nearly resembles the arena of international politics than a group of disciplined subordinates responsible to the control of common superiors." Two points stand out: the size of the President's job and the pluralism of interests that may be reflected in the federal executive establishment.

The sheer size of the President's job, the heavy burden of work, and the limited amount of time available to cope with any single problem combine to complicate his relations with the bureaucracy. Only on the most pressing matters does a Chief Executive have more than an occasional opportunity to check closely on what has actually happened since he issued an order. Of necessity he must rely heavily on his subordinates to carry out his wishes; and these officials in turn must rely on their own subordinates to complete the tasks. "Like our governmental structure as a whole," Neustadt has observed, "the executive establishment consists of separated institutions sharing power. The President heads one of these; Cabinet officers, agency administrators, and military commanders head others. Below the departmental level, virtually independent bureau chiefs head others."[19]

Furthermore, since a President can inform himself personally of only a few problems, he is dependent on others to provide the information he needs to make decisions. Even when there is no conscious effort at deception or deviousness, this is no easy role to fulfill. A fact omitted from a briefing because a subordinate thought it unimportant, forgot about it, or was simply unaware of it can have a significant influence on the way a President views the alternatives open to him.

Adding to the President's burdens is the pluralism of interests that may exist within the bureaucracy. Career civil servants at the senior level have usually been working for many years in specialized fields and often feel that they, not their appointed or elected superiors who stay for only relatively short periods, really know what policies are best. Heel-dragging by these people can hamper execution of many policies. "Were the Presidents of the last fifty years to be polled on this question," Clinton Rossiter[20] claims, "all but one or two, I am sure, would agree that the 'natural obstinacy' of the average bureau chief or commissioner or colonel was second only to the 'ingrained suspicions' of the average congressman as a check on the President's ability to do either good or evil."

A similar situation may obtain where appointed officials are concerned. To gain nomination and win election a President may have had to promise certain appointments in exchange for support. These appointees may not necessarily

---

[18] Robert A. Dahl and Charles E. Lindblom, *Politics, Economics, and Welfare* (New York: Harper & Row, Publishers, 1953), p. 342.

[19] P. 39.

[20] *The American Presidency,* 2d ed. (New York: Harcourt, Brace & World, Inc., 1960), p. 59.

agree with him on policy matters, but as long as they retain their base of political support and conduct their opposition with circumspection a President may find it inexpedient to fire them. In addition, some appointees may feel that they owe their position not to the President but to some other person, perhaps a governor, senator, or member of the party's national committee, and give their loyalty to one of these men.

As discussed in Chapter 6 on the party system, an administrator may find that the White House is unable to protect him in dealing with Congress. In order to carry out his policy aims—which may or may not be those of the President— he must enter into an alliance with some legislators and perhaps also with certain interest group leaders. "The conditions which a system of fragmented power sets for the success and survival of a Cabinet officer," Richard F. Fenno, Jr.,[21] has observed, "encourage him to consolidate his own nexus of power and compel him to operate with a degree of independence from the President." This point is no less true of high level officials below Cabinet rank.

Ambition may also enter the picture. Charles G. Dawes, Budget Director under President Hoover and Vice President under President Coolidge, used to say that Cabinet members were a President's natural enemies. Dawes may have been exaggerating, but it has not been unknown for a Cabinet officer, or even a lesser-ranking official, to harbor hopes of seeing himself one day in the White House or on Capitol Hill. Such a man is apt to look on the President more as a dangerous rival than a revered commander-in-chief.

Judges and State Officials

The Constitution makes federal judges virtually independent of presidential control once they are nominated and confirmed, and many executive policies face major tests before the courts. There judges may be asked to pass on the constitutionality of legislation or executive orders or to interpret a statute to determine whether Congress in fact has authorized a particular course of action.

State officials may also check presidential policies. Chapter 6 stressed the federal nature of American political parties and pointed out that state and local officials can help shape the reactions of senators, legislators, and even administrators to presidential proposals. Conversely, again in part because of the federal nature of the party structure, the success of many supposedly national programs depends on the cooperation of state and local officials.

INSTRUMENTS OF PERSUASION

Despite these interlocking checks, a President is still in a position of immense influence—provided he has the desire, energy, and ability to exploit his opportunities for persuasion. He has at his command a

---

[21] "President-Cabinet Relations: A Pattern and a Case Study," *American Political Science Review,* 52 (June 1958), p. 404. (Italics omitted.)

number of instruments, not the least of which are the availability of evidence to support his arguments and the use of reason in convincing others. In addition, he has the respect and prestige of his office, unequaled access to the mass media, and certain specific constitutional grants such as the appointing power. He also possesses personal charm and skill in human relations. None of these instruments is likely to be effective alone, but if several of them are combined expertly they may yield some measure of success.

To a certain extent a President may be hampered by the Twenty-second Amendment, which stipulates that a President may not serve for more than two full terms.[22] In his second term and especially in his last year, rival candidates for the nomination may attract considerable political support to themselves and away from the incumbent. But, by using his instruments of persuasion to control his party's choice of a candidate, a President may still retain much of his power during this bowing-out period.

Molding Public Opinion

We have seen that the President has unrivaled capacity to mold public opinion. The mass media are at his disposal: For important speeches he may preempt prime television and radio time, newspapers carry his remarks on their front pages, magazines publish feature articles on him and his family. His press conferences allow him to engage in give-and-take discussions with news analysts from all over the country. By displaying confidence, knowledge, wit, and mental agility, an adroit President may do much at these conferences to build up a highly favorable public image that will affect not only newspaper readers the next day but also the stories that reporters will write for months to come. President Kennedy made full use of his quick wit by having his press conferences televised.

Since a President finds it difficult to escape publicity, he must be wary of overexposure. Everything he or his family does is newsworthy; the trivial as well as the important events are faithfully reported. Whether he tries to take a long walk, golf, sail, drive at breakneck speed around the countryside, or hold a Beagle puppy by the ears, the very next day a President is likely to see a picture of himself in action.

Influencing Congress

To induce members of Congress to cooperate or at least compromise a President has a number of instruments. First is his party organization. He may invoke party loyalty in an effort to rally support on Capitol Hill. While party loyalty may be a sometime thing for most senior legislators, it can tug on their self-interest as well as their emotions. Even if their

---

[22] The amendment allows a person who succeeds to the Presidency and serves for not more than two years to run twice for election on his own; if such a person serves an unexpired term of more than two years he can run only once. Thus a President may serve not more than ten years in the White House.

own reelection is certain, if their party does not win the Presidency again, the congressmen's ability to influence appointments may vanish. If their party does not retain control of Congress, their leadership positions and committee chairmanships will go to men from the other party.

Still, the weak, decentralized structure of both major parties cannot be depended upon to bridge by itself the gap between the executive and legislative branches. Far more often than not, only by means of bipartisan majorities is the President able to get measures through Congress. Piecing these majorities together is delicate work. On almost every issue the President is likely to be opposed by some members of his own party who are in genuine disagreement with him on substantive grounds and to whom considerations of party loyalty are not sufficiently strong to outweigh their distaste for the President's position. Contrariwise, some members of the opposition party may agree with the President on substantive grounds, but will nonetheless vote against him because the opportunity to embarrass him politically is too strong to be resisted. And yet, if the President is to secure the legislation he wants, he must persuade some members of one or the other of these groups to abandon their inclination to vote against him. Often it is the opposition congressman, rather than the member of the President's own party, who decides to go along with the White House.

The Constitution explicitly provides three instruments of presidential persuasion: the message power, the veto power, and some measure of control over sessions of Congress.

Article II specifies that the President shall "give to the Congress information

President John F. Kennedy delivers a State of the Union Message before a joint session of Congress. In his State of the Union speech, customarily given at the beginning of each legislative session, the President outlines the problems confronting the nation and recommends legislative solutions. (Cornell Capa from Magnum)

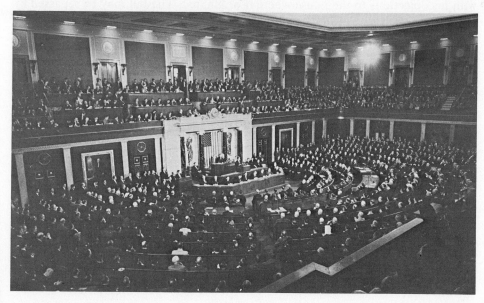

of the state of the Union," and "recommend to their consideration such measures as he shall judge necessary and expedient." In practice there has been considerable variation in the exercise of this power by different Presidents. All Presidents have used the opening of each regular session of Congress as the occasion for a State of the Union message, but there the uniformity ends. Woodrow Wilson revived the practice of delivering this message in person before a joint session of the two houses, although since Thomas Jefferson the practice had been to send the message in writing to be read by clerks. In their annual message some Presidents have chosen to present numerous specific requests for legislative action. Others have chosen to make the State of the Union message a general speech addressed as much to the people as to Congress, following it up with a series of special messages making recommendations on specific measures. Recent Presidents have increasingly adhered to this practice.

A presidential message to Congress is almost always intended to bring about the enactment of some piece of legislation. But the Constitution also gives the President a powerful weapon to prevent the enactment of a law that meets with his disapproval. This is the veto power. Here, too, the Constitution is specific in its provisions: Every bill, order, resolution, or vote to which the concurrence of the Senate and the House of Representatives may be necessary (except a question of adjournment) shall be presented to the President of the United States for his approval or disapproval. Although the language of the Constitution seems to permit only the exception just noted to the requirement, others have been added. Concurrent resolutions need not be submitted to the President, and the same is true of proposed constitutional amendments.[23]

Under the Constitution the President has four choices when he receives a bill. The first and most obvious is to sign it, in which case the bill becomes law. If the President disapproves the bill, he may return it without his signature and with his objections to the house where it originated. The bill may be repassed by each house with a two-thirds majority, whereupon it becomes law without the President's approval; otherwise the veto holds and the bill dies. Or the President may let a bill remain on his desk ten days without either signing it or returning it to Congress; in this case it becomes law without his signature. Presidents have not often done this. The fourth possibility is a variation of the third: if during the ten-day period that the President holds a bill without signing it Congress ends its session and adjourns, the bill automatically dies instead of becoming law. This is the so-called pocket veto. It is the most effective veto from the President's point of view, for adjournment of Congress eliminates any possibility of his veto's being overridden. Since Congress, like many state legislatures, tends to pass a great many bills during the closing days of a session, a President is apt to have extensive opportunity to use the pocket veto.

The veto has had a long, varied, and controversial history. Early Presidents made very sparing use of the veto power, and until the time of the Civil War most vetoes were justified on the ground of a bill's doubtful constitutionality. In fact,

---

[23] See *Hollingsworth v. Virginia,* 3 Dallas 378 (1798).

it was even contended by some that this was the only reason for which a President should exercise the power. Since the Civil War, however, Presidents have based their objection to a bill far more often on its lack of wisdom or expediency. Eight Presidents vetoed no bills at all during their terms of office. Two Presidents, Grover Cleveland and Franklin Roosevelt, account for over half of all vetoes since George Washington. Each man vetoed more than five hundred bills; indeed, Roosevelt wished to exercise this power to the fullest possible extent and instructed his staff to take special care to search out bills he could veto.

Relatively few bills are ever repassed over the President's veto. The Constitution makes reconsideration mandatory, but this requirement is fulfilled by mere reference of the bill back to the standing committee that reported it to the house in which it originated. In the first 100 years of the American republic there were 451 vetoes, 29 of which were overridden. But of these 29 over half occurred in Andrew Johnson's administration.[24] During the twelve years of his Presidency Franklin Roosevelt vetoed 631 bills, only 9 of which were overridden. Harry Truman fared less well than his predecessor, since 12 of his 251 vetoes were overridden. During his two terms in office Dwight D. Eisenhower used the pocket veto 107 times and his regular veto power on 74 occasions. Only two of the latter were overridden. During his time in the White House President Kennedy vetoed only 21 bills; and Johnson used the veto power even more sparingly, largely reserving it for private rather than public bills. No serious efforts were made to override any of Kennedy's vetoes or through the end of the first session of the Ninetieth Congress any of Johnson's.

The President does not possess an item veto power, as do the governors of some American states. Accordingly, he must accept or reject a bill in its entirety. Any sweeping grant of an item veto power would require a constitutional amendment, although it seems permissible for Congress to write into each appropriation bill a clause authorizing the President to suspend items from operation if he wishes. But Congress has shown little inclination to give the President any such discretionary power. Presidents, however, have occasionally exercised this kind of power simply by declining to spend money on projects authorized by Congress.

The veto power is of far greater importance than the mechanics of its operation indicate. Its use by modern Presidents has led Congressmen to have great respect for the veto. The mere threat of its exercise frequently influences congressional action during the stages when legislation is being formulated. In other words, the veto power has come to have a positive as well as a negative significance. By judiciously reminding Congress of the possibility that he may use it, a President is frequently able to persuade Congress to shape the language of a bill to his liking. This is precisely the strategy that President Roosevelt followed in asking his staff to find bills for him to veto.

A third and less important constitutional grant allows the President a measure of control over the sessions of Congress. The Constitution provides for an

---

[24] Many of these data are taken from Katherine A. Towle, "The Presidential Veto since 1889," *American Political Science Review,* 31 (February 1937), p. 51, and George C. Robinson, "The Veto Record of Franklin D. Roosevelt," *American Political Science Review,* 36 (February 1942), p. 75.

automatic beginning of the annual sessions of Congress in January. But the President alone has power to call Congress in special session. In the past some of the most notable sessions of Congress have been special ones. For example, the hundred-day session in 1933 was a special session called by President Roosevelt immediately after he took office. Under the Twentieth Amendment, which was ratified in 1933, Congress now meets in regular session in January of every year and seldom adjourns before August 1. Often, its sessions run well beyond that date. Thus the interval between regular sessions rarely exceeds five months, and the need for special sessions has been greatly lessened.

The Constitution provides that the two houses of Congress must agree before either house can adjourn or recess for more than three days, and then adds the provision that, in case of the inability of the two houses to so agree, the President may order an adjournment of Congress, "to such time as he shall think proper." There is not a single instance of the use of this power. It seems likely that the political repercussions that might well follow will continue to dissuade Presidents from exercising it in any but a grave emergency.

To lead Congress a President must also utilize less formal methods of persuasion. He must learn to be a consummate manipulator of men, alternately friendly and firm, now shrewd and calculating, now open and frank, by turns the suppliant and the bully, the flatterer and the threatener. He has a wide field on which to practice such talents. Because of the way power is divided in Congress, he must deal with majority and minority leaders and committee chairmen, as well as with influential members of the rank and file; he must weld them into an effective team when possible, play them off against each other when necessary, and somehow persuade them that his program is good for the country, good for their constituents, and therefore good for themselves.

Modern Presidents have all gone out of their way to woo congressmen through friendly gestures and sociability. President Coolidge invited Republican congressmen to the White House for breakfast; President Roosevelt entertained Democratic congressmen at clambakes on an island in Chesapeake Bay; President Truman now and then appeared suddenly at the Capitol and modestly asked to eat lunch with some of his old colleagues; President Eisenhower offered lunch at the White House to Republicans and Democrats alike. President Kennedy often extended the hospitality of a formal White House dinner with vintage wine, French cuisine, and music from the Marine band. President Johnson uses the telephone to keep in touch with members of Congress at all hours of the day—and night. His entertaining is more folksy than that of his two immediate predecessors. The most coveted invitation is to the President's Texas ranch for huge outdoor barbecues.

It is doubtful that these gestures have often paid off in bills passed or not passed by Congress. But no President can afford to ignore the friendly gesture as part of his program to lead Congress. There are so many occasions when he must play the role of the stern taskmaster that he must seize every opportunity to persuade congressmen that he is a decent human being, not a harsh tyrant.

The President may also use public opinion to influence congressmen. By utilizing his access to the mass media of communications, he can do more than increase his own popularity or his party's chances at the next election. More immediately—if he does not try this tactic too often or too crassly—he can cause constituents to put heavy pressure on members of Congress.

Sometimes the President can trade measures with members of Congress. A promise of support for a congressman's pet bill, or a threat of presidential opposition to it, may produce support for the President's own program. Frequently the President must bargain with congressmen about the details of his own measures. One of the chief purposes of the regular consultations between the President and congressional leaders is to determine whether the lines can be held fast for the President on one of his proposals or whether compromise, and if so, how much, is in order.

Perhaps the most famous of the President's informal powers for use in influencing Congress is distribution of patronage. Use of the appointing power by the President to win favor with members of Congress dates back to George Washington. This does not mean that Presidents have often indulged in a crude business of purchasing votes in Congress for legislation by offering to make appointments according to the wishes of congressmen. A President is likely to use the patronage power more subtly as a means of cultivating friendly relations with members of Congress, thereby encouraging sympathetic consideration of executive proposals. This kind of approach was illustrated in the special session of Congress in 1933 at which many of the most important of Roosevelt's New Deal measures were passed. The administration let it be understood that the patronage would not be distributed until after the session had come to a close. In this way congressmen eager to control certain appointments were compelled to give favorable consideration to the President's legislative requests.

In recent decades the development of the merit system has lessened the value of patronage as a means of influencing Congress, as has the fact that long years of prosperity have eased much constituent pressure on legislators for government jobs. The large turnover in government personnel that used to mark the beginning of a new administration has now been greatly reduced. The Eisenhower Administration had so little patronage to distribute in 1953 that it experienced difficulty in meeting congressional requests for favors that were exceedingly modest by past standards. Still, there are certain types of federal offices—district judgeships, for example—that become vacant from time to time and which are then filled in such a way as to curry favor with congressmen in the states in which these federal officers serve.

Presidents have also come to realize that patronage is a two-edged sword. For one thing, an appointment that pleases one congressman may irritate other legislators as well as disappointed candidates. Second, by trading patronage for congressional votes a President may be weakening his control over administration, since the appointees may feel a stronger loyalty to members of Congress than to the Chief Executive. President Taft summed up these problems in his lament that every time he made an appointment he created nine enemies and one ingrate.

A promise of presidential support at the next election campaign can be an effective instrument of persuasion. In extreme circumstances the President may threaten political reprisals against uncooperative congressmen. But he must think twice before he takes this step, for the institutional arrangement is not entirely in his favor. He cannot threaten to dissolve Congress or to call a new election. Even though a regular election may be impending, if his quarrel is with members of his own party he cannot very well ask for the election of members of the opposite party. To secure the defeat of his own party colleagues he must go into state primaries and conventions and try to persuade party voters to replace these men with new men who will be more loyal to him. President Roosevelt discovered to his sorrow in 1938 that this is not easily done.

Directing the Bureaucracy

Viewed from the White House, the loose organization of almost 3 million employees in the various federal agencies may make the bureaucracy appear to be a massive jungle. But if it is a jungle, it is one that can be controlled if not conquered. As in all aspects of his work, one of the most useful instruments a President has is himself—his reputation for knowing what to do and how much can be done and his willingness to put his whole energy into the task. Professional respect may not win over all doubters, but it does greatly increase the likelihood that they will listen attentively.

A President can try to keep his patronage promises to a minimum so he retains as much control as possible over his appointments. While he may not in this way be able to eliminate all problems in dealing with Cabinet officers and agency heads—after all he does not want assistants who have no strong views of their own—a President can reduce his difficulties if he chooses men of ability who think as he does on basic policy issues and who know that they owe their positions to him.

A President may also take advantage of his appointing power to build a personal staff of old acquaintances who owe deep allegiance to him. Both Kennedy and Johnson brought to the White House a group of aides who had worked with them for years in the Senate. Although Congress has now allowed the President a considerably larger White House staff than in past decades, a President might still prefer that one or more of his most trusted advisers not hold any public office at all.

A President may use these advisers to give him insights that professional politicians might lack, as Kennedy used Arthur M. Schlesinger, Jr.; to act as a personal emissary, as Roosevelt used Harry Hopkins; to screen him from unpleasant details, as Eisenhower used Sherman Adams; or to coordinate the work of several departments and agencies, as Kennedy and Johnson used McGeorge Bundy. Even in his relations with his personal staff of advisers, a President has to be wary, not merely in choosing but also in retaining them. As Neustadt[25] points out, "Any aide who demonstrates to others that he has the President's

---

25 P. 42.

consistent confidence and a consistent part in presidential business will acquire so much business on his own account that he becomes in some sense independent of his chief."

A President may also employ his authority as Chief Executive to assign to various people or agencies in whom he has great trust special missions that may appear to be outside their normal jurisdiction. In addition, he may use this same authority to construct several overlapping networks of responsibility and information. This tactic may make for disorderly organization charts, but it also provides the President with access to different sources of information and at the same time establishes several lines of competition in executing programs. If one fails, the other may succeed, and in any case the existence of competition may spur each on to do a better job. Franklin Roosevelt delighted in this tactic. "His favorite technique," Arthur M. Schlesinger, Jr.,[26] has written,

was to keep grants of authority incomplete, jurisdictions uncertain, charters overlapping. The result of this competitive theory of administration was often confusion and exasperation on the operating level; but no other method could so reliably insure that in a large bureaucracy filled with ambitious men eager for power the decisions, and the power to make them, would remain with the President.

Persuading Judges and State Officials

In dealing with state officials a President can use almost the same instruments and tactics that he employs with Congress —reason, prestige, publicity, personal charm, promises of campaign support, patronage, and old-fashioned bargaining. In contrast, a President has as little chance of charming judges into agreement as he does of overawing them with his prestige or with promises of patronage. Of course, since federal judges do not stand for election, campaign support is of no value to them. Reasoned argument, usually presented by the solicitor general and members of his staff from the Department of Justice, is the instrument most often used in dealing with judges. But a President's appointing power can also be important, both in selecting men to run the solicitor general's office and choosing, insofar as he can, judges whose basic views tend to coincide with his own.

In addition, if courts hand down a decision or series of decisions that threaten his policy objectives, the President may deploy his instruments of persuasion against Congress to obtain some counteraction—perhaps a constitutional amendment, a more clearly worded statute, a change in the kind of cases the courts can hear, or an increase in the number of judges. As a last resort a President may refuse to enforce a court decision, as Lincoln declined to do during the Civil War when Chief Justice Roger B. Taney ordered a southern sympathizer released from a military prison.[27]

---

[26] *The Age of Roosevelt,* Vol. 2, *The Coming of the New Deal* (Boston: Houghton Mifflin Company, 1959), p. 523.

[27] *Ex parte Merryman,* 17 Fed. Cases 144 (1861).

It should also be kept in mind that in influencing public opinion in general a President may also influence judges, not in the crude sense of courts following election returns but in the deeper sense of creating a climate of opinion in which all citizens must live. "The great tides and currents," Justice Cardozo[28] once said, "which engulf the rest of men do not turn aside in their course and pass the judges by."

STATESMANSHIP AND POLITICS

This chapter has stressed the political nature of the Presidency. Emphasis on the necessity of manipulation and maneuvering does not in any way question the necessity of a President's having, or being receptive to, creative policy ideas that have great substantive merit. Rather, the point is that many other government officials, officials who have power to check the President, also have firm policy views of whose worth they are sincerely convinced. Faced with these conditions and armed with only a limited authority to command, a President must persuade, negotiate, even bargain and manipulate, if he wants to achieve a positive program.

Knowing what policies to pursue requires the vision of a statesman; putting those policies into actual operation requires the talents of a masterful politician. A successful President needs not only strength of character and a thorough understanding of the long-run needs of the nation but also professional political skills, personal charm, a feel for shifting winds of public opinion, and a delicate sense of timing. He must be able to distinguish among what is worth fighting for to the bitter end, what is worth compromising on, and what is worth only capitulation. He must know when to move and when to wait, when to argue and when to agree, when to stand firm and when to compromise, when to reason and when to bargain, when to cajole and when to command. Without a doubt, such paragons are rare. The amazing thing is how often they have made their way through the labyrinthine paths of American politics to the White House.

Selected Bibliography

Binkley, Wilfred E., *President and Congress,* 3d ed. (New York: Random House, Inc., 1962). An historical account of presidential-congressional relations.

Blum, John M., *The Republican Roosevelt* (Cambridge, Mass.: Harvard University Press, 1954). A sparkling study of Theodore Roosevelt as President.

Donovan, Robert J., *Eisenhower: The Inside Story* (New York: Harper & Row, Publishers, 1956). An examination of the operation of the Eisenhower Administration during its first few months in office.

Evans, Rowland, and Robert Novak, *Lyndon B. Johnson: The Exercise of Power* (New York: The New American Library, 1966). A critical analysis of Johnson the politician and President by two veteran reporters.

Fenno, Richard, *The President's Cabinet* (Cambridge, Mass.: Harvard University Press, 1959).

---

[28] Benjamin N. Cardozo, *The Nature of the Judicial Process* (New Haven, Conn.: Yale University Press, 1921), p. 168.

A thorough study of the cabinet and an explanation of why it cannot be an effective governing device for presidential purposes.

Koenig, Louis W., *The Invisible Presidency* (New York: Holt, Rinehart and Winston, Inc., 1960.) Interesting portraits of persons who have wielded "behind-the-scenes" power in the White House, including Hamilton, Van Buren, Loeb, House, Cocoran, Hopkins, and Adams.

Laski, Harold, *The American Presidency* (New York: Harper & Row, Publishers, 1940). A provocative account of the Presidency, with a strong argument for an expansion of presidential power.

Neustadt, Richard E., *Presidential Power: The Politics of Leadership* (New York: John Wiley & Sons, Inc., 1960). An impressive, path-breaking study that deals not with the Presidency as an institution, nor with its legal and constitutional position, nor with the politics of winning nomination and election, but rather with the President's problem of obtaining power for himself while holding office. Told in terms of three case illustrations.

Schlesinger, Arthur M., Jr., *The Age of Roosevelt,* a 3-volume history of the years preceding and during F.D.R.'s administrations: Vol. 1: *The Crisis of the Old Order;* Vol. 2: *The Coming of the New Deal;* Vol. 3: *The Politics of Upheaval* (Boston: Houghton Mifflin Company, 1957, 1959, 1960). A distinguished history, colorful and brilliant, illuminating an exciting era of ideas, events, and personalities.

————, *A Thousand Days* (Boston: Houghton Mifflin Company, 1965). A controversial but lively insider's analysis of Kennedy's Presidency.

Sherwood, Robert, *Roosevelt and Hopkins* (New York: Harper & Row, Publishers, 1948). An extraordinarily rich biographical study of the Roosevelt Administration.

Sorensen, Theodore C., *Kennedy* (New York: Harper & Row, Publishers, 1965). A well-written and thoroughly detailed account of Kennedy as a senator and President, written by his former Special Counsel.

Tugwell, Rexford G., *The Democratic Roosevelt* (New York: Doubleday & Company, Inc., 1957). A reliable and interesting account of President Roosevelt by one of his early advisers.

15

The presidential establishment

President Kennedy[1] once wrote:

The American Presidency is a formidable, exposed, and somewhat mysterious institution. It is formidable because it represents the point of ultimate decision in the American political system. It is exposed because decision cannot take place in a vacuum: the Presidency is the center of the play of pressure, interest, and idea in the nation; and the presidential office is the vortex into which all the elements of national decision are irresistibly drawn. And it is mysterious because the essence of ultimate decision remains impenetrable to the observer —often, indeed, to the decider himself.

It is a truism today that the President is the focal point of the American political system. In its institutional sense the Presidency embraces hundreds of persons, but it is the President himself and his capacity for leadership more than any other individual or institution that determines the shape, tempo, and character of American governmental action. Because the President's influence on American

[1] Foreword to Theodore C. Sorensen, *Decision-Making in the White House* (New York: Columbia University Press, 1963), p. xi.

politics and on public policy can scarcely be exaggerated today, the Presidency is preeminently a place for men of politics who can readily become experts in the mobilization and use of political power. In his drive to reach a high level of expertness in the search for political power the President may be helped, if he wishes to be helped, by the apparatus of the executive office and especially by close personal aides. But he cannot share presidential power with subordinates except at the price of undermining that power. The rapid development of the presidential establishment since 1939 has not reduced the significance and impact of the President as a person. Paradoxically it has only cast in sharper relief the strategic importance of personalized presidential power.

A great President, President Kennedy's Special Counsel Theodore Sorensen[2] has said, is "not the product of his staff but the master of his house."

THE PRESIDENT NEEDS HELP

The Presidency is, among other things, a delicate balance between the delegation of authority and the maintenance of authority, between the sharing of burdens and the holding of burdens. Today the executive branch of the federal government is a vast organization with staggering managerial problems. It comprises about 3 million civilian workers and 3 million members of the armed forces. The annual civilian payroll and the cost of military personnel each runs over $15 billion. Every year over $40 billion worth of goods are bought. Annual payments in pensions and grants to individuals approach $40 billion per year. There are twelve departments headed by secretaries of Cabinet rank, about fifty agencies and commissions, many special advisory commissions, and a vast number of interdepartmental committees. This is the organization that the President "heads" and that he is expected to "run."

The President obviously must have a great deal of help if he is to keep control of the significant activities of this mammoth structure. The heads of departments traditionally were the President's principal aides, individually and as members of his Cabinet. But with the growth of the departments and the increased scope and complexity of their activities, the management of departmental affairs has become a full-time job and, of course, the preoccupation of departmental heads. More than 1600 people now work in the executive office of the President, including 300 senior assistants and clerical workers in the White House office, but excluding the staff of the Office of Economic Opportunity.

Before examining each of these "presidential help" agencies, a brief statement about the origin of the Executive Office of the President is warranted. Not long after he assumed office, Franklin Roosevelt appointed a group to study the problem of how the Presidency might be more efficiently organized from the standpoint of the administration of the federal government. The 1937 *Report of the President's Committee on Administrative Management* has become one of the landmarks in the evolution of the presidential office. Its theme was *the President*

---

[2] P. 87.

President Johnson discusses the annual budget with several White House aides. (UPI)

needs help. And it recommended, among other things, the appointment of six administrative assistants to work directly with the President, and the establishment of the Executive Office of the President, with separate offices for personnel management, budgeting and finance, and planning. In 1939 the Executive Office was established. To it was transferred immediately the Bureau of the Budget, which had been a part of the Treasury Department since its creation by the Budget and Accounting Act of 1921. Subsequently were added the Council of Economic Advisers, created by the Employment Act of 1946; the National Security Council, established by the National Security Act of 1947; the Office of Emergency Planning, created initially as part of the Executive Office in 1950 and called the Office of Defense Mobilization, and changed in 1958 to the Office of Civil and Defense Mobilization; the National Aeronautics and Space Council, established by the National Aeronautics and Space Act of 1958; the Office of Science and Technology, created by President Kennedy's Reorganization Plan No. 2 of 1962; the Office of Special Representative for Trade Negotiations, and several presidential commissions.

The White House staff is a recent development. Before William McKinley's administration, Presidents had "personal" or "private" secretaries to help with correspondence, but these were not recognized as "officials" of the government. This arrangement was consistent with the principle that all "official" matters were referred to appropriate departments for action and that the correspondence of the President was "personal."

Abraham Lincoln handled White House problems with the help of two or three correspondence clerks. Grover Cleveland answered his own telephone and wrote most of his papers in longhand. President Taft thought it remarkable that the volume of business in his day required the assistance of twenty-five clerks and stenographers. From McKinley's administration until the close of Herbert Hoover's term, one man, Ira Smith, was able to take care of all the mail that came to the White House. Calvin Coolidge used to sit on the corner of Smith's desk while Smith opened the envelopes and passed him his letters. Before Smith retired in 1948, after fifty-one years of service, he had a staff of fifty clerks to help him with the mail. For twelve years under Franklin Roosevelt, an average of 5000 letters was delivered to the White House each day, and as many as 175,000 letters on a single day. Over 4000 letters now come to the White House each week.

The recent increase in the number of presidential assistants is equally dramatic and of greater significance. In 1915 Woodrow Wilson was operating the White House with the help of three immediate aides. Herbert Hoover had a personal staff of five, the same number that worked with Theodore Roosevelt in 1907. Under Franklin Roosevelt, the number of administrative assistants varied from six to fourteen. In 1952 the White House staff included fifteen personal assistants to President Truman, and it increased rapidly under President Eisenhower. In 1953 he had twenty-four senior assistants, and forty-six to fifty during the period 1958–1960. The number declined under Presidents Kennedy and Johnson but still remains substantial.

Under President Eisenhower, "the Assistant to the President," a position which under Mr. Truman had been simply that of a very senior assistant, became to all intents and purposes the "Assistant President." President Eisenhower's own preferences were clearly in the direction of delegating large responsibilities to an aide in whom he had complete confidence. But a major factor was undoubtedly the combination of special qualities that Sherman Adams brought to the job. Adams possessed in unusual degree the quality that is most essential for effective service as a presidential aide—consuming loyalty to the President and self-sacrificial devotion to his service. The position was not revived by Presidents Kennedy or Johnson.

Several senior assistants normally work on problems concerned with the general operation of the Presidency. The press secretary long ago became one of the most influential members of every White House entourage. The appointments secretary is likely to see the President very frequently. It is his

Tom Little. © 1958 by the New York Times Company.
Reprinted by permission.

job to select from the dozens of daily requests for appointments the few whom it is desirable for the President to see. Other assistants may be assigned to economic affairs, national security problems, patronage questions, presidential speech-writing, congressional liaison, and other areas.

Presidents usually have felt the need for intimate association with men outside the immediate circle of official aides. This practice goes back at least as far as Andrew Jackson's famous "kitchen cabinet"—a group of personal friends whom he consulted and relied upon more heavily than he did the members of his Cabinet. Abraham Lincoln found such a group invaluable. Woodrow Wilson called upon Colonel House to carry out missions that he considered too vital to entrust to government officials. And during Franklin Roosevelt's administration, especially during the war years, Harry Hopkins exercised enormous influence as the President's personal and confidential assistant. Although a few of President Truman's intimates were poorly equipped for this service, their indiscretions did not destroy a President's need for personal advisers. No one clearly emerged as President Eisenhower's Colonel House or Harry Hopkins, perhaps because of his development and use of the White House staff. President Kennedy relied heavily on his official White House staff, while President Johnson appeared to count on advice and counsel from congressional leaders and old-time political associates.

Among recent Presidents, only President Eisenhower might be described as an antipolitician. He achieved national support as a great war hero and father-figure, but he often was unable to utilize this support to achieve political or public objectives. In his attempt to place the Presidency "above politics," Eisenhower put heavy emphasis on tidy administrative arrangements and careful staff work, and relied on assistants for information, ideas, analyses, and insights. The staff system, as developed by Eisenhower, gave him the help he wanted and made the President's tasks, as he perceived them, more manageable. But in the process "he became typically the last man in his office to know tangible details and the last to come to grips with acts of choice."[3]

President Eisenhower found it very difficult to work except through orderly procedures carefully laid down in advance. Most of the biographical evidence suggests that considerations of personal advantage played little, if any, role in the President's conduct. Given the irrelevancy of military experience for White House occupants, Eisenhower's insensitivity to political factors and forces is explainable. To paraphrase Neustadt, Eisenhower sought national unity, not personal power; he disliked the political process and partisan politics; his role was to reconcile differences among Americans and among nations. As an "antipolitician," he preferred to moderate rather than to initiate proposals.

From the moment he assumed office President Kennedy gave every indication of loving his job. Reporters repeatedly described him as a constant source of fresh ideas and energy, as the focus of attention in American politics, and as a center of action. Kennedy maintained and even expanded an enormous command of information on a wide range of matters and issues. Impatient with large staff meetings and regularly scheduled Cabinet sessions, he preferred direct exposure to the free flow of argument. He resisted summaries and synopses of reports and memoranda and readily absorbed details.

---

[3] Richard E. Neustadt, *Presidential Power* (New York: John Wiley and Sons, Inc., 1960), p. 159.

The Kennedy White House staff reflected directly the habits, talents, and preferences of its chief. While President Eisenhower functioned more like a chairman of the board, waiting for the staff and advisers to resolve policy controversies and bring to him for ratification decisions commanding wide agreement, President Kennedy restlessly tackled problems personally, seeking out information, reading half a dozen newspapers thoroughly every day. Presidential assistants had no carefully staked out areas of concern or operation, although they may have tended to concentrate in one area rather than another. They obviously worked *with* the President and never *instead of* him in disposing of White House business.

A political reporter[4] has commented:

President Kennedy and his staff have brought a new style and tempo to the White House. Under the Eisenhower concept, teamwork was conducted much in the manner of a football game—frequent huddles, great attention to co-ordinating everybody, and interminable periods between plays. The Kennedy concept seems to be more along the lines of basketball. Everybody is on the move all the time. Nobody has a very clearly defined position. The President may throw the ball in any direction and he expects it to be kept bouncing.

President Kennedy's White House office was not very tidy. As one Washington observer stated, coordination was a minor pastime, and failures of coordination may have had disastrous consequences, as the crushing defeat at the Bay of Pigs in 1961 illustrated. The President actively fought against the diffusion of leadership through layers of committees, and he often cut across normal administrative channels to keep informed about developments or to communicate ideas to others.

A leader by temperament, President Johnson had worked closely with Presidents and statesmen for twenty-five years before he assumed the Presidency on the death of President Kennedy on November 22, 1963. During the Eisenhower years Johnson had acquired a reputation for political genius in his astute management of the Democratic majority in the Senate. Probably none of the other seven Vice Presidents who succeeded to the Presidency upon the death of Presidents was as thoroughly prepared for the highest office. Starting as a country schoolteacher in the Texas hills, he had been known for cyclonic energy, a zest for crisis reminiscent of the Roosevelts, and an iron will in facing up to tough decisions. Whereas President Kennedy tended to be dashing and even electric in style, Johnson was flamboyant and emotional, yet acutely sensitive to the "art of the possible" in domestic politics. Like Franklin Roosevelt, he displayed, until he deeply committed himself to massive military involvement in Vietnam, a highly developed sense of the limitations of political power. He began office with a belief in a strong Presidency, an immense reserve of congressional good will, and a respected capacity for designing accommodations needed to reach majority agreement. A man of many moods, he was often described as a bundle of paradoxes, easy to caricature but impossible to paint. His decision not to run in 1968 was just one more unexpected piece in an incomplete jigsaw puzzle.

With the crucial exception of Vietnam, criticism was directed more at John-

---

[4] Douglass Cater, *The Reporter*, March 16, 1961, pp. 28–29.

son's style and operating methods than his policies. As one journalist[5] summarized the complaints heard in Washington:

> The President drives people too hard, is too high-handed and arrogant, doesn't really want argument and independent points of view . . . he is too preoccupied with his popular image, is too sensitive to criticism, spends too much of his time answering attacks he should ignore . . . he tends to whine over his troubles and blame others for his mistakes . . . when things go truly wrong, he frequently turns nasty.

Whatever validity there may have been in such criticism, it is clear that Johnson lacked the warmth of Eisenhower and the wit and grace of John F. Kennedy. He was rather the clever, hard-driving, purposeful and somewhat ornery Texan.

While President Johnson typically worked his staff very hard, he tended to rely heavily on department and agency heads. He permitted no one to interpose himself as an Assistant President between himself and his Cabinet secretaries. In working with his immediate staff he alone set the schedule and determined the priorities. As a top aide[6] concluded:

> By this avoidance of commitments, by the avoidance of fixed routines of government, a President is able better to keep on top of a job that, if he submits himself to routines, can quickly become so burdensome, so time consuming, that he himself can never apply any new initiatives to the job.

The President's Cabinet

Although the Constitution does not specifically provide for a Cabinet, the Founding Fathers clearly contemplated that the President would look to the heads of departments for advice and counsel. Washington established the tradition of meeting with these officials as a group, thus creating the Cabinet. But it is not a cabinet in the sense in which that term is used in a parliamentary system such as Britain's.

The members of the President's Cabinet do not share with him a constitutional, collective responsibility for policies and decisions on major policy questions. A President is not even bound to consult them. For example, during the Civil War Lincoln met infrequently with the Cabinet, apparently did not insist that members make a point of being present, and did not always attend himself. Theodore Roosevelt and Woodrow Wilson both regarded their Cabinet members as administrators rather than as a group of policy advisers concerned with the broad strategy of affairs. Wilson did not read his war message to the Cabinet because he did not want to subject its language to review and discussion. Although at first Franklin Roosevelt apparently thought of using his Cabinet more systematically, in the later years the meetings did not amount to much. To Secretary of War Stimson,[7] for example, they "were useful principally as a way of getting

[5] Alan L. Otten, *The Wall Street Journal,* July 6, 1965, p. 16.

[6] Douglass Cater, quoted in Tom Wicker, "Lyndon Johnson Is 10 Feet Tall," *New York Times Magazine,* May 23, 1965, p. 91.

[7] Henry L. Stimson and McGeorge Bundy, *On Active Service* (New York: Harper & Row, Publishers, 1947), p. 561. Also, Harold L. Ickes, *The Secret Diary of Harold L. Ickes* (New York: Simon & Schuster, Inc., 1953).

into the White House to have a word with the President in private after the meetings were over. . . ."

President Truman tried to make the weekly Cabinet meetings more useful by having the agenda distributed in advance and a record made of the points agreed to after discussion.

President Eisenhower extended these innovations by establishing a "Cabinet secretariat." Members who wished to have the Cabinet discuss a problem submitted the item to the Cabinet secretary for inclusion in the agenda. Before scheduling it, the secretary or his assistant generally discussed the proposed item with several interested officials in various departments and attempted to screen out minor problems. If the matter was to be discussed, a memorandum was prepared analyzing the problems, including relevant information, the most practicable alternatives, and perhaps a recommendation. The secretariat might rehearse the Cabinet member so that his presentation would be as succinct as possible. Prior to the Friday meetings of the Cabinet the secretary went over the agenda with the President. After the meeting the secretariat met with "special assistants for cabinet co-ordination" in each department to see that the decision was carried out.

President Kennedy openly minimized the importance of Cabinet meetings. The practice of calling Cabinet members together at the Cabinet table was declared "unnecessary and a waste of time." President Johnson falls somewhere between the Eisenhower and Kennedy positions; Cabinet meetings under him became more frequent and members were expected to offer the President advice on matters falling outside their respective departmental jurisdictions.

The role of the Cabinet is determined by usage rather than by constitutional specification. Each President makes of it what he wishes. His own working methods determine the procedures of the Cabinet and, within the scope permitted by the Constitution, its contribution as a unifying and creative force in the affairs of the executive branch. The critical fact is, of course, that it is the President, not the Cabinet, who bears the responsibility and must make the crucial decisions.

A President weighs many factors in selecting Cabinet members. He must consider groups and individuals whose support contributed significantly to his election. If his party is badly split, or if there is a national crisis, he may wish to appoint one or two representatives of an opposing faction or party. Lincoln selected two of his rivals for Cabinet membership, and Franklin Roosevelt brought into his war Cabinet two prominent Republicans, Henry L. Stimson and Frank Knox, to head the War and Navy departments to solidify the nation. Since the President must work closely with members of his Cabinet, the question of compatibility is important. Woodrow Wilson sought, in general, men who shared his ideas and philosophy. The result was an able and congenial group with relatively little political prestige or influence. A President is not compelled to choose party leaders or men who are widely known and respected for their competence or for their views on public affairs. It is not traditional, either, to appoint as head of a department a man who is an expert in the activities for which he will be responsible.

Bureau of the Budget

Next to the White House staff the Bureau of the Budget is the most important of the agencies whose primary mission is to help the President manage the executive branch. It did not acquire its present significance until it was transferred in 1939 from the Treasury Department to the executive office of the President. In terms of employees, this development is indicated by an increase from 40 in 1939 to over 500 today. The Bureau is headed by the Director of the Budget, who is appointed by the President without Senate confirmation.

The Bureau of the Budget has three main jobs. Its primary activity is the formulation and execution of the federal budget, which today is accepted as a major responsibility of the Chief Executive. Before the passage of the Budget and Accounting Act of 1921, departments and agencies presented estimates of their financial requirements directly to Congress. There was no general budget for the executive branch until an employee of the House Appropriations Committee assembled the separate budgets submitted by the several departments. Under this system even the most experienced legislators had difficulty in determining the relative needs of competing departments.

The President was under an even greater handicap. He could not supervise and control departments that received directly from Congress money to carry on activities he thought should not be undertaken at all. He lacked the most useful of managerial tools, fiscal control. Yet under the Constitution he was held responsible for the operations of all of the executive establishment.

The Budget and Accounting Act requires all executive agencies to submit budget estimates to the President and authorizes the Bureau of the Budget, on behalf of the President, "to assemble, correlate, revise, reduce, or increase the estimates." Thus the Act gives the President the authority he needs to control expenditures of the executive branch, and it provides a group of specialists to help him use this authority intelligently. By reducing or eliminating funds requested to carry out programs that the President does not support, the Bureau helps to keep departmental activities within bounds set by the President. Congress can, of course, override these decisions.

Another major task of the Bureau of the Budget is to help improve the organization and management of the executive branch, which it does in two ways. First, the Bureau provides technical assistance in preparing plans for the reorganization of executive agencies. This phase of its work is especially important when the President is given authority by Congress to carry out extensive structural changes.

Second, the Bureau assists executive departments and agencies to improve their internal organization and operating procedures. The executive establishment is so vast that it cannot be directed and controlled solely from the executive office of the President. Long-run improvements in organization and operations depend in large part upon the ability of each agency to search out and correct its weaknesses. The staff of the Bureau of the Budget is useful in making departments sensitive to opportunities for improvement and in informing all agencies of the best methods in use throughout the government.

A third activity of the Bureau of the Budget is to help the President control legislative requests made by executive departments and agencies. With information provided by the Bureau of the Budget, the President is able to tell legislative leaders whether a particular bill has his support, whether he is indifferent, or whether it is contrary to his program. In the process of compiling information, the Bureau's staff points out conflicts in proposals from different departments and in other ways prevents competing or ill-advised proposals from being submitted to Congress as "administration bills." Congressmen find it useful to know that legislative proposals dealing with a single subject but emanating from different departments have at least been considered side by side and that an effort has been made to examine them from an over-all point of view.

The Bureau also keeps the President informed about bills pending in Congress and those that have been passed. The Bureau's staff surveys interested departments and agencies to find out how they would be affected by a bill that has been passed and on which the President must act. If the consensus is against the bill, the President is informed and probably provided with a draft of a veto message. The President, of course, consults legislative leaders as well as executive officials. If the advice of the legislators conflicts with that of the executive departments, he finds it easier to make up his own mind because of the background of information assembled by the Bureau of the Budget.

The Council of Economic Advisers

The Employment Act of 1946 requires the President to send an economic report to Congress soon after the opening of each regular session and created the Council of Economic Advisers to help him prepare it. The President's economic report describes the economic state of the nation, discusses trends in employment and production, and appraises federal economic programs. It also recommends actions necessary to maintain the objectives stated in the act—maximum employment, production, and purchasing power. The Council is composed of three members appointed by the President, by and with the advice and consent of the Senate. Apparently it is succeeding in giving the President and Congress useful information and advice about the nation's economic welfare.

During its early years the Council met with President Truman from time to time and with the President and Cabinet at a regular meeting held four times a year. In the first years of the Eisenhower Administration the chairman of the Council met weekly with the President or his principal assistants and, as required, with the Cabinet. These weekly meetings were given up following the President's heart attack. Moreover, with the appointment of a new chairman of the Council, the President relied more and more on his special assistant for economic affairs. Under President Kennedy the Council became more active, and under President

Johnson its influence in developing the Administration's economic policies increased substantially. In recent years the chairman of the Council has served as one of the President's closests advisers and his mentor in economic matters.

The National Security Organization

Radical changes in the character of war and diplomacy have required a major reorganization of the Presidency insofar as national security is concerned. The *Secretary of Defense* is the President's principal assistant in matters involving the armed services. Although the departments of Army, Navy, and Air Force are each headed by a secretary, these officials are not members of the President's Cabinet. Under the National Security Act of 1947 they are subject to general supervision by the Secretary of Defense. The primary objective of Congress in establishing the Department of Defense in 1947 was to strengthen unified, civilian direction of the three services without, however, merging them into a single service. While many steps were taken from 1947 to 1960 to coordinate defense activities, it was not until Robert McNamara became Secretary of Defense in 1961 that central control in the Secretary's office began to realize the promise of the 1947 reorganization. Under McNamara the office has been a strong and controversial one.

In the overlapping area of foreign and military policies the President has the guidance of the *National Security Council.* Next to the grouping of the separate armed services under a single secretary, the establishment of the NSC was perhaps the outstanding feature of the National Security Act of 1947. The President is chairman of the Council; the other statutory members are the Vice President, the secretaries of State and of Defense, and the director of the Office of Emergency Planning. The President may, with the Senate's approval, appoint others to the Council.

The Council is charged by Congress to "advise the President with respect to the integration of domestic, foreign, and military policies relating to national security" and to "assess and appraise the objectives, commitments, and risks of the United States in relation to our actual and potential military power, in the interest of national security." Its unique task is to bring together all significant military and political factors in planning for national security. It cannot do this without the services of persons trained and widely experienced in the complexities of political-military strategy. These services are provided by a staff drawn from the Policy Planning Committee of the State Department, the Central Intelligence Agency, the Office of Emergency Planning, and the Army, the Navy, and the Air Force.

The military departments are responsible for mobilizing the fighting strength of the nation. The *Office of Emergency Planning,* one of the units of the executive office of the President, has the task of planning the mobilization of civilian resources for national security. Its principal concern is how the industrial and economic resources of the nation can be used to meet the total needs of the armed forces and the civilian economy for manpower and equipment. Its director is the

President's principal civilian adviser on mobilization matters and serves on the National Security Council.

When Congress enacted the National Aeronautics and Space Act of 1958 it created a *National Aeronautics and Space Council,* headed by the Vice President, to advise and assist the President on space programs, policies, and plans. The Council was empowered to fix the responsibilities of government agencies engaged in aeronautical and space activities. Its other members are the secretaries of State and Defense, the administrator of the National Aeronautics and Space Administration, and the chairman of the Atomic Energy Commission.

The *Office of Science and Technology* was established in June 1962 under a presidential reorganization plan with congressional approval. The plan provides a small permanent staff to advise and assist the President in coordinating federal policies to promote basic research and education in the sciences and to evaluate scientific research programs undertaken by federal agencies. Since 1965, these latter activities have cost around $15 to $16 billion annually.

ROLE OF THE VICE PRESIDENT

The search for ways of easing the President's burdens inevitably turns to a consideration of the role of the Vice President. In the American political system the office generally has not attracted able and vigorous men who could render substantial service as a member of the President's working team. Until recently a candidate for the Vice Presidency was selected not for his ability to serve the President or for his promise as a possible successor to the Presidency, but to reward an "elder statesman," to placate or weaken a party faction, or to sidetrack a rival candidate. Second, the Constitution makes the Vice President the presiding officers of the Senate. If this is not in itself a full-time job, it at least makes it difficult for the Vice President to accept any other fixed and taxing responsibilities. From time to time Presidents have attempted to utilize the services of VicePresidents, but with uneven success. Franklin Roosevelt used John N. Garner's talents in the early New Deal days to help get his legislative program through Congress; and he gave Henry Wallace important administrative duties in World War II. President Truman, by statutory authority, appointed Alben Barkley a member of the National Security Council. After President Eisenhower's illness in September 1955, many ceremonial activities were assigned to Vice President Richard Nixon. In the absence of the President, he presided over meetings of the Cabinet and the National Security Council, but he was not given any important executive responsibility. The vacuum caused by the President's temporary inability was not filled by the Vice President but by the White House staff and key Cabinet officers.

The Constitution does not give the Vice President the position or powers of an Assistant President. Heads of departments and other top officials expect presidential decisions, not the advice and direction of the Vice President. A President normally prefers to have as his chief subordinate a man of his own choosing with whom he works easily and whom he can discard if he is so minded.

The Vice President can and should take over a great many more of the President's ceremonial duties—meeting foreign dignitaries at the National Airport and Union Station; attending public dinners; making good will trips here and abroad; receiving groups at the White House; and so on. But unless there is a radical change in the constitutional position of the Vice President, this office is not likely to ease greatly the most wearing presidential burden: the responsibility for executive leadership and decisions on the most vital questions affecting the nation.

The considerations that led President Nixon to select Spiro Agnew as his running mate in 1968 may never be completely revealed. It is a reasonable conclusion, however, that the qualities the President perceived in Agnew as a possible successor in the event of his own disability or death did not play as significant a role as in Johnson's choice of Humphrey in 1964 or Kennedy's choice of Johnson in 1960. Like most of his predecessors, President Nixon announced immediately after his election that he planned a large and important role for the Vice President. Still, it is not likely that Agnew, any more than previous Vice Presidents, will be allowed to develop a national political following of his own.

PRESIDENTIAL INABILITY

An emergency arises in the Presidency when a President dies in office or is incapacitated by illness. In order to maintain political stability there must be an accepted and orderly procedure for transferring power when it is necessary to replace the Chief Executive. A state that does not have such a procedure invites political crises, struggles for power, and even revolution.

The United States Constitution, in Article II, section 1, states that the Vice President shall succeed to the Presidency upon the removal, death, resignation, or inability of the President to discharge his duties and authorizes Congress to provide by law for the succession in the event that the Vice President is unable to carry on the office. Two questions arise under these provisions: Who determines whether the President is unable to discharge his duties? Who succeeds the Vice President in the event that both the President and the Vice President die, resign, or are removed?

Two cases have arisen in which Presidents have been incapacitated for extended periods. President Garfield was unable to discharge the duties of his office for several weeks after he was shot, and President Wilson was disabled for several months following a cerebral hemorrhage in September 1919. On both these occasions there were extended discussions about the steps that should be taken. It was variously suggested that the Vice President decide whether the President was able to work, that it be decided jointly by the Vice President and Congress, and that it be decided by Congress alone. In each case, what happened was that the President's family and intimate associates determined he was able to carry on his duties, even though the evidence indicated that he was disabled.

The determination of when a President is in fact unable to serve remains a critical question today. In 1958, President Eisenhower and Vice President Richard M. Nixon made a private agreement about the assumption of the President's duties by the Vice President should the President become incapacitated. In August 1961, President Kennedy and Vice President Lyndon B. Johnson made a similar agreement, as did President Johnson and Vice President Humphrey in 1965. It provided that the Vice President shall serve as acting President if the President asks him to do so or if it is otherwise clear that the President cannot function. The decision as to his inability is left to the President himself. Thus there was still no provision for action in a case where the President is not fitted to serve but is unwilling to relinquish the powers and duties of his office.

The further possibility that a President and key officials might be obliterated in a sudden and devastating attack on Washington has not received the consideration it deserves, but the law at least is clear. The Speaker of the House of Representatives acts as President upon the death, removal, or resignation of both the President and the Vice President. Next in the line of succession are the President *pro tempore* of the Senate and the Cabinet members. A Cabinet member may serve only until a Speaker of the House or a President *pro tempore* of the Senate is available and qualified to supersede him. This line of succession raised further doubts when immediately following the assassination of President Kennedy it was rumored that Vice President Johnson was dead also. This left the Presidency to an elderly Speaker and an even more elderly President *pro tempore*.

Twenty-fifth Amendment

In 1965, Congress approved a proposed constitutional amendment spelling out a specific procedure that permits the Vice President to become acting President if the President is disabled and providing for filling a vacancy in the office of Vice President. By 1967, thirty-eight state legislatures had ratified the proposal, which became the Twenty-fifth Amendment to the Constitution. Under the amendment the President is to inform the Speaker and the President *pro tempore* of the Senate that he is unable to perform the duties of the Presidency; in that event the Vice President would serve as acting President until the President sends a written declaration to the contrary to the Speaker and the Senate leader.

Under the amendment the Vice President is authorized to assume the office of acting President whenever he and a majority of the Cabinet—or a majority of another body to be prescribed by Congress—declare the President to be disabled. Under these circumstances the President could resume power upon declaring his disability ended, unless the Vice President and a majority of the Cabinet disagreed and informed Congress of their disagreement within four days. If this happened, Congress would decide the issue. If, within twenty-one days, Congress decided that the President was unable to resume his duties, the Vice President would continue as acting President. Otherwise the President would resume his office. The new amendment also provides that a vacancy in the office of Vice President may be filled by a person nominated by the President and confirmed by a majority vote of both houses of Congress.

Presidential Transitions

For the great body of American voters the inaugural ceremony at noon on January 20 every four years signifies the orderly transfer of constitutional authority from the outgoing President to the President-elect. In fact, the ritual of oath-taking on inauguration masks a complex and uncertain process through which the President and the President-elect have prepared for the transfer of political power.

This transfer involves two broad requirements. The first is the continuity of presidential leadership in national and international affairs and the stability of administrative performance by the machinery of government. Because of the enormous increase in the significance of the international position of the United States and the strategic role played by government decisions and actions in the economic life of the country, the instabilities of a presidential transition generate powerful pressures that threaten the continuity of responsible leadership and expert management. The second requirement concerns the responsiveness of the government to new political leadership. In addition to continuity in presidential leadership and administrative performance, it is equally important that the incoming President be given a fair chance to bring about changes in policies reflecting his objectives.

From 1933 to 1952 unbroken control of the White House by the Democrats reduced the problems of transferring presidential power. But in more recent years the old, improvised ways of ushering in a new administration, ready to govern, have been increasingly regarded as inadequate and impractical.

The first modern President to consult with his successor shortly after election day was Herbert Hoover. Generally, both Presidents Franklin D. Roosevelt and Harry S. Truman, while running for reelection, permitted their subordinates to maintain informal confidential communication with rival presidential candidates. The first organized attempt to achieve an orderly transfer of presidential power came in 1952 when President Truman arranged, during the election campaign, to keep the candidates informed about critical matters facing the nation. Truman should also be credited with establishing the precedent that the outgoing President must accept responsibility for facilitating the transfer of power to his successor, a precedent that both Presidents Eisenhower and Johnson followed. Eisenhower and Johnson also continued the practice of giving intelligence briefings to rival party candidates in 1956, 1960, 1964, and 1968.

Outgoing Presidents tend to be more concerned about an orderly presidential transition than are Presidents-elect. In the future, as the experience of President John F. Kennedy suggests, incoming Presidents may make arrangements for temporary staff headquarters for the period of two and one half months between election day and their inauguration. Some of the urgent matters that require staff attention as early as possible are preparation of the presidential messages that are expected of a new administration; consultations with leading congressmen and senators looking toward a timetable of legislative action; and the filling of Cabinet and other key posts. In 1964, President Johnson followed President Kennedy's practice of charting with the help of task forces the political course of action that the President may take in critical areas of public policy.

MANAGING PRESIDENTIAL BURDENS

Delegation of Presidential Duties

The American Presidency has been remarkably flexible and adaptable. Created in a period of distrust of executive power and subjected to a system of checks and balances, it approaches a constitutional dictatorship when national security requires extraordinary governmental action. When the crises are over, it reverts to a normal power relationship with Congress. The Presidency is above all things a center of activity. As Alexander Hamilton wrote in *The Federalist,* "Energy in the Executive is a leading character in the definition of good government." How can the needed energy be provided?

The energy of Presidents could be more usefully employed, it is often said, if routine duties could be delegated to others. Many of the President's ceremonial functions as chief of state might be taken over by the Vice President. The possibilities of shifting other duties may be just about exhausted. In a series of cases extending back more than a hundred years, the Supreme Court has approved the delegation of presidential powers to others, excepting only those that the Constitution specifically vests in him. For the most part, these constitutional obligations are mechanical and not too taxing. Congress, too, has done its part. A law enacted in 1950 allows the President to delegate to any executive official whose appointment is confirmed by the Senate any duty that Congress has vested in the President, *if* the President retains responsibility for his subordinate's actions and the delegation is not expressly prohibited by law. All Presidents have subsequently availed themselves of this authority and delegated hundreds of their duties.

The provision of staff assistants is another principal approach to the problem of making the Presidency manageable and endurable. The "staff system" is neither new nor experimental. Military and other big organizations could not possibly function without versions of the staff concept, and it was introduced into the Presidency by establishment of the executive office of the President in 1939.

A President's staff can help him in several ways. It can screen the matters coming to the White House, so that trivial matters, or important matters that can be handled by other officials, do not get on the President's desk. The staff can do the preliminary investigation and analysis of problems that should have the President's attention. It can see that the President's decisions are actually carried out. And the staff can plan ahead—anticipate problems that have not yet emerged, get the proper officials thinking about them, formulate actions that may prevent their arising. This service can make the difference between a President who is master of his job and one who, like Coolidge, simply keeps his desk clear.

At the same time, the staff can weaken rather than strengthen the President if it attempts to make decisions that he should make himself. It is always tempting for men close to great power to act as though they are in fact the holders of the power. A little of this is human and tolerable; but the "palace guard" mentality is not. The question of what should go to the President is undoubtedly one of the most perplexing questions the staff has. The answer probably has to be worked out by experience, depending upon the time, circumstances, and the working habits and desires of each President.

The most effective staff system cannot reduce the volume of work the President has to do. It is axiomatic in administration that the more assistants an executive has, and the higher their quality, the more work they will make for him. The staff, however, can change the type of activity that absorbs his time. A good staff can manage his office so that his energy is released for matters of first importance and brought to bear upon them at the most propitious time. But the staff itself requires a considerable amount of the President's attention. He must keep himself informed of its activities, check the quality of its work, and in general see that it is doing what he wants it to do.

The Presidential Perspective

Discussions of the presidential establishment often run the risk of suggesting that the process by which the President makes decisions can be systematized or that certain staffing arrangements and organizational schemes will improve the quality of presidential judgments. Such suggestions are misguided and misleading. How-to-do-it guides to improved executive management—so common in business management literature today—are wholly inappropriate to presidential management because of the breadth and scope of presidential decisions. No corporation executive begins to match the President in terms of multiple responsibilities and the complex issues requiring decisions. No other executive in public or private life anywhere in the world must resolve so many issues fraught with conflict—with Congress, between departments and expert advisers, with other nations, and with interest groups.

Cabinets may be useful to some degree to a President seeking advice, but the President can never lose sight of the fact that each department has its own interests, its own relations with Congress and powerful interest groups, and its own clientele. Inevitably the secretaries as political leaders of their departments reflect some degree of bureaucratic parochialism in their advice to the President. White House staff advisers, on the other hand, may see problems in a wider context than a Cabinet secretary, but their contact with Congress, interest groups, and actual operations is less. Their views are apt to be less parochial than a secretary's but they may also be less sensitive to the immediate political and administrative setting of the problem under analysis.

Even if the Presidency is stripped of its routine duties and the Office is provided with the best staff assistance, the President's job necessarily remains enormously burdensome. For he cannot delegate to others the duties that make the greatest demands upon human wisdom and energy.

The President cannot escape the necessity of political leadership. He must lead his political party constructively in the service of truly national needs. Nor can he escape the necessity of formulating imaginative solutions for the most pressing public problems and of taking an active role in getting these solutions enacted into law. Above all, he cannot pass to others the incredibly perplexing task of leading this nation and her allies steadily and cooperatively forward to a reasonably stable world order.

As presidential and other memoirs make abundantly clear, the presidential perspective is necessarily immodest. No one else approaches the President in the gravity of the decisions he must personally make. Sorensen[8] has written:

A President knows that his name will be the label for a whole era. Text books yet unwritten and school-children yet unborn will hold him responsible for all that happens. His program, his power, his prestige, his place in history, perhaps his re-election, will all be affected by key decisions. His appointees, however distinguished they may be in their own rights, will rise or fall as he rises or falls. Even his White House aides, who see him constantly, cannot fully perceive his personal stakes and isolation. And no amount of tinkering with the presidential machinery, or establishment of executive offices, can give anyone else *his* perspective.

No other position in American public or private life can in itself be held to qualify a candidate for the post of Chief Executive. Richard Neustadt[9] reminds us that Justice Holmes once characterized Franklin D. Roosevelt as a "second-rate intellect but a first-rate temperament." "Perhaps," Neustadt adds, "this is a necessary combination. The politics of well-established government has rarely been attractive to and rarely has dealt kindly with the men whom intellectuals regard as first-rate intellects." The persistent mystery of American politics is the nature of the temperament that develops expertness in presidential power.

Perhaps the President's tasks would be simplified if the major political parties developed distinctive ideologies that commanded the loyalty and devotion of those who voted for their candidates. But there is very little evidence that parties will be soon transformed into truly national parties replacing the varied sectional clusters of voters that constitute the cores of the major parties today. The party of the President is not likely to become one with the congressional unit of his party, even though the party labels are the same. In this setting the President who hopes to achieve his goals must become a supreme bargainer in a political system that diffuses responsibility and authority and fragmentizes political power.

Selected Bibliography

Corwin, Edward S., *The President: Office and Powers,* 4th ed. (New York: New York University Press, 1957). The authorative study of the presidency from a constitutional and legal perspective.

Fenno, Richard, *The President's Cabinet* (Cambridge, Mass.: Harvard University Press, 1959). The most thorough account of the Cabinet as an institution, pointing up its weaknesses as a policy-making body.

---

[8] Sorensen, pp. 83–84.
[9] Neustadt, p. 182.

Jackson, Henry M., *The National Security Council: Jackson Subcommittee Papers on Policy-making at the Presidential Level* (New York: Frederick A. Praeger, Inc., 1965). A valuable set of essays that describe and evaluate the National Security Council and discuss the general problems of presidential policy-making on foreign and defense questions.

Koenig, Louis W., *The Chief Executive* (New York: Harcourt, Brace & World, Inc., 1964). The best general introduction to the Presidency, discussing all the major aspects of the office, although the absence of notes reduces the usefulness of the book.

Polsby, Nelson, and Aaron Wildavsky, *Presidential Elections: Strategies of American Electoral Politics* (New York: Charles Scribner's Sons, 1964). The best analysis of the selection process for the Presidency, including nominating, campaigning, and election procedures.

Schlesinger, Arthur M., Jr., *A Thousand Days: John F. Kennedy in the White House* (Boston: Houghton Mifflin Company, 1965). An historical account of the Kennedy administration by one of the participants.

Sorensen, Theodore C., *Kennedy* (New York: Harper & Row, Publishers, 1965). A general account, dealing with President Kennedy's entire political career, but emphasizing the organization and procedures used during his years in the White House.

Williams, Irving, *The Rise of the Vice-Presidency* (Washington, D.C.: Public Affairs Press, 1956). Still the best account of the office, although seriously outdated by important developments in the decade since its publication.

16

The executive
branch at work

THE ADMINISTRATIVE PROCESS

A democratic government earns its daily bread by doing the things its people want and expect to have done. If a citizen works for someone or if he runs a business or a farm, he wants a prosperous economy and he expects the government to *do* something if times get hard. He also expects the government to deliver letters promptly and below the cost of service; to provide reasonably adequate payments to the aged, to the unemployed, and to widows and their families. He expects foreign and military policies that will give maximum security against war and ensure victory if war comes.

If things that people want are done, they do not get done simply by Congress's enacting laws or by the President's issuing orders—by such abstractions as the "legislature" and the "executive." They are the accomplishments of thousands of government employees in many different places, working together to stimulate economic growth, develop highways and transit facilities, and overcome urban decay, among other things. The concerted activity of these groups is the "administrative process," or, more simply, "administration."

When a federal department or agency administers a program it is the *government* that acts, not simply a particular agency or the executive branch. Administration involves a wide range of concerns. What does the law allow or require a citizen to do? How has the agency interpreted the law in similar cases? Have the courts rendered any decisions that should be considered? What have congressional committees said about the matter? Have the representatives and senators whose constituents are affected expressed any views? Would it be prudent or essential to consult certain interest groups? a political party leader? Is there a political factor of interest to the President? Is there another executive agency concerned with the problem or contemplating action under a different law? Does the problem concern a state or local government? What action would most nearly satisfy the interest of all government—federal, state, and local—and be fairest to the private citizens involved? Congress, the courts, political parties, interest groups, state and local governments, and individual citizens—all are involved in administration. In this sense, administration is intermingled with the whole process of government.

Policy-making and Administration

Any governmental activity involves policy-making decisions about what is to be done and administration-taking actions to carry out the decisions. These elements may at first seem distinct, but on closer scrutiny they appear to merge. Are policy and administration distinct and separable or are they simply different aspects of the intricate processes of governing? It is Congress *alone* that formulates policy, and the executive *alone* that administers policy? It is the Cabinet secretary who decides and the career civil servants who execute decisions?

Broadly speaking, there are two views. One is that policy-making and administration are different processes and that each process should be the responsibility of a distinct group. Thus under the separation of powers the characteristic function of Congress is the formulation of policy; the characteristic function of the executive is the administration of policy. The other view, and the one adopted here, is that policy and administration are so intermingled that those who exercise the powers of government inevitably make *and* execute policy. For example, in carrying out its role of policy-maker, Congress intervenes in a host of ways in administrative matters.

When Congress decides that a new activity should be undertaken it also determines how the activity is to be administered. A new agency may be created, or an existing agency may be given a new task. Congress also determines how the new law is to be enforced. Through its power of the purse it controls the expenditure of funds by government agencies and directly influences the organizational structure, operating methods, and work load of these agencies. Congressional committees advise and influence administrative officials on policy matters that arise in day-to-day administration. This practice is so pervasive that some observers have concluded that in terms of actual supervision, executive departments and agencies receive more guidance from Congress and its committees than they receive from the President.

The President is the most strategic policy maker in the government. His policy role is paramount in military and foreign affairs. As head of the executive branch, he gives general direction to the work of administrative agencies. As we have said in Chapter 14, limitations of time and energy mean that some agencies receive little presidential attention. But the President does attend personally to many departmental and agency questions affecting broad national interests. In some instances the President makes the decisions himself after consultations with administrative officials; in other cases, he approves decisions made by subordinates.

Judges are also concerned with policy and administration. Although only a small proportion of administrative decisions are reviewed by the courts, these decisions often concern matters of broad policy and are a major factor in the subsequent activity of an agency. The courts may also review the procedures used by administrative agencies when it is alleged that statutory or constitutional requirements have not been followed.

Finally, the people responsible for administering governmental activities make policy decisions in the course of their work. These decisions have varying significance. If the question concerns an entire department, or several departments, the decision may be made by the highest department officials or by the President or one of the White House staff. If the question is limited to a small unit within a department, the decision is normally made by the persons accountable for the unit's work. Matters of intermediate significance are handled within the organization by officials with the knowledge and judgment that their disposition requires.

Political Influence in Administration

Political influence in administration is inevitable, for two reasons. First, the vital character of the work of administrative agencies invites political pressure. When personal interest is intense, it is natural to reinforce arguments for favorable treatment with whatever political influence can be mustered. Second, political influence is inevitable because administrators are influenced indirectly by the electorate. The President is the political leader elected by the people, and he is also head of the executive establishment. Members of Congress are popularly elected and exercise, as a legislative body and as individuals, enormous influence in administrative agencies. The heads of departments and agencies are usually appointed by the President with the approval of the Senate. Whether politicians or not, they must be acutely aware of political factors that are important to the President or to the members of Congress to whom they look for support. If for no other reason than to keep in the good graces of powerful congressional committees, administrators frequently seek the advice of congressmen on questions relating to the work of their agencies. The gradual extension of the civil service to the higher positions in the executive branch has reduced, but not eliminated, points of political pressure.

In the process of acquiring information a member of a congressional committee may express views about matters for which executive officials are responsible and by this means try to get administrators to do as the congressman thinks

Washington: Johnson's Administrative Monstrosity

By James Reston

WASHINGTON, Nov. 22 —As President Johnson starts his fourth year in the White House, one fact is not only clear but undisputed: his Administration is poorly organized to administer the domestic programs he has introduced, and the administrative chaos of the state and local governments is even worse.

The reasons for this are fairly clear. The Administration has put through more social and economic programs in the last two years than it can absorb. The 89th Congress alone passed 21 new health programs, seventeen new educational programs, fifteen new economic development programs, twelve new programs for the cities, seventeen new resource development programs, and four new manpower training programs.

Help! Help!

These programs are administered by such a variety of different Federal agencies that, as Senator Robert Kennedy of New York remarked here this week, it is almost impossible for small town officials to know what money is available for what purposes or even where to go for information.

Senator Edmund S. Muskie of Maine, who is exploring this thicket, recently observed that Federal aid expenditures to the states and municipalities have risen from $1 billion in 1946 to $15 billion this year and are expected to go up to $60 billion by 1975. There are now, he noted, 170 different Federal aid programs on the books, financed by over 400 separate appropriations, and administered by 21 Federal departments and agencies aided by 150 Washington bureaus and over 400 regional offices empowered to receive applications and disburse funds.

This has created something almost unheard of here. Criticism of the system, cries of growing domination by the Federal Government, complaints about administration confusion and waste are now coming not alone from the Administration's critics or from observers in the state capitals but from leading officials of the Johnson Administration itself.

The Local Mess

"In almost every domestic program," Secretary of Health, Education and Welfare John W. Gardner told the Muskie committee, "we are encountering crises of organization. Coordination among Federal agencies leaves much to be desired. Communication between the various levels of Government —Federal, state and local— is casual and ineffective. State and local government is in most areas seriously inadequate."

Washington obviously cannot solve this problem by itself. There are now over 80,000 separate local governments in the United States, few of them large enough in population, area, or taxable resources to get adequate personnel or funds to apply modern methods in solving present and future problems.

Overlapping layers of local government, ineffective popular control, weak policy-making mechanisms, antiquated administrative machinery and underpaid and undertrained personnel—all these are keeping the state and local governments from forming an effective partnership with the Federal Government, which now provides 20 per cent of the total annual revenues of the states.

Yet it is probably unrealistic for Secretary Gardner to call on "the American people" to correct these deficiencies. The remedy must begin in Washington. The interdepartmental committee system, designed to coordinate the activities of the various departments and agencies in the poverty program—to take just one example—has not worked.

"We have a President who is keenly interested in the problem," Secretary Gardner told the Muskie committee. But we also have a President who is poorly organized himself, reluctant to delegate power over these home-front activities to the Vice President or anybody else, and suspicious of political institutions of any kind.

The One-Man Band

He did not work easily with the Democratic caucus when he was in the Senate. He has not made an effective instrument out of the Cabinet or the National Security Council. He all but wrecked the Democratic National Committee after he got into the White House, and he is still trying to run the Presidency as if it were a Senator's office on Capitol Hill.

The problems, however, are monumental. They are getting bigger and more complicated all the time, and while the President talks about creating a new partnership with the states and municipalities and expounds on what he calls "creative federalism," the fact is that he has not created the machinery to carry this out. He has an administrative monstrosity on his hands, and even his own people are beginning to criticize it in public.

they should. Questions like these may be asked: "I understand that you are going to establish several new field offices. I think that it is very important that one of them be in the southern part of my state. Can this be done, and if not, why not?" Or, to a Democratic Cabinet member, "Is John Persons still working in your office? I know that he attended the Lincoln Day dinner, and the last time you were before the committee you said that you would look into it. What did you find out and what are you going to do?" Or, "Can you award a contract to the White Company? They can do the work, their orders are falling off, and they are operating only three days a week."

Interest groups, such as the National Association of Real Estate Boards, the National Association of Manufacturers, and the AFL-CIO, try to influence the administration of laws affecting their members. They are no less active in the executive than in the legislative branch. Claiming hundreds of thousands of members, group leaders are quick to express their points of view to congressmen, to administrative officials, and to the President. Frequently a congressional committee can be persuaded to make a recommendation to the agency that is favorable to an interest group. Representation of such groups has increased with the expansion of governmental activities. Their representatives often perform a useful function in helping citizens to find their way through the maze of government agencies. Agency officials find interest groups a valuable source of information about practices that affect administrative problems and about the attitudes of their organizations toward government policy.

Political parties have not acquired a role in administration comparable to that of interest groups. For the most part party influence is confined to officials appointed by the President. Reluctance to see an extension of party activities is due in part to general acceptance of the merit principle in the appointment of administrative personnel. This attitude is also prevalent among government administrators, who seem to prefer to deal with leaders of interest groups rather than with party officials. As a result, administration in the executive branch tends to be shielded from the influence of political parties on which so much of the process of government now depends.

THE PRESIDENT AS ADMINISTRATOR-IN-CHIEF

As administrator-in-chief of the national government, the President's dilemma is that he is generally accountable for the whole executive establishment but lacks control over many of its parts. The President strives for unity, for government-wide standards, and for responsiveness to his administration's goals and policies, but department and agency heads "have an inherent drive toward greater operating autonomy even though they face the same problems of coordination and control over their bureaus and divisions that the President faces in his relationship to them."[1]

Presidents have attempted to improve their capacity to direct and control

[1] Marver H. Bernstein, *The Job of the Federal Executive* (Washington, D.C.: The Brookings Institution, 1958), p. 65.

their administration by formulating reorganization plans reducing the number of executive agencies. Another favorite presidential device has been to improve management by staffing the White House office with highly competent assistants. A third device has been mobilization of facilities for coordination and policy guidance in the Bureau of the Budget, the Council of Economic Advisers, and the Office of Science and Technology.

The impact of presidential staffs on departmental and agency staffs varies greatly. Some agency heads may defer weakly to the executive staff while others stoutly resist. Some learn to develop cooperative responses in the presidential establishment, and some also develop imaginative ways of surmounting the procedures imposed by the executive office of the President. Some devote assiduous attention to cultivating political support in congressional committees and interest group constituencies in order to counteract presidential influence. Indeed, a persistent theme has been the pervasive development of clusters of power comprising government offices and bureaus, congressional committees, and interest groups. As one commentator[2] has stated, interest groups attempt

> to create autonomous and controllable fragments of government, each with a jurisdiction corresponding to the area and scope of the pressure group's interest—autonomous, that is to say, in the sense of independence from the rest of the government, and controllable from the point of view of the pressure group.

Presidential success in combating the drives of individual administrators for maximum autonomy also varies greatly. Some agencies operating in areas relatively unimportant from the point of view of the President's program do not warrant much effort to bring them into line. Others carry on programs that are at the heart of the administration's goals, but even here presidential control may be problematical. A reasonable degree of control can be achieved only by a highly skillful President. Here, as in other aspects of the American political system, powerful centrifugal forces complicate infinitely the art and process of governing. Only political leadership at the most effective level can overcome the splintering of authority, responsibility, and political power that characterizes American politics. Viewed in this perspective a high premium has been placed on the unifying influence of the President.

Departments and Agencies

The major organizations within the executive branch are the twelve Cabinet-level departments: State; Defense; Treasury; Justice; Post Office; Interior; Agriculture; Commerce; Labor; Health, Education and Welfare; Housing and Urban Development; and Transportation. Each department is headed by a secretary who is responsible directly to the President for the satisfactory performance of the activities of his department and is a member of the President's Cabinet. Roughly 85 to 90 percent of all civilian employees of

---

[2] Harvey C. Mansfield, "Political Parties, Patronage, and the Federal Government Service," The American Assembly, *The Federal Government Service: Its Character, Prestige, and Problems* (1954), p. 106.

the federal government work in these twelve departments, and 65 percent work in the Department of Defense and the Post Office Department alone.

In addition, there is a highly varied group of more than fifty organizations— agencies, corporations, administrations, commissions, authorities—the heads of which report directly to the President but are not members of his Cabinet. Agency heads are directly responsible for such large organizations as the Veterans Administration, the General Services Administration, the Civil Service Commission, the Panama Canal Company, the Tennessee Valley Authority, the Atomic Energy Commission, the National Aeronautics and Space Administration, and the Selective Service System.

Independent regulatory commissions are part of the executive branch, but they have a special relation to the President. These agencies were establishd by Congress to regulate such activities as radio, television, and satellite communications, interstate transportation by railroads and trucks, ocean shipping, trade practices, and the interstate distribution of electricity. The statutes under which these commissions operate authorize them to issue rules and regulations having the effect of law as far as private citizens are concerned, and to decide cases arising under the regulations.

Organization and Reorganization

The organization of the executive branch is constantly changing. The *United States Government Organization Manual* is published annually, but is often already out of date when it comes off the press. As the federal government takes on new activities, a place must be made for them in the organization structure. For example, in 1958, Congress created the Federal Aviation Agency in the hope of stimulating more effective performance of many government programs affecting air transport, and the National Aeronautics and Space Administration to conduct space research and develop, test, and operate space vehicles for research purposes. In 1961, Congress established the Arms Control and Disarmament Agency to advise the President on arms controls and disarmament matters, including conduct of research on nuclear detection, reduction of the armed forces, and elimination of the danger of war by accident or miscalculation. The Equal Employment Opportunity Commission was established under the Civil Rights Act of 1964 to investigate complaints of discrimination in employment. In recent years there has been agitation to create several new Cabinet departments dealing with activities that many feel deserve high priority, such as science and technology, transportation, and urban affairs. Citizen groups interested in particular programs like to see them given the prestige of departmental status.

Nor is adding to the number of government agencies the only way of reflecting changing needs in the organizational structure of government. Desires to reduce governmental costs and to ease the President's responsibility for over-all management of the executive branch are perhaps the best reasons for the continuing re-examination. Beginning in 1932, Congress passed several acts authorizing the

President to improve the efficiency of the executive branch by means of reorganization. Presidents have often appointed commissions to study the problem and to recommend improvements. The President's Committee on Administrative Management reported in 1937; another, the Commission on Organization of the Executive Branch of the Government, popularly known as the Hoover Commission, in 1949; and a third, also headed by former President Herbert Hoover, completed its work in 1955. As a result of these and other studies, some improvements have been made, and there is general agreement about other changes that would ease the President's managerial tasks and improve the operations of the executive branch. Most students of these problems agree that three principal weaknesses should be corrected. First, the President is expected to supervise directly and personally too many people. He is responsible for organizations ranging in importance from the Department of Defense to the Indian Claims Commission. Second, too many agencies having some degree of independence have been established by Congress. Third, Congress has often weakened the President's power by specifying the way in which the authority of subordinate executive officials must be exercised.

Nevertheless, it is often hard to get congressional consent to specific proposals for correcting these difficulties. Congress tends to suspect that a President who seeks reorganization of the executive branch is interested in increasing his own power. President Hoover's sweeping reorganization plan was rejected by Congress; charges of dictatorship greeted President Roosevelt's support of the recommendations of his Committee on Administrative Management; and some of President Truman's proposals were turned down for this reason. Moreover, government bureaus and the interest groups that work with them develop vested interests in the existing organization and procedures and oppose reorganization proposals. For example, no President has overcome the opposition of the transport interests to presidential designation of the chairman of the Interstate Commerce Commission.

In recent years reorganizations have been authorized under the terms of the Reorganization Act of 1949, which grew out of the recommendations of the first Hoover Commission. Under this act the President may submit a reorganization plan to Congress involving a shift of an agency from one department to another or a regrouping of functions within a department or agency. If Congress does not take negative action within sixty days, the plan goes into effect. A simple majority of either the House or the Senate is sufficient to vote a reorganization plan. In the two decades since 1949 about 80 plans were submitted by Presidents, three fourths of which were accepted by Congress.

EXECUTIVES FOR GOVERNMENT

The Dual-Personnel System

For decades the system by which the federal government recruits and retains executives to manage federal agencies and offices has remained more or less the same. The system draws on two groups.

There are 5000 or more experienced career executives with permanent civil service status who serve as government executives through changes of party control in the President's administration. They are professional administrators providing expert knowledge not only about specific programs but also about the complexities of the political environment. Above this relatively permanent body of career executives are about 500 presidential appointees, or political executives.

The 500 top political executives include the secretaries and assistant secretaries of departments, agency heads and their deputies, heads and members of boards and commissions, and chiefs and directors of major bureaus, divisions, and services. These men and women bear the brunt of translating the aims and philosophy of the administration into operating programs.

The large group of about 5000 civilian career executives and professionals occupy the so-called supergrade positions or their equivalents. These include the three top grades under the Classification Act (GS-16, GS-17, and GS-18), equivalent grades in the postal field service, high posts under Public Law 313 (which was enacted to encourage recruitment of needed scientists or those with scarce specialized skills), and equivalent positions in special merit systems in such agencies as the Atomic Energy Commission, the Tennessee Valley Authority, and the U.S. Public Health Service. About 500 other positions are so-called schedule C jobs that lack standard civil service tenure protections; however, about half of these positions are actually filled by career employees who can return to their civil service status, while the remaining 250 are political appointees.

The posts occupied by these 6000 top political and civilian career executives in federal administration tend to fall into three groups roughly equal in number. About one third serve as agency heads, bureau chiefs, and office and division directors and are responsible for a specific governmental program or operation. Another third are supporting staff specialists, officials who serve as deputies or executive assistants to program heads or who provide managerial services in budgeting, fiscal operations, personnel, management analysis, and general administration. And finally, about a third provide professional services. Typically, they are experts in professional or technical areas—lawyers, economists, physicists, marine biologists.

Career Executives and Politics

Career executives are expected to serve different presidential administrations and different political bosses loyally and without regard to party designations. But they cannot help becoming involved in policies and in political matters, for they provide expert political and substantive knowledge and experience that their temporary political chiefs often lack. Although political involvement runs counter to the principle of the politically neutral professional administrator—a central tenet of the civil service faith—the dual-personnel system often imposes a burden upon the careerist to guide his political superiors through the treacherous jungles and bypaths of Washington politics. The difference between a skillful career executive and an inadequate one is often the former's ability to provide a substantial measure of political skill without becoming excessively involved in partisan politics. As a prominent management consultant[3] concluded:

... large numbers of bureau chiefs cannot avoid making policy or carrying political responsibility. The real trick is to work conscientiously to promote the political policies of the party in power, both parties being presumed to operate in the public interest. Most career executives are better politicians—in the best sense of the word—than are their political supervisors. The present [Eisenhower] administration talked a good deal about a Washington housecleaning in the early months of the first term. While political appointees were changed, and properly, few significant changes were made in the career service. This is not a failure on the part of the administration but rather is evidence that a large number of permanent professionals must be in important posts if our government is to function.

A Profile of Political Executives

From March 1933 to April 30, 1965, five American Presidents made 1567 appointments to fill about 200 top federal executive positions as secretaries, undersecretaries, assistant secretaries, and general counsels of the cabinet and military departments; as commissioners of the independent regulatory commissions; and as administrators and deputy administrators of the larger, single-headed agencies. Since some persons received appointments to two or more positions, the number of persons holding these positions totaled only 1041.[4] Normally these top political executives serve only one administration. They come primarily from urban backgrounds and more likely from eastern sections of the United States. As a group they are well educated and about 48 years old when they take up their initial political appointments. Occupationally these executives come mostly from government service, law, and business; a few are educators; very few are scientists and engineers. While evaluations of performance are hazardous and impressionistic, executives with some previous government service have been more effective than those coming exclusively from the private sector.[5]

On the average these executives stay in their jobs for only two to three years (other than regulatory commissioners, whose median service is longer). Short tenure can be traced to such factors as crushing work load, administrative frustrations, poor congressional relations, difficulties with news media, family problems, fear of loss of promotional prospects and fringe benefits in their interrupted private careers, and salary problems. As Stanley, Mann, and Doig[6] conclude: "The short tenure of many subcabinet officers creates serious obstacles to effective political leadership in federal agencies."

[3] Richard M. Paget, "Strengthening the Federal Career Executive," *Public Administration Review,* 17 (Spring 1957), p. 93.

[4] Data in this section are taken from David T. Stanley, Dean E. Mann, and Jameson W. Doig, *Men Who Govern* (Washington, D.C.: The Brookings Institution, 1967).

[5] For corroboration of this view, see Dean E. Mann, with Jameson W. Doig, *The Assistant Secretaries: Problems and Processes of Appointment* (Washington, D.C.: The Brookings Institution, 1965), p. 247.

[6] P. 6

Obstacles to Executive Recruitment

It is not difficult to account for the federal government's disadvantage in obtaining and retaining a fair share of the best executive talent. Opportunities for executives outside government have been plentiful in recent years. Although government salaries at lower and middle levels of employment compare favorably with those in private business, government can never expect to compete with private business in terms of salaries for executives. Its personnel program must of necessity be based on a recognition of this fact of public life. Moreover, the environment of government is so different from that of the business world that there is little or nothing in nongovernmental work that prepares a person for executive work in government. Above all, it is the public nature of the government's business that differentiates it so clearly from nongovernmental enterprise. As the promoter of the public interest, government must be staffed by executives whose perspective is broader than that of a person in private employment. Virtually nothing that government does is immune from public scrutiny and debate. Matters of administrative detail in government are often the subject of criticism and investigation in Congress, in the press, and over television. Government executives are accountable publicly for what they do or fail to do. Yet Congress has drastically limited the authority of executives by restricting their freedom to organize their offices, hire and fire employees, spend public funds, purchase supplies, and develop new procedures and methods of carrying on their activities. Executives serving temporarily in Washington are usually impressed with the restrictions on their power compared with their former employment.

In size and complexity no enterprise in the United States can compete with the federal government. In 1968 nearly 6 million civilians and personnel on active military duty were employed full-time by the federal government, compared to 800,000 employed by the largest private employer, the American Telephone and Telegraph Company, and 600,000 by General Motors. There are about 350 major operating bureaus below the departmental and agency level, along with over 60 separate departments, agencies, boards, commissions, and corporations.

The federal government not only employs more people than any large corporation but it employs them in more different occupations. About two out of three government civilian employees are white collar workers, while one out of three is a "blue collar" worker or a skilled or semiskilled laborer. About one fourth of federal workers are women.

One overriding consequence of the size of the governmental establishment is that important matters are rarely the concern of a single agency. As a result, a government executive rarely has final authority to handle matters without consulting a host of other officials with different and often competing interests. A related consequence is a continuing need to provide a variety of coordinating devices to mesh the activities and programs of federal agencies. Former Secretary of the Treasury George Humphrey[7] found the interpenetration of government activities to be the most distinctive characteristic of the executive branch:

Government is vast and diverse, like a hundred businesses all grouped under one name, but the various businesses of government are not integrated nor even directly related in fields of activity; and in government the executive management must operate under a system of divided authority . . . when a government executive decides on a course of action not already established under law, he must first check with other agencies to make certain his proposal does not conflict with or duplicate something being done by somebody else. It is common in government, much too common, for several agencies to be working on different facets of the same activity. The avoidance of overlapping or conflict calls for numerous conferences, for painstaking study of laws and directives, for working out in tedious detail so that what one Cabinet officer does will not bump into what another is doing—or run counter to our interests and activities abroad. . . .

Before coming to Washington, I had not understood why there were so many conferences in government, and so much delay. Now I do. Everything is more complex. . . .

Moreover, in order to accept government employment, an executive must not only be willing to undergo financial sacrifices; he must also expect little status and considerable abuse and harassment from Congress and the public, who will occasionally question his integrity, the sincerity of his convictions, and his suitability for public employment.

Finally, among the many restraints that tend to deter executive recruitment are a number of statutes know as conflict-of-interest laws. These are discussed more fully below.

The quality of the service rendered by the government is a direct result of the quality of men and women it employs. These public servants represent a fair cross section of America. Only about 11 percent work in the Washington, D.C., area; 83 percent work in the various states; and 6 percent are located abroad. Slightly over half of all white collar civilian jobs are professional or technical, not clerical, and the proportion will increase as a result of automation. In 1955 one out of every three civilian employees at all levels of government worked for the federal government, but by 1965 the ratio of federal to state and local employees was one to four, and it continues to drop with increases in state-local employment.

The civil servant engages in most of the occupations found in private life. The federal government, for example, employs doctors, lawyers, engineers of all kinds, chemists, botanists, physicists, economists, sociologists, political scientists, historians, aerial photographers, social workers, teachers, nurses, and dentists. Thousands of clerks, stenographers, messengers, telephone operators, janitors, and skilled and unskilled laborers are also required.

The vast majority of federal workers get their jobs under the provisions of a merit system. When the Civil Service Act was passed in 1883 about 10 percent of the employees in the executive branch were brought into the merit system, the great majority remaining under the spoils system. Through the years the system

---

[7] George M. Humphrey, with James C. Derieux, "It Looked Easier on the Outside," *Collier's,* 133 (April 2, 1954), p. 31.

A Peace Corps volunteer in Gana, a "satellite city" near Brasilia, Brazil. In the words of President Kennedy, the Peace Corps was established in 1961 "to help foreign countries meet their urgent needs for skilled manpower." Volunteers have gone to almost all parts of the world to participate in many tasks and to live with and at the level of the native-born. (Paul Conklin from Peace Corps)

has been extended to more and more positions, so that today about 84 percent of all federal positions are in the competitive civil service. Moreover, a few agencies that do not come within the Civil Service Act, principally the Atomic Enery Commission, the Peace Corps, the Tennessee Valley Authority, the Federal Bureau of Investigation, the Public Health Service, the Veterans Administration, and the Foreign Service of the Department of State, are under separate merit systems.

Recruitment of Civil Servants

The recruitment of federal workers is a responsibility of the Civil Service Commission. The magnitude of the task of finding suitable candidates is indicated by the fact that the government hires about a quarter of a million annually. If the quality of the civil service is to be improved steadily, there must be an active and imaginative program for attracting competent people to government employment.

The Civil Service Commission generally has not exerted itself to *find* the best-qualified people; traditionally it has been content to discover the most competent among the candidates who voluntarily present themselves. Above all, it seeks to prevent government employment of the patently unfit. This essentially negative philosophy is an outgrowth of the commission's origin and of the American tradition of equality of opportunity. When the commission was established the central problem was to combat the spoils system, to prevent departments and agencies from selecting personnel for political or other extraneous reasons. This reform objective was proper in the early years of the commission, but today the problem is quite different.

The Civil Service Commission uses examinations to screen qualified applicants. Written examinations are most useful for positions that involve relatively simple duties. The examination for higher positions consists of an appraisal of the candidates' previous experience on similar jobs, general training and background, personality, judgment, character, and other factors that cannot be measured by written examinations. Candidates are ranked according to grades. The Commission then compiles a list, or "register," of persons who passed the examination and are eligible for appointment, with adjustments made for men and women whose veterans' status entitles them to additional points. Today half of all male federal employees are veterans. When a government agency has a vacancy to fill it asks the Civil Service Commission for the names of candidates available for appointment. Agency officials then select from the persons certified by the commission the one who seems to meet their requirements most fully.

Specialized Expertness: A Key Characteristic of the Federal Service

One of the persisting characteristics of the federal career executive is the narrow range of federal programs in which he operates during his career. The doctrine of the federal merit system calls for the establishment of a career service for the entire federal government. In practice, however, a series of "closed" career groups anchored in particular bureaus have been created over the years, and new entrants are normally admitted only at junior levels. The career system in the operating bureaus have, typically, placed the highest value on technical, specialized training. Consequently, the transferability of administrative skills from one program to another and job mobility across bureau and departmental lines have been minimized. As one expert observer notes:[8]

... our traditional principles have not merely made it difficult to get for government a fair share of the top administrative talent, but they have forced the able men in government careers to concentrate their talents on the interests of particular bureaus or services. And so we have made it almost impossible for the career service to do its main job—which is to look ahead at the great problems that confront the nation, to devise and recommend policies to meet them, and to see that the various departments are effectively coordinated in carrying the decisions of responsible political authorities.

---

[8] Don K. Price, "Administrative Leadership," *Daedalus,* Journal of the American Academy of Arts and Sciences, 90 (1961), p. 752.

One of the fundamental governmental needs for the future is administrative talent. Sources of talent within the government may be discovered by broadening the base of education and training and by deemphasizing technical and specialized expertness and parochial assignments within the service. Sources of talent outside the government can be tapped if more effective ways can be found to promote the interchange of talent between government and private employment.

Before World War II the compensation of civil servants in the lower brackets was relatively favorable/as compared with other employment. In the mid-40s the government's position was still reasonably satisfactory. But ten years later business was competing vigorously for the best college graduates, offering salaries relatively higher than those available under civil service or those paid young faculty members by most educational institutions. In 1967, a college graduate entering the federal service without previous experience or graduate study normally received a starting salary of $6450.

In an effort to make the federal service more competitive, Congress in 1949, and by amendments since that time, substantially increased the salaries of top officials, including Cabinet officers, heads of agencies, and some of the principal departmental officials.

In 1962, President Kennedy proposed a two-stage increase in federal salaries. In support of his plan, the President noted that top career salary rates in several states and localities exceeded current federal salary levels. And salaries of school superintendents and city managers often exceeded the 1962 salary of $25,000 for a Cabinet post. Although Congress rejected some of the President's recommendations, it went far toward making federal employment more attractive by raising all federal civil service salaries and increasing the number of supergrade positions. Further increases were enacted by Congress in 1964 and 1966. Top salaries in 1967 were:

Vice President	$43,000
Speaker of the House	43,000
Chief Justice, Supreme Court	40,000
Associate Justices, Supreme Court	39,500
Cabinet Secretaries	35,000
Members of Congress	30,000
Agency heads	30,000
Deputy and Under Secretaries	28,500
Supergrade positions, GS-16–GS-18	20,075–25,890

Government service has perhaps fewer of the risks that go with responsible positions in industry. Aside from the heads of departments and agencies and their aides, a competent civil servant who does his job well and avoids involvement in political activity has a position that is reasonably secure for life. He is not protected, of course, if the agency in which he works, or his job, is abolished. But even in these cases he enjoys a priority that normally means he will be appointed to another position within a relatively short period of time.

The federal service also provides liberal vacation, sick leave, insurance, and retirement benefits. After a year of service an employee is entitled to approximately a month's vacation with pay each year. Also, he is entitled to two weeks of sick leave. An employee who makes the federal government service his lifework may also count upon a reasonably adequate pension upon retirement. The benefits have been liberalized from time to time, and the government shares the cost with the employee.

Dismissal of Federal Civil Servants

A fundamental principle of the federal civil service is that the head of a department should have final authority to determine the fitness and capacity of his employees. Thus it is the department that makes appointments and the department that has authority to dismiss employees, even those with civil service status.

Under federal law[9] no civil servant may be removed from the classified civil service "except for such causes as will promote the efficiency of said service. . . ." Dismissal for incompetence is supposedly simple, but in practice has proved to be time-consuming and difficult, and some supervisors lack the courage or tenacity to fire incompetent employees.

When Congress reduces a departmental appropriation, it may be necessary for the department to resort to the "reduction-in-force" procedure for dismissing employees. This procedure is controlled by the Civil Service Commission under the terms of the Veterans' Preference Act of 1944, and it is designed to give due weight to seniority, tenure status, veterans' preference, and performance ratings in designating the employees to be dismissed.

Since 1940, one of the most perplexing problems of the civil service has been the question of what needs to be done to safeguard the government against employees who are disloyal or who are security risks, perhaps vulnerable to blackmailing pressures. During World War II the principal concern was with employees who were sympathetic toward Germany, Italy, and Japan. With the Cold War, however, attention shifted to the Communists, and it was feared that Communist party members might advance to strategic federal positions where they could work for the interests of the Soviet Union. In 1947, President Truman issued a "loyalty order" designed to protect the government against this kind of infiltration. In 1950, Congress authorized the dismissal by department heads of any employee when deemed necessary in the interest of national security; and in 1953, President Eisenhower issued a more detailed executive order designed to cope with this problem.

The evidence is conclusive that the overwhelming majority of civil servants are honest, sober, and loyal. On the other hand, the government must take into account the fact that deceit, deception, subversion, and sabotage are standard tactics of international politics. Under President Truman the loyalty-security program was scarcely a model of fairness; and during the early years of the Eisenhower Administration the security program was recklessly administered, under the stim-

---

[9] The basic requirements are contained in the Lloyd-LaFollette Act of 1912 (37 *Stat.* 539). The Veterans' Preference Act provision is § 14 of 58 *Stat.* 387.

ulus of the late Senator Joseph McCarthy. The result was considerable damage to the morale and general efficiency of the career service. By 1957, however, that particular storm had been weathered.

The Spur of Politics

In principle, permanent civil service employees do not engage actively in party politics, and if they have strong political beliefs, do not act upon them insofar as their official duties are concerned. The political activities of federal employees are limited by the Hatch Act of 1940. Under the doctrine of political neutrality, the civil servant is expected to carry out faithfully the policy instructions of his superiors. Consequently, it is not necessary for a party recently come to power to replace the rank-and-file government employees with men of their own party and choice.

In fact, however, the relationship is not quite this clear-cut. Men who spend a lifetime on a particular job cannot help acquiring the attitude that they know more about the work and what ought to be done than a department head whose tenure ends with the President's. For this reason, department heads may find that their subordinates are not very responsive to new ideas and policies. In unusual cases, subordinate officers of a department may oppose policies that have the support of the department head, the President, and the general public.

Viewed in these terms, the relationships between civil servants and policy officers pose a basic issue. Progressive extension of the career service to important executive positions has created opportunities for competent men and women and thereby has improved the quality of government personnel. At the same time it has become difficult for department heads to inject new ideas and new policies. There is need for some adjustment of the patronage and merit systems that will preserve the values of the career service and maximize the responsiveness of the civil servant to democratic influences.

Conflict of Interest in Federal Employment

After each major war attention in the United States has focused on problems of ethics and morality in government. After World War II almost all barriers to federal employment were removed or simply overlooked. Despite the anxious concern of a handful of men, some dollar-a-year men played influential roles in policy matters affecting their own industries and occasionally their own companies. Statutes and regulations prohibiting federal employees from carrying on certain forms of outside economic interests were largely ignored.

The 1951 Report on Ethics in Government of the Douglas subcommittee of the Senate Committee on Labor and Public Welfare was the first attempt to provide, in a public document, a broad perspective on problems of morality in government. The gradual unfolding during the Eisenhower Administration of tales of vicuna coats, Air Force stationery, travel expenses, and illicit traffic in allocating television channels helped to direct attention toward a more specific inquiry into problems of conflicting interests. Such concern cannot be regarded as evidence of depravity and declining morality in the executive branch. Indeed, standards of behavior in federal employment have probably never been higher.

Conflicts of interest constitute one of the many types of ethical problems of federal employees: the problems of dual economic allegiance. Federal statutes and regulations prohibit certain forms of employee behavior that bring official duty into conflict with personal economic interests outside the government. They cover conduct that might not be offensive on the part of private citizens but that is intolerable in a position of public trust. Contacts between citizens and the government, between private economic interests and governmental programs, have multiplied and government's pervasive role in the nation's economic life has been accompanied by innumerable direct and indirect impingements on private economic interests. In a simpler world the line between public and private was reasonably easy to define. As the line blurs into a broad gray band, the problem of preventing dual economic allegiance becomes critical. Two examples may be cited.

The first is the case of the individual in private life whose expert consultant or advisory services are in demand by one or more government agencies. As an intermittent government employee, he becomes uncertain about the line between his public duties and his private interests. He can scarcely be required to renounce his private interests as a price of serving his government from time to time. And the government sharply lowers its capacity to draw on private individuals for advice, counsel, and temporary staff services if it requires them to divorce themselves entirely from private economic interests.

The second case is that of the scientist. He may be a physicist on a university faculty. Because of the nature of his expertness, he has many opportunities to consult with government agencies and with private firms, many of whom have contracts with government agencies. His expertness may be based primarily on research experience that has been financed largely by government grants to him or to his university. He may be successful, moreover, in developing a gadget that becomes an essential ingredient of a complex weapon or instrument needed by the government. Such a scientist eventually reaches a point where he can scarcely tell when he is acting in a public or a private capacity. His scientific learning and experience can scarcely be compartmentalized and labeled as either.

Until 1962, there were seven statutes dealing with behavioral problems falling within the range of conflicting public and private interests. Three were aimed directly at preventing public employees or ex-employees from assisting others in the prosecution of claims against the United States. A fourth forbade the employee to assist another for pay in any matter that is before an agency of the executive branch and in which the United States is interested. The fifth statute prohibited a government official from acting for the government in transactions with a business entity in which he had an economic interest. The sixth forbade the official from receiving pay from nongovernmental sources "in connection with" his official services. And the seventh forbade the official from receiving pay for assisting another in obtaining a government contract. From these provisions a tangle of legal complexities resulted.

Congressional committees, spurred by the Kennedy Administration, demonstrated active concern for conflicts of interest in the executive branch and the military services. By the close of 1962 they had succeeded in working out a more satisfactory pattern of statutory restraints. The new statute[10] consolidates and strengthens conflict-of-interest laws governing full-time federal employees and makes special provisions for part-time and temporary employees in an effort to draw more consultants and experts, especially in scientific fields, to intermittent government service. Its provisions do not apply to members of Congress. This statute's notable advance in modernizing and clarifying restraints upon conflicting interests focuses attention more sharply on Congress itself. As former Senator Kenneth B. Keating of New York remarked, Congress should not be exempted "from the same high ethical standards we intend to impose on the officers and employees of the other branches of the Government."

Civil Service Opportunities

The limited appeal that the federal service has for college graduates is a serious obstacle to the improvement of the career service. In spite of some negative aspects, the federal government does offer rich opportunities for outstanding young men and women. One of its attractions is the magnitude of the problems that officials are called upon to solve. In terms of complexity and interest, these opportunities in government cannot be matched in business. It has not been unusual for businessmen to find, after service in the government, that their old jobs were relatively simple and dull.

A young college graduate without previous experience does not, of course, move immediately into a position with great responsibility. Nevertheless, the best young government employees are given important assignments early in their careers, and even routine assignments are likely to be more significant, in terms of lives and money, than would be true in private employment.

The opportunity for public service should be the primary appeal of a career in public affairs. As Dean G. Acheson,[11] who spent years in the federal service, ultimately as Secretary of State in the Truman Administration, wrote:

I am all for young (and also old) men of quality going into public life and government service. . . . Why? Not because I see the gleam of a halo forming about their heads . . . but because there is no better life for a man of spirit. The old Greek conception of happiness is relevant here: "The exercise of vital powers along lines of excellence."

This is the Geiger counter which tells us where to dig. It explains also why to everyone who has ever experienced it, the return from public life to private life leaves one feeling flat and empty. Contended, interested, busy—yes. But exhilarated—no. For one has left a life affording scope for the exercise of vital powers along lines of excellence.

---

[10] Act of Oct. 23, 1962, 87th Congress, 2d Sess., 18 U.S.C., § 201–218.

[11] Part of a letter reprinted by James Reston, *New York Times,* February 2, 1958.

Selected Bibliography

Bernstein, Marver H., *The Job of the Federal Executive* (Washington, D.C.: The Brookings Institution, 1958). Based on discussions among federal executives about their activities and the political context in which they operate.

Hitch, Charles J., *Decision-Making for Defense* (Berkeley, Calif.: University of California Press, 1965). The best introduction to the nature and purposes of the managerial innovations introduced into the Defense Department and now being extended to other areas of government activity.

Stanley, David T., *Changing Administrations: The 1961 and 1964 Transitions in Six Departments* (Washington, D.C.: The Brookings Institution, 1965). A study of executive transitions that contains valuable insight into the general organization and operation of the departments treated.

————, *The Higher Civil Service: An Evaluation of Federal Personnel Practices* (Washington, D.C.: The Brookings Institution, 1964). An empirical study of the backgrounds, career patterns, and behavior of civil servants in the senior grades.

Stein, Harold, ed., *Public Administration and Policy Development* (New York: Harcourt, Brace & World, Inc., 1952). A collection of thorough case studies of government in action.

U.S. Government Organization Manual (Washington, D.C.: Government Printing Office, published annually). The best source book on the organization, functions, and personnel of government agencies.

17

The scope
of government
activities

THE EXPANDING ROLE OF GOVERNMENT

The most striking fact about the government of the United States is the breadth of its activities. They range from eradication of plant pests to international warfare; from control of food and drugs to regulation of railroad rates; from construction of flood-control and power dams to lunar probes; from sale of postage stamps to sale of nuclear energy; from protection of migratory birds to support of widows and orphans; from education of Indian children to stimulation of basic scientific research; from provision of old-age pensions to promotion and maintenance of a healthy economy; from negotiations with prime ministers to diplomatic representation in hundreds of cities all over the world.

The program of the federal government is so vast today that it entails expenditures of more than $130 billion each year, the services of about 3 million civilian employees, and the operation of 1800 departments, agencies, bureaus, commissions, corporations, sections, and units. Since 1965 it has cost more to

331

pay the interest on the national debt than it did to finance the total cost of the federal government in 1940. In concluding its survey of federal governmental activities, the first Hoover Commission reported in 1949:[1]

> It is almost impossible to comprehend the . . . problems of the Federal Government unless one has some concept of its hugeness and complexity. The sheer size, complexity, and geographical dispersion . . . almost stagger the imagination. As a result of depression, war, new needs for defense, and our greater responsibilities abroad, the Federal Government has become the largest enterprise on earth.

Two decades later, the evidence supporting this judgment has mounted geometrically.

Big Economy, Big Government

American industrial society has tended to concentrate and centralize economic and political power; the growth of government followed the growth of private economic power. Bigness in economic enterprise is encouraged by competition and by technological advances. During the nineteenth century the competitive drive for profits led to the widespread adoption of mass production methods based upon new inventions and specialization of labor. Large-scale production in turn stimulated new inventions. Big producing units were able to increase output, reduce costs, and therefore prices, and still make higher profits.

Gradually corporations replaced simple proprietorships, which seldom could command sufficient capital to finance large-scale enterprise, as the dominant form of business organization. The growth in the number of corporations meant an increasing concentration of wealth in relatively few business firms. An authoritative work reported in 1932[2] that 200 of the largest corporations controlled half of all corporate wealth (other than banking) and exercised control over business generally through trade associations, informal agreements, interlocking directorates, and other devices. Today the 200 largest corporations strongly influence half and perhaps as much as three fourths of American business life.

The growth of machine industry and corporate power had its counterpart in the development of the labor movement. The individual worker was no match for his corporate employer in bargaining over wages, hours, and other conditions of employment. Workers resorted to collective efforts to obtain more favorable working conditions; the strike was their ultimate weapon. Labor organizations grew in size, power, and militancy as the number of industrial wage earners increased. But they had not yet become strong determinants of economic policy. During the 1920s, when industrial activity was at a high level, employers were generally disposed to share the system's benefits with their employees, but on

---

[1] United States Commission on Organization of the Executive Branch of the Government, *Concluding Report* (Washington, D.C.: Government Printing Office, 1949), pp. 3–4.

[2] A. A. Berle, Jr., and Gardiner Means, *The Modern Corporation and Private Property* (New York: Crowell-Collier & Macmillan, Inc., 1932).

their own terms. During the depression years 1929–1933, labor organizations grew relatively weak, but in the next ten years there was a tremendous resurgence of labor's power, and by 1942 from 8 to 10 million workers in major industries had been brought into collective bargaining units. Particularly as a result of government policies during World War II, labor unions continued to grow in size and power. By 1950, approximately 15 million workers belonged to unions, and Congress had found it desirable to enact legislation to curtail their power.

The effect of the situation in agriculture has been somewhat different. There has been a steady decline in the number of Americans who earn their living by farming. Moreover, agriculture as a commercial enterprise is dominated by a relatively small proportion of independent farmers. Two thirds of all farmers produce only 10 to 15 percent of the volume of crops distributed commercially. Many of these are only part-time farmers, and more than two thirds of all farms do not provide the major source of income for the farm family. As the relative importance of agriculture in the economy declined, several million farmers looked to the government to ease the effects of uncontrolled competition.

Democratic Influences and Ideas

The opportunities of American citizens to participate in governmental processes expanded as their individual ability to control economic forces and institutions declined. Gradual extension of the right to vote, the development of vigorous political parties and interest groups, the popular election of senators, and, in effect, of the President, all resulted in the strengthening of popular government by creating a more direct relationship between individuals and government officials. When the problem of coping with competitive interests became too great citizens had an opportunity to present their case to elected public officials, whose continuation in office depended upon satisfying the electorate. By joining with others who had similar problems and objectives a citizen might sufficiently magnify his power to bring the government to support his position. The growth and concentration of power in the economy, the strengthening of democratic institutions, and the expansion of governmental activities were thus parallel developments.

The American government undertakes activities in response to what it perceives to be the wishes and needs of the people. Generally the government acts in response to pressures created by the misfortunes or dissatisfactions of groups of citizens. Since democracies usually take action gradually, the government's response is slow rather than rapid, reluctant rather than eager, and piecemeal rather than planned. Demands from individuals and groups for governmental services exceed the government's ability to plan, organize, and finance the desired activities.

Any policy decision of national significance must have the support of a legislative majority. The President on occasion may set a course of national action without the guidance of legislation, but before the action is very far advanced it is generally necessary to obtain legislative approval in the form of appropriations of funds. This makes political parties and interest groups work continuously to convince congressmen of their views of what should or should not be done. All these points of view—of officials in the three branches of government, of economic and professional interests as expressed through political parties and pressure groups, of state and local political leaders, and of the electorate as a whole—interact to influence the response of government.

A MIXED ECONOMY
OF PUBLIC AND PRIVATE ENTERPRISE

One of the primary areas of governmental activity in the United States is the economy. The idea of government support of the economy was conceived by the Founding Fathers. The delegates to the Constitutional convention in 1787 believed that the powers of the national government should be strengthened to promote economic welfare. Under the leadership of Alexander Hamilton, George Washington's Administration took steps to promote trade, to protect struggling American industry from foreign competition, and to establish a stable currency and banking system without which business could not flourish. Before the Civil War the states chartered corporations in order to promote industries whose operations were considered to be in the public interest. To stimulate "internal improvements" state legislatures sometimes authorized the purchase of stock of private corporations by their state governments.

Contrary to many current popular notions, throughout American development relations between government and business have usually been close. Since colonial times Americans have maintained a dynamic economic system with changing mixtures of public and private enterprise and changing forms and degrees of governmental interference and noninterference. Sooner or later we have called upon government to protect the private economy from destroying itself by its indulgence in greed or avarice and to help the economy in other ways when it appears to be unable to take care of itself. As government grew along with business and labor, its activities became more significant for the economy. Big government today is deeply involved in economic problems. Business, both small and big, has attempted to use government to bolster its economic position. The small business man understandably wants an economy made up of small-scale businesses operating in a truly competitive manner and therefore wants vigorous enforcement of the antitrust laws. The big business man generally agrees that large corporations do exercise great power, but he wants to be regarded as a trustee who acts in the public interest. Thus he wants to be free from government attempts to hold him accountable.

With different business groups exerting opposing pressures, how does this mixture of public and private enterprise work? What is the American economic system? Its fluid elements make it difficult to describe; economists themselves do not entirely agree on a theory that adequately explains even its "normal" behavior, much less on how to deal with the problems that occur during an economic crisis.

The Concept of Laissez Faire

In the nineteenth century the popular view of the American economic system was based on the concept of laissez faire. According to this concept competition is the great economic stimulus. Under its spur the individual develops his latent capacities to the utmost; he exploits every opportunity that presents itself or that he creates. The value of each man's services is fixed in the market place, in competition with other men performing like services. Those who plan most carefully and work the hardest receive the largest share of the available wealth.

The theory assumed that men are rational and can be expected to temper selfishness with enlightenment and, further, that conflicts between individuals are harmonized by a universal law that maximum wealth for society will be produced by each individual striving for selfish gain. Since the primary objective of society is to produce wealth, competition between individuals should not be discouraged by government interference.

The doctrine of laissez faire received its first systematic statement in Adam Smith's *Wealth of Nations,* published in 1776. Smith opposed all government activities that restricted free enterprise, but he favored government activities to promote the general welfare. Government enforcement of contracts by which men, materials, and facilities are organized in the production system, the maintenance of patent rights, and the provision of a stable money system he regarded as essential to a laissez-faire economy.

The idea that business activities should be free from government restrictions was given a new twist by Herbert Spencer, who applied certain Darwinian concepts of biology to economic behavior. To Spencer the survival of the fittest was applicable to society as well as to the biological world. Those too weak to survive in the competition for the means of existence perished, and their elimination hastened progress. Any effort on the part of government to take care of the poor and distressed was contrary to this law and an obstacle to progress, and any effort to regulate economic life through social planning and public control would lead to disaster. As the Beards[3] summarized this view, "individuals, government, and society stood in the presence of an unconscious, largely automatic, self-adjusting system, akin to the mechanism of nature."

The Changing Mixture

Whether a true laissez-faire system ever existed is debatable. In any event, the American economic system today is a combination of private and public enterprise, of monopoly and competition. Most of the nation's business is private in character; it is financed by private capital rather than by public funds; and it is controlled by private persons rather than by government officials. But the balance between privately and publicly controlled

---

[3] Charles A. Beard and Mary R. Beard, *America in Midpassage* (New York: Crowell-Collier & Macmillan, Inc., 1939), II, p. 871.

enterprise is not firmly fixed. Private economic interests in the fields of business, agriculture, and labor have frequently changed their minds concerning government intervention in private enterprise. Severe economic depressions, natural disasters such as floods, earthquakes, and fires, and, above all, wars have also created irresistible pressures upon government to promote and regulate economic activity in the public interest. The American economy remains essentially private in character, but it depends substantially upon government activity and control to safeguard and promote the public interest and to maintain private enterprise.

The mixture of governmental and private economic activity is influenced by the development of public policies in five major ways.

1. As purchaser of goods and services the federal government accounts directly for one tenth of all economic activity in the country.

2. As entrepreneur the federal government operates a vast postal system, maintains a monopoly on most nuclear energy developments, runs electric generating plants, railroads, and steamship lines, manufactures clothing, and operates many retail and service enterprises for military personnel. It has used federal funds to establish new nonprofit institutions to perform tasks once handled by government staffs or business firms.

3. As regulators of business enterprise federal agencies directly influence or control business decisions on prices, services, advertising of products, and corporate financial structure.

4. Throughout American history the federal government has used public funds to promote and subsidize various business and economic activities. Ship operators and airlines, publishers and direct mail advertisers who use second and third class mail, mineral producers who supply materials for the defense stockpiles, farmers, grazers, and many other groups are the recipients of federal subsidies or financial aid. By lending money and guaranteeing loans to urban developers, college students, farmers, underdeveloped nations, small businesses and others, the federal government promotes economic life. In other ways—dredging harbors, financing airport construction, making grants to states for highway construction, and maintaining protective tariffs—federal programs stimulate, protect, and promote economic activities.

5. By encouraging foreign trade and investment by American business through loans, guarantees, and tax concessions the federal government has increasingly affected the international activities of American firms.

Increases in the government's role in the mixed American economy plus changes in the character of some of its ingredients seem inevitable in the years ahead. It remains to be seen whether the extension of governmental authority can be accomplished without placing further limits on the freedom of decision by individual businessmen.

The Public Economy

One of the most significant trends in twentieth-century America is that more people carry more public responsibility than before. No longer can the public official be distinguished from the private executive merely by determining whether he works for a "public" agency. Today in almost all large organizations, governmental and nongovernmental, the line between what is public and what is private has become blurred. Perhaps the major factor accounting for this change is the growth in size and influence of large-scale private organizations—industrial corporations, banks, universities, private foundations. The decisions and actions of these "private" agencies deeply affect the public interest and in turn are heavily affected with the public interest. Decisions in contemporary society about involvement in the affairs of other nations, flights to the moon, urban ghettos, labor-management relations, or atomic testing are made by nongovernmental executives as well as public officials.

The battering down of barriers between public and private actions and decisions comes from both sides. Private enterprise often seeks governmental involvement in its affairs, many times to bail business out when things go wrong through poor managerial judgment, and sometimes to put the stamp of public approval on private behavior. And government agencies contract with private organizations to carry out more and more public functions.

In the economic arena the American system of private enterprise may be just as enterprising as it was a generation ago. But what has gradually come into being is a *public economy* in which the relations between public and private actions and interests are becoming more subtle and more dynamic. As a result, traditional analysis and description of the American economy have become unusable as a realistic explanation of the American economy today. In determining economic policy, holding fast to such concepts as laissez faire has yielded to the imperatives of national security at home and of economic and political developments in emerging countries.

NATIONAL SECURITY
AND INTERNATIONAL AFFAIRS

No description of any modern government in action is valid without stressing national security and international affairs. In personnel employed, materials utilized, and money spent, military and defense activities and the conduct of foreign affairs have accounted for much more than half of the expenditures of the U.S. federal government in recent years and for one third of the total federal, state, and local governmental expenditures, capital assets, and workers. Fifty years ago national defense accounted for only 10 percent of government's total expenditures.

Peace and war are no longer easily separable. Since the end of World War II the great nations of the world have had to devote a major share of their economic and human resources to developing and maintaining military strength. Ever since the Korean conflict the United States has given increasing attention to defense requirements. Expenditures for defense totaled $13 billion in 1949, reached a peak of $50 billion during the Korean period, but never fell below $38 billion. Since 1962 federal expenditures for national defense have exceeded $50 billion annually and reached $60 billion by 1967. Together with the cost of the international activities of the federal government they account directly for roughly 10 percent of gross national product.

Foreign policies have similarly been motivated primarily by desires to strengthen national security and to win the friendship and support of allies. Today national security involves not merely the training of combat forces but also the maintenance of a stable economy capable of industrial production at high levels. National security includes the education of a nation's youth and the continued development of scientific facilities and research in nuclear fission, space technology, guided missiles and satellites, supersonic aircraft, and other fields. It may require the mobilization of the economy and man power of the nation for all-out concentration on war or defense. Military power for national security involves almost all the activities of a society at peace. The peacetime concern for a prosperous and productive agriculture, for example, becomes a vital consideration in developing military strength. The general well-being of various age groups, the effective operation of manufacturing industries, the development of technical and vocational skills of high school and college graduates, the use and conservation of natural resources—all affect a nation's ability to defend itself against military aggression.

ECONOMIC SECURITY AND WELFARE

American governments provide the citizen with a great variety of services, many of which increase his status and security as an individual, and some of which may place restraints upon his freedom to act. These services include public school facilities for educating children and young men and women; insurance against loss of income during old age; public health programs; financing housing for low-income groups; insurance against unemployment; assistance to the aged, dependent children, widows, orphans, and the blind; and services and benefits for veterans, including special insurance, medical care, educational benefits, and business advice. The government providing such welfare services is often called a welfare state.

The term "welfare state" came into general use in the United States after World War II, probably as the result of the publicity concerning the famous report of Lord Beveridge in England on the responsibility of government to support human welfare. But the controversy in the United States about the extent to which government should assume this responsibility goes back at least as far as the Continental Congress. Since the enactment of the Northwest Ordinance of 1787, which set aside a part of every land section between the Ohio and the Mississippi rivers to support education, government activity in behalf of the welfare of its citizens has been extended to include education, housing, social security, medical treatment, social work, human rehabilitation, and promotion of equal opportunities for all individuals regardless of race, color, or creed.

Vast shifts in the country's population in recent decades have produced pressures for more schools, bigger pensions, improved medical facilities, and other social needs. Republicans and Democrats alike who hope to remain in office will probably find it necessary to shape governmental welfare policies along lines indicated by population trends.

The welfare services provided by the federal government continue to increase. In 1965, Congress passed a body of domestic legislation unparalleled since the early years of the New Deal. Forming the broad outlines of President Johnson's Great Society program, this legislation was designed to improve the education, health, and productivity of all who work and to break down barriers to the full development of each citizen's abilities. These programs, which are described in Chapter 25 together with earlier ones in social security, labor, and welfare, now require an annual outlay of about $40 billion, partly in direct expenditures and partly in cash payments to various categories of recipients.

LABOR POLICY

In 1902, President Theodore Roosevelt tried to end a coal strike that threatened to leave the nation without fuel in the winter. The unions welcomed the President's support of their cause, but the coal operators, led by George Baer, president of the Reading Railway, refused to negotiate with the miners. Baer[4] insisted that a workingman has no right to control a business "in which he has no other interest than to secure fair wages for the work he does." He wrote to one labor sympathizer:

The rights and interests of the laboring man will be protected and cared for—not by the labor agitators, but by the Christian men to whom God in his infinite wisdom has given the control of the property interests of the country, and upon the successful Management of which so much depends.

Louis Brandeis,[5] before he became a justice of the Supreme Court, pointed out, however, that the unorganized worker has no effective voice in improving his position and falls victim to the "industrial absolutism" of giant corporations:

It is not merely the case of the individual worker against employer which, even if he is a reasonably sized employer, presents a serious situation calling for the interposition of a union to protect the individual. But we have the situation of an employer so potent, so well-organized, with such concentrated forces and with such extraordinary powers of reserve and the ability to endure against strikes and other efforts of a union, that the relatively loosely organized masses of even strong unions are unable to cope with the situation. . . . There develops within the State a state so powerful that the ordinary social and industrial forces existing are insufficient to cope with it.

The railway president and the liberal lawyer typify the sharp differences of opinion concerning the relative rights and privileges of labor and management. In the twentieth century government has played a dominant role in etching out public policies affecting labor and management that have drastically altered em-

---

[4] The letter, dated July 17, 1902, is photostated in Mark Sullivan, *Our Times, The United States 1900–1925* (New York: Charles Scribner's Sons, 1927), II, p. 425.

[5] From Brandeis' testimony before the U.S. Commission on Industrial Relations, *Final Report and Testimony,* VIII, 1916 (Senate Document No. 415, 64th Cong., 1st Sess.), p. 7660.

ployer-employee relations. The employer wants an adequate number of responsible and effective workers so that he can operate his business at a profit. The employee wants a job that pays fair wages, provides reasonable working conditions, and offers some security of employment. The public interest in labor policy is to find ways to harmonize these sometimes conflicting objectives in order to promote and maintain economic progress for all and security for workers.

In mediating labor-management conflicts government policy has several goals. First, there must be an adequate supply of needed commodities and services to maintain a modern industrial society. Second, public policy is expected to increase equality of opportunity for all citizens and to establish a minimum level of existence below which they will not be permitted to fall. Additionally, workers must be protected from exploitation by employers. In the past such exploitation resulted inevitably from the weaker economic position of the worker. Finally, there is today little or no dispute about the duty of the government to help workers and management to resolve conflicts that curtail production and employment, although there is considerable controversy about the means to achieve this end.

Protecting Workers against Exploitation

Exploitation of workers by employers historically took the form of long working hours under unsafe or unhealthy conditions and at very low wages. Sometimes particular groups were singled out for grossly discriminatory treatment—notably women, children, Negroes, and migrants. Remedial legislation was largely the product of the progressive ferment in American politics from the turn of the century to World War I. It was during this drive for social justice that the first practical steps were taken to forbid the employment of children under sixteen in factories and to establish other protections governing dangerous employment (in mining, for example) and jobs that interfered with education. But, because of Supreme Court decisions sharply limiting the meaning of the interstate commerce clause of the Constitution, the federal government did not successfully regulate child labor until 1938.

Nineteenth-century efforts to protect women workers failed, and not until 1908 did the Supreme Court, under the impact of Louis Brandeis' celebrated brief on the deterioration of health caused by long hours of work, uphold state legislation fixing maximum hours of employment for women. State minimum-wage laws were not fully validated by the Supreme Court until 1937. Migrant workers, especially those employed as seasonal farm workers, were largely unprotected until recent years, and enforcement of state minimum requirements for housing and wages has been very difficult.

Although Negro and white workers share many problems, the former find job opportunities more restricted and encounter more difficult and more pervasive forms of discrimination. A few states have adopted fair-employment–practice laws that forbid employers to discriminate against any person in terms, conditions, or privileges of employment because of color, race, creed, or national origin.

Attempts of states to limit hours of labor have been meager. In 1905, in the

A contract agreement between the United States Steel Corporation and the United Steel Workers. (UPI)

famous *Lochner* case, the Supreme Court held that a New York statute limiting the working hours of bakers violated the baker's freedom of contract.[6] On the other hand, an Oregon statute limiting employment in factories to ten hours a day was upheld in 1917.[7] In interstate commerce or where federal activity was clearly involved, however, the federal government was more successful. Finally, in 1938, general federal regulation of hours of persons employed in interstate commerce was achieved by the Fair Labor Standards Act, which also fixed minimum wages of persons employed in interstate commerce. As the possibility of serious injuries to workers increased with the growing complexity of a technological society, states began in the last century to extend the liability of employers for industrial accidents. Today, under workmen's compensation laws, workers receive payments or medical benefits for injuries incurred on the job.

Protecting Labor's Right to Organize and Bargain Collectively

Until 1933, there were almost no restraints upon American employers in their dealings with labor unions and employees. The judiciary held tenaciously to the dogma that the unorganized worker was as free as his employer to influence the terms of his labor contract. Such restrictive doctrines meant that employers could refuse to recognize unions as bargaining

---

[6] *Lochner v. New York,* 198 U.S. 45 (1905).
[7] *Bunting v. Oregon,* 243 U.S. 426 (1917).

agents for workers, could discharge a worker for joining a union, and could oppose union activity by lockouts, strikebreaking, private police systems, labor spies, black-listing, and company-dominated unions. Under the impact of the depression, however, Congress in 1933, in section 7(a) of the National Industrial Recovery Act, guaranteed the right of employees to organize unions and bargain collectively over terms and conditions of employment. When the NIRA was declared unconstitutional in 1935[8] it was replaced by the National Labor Relations Act, commonly known as the Wagner Act.

The two major aims of the Wagner Act were to encourage collective bargaining and to guarantee each worker the right to join or not to join a union, with the emphasis on joining. From the beginning the act was the target of criticism by management groups and unsuccessful unions. Critics alleged that it permitted certain union practices to threaten the free enterprise system. Charges of labor racketeering, featherbedding, and dictatorial control of unions were cited to support demands for reducing the power of unions and treating the employer more fairly. In the continuing search for a balance of interests in labor-management relations, Congress passed the Labor-Management Relations (Taft-Hartley) Act in 1947, which imposed new restrictions on unions and outlawed certain union practices as unfair. In its attempt to give the employer a measure of protection against union activity, this act somewhat increases government intervention in collective bargaining.

Settling Labor Disputes

Labor's principal weapon in enforcing demands on employers is the strike. The right to strike has been curbed by judicial decisions, by statutes, by voluntary restraint during periods of national emergency, and by labor-management agreement. The Taft-Hartley Act provides some complicated machinery for delaying strikes. Generally, either party to a labor dispute affecting interstate commerce must give the other party a sixty-day notice of intention to terminate or modify a labor contract. During this cooling-off period strikes are forbidden while the government attempts to mediate the dispute. When a strike affects an industry so that national health or safety is imperiled the Attorney General may ask a federal judge to forbid a strike for eighty days while a presidential board attempts to settle the dispute. These emergency provisions of the Taft-Hartley Act have been invoked in recent years against strikes in atomic energy, coal, shipping, steel, telephone service, and airlines.

Protecting the Freedom of Workers

In the 1930s great issue in labor-management relations was the right of workers to form "unions of their own choosing." But since the government guaranteed the worker's right to organize and bargain

---

[8] *Schechter v. United States,* 295 U.S. 495 (1935).

collectively, the national economy has undergone revolutionary change. Business practices have been subjected to wide-ranging supervision by government; Congress has committed the nation to a policy of promoting high levels of production and employment; government-sponsored security measures 'for workers and farmers have multiplied; and "managerial prerogatives" of employers have been substantially modified as labor organizations have prospered. By the 1950s, unions had become well established in most major industries. They had succeeded in affecting the income, leisure, job opportunities, security, pace of work, discipline, and retirement of workers, and their influence extended even into the political life of the nation. Unions had come of age, but a few of them had also become corrupt. The remarkable change in the role of labor in the American economy is demonstrated by the Labor-Management Reporting and Disclosure Act of 1959, which establishes a "Bill of Rights of Members of Labor Organizations" and attempts to enforce a system of financial and organizational accountability for union officers. Unions have come a long way since the 1920s. It is a measure of their growth that American society has become less concerned with their impact on employers and production and more with their impact on the freedom of workers.

AGRICULTURAL POLICY

From the time of the Constitutional convention to the present day the farmer's problems have been both acute and persistent, and at least since the Civil War he has never hesitated to turn to the government for help. The reason for his chronic distress is not hard to find. Agriculture is the oldest and most essential of man's economic activities, yet it has inherent qualities that seem to throw it out of balance with the rest of the nation's economy. Farming is a risky business. On the one hand the farmer is threatened by natural hazards over which he has no control: too much or too little rain, sun, or wind and too many insects. On the other hand, when the good years finally come, the farmer seems to grow too much, and the resultant surpluses depress the market and once more deny him a fair return. In the face of falling prices a businessman cuts production, but the farmer's natural inclination is to try to grow more and thus hold up his income. Faced with the possibility of economic ruin by forces beyond his control, the farmer long ago found that he could turn to government and exert enough political pressure to secure the adoption of beneficial public measures. Undoubtedly, much of the farmer's problem today is the cumulative consequence of his inability to adjust to the forces of change. Under the impact of rapidly advancing technology, rising capital requirements, overhanging surpluses, and declining income, his turning to government and to politics for answers to his economic problems has become a staple of the American political system.

Farming was once the major occupation of Americans. In 1910 more than a third of the population lived on the land and were engaged in farming. By 1965, farm people totaled less than 13 million and made up 6.4 percent of the population; over a million people were leaving farms each year. Today American agriculture consists of two sectors, one expanding and one diminishing. The former, which is growing rapidly, is made up of farms with annual gross sales in excess of $10,000. In 1965, there were slightly over 1 million of these farms, or 31 percent of all farms, and their share of total farm marketing was an estimated 83 percent. These were typically family farms using very little hired labor and requiring greatly increased amounts of capital. The declining sector comprised in 1965 about 2 million farms, whose contribution to farm production was rather negligible. Many of these families were underemployed in agriculture, seriously undercapitalized in equipment and livestock, and living in poverty. Families on these farms derived little benefit from governmental price- and income-support programs.

In terms of growth in productivity, agriculture is a highly progressive segment of the American economy. Yet farm income is low relative to incomes earned in other occupations, and farm employment is steadily declining. Commercial farms have a total capacity to produce far in excess of the market demand for produce at reasonable prices. As inputs of machinery, insecticides, and fertilizers have become more important in farm production, crop production per acre in 1965 soared 18 percent over the 1959–1961 average.

Objectives of Agricultural Policy

The major long-term goals of government agricultural policies may be summarized as follows:

1. The prime objective of any nation's agricultural policy is, of course, to achieve abundant and continuous supplies of food and fiber for consumers. A related objective is the expansion of domestic consumption of food, not only quantitatively but also in terms of better-balanced diets of higher nutritive content. Securing abundant food production is closely related to general economic conditions. If family incomes can be increased, food consumption will rise and farmers will be able to sell more commodities at favorable prices.

2. Because of the political strength of farm groups, the major goal of American agricultural policy is to improve the economic position of farmers. This can be achieved by assuring them a higher and more stable income. The objective can be summarized as a fair share of the national income for farm families and a fair exchange value for farm products. Agricultural policy has been largely shaped by the belief that agriculture has not—at least since 1909–1914—had a fair share of the national income as compared with industry and labor. This is the objective with which farmers are principally concerned.

3. Another objective of agricultural policy is to provide for the conservation and wise use of agricultural resources. Much land in the United States has been ruined or damaged by erosion. Farms have been worn out through destruction of the soil, overgrazing by cattle, and wasteful practices in cutting timber. Families were permitted to settle on poor land or on plots too small to be operated efficiently. Large areas of grassland and forest were mistakenly opened up to farming, and land speculation encouraged wasteful management of soil resources. Incentives to conserve land developed only after cheap and abundant land was ex-

hausted. In agricultural policy conservation is closely linked to the objective of economic security. The government assists farmers to earn a fair share of the national income but insists in return upon their adopting soil-conserving practices.

4. Agricultural policy also aims to eliminate rural poverty and to rehabilitate disadvantaged farm groups. Not only does the government hope to raise farm income above the poverty line for all farmers but it also hopes to encourage farm ownership to improve the status of farm tenants, and to develop rural institutions capable of providing adequate social services.

Parity, Price Supports, and Soil Banks

During the election campaign of 1932 the Democrats promised to find a solution to agricultural problems and to put an end to farm bankruptcies and land foreclosures. Accordingly, the New Deal established a series of farm-aid programs based on the view that the national government had a responsibility to help farmers get fair prices for their products. These programs established a standard for farm prices that, its sponsor said, was equally fair to farmers and to those who bought farm products. This standard was named *parity*. It was designed to establish farm prices that were on a par, in terms of buying power, with prices farmers had received in some period in the past when their general position was good. For example, if three bushels of wheat had bought a pair of pants in this earlier period of farm prosperity, then, according to the principle of parity, farm prices should be such that three bushels of wheat would continue to buy a pair of pants.

Farm legislation developed a formula for determining parity prices for many farm commodities. Under the formula parity, or "fair," prices rise and fall with changes in the prices of things farmers buy in such a way that equality of price is maintained between the farm product and the nonfarm product. Until recently parity was based on the relation between farm and nonfarm prices in the years 1909–1914, a period of unprecedented farm prosperity. Parity prices actually are only a rough attempt to rationalize a policy of keeping farm prices from falling below certain levels.

Since the early 1940s the government has supplemented previous programs with an elaborate system of *price supports,* which places a floor under agricultural prices. Basically, the plan requires the government to make loans to farmers on those portions of their crops that are held off the market. This makes it necessary for buyers of farm produce to match the price-support loan rate in order to buy from farmers. The program works like this: The government offers to make loans to farmers on a particular commodity. When the market price falls below the price-support loan the farmer may store his grain and receive a loan from the Commodity Credit Corporation figured at the higher price-support rate. If the market price remains below the price-support level, the farmer may then leave his crop permanently with the CCC, which accepts it as repayment of the loan. As long as the crop is stored under the commodity loan it is not available for the market.

Price supports are tied to the parity formula. In recent years many commodities have been supported by prices equivalent to 75 to 90 percent or more of parity. During periods when expansion of production is required price supports are useful as a guide to farm production. Floors under prices lessen risks and encourage production of needed crops. In periods of declining prices, however, price-support loan programs force the government to buy and store huge quantities of commodities in order to maintain prices. In recent years legislation has continued a trend in farm policy toward lower price supports, supplemented by direct government payments to farmers growing wool, sugar, feed grains, wheat, and cotton.

GOVERNMENT REGULATION OF BUSINESS

Historical Development

Most regulatory or promotional activities of government have originated at the state or local level. An exception may be seen in the case of a totally new form of enterprise, such as the production and use of atomic energy, which emerges so suddenly and upon such a broad scale that national control is immediately necessary. But in times past, when economic enterprise was conducted almost exclusively upon a local scale, it was only natural that pressure for government activity to promote or to regulate enterprise was felt first at the local level. So long as businesses remained relatively small and produced goods and services for local markets, local units of government were able to devise and administer regulatory policies with a considerable degree of success. But as business enterprise expanded beyond the political boundaries of single communities, local government controls became less effective and the pressure for regulation soon spread to the states.

Before the Civil War, such government regulation or promotion of the economy as existed was primarily local or state. Thereafter, until the close of the nineteenth century, state governments assumed increasing responsibility for the satisfactory handling of economic problems. As transportation facilities improved, business enterprise burst through state boundaries, and goods were soon being sold and consumed thousands of miles away from the places where they had been produced. Many businesses hitherto local or state-wide in scope now expanded and entered regional or national markets. The corporate form of business enterprise was perfected and eased the transition from locally owned and managed establishments to the great national concerns of today owned by hundreds of thousands of security holders and operated by professional managers. The state inevitably found the regulation of these new forms of business enterprise increasingly difficult, and beginning around the turn of the century demands were made that Congress undertake to establish necessary national controls.

Government policies concerning economic enterprise in the United States have not developed according to a carefully conceived plan or systematic philosophy. Instead, they have been evolved through trial and reflect the traditional experimental approach that has prevailed in almost all phases of American social development. Regulation of economic enterprise has certainly not been established as the result of any master plan to destroy capitalism or free enterprise. The immediate motivation of governmental control has usually been a desire to protect the free enterprise system against forces or conditions threatening to destroy it from within. For example, antitrust regulation is designed to protect small enterprises against monopoly. Moreover, the pressure for such a policy has come largely from businessmen themselves. As a result of the unplanned development of government economic controls, the relations between business and the government are not orderly and do not follow any comprehensive philosophy. Instead, it has been possible to adjust the solutions of particular problems to "felt abuses" and "specific evils."

Although executive, legislative, and judicial branches of government have all participated—and still do—in formulating and administering public economic controls, the role played by legislatures has declined and that of administrative agencies has become more important. Before 1860, most government control of the economy in the United States was the work of city councils and state legislatures, with very little assistance from executive agencies. But as the economy became increasingly industrialized after the Civil War, legislatures soon found themselves unable to cope with the burden of regulatory activity. Led by Massachusetts in 1869, the states began to establish commissions to administer regulatory statutes. The first federal regulatory agency, the Interstate Commerce Commission, was established by Congress in 1887. This step marked a new era in government regulation of business—an era characterized by greater federal participation in economic regulation and by increasing use of administrative bodies as the agencies of control.

The Courts and Government Regulation of the Economy

The courts have always played an important part in government control of the economy. Even before legislatures or administrative agencies, they were actively engaged in regulating and promoting economic enterprise in England and America. An important function of the common law court in England was to settle litigation growing out of business conflicts between private persons, particularly those having to do with contractual obligations.

The Commerce Clause of the Constitution

As early as 1824, in the case of *Gibbons v. Ogden,* the Supreme Court of the United States profoundly affected the course of government control of the economy. The Court canceled a monopoly in the operation of steamboats in New York-New Jersey waters that had been granted by the New York legislature and upheld the license that a competing firm had obtained from the federal government. The court ruled that the federal commerce power established prior right of Congress to control such navigation, and it upheld a federal statute providing for the free issuance of licenses to coastal vessels while invalidating a state law granting a monopoly to such a vessel.[9] It has been said that this ruling marked the beginning of a federal antitrust policy.

The commerce clause of Article 1 of the Constitution and the due process of law clauses of the Fifth and Fourteenth Amendments have been widely used to review the validity of legislative and administrative controls of the economy. During the nineteenth century, on the basis of the commerce clause, the courts invalidated state controls by asserting that they encroached upon power delegated by the Constitution to the federal government. In the present century, as the center of control shifted from the states to the national government, conservative judges reversed this reasoning and held that federal use of the commerce power had become so broad as to encroach upon powers reserved to the states by the Constitution—in particular, the power to regulate intrastate commerce. At times the courts succeeded in creating a twilight zone in which neither the states nor the federal government could act effectively.

The Due Process Clauses and Government Control of the Economy

The Fifth and Fourteenth Amendments forbid the national government and the states, respectively, to deprive any person of liberty or property without due process of law. Near the end of the nineteenth century lawyers, acting on behalf of businessmen, succeeded in persuading the courts to define "person" to include corporations and to interpret "due process of law" so as to invalidate progressive regulatory legislation. For example, maximum railroad rates established by statute or administrative regulation were frequently invalidated by the courts on the ground that they were fixed so low that they prevented the railroads from earning a fair profit and thus deprived them of their property in unreasonable or arbitrary fashion—that is, without due process of law.

Through narrow interpretation of the commerce and due process clauses and of statutes enacted under them the courts obstructed government regulation of the economy in the half-century following 1885. One branch of the government thus set itself in opposition to the two other branches, and for many years the development of an orderly, progressive program of government control of the economy was difficult if not impossible. In the middle of the 1930s, in a fundamental reversal of judicial policy, the Supreme Court reinterpreted the two clauses so as to virtually end their use as barriers to state and federal regulation of economic enterprise.

GOVERNMENT AND SCIENCE

The twentieth-century revolution in science and technology has brought about a rapid proliferation of governmental financing of university and industrial research and development. Not only has the

---

[9] Wheaton 1 (1824).

traditional wall between what is public and what is private been further breached but also the nature of modern science has blurred the traditional line between the policy-maker and the technical adviser.

Most of the scientific activities of the government today have their precedents in the nineteenth century. In that period government action consisted of support for and use of science and technology to achieve governmental aims and cooperation with professional scientific societies. The first federal scientific program can be traced to 1790, when the Patent Office was created, the decennial census was inaugurated, and a uniform system of weights and measures was established. Perhaps the first federal grant for experimental research was made in 1832 to the Franklin Institute for an investigation of explosions in steam boilers. The Smithsonian Institution was incorporated as a national foundation in 1846. After the Civil War a major expansion of federal scientific activities came with the development of the land-grant colleges and a vast federal-state cooperative system of education and research in agriculture.

The use of science in many government programs concerned with the exploration of the American frontier gave added impetus to government's developing role in science. Federal support was extended to the Lewis and Clark expedition; an engineering school was established at West Point; and the Naval Observatory was one of the earliest federal agencies to support basic research. A reflection of the growing cooperation between scientists and government officials was the chartering of the National Academy of Sciences in 1863. In 1901, the National Bureau of Standards was established, followed by the National Advisory Committee for Aeronautics in 1951 and the National Research Council in 1918.

Until World War II the scientific activities of the federal government were not based on a general policy but were developed in connection with specific governmental operations, such as the survey activities of the Geological Survey and the testing and measurement activities of the National Bureau of Standards. As a result, there was heavy emphasis in all government activities on applied research and almost no support of basic research, for which it was generally assumed the federal government could not properly take any responsibility.

The experience of World War II drastically altered government-science relations. Universities and industrial laboratories for the first time received public funds on a contractual basis, and wholly new nongovernmental bodies working almost entirely on governmental projects were created. The patterns of cooperation developed then persist in contemporary science organization.

The first general-purpose federal science agency was the National Science Foundation, created in 1950 to develop a national policy for the promotion of basic research and education in the sciences. Almost every year its appropriation has been increased by Congress. In 1957, President Eisenhower created the Office of the Special Assistant for Science and Technology, a Science Advisory Committee composed of some of the nation's most eminent scientists, and a Federal Council for Science and Technology. These agencies increased the potential for government-wide coordination of science policy, but many critics argued that only the creation of a Department of Science and Technology could provide effective central direction. President Kennedy's solution, as accepted by Congress, was the

This photograph, taken by a Gemini XI astronaut, shows a view of India and Ceylon from a distance of 540 nautical miles above the earth's surface looking north, with the Bay of Bengal to the right and the Arabian Sea to the left. (NASA)

creation in 1962 of an Office of Science and Technology in the executive office of the President.

In this way science came increasingly to be regarded by governmental officials as a major national resource requiring continuing federal support and encouragement; scientists were treated as a very special type of public official; the war-born partnership with business and the educational community was extended; and science as a part of the policy-making machinery of the government was given higher status in the federal hierarchy.

This pattern continues today. In 1938, federal expenditures on scientific research and development totaled $48 million. In 1967, federal spending for scientific research and development reached $16 billion. Although the government now provides 60 percent of national expenditures for research and development, the bulk of scientific work is done in the laboratories of industrial companies and universities, most of it under government contract.

The agencies spending the largest sums for scientific research and development, in order of magnitude, are: the U.S. Department of Defense, the National Aeronautics and Space Administration (NASA), the Atomic Energy Commission (AEC), the U.S. Department of Health, Education and Welfare, the National Science Foundation, the Department of Agriculture, and the Department of the Interior. Annual expenditures for scientific purposes by the Department of Defense and NASA today exceed $5 billion each and account for about 80 percent of all federal expenditures for scientific research and development.

Government by Contract

One of the most striking changes in the American system of government in recent years has been the growth of government contracting, by means of which the government uses nongovernmental agencies to provide various services. Government by contract has developed without explicit policy guidance from Congress or the Presidency. The causes of this growth are reasonably clear. Contracting has been viewed as one way to meet some crucial needs of society without building up the personnel and physical resources of the government itself, to stimulate private economic activity, to get around rigid civil service salary schedules, to compete for scarce talent, to recognize that many Americans prefer to work for nongovernmental agencies, and so forth. We know very little, however, about the conditions under which the contract system works satisfactorily.

The contract is not the traditional market affair. It is not let on competitive bids, the product cannot be specified, the price is not fixed, the government supplies much of the plant and capital, and the government may determine or approve the letting of subcontracts, the salaries of key executives, and a host of other managerial matters. A sizable proportion of the government's (and the nation's) business is done this way; and any one of six industrial corporations spends more federal tax dollars than any of the four smallest executive departments.[10]

The Korean war greatly stimulated the use of contracting by the federal government. Since 1950 American experience indicates that the system creates many difficult problems while solving others. Contracting gives rise to an enormous range of group pressures on the government. A state university that has expanded its facilities to handle a government contract may regard the continuation of the contract as vital to its status and program, and the federal agency may find it most difficult to allow the contract to expire. Employees of contracting firms may press hard for the extension of the protections and benefits of civil service on the ground that they are government employees as well as private employees. Sometimes the government may be able to obtain the services of an expert on a contractual basis when it would be prevented from employing that person directly by the federal conflict-of-interest statutes. At the same time, government by contract may, under certain conditions, be the only way, or the best way, for the government to obtain needed services. But it has also produced a new type of corporation, the "kept" corporation, a nonprofit firm whose business is entirely or mainly with the government, whose operations may be carried out in public buildings, and whose income is in the form of fixed fees over costs. Such organizations hardly qualify as "private."

The New Federalism

The decentralized character of governmental programs in scientific research and development reflects what may be called the New Federalism of the postwar era. Just as the grant-in-aid system established new patterns of administration and provided a workable compromise between federal centralization and state autonomy in handling problems of national scope, so does the contractual scheme make possible dominant federal support for scientific and technological developments without centralizing operations in Washington. Today the California Institute of Technology can undertake major

[10] Don K. Price, "The Scientific Establishment," *Science,* 136 (1962), p. 1104.

responsibility for rocket research; the University of California for jet propulsion; the Institute for Defense Analyses for weapons system evaluation; and the Aerospace Corporation for space technology, while major industrial giants such as Union Carbide, DuPont, Monsanto, General Electric, and others build facilities to produce military hardware and carry out other research programs. Several major universities today administer special atomic and nuclear programs for the government and consequently draw 50 to 85 percent of their budgets from government. Certain private institutions, such as Yale, Harvard, and Princeton, now get a larger proportion of their operating revenues from federal research funds than do such land-grant universities as Illinois, Kentucky, and Maryland.

It is difficult to exaggerate the significance of the New Federalism. Industrial corporations now maintain Air Force bombers and missile ranges under contract, universities administer technical assistance programs all over the globe, dozens of manufacturing firms work with the National Aeronautics and Space Administration on manned lunar landings, and private research institutes prepare studies for congressional committees on aspects of American foreign policy. One result of these new relations between public and private institutions is the breaking down of some of the political opposition to federal programs. Don Price[11] has described the alteration of the general attitude of corporate industry toward government:

Now that the atomic energy and space and military programs support such a large share of the nation's business, and so much of its enterprise and innovation come from research and development financed by federal funds, and so much of that innovation and enterprise spills over quite naturally into related commercial fields, it is no wonder that private business corporations are less jealous of government. More accurately, their jealousy no longer takes the form of fighting socialism, but of haggling over the administrative provisions of contracts. A great deal of private enterprise is now secreted in the interstices of government contracts. In short, what the grant-in-aid programs did to the argument for states' rights, the new contractual systems are doing to those for private enterprise.

Problems in Science Policy

Beginning with World War II the strategic nature of much scientific work led to the establishment of regulations to protect national security and to ensure the loyalty of scientists working on military matters. Under the contract system of the New Federalism these problems are now shared with universities and business corporations. Personal loyalty requirements have proved distasteful to many scholars and scientists, and universities have grave difficulties squaring security requirements with free scientific inquiry.

A second problem of growing importance concerns the impact of federal activities on the universities. Some problems evolve out of the intricacies of government-university relationships and the government's need for strict accountability of the way public funds are spent. But the more significant problems reflect the growing dependence of universities upon federal grants, which have an increasing share of their operating budgets. A third problem area reflects a controversy about

---

[11] P. 1104.

both the real and the alleged impact of government research and development on economic growth. For example, some economists have argued that the contract system tends to foster concentration of economic control in the hands of large corporations. The sheer size of many contracts gives the government enormous power—both in the granting and withholding of contracts—to influence the economic life of the country. Finally, potential danger lies in the expectation of the public that the scientific community can supply infallible answers to all problems. As a noted scientist has stated:[12]

Science moves from puzzled observation, through inspired guesswork, to established conclusions. The process may take centuries, as in the case of the heliocentric explanation of the solar system; or a few years, as with the fission of uranium. The degree of certainty with which scientists can answer a question depends on the stage in this process which they have reached.

According to this scientist, scientists advising the government should "learn to label their statements—to put them into categories of reliability: (1) This we know . . . (2) This we believe . . . (3) This we guess. . . ."

Selected Bibliography

Bauer, Raymond A., Ithiel de Sola Pool, and Lewis A. Dexter, *American Business and Public Policy: The Politics of Foreign Trade* (New York: Atherton Press, 1963). A discussion of the role of private groups in the policy-making process, including generalizations beyond the specific issue on which it focuses.

Levitan, Sar A., *Federal Aid to Depressed Areas* (Baltimore, Md.: The Johns Hopkins Press, 1964). A study of the legislative origin and early operation of the Area Redevelopment Administration.

Price, Don K., *The Scientific Estate* (Cambridge, Mass.: Harvard University Press, 1965). A brilliant theoretical discussion of the impact of scientific developments on governmental activities and the difficulties of policy-making in areas heavily affected by scientific and technological considerations.

Smith, Bruce L. R., *The RAND Corporation: A Case Study of a Nonprofit Advisory Corporation* (Cambridge, Mass., Harvard University Press, 1966). A perceptive account of an important new organizational concept for assisting the government in new areas of interest.

U.S. Bureau of the Budget, *The Federal Budget in Brief* (Washington, D.C.: Government Printing Office, published annually). A summary of the President's proposals for government programs for the coming year.

Van Dyke, Vernon, *Pride and Power: The Rationale of the Space Program* (Urbana, Ill.: University of Illinois Press, 1964). A critical discussion of the motivations, organization, and decision-making procedures supporting the space program.

Wiesner, Jerome B., *Where Science and Politics Meet* (New York: McGraw-Hill, Inc., 1965). A general treatment of the growing role of scientists in government by one of the important participants in recent policy-making in this field.

---

[12] *Henry De Wolf Smyth,* "This Science Knows—and This It Guesses," *New York Times Magazine,* May 13, 1962, pp. 16, 101.

Part 5 Establishing Justice

Summary of Supreme Court's Actions

SPECIAL TO THE NEW YORK TIMES

WASHINGTON, June 6— The Supreme Court took the following actions today:

Antitrust

Upheld the Federal Trade Commission's ruling that a franchise granted by the Brown Shoe Company to retailers, under which the retailers agreed to concentrate on the Brown Shoe lines, amounted to unfair competition with other manufacturers (No. 118, Federal Trade Commission vs. Brown Shoe Company Inc.).

Contempt

Upheld, 6 to 2, the power of a Federal judge to give a six-month prison sentence for criminal contempt and a $100,000 fine for criminal contempt of court in violating a Federal Trade Commission order, with six Justices stating that a judge cannot give such a sentence for a term of more than six months without a trial by jury (No. 67, Cheff vs. Schnackenberg).

Ruled, 7 to 1, that contempt sentences against two New York crime syndicate figures for refusing to testify under grants of immunity before a grand jury were civil and not criminal contempt, and that the men must be released from jail because the life of the grand jury had expired (No. 412, Shillitani vs. United States; No. 442, Pappadio vs. United States).

Criminal Law

Threw out, by an 8-to-1 vote, the second-degree murder conviction of Samuel H. Sheppard, osteopathic surgeon from Cleveland, on the ground that "massive" publicity had denied him a fair trial (No. 490, Sheppard vs. Maxwell).

Let stand the 18-month prison sentence of Lawrence W. Medlin of Nashville, Tenn., for offering a $10,000 bribe to a juror to vote for acquittal in the 1962 trial of James R. Hoffa, president of the Teamsters International Union (No. 1228, Medlin vs. United States).

Divorce

Let stand a decision of the New York Court of Appeals that recognized the validity of a "quickie" Mexican divorce, in which one spouse had gone to Mexico to obtain the divorce with the consent of the other (No. 1242, Rosenstiel vs. Rosenstiel).

Government Contracts

Ruled unanimously that, when the Board of Contract Appeals erroneously dismisses an appeal before it as untimely and the Court of Claims reverses, the case should be sent back to the board to make a record on the disputed issue, rather than having this done before the Court of Claims (No. 439, United States vs. Anthony Grace & Sons, Inc.).

Ruled unanimously that disputes settled by administrative decisions under a Government procurement contract are not subject to new review by the Board of Contract Appeals in an appeal of other disputes under the contract (No. 440, United States vs. Utah Construction and Mining Co.).

Labor

Let stand a lower court ruling that horseshoers at Maryland race tracks are independent contractors and not employes of race horse owners, so that the horseshoers' efforts to establish a minimum rate for shoeing of horses could be a violation of Federal antitrust laws (No. 1175, Local No. 7, International Union of Journeymen Horseshoers of U.S. and Canada vs. Taylor).

Agreed to decide whether a provision in a collective bargaining contract that the employer shall not purchase prefabricated materials incorporating work that his employes had traditionally performed violated the prohibition of the National Labor Relations Act against "hot cargo" clauses (No. 1247, National Labor Relations Board vs. National Woodwork Manufacturers' Assn.; No. 1238, National Woodworks Manufacturers' Assn. vs. National Labor Relations Board).

Agreed to decide whether a union can be liable in damages for refusing to take a member's grievance against the employer to arbitration in the good-faith belief that it lacked merit (No. 1267, Vaca vs. Siples).

Let stand the New York Court of Appeals' denial of a court order requiring District Attorney Frank S. Hogan of New York County to disclose whether he has planted, under a court eavesdropping order, electronic eavesdropping devices in the premises of Hyman S. Siegel, an attorney indicted in connection with bribery of state liquor authority employes (No. 1236, Siegel vs. New York).

Taxation

Ruled, 8 to 1, that a Federal tax lien, recorded prior to default on a mortgage, is entitled to priority over the mortgagee's claim for an attorney's fee fixed by statute and taxed as costs in the foreclosure action (No. 645, United States vs. The Equitable Life Assurance Society of the United States).

Agreed to decide whether an expired Federal tax lien is extended indefinitely by means of an undocketed tax judgment (No. 1106, Hodes vs. United States).

18

The judicial process and the American court system

THE NATURE AND GROWTH OF LAW

Law consists of those formal rules by which human conduct is governed in an organized society, and, in particular, of those formal rules that are recognized and enforced by courts. These rules are concerned both with man's dealings with his government and his relations with his fellow men. Law covers basic human relations involving ownership of property, titles to land, making and enforcement of contracts, organization of business enterprises, employment of labor, buying and selling of goods, marriage and divorce, inheritance of estates, and commission of antisocial acts such as murder, arson, and burglary. Law should give men advance notice of their rights and responsibilities, and it also should warn them that government will enforce the regulations upon which these rights and responsibilities rest.

Anglo-American Law: Common Law, Equity, and Statutes

Anglo-American law had its origins not so much in statutes enacted by legislative bodies as in customs, church teachings and practices, as well as decisions rendered by judges. In England during the centuries after the Norman Conquest judges were called upon to referee disputes that arose between individuals in their daily lives. They rendered decisions based in part upon customary usages and in part upon their own common sense or personal prejudices, or on a need to serve the interests of the king, the nobility, the church, or some other class institution. In this way there came into being a body of judicial rulings, said to be derived from "the common custom of the realm," which became known as *common law*. The law was common in the sense that it had replaced the systems of local law or custom formerly prevailing in different parts of England and also in the sense that it differed from special law, such as the canon law of the church.

At an early stage in the development of common law the quest for certainty led to the appearance of the rule of *stare decisis* (which means "adhere to the decisions"). When a case had a counterpart in previous litigation judges felt that the decision in the earlier case should constitute a precedent and should govern disposition of the later one. In this way the administration of justice took on a degree of historical continuity—as opposed to a system in which judges might render justice in each case anew without regard to what had gone before. By means of *stare decisis* "as cases grew in number and variety they became a storehouse of knowledge and understanding, representing the cumulative experience of the bench in resolving the tangles of human affairs."[1]

Through the centuries the common law developed as a judge-made, national system of law covering most of the social and economic problems existing in English society. But gradually the common law tended to harden into a more or less permanent set of forms of action that enabled people to obtain relief in court only in standard situations. This rigidity prevented the common law courts from hearing cases that lay outside the fixed pattern. But the English social system was still evolving, and strong pressures arose for the establishment of judicial machinery that would make it possible to obtain justice in situations in which the common law was inadequate. Accordingly, petitions to the king for justice in such cases were increasingly referred to a member of the king's executive council, the chancellor. This official's department, the chancery, developed into a court, separate and apart from the common law courts, possessing jurisdiction over cases the latter could not hear. The law enforced in this court came to be known as *equity*.

The chief common law remedy in civil suits was an award of money damages to compensate for a wrong; the common law could do little or nothing to prevent or abate the wrong itself. For example,

Suppose that X has a house on the edge of his land, with windows looking over the land belonging to Y, and that X has acquired a right to light, sometimes called "ancient lights." If Y

---

[1] Walton H. Hamilton, "Judicial Process," *Encyclopaedia of the Social Sciences,* 8, pp. 450, 452–453.

builds on his land so as to block X's windows, then Y has infringed X's rights: X's remedy at common law is to sue Y and recover damages. The remedy in equity would be to ask the court to grant an injunction prohibiting Y from erecting the building, or if the building is already erected, to command Y to pull it down.[2]

In this situation, then, the common law could provide only remedial justice, whereas equity could give preventive or corrective justice. Serving as a sanction to enforce orders in equity was the threat of a citation for contempt of court.

Equity was thus a force for reform of the law. It provided a means of adapting legal rules to a changing society, at a time when the common law seemingly could not. The origin of rules of equity, like the origin of common law rules, remains obscure. Since there were no precedents to follow, early equity cases were said to be decided on the basis of "natural justice." But equity soon began to accumulate precedents, and these rulings soon had much the same vitality in equity that similar rulings had in the common law.

For many centuries courts of law and courts of equity remained separate institutions, following different procedures. For example, equity cases were tried without a jury, and, on appeal, were tried anew both as to the facts and the law; common law cases were usually tried with a jury and, on appeal, were subject to a review as to questions of law only. But by the middle of the nineteenth century the historic reasons that had brought about the existence of these two systems administered by separate courts had ceased to exist, and Parliament established a single-court system. In this regard the British were following American precedent. Since 1789, federal courts have been authorized to decide both common law and equity cases, a practice generally, though not universally, accepted today in the states.

Today a great deal of law is embodied in statutes. Much statutory law, however, is of quite recent origin. Legislation as a basis of English law "played no highly significant part . . . until the second quarter of the nineteenth century."[3]

Like equity at an earlier time, statutes were generally a progressive force in the development of the law. By the nineteenth century the common law had again become conservative. It served to protect private property and to exalt the spirit of economic individualism. In so doing it enabled the individual to use his property as he saw fit, regardless of the social consequences. Accordingly, as considerations of social welfare came to play a more important role in English and American society, legislatures altered the rules of common law to safeguard and enhance the public interest. For example, a striking change in the common law made by modern statutes concerns the degree to which an employer is liable for injuries suffered by his workers while on the job. The common law excluded such liability where an injury resulted solely from the negligence of a fellow worker and the employer was not at fault. Today, however, in the interest of protecting workers against the hazards of industrial employment, many statutes provide that an employer shall compensate an injured worker under such circumstances.

---

[2] R. Jackson, *The Machinery of Justice in England* (Cambridge: Cambridge University Press, 1940), p. 10.

[3] J. A. Corry, *Elements of Democratic Government* (New York: Oxford University Press, 1947), p. 321.

Statutes and Judge-made Law

There is no doubt about the constitutional or political power of a British or an American legislature to replace judge-made law by statute law. But it is impossible to make statutory law so comprehensive that it will cover all cases arising under it. In the end, "law" is a mixture of statutes, common law, and equity. For one thing, when a legislature passes a statute it may be strongly influenced by common law and attempt merely to give more definite form to an essentially similar rule originally made by judges and long applied by them. Moreover, following the enactment of a statute, there is almost always a necessity for further growth of the law. Years go by and courts render hundreds and even thousands of decisions under this statute. Judges often interpret it in the light of new conditions and problems which have arisen, and, as a result, the law that actually operates and controls is something more than the original statue.

In general, courts do not act on their own initiative, nor do they function continuously or systematically as law-enforcement agencies. Instead, the judicial wheels begin to turn only when specific business is brought to the courts from outside. Requests that courts bring their powers into play by hearing cases and rendering judgments come from two sources—from private citizens who bring their civil disputes to the courts for solution and from public officers who are responsible for law enforcement.

A great deal of litigation gets settled without ever being brought to trial. Lawyers advise clients about the rules that cover their activities, thereby enabling them either to avoid legal difficulties or to settle many conflicts without going to court. The trial process is a costly one and the incentive to avoid a final showdown in the courtroom is strong. In other words, the law and the courts often serve their function merely by existing.

THE AMERICAN DUAL-COURT SYSTEM

An outstanding characteristic of the American judiciary is the existence, side by side, of two entirely separate court systems. On one side is the federal judiciary consisting of some one hundred trial and appellate courts scattered throughout the nation. On the other side are the judiciaries in the fifty states, with the total number of trial and appellate courts running into the thousands. This dual system is, of course, a result of a federal system of government in which both national and state governments make and enforce laws. If the federal and state courts are to be confined to separate spheres of activity, the jurisdiction of each system of courts must be defined with reasonable precision. The Constitution makes a beginning toward a solution of the problem by spelling out the maximum limits of the jurisdiction of federal courts and, through the Tenth Amendment, reserving to state courts jurisdiction in all other kinds of cases.

Federal Jurisdiction under the Constitution

Article III expressly sets forth federal jurisdiction in one of the most succinctly worded paragraphs of the Constitution. To begin with, jurisdiction is limited to "cases" and "controversies." This means that the federal courts must confine their work to the settlement of bona fide disputes between opposing parties who have a true conflict of legally protected interests. The settlement of friendly or collusive suits and the rendering of advisory opinions are beyond the authority of the federal courts.

Article III then enumerates the specific types of jurisdiction that may be exercised by federal courts. These fall roughly into two categories: one type of case that depends upon the nature of the subject matter being litigated and a second that depends upon the nature of the parties to the litigation. In all, there are nine kinds of "cases" or "controversies" that may be heard in federal courts. These are:

A. Nature of the Subject Matter
  1. Cases arising under the federal Constitution, or a federal statute or treaty;
  2. Cases falling within the fields of so-called admiralty and maritime law.
B. Nature of the Parties
  3. Cases affecting ambassadors and other agents of foreign governments;
  4. Controversies to which the federal government itself is a party;
  5. Controversies between two or more state governments;
  6. Controversies between a state government and citizens of another state, where the state is the plaintiff;[4]
  7. Controversies between citizens of different states;
  8. Controversies between citizens of the same state claiming lands under grants of different states;
  9. Controversies between a state government or citizens of a state and a foreign government or its citizens or subjects.

This is a full statement of federal jurisdiction. Unless a case falls within one of these nine categories it may not under any circumstances be heard by any federal court. It does not follow, however, that federal courts will always take jurisdiction over all such cases. The language of Article III clearly indicates that Congress may (1) assign some, or all, of this jurisdiction to the state courts on a concurrent or even an exclusive basis and (2) distribute this jurisdiction in any way it sees fit among different federal courts. The only exception is that Congress may not alter the original jurisdiction of the Supreme Court to hear cases affecting ambassadors and other foreign agents and cases to which a state government is a party, but this last has come to have a restricted meaning. (See p. 364.)

The Supreme Court is the only federal court specifically mentioned in Article III. Thus it is necessary to turn to federal statutes for detailed information about the federal court system. Congress has provided for the organization and operation of federal courts in a series of judiciary acts. The first of these was passed in 1789 and determined the initial organization of the federal judiciary. Many of the current provisions of the federal judicial code can still be traced back to this act of 1789, but at irregular intervals since that date Congress has passed further legislation dealing with the judiciary.

---

[4] The qualifying clause was added to the Constitution by the Eleventh Amendment.

Overlapping Federal and State Jurisdiction

Under this dual judicial system it is not always easy to draw the line between a case that may be heard in the state courts and one that may be heard in the federal courts. In the first place, the subject matter of a case may involve both state and federal laws and so fall within the jurisdiction of both courts. For example, kidnapings or automobile thefts that involve the crossing of state lines are crimes under both state and federal laws. Depending upon who arrests him, a kidnapper or an automobile thief may be prosecuted in either a state or a federal court. He may even be prosecuted in both, for by his single action he may have committed two crimes—one against state law and one against federal law.

In the second place, Congress has deliberately allowed state courts to exercise some "federal jurisdiction." To limit the work of federal judges and to channel much of the everyday litigation between private persons into the state courts, Congress has provided that federal district courts may take jurisdiction over civil suits between citizens of different states, or arising under federal statutes, only if the amount in controversy exceeds $10,000.[5] Even if the amount does exceed $10,000, the parties to a case, though they are citizens of different states, may choose to take their dispute to a state court rather than to a federal one. Congress has also provided that corporations shall be regarded as "citizens" of the states in which they have their "principal place of business" as well as the states in which they are incorporated. This prevents a corporation from bringing cases in the federal courts against parties who are citizens of either the state in which it is incorporated or has its principal business.

On the other hand, Congress has provided that federal courts shall exercise exclusive jurisdiction in a number of areas. This is true, for example, of all cases arising under federal patent or copyright statutes, all proceedings in bankruptcy, and all suits against ambassadors and foreign agents.

Trial and Appellate Courts

The English and American court systems are arranged in hierarchal fashion with two main levels. At the lower level are the courts of original jurisdiction, known as trial courts. These courts hear and decide cases in the first instance. At the upper level are courts of appellate jurisdiction, known as courts of appeals. These courts review the judgments of the trial courts, affirming, reversing, or correcting them.

A trial court is concerned with the drama of human affairs. Contending attorneys argue, witnesses testify, and jurymen listen and ponder so that the facts

---

[5] There are a few exceptions. See section 41 of title 28 of the United States Code. Title 28 is entitled "Judicial Code and Judiciary" and contains all federal statutory provisions relating to the courts. Section 41 enumerates twenty-eight types of federal district court jurisdiction.

of a controversy may be ascertained and justice rendered under law. Presiding over the trial, but in a sense detached from the proceedings, is the judge. His functions are to insure that proper forms are observed and customary procedures followed and that the litigants and the jury are never at a loss for authoritative legal advice and rulings.

An appellate court presents a very different scene. There are no witnesses or jury. Attorneys discuss disputed points of law by means of written briefs and limited oral arguments. Human drama is at a minimum; the atmosphere of the courtroom is quiet and scholarly. The trial judge is often limited at the end of a case to the mere pronouncing of a *judgment* already clearly indicated by the verdict of the jury, but the appellate judge hands down a legal *decision* supported by a written *opinion*.

THE FEDERAL COURT SYSTEM

The United States District Courts

The trial courts of the federal judicial hierarchy are the district courts, which were established by Congress in 1789. The fifty states are divided into eighty-eight districts, with one court for each district. For the most part the districts coincide with states, but some states have been divided into two or more districts. No district crosses state boundaries. Two additional district courts have been provided for the District of Columbia and Puerto Rico. A district court is usually presided over by a single judge, as are most other trial courts. A district may, however, have as many as 24 judges who hold court simultaneously in different places. The number of federal district judges was 333 in 1967, each judgeship having been authorized by Congress.

District courts have original jurisdiction only. They are, as we have said, the trial courts of the federal government. Here most of the ordinary litigation between private persons that falls within federal jurisdiction—such as disputes between citizens of different states or cases arising under federal statutes—is finally settled. And here prosecutions under federal criminal statutes take place. Since the Constitution guarantees the right to trial by jury in both civil and criminal cases, the district court frequently sits with a jury.

The United States Courts of Appeals

At the first stage of the appellate level of the federal judiciary are the courts of appeals, established by Congress in 1891. The fifty states are divided into ten numbered circuits, with one of these courts for each circuit. The District of Columbia also has a court of appeals. In 1967 the personnel of these eleven courts consisted of eighty-four judges, the usual procedure being for three judges to sit together in reviewing a case. These courts, as the name suggests, have appellate jurisdiction only. Certain kinds of cases may be appealed directly from a federal district court to the Supreme Court, but the great majority of district court judgments—in civil and criminal cases alike—if they are reviewed at all, are reviewed by a court of appeals and go no higher. The courts of appeals also review certain orders of administrative agencies, such as the Interstate Commerce Commission and the Federal Trade Commission, the district courts being by-passed in these instances.

The United States Supreme Court

At the top of the appellate level of the federal judiciary is the U.S. Supreme Court. The Supreme Court is mentioned in the Constitution by name only and depends for its actual organization upon congressional legislation. The Supreme Court is almost exclusively an appellate court. Of the two kinds of cases over which it has original jurisdiction under the Constitution, those that affect ambassadors and foreign agents almost never arise. And those to which a state is a party are not very numerous because the Eleventh Amendment has been used to restrict such cases largely to those in which a state is a plaintiff, suing another state or an agency of the federal government.

The procedure by which cases reach the Supreme Court under its appellate jurisdiction is technically complex because of the double stream of litigation coming both from state and federal courts. Generally speaking, cases reach the Supreme Court in one of three ways: certification, appeal, or certiorari. Judges of a U.S. court of appeals may "certify" to the Supreme Court a question of federal law in a case before them, a question that the judges feel is of such importance or difficulty that it should be resolved immediately by the highest tribunal in the country. This procedure is infrequently used.

Appeal is more often resorted to in trying to obtain review. Under existing statutes a losing party may appeal his case to the Supreme Court: (1) where a federal court has declared a state law unconstitutional or has issued an injunction against the enforcement of an act of Congress; (2) the highest court of a state has declared unconstitutional a federal statute, executive order, or treaty, or has sustained the validity of a state law against a substantial challenge that it violates the U.S. Constitution. Jurisdictional statutes appear to oblige the Supreme Court to hear these kinds of appeals, but the justices dismiss most of them on the grounds that the challenges are insubstantial.

The bulk of cases are brought to the Supreme Court by a writ of certiorari (from the Latin, "to be made more certain"). The losing party in a U.S. court of appeals or in the highest court of a state, if his claim involves a question of federal law, may petition the Supreme Court to review his case. Granting certiorari, that is, agreeing to hear the case, is strictly a matter of discretion. The justices vote on whether or not to take each of these cases, four votes, one less than a majority, being necessary to accept the dispute. Each year the Court receives about 1000 such petitions from state courts and an equal number from U.S. courts of appeals. The justices usually consent to hear less than 200 of these.

Three Special Federal Courts

There are also three federal courts of special jurisdiction: the customs court, the court of customs and patent appeals, and the court of claims. The customs court hears appeals from the rulings of customs collectors concerning the appraisal of imported goods and the collection of import duties. The court of customs and patent appeals reviews the rulings of the customs court, hears appeals from some rulings of the U.S. Patent Office, and also reviews certain findings of the U.S. Tariff Commission as to unfair practices in the import trade. The court of claims has jurisdiction over most cases involving suits against the government for damages. Decisions of these courts are reviewable by the Supreme Court under much the same procedures as cases from other federal courts.

THE WORK OF TRIAL COURTS

Civil and Criminal Cases

Federal district courts and state courts of original jurisdiction hear both civil and criminal cases. In civil cases the plaintiff and the defendant are ordinarily private persons. The government prescribes the laws governing the civil relations of men and it provides the machinery whereby controversies arising under these laws may be settled; but the decision whether or not to make use of this law and machinery is left to private citizens. In criminal cases, on the other hand, the government is the plaintiff and an accused individual the defendant. Here the government not only prescribes law governing human conduct but it also seeks in a positive way to enforce the law. A trial court tries to accomplish three things in the course of an ordinary case, whether civil or criminal: to determine the nature of the conflict and the point or points at issue; to obtain an accurate account of the factual side of the conflict; to apply law to the issue in the light of the facts and to pronounce judgment.

Procedure

Procedure in federal and most state courts is based upon statutory codes, which are, however, derived in good part from common law traditions. Under these codes a civil case is divided into two parts: a written or pleadings stage and an oral or trial stage. The purpose of the pleadings is to frame an issue for proper trial. The plaintiff, who thinks he has suffered an injury from an unlawful act of the defendant, invokes the law and asks for the aid of a court. He does this by filing with the court a *complaint* in which he states his case as he sees it. The court then notifies the defendant and directs him to submit an *answer,* in which he sets forth the case as *he* sees it. Thereupon various counterclaims and amendments may be filed, and the court ultimately fixes a date for trial.

The second, or trial, stage consists of a series of formal steps. After a jury has been selected (unless the parties elect to waive a jury trial, in which case the judge not only applies the law but also passes upon the evidence) attorneys deliver their opening speeches, present evidence for their respective parties by marshaling their own witnesses and exhibits and cross-examining those of the other side, and finally make their closing speeches to the jury. Then the judge instructs the members of the jury about the proper legal rules and charges them to apply these rules to the facts as they see them. The jurymen deliberate, and, if they can reach agreement (which must usually be unanimous), return a verdict. Finally, the judge pronounces judgment in accordance with the jury's verdict.

In criminal cases the procedure runs somewhat as follows: (1) A person suspected of crime is arrested and evidence against him is seized. (2) A preliminary hearing is given this person before a police magistrate or a justice of the peace. If there seem to be sufficient grounds for further proceedings, the suspect is "bound over" to the proper authorities. (3) Bail is fixed and by this device the accused is usually permitted to remain at liberty between the time of his arrest and his trial. (4) The accused is indicted. Specific charges are lodged against him; some, at least, of the evidence against him is indicated; and either by grand jury action or by decision of the public prosecutor he is ordered held for trial. (5) The trial takes place and the guilt or innocence of the accused is determined.

Trial Judge and Jury

The judge "presides" over the trial of a case. He helps the parties define and clarify the legal points at issue, he sees that evidence and arguments are adduced in accordance with prescribed rules, he advises the jury on the law, and he pronounces sentence or renders a judgment after the jury has returned its verdict. The jury, on the other hand, considers and evaluates the evidence. By listening closely to testimony of witnesses and arguments of attorneys it must determine which party has the stronger factual "case." The historic rationale for trial by jury is that a group of laymen is better qualified to render a verdict on the facts of a dispute involving some

"Evidence? Just look at those shifty eyes"

Drawing by Mulligan. © 1957 the *New Yorker* Magazine, Inc.

A jury in Yancy County, North Carolina. (Flip Schulke from Black Star)

everyday situation, such as a disputed title to land, broken contract, or a burglary, than are trained legal experts.

In practice, no such careful separation of functions has been maintained. The law often allows the judge to comment on the evidence to the jury and even in extreme cases to set aside a jury's verdict if he feels it is contrary to the weight of the evidence. Likewise, juries necessarily apply a good deal of law in reaching their verdicts, for law and fact are often so mingled in a case that it is impossible to separate them. Moreover, where trial by jury is waived, the judge must pass on the facts as well as determine the law.

The late Judge Jerome Frank,[6] one of the most articulate of recent American jurists, viewed the jury as an outmoded and unsuccessful means of determining facts in a case: "To my mind a better instrument than the usual jury trial could scarcely be imagined for achieving uncertainty, capriciousness, lack of uniformity, disregard of the [rules,] and unpredictability of decisions." Others have argued that the tendency of juries to ignore both law and evidence in reaching "common sense" or "just" decisions often serves a good purpose. They claim that a too rigid adherence to the letter of the law or even the weight of "facts" sometimes produces unfortunate results and that it is desirable that some agency, such as the jury, be in a position to soften the harsh results of the judicial process. Justice Oliver Wendell Holmes,[7] while observing that he had not found juries "specially inspired for the discovery of truth," or "freer from prejudice" than judges, noted that they "introduce into their verdict a certain amount—a very large amount, so far as I

---

[6] *Courts on Trial* (Princeton, N.J.: Princeton University Press, 1950), p. 123. The excerpts quoted from this work are used by permission of the Princeton University Press, publishers.

[7] Oliver Wendell Holmes, Jr., *Collected Legal Papers* (New York: Harcourt, Brace & World, Inc., 1920), pp. 237-238. Excerpts reprinted from this work are used by permission of Harcourt, Brace & World, Inc., publishers.

have observed—of popular prejudice, and thus keep the administration of the law in accord with the wishes and feeling of the community." More recent and systematic studies of juries indicate that their decisions are closer to those of the judges who presided at the trials than most people had previously thought.[8] In fact, the most complete analysis indicates that judges and jurors agree in more than four out of five criminal cases. In any event, trial by jury is used less extensively than in the past. In England trial by jury in civil cases has declined to a point where it is now used in fewer than 10 per cent of the cases.[9] In the American federal courts the Constitution guarantees the right to trial by jury in civil as well as criminal cases. Jury trial may, however, be waived by the parties, and this is often done today, particularly in civil cases.

Trial Court Discretion

Judge Frank also once described the conventional theory of the trial process in these words:[10]

For convenience, let us symbolize a legal rule by the letter R, the facts of a case by the letter F, and the court's decision of that case by the letter D. We can then crudely schematize the conventional theory of how courts operate by saying

$$R \times F = D$$

The determination of the R factor in a trial court case is very similar to the function that an appellate court performs. Indeed, the issue confronting an appellate court when it reviews a case is whether the right law has been applied by the trial court. The factors that introduce an element of choice or uncertainty in the judicial process at the appellate level will be examined later in this chapter, but it may be noted here that they are also present, to at least the same degree, in the trial courts. Indeed, the trial court judge faces certain special difficulties in determining the R factor. He may have less judicial experience than the appellate court judge; often he must make his legal rulings with less opportunity for study and reflection; and sometimes he finds it necessary to apply the law (or "make law") in a situation that is under judicial analysis for the first time.

But it is the F factor that introduces the largest measure of uncertainty into the work of trial courts. In the original trial of every case the foremost and, usually, the most difficult, question is, What are the facts? Did John Doe commit the burglary with which he is charged? Has Richard Roe been cruel to his wife to the point where she is entitled to a divorce? Does Super Foam's share of the national detergent market restrain trade? The answers to these typical problems, which are the everyday concern of the trial courts, are often uncertain in the highest degree.

---

[8] Harry Kalven and Hans Zeisel, *The American Jury* (Boston: Little, Brown & Company, 1966).
[9] See Jackson, pp. 62–63.
[10] P. 14.

THE WORK OF APPELLATE COURTS

When a case is carried to a federal court of appeals or to a state court of appellate jurisdiction the primary purpose is to secure a careful review of the way in which the law has been applied. To obtain a reversal in a higher court a litigant must show that the trial court has either misconstrued the nature of the conflict, committed procedural errors, applied the wrong law to the facts as ascertained, or pronounced an improper judgment in light of the evidence. The appellate court is not asked to check the factual side of a controversy or to retry a case, though it may send a case back to a court of first instance for a retrial. As at the trial level, however, the distinction between law and facts may be exceedingly fine in appellate proceedings, and appellate judges may sometimes have to decide for themselves what were the facts in a case before them.

Two factors support the idea of appeal. The first grows out of the interests of the individual parties to litigation and the need to safeguard the element of justice in the decision. Because trial courts may err, it is desirable to allow a limited appeal to higher courts so that errors may be corrected and justice served.

As Lawmaking Agencies

The second reason for appeal grows out of the fact that courts not only decide cases involving specific individuals, but in so doing also state the law that governs other persons. It is clearly desirable that law should operate uniformly. If a state had but a single court, a uniform interpretation of the law would result automatically, but as soon as there are two or more trial courts the possibility arises that law will be made or interpreted by different judges in different ways. By providing for an appeal of those cases in which the meaning of law is involved, ultimately if not directly to a single court of highest jurisdiction, an authoritative ruling as to the doubtful legal issue can be obtained and thereafter followed by all the lower courts.

If such an arrangement is to prove workable, some sort of winnowing process is necessary so that the volume of business at the appellate level may be held within manageable limits. In the Anglo-American court systems this selection is customarily accomplished by limiting review to those cases in which the law at issue has not already been clearly interpreted or defined or to those judgments of lower courts in which it can be shown that errors have been committed that are resulting in substantial injustices to the parties to the litigation. In this latter respect, however, it has been found necessary to distinguish between errors of law and errors of fact. Unless a court of appeals were to try a case anew, listen to all the witnesses and consider all the evidence, it could not have as good a basis for evaluating facts as did the trial court. For this reason appeal has been limited in common law cases to errors of law. In most cases not tried by juries, however, such as cases in equity, a broader appeal, both as to issues of fact and issues of law, has traditionally been permitted. As already noted, there are exceptions to the rule that a court of appeals is concerned only with disputed *legal* points, but the principle still has much vitality and does help to hold down the volume of appellate business.

Appellate Court Discretion

Since it is the business of appellate courts to interpret and clarify the law as applied to specific situations, it follows that the judges of these courts necessarily exercise a measure of discretionary power. Perhaps the most careful weighing of the element of judicial discretion at the appellate level was made by Justice Cardozo.[11] He wrote: "I take judge-made law as one of the existing realities of life." And again:

I was much troubled in spirit, in my first years upon the bench, to find how trackless was the ocean on which I had embarked. I sought for certainty. I was oppressed and disheartened when I found that the quest for it was futile. . . . As the years have gone by, and as I have reflected more and more upon the nature of the judicial process, I have become reconciled to the uncertainty, because I have grown to see it as inevitable.

Why did Cardozo reconcile himself to the inevitability of uncertainty in the law? Why do appellate judges necessarily exercise some measure of discretion in deciding cases? Why can't the law be made so clear and precise that judicial power may become, as Chief Justice John Marshall once put it, a mere instrument through which "the will of the law" is expressed? Answers to these and similar questions are not difficult to provide. The total body of law—statutory, judge-made, or otherwise—has become very extensive and detailed indeed. But life in present-day industrial civilization has become so varied and intricate that no body of law can possibly provide a specific rule for the settlement of every serious problem. The law can be, and is, sufficiently complete to deal in a general way with most basic issues. But it cannot be so detailed as to make its application to any particular variant an automatic operation. If law is to provide the means for a just—or even a workable—solution of each case as it arises, it must have flexibility. "The life of the Law," Justice Holmes once said, "has not been logic: it has been experience." [12]

A further reason for flexibility—and thus uncertainty—is that law must be kept adaptable to the needs of changing times. The law of corporations must be adjusted to enterprises utilizing atomic energy; the law of bankruptcy must be altered to ease the plight of unprofitable but socially useful enterprises, such as the railroads; the law of communications must be made to fit the needs of television and relay satellites; the law of property must be broadened to include

---

[11] Benjamin Cardozo, *The Nature of the Judicial Process* (New Haven, Conn.: Yale University Press, 1921), pp. 10, 166. The excerpts quoted from this work are used by permission of Yale University Press, publishers.

[12] Oliver Wendell Holmes, *The Common Law* (Boston: Little, Brown & Company, 1881), p. 1.

the use of the air for aviation purposes. Some of this growth in the law is bound to come through court decisions as well as through legislative enactments.

It is important not to exaggerate judicial discretion and uncertainty concerning the outcome of cases. For example, Benjamin Cardozo,[13] while emphasizing judge-made law as a reality of life, was careful to delimit the discretionary power that he believed judges in fact exercise: "In countless litigations, the law is so clear that judges have no discretion. They have the right to legislate within gaps, but often there are no gaps." And speaking of his experience as a member of the highest court of appeals in New York state he reported: "Of the cases that come before the court in which I sit, a majority, I think, could not, with semblance of reason, be decided in any way but one. The law and its application alike are plain."

THE COURTS AND THE ATTORNEY GENERAL

The extent of the work of judges depends upon the initiative of nonjudicial personnel. Unless these people, who range all the way from the President of the United States to a local policeman on his beat to a private citizen who has a grievance against his neighbor, take steps to enforce law, the courts are powerless, by and large, to play any part in the governmental process. More often than not the government initiates court action through a specialized legal agency staffed with public attorneys. At the local level the head of this agency is known as the prosecuting attorney, county attorney, district attorney, or state's attorney; at the state and federal level he is known as the attorney general. At the federal level the Attorney General is assisted in each federal judicial district by a "U.S. attorney" who represents the national government in starting court actions under federal law.

Broadly speaking, the functions of the Attorney General of the United States are twofold. He acts first as legal adviser to the executive branch of the government, providing rulings or "opinions" on points of law at the request of the President or other executive officers. Second, he has the duty of prosecuting suits for the U.S. government and of representing the government in any litigation to which it is a party. This includes initiating criminal proceedings against persons who break the law, undertaking civil actions in the name of the government, and defending governmental action in lawsuits initiated by others. This work brings the Attorney General into close personal relations with the courts. There is, however, no formal connection between the Department of Justice, which the Attorney General heads, and the federal judiciary. Indeed, their separation reflects the Anglo-American tradition that there shall be no direct tie between prosecutor and judge, a tradition that runs counter to that of many other nations, especially those of continental Europe.

---

[13] P. 129.

Selected Bibliography

Cardozo, Benjamin N., *The Nature of the Judicial Process* (New Haven, Conn.: Yale University Press, 1921). These essays are among the most revealing descriptions of the judicial process ever published.

Carr, Robert K., *The Supreme Court and Judicial Review* (New York: Holt, Rinehart and Winston, Inc., 1942). A brief analysis of the role of the Court in judicial review of legislation and governmental action.

Frank, Jerome, *Law and the Modern Mind* (New York: Brentano's, Inc., 1930). A brilliant and provocative analysis of the role of law in modern society.

Haines, Charles Grove, *The American Doctrine of Judicial Supremacy* (Berkeley, Calif.: University of California Press, 1932). A leading study of the operation of judicial review.

Holmes, Oliver Wendell, *The Common Law* (Boston: Little, Brown & Company, 1881). An outstanding analysis of the judicial process by one of the most famous American legal scholars and Supreme Court justices.

Hurst, Willard, *The Growth of American Law: The Law Makers* (Boston: Little, Brown & Company, 1950). A penetrating historical analysis of the development of law in the United States, emphasizing the role of lawmaking agencies.

Kalven, Harry, and Hans Zeisel, *The American Jury* (Boston: Little, Brown & Company, 1966). A fascinating empirical study of the work of juries and how their decisions differ from those of judges.

McWhinney, Edward, *Judicial Review in the English-Speaking World,* 3d ed. (Toronto: University of Toronto Press, 1966). An excellent introduction to judicial review as it operates in seven countries.

Murphy, Walter F., *Elements of Judicial Strategy* (Chicago: University of Chicago Press, 1964). An analysis of the political power of the Supreme Court based on the private papers of several justices.

————, and C. Herman Pritchett, *Courts, Judges, and Politics* (New York: Random House, Inc., 1961). An introduction to the judicial process in the United States.

Peltason, Jack W., *Federal Courts in the Political Process* (New York: Random House, Inc., 1955). A stimulating analysis of the role that judges play in American government.

19

The Supreme Court at work

From the time of Chief Justice John Marshall to the present, the Supreme Court has had a significant share in the power to govern, and it has profoundly influenced the course of American life in at least three ways. It has helped shape the main outlines of the political system by giving vitality to fundamental constitutional principles, for example, in giving specific meaning to the principles of federalism and separation of powers. Second, the Court has helped provide a uniform set of rules governing those aspects of human relations that are subject to federal control. Although Congress has tried increasingly to pass statutes to give order to life in a complex modern society, legislation can but indicate the main directions of public policy. Administrators and judges must then give detailed meaning to these initial policy statements and shape them to everyday needs. The Supreme Court has interpreted virtually every major statute enacted by Congress, so that lesser courts and administrative agencies might have authoritative guidance in applying law to specific situations. Finally, the Supreme Court has profoundly influenced the formation of the American concept of justice. Some sense of the spirit of fairness that the Court has fostered is felt in reading

373

the words of Justice Hugo Black[1] in the Court's opinion in *Chambers v. Florida,* a case in which four Negroes were saved from a sentence of death pronounced by a Florida court after they had been bullied into a confession by third-degree methods:

> Under our constitutional system courts stand against any winds that blow as havens of refuge for those who might otherwise suffer because they are helpless, weak, outnumbered, or because they are nonconforming victims of prejudice and public excitement. Due process of law, preserved for all by our Constitution, commands that no such practice as that disclosed by the record in this case shall send any accused to his death. No higher duty, no more solemn responsibility, rests with this Court, than that of translating into living law and maintaining this constitutional shield deliberately planned and inscribed for the benefit of every human being subject to our Constitution—of whatever race, creed, or persuasion.

THE NATURE AND ORIGIN OF JUDICIAL REVIEW

A special function performed by American courts is known as judicial review. It may be defined as a process by which courts test the acts of other governmental agencies—legislatures particularly—for compliance with fundamental constitutional principles, and declare null and void those acts that fail to meet this test. A great many American courts, both federal and state, have and from time to time exercise this power. Any federal court can declare any statute—state or federal—invalid under the federal Constitution and refuse to enforce it. Similarly, state courts can declare federal statutes invalid under the federal Constitution, or state statutes invalid under either the federal or a state constitution. In the end, however, it is the Supreme Court of the United States that, with few exceptions, determines whether or not a federal statute is in conflict with the federal Constitution.

The Intention of the Framers

There has been much controversy concerning the origin of judicial review in the United States. It is clear that the Constitution itself does not *in so many words* authorize judges to declare acts of Congress unconstitutional. Whether the framers of the Constitution intended the federal courts to invalidate acts of Congress is a historical puzzle that will probably never be solved, since the debates of the Philadelphia convention throw very little light on the matter. Judicial review has had to find its official basis, then, not so much in the words of the Constitution or in historical evidence as in rationalization and constitutional interpretation. The beginnings of what may be called the official theory supporting judicial review may be seen in *The Federalist,* the papers published during the struggle over the ratification of the Constitution. In Number 78 of the papers Alexander Hamilton specifically defended judicial review.[2]

---

[1] 309 U.S. 227, 241 (1940).
[2] *The Federalist,* Henry Cabot Lodge, ed. (New York: G. P. Putnam's Sons, 1888), pp. 485–486.

The interpretation of the laws is the proper and peculiar province of the courts. A constitution is, in fact, and must be regarded by the judges, as a fundamental law. It therefore belongs to them to ascertain its meaning, as well as the meaning of any particular act proceeding from the legislative body. If there should happen to be an irreconcilable variance between the two, that which has the superior obligation and validity ought, of course, to be preferred; or, in other words, the Constitution ought to be preferred to the statute, the intention of the people to the intention of their agents.

Marbury v. Madison

A few years later this statement provided inspiration for the Supreme Court's own position. In 1803, in *Marbury v. Madison,*[3] the Court for the first time declared unconstitutional a provision of federal law. The narrow point at issue was the Court's own jurisdiction. William Marbury, who had been appointed to the office of justice of the peace in the closing days of the Adams Administration, asked the Court to take original jurisdiction over his case under a provision of the Judiciary Act of 1789 and to issue a writ of mandamus ordering Madison, the new Secretary of State under Jefferson, to deliver Marbury's commission to him. The Supreme Court, speaking through Chief Justice John Marshall, found a conflict between Article III of the Constitution, which limited the Court's original jurisdiction to two situations, and the act of 1789, which seemed to the Court to give it such jurisdiction in a third situation. Assuming that such a conflict between Constitution and statute existed, did it follow that the Court must invalidate the statute? Marshall believed that it did, and his argument ran something like this: *It is one of the purposes of a written constitution to define and limit the powers of the legislature. The legislature cannot be permitted to pass statutes contrary to a constitution, if the latter is to prevail as superior law. A court cannot avoid choosing between the Constitution and a conflicting statute when both are relevant to a case which the court is asked to decide. Since the Constitution is paramount law, judges have no choice but to prefer it to the statute and to refuse to give effect to the latter.* To buttress this general line of reasoning Marshall cited Article III of the Constitution, which authorizes judges to decide cases "arising under this Constitution," and Article VI, which requires them to take an oath to support the Constitution. The Court therefore concluded that the provision in the act of 1789 was invalid and that it must refuse to take jurisdiction over the case.

The fundamental point in the Chief Justice's logic—that a judge confronted with a conflict between a statute and the Constitution must necessarily uphold the Constitution and declare the statute null and void—is not unassailable. Justice John B. Gibson of the Pennsylvania supreme court used the same kind of reasoning to reach an exactly opposite conclusion in a dissenting opinion in the 1825 case of *Eakin v. Raub*. His reasoning runs as follows:[4] *Granted that a judge may be asked in a specific case to enforce a statute that he believes to be in conflict with*

---

[3] 1 Cranch 137 (1803).

[4] 12 Sergeant and Rawle 330 (1825). Reprinted in Robert E. Cushman, *Leading Constitutional Decisions,* 10th ed. (New York: Appleton-Century-Crofts, 1955), p. 252.

constitutional principles, there is nothing in the judge's oath or in his duties of office that requires him to determine a statute's constitutionality before he proceeds to apply it. It is the business of courts to interpret and apply statutes, not to determine whether the legislature erred in passing them. If a legislature has in fact passed an unconstitutional statute, the responsibility rests exclusively with the legislators. Judges have no positive duty to correct the error; neither do they commit any unconscious wrong in giving effect to such a law. If an error has been committed, the voters, the sovereign people, may turn the legislators out at the next election.

THE EXERCISE OF JUDICIAL REVIEW

Following *Marbury v. Madison* the power to invalidate a federal statute was not used again by the Supreme Court until the *Dred Scott* case in 1857, over half a century later. In the meantime, the Court first held a state law void under the federal Constitution in *Fletcher v. Peck* in 1810.[5] Up to the Civil War only two federal statutes and fewer than twenty state laws were invalidated. Not until about 1890 did the Court begin to invalidate federal or state laws with any regularity, and even in the present century the number of laws rejected has been far smaller than is often supposed. To the present day the Supreme Court has invalidated provisions of federal laws in about eighty cases.[6] (Since 1789, Congress has passed about 40,000 public acts.[7])

Until about 1890 most state laws invalidated by the Supreme Court were held to contravene one, or sometimes both, of two clauses of the original Constitution. The first of these was the clause in section 8 of Article I, which grants to Congress the power to regulate commerce "among the several states" and with foreign nations; the second was the clause in section 10 of the same article, which forbids the states to pass laws "impairing the obligation of contracts." After 1890, however, the second clause was cited less often, and a large number of state measures were struck down on the ground that they deprived persons of life, liberty, or property without due process of law or denied persons equal protection of the law and thereby violated the Fourteenth Amendment.

With respect to federal legislation, the Court has seldom chosen to invalidate a measure solely because it deprives persons of their liberty or property without due process of law, as forbidden by the Fifth Amendment. Instead, the justices have preferred to hold that in enacting certain laws Congress has exceeded the limits of the positive legislative powers expressly granted to it in section 8 of Article I of the Constitution. But here the Court has been highly selective in its

---

[5] 6 Cranch 87 (1810).

[6] It is rather difficult for technical reasons to be absolutely accurate in presenting such statistics. See Norman J. Small, ed., *The Constitution of the United States: Analysis and Interpretation* (Washington, D.C.: Government Printing Office, 1964), pp. 1385–1402, for a listing of cases in which the Supreme Court invalidated provisions of federal statutes.

[7] Between 1789 and 1945 Congress passed a total of 64,446 laws. Of these, 28,237 were public acts and 36,209 were private acts. George B. Galloway, *Congress at the Crossroads* (New York: Thomas Y. Crowell Company, 1946), pp. 147–149.

references to the specific powers said to have been exceeded. Even during the period 1890–1937 when the Court was most active in invalidating federal statutes, the justices were much more likely to find that Congress had gone beyond its authority to regulate commerce than to strike down laws based upon the taxing, spending, postal, or war powers.

The full restraining influence of judicial review is not to be measured only in terms of the number of statutes that have actually been declared unconstitutional. Undoubtedly, judicial review has had a further effect in that legislatures, federal, state, and local, have been deterred from passing laws because of the belief that they might be invalidated by the courts.

As already indicated, judicial review is not limited to legislative enactments. From time to time the Supreme Court has invalidated acts or rulings of the President or of his

"My first official act is to call for the impeachment of Earl Warren."

Reproduced by permission of *Esquire* Magazine.
© 1966 by Esquire, Inc.

subordinates in the executive branch of the government. Thus in the *Steel Seizure* case[8] the Court found that President Truman had exceeded his powers in authorizing the Secretary of Commerce to seize the steel mills to prevent a nationwide strike. Such decisions are, however, more often based upon a finding that the President or one of his subordinates has exceeded his authority under particular statutes than on a finding that he has violated the Constitution.

Judicial Choice

There has been much disagreement about the *kind of power* the Supreme Court exercises when it declares a statute unconstitutional. Does it exercise an automatic power by which it does only what the logic of constitutional principles requires it to do? Or does it exercise a discretionary power by which the justices determine the fate of a statute either way?

Many people believe that the Court's exercise of its power of judicial review is mechanical. In the majority opinion in *United States v. Butler,* the case in which the first Agricultural Adjustment Act was declared unconstitutional by a six to three vote, Justice Owen J. Roberts endorsed this notion. He said:[9]

---

[8] *Youngstown Sheet & Tube Co. v. Sawyer,* 343 U.S. 579 (1952).
[9] 297 U.S. 1, 62–63 (1936).

There should be no misunderstanding as to the function of this court. . . . It is sometimes said that the court assumes a power to overrule or control the action of the people's representatives. This is a misconception. The Constitution is the supreme law of the land ordained and established by the people. All legislation must conform to the principles it lays down. When an act of Congress is appropriately challenged in the courts as not conforming to the constitutional mandate the judicial branch of the Government has only one duty—to lay the article of the Constitution which is invoked beside the statute which is challenged and to decide whether the latter squares with the former. All the court does, or can do, is to announce its considered judgment upon the question.

Other authorities have emphasized the very large element of choice that is usually present in a constitutional case. The language in which principles find expression in the Constitution, and against which the validity of a statute must be determined, is for the most part exceedingly vague. For example, while still a professor of law, Felix Frankfurter[10] wrote of the due process and equal protection clauses of the Fourteenth Amendment that

these broad "guarantees" in favor of the individual are expressed in words so undefined, either by their intrinsic meaning, or by history, or by tradition, that they leave the individual Justice free, if indeed they do not actually compel him, to fill in the vacuum with his own controlling notions of economic, social and industrial facts with reference to which they are invoked. These judicial judgments are thus bound to be determined by the experience, the environment, the fears, the imagination of the different Justices.

At this late date in American history it is impossible to deny that the Supreme Court must exercise some measure of discretion in the way in which it shapes law and decides cases. But the exact degree of discretion that the Court has in fact exercised, or ought ideally to exercise, remains an extremely controversial issue. Even the nine justices have at times disagreed vigorously with one another on this point.

CONTROVERSY OVER JUDICIAL REVIEW

The exercise of the power of judicial review by the Supreme Court has never long been free from controversy. The attacks of recent years on the Court provoked by its decisions in the school prayer and reapportionment cases are only the latest in a long line. In this continuing controversy all sections of the country, all economic groups, and all political parties have sooner or later added their voices to the chorus of criticism, for no one faction has been consistently the Court's champion or critic. Indeed, since 1803, there has been an almost constant stream of proposals to alter the Supreme Court or its powers. These proposals can be grouped roughly into four categories: (1) those affecting Court personnel; (2) those affecting Court structure and jurisdiction; (3) those affecting Court procedure; and (4) those affecting particular Court rulings.

Following a series of decisions in which the Supreme Court invalidated several of the key statutes enacted by Congress during Franklin Roosevelt's first

---

[10] *Law and Politics* (New York: Harcourt, Brace & World, Inc., 1939), p. 13.

term, the President in 1937 advocated that the Court be enlarged by act of Congress so that its views on the Constitution might be changed through the appointment of new justices. Although Congress rejected the proposal, the size of the Court had previously been changed by act of Congress several times. The Court originally consisted of six members. It was reduced to five in 1801, increased to six in 1802, to seven in 1807, to nine in 1837, and to ten in 1863. In 1866, it was reduced to seven, and fixed at nine in 1869. In every one of these instances there is evidence that the change was designed, in part at least, to influence the Court's decisions.

Several reform proposals have been based upon Congress' undeniable power to control the structure and jurisdiction of the federal courts. It is true that the Constitution provides that there shall be one Supreme Court, but Congress might attempt to abolish the existing Court and replace it with another. In 1861, as part of the attack upon the Supreme Court occasioned by its decision in the *Dred Scott* case, Senator John P. Hale of New Hampshire introduced a resolution embodying just such a proposal. The resolution was not adopted. The Constitution also gives Congress authority to fix by law the classes of cases that the Supreme Court may hear. In 1868, Congress passed a law curtailing the appellate jurisdiction in such a manner as to prevent the Court from taking jurisdiction over a case that raised the issue of the constitutionality of the Reconstruction Acts.[11]

Angered by a series of Supreme Court decisions in cases involving national security questions, Senator William Jenner of Indiana introduced a bill in the Senate during 1957 to deprive the Court of its appellate jurisdiction to review five classes of cases. The bill provided that the Supreme Court should exercise no jurisdiction over (1) cases arising out of congressional investigations; (2) cases involving loyalty or security proceedings in the executive branch of the federal government; (3) cases arising out of the enforcement of state antisubversive activity laws; (4) cases arising out of efforts by local school boards to curb subversive activity; and (5) state policies and practices governing admission of persons to the practice of law. If the Jenner bill had become law, all such cases would have been finally settled in the lower courts. Although it was not passed, the bill commanded a surprising amount of support both in and out of Congress.[12] Similarly, a bill to remove jurisdiction from all federal courts to hear reapportionment cases passed the House of Representatives in 1964 but died in the Senate.

Other proposals have been directed at five to four decisions. One line of attack has proposed that a larger majority be required for the invalidation of federal laws. It has been suggested that a six to three or a seven to two vote be required. Whether such a change would require a constitutional amendment or could be effected by act of Congress or even a rule voluntarily adopted by the Court is subject to argument. An alternative proposal that has several times been made is that the Constitution be amended to empower Congress to repass a law over an adverse decision of the Supreme Court. This proposal has sometimes been

---

[11] See Ex Parte *McCardle,* 7 Wallace 506 (1869).

[12] See Walter F. Murphy, *Congress and the Court* (Chicago: University of Chicago Press, 1962).

qualified by requirements that a national election intervene between the Court ruling and the repassage of the law, or that reenactment be by a two thirds vote in both houses of Congress.

Finally, many proposals have been made that adverse Supreme Court decisions be overcome by constitutional amendment dealing with the substance of the disputed issue rather than with the mechanism of judicial review. The Sixteenth Amendment expressly authorized a federal income tax, thus repudiating the adverse ruling of the Court in *Pollock v. Farmers' Loan and Trust Co.* in 1895.[13] Similarly, the Eleventh and Fourteenth Amendments reversed Supreme Court rulings. The public school prayer decisions in 1962 and 1963 inspired a spate of indignant demands that the decisions be overturned by means of an amendment to the Constitution.

Legitimation

In assessing the work of federal judges it is all too easy to emphasize only the negative side—to remember only those statutes and executive orders courts held unconstitutional or to think of those countless other policies that were stillborn because of anticipated judicial decisions. There is, however, also a positive side to judicial review. First, in saying no to some kinds of governmental action judges often foster positive policies. The reapportionment decisions, for instance, have spurred legislative redistricting all around the country, just as the *School Segregation Cases* have bolstered the cause of Negro civil rights in the executive and legislative processes as well as in the courts.

In another sense, judges may also further positive action and at the same time contribute to political stability. When faced with a crisis, Congress or the President frequently adopts a new policy that is quite different from those in effect earlier. Opposition groups protest that the new policy is not only unwise but also unconstitutional, throwing into doubt the legitimacy of the governmental action. If the crisis is in domestic politics, the odds are high that the groups who lost in the legislative or executive process will go to the courts and there challenge the constitutionality of the new policy. The odds are also high that the Supreme Court will eventually hold that the policy is constitutional; for, despite the publicity that always surrounds a declaration of unconstitutionality, such decisions are rather unusual. As a matter of fact, in less than a dozen cases in the thirty years between 1937 and 1966 did the Court invalidate parts of acts of Congress, and none of these rulings involved statutes of outstanding importance. While a validating or legitimizing decision by the Supreme Court does not automatically remove all doubts, it can be a major factor in promoting acceptance of novel and controversial policies, and it can have this impact in large part because the justices are willing and able to declare policies unconstitutional.

---

[13] 157 U.S. 429; 158 U.S. 601 (1895).

Politics and People

Thorny Thickets

By Alan L. Otten

WASHINGTON—The Supreme Court, having plunged headlong into one political thicket, stands hesitating before an even thornier one. Clearly it doesn't want to enter. And yet it may.

The first political thicket—to use the late Justice Frankfurter's term—involved the wide differences in population in state legislative and Congressional districts. In the wake of the Court's one-man-one-vote rulings, legislative reapportionment and Congressional redistricting have been fast and far-ranging. Practically every state legislature next year will have districts importantly different from those of just a few years back, and 28 states have overhauled Congressional boundaries to greater or lesser extent. Many states are under court order for further change.

All this activity, though, has also encouraged record resort to a fine old American political art—the gerrymander. Gerrymandering simply seeks to manipulate district boundary lines, frequently in rather outlandish fashion, to gain a particular end: To maximize the representation of the party in power and deprive the out-of-power party of its fair share of seats, to maximize the influence of one group (say, farmers) or minimize the influence of another (say, Negroes), or perhaps merely to keep in office the largest possible number of incumbents.

The gerrymander is the new thicket confronting the court—one it seems anxious to avoid if possible but one which it has indicated it will attack if the states don't behave.

As most high-school students know and most adults have forgotten, the word was coined in Massachusetts in 1812, when the Democratic Party artfully laid out state legislative boundaries to hold Federalist seats to a bare minimum. An alert cartoonist noted that one weirdly mapped district resembled a prehistoric monster standing erect; he drew it as a huge salamander with forked tongue and claws, and, adopting the name of Gov. Elbridge Gerry, called it a gerrymander.

The historic ability of states to create districts of widely different population reduced somewhat their need for tricky gerrymandering. Now, however, required to work out districts of substantially equal population, the legislatures are turning to the gerrymander more than ever, deeply aware that every line drawn on the map can give important partisan or racial advantage.

Conservative Texas Democrats, for example, drew new state legislative and Congressional districts in fishhooks and other outlandish shapes to minimize both Republican and liberal Democratic opportunities.

To even out population among Congressional districts and still keep in office three senior Democrats, a Maryland court added small chunks of Baltimore suburbs to each of the three's central city district. The suburban areas are mere appendices to the urban core of each district; logic clearly would have dictated two strictly urban districts and one combined urban-suburban area with greater suburban weight.

As in Maryland, today's gerrymandering frequently seeks to safeguard incumbents. One student gibes that the motto is S.O.S. —Save Our Seats.

In a number of states, particularly in the South, the one-man-one-vote requirement has led to increasing use of larger, multimember districts in lieu of several smaller, single-member districts. The latter, obviously, might more easily have Negro majorities.

The Supreme Court thus far has shied from stepping into the gerrymander thicket, though there are signs an outrageous instance might bring action. The Court found grounds to avoid a direct ruling in one Georgia case, for instance, but Justice Brennan warned that a multimember system might be suspect if it operated "to minimize or cancel out the voting strength of racial or political elements of the voting population."

Lower courts have been more forthright. A North Carolina Federal court, setting aside a Congressional redistricting plan recently, cited population inequality, "The tortuous lines which delineate the boundaries, (and) the resulting lack of compactness and contiguity." An advisory opinion of the Rhode Island Supreme Court argued that political gerrymandering was clearly unconstitutional.

The courts seem to be saying that they want the legislatures themselves to keep gerrymandering within reasonable bounds. But they also seem to be saying that if this doesn't happen, they stand ready to enter the thicket, however thorny.

STATUTORY INTERPRETATION

Less dramatic but not necessarily less significant are those cases in which judges decide issues of statutory rather than constitutional interpretation. Litigants constantly ask the Supreme Court to explain in a specific factual context the meaning of statutes such as the Sherman Antitrust Act, the Fair Labor Standards Act, and the National Labor Relations Acts. Repeated judicial interpretations of a single statute can build up a patina over the law that is as important as the original words of Congress. Moreover, no less than in constitutional clauses, statutory language may be broad, vague, or obscure; and this problem returns us again to the matter of judicial discretion.

THE HUMAN FACTOR AND THE COURT

A judge, like a legislator or an administrator, has a point of view. When he is called upon to exercise choice in the settlement of human conflicts his personal scheme of values is likely to serve as a frame of reference. Some judges have been frank and realistic enough to admit this. "There is in each of us a stream of tendency," Benjamin Cardozo[14] said, "whether you choose to call it philosophy or not, which gives coherence and direction to thought and action. Judges cannot escape that current any more than other mortals." More specifically, he spoke of forces "deep below consciousness," "the likes and the dislikes, the predilections and the prejudices, the complex of instincts and emotions and habits and convictions, which make the man, whether he be litigant or judge."

What are these personal factors, "emotions," "habits" and "convictions" that may influence a judge as he decides a case? His own struggle to make a way in life may have given him a deep respect for the dignity and liberty of the individual against all material considerations of wealth and power. Or he may be a doctrinaire liberal, as incapable as the doctrinaire conservative of arriving at a sophisticated understanding of human nature and institutions. At least some of a judge's experiences, characteristics, and loyalties can be discovered and their influence upon his judicial career considered. Among these are his legal training and experience, his political beliefs and activities, and his age.

Legal Training and Professional Experience

Law schools, with a few notable exceptions, do not devote a great deal of attention to training future judges. Present-day legal education places much reliance on the case method, originally introduced at the Harvard Law School by Dean Christopher Langdell in the nineteenth century. This method sharpens the minds of law students and prepares them well

---

[14] *The Nature of the Judicial Process* (New Haven, Conn.: Yale University Press, 1921), pp. 12, 167, 168.

*The United States Supreme Court.
From left seated, are Justices John
M. Harlan, Hugo L. Black, Chief
Justice Earl Warren, William O.
Douglas, and William J. Brennan,
Jr. Standing are Justices Abe
Fortas, Potter Stewart, Byron R.
White, and Thurgood Marshall.*
(Wide World Photos)

for private practice. But whether it supplies future judges with everything they need to know about human nature and social problems is less certain. It is necessary to remember that "in the common law system the judges are recruited from the legal profession, without . . . any special training for the function."[15]

After graduation from law school and admission to the bar, a lawyer who would one day become a judge finds several paths open to him. Some Supreme Court justices, such as Stanley Matthews, Melville Fuller, Pierce Butler, and Owen Roberts, were, before their appointment, highly successful practicing lawyers whose services were much sought after by clients. Others, such as Harlan Stone, Felix Frankfurter, William Douglas, and Wiley Rutledge, were teachers of law. Some, such as Oliver Wendell Holmes, Benjamin Cardozo, William Brennan, and Potter Stewart, were lower-court judges who came up the judicial ladder to the High Court. Finally, some, such as George Sutherland, Hugo Black, Harold Burton, Tom Clark, Earl Warren, and Byron White, were practicing politicians. Supreme Court justices of course, may have varied backgrounds, but almost all have at some time been active in politics before going to the bench. When Charles Evans Hughes was appointed Chief Justice in 1930 he had been governor of New York, an Associate Justice of the U.S. Supreme Court, Republican nominee for President, Secretary of State under two Presidents, a law school lecturer, and a highly successful practicing attorney. At the time of his appointment as Chief Justice, Fred M. Vinson had served in all three branches of the federal government —as a member of the House of Representatives from Kentucky, as a judge of the court of appeals for the District of Columbia, and as Secretary of the Treasury, in addition to filling several other administrative posts. Chief Justice Earl Warren is a veteran of state politics. He served for many years as attorney general and

---

[15] A. A. Berle, Jr., "Modern Legal Profession," *Encyclopaedia of the Social Sciences,* 9, p. 340.

then governor of California, and was several times a candidate for the Republican presidential nomination. In 1948, he was Thomas Dewey's running mate as Republican candidate for the Vice Presidency.

A Judge's Political Beliefs

It is significant that Presidents have from the time of George Washington made most of their appointments to the federal judiciary from their own party ranks. Professor Charles G. Haines says that Washington "exercised peculiar care" to name only supporters of the new Constitution to the Supreme Court, and that without exception these proved to be "ardent Federalists." Thus Washington himself "initiated the system of appointing political adherents, and political adherents only to places on the Supreme bench. That system has seldom been departed from."[16] Only two of the fourteen men who have served as Chief Justice, Edward White and Harlan Stone, belonged to a different political party from the party of the Presidents who appointed them. Moreover, federal judges have frequently been selected from among the most active and loyal groups of party workers, and not from groups whose members were only nominally party men. This has been particularly true of federal district judges, whose appointment is frequently subject to senatorial courtesy and thereby to the operation of the spoils system. Such Supreme Court justices as John Marshall, Roger Taney, Salmon Chase, James McReynolds, George Sutherland, William Howard Taft, Charles Evans Hughes, Hugo Black, Frank Murphy, Fred Vinson, Sherman Minton, Tom Clark, Earl Warren, Byron White, and Arthur Goldberg were all loyal and vigorous workers in the parties of the Presidents who appointed them.

Supreme Court justices have by no means always suspended their party interests once they have gone on the bench. Frequently a justice's decisions have been in harmony with the traditions and interests of his own party. This can be seen in the opinions of Chief Justice John Marshall in such cases as *McCulloch v. Maryland, Gibbons v. Ogden,* and *Dartmouth College v. Woodward,* which coincided closely with the Federalist position; in the opinions of Chief Justice Roger B. Taney, which often adhered closely to Democratic principles; and in the decisions of Chief Justice William Howard Taft, which seldom departed from the prevailing Republican philosophy. A recently published biography of Taft reveals that he engaged in Republican party politics to a striking degree while serving as Chief Justice.[17] In this respect Taft was unusual but hardly unique.[18]

It is possible, however, to overemphasize the importance of *party* politics

---

[16] *American Doctrine of Judicial Supremacy,* pp. 345–346. Haines is quoting W. D. Coles, "Politics and the Supreme Court of the United States," *American Law Review,* 27 (March–April 1893), p. 183.

[17] Alpheus T. Mason, *William Howard Taft: Chief Justice* (New York: Simon and Schuster, Inc., 1964).

[18] See Walter F. Murphy, *Elements of Judicial Strategy* (Chicago: University of Chicago Press, 1964).

in a judge's work. More often than not the personal frame of reference a judge uses in deciding cases is one in which pure party politics is only a factor, and probably not the strongest. For example, the four conservative justices of the Supreme Court who so often stood together in opposition to the New Deal in the 1930s—James McReynolds, Pierce Butler, George Sutherland, and Willis Van Devanter—divided evenly in their party affiliations, the first two Democrats, the others Republicans. The Supreme Court of the early 1950s, all nine of whose members were appointed by Democratic Presidents and only one of whom was a Republican, was the most divided Court in American history.

HOW THE COURT OPERATES

The Supreme Court is in session from the first Monday in October until some time in late June or early July. The justices normally hear arguments for two weeks, then recess for two weeks to brood, research, and prepare opinions. During the weeks when cases are being heard Court opens at 10 A.M., Monday through Thursday. The first order of business is admission of new members of the Supreme Court bar, then any opinions or rulings that are ready are announced. Thereafter the Court hears oral arguments in pending cases. Oral argument is usually restricted to an hour, or perhaps even a half hour, for each party to a case. Actually, for a systematic presentation of the arguments, the justices depend heavily on written briefs submitted by the parties.

Much of the time for oral argument in a case is frequently consumed by questioning of the attorneys by the justices. Fortunate indeed is the attorney who is permitted to present his oral argument without interruption. Such a policy of interruption has, to be sure, much to commend it; as Felix Frankfurter and James M. Landis[19] pointed out, "questioning, in which the whole Court freely engage, clarifies the minds of the justices as to the issues and guides the course of argument through real difficulties." Not surprisingly, when he became a member of the Court, Justice Frankfurter was one of the leading exponents of the "Socratic method" during oral argument.

Friday of each week is set aside for a conference, at which the justices discuss the cases already argued and decide how to dispose of them. By tradition the Chief Justice is the first to voice his opinion and the last to vote when the decision is being determined. Conversely, the junior member of the Court is the last to speak and the first to vote. By speaking first, the Chief Justice and the senior associate justices can influence the direction of the discussion, and by voting last they can note the tentative line-up in a divided case and, if they wish, let that be a factor in determining their own stands. Little is known of what goes on in these Supreme Court conferences, for there are no formal reports and the justices themselves have usually been very discreet about preserving their confidential character. The informal notes that Justice Frank Murphy kept of the conferences in

---

[19] *The Business of the Supreme Court* (New York: Crowell-Collier & Macmillan Inc., 1927), p. vii.

which he participated from 1940 to 1949 are the best account to date. They indicate that discussion is informed, lively, and not infrequently both long and heated.

The Chief Justice assigns preparation of the Court's opinion to one of the justices who voted with the majority. If a justice does not approve the decision, he may note his disagreement, and, if he wishes, write a *dissenting opinion*. Other opposed justices may either join in this opinion or prepare separate dissenting opinions. If the Chief Justice aligns himself with the dissenters, the senior justice in the majority group assigns the task of writing of the majority opinion. The justices within the majority group sometimes differ among themselves about the reasoning by which the group should justify its decision. If his differences are serious, a justice may file a separate opinion agreeing with the result but dissociating himself from the reasoning employed by the majority. This is known as a *concurring* opinion. First drafts of opinions are circulated among the justices, and a considerable measure of revision may occur at this stage. A good deal of watering down of original drafts to make them palatable to all concurring justices is often necessary. Justice Oliver Wendell Holmes once referred to this diluting process as "pulling out all the plums and leaving the dough."

The written opinions, majority and dissenting, of the Supreme Court constitute one of the most valuable original sources of information about the governmental process. As Walton Hamilton[20] has suggested, the Court opinion "serves the multiple purpose of helping the bench to be critical of its own intellectual processes, keeping lower courts in order, announcing legal standards for acceptable human conduct, extending the courtesy of an answer to arguments which do not prevail and affording an opportunity to justify a judgment."

There has been much controversy concerning the dissenting opinion. Although dissents among Supreme Court justices have been at an all-time high in recent years, the tradition has always been an honored one. Criticism of dissent rests on a number of grounds. Those who believe in the certainty of the law and who think that there is only *one* "correct" solution to any legal problem are, of course, hostile to dissenting opinions. "Judicial dissent often is blamed," Justice Holmes[21] once said, "as if it meant simply that one side or the other were not doing their sums right, and, if they would take more trouble, agreement inevitably would come." As Holmes implied, this criticism ignores the high degree of uncertainty, particularly in constitutional law.

More sophisticated critics of dissenting opinions hold that, although differences among justices are frequently legitimate on intellectual grounds, the desirability of giving law a seeming unity should persuade minority justices to abandon their dissenting views in favor of a unanimous stand. This, it is argued, would lead to greater public respect for courts and would make for a more law-abiding citizenry. However, the degree of uncertainty in the law is sometimes so great that there is always a chance that a dissenting position may prove ultimately to

[20] "Judicial Process," *Encyclopaedia of the Social Sciences*, 8, pp. 450, 455.
[21] Oliver Wendell Holmes, Jr., *Collected Legal Papers* (New York: Harcourt, Brace & World, Inc., 1920), p. 180.

be sounder than the position of the majority and thus be adopted by a later Court. Chief Justice Hughes once stated:[22] "A dissent in a court of last resort is an appeal to the brooding spirit of the law, to the intelligence of a future day, when a later decision may possibly correct the error into which the dissenting judge believes the court to have been betrayed." Still another justification for dissenting opinions has been pointed to by a present member of the Supreme Court, Justice William O. Douglas:[23] "When judges do not agree it is a sign that they are dealing with problems on which society itself is divided. It is the democratic way to express dissident views. Judges are to be honored rather than criticized for following that tradition, for proclaiming their articles of faith so that all may read."

Closely related to the matter of dissent is the practice by which the Supreme Court occasionally reverses previous decisions and alters a legal principle, despite the rule of *stare decisis*. For example, in the ten-year period from 1937 through 1946, the Supreme Court overruled thirty-two previous decisions.[24] In many of these reversals the new position of the majority closely approximated an earlier position taken by dissenting justices, thus supporting Hughes's thesis that a dissenting opinion may sometimes appeal successfully to the intelligence of a later day. It is not surprising that legislators and judges alike have been compelled to revise old laws and make new ones for the better control of social conflicts and problems.

SELECTION AND TENURE OF FEDERAL JUDGES

In the United States all federal judges are appointed by the President, by and with the advice and consent of the Senate. About three quarters of the states choose their judges by popular election. The remainder of judges are appointed—sometimes by the governor, sometimes by the legislature, and in Missouri, California, Kansas, and Alaska by a combined appointive-elective method involving initial appointment by the governor and reelection after a period of years by the voters.

Federal judges hold office for life "during good behavior." They are subject to impeachment and removal from office by Congress for treason, bribery, or other high crimes or misdemeanors. Indeed, nine of the twelve federal officers who have been impeached by the House of Representatives were judges. All four of the impeached officers who have been convicted by the Senate were judges. The corrupt federal judge has been rare, however. The real problem with life tenure has been caused by judges who because of age or health are unable efficiently to perform their duties yet insist on remaining on the bench. It has been

[22] Charles Evans Hughes, *The Supreme Court of the United States* (New York: Columbia University Press, 1928), p. 68.

[23] Address delivered to the American Bar Association as reported in the *New York Times,* Sept. 9, 1948, p. 32.

[24] C. H. Pritchett, *The Roosevelt Court* (New York: Crowell-Collier & Macmillan Inc., 1948), pp. 57, 300–301.

most noticeable in the Supreme Court, where many justices stayed on after their faculties had begun to decline, sometimes with unfortunate results.[25] For example, Justice Stephen J. Field cast the deciding vote in the controversial five to four income tax case at the age of seventy-eight, years after his mental faculties had begun to fail. Charles Fairman[26] has stated: "No rationalization can justify a system whereby the powers of government in a matter of such high moment are finally determined by a mind so somnolent and prepossessed as Justice Field's had become by that time."

Impeachment of an aged judge has always seemed a harsh remedy to members of Congress. Several other solutions have been offered. It has frequently been proposed that the Constitution be amended to provide for the compulsory retirement of federal judges at some fixed age, such as seventy or seventy-five. In 1954, an amendment making mandatory the retirement of federal judges at seventy-five actually passed the Senate. The amendment, which also fixed the size of the Supreme Court at nine—thus denying to Congress the power to change the Court's size by statute—was not acted upon by the House of Representatives.

A second solution is to encourage judges to retire voluntarily. As a result of the controversy in 1937 over the more drastic Roosevelt proposals for court reform, Congress augmented earlier statutes by providing that a judge who reaches seventy and has ten years of service may retire to inactive duty (rather than resign outright) on full salary. If a judge is in bad health, both the age and years of service requirements may be waived. A number of justices of the Supreme Court have retired under the 1937 law, but most delayed their departures until they were over seventy. As Charles Evans Hughes[27] once remarked, "It is extraordinary how reluctant aged judges are to retire and to give up their accustomed work. They seem to be tenacious of the appearance of adequacy." In spite of this observation and in spite of the fact that he had once publicly recommended that judges retire at seventy-five, Hughes himself did not leave the bench until he was seventy-nine.

Many lawyers have contended that the Constitution permits Congress to use means other than impeachment to remove judges who have committed no crimes but are performing ineffectually. Even well-intentioned ineffectiveness, these experts maintain, is not "good behavior." A number of bills to provide machinery alternative to impeachment have been introduced in Congress, but no such explicit measure has been enacted into law.

On the other hand, it may be that Congress has implicitly established a similar procedure, at least for lower-court judges. A federal statute[28] provides that there should be within each judicial circuit an annual meeting of a group known as the judicial council, comprising the judges of the court of appeals for that circuit and representatives of the district judges and of the bar. This council is authorized

---

[25] See Charles Fairman, "The Retirement of Federal Judges," in *Selected Essays on Constitutional Law* (Chicago: The Foundation Press, Inc., 1938), 1, p. 885; originally published in *Harvard Law Review*, 51 (January 1938), p. 397.

[26] Pp. 885, 910.

[27] P. 75.

[28] 28 U.S. Code § 332.

to "make all necessary orders for the effective and expeditious administration of the business of the courts within its circuit." In 1965, the judicial council of the tenth circuit ordered that a district judge accused of inefficiency should not hear any additional cases or proceed further with cases already on his docket. The judge thus retained his office and salary but was stripped of his formal authority.

A number of critics, including members of Congress and two Supreme Court justices, expressed serious objections to this method on the grounds that it violated the independence of federal judges and was procedurally unfair. The Supreme Court, however, refused to hear the judge's case on the grounds that the judicial council's order was only temporary and would not become permanent until the council had completed a further inquiry into his conduct.[29]

Selected Bibliography

Beveridge, Albert J., *The Life of John Marshall* (Boston: Houghton Mifflin Company, 1916). The first major biography of a Supreme Court justice: now a modern classic.

Jackson, Robert H., *The Supreme Court in the American System of Government* (Cambridge, Mass.: Harvard University Press, 1955). Short, trenchant essays on the Court by a late justice.

Mason, Alpheus T., *Harlan Fiske Stone: A Pillar of the Law* (New York: The Viking Press, 1956).

———, *William Howard Taft: Chief Justice* (New York: Simon and Schuster, Inc., 1965). Two of the leading biographical studies of Chief Justices of the United States.

Pritchett, C. Herman, *The Roosevelt Court: A Study in Judicial Politics and Values, 1937–1947* (New York: Crowell-Collier & Macmillian Inc., 1948). One of a series of studies of the Supreme Court by a leading scholar.

Schmidhauser, John R., *The Supreme Court* (New York: Holt, Rinehart and Winston, Inc., 1960). A useful analysis of the Supreme Court justices and the personality factor in decision-making.

Twiss, Benjamin R., *Lawyers and the Constitution: How Laissez-Faire Came to the Supreme Court* (Princeton, N.J.: Princeton University Press, 1942). A unique study of the influence on the Court of lawyers who have argued cases before it.

Warren, Charles, *The Supreme Court in United States History* (Boston: Little, Brown & Company, 1922), 2 vols. A leading general history of the Court, written from a sympathetic point of view.

---

[29] *Chandler v. Judicial Council*, 382 U.S. 1003 (1966).

Part **6** **Civil Liberties**

Police vs. 'Miranda'

Has the Supreme Court Really Hampered Law Enforcement?

By Wayne E. Green

Last summer the Supreme Court sharply broadened its interpretation of the rights due an accused person; immediately, police and prosecuting attorneys damned the decision as a blow to effective law enforcement. . . , What does the record show?

It shows that the critics considerably overstated their case. Some of the evidence for this assessment comes from neutral legal scholars or from supporters of the Court. But much other evidence, surprisingly, comes from statistics compiled by the critics themselves. . . .

The assault intensified last June when the Court threw out a written confession and freed Ernesto Miranda, an indigent Mexican-American convicted by a lower court of kidnaping and rape. The High Tribunal ruled in Miranda vs. Arizona that before police can interrogate a suspect taken into custody they must advise him of his right to remain silent and to consult a lawyer. Because Mr. Miranda wasn't forewarned, his signed confession was held invalid and his conviction overturned.

Law men were already complaining that prior Supreme Court opinions had severely restricted the use of confessions in police work. Miranda would not only abolish the confession but would eliminate interrogation and investigation as well.

Despite these charges, confessions still abound and investigation continues, in a gradually more sophisticated way. Many legal experts now believe that Miranda merely clarified what the Court intended to say in Escobedo vs. Illinois. In that case the High Court reversed Danny Escobedo's death sentence for murder because he wasn't allowed to see his attorney before confessing.

Typically, both prosecutors and policemen have argued that confessions are essential to effective law enforcement. . . .

Thus, it was no surprise that law enforcement officials wailed loudly when the Miranda opinion was handed down. They complained that any suspect warned of his rights not only wouldn't confess, he wouldn't say anything at all. Confident of their contentions, many policemen and prosecutors began keeping statistics to prove their point.

To their dismay, the results are leaving the confession arguments in shambles. Not the least significant is a major statistical study covering more than 1,000 felony cases in Los Angeles County, which has the nation's largest caseload. This report, made public recently by District Attorney Evelle J. Younger, showed that half the suspects in those cases were confessing despite warnings from the police—a 10% increase over the number of confessions found in a similar survey before the Miranda case. . . .

Mr. Younger's Los Angeles study also struck hard at the argument that confessions are essential to good law enforcement. The report claimed that confessions were needed for successful prosecution in fewer than 10% of the more than 1,000 cases checked. . . .

One apparent effect of these statistics is that many law officers are assaulting Miranda from a different direction. Shying from Miranda's effect on confessions, many officials instead contend that case rules out reasonable interrogation. . . .

Civil libertarians reply that law enforcement officials are trying to stir up public concern by reading Miranda too broadly. . . . Read closely, there seems little question that the Miranda case leaves room for interrogation. It specifically permits station-house questioning, even in the absence of counsel, if a properly advised suspect intelligently waives his rights. In addition, the opinion indicates that a person need not be advised of his rights before submitting to some questioning outside the police station unless he "is taken into custody or otherwise deprived of his freedom by authorities."

And, despite charges to the contrary, the court specifically notes that any statement "given freely and voluntarily without any compelling influences is, of course, admissible in evidence.". . .

Few doubt the Miranda decision at least temporarily will complicate law enforcement, however. For one thing, it will require more time, both in investigation and pre-trial procedures. . . .

The Miranda decision also requires that, before a suspect's statement can be introduced as evidence, it must be proved at trial that he was warned of his rights and "knowingly and intelligently" waived them. . . .

The Miranda case appears to bring closer to reality the Supreme Court's long-sought goal of protecting the individual at no cost to effective law enforcement.

20

Liberty and authority: safeguarding fundamental freedoms

RECONCILING LIBERTY AND AUTHORITY

At the beginning of the Civil War Abraham Lincoln asked, "Must a government of necessity be too *strong* for the liberties of its own people, or too *weak* to maintain its own existence?" Lincoln was referring to the immediate problem with which he had to deal, but in a deeper sense his question touches one of the most basic problems of a democratic society: finding a satisfactory balance between the liberty of an individual to live his life as he will and the authority of society to protect and enhance the welfare of all people. The United States was founded and settled chiefly by people seeking greater liberty. Many of the subsequent events in American history—the Revolutionary War, the settlement of the West, the coming of tens of millions of immigrants, the participation in two world wars—have had liberty as their motivating force. Americans frequently proclaim that every person has a dignity and an integrity that society must respect, that every person should enjoy a fair and equal opportunity to realize his potentialities, and that to achieve these goals each man should enjoy a large measure of freedom and should be subject to a minimum of social restraint. This attitude toward the importance of the individual meets such

393

ready acceptance today, at least in principle if not always in practice, that most Americans are almost inclined to take it for granted.

Acceptance of authority has also been a strong American tradition. Three centuries ago the newly arrived colonists immediately established authority, whether in the form of organized church, town government, or cooperative farm. Those who advocated revolution in 1776 claimed that life, liberty, and the pursuit of happiness were unalienable rights, but they hastened to add that governments were instituted among men to secure these rights. A century later western pioneers, famed for their individualism, nonetheless depended on government for protection against Indian and outlaw and for development of public services such as roads and schools.

Choosing between authority and liberty creates a dilemma for the architects of government as well as the poets of human freedom. Where men have felt they had to make such a choice, they have tended to prefer authority to liberty. But men have often refused to concede that such a choice had to be made. Indeed, the evolution of democratic institutions has been largely concerned with a search for a satisfactory equilibrium between governmental authority on the one hand and individual liberty on the other. The effort of the American Founding Fathers to draft a constitution was a part of that search. As the Beards[1] have put it, the framers were confronted with this fundamental problem: "How to set up a government strong enough to serve the purposes of the Union and still not too strong for the maintenance of the liberties of the people." Abraham Lincoln's question merely echoed this problem.

Paradoxically, one of the most powerful forces leading to the creation of political authority has always been a desire to preserve and protect liberty, for a person's freedom can be threatened not only by government officials but also by other individuals. The activity of lone criminals and organized crime syndicates —or of white or black lynch mobs—testifies to the necessity of government's securing the rights of most citizens against the greed and cupidity of other citizens. But a free people must be on guard lest this truth be used to justify unnecessary encroachments by government upon individual freedom. As Edmund Burke,[2] the great English statesman, said:

Liberty, too, must be limited in order to be possessed. The degree of restraint it is impossible in any case to settle precisely. But it ought to be the constant aim of every wise public counsel to find out by cautious experiments, and rational, cool endeavors, with how little, not how much, of this restraint the community can subsist. . . .

Liberty: A Relative and Changing Concept

The conclusion that liberty and authority are not in any final sense irreconcilable is further strengthened when one understands that every right is exercised within limits. Freedom of speech stops short

[1] Charles A. Beard and Mary R. Beard, *A Basic History of the United States* (New York: New Home Library, 1944), p. 131.
[2] R. J. S. Hoffman and P. Levack, eds., *Burke's Politics* (New York: Alfred A. Knopf, Inc., 1949), p. 109.

of the right to call a man a racketeer or a Fascist; freedom of religion in a Western society does not include the right to engage in public sex orgies; freedom of assembly does not justify holding a street meeting in the midst of a race riot. Moreover, two rights are often found to be in conflict with each other, and in resolving the conflict one or both may have to be limited. A good example involves a conflict between freedom of the press and the right to a fair trial. Irresponsible or malicious newspaper reporting of judicial proceedings may endanger the right of litigants to obtain justice.[3]

It is unlikely that any particular balance between liberty and authority can be permanently satisfactory. Objective conditions and subjective attitudes change too much. Some public problems are solved and a given exercise of authority may no longer be necessary; but new problems will arise and different kinds of authority may be needed to deal with them. American economic policy in the nineteenth century, for instance, was based on the premise—established in an earlier, agricultural society—that liberty includes the right of employers and employees to enter into any sort of labor contract they can agree on. Whatever its original value, this right was useless to an individual worker with a large family trying to bargain with a wealthy factory owner. Under the prodding of economic crises and the power of the labor vote, public officials were gradually convinced that society could not afford the luxury of costly and disruptive battles between unrestrained capitalists and workers. Therefore, they insisted as a matter of law that employers recognize labor unions and bargain collectively with them and that workers desist from such practices as secondary boycotts or picketing in a context of violence. Liberty, here, had to give ground to authority; and rights, once widely recognized, were curbed by law.

The reconciliation of liberty and authority is also made somewhat easier by the fact that liberty is of value to a democratic society as a whole, that is, the individual does not have to fight a lone battle against society to safeguard his civil liberties. Freedom of speech and press enable the individual to express himself; but they are also the means by which society tests out competing ideas in its search for more satisfactory public standards and policies. When intimidation and violence are used to keep certain voters away from the polls, the individual loses his rights and society its ideals, perhaps even its purpose.

FEDERALISM AND FUNDAMENTAL LIBERTIES

The American federal system complicates protection of civil rights. On the one hand, complete uniformity in all details of law and politics in each of the fifty states would be as dull as it would be unworkable. On the other hand, if the United States is to be a nation rather than a confederation and if American citizenship is to have real meaning, certain rights have to be protected in every part of the country, and protected against state as well as federal violation.

---

[3] Three recent cases in which the Supreme Court has recognized the existence of this conflict between two liberties are *Marshall v. United States,* 360 U.S. 310 (1959); *Estes v. Texas,* 381 U.S. 532 (1965); and *Sheppard v. Maxwell,* 384 U.S. 333 (1966).

Over the years the Supreme Court, and less often framers of constitutional amendments, have tried to distinguish between rights that are and those that are not absolutely essential to citizens in a democratic society. Drawing this line is difficult, for such a distinction must necessarily be based on values that are not universally shared.

Historically, the problem of finding national protection for rights deemed basic has also been difficult, for the original Constitution imposed few restrictions on the authority of a state vis-à-vis its own citizens. Section 10 of Article I forbade states to impair the obligation of contracts, or pass bills of attainder[4] or ex post facto laws.[5] Section 2 of Article IV declared that citizens of each state shall be entitled to the privileges and immunities of the citizens in the several states, a vague statement that has never had much practical effect. More important, the Supreme Court ruled in 1833 that the Bill of Rights limited only the federal government.[6]

There the matter rested until the adoption of the Fourteenth Amendment after the Civil War. Section 1 provided:

All persons born or naturalized in the United States, and subject to the jurisdiction thereof, are citizens of the United States and of the State wherein they reside. No State shall make or enforce any law which shall abridge the privileges and immunities of the citizens of the United States; nor shall any State deprive any person of life, liberty, or property, without due process of law; nor deny to any person within its jurisdiction the equal protection of the laws.

This definition of citizenship overruled the Supreme Court's decision in the famous *Dred Scott* case[7] that Negroes could not be American citizens. The command of equal protection of the laws forbade unreasonable discrimination among persons; and the privileges and immunities and due process clauses laid the basis for an argument that this amendment had "incorporated" the Bill of Rights and thus made those protections effective against the states.

Some justices have completely rejected this argument; others have completely accepted it. The result has been a slow process of inclusion and exclusion of specific rights. In 1925, for instance, the Supreme Court held that the due process clause protects freedom of speech against state action.[8] It should be kept in mind that one of the peculiarities of American constitutional law is that the term "state action" covers any official act by a state officer or an officer of local government, county, city, town, school district, or any other level whatsoever.

In the course of American constitutional development eight sets of liberties

---

[4] A bill of attainder is an act of the legislature that convicts a person of a crime and imposes punishment without allowing that person a judicial trial. See *Cummings v. Missouri,* 4 Wallace 277, 323 (1867).

[5] An ex post facto law is a statute that makes an act, legal when it was committed, a crime, or retroactively increases the punishment for a criminal act, or lowers retroactively the standards of proof required to convict a person of a particular crime. See *Calder v. Bull,* 3 Dallas 386 (1798).

[6] *Barron v. Baltimore,* 7 Peters 243 (1833).

[7] *Dred Scott v. Sandford,* 19 Howard 393 (1857).

[8] *Gitlow v. New York,* 268 U.S. 652 (1925).

have emerged as fundamental: the right to freedom itself; the right to equal treatment under law; the right to citizenship and its corollary the right to vote; freedom of conscience and religion; freedom of expression and assembly; freedom of movement; the right to privacy; and the right to justice when accused of crime. Chapter 8 analyzed the right to vote and Chapter 21 will take up problems of equal treatment under law, privacy, and criminal justice. This chapter will discuss the remainder of these fundamental rights. In both this and the following chapter we shall indicate the extent to which the Supreme Court has made specific facets of these rights binding on the states as well as the federal government.

THE RIGHT TO FREEDOM AND THE RIGHT TO CITIZENSHIP

The Thirteenth Amendment of the Constitution provides for the right to freedom. This particular right, unlike so many others guaranteed by the Constitution, operates against encroachment not only by government but also by private persons.

Neither slavery nor involuntary servitude, except as a punishment for crime whereof the party shall have been duly convicted, shall exist within the United States, or any place subject to their jurisdiction.
Congress shall have power to enforce this article by appropriate legislation.

Most of the controversies that have arisen under the Thirteenth Amendment have centered about real or alleged instances of "involuntary servitude" rather than "slavery." In 1867, Congress passed an Antipeonage Act, making it a federal crime to hold persons in involuntary servitude. Peonage has been defined by the Supreme Court as "a status or condition of compulsory service, based upon the indebtedness of the peon to the master."[9] Thus attempts to force a man against his will to work off a debt are outlawed. As the Supreme Court has said: "The undoubted aim of the Thirteenth Amendment as implemented by the Antipeonage Act was not merely to end slavery but to maintain a system of completely free and voluntary labor throughout the United States."[10]

In a world divided into hundreds of nations, citizenship is closely allied to freedom. Citizenship, Chief Justice Warren has observed, is "the right to have rights."[11] In recent years the Supreme Court first rejected then reversed itself and accepted the doctrine that an American can lose his citizenship only by voluntarily renouncing it. A majority of the justices have held that neither desertion from the armed forces in wartime nor voting in a foreign election is conclusive evidence of repudiation of American citizenship.[12]

---

[9] *Bailey v. Alabama,* 219 U.S. 219, 242 (1911).
[10] *Pollock v. Williams,* 322 U.S. 4, 17 (1944).
[11] *Trop v. Dulles,* 356 U.S. 86, 102 (1958).
[12] *Perez v. Brownell,* 356 U.S. 44 (1958), ruled that Congress could revoke a man's citizenship for voting in a foreign election. *Trop v. Dulles,* 356 U.S. 86 (1958), held unconstitutional a federal statute permitting revocation of citizenship as punishment for wartime desertion. After several intervening cases, the Court overruled *Perez* in *Afroyim v. Rusk,* 387 U.S. 253 (1967).

FREEDOM OF RELIGION

The First Amendment to the Constitution states: "Congress shall make no law respecting an establishment of religion, or prohibiting the free exercise thereof. . . ." The third section of Article VI of the original Constitution also provides that "no religious test shall ever be required as a qualification to any office or public trust under the United States." Freedom of religion, as defined in the First Amendment and made binding on the states by the Fourteenth, is a two-pronged right. First, the government is forbidden to establish directly or indirectly a religion. This is what is meant by the phrase "separation of church and state." Second, the government is forbidden to interfere with or regulate religion.

Public Aid to Parochial Schools

The Supreme Court did not pass upon the meaning of the "establishment of religion" clause of the First Amendment until 1947, when by a five to four vote it held that use of public funds to transport pupils to a parochial school was not improper. The majority felt that this use of public funds was intended to ensure the safety of children going to and from school rather than to give support to church schools. However, in an oft-quoted passage in the majority opinion, Justice Hugo Black[13] asserted:

The "establishment of religion" clause of the First Amendment means at least this: Neither a state nor the Federal Government can set up a church. Neither can pass laws which aid one religion, aid all religions, or prefer one religion over another. . . . No tax in any amount, large or small, can be levied to support any religious activities or institutions, whatever they may be called, or what ever form they may adopt to teach or practice religion. Neither a state nor the Federal Government can, openly or secretly, participate in the affairs of any religious organizations or groups and vice versa.

The four dissenting justices all believed that the expenditure in question did give aid to religion as well as protect the welfare of children. Some twenty years earlier the Court had upheld the use of public funds to purchase textbooks for children attending private and parochial schools as well as public schools. The Court had not, however, considered the constitutional issue of separation of church and state in rendering this decision.[14] Whether the Court will draw a line between expenditures of public funds for transportation or school books on the one side and public aid to parochial schools for the payment of teachers' salaries and the construction of school buildings on the other remains to be seen.

"Released Time" Religious Education

A second problem under the "establishment of religion" clause concerns the constitutionality of religious education in the public schools. Since it is quite clear that the Constitution forbids direct and

---

[13] *Everson v. Board of Education of Ewing*, 330 U.S. 1, 15–16 (1947).
[14] *Cochran v. Louisiana State Board of Education*, 281 U.S. 370 (1930).

outright efforts at religious indoctrination by public school teachers, a formula, known as released time has been worked out to permit religious instruction for public school children. The problem first came to the Supreme Court in 1948 in a case from Champaign, Illinois. Here, at their parents' request, school children were released from regular classwork for a scheduled time each week to receive religious instruction in the school building from outside teachers supplied by the Champaign churches. These teachers were not paid from public funds, but the school's compulsory attendance system was used to require attendance at religious education classes by those pupils whose parents wanted them to attend. The Court thought that these facts showed a "close cooperation between the school authorities and the religious council in promoting religious education," concluded that this "is beyond all question a utilization of the tax-established and tax-supported public school system to aid religious groups to spread their faith," and held the program unconstitutional.[15]

Four years later, however, the Court modified somewhat the effect of its Champaign decision when, by a six to three vote, it upheld a "released time" program in New York state.[16] The New York system differed from that of Champaign in only one important respect—classes in religious education were not held in school buildings.

Prayers and Bible Readings in Public Schools

It has long been customary in many public schools to offer prayers or to read passages from the Bible.[17] This has been done on every possible basis, ranging from wholly voluntary and intermittent action by individual teachers to a uniform requirement prescribed by state authorities. For years the Court avoided a direct decision on the constitutionality of these practices,[18] but in 1962 the justices invalidated a school-prayer requirement. The case arose in New York, where the state Board of Regents had composed the following prayer and recommended it to local school district authorities: "Almighty God, we acknowledge our dependence upon Thee, and we beg Thy blessings upon us, our parents, our teachers, and our country." The New Hyde Park Board of Education ordered the prayer to be recited at the beginning of each school day, with a provision that any student might be exempted from the requirement if his parents objected. In spite of this exemption, the parents of ten students challenged the prayer in the courts. The Supreme Court majority ruled that the prayer violated the Constitution. Speaking through Justice Hugo Black,[19] the majority declared:

It is neither sacrilegious nor antireligious to say that each separate government in this country should stay out of the business of writing or sanctioning official prayers and leave that purely

---

[15] *McCollum v. Board of Education,* 333 U.S. 203, 209–210 (1948).

[16] *Zorach v. Clauson,* 343 U.S. 606 (1952).

[17] It is interesting to note that the framers rejected a motion made by Benjamin Franklin in the Philadelphia Convention that regular prayers be offered.

[18] See *Doremus v. Board of Education,* 343 U.S. 429 (1952).

[19] *Engel v. Vitale,* 370 U.S. 421, 435 (1962).

religious function to the people themselves and to those the people choose to look to for religious guidance.

The following year a majority of eight extended this ruling to strike down a Pennsylvania requirement of daily reading in public schools of verses of the Bible and recitation of the Lord's Prayer. Justice Clark[20] wrote for the Court:

> The place of religion in our society is an exalted one, achieved through a long tradition of reliance on the home, the church and the inviolable citadel of the individual heart and mind. We have come to recognize through bitter experience that it is not within the power of government to invade that citadel, whether its purpose or effect be to aid or oppose, to advance or retard. In the relationship between man and religion, the State is firmly committed to a position of neutrality.

Jehovah's Witnesses

Where the government has been accused of violating the second part of the religious freedom guarantee, that is, "prohibiting the free exercise" of religion, the case has usually concerned some small religious group. In the mid-nineteenth century the Mormons' practice of polygamy inevitably brought them into conflict with conventional social beliefs and marriage customs. Congress outlawed the practice of polygamy in the territory of Utah, and the Supreme Court unanimously upheld the constitutionality of such legislation.[21] In one of the Mormon cases the Court said:[22]

> With man's relations to his Maker and the obligations he may think they impose, and the manner in which an expression shall be made by him of his beliefs on those subjects, no interference can be permitted, provided always the laws of society, designed to secure its peace and prosperity, and the morals of its people, are not interfered with. However free the exercise of religion may be, it must be subordinated to the criminal laws of the country, passed with reference to actions regarded by general consent as properly the subjects of punitive legislation.

Had the Mormon movement occurred a century later and had its leaders advocated merely "serial polygamy," that is, many wives but only one at a time, they would have had no trouble with American law and probably would have been unnoticed except by judges and divorce lawyers.

More recently the Jehovah's Witnesses have time and again run into difficulties with the law. They discourage participation in political affairs and refuse to support war. They are opposed to the worship of images and accordingly will not salute the flag. Every Witness regards himself as an ordained minister, and he is expected to be an active proselytizer. The persistent views and practices of the sect have subjected its members to prosecution for violation of law and to persecution for flouting customs. Under local ordinances they have been charged with distributing literature or soliciting funds without a permit, engaging in disorderly

---

[20] *Abington School District v. Schempp,* 374 U.S. 203, 226 (1963); see also *Chamberlin v. Dade County,* 377 U.S. 402 (1964).

[21] *Reynolds v. United States,* 98 U.S. 145 (1879); *Davis v. Beason,* 133 U.S. 333 (1890).

[22] *Davis v. Beason,* 133 U.S. 333, 342 (1890).

conduct on the streets, parading without a license, using children to solicit funds, and with failure to salute the flag. The sect has appealed adverse local rulings to the Supreme Court of the United States, arguing that the Constitution has been violated, and the Court has invalidated many of the challenged ordinances.

The refusal of the Jehovah's Witnesses to comply with laws providing for a compulsory flag salute occasioned the most notable constitutional controversy involved in the many cases pertaining to the sect. Moreover, it resulted in one of the most remarkable about-faces by the Supreme Court in its history. The problem was admittedly borderline. Was the requirement of the flag salute of sufficient importance in encouraging patriotism to outweigh an individual's religious scruples? In 1940, by an overwhelming eight to one majority, the Court upheld a requirement of this type, with Justice Harlan Stone the lone dissenter.[23] Three years later the Supreme Court took jurisdiction over a second flag-salute case and agreed to reconsider the problem. Four of the justices who had participated in the first decision were now ready to invalidate compulsory flag-salute legislation. They were joined by two new members of the Court to make up a six to three majority that held legislation requiring the flag salute to be an unconstitutional interference with religious freedom.[24]

"Blue" Laws and Test Oaths

In 1961, the Supreme Court faced the issue of the constitutionality of laws requiring the closing of many businesses on Sunday. In a series of cases a sharply divided Court upheld the Sunday closing laws of three states, rejecting arguments that these laws established religion or interfered with religious freedom. The first argument was rejected on grounds that the purpose and effect of the statutes was not to aid religion but to set aside Sunday as a day of rest and recreation. The second argument was rejected on the ground that the statutes caused either no, or minimal, interference with the religious freedom of the persons (primarily Jewish merchants prevented from operating their businesses on Sunday) challenging the laws.[25] On the other hand, the Court held unconstitutional South Carolina's denial of unemployment compensation to a Seventh Day Adventist who refused to accept a job that required him to work on Saturdays.[26]

In *Torcaso v. Watkins* a unanimous Court invalidated a provision in the Maryland state constitution that required all persons holding offices of profit or trust in the state to declare a belief in the existence of God. Torcaso had been denied a commission as a notary public because of a refusal to make such a declaration. The Court[27] said, "This Maryland religious test for public office uncon-

---

[23] *Minersville School District v. Gobitis,* 310 U.S. 586 (1940).

[24] *West Virginia State Board of Education v. Barnette,* 319 U.S. 624 (1943).

[25] *McGowan v. Maryland,* 366 U.S. 420 (1961); *Gallagher v. Crown Kosher Super Market,* 366 U.S. 617 (1961); *Two Guys From Harrison-Allentown v. McGinley,* 366 U.S. 582 (1961); *Braunfeld v. Brown,* 366 U.S. 599 (1961).

[26] *Sherbert v. Verner,* 374 U.S. 398 (1963).

[27] 367 U.S. 488 (1961).

stitutionally invades the appellant's freedom of belief and religion and therefore cannot be enforced against him." The justices were doing little more here than recognizing that freedom to believe in God is not true freedom unless it includes the right not to believe.

Military Service and Conscientious Objectors

Governmental authority to raise armies by means of compulsory service can endanger the religious freedom of citizens who are opposed to war on theological grounds. Here two rights may come into direct conflict, that of society to defend itself and that of the individual not to violate his conscience. The problem is made more complex by the difficulty of ascertaining whether a man is truly opposed to war on moral principles or is merely trying to avoid risking his life.

Even in Colonial times the states made some provision for exempting conscientious objectors from service in the militia. And when the federal government first instituted a draft during the Civil War, Congress followed this state practice, though the exemptions were narrow. Again, in World War I, Congress excused from combat service members of any "well-recognized religious sect" whose tenets forbade participation in war.[28]

In 1940, Congress widened the limits to include any person "who, by reason of religious training and belief, is conscientiously opposed to participation in war in any form."[29] Eight years later Congress added that "religious training and belief in this connection means an individual's belief in a relationship to a Supreme Being involving duties superior to those arising from any human relation, but does not include essentially political, sociological, or philosophical views or a merely personal code."[30]

The Supreme Court has liberally interpreted these provisions. In *United States v. Seegar* the justices unanimously reversed draft-evasion convictions of three men, two of whom expressed beliefs in a Supreme Being and vaguely related these beliefs to moral objections to war. The third defendant claimed that he was opposed to war on religious grounds but admitted skepticism regarding the existence of a Supreme Being. Rather, he based his opposition to war on a "belief in and devotion to goodness and virtue for their own sakes, and a religious faith in a purely ethical creed." The justices found that this statement, if sincerely made, entitled him to exemption under the law. In reversing these convictions, the Court tried to formulate two general tests to determine whether individuals who do not belong to sects such as the Quakers should be exempt from military service. The first test is: Does the claimed belief occupy the same place in the life of the objector as an orthodox belief in God holds in the life of one clearly qualified for exemption?[31] The second test is more difficult and factual: Does the objector sincerely believe in the pacifist views he proclaims?

---

[28] 40 *Stat.* 76.
[29] 54 *Stat.* 885.
[30] 62 *Stat.* 613.
[31] 380 U.S. 163, 184 (1965).

In 1967 Stokely Carmichael and Nobel Prize winners Dr. Martin Luther King and Dr. Linus Pauling addressed a crowd gathered at the UN to protest the United States' participation in the Vietnam War. Estimates of the crowd ranged from 100,000 to over half a million. (Laurence Bosworth from PIX, Inc.)

FREEDOM OF EXPRESSION

Almost the first words of the Bill of Rights provide that: "Congress shall make no law . . . abridging the freedom of speech or of the press." The command is peremptory. Congress—and, through the Fourteenth Amendment, the states—shall make no law restricting this right. While most people may believe that freedom of speech and press is vital to democracy, few can agree on the precise meaning of this freedom in everyday life. New modes of expression, such as motion pictures, radio, and television, have raised difficult issues concerning its coverage. No right, however basic, better illustrates the *relativity* of freedom in the modern state. The Supreme Court has consistently taken the view that it is not the purpose of the First Amendment to protect unbridled freedom of expression. The Court has also held that the proper limits of this freedom are to be found by seeking its practical meaning in its historical context and in its application to the changing circumstances and problems of the present day.

Not all Supreme Court justices have agreed with this approach. Justice Hugo Black,[32] in particular, has argued that freedom of expression under the First Amendment is an absolute right. "It is my belief," he has said, "that there *are* 'absolutes' in our Bill of Rights, and that they were put there on purpose by men who knew what words meant, and meant their prohibitions to be 'absolutes.'" And he added, "Our First Amendment was a bold effort . . . to establish a country with no legal restrictions of any kind upon the subjects people could investigate, discuss, and deny."

---

[32] "Absolutes, Courts, and the Bill of Rights," *New York University Law Review,* 35 (April 1960), p. 865.

What, then, are the kinds of protection the Constitution establishes for speech and publication? First, the government may not establish a system of advance censorship or "previous restraint," which curbs ideas *before* they are expressed. Punishment after an act is one thing; to seek to prevent an expression is another. There may be rare exceptions to this rule insofar as speech and press are concerned. For example, Supreme Court decisions imply that the government may establish a considerable measure of press censorship in time of war if it chooses to do so.[33]

Second, the Constitution provides a large measure of protection against punishment *after* words are uttered. Freedom of expression would have little value if it protected the individual only against previous restraint and left him to take the consequences for words actually uttered. Obviously, to have any practical value, freedom in this respect must operate both after as well as before the act. Persons, however, may be punished under law if their actual remarks, spoken or printed, are in certain ways inimical to the public interest.

Punishment for Libel and Slander

Libel and slander may be defined as words (*printed* in the case of libel, and *spoken* in the case of slander) used with a malicious intent to defame the character of an individual or to expose him to public hatred, contempt, or ridicule. For centuries English law and American law have regarded such conduct as harmful to the individual and dangerous to the public welfare and have provided civil and criminal remedies against it. In either case the aid of the courts may be invoked under the law to penalize an individual for the way in which he has expressed ideas, and the courts have not yet held that such penalties violate the constitutional guarantee of freedom of expression.

As part of his general political philosophy, Justice Black has taken the position that the First and Fourteenth Amendments forbid libel and slander laws, no matter how carefully drawn.[34] The closest the Supreme Court has ever come to endorsing this absolutist position was in a 1964 decision, *New York Times v. Sullivan*. There the Court reversed a state libel judgment against the *Times* for publishing an advertisement attacking Birmingham, Alabama, officials for mistreating Negroes. Conceding that some information in the advertisement was false, a majority of the justices nevertheless ruled that good faith criticism of government officials was so important to a democracy that the Constitution "prohibits a public official from recovering damages for a defamatory falsehood relating to his official conduct unless he proves that the statement was made with 'actual malice'—that is with knowledge that it was false or with reckless disregard or whether it was false or not."[35] Justices Black, Douglas, and Goldberg would have held that in criticizing a public official a newspaper has absolute immunity from a libel suit.

---

[33] *Near v. Minnesota,* 283 U.S. 697, 716 (1931).

[34] "Justice Black and First Amendment 'Absolutes': A Public Interview," *New York University Law Review,* 37 (June 1962).

[35] 376 U.S. 254, 279–280 (1964); see also *Garrison v. Louisiana,* 379 U.S. 64 (1965); and *Rosenblatt v. Baer,* 383 U.S. 75 (1966); which follow the *New York Times* doctrine.

Punishment for Obscenity

The courts have sustained the constitutionality of a number of state and federal laws forbidding the uttering of obscene words or the printing and distributing of obscene literature and materials. The line between obscenity and frank but proper discussion of some topics is, however, anything but clear. There is always a danger that idiosyncratic or outmoded standards of morality may be used to inhibit creativity in the arts or literature. To date, the Supreme Court has never declared unconstitutional a federal law restricting obscenity, although the Court has occasionally held that the Postmaster General has in a particular case exceeded the authority Congress has given him to ban certain material from the mails.[36]

In recent years the Supreme Court has subjected state obscenity laws to more exacting scrutiny under the Fourteenth Amendment and has invalidated a number of them.[37] In 1957, for example, the justices struck down a Michigan statute that made it a criminal offense to offer the general reading public a book that might have a potentially deleterious effect on youth. The Court said that the law was "not reasonably restricted to the evil with which it is said to deal. . . . The incidence of this enactment is to reduce the adult population of Michigan to reading only what is fit for children." "This," the Court observed, "is to burn the house to roast the pig."[38]

Roth v. United States, also decided in 1957, was a landmark case in the law of obscenity. There the justices wrestled with problems of defining obscenity and of establishing a test to distinguish constitutionally protected speech and writing from that which is not protected. The Court emphasized that "sex and obscenity are not synonymous" and defined the latter as "material which deals with sex in a manner appealing to prurient interest." The Court expressly rejected a Victorian test of obscenity to the effect that a book might be judged obscene because of isolated passages. In its place the Court established this test of obscenity— "whether to the average person, applying contemporary community standards, the dominant theme of the material taken as a whole appeals to prurient interest."[39]

In 1966, the justices elaborated on their test of obscenity to include three elements:[40] "(a) the dominant theme of the material taken as a whole appeals to a prurient interest in sex; (b) the material is patently offensive because it affronts

---

[36] *Hannegan v. Esquire, Inc.,* 327 U.S. 146 (1946); *Walker v. Popenoe,* 149 F. 2d 511 (1949); also relevant is *Lamont v. Postmaster General,* 381 U.S. 301 (1965), which invalidated on First Amendment grounds an act of Congress authorizing the Postmaster General to detain and destroy unsolicited mail that he deemed to be Communist propaganda, unless the addressee requested delivery.

[37] *Roth v. United States,* 354 U.S. 476 (1957). See also *Kingsley Books v. Brown,* 354 U.S. 436 (1957); *Smith v. California,* 361 U.S. 147 (1959); *Marcus v. Search Warrant,* 367 U.S. 717 (1961); *Manual Enterprises, Inc., v. Day,* 370 U.S. 478 (1962); *Bantam Books v. Sullivan,* 372 U.S. 58 (1963); *A Quantity of Books v. Kansas,* 378 U.S. 205 (1964).

[38] *Butler v. Michigan,* 352 U.S. 380, 383 (1957).

[39] 354 U.S. 476, 487, 489 (1957).

[40] *Memoirs v. Massachusetts,* 383 U.S. 413, 418 (1966).

Publisher Ralph Ginzburg was convicted in June 1963 by the State of Pennsylvania for sending obscene materials through the mails. These included Eros *magazine,* Liaison *newsletter, and* The Housewife's Guide to Selective Promiscuity. *His conviction was upheld by the Pennsylvania Court of Appeals in 1964 and by the U. S. Supreme Court in 1965. In March 1967, Ginzburg was sentenced to five years in prison and fined $42,000.* (Daily News)

contemporary community standards relating to the description or representation of sexual matters; and (c) the material is utterly without redeeming social value."

Unfortunately, in none of their decisions have the justices been able to agree as to whether "contemporary community standards" are those of the nation as a whole or those of a particular locality.[41] A majority, however, have held that it is legitimate for government officials to consider the way in which an item is advertised as a factor in determining whether its appeal is mainly to prurient interests. Thus the Court upheld the conviction of the publisher of the magazine *Eros* after a trial had brought out that the defendant had used advertising methods that were permeated by the "leer of the sensualist" and had, for obvious publicity reasons, tried to get his material mailed from two Pennsylvania towns, Intercourse and Blue Ball. Failing in this he had settled on Middlesex, New Jersey.[42]

Punishment for Incitement to Crime or Violence

Closely analogous to legislation curbing obscenity are laws designed to protect the public from the harmful effects of lurid publications dealing with crime and bloodshed. In 1948, the Supreme Court heard a case challenging the constitutionality of a New York law that made it an offense

---

[41] *Jacobellis v. Ohio,* 378 U.S. 184 (1964); *Ginzburg v. United States,* 383 U.S. 463 (1966), dissenting opinion of Justice Black.
[42] *Ginzburg v. United States,* 383 U.S. 463 (1966).

to publish or sell periodicals or books dealing principally with crime and blood-shed that so "massed" this material as to incite violent and depraved crimes. The majority ruled that the statute was invalid because it failed to define the forbidden conduct with sufficient precision. The decision implies that freedom of expression may be limited as a means of preventing crime, but the limitation must be care-fully spelled out.[43] Many states and municipalities have enforced more carefully drawn laws. In particular, comic books and similar literature designed for juvenile consumption are being increasingly subjected to statutory control. Many of these regulations are enforced, particularly at the local level, without effective challenge in the courts.

Contempt of Court as a Restraint upon Freedom of Expression

A further restriction upon speech or press is the authority of judges to cite individuals for contempt of court and to impose punishment for remarks or publications that may impede the work of the courts. Thus to alter somewhat Justice Oliver Wendell Holmes's famous aphorism, no man can claim the right to cry out in a courtroom that the presiding judge is dis-honest. The Supreme Court has allowed state and federal judges great leeway in punishing contemptuous acts committed in the courtroom,[44] but the justices have restricted the authority of judges to punish newspapers or private citizens for making, outside of the courtroom, statements critical of judicial conduct. It is not enough, the Court has said,[45] that criticism be vehement. To be punishable it must also "constitute an imminent, not merely a likely, threat to the administration of justice. The danger must not be remote or even probable; it must immediately imperil."

Punishment for Seditious Utterances

A further exception to freedom of ex-pression allows punishment of persons who make seditious utterances. Sedition consists in the use of words to incite persons to engage in unlawful action against the government or public officers. The first federal sedition act was passed by Congress in 1798. The two world wars of the present century and the general inter-national unrest of contemporary times led Congress to pass several new sedition acts that place important curbs upon freedom of expression. The states have also enacted much legislation of this type in recent years. These laws will be examined more carefully later in this chapter as part of the problem of balancing the interests of national security and individual freedom.

---

[43] *Winters v. New York,* 333 U.S. 507 (1948).

[44] *Fisher v. Pace,* 336 U.S. 155 (1949); *Sacher v. United States,* 343 U.S. 1 (1952): see, however, *Offutt v. United States,* 348 U.S. 11 (1954).

[45] *Craig v. Harney,* 331 U.S. 367, 376 (1947). See also: *Nye v. United States,* 313 U.S. 33 (1941); *Bridges v. California,* 312 U.S. 252 (1941); and *Pennekamp v. Florida,* 328 U.S. 331 (1946).

Incidental Restraints on Freedom of Expression

Freedom of expression may be indirectly affected by general statutes that do not on their face purport to control this freedom. For example, a newspaper publishing company may properly be subjected to laws regulating ordinary businesses. There is no reason why such a company should not pay taxes, observe the local building code, maintain safe working conditions in its plant, or meet various labor standards concerning wages, hours, and collective bargaining.[46] On the other hand, if such a seemingly general statute actually interferes with the free operation of a newspaper, or discriminates against the press, it is likely to be invalidated. During the Huey Long era, for instance, the Louisiana legislature placed a tax of 2 percent on the gross receipts of newspapers having a circulation of more than 20,000 a week. The Supreme Court[47] recognized that this tax was intended to harass big city newspapers hostile to the Long machine and struck down the law as an interference with freedom of the press.

Motion Pictures, Radio, and Television

None of the new media of expression such as motion pictures, radio, and television has yet been able to secure the same measure of constitutional protection as newspapers have. All have been subjected to substantial measures of government regulation. In particular, state and local governments long ago set up machinery to censor motion pictures. Such censorship was quickly challenged as unconstitutional, but in 1915 the Supreme Court ruled that, like the stage, motion pictures were primarily media of entertainment rather than of expression and thus were not protected by the Constitution.[48] In 1952, however, in *Burstyn v. Wilson*,[49] the Court changed its mind and declared that movies were protected by the First and Fourteenth Amendments, though the justices added the qualification that movies were not "necessarily subject to the precise rules governing any other particular method of expression."

In *Burstyn* the Court invalidated a New York state system that authorized banning films because of sacrilegious content. For several years thereafter the justices extended this ruling by striking down state censorship designed to ban films held to be "immoral," "harmful," or "tending to corrupt morals."[50] But in 1961, a five-judge majority returned to the precise holding of the *Burstyn* case, and in *Times Film Corporation v. Chicago*[51] upheld an ordinance requiring submission of all films for examination by city officials before permits for public exhibition could be obtained. The majority was unwilling to hold that *any* general advance

---

[46] *Associated Press v. NLRB,* 301 U.S. 103, 132–133 (1937).

[47] *Grosjean v. American Press Co.,* 297 U.S. 233 (1936).

[48] *Mutual Film Corp. v. Ohio Industrial Commission,* 236 U.S. 230 (1915).

[49] 343 U.S. 495, 503 (1952).

[50] *Superior Films v. Ohio,* 346 U.S. 587 (1954); *Kingsley International Pictures Corp. v. New York,* 360 U.S. 684 (1959).

[51] 365 U.S. 543 (1961).

censorship or prior restraint of motion pictures, like prior restraint on newspapers, is unconstitutional.

Four years later, in *Freedman v. Maryland,*[52] the justices further explained that the holding that any prior restraint on movies was not unconstitutional did not mean that any prior restraint was constitutional. To be valid a movie censorship system must offer at least three procedural safeguards: (1) the burden of proof that a film is obscene or otherwise objectionable must rest with the censor; (2) the censor must quickly either issue a license or go to court and ask for an order forbidding the showing of the picture; (3) there must be a provision for a prompt and final court review of any action taken by the censor.

In the case of radio and television Congress has provided for a drastic measure of control of broadcasting by the Federal Communications Commission, including the licensing of all stations and the allocation of wavelengths. The national government has not attempted to establish any systematic censorship over the content of radio or television programs. At the same time, the FCC is authorized to use its discretion in licensing stations by giving attention to the "public interest, convenience, or necessity." Moreover, licenses are subject to cancellation or renewal every three years. In granting such renewals the Commission has given consideration to the content of radio and television programs, and in a few instances renewals have been refused because of objectionable programs or objectionable practices. Thus, although there is little evidence that the FCC has exercised any substantial supervision over the broadcasting of controversial political or social information, a limited measure of supervisory censorship undoubtedly exists. The Supreme Court[53] has upheld this control:

The right of free speech does not include, however, the right to use the facilities of radio without a license. The licensing system established by Congress in the Communications Act of 1934 was a proper exercise of its power over commerce. The standard it provided for the licensing of stations was the "public interest, convenience, or necessity." Denial of a station license on that ground, if valid under the Act, is not a denial of free speech.

FREEDOM OF ASSEMBLY AND PETITION

The First Amendment also provides that "Congress shall make no law . . . abridging . . . the right of the people peaceably to assemble, and to petition the government for a redress of grievances." In its broadest aspects this constitutional provision guarantees the right of the American people to assemble to discuss political questions and to organize to secure political action. More specifically, they may form political parties to bring about the adoption of specific governmental policies, and they may form interest groups and petition public officers, including judges, to influence governmental programs.

Use of public streets and parks for outdoor political rallies and religious meetings has a long tradition; but the courts have interpreted the Constitution as

---

[52] 380 U.S. 51 (1965).
[53] *National Broadcasting Co. v. United States,* 319 U.S. 190, 227 (1943).

not guaranteeing to any group a right to conduct an open-air meeting on public property if traffic will be disrupted or lives endangered. At the same time, judges have also often rejected police claims of "public order" when this claim has been used to restrict the activities of groups espousing unpopular causes.

Since 1940, the Supreme Court has decided a large number of difficult cases concerning freedom of assembly and petition.[54] A classic instance was that of *Edwards v. South Carolina* in 1963.[55] One hundred eighty-seven Negro high school and college students, carrying placards protesting against segregation policies, walked around the state capitol grounds. Local police at first merely watched the demonstration. Then, when a crowd of several hundred persons gathered and traffic in the area was being slowed, police, fearing a clash between the demonstrators and the crowd, told the students to disperse. Instead of leaving the capitol, the students began singing patriotic and religious songs while clapping their hands and stomping their feet. The police promptly marched the demonstrators off to jail, and later the students were convicted for breach of the peace. The Supreme Court reversed the convictions, pointing out that the students had done no more than exercise their constitutional rights of assembly and petition. The Court stated that the very purpose of these rights was to invite dispute, even perhaps to stir anger and bring about unrest. As long as the students had demonstrated peacefully and had not caused a major traffic obstruction, they could not be punished.

In an interesting case parallel except in that demonstrators were protesting outside a state courthouse, the Supreme Court sustained the constitutionality of a Louisiana statute prohibiting picketing "near" a court. The justices reversed the convictions in this instance on several technical grounds, but they were careful to point out that a state could protect a court not only from interference but also from any situation that might give rise to a belief that the judge and jury might have been unlawfully swayed in their judgment.[56]

Lobbying is another and usually more subtle form of influencing public officials, an approach widely used by interest groups and individual citizens alike. There is no question that lobbying is protected by the First and Fourteenth Amendments, but it is also a right that can easily degenerate into efforts at bribery or illegal threats. As discussed in Chapter 7, Congress in 1946 passed the Regulation of Lobbying Act to curb some of the more obvious abuses. This federal statute does little more than to require certain lobbies seeking to influence Congress to register with the federal government and to disclose information about their income and expenditures, including the names of large donors and persons to whom expenditures are paid. Doubts were raised, however, as to whether even this modest requirement did not infringe the right to petition the government for a redress of grievances, as set forth in the First Amendment. The act reached the Supreme Court in 1954. By greatly narrowing the law's application, to a point where it covers

---

[54] See, for example: *Cox v. New Hampshire,* 312 U.S. 569 (1941); *Terminiello v. Chicago,* 337 U.S. 1 (1949); *Feiner v. New York,* 340 U.S. 315 (1951); *Fields v. South Carolina,* 375 U.S. 44 (1963); *Henry v. Rock Hill,* 375 U.S. 6 (1963).

[55] 372 U.S. 229 (1963).

[56] *Cox v. Louisiana,* 379 U.S. 536 (1965); *Cox v. Louisiana,* 379 U.S. 559 (1965).

only persons who solicit or receive money to be used to influence legislation through direct communication with members of Congress, the Court by a five to three margin upheld its constitutionality.[57]

INDIVIDUAL FREEDOM
AND NATIONAL SECURITY

A democratic nation always finds itself in something of a dilemma in dealing with threats of subversion. On the one hand, unless it protects itself against efforts to overthrow the established order by violent, unconstitutional means, democracy may be destroyed. On the other hand, if it suppresses ideas, even revolutionary ideas, as opposed to revolutionary action, government runs the risk of destroying the very values it seeks to protect.

Protecting National Security:
The Milton-Jefferson-Holmes Approach

The methods that have been used in the last twenty years to meet the threat of domestic communism have stirred a storm of controversy, and many Americans see in them a serious threat to civil liberty. Critics of these methods recall the advice frequently offered in the past that a democracy must tolerate revolutionary ideas and combat them only through freedom or discussion. Three hundred years ago in the midst of a bitter revolutionary period in English history John Milton[58] voiced this argument:

And though all the windes of doctrin were let loose to play upon the earth, so Truth be in the field, we do injuriously by licensing and prohibiting to misdoubt her strength. Let her and Falshood grapple; who ever knew Truth put to the wors in a free and open encounter?

Thomas Jefferson[59] echoed Milton in his first inaugural address:

If there be any among us who wish to dissolve this union, or to change its republican form, let them stand undisturbed as monuments of the safety with which error of opinion may be tolerated where reason is left free to combat it.

Finally, members of the United States Supreme Court have again and again repeated the same idea. Justice Oliver Wendell Holmes,[60] for example, said:

If in the long run the beliefs expressed in proletarian dictatorship are destined to be accepted by the dominant forces of the community, the only real meaning of free speech is that they should be given their chance and have their way.

What this position comes to is that as long as revolutionaries are content to use words, rather than acts, to win their purpose, a democracy must leave them

---

[57] *United States v. Harriss,* 347 U.S. 612 (1954).

[58] John Milton, *Areopagitica,* Hales, ed. (New York: Oxford University Press, 1917), pp. 51–52.

[59] *Messages and Papers of the Presidents,* compiled by James D. Richardson (New York: Bureau of National Literature and Art, 1903), 1, pp. 321–322.

[60] *Gitlow v. New York,* 268 U.S. 652, dissenting opinion 673 (1925).

alone. Unfortunately, it has never proved possible to define the proscribed area of human conduct by drawing quite so sharp a line between words and acts. Men long ago learned that words can be an incitement to criminal acts. As Judge Learned Hand observed, "words are not only the keys of persuasion but the triggers of action."[61] The Supreme Court employed much the same reasoning implicit in Learned Hand's phrase when five decades ago it enunciated the famous "clear and present danger" test concerning freedom of speech.[62] The test says that when men are using speech in such a way as to create an immediate danger that criminal acts against which society has an undoubted right to protect itself will follow, then the words themselves can be declared unlawful and those who utter them punished.

Protecting National Security: Subversive Conduct

Statutes defining such subversive *acts* as espionage and sabotage have long been on the statute books, and their enforcement has involved very little danger to civil liberty. After all, persons who engage in such acts as these have definitely broken with the established order and can hardly expect to escape punishment if they are apprehended. Further statutes outlaw conspiracy and sedition. These vague crimes are difficult to define with precision. Conspiracy involves preliminary *planning,* by two or more persons, of criminal acts. Sedition involves efforts to incite other people to commit criminal acts against the state. As has already been seen, the clear and present danger test recognizes that a sedition statute does not necessarily violate freedom of speech. According to this test, a speaker may be punished when he is clearly inciting immediate commission of unlawful acts. Similarly, courts have long held that government officials need not wait for overt acts before moving against those conspiring to commit criminal acts.

Although society may have good reason to protect itself against both sedition and conspiracy, statutes directed against these offenses are particularly prone to result in abuse of public power. In the hands of public officials who are honest but who suspect that those disagreeing with them are subversives, such statutes can readily become dangerous instruments for the persecution of people whose crimes consist in being unpopular or in expressing radical ideas.

Congressmen have been slow to enact sedition laws. In 1798, under the leadership of the Federalist party, Congress passed the Alien and Sedition Acts.[63] The latter act made it a crime to publish false, scandalous, or defamatory writings with an intent to discredit the government, the President, or Congress, or to excite hatred against them, to stir up sedition, to excite resistance against the law, or to aid hostile foreign designs against the United States. For a year or two the act was

---

[61] *Masses Publishing Co. v. Patten,* 244 F. 535, 540 (1917).
[62] *Schenck v. United States,* 249 U.S. 47, 52 (1919). See also *Whitney v. California,* 274 U.S. 357, 376–377 (1927).
[63] 1 *Stat.* 570, 596.

vigorously enforced. In all, some twenty-five persons were prosecuted, ten of whom were convicted.[64]

A New Jersey editor was fined $100 for hoping in print that the wad of a cannon fired in a presidential salute might hit President Adams on the seat of the pants. A Vermont Jeffersonian, who accused the President of "unbounded thirst for ridiculous pomp, foolish adulation and a selfish avarice," received a thousand dollar fine and four months in jail.

This early peacetime attempt to develop a statutory crime of sedition contributed to the defeat of Adams and the Federalists in the election of 1800. When Jefferson became President in 1801, he pardoned all persons imprisoned under the Sedition Act, and Congress ultimately ordered all fines repaid. The act itself was allowed to expire on March 3, 1801.

More than a century elapsed before Congress once more placed a sedition law on the federal statute books. However, during the Civil War Congress did enact a statute aimed against conspiracy to overthrow the government by force, and this statute is a part of federal law today.[65] During World War I Congress enacted a new sedition statute making it a crime to interfere with the draft, obstruct recruiting, encourage disloyalty, incite insubordination in the armed services, hinder sale of U.S. bonds, or "willfully utter, print, write, or publish any disloyal, profane, scurrilous, or abusive language about the form of government of the United States or the Constitution . . . or to bring the form of government . . . or the Constitution . . . into contempt. . . ."[66]

The operation of this far-reaching restraint upon speech and press was limited by Congress to periods of actual warfare. Nearly 2000 persons were convicted and sent to prison under this and similar laws during the period of World War I, although presidential pardons were granted to many of those still in jail after the close of the war.

In 1940, in the face of new international tensions, Congress enacted the first peacetime sedition law since the act of 1798. This was the Alien Registration Act, more popularly known as the Smith Act.[67] This act defined three offenses: knowingly advocating the overthrow of government by force or violence; helping organize a society that engages in such advocacy or becoming a member of such a society, knowing its purposes; and conspiring with others to commit either of the first two offenses.

In 1951, by a six to two vote, the Supreme Court declared that the Smith Act did not violate the Constitution—in particular, that it did not abridge freedom of speech.[68] Eugene Dennis and ten other national leaders of the Communist party of the United States were charged with conspiring to teach and advocate the overthrow of government by force and violence, and of conspiring to organize the Communist party to teach and advocate the same result.

[64] Arthur M. Schlesinger, Jr., *The Vital Center* (Boston: Houghton Mifflin Company, 1949), p. 193.
[65] 12 *Stat.* 284.
[66] 40 *Stat.* 217, 553.
[67] 54 *Stat.* 670.
[68] *Dennis v. United States,* 341 U.S. 494 (1951).

The evidence consisted largely of quotations from classics of Communist literature asserting the inevitability of force to overthrow the established order in capitalist states and the testimony of ex-Communists that they had heard the accused advocate the use of force. The defendants argued that they could not be found guilty unless the government proved that their activity had resulted in a clear and present danger of a substantive evil, namely, the forcible overthrow of the government.

The six justices in the majority could not agree on the reasoning necessary to uphold the convictions and wrote three separate opinions. In the opinion of Chief Justice Fred Vinson, in which three other justices concurred, the clear and present danger test was reinterpreted to become a "grave and probable" danger test. In other words, these justices held that where speech is used to create a particularly grave danger of overthrowing the government it is sufficient that there should be a probability that the evil result will transpire.

In their dissenting opinions Justices Hugo Black and William Douglas protested against what they regarded as a drastic dilution of the clear and present danger test. Granting that the "ugliness of Communism" and "its deceit and cunning" were present in the Marxist books used by the accused, the dissenters did not feel that the government had proved that the defendants had used speech, or were planning to use speech, in such a way as to create a clear and present danger to the established order.

Following the Supreme Court decision in the *Dennis* case, the federal government proceeded with the prosecution of several score lesser Communist leaders. Virtually all of these defendants were convicted. In 1957, however, in *Yates v. United States,* the Supreme Court set aside convictions of fourteen persons in one of these trials. The majority interpreted the Smith Act as forbidding only advocacy of *action* to achieve the forcible overthrow of government and held that it did not encompass advocacy of the mere abstract *doctrine* of the desirability or inevitability of forcible overthrow. Since the trial judge had failed to charge the jury that the evidence must show that the defendants advocated *action* to overthrow the government, the Court set aside the convictions. It also held that the term "organize," as used in the statute, referred only to the act of founding or establishing an organization and not to the continuing process of carrying on the affairs of an already existing organization. Since it was agreed that the Communist party was finally "organized" no later than 1945, the indictment of the defendants in 1951 was improper under the federal statute of limitations requiring that persons accused of such an offense be prosecuted within three years of the time the alleged offenses were committed.[69] In 1962, Congress amended the Smith Act to include within the word "organize" recruitment of new members and formation of new units of the Communist party, thus reading into the law the meaning rejected by the Supreme Court in the *Yates* case.

In 1961, in *Scales v. United States,* the Court finally passed on the constitutionality of the so-called membership clause of the Smith Act, which makes it a

---

[69] 354 U.S. 398 (1957).

criminal offense to become a member of a society knowing that it advocates over-throw of government by force or violence. In upholding both the validity of the clause and the conviction of Scales under it, the Court ruled that the act reaches only "active," and not merely "nominal" or "passive," members.[70] In a companion case the justices reversed a conviction on membership grounds because the evidence had not been sufficient to show that the particular Communist party unit to which the accused belonged had engaged in advocacy not merely of abstract doctrine of forcible overthrow but of action to that end. And the Court reiterated "the premise that Smith Act offenses require rigorous standards of proof."[71] Thus, though the Court in the end upheld the constitutionality of all phases of the Smith Act brought before it, it has substantially narrowed the act through interpretation, and it now requires the government to carry a heavy burden of proof in winning convictions. The Court's rulings make it very difficult to secure convictions under the Smith Act; and these decisions came at a time when federal officials in the executive branch had pretty well concluded that Smith Act prosecutions were a poor way of combatting communism.

In 1950, Congress passed, over President Truman's veto, another major statute aimed at "subversives," the Internal Security Act, popularly known as the McCarran Act.[72] Although portions of the act apply to all "totalitarians," its primary target is Communists. The statute requires all "Communist-action" and "Communist-front" organizations, and individual members of the former, to register with the federal government. The act also created a Subversive Activities Control Board to decide what organizations are required to register. Members of such organizations are subject to varying prohibitions; for example, they may not hold government jobs. The act also provides for internment of Communists in time of emergency, and it places severe immigration and naturalization restrictions upon Communists.

The McCarran Act has remained a largely unenforced statute. Enforcement of the registration system bogged down for a decade in a seemingly never-ending effort to compel the Communist party to register. Finally in 1961, in a five to four ruling, the Supreme Court held that the registration section of the act was constitutional and that the Communist party was properly required to register under it. The Court postponed, however, a ruling on the validity of the consequences of such registration on party members.[73] Party officials still refused to register, and eventually their case again reached the Supreme Court in 1965. The Court then ruled, eight to zero, that the registration requirements for individual party officers violated the Fifth Amendment's ban against compulsory self-incrimination.[74]

The last major statute directed against "subversives" is the Communist Control Act of 1954.[75] It begins with legislative "findings of fact" that the Com-

---

[70] 367 U.S. 203 (1961).
[71] *Noto v. United States,* 367 U.S. 290 (1961).
[72] 64 *Stat.* 987.
[73] *Communist Party v. Subversive Activities Control Board,* 367 U.S. 1 (1961).
[74] *Albertson v. SACB,* 382 U.S. 70 (1965).
[75] 68 *Stat.* 775.

munist party of the United States is "a conspiracy to overthrow the Government of the United States" and that "its role as the agency of a hostile power renders its existence a clear present and continuing danger to the security of the United States." On the basis of this finding, the act then denies the party all "rights, privileges, and immunities" customarily possessed by American political parties under federal or state law. Moreover, any person who "knowingly and willfully becomes or remains a member of . . . the Communist Party" is made subject to all penalties of the McCarran Act. What this act adds to the laws of 1940 and 1950, as interpreted and applied by the Supreme Court, is difficult to say, particularly since the government has made no real effort to enforce it as a separate statute.

Everything considered, the laws of 1940, 1950, and 1954 were undoubtedly a factor in the sharp decline in the fortunes of the American Communist party in the years following World War II. Yet it seems equally clear that much of this decline can properly be attributed to postwar events on the world scene and the growing sophistication of the American people regarding the nature of communism. On the whole, it is hard to find in these statutes an intelligent or effective approach to the problem of controlling subversive activity. In spite of the fact that many authorities on constitutional law expressed grave doubts about the validity of many features of these laws, the Supreme Court has declared unconstitutional only two sections of the Internal Security Act of 1950, the registration provision and another regarding passports. The Court has, however, narrowed the scope and application of these laws through its power to interpret them and to prescribe the weight of evidence necessary to convict an accused. As has been typical in American history, the justices have avoided a frontal challenge to Congress' attempt to deal with an important problem; nevertheless, they have played an important part in shaping details and lessening the impact of congressional policy.

It should again be noted that federal statutes dealing with such traditional offenses as espionage and sabotage have remained in effect. For example, the members of the Rosenberg spy ring were prosecuted and convicted under the Espionage Act.

Protecting National Security: Loyalty-Security Programs

The executive and legislative branches of the federal government have also tried to protect national security by means of loyalty tests and security checks. Millions of Americans, both in government jobs and in private employment, have been compelled to swear oaths or to pass tests with respect to their loyalty or dependability. For example, under state and local law a considerable part of the teaching profession, both in public and private schools, has been required to sign loyalty oaths.

By an executive order issued by President Truman in 1947, all federal employees, actual and prospective, were compelled to pass a loyalty test. As revised during the Eisenhower Administration, the test provided that the employment of a person by the federal government shall be "clearly consistent with the interests of the national security."[76] Although wider in scope, this test has been less severe in practice than the former in that it has allowed the government to discharge an official without branding him as disloyal because, for example, he has relatives behind the Iron Curtain and his concern for their safety might be used to blackmail him into betraying secrets. It is probable, however, that many persons still confuse loyalty and security, and that the loyal official who has become a security risk may be subjected to social stigma. In any event, in 1956, by a six to three vote, the Supreme Court ruled that insofar as the test was based on the Summary Suspension Act of 1950, it could validly be applied only to persons occupying so-called sensitive posts in the government service, since Congress had indicated such an intention in the statute.[77]

Closely associated with loyalty testing has been the promulgation by various governmental agencies of lists of private organizations deemed subversive. Thereafter, membership in such a proscribed organization is regarded as a black mark against any person subject to a loyalty test or security check. The most famous of these lists is the one that the U.S. Attorney General has maintained since the federal loyalty program was originally established in 1947. Such lists pose hazards to civil liberty unless great care has been taken to include only organizations that have engaged in subversive activity or in fact have such aims. There is danger that, unless organization officers are given notice and allowed to defend themselves, groups will be listed merely because they are unpopular.[78] In addition, there is always the possibility that some people remained members of organizations being infiltrated by Communists in the hope of keeping or winning back control.

Loyalty testing has met with a varied reception in the Supreme Court. When lower-court judges ruled the federal program constitutional the Supreme Court did not reverse these decisions, though, as in the *Yates* case interpreting the Smith Act, the justices have narrowed the scope of the program.[79] The Court has been more exacting in its scrutiny of state programs. During the McCarthy era the Court sustained several state loyalty-security statutes,[80] but even then it invalidated an Oklahoma law that made membership, whether knowing or innocent, in any organization on the Attorney General's list a bar to holding state office.[81] More recently the Court has struck down, as too vague, state requirements that each government official swear that he is not a "subversive person,"[82] or that he has never "knowingly" lent his "aid, support, advice, counsel or influence to the Com-

---

[76] See Executive Order 9835, 12 *Federal Register* 1935 (March 21, 1947); Executive Order 10,241, 16 *Federal Register* 3690 (April 28, 1951); Executive Order 10,450, 18 *Federal Register* 2489 (April 29, 1953).

[77] *Cole v. Young,* 351 U.S. 536 (1956); see also *Vitarelli v. Seaton,* 359 U.S. 535 (1959); and *Cafeteria and Restaurant Workers v. McElroy,* 367 U.S. 886 (1961).

[78] *Joint Anti-Fascist Refugee Committee v. McGrath,* 341 U.S. 123 (1951).

[79] See *Bailey v. Richardson,* 182 F. 2d 46 (1950). See also *Peters v. Hobby,* 349 U.S. 331 (1955); *Cole v. Young,* 351 U.S. 536 (1956); *Greene v. McElroy,* 360 U.S. 474 (1959).

[80] *Garner v. Board of Public Works,* 341 U.S. 716 (1951); *Gerende v. Board of Supervisors,* 341 U.S. 56 (1951); *Adler v. Board of Education,* 342 U.S. 485 (1952).

[81] *Wieman v. Updegraff,* 344 U.S. 183 (1952).

[82] *Baggett v. Bullitt,* 377 U.S. 360 (1964).

munist party."[83] This latter oath could well have disqualified for government work a man who fought in World War II against Nazi Germany.

Advocates of loyalty testing have argued that subversive agents who have penetrated to the heart of sensitive areas of employment, whether public or private, can do serious damage to the national security, and they insist that there is good reason to believe that many such agents are to be found in these sensitive areas. Opponents have doubted that there are large numbers of disloyal persons scattered through the civil service or in such a profession as teaching and have questioned whether the few disloyal persons who may be there can be caught by large-scale, indiscriminate loyalty testing. Such testing is also criticized on the ground that insofar as disloyalty is measured by membership in allegedly subversive organizations, the traditional Anglo-American standard of personal guilt is being replaced by a new standard of "guilt by association." A reply to this argument is made that it is also traditional in evaluating a person's over-all competence to hold a job of some professional importance to take notice of "the company he keeps." In any event, almost no truly subversive persons have been turned up in the public service solely by means of loyalty tests or security checks. Where such persons have been found, it has usually been through traditional police work by intelligence agencies. About the most that can be said for loyalty tests and security checks is that a certain number of untrustworthy or "potentially dangerous" persons have been denied posts in which they might have done the nation harm.

FREEDOM OF MOVEMENT

The Constitution of the United States does not in so many words guarantee freedom of movement. But the right is implicit and in the main has been upheld by the Supreme Court. For although the justices have recognized that freedom of movement must give way to the power of Congress to regulate immigration and even to restrict foreign travel by American citizens,[84] they have several times thwarted efforts of the states to restrict the movement of people across their boundaries. Shortly after the Civil War the Court invalidated a Nevada statute that sought to stem the loss of the state's population by taxing the railroads for every passenger carried out of the state.[85] During the depression of the 1930s California and other states enforced laws designed to exclude persons who might become a burden on local relief systems. The California statute was invalidated in 1942 by a unanimous Supreme Court. Five justices, somewhat strangely, chose to base their decision on a finding that the state was interfering with interstate commerce. The other four more boldly stated their belief that the statute robbed citizens of their privileges and immunities as protected by the Fourteenth Amendment.[86]

---

[83] *Cramp v. Board of Public Instruction,* 368 U.S. 278 (1961). See also *Elfbrandt v. Russell,* 384 U.S. 11 (1966). Compare, however, *Beilan v. Board of Education,* 357 U.S. 399 (1958); and *Lerner v. Casey,* 357 U.S. 468 (1958).

[84] *Zemel v. Rusk,* 381 U.S. 1 (1965).

[85] *Crandall v. Nevada,* 6 Wallace 35, 44 (1868).

[86] *Edwards v. California,* 314 U.S. 160 (1942).

In the modern world the passport has become a universal requirement for international travel. The power to grant or withhold such a license to travel necessarily rests in administrative officers, subject to statutory control, and is peculiarly susceptible to abuse. In recent years denial of passports to Communists has been a controversial issue in the United States. Acting under authority purportedly conferred upon him by Congress, the Secretary of State early in the Eisenhower Administration refused to grant passports to persons believed to be members of the Communist party. The Supreme Court in a five to four decision in 1958 set aside this action on the ground that the laws in question did not delegate to the Secretary any such discretionary authority. Speaking for the majority, Justice William Douglas[87] observed that "the right of exit is a personal right included within the word 'liberty' as used in the Fifth Amendment":

Where activities or enjoyment, natural and often necessary to the well-being of an American citizen, such as travel, are involved, we will construe narrowly all delegated powers that curtail or dilute them.

The Internal Security Act of 1950, discussed earlier in this chapter, subjects members of Communist-action and Communist-front groups to various disabilities. Included is a provision that makes it a felony for a member of such a group even to apply for a passport. In 1964, the Supreme Court invalidated this section of the act. While recognizing the authority of Congress to some control over issuance of passports, six justices found that the statute "sweeps too widely and too indiscriminantly across the liberty guaranteed by the Fifth Amendment." In making it a crime for a Communist under any circumstances to apply for a passport, Congress, the justices felt, had punished innocent as well as potentially subversive conduct. "Precision," the majority stated, "must be the touchstone of legislation so affecting basic freedoms."[88]

In the 1960s, activities of "freedom riders" also brought into sharp focus the meaning of freedom of movement. These riders, white and Negro alike, made trips into the Deep South, usually by bus, to dramatize the discrimination still practiced against Negroes in waiting rooms, restaurants, and other facilities related to interstate transportation. In many instances they encountered resistance from state and local law-enforcement officials in the South who arrested them and charged them with such offenses against local law as "breach of the peace" and "incitement to violence." Indeed, violence was used against some of the "freedom riders." Whatever the wisdom and effectiveness of their activity, however, the riders were exercising a constitutionally protected right to travel freely within the United States. In weighing this right against the alleged right of communities to protect themselves against disturbances of the peace, southern courts in which the prosecutions were brought almost always voted for conviction. But relief against these adverse judgments was usually obtained through habeas corpus proceedings in the federal courts or appeals to the Supreme Court.

---

[87] *Kent v. Dulles,* 357 U.S. 116, 129 (1958); see also *Dayton v. Dulles,* 357 U.S. 144 (1958).

[88] *Aptheker v. Rusk,* 378 U.S. 500 (1964); see also *United States v. Lamb,* 385 U.S. 475 (1967).

Selected Bibliography

Becker, Carl, *Freedom and Responsibility in the American Way of Life* (New York: Alfred A. Knopf, Inc., 1945). A beautifully written analysis of the compatibility of political authority and individual liberty.

Berns, Walter, *Freedom, Virtue and the First Amendment* (Baton Rouge, La.: Louisiana State University Press, 1957). A vigorous attack on the American tradition of freedom of expression.

Brown, Ralph S., Jr., *Loyalty and Security* (New Haven, Conn.: Yale University Press, 1958). A thorough and comprehensive analysis of the loyalty-security problem.

Chafee, Zechariah, *Free Speech in the United States* (Cambridge, Mass.: Harvard University Press, 1941). A classic in civil rights literature, by a noted legal scholar and defender of human liberty.

Lasswell, Harold D., *National Security and Individual Freedom* (New York: McGraw-Hill Book Company, Inc., 1950). An analysis of the dangers of the garrison state; what happens when liberty is conceived as an expendable luxury when national security is under attack.

Meiklejohn, Alexander, *Free Speech and Its Relation to Self-Government* (New York: Harper & Brothers, 1948). A provocative thesis that in the area of political discussion freedom of speech should be an absolute right.

Mill, John Stuart, *On Liberty* (New York: Appleton-Century-Crofts, 1947). Originally published in 1851; a famous attempt to define the proper limits of liberty and authority.

Russell, Bertrand, *Authority and the Individual* (New York: Simon and Schuster, Inc., 1949). An effort to reconcile political authority and individual freedom, by the noted British philosopher.

Thoreau, Henry D., *On the Duty of Civil Disobedience* (New Haven, Conn.: Yale University Press. 1928). Originally published in 1849; an impassioned statement of the duty of the individual to resist unjust governmental authority.

21

Equal justice
and equal
opportunity

TWO ASPECTS OF EQUALITY

"All men are created equal," Thomas Jefferson wrote in the Declaration of Independence, and since 1776 this statement has been echoed by generations of school children and public officials. Yet there has been no more controversial concept in American social and political history. Neither Jefferson nor his ideological successors believed that all men are born equal in talent or virtue. Rather, in the American context, equality has had two aspects: It means, first, that government should not discriminate among citizens by establishing legal classes, but should treat all persons alike, especially in matters of discipline. This is the traditional interpretation of the phrase in the Fourteenth Amendment: "nor [shall any state] deny to any person within its jurisdiction the equal protection of laws."

In the abstract there is some but not great opposition to equality under the law. Practice, of course, is another matter, as one glance at race problems shows. Far more controversial is the second aspect of equality, that each man should be free to develop his talents to the limit of his ability. This ideal, equality of opportunity, is also cherished in America, but it means that freedom is in tension with equality. For, in a free society populated by men of unequal capabilities, advantages and disadvantages inevitably hamper equality of opportunity. Wealth confers advantages not only on those who earned it but on those to whom it is passed. The son of a millionaire obviously has a greater opportunity to obtain a university education and achieve financial success than has an equally intelligent and motivated son of an illiterate sharecropper.

Especially in this century the belief has been strong that government should do more than not discriminate, that it should act positively to ensure that each citizen has a fair if not completely equal chance to maximize his talents. Free public education and antidiscrimination laws are relatively old examples of positive governmental action to further equality of opportunity. The various programs of the Johnson Administration lumped together under the heading "the war on poverty" constitute more recent illustrations. One might also recall that at the turn of the century many of the supporters of the income tax had high but vain hopes that this levy, designed to take proportionately more from the rich than the poor, would redistribute wealth.

In this chapter we shall look at both aspects of equality. The first part deals with problems of criminal justice, the substantive and procedural rights that the American constitutional system guarantees to those accused of having committed a criminal act. The second part of the chapter discusses positive efforts toward equality, in particular the efforts of federal officials and some state officers to make sure that neither public officials nor private citizens discriminate against minority racial groups. The war on poverty programs are discussed in Chapter 25.

BASIC TENETS OF ANGLO-AMERICAN LAW

"The quality of a nation's civilization," the Chief Justice of Illinois has written, "can be largely measured by the methods it uses in the enforcement of its criminal law."[1] On the one hand, there will always be a public demand—and a public necessity—that government protect peace and good order by apprehending and punishing or rehabilitating criminals. On the other hand, there is a concomitant necessity, though not always an equal demand, that government officials follow certain rules when enforcing the law. As Justice Oliver Wendell Holmes once remarked, "for my part I think it a less evil that some criminals should escape than that the government should play an ignoble part."[2] Despite the fact that criminal cases so often involve "not very nice people,"[3] Anglo-American law has resolved these competing demands and necessities in favor of the accused.

---

[1] Walter Schaefer, "Federalism and State Criminal Procedure," *Harvard Law Review,* 70 (Nov. 1956), pp. 1, 26.

[2] *Olmstead v. United States,* 277 U.S. 438, dissenting opinion, 470 (1928).

[3] Justice Frankfurter dissenting, *United States v. Rabinowitz,* 339 U.S. 56, 69 (1950).

The basic tenets of criminal justice in British and American jurisprudence are:

1. Government must clearly define by law all criminal offenses.

2. An accused person shall be presumed innocent until proved guilty in a court of law; thus the burden of proof is on the prosecution.

3. Guilt must be established beyond a reasonable doubt.

4. Guilt is personal; no man shall be convicted because of the wrongdoing of others.

5. A trial shall always be conducted in accordance with set procedures and guilt or innocence determined by an impartial legal tribunal.

SUBSTANTIVE RIGHTS

In discussing criminal justice jurists typically distinguish between the substantive and procedural rights of the accused. Substantive rights refer to what a person is protected against; procedural rights to the rules that government must follow in taking action against an accused. The original Constitution contained few guarantees regarding either class of rights. Most important among the substantive liberties are protections against bills of attainder and ex post facto laws, as well as a restrictive definition of treason.

Sections 9 and 10 of Article I of the Constitution forbid both Congress and state legislators to pass any legislative act that, without judicial trial, inflicts punishment on persons either named or easily ascertained. Such bills of attainder had frequently been passed by the British Parliament to order the execution of political offenders without allowing the accused a trial before a judicial tribunal. Bills of attainder have been relatively rare in the United States since the adoption of the Constitution, though they were common before then, especially during the Revolutionary War.

Most of the American cases have involved statutes on the borderline between general laws and bills aimed at punishing specific people. None has been so crass as the typical English bill of earlier years. Shortly after the Civil War the Supreme Court held invalid a clause in the Missouri constitution that denied to any person who had failed to support the Union the right to hold public office or to become a lawyer or a minister. Five of the justices thought this to be a bill of attainder.[4] A similar act of Congress, requiring attorneys wishing to practice before federal courts to take an oath that they had been loyal to the Union, was also struck down as a bill of attainder.[5] Again in 1946 the Court interpreted as a bill of attainder a provision in an appropriation act that no salary could be paid to three named federal employees because of alleged subversive activities.[6] Most recently, a five-judge majority held in 1965 that the section of the Labor Management Reporting

---

[4] *Cummings v. Missouri,* 4 Wallace 277, 323 (1867).

[5] *Ex Parte Garland,* 4 Wallace 333 (1867).

[6] *United States v. Lovett,* 328 U.S. 303 (1946).

Act of 1959 making it a crime for a Communist to hold any important union office was a bill of attainder. The majority believed this statute penalized a specific group of people without allowing a court to determine if any individual Communist was in fact committing acts that Congress could proscribe.[7]

Sections 9 and 10 of Article I also forbid Congress and state legislatures to pass ex post facto legislation. In one of its first cases the Supreme Court held that these clauses prohibit only retroactive criminal laws and not all laws that may have a retroactive effect.[8] In other words, an ex post facto law is one that (1) makes criminal an act that when committed was innocent; or (2) increases punishment for a crime after the alleged act was committed; or (3) lowers the degree of proof for a crime, again after the alleged act was committed.

The third substantive right mentioned in the Constitution itself involves the crime of treason. The men who drafted the Constitution were aware that false accusations of treason had been used as a weapon against nonconforming persons during the troubled times of the preceding centuries in England. To prevent any such arbitrary action in America they narrowly defined treason in Article III of the Constitution:

Treason against the United States shall consist only in levying war against them, or in adhering to their enemies, giving them aid and comfort. No person shall be convicted of treason unless on the testimony of two witnesses to the same overt act, or on confession in open court.

The Congress shall have power to declare the punishment of treason, but no attainder of treason shall work corruption of blood or forfeiture except during the life of the person attainted.

This constitutional restraint has had less significance than might have been expected because, despite this narrow definition, Congress is not prevented from broadening laws against subversive activity by using other nomenclature. Thus Congress has defined such crimes as sedition, espionage, and conspiracy so as to include acts that cannot be regarded as treason.

Most substantive—and many procedural—rights have their origin in the due process clauses of the Fifth and Fourteenth Amendments. The Fifth Amendment forbids the federal government, and the Fourteenth the states, to deprive a person of his "life, liberty, or property without due process of law." Although the phrase "due process of law" once meant only "according to generally accepted procedures," since shortly before the Civil War American judges have been holding that this phrase also encompasses certain substantive as well as procedural rights. For instance, the Supreme Court has interpreted the Fourteenth Amendment to mean that states must respect most of the rights discussed in the last chapter, such as speech, press, and religion.

One of these, the right to a fair trial, is the keystone in any analysis of procedural rights of the accused. In an appeal judges will look beyond procedure to what actually happened at a trial and will not allow a conviction to stand if, for instance, it was based on perjured testimony, if the trial judge was grossly preju-

---

[7] *United States v. Brown*, 381 U.S. 437 (1965).
[8] *Calder v. Bull*, 3 Dallas 386 (1798).

diced, if the evidence was insufficient to prove guilt beyond a reasonable doubt that judges think reasonable men should have had, or if the statute under which the accused was tried was so vague as not to give fair warning of its prohibitions.

PROCEDURAL RIGHTS

Constitutional Amendments Four through Eight catalog a series of procedural rights that the federal government must observe; and the Supreme Court has ruled, again through the Fourteenth Amendment, that states must respect many, though not all, of these. State constitutions, however, sometimes contain similar or even more broadly protecting language than the U.S. Constitution, and the Supreme Court has never objected if a state wishes to require its officials to give greater protection to civil liberties than the minimum standards of the Bill of Rights.

Freedom from Unreasonable Searches and Seizures

The Fourth Amendment to the federal Constitution provides:

The right of the people to be secure in their persons, houses, papers and effects, against unreasonable searches and seizures, shall not be violated, and no warrants shall issue, but upon probable cause, supported by oath or affirmation, and particularly describing the place to be searched, and the persons or things to be seized.

The search warrant clause was designed to outlaw "general" warrants that enabled officers of the law to engage in "fishing" expeditions in searching private homes for evidence. Yet from the very beginning courts have permitted police, without a warrant, to arrest a lawbreaker at the scene of a crime and to seize such evidence as may be at hand. The purpose of the Fourth Amendment is to protect privacy only against "unreasonable searches and seizures," not against all government inquiries.

The difficulty of drawing a line between reasonable and unreasonable searches and seizures has increased because of the character of machine civilization. For example, the extent to which people now transact business and discuss their personal affairs over the telephone allows police officers to obtain evidence of criminal wrongdoing by means of wire tapping. Are such intercepted communications when obtained without a search warrant admissible as evidence in a criminal trial? This question first came to the Supreme Court in the 1920s in a case in which federal agents, by listening in on telephone conversations over a five-month period, had obtained evidence against a large ring of bootleggers. By a five to four vote the Court ruled that the Fourth Amendment does not bar wire tapping.[9] In the Federal Communications Act in 1934,[10] however, Congress decreed: "No person not being authorized by the sender shall intercept any communication and

---

[9] *Olmstead v. United States,* 277 U.S. 438 (1928).
[10] 48 *Stat.* 1063, § 605.

divulge or publish the evidence, contents, substance, purport, effect or meaning of such intercepted communication to any person." The Supreme Court has interpreted this statute to make wire tapping a federal crime and has refused to allow use, in federal courts, of evidence obtained by wire tapping.[11] For years, however, the Court did not go so far as to deny states authority to introduce wiretapping evidence at trials. Then, in 1967, *Berger v. New York* held unconstitutional a state law authorizing wiretapping, even though the statute required police to obtain a warrant, and further declared that evidence so obtained was inadmissible in court.[12] While the justices did not fully spell out the implications of this ruling, Justice Douglas, who voted with the majority, claimed that the Court was overruling the *Olmstead* decision.

Despite the Federal Communications Act and Supreme Court decisions, Presidents have authorized the FBI to tap telephone lines in certain very serious cases, such as those involving kidnapping or national security. It became clear in the mid-1960's, however, that a number of federal agencies, including the Internal Revenue Service, were widely using wiretaps and various kinds of electronic surveillance in investigating less serious crimes. To correct what was bordering on a national scandal, Attorney General Ramsey Clark issued in the summer of 1967 instructions to the heads of all federal agencies informing them that federal law forbade wiretapping and the Fourth Amendment prohibited many other forms of eavesdropping. The Attorney General required that, except in emergencies, any agency except those involved in national security work wishing to use electronic surveillance equipment obtain his written permission. This new policy thus provides for centralized control over rather than elimination of wiretapping and eavesdropping by federal officers.

Anglo-American law has sometimes made a rather curious distinction between prohibiting an unreasonable seizure of evidence and prohibiting use of improperly seized evidence in a criminal trial. As early as 1914, the Supreme Court rejected this distinction in federal criminal cases, ruling that evidence seized in violation of the Fourth Amendment could not be used in prosecuting persons.[13] Four decades later, in a highly controversial decision in *Wolf v. Colorado,* the Court extended the Fourth Amendment's ban against unreasonable searches and seizures to the states under the Fourteenth Amendment, but then made this extension quite meaningless by holding that the Constitution did not prevent a state from using such tainted evidence in prosecuting someone accused of a state crime.[14]

In 1961, in *Mapp v. Ohio,* the Court by a six to three vote repudiated the distinction in *Wolf v. Colorado.* The majority declared that the Fourteenth Amendment both forbids the states to engage in unreasonable searches and seizures and to introduce such evidence in a criminal trial.[15]

---

[11] *Nardone v. United States,* 302 U.S. 379 (1937); 308 U.S. 338 (1939).
[12] *Berger v. New York,* 384 U.S. 41 (1967).
[13] *Weeks v. United States,* 232 U.S. 383 (1914).
[14] 338 U.S. 25 (1949).
[15] 367 U.S. 643 (1961).

Freedom from Excessive Bail

The Eighth Amendment in its first clause makes this terse statement: "Excessive bail shall not be required. . . ." This provision has not presented unusual difficulties of interpretation. It is clearly a relative right. For example, it does not prevent complete denial of bail in cases involving capital offenses. In fixing bail in other cases courts ordinarily take into account the severity of the offense, the ability of the accused to meet the amount imposed, and the possibility that he will fail to appear at his trial if he is released on bail. It is difficult for an accused person successfully to invoke this constitutional provision in seeking any relief from bail actually imposed in his case.[16] The Supreme Court has not yet ruled on whether states are bound by this provision of the Bill of Rights.

Another defect of this right is that, even when bail is reasonable, a poor person may have difficulty raising the money or getting a professional bondsman to put it up. Because, many people have had to stay in jail for long periods while awaiting trial, and after several pilot studies showed that an overwhelming majority of persons released without bail would show up for trial, Congress passed the Bail Reform Act of 1966.[17] This statute, affecting only federal criminal procedure, requires that a judicial officer[18] release those accused of noncapital offenses who are unable to raise bail, unless he has strong reason to believe that the accused will not appear for trial. The statute also authorizes, but does not require, judicial officials to apply the same procedure to persons accused of capital offenses. In addition, Congress provided for swift appellate court review of decisions refusing release of an accused and ordered the Attorney General henceforth to give credit toward any prison sentence for time a defendant spent in custody awaiting trial.

The Right to Indictment by a Grand Jury

The first clause of the Fifth Amendment provides: "No person shall be held to answer for a capital, or otherwise infamous crime, unless on a presentment or indictment of a grand jury. . . ." The purpose of this clause, historically, has been to protect innocent persons against governmental harassment. It is to the grand jury that a prosecuting officer presents the evidence he has collected against a person suspected of crime. If this group is convinced that the evidence is sufficient to indicate that the accused person should stand trial, it returns "a true bill," or "indicts" him. The reference in the Fifth Amendment to

---

[16] See *Stack v. Boyle,* 342 U.S. 1 (1951); *Carlson v. Landon,* 342 U.S. 524 (1952).

[17] 80 *Stat.* 214.

[18] The term "judicial officer" is used here because in federal district courts a commissioner appointed by the district judge, rather than the judge himself, normally issues search warrants, hears charges against an accused, informs him of his constitutional rights, and sets bail. A commissioner cannot, however, preside at a trial or impose punishment.

"capital" and "infamous" crimes limits the grand jury requirement to cases in which the penalty involves death, hard labor, or a penitentiary term. In general, a person may be brought to trial for a "misdemeanor," that is, a minor offense, without having been indicted by a grand jury.

The grand jury system has been increasingly criticized in modern times, and some students of criminal procedure advocate its abolition. In its place they would allow the public prosecuting official to file an "information" against a person. The right to a grand jury hearing is one of the civil liberties that the Supreme Court has held does not restrict state governments, and in about half of the states grand jury indictment has been replaced in whole or in part by the information.

The Right to the Writ of Habeas Corpus

One of the most important rights guaranteed by the original Constitution is the right to the writ of habeas corpus. Section 9 of Article I of the Constitution provides: "The privilege of the writ of habeas corpus shall not be suspended, unless when in cases of rebellion or invasion the public safety may require it."

Sometimes called "the great writ of liberty," habeas corpus was especially designed to prevent arbitrary arrest or unlawful imprisonment. Where this right is available, any person who is being held by state or federal officers, or the lawyer or friend of the prisoner, may ask the nearest court for such a writ. The writ orders the officers who have a person in their custody to bring him into court and show legal cause for holding him—in other words, to charge formally that he has violated a specific provision of a statute and to offer at least some evidence that he should be held for trial on that charge. If such cause is not shown or if a charge is not brought, the court will order the person released.

Much controversy has centered about the suspension of the writ of habeas corpus. The Constitution does not make clear whether suspension must be limited to those areas immediately affected by rebellion or invasion, and it does not specify the agency of government that may order the suspension, though the clause occurs in the article describing congressional authority. Early in the Civil War, without any congressional authorization, President Lincoln suspended the writ in various parts of the country, both in and outside of combat areas. This action was challenged by Chief Justice Roger Taney, who, sitting as a trial judge, as Supreme Court justices then also had to act, ruled in *Ex Parte Merryman* that power to authorize suspension of the writ rested exclusively with Congress.[19] Thereafter Congress passed legislation specifically authorizing the President to suspend the writ when in his judgment such action was necessary.

Just after the Civil War, in the case of *Ex Parte Milligan*,[20] the Supreme Court faced the question of the constitutionality of a suspension of habeas corpus in an area outside an actual theater of war or rebellion. All nine justices agreed that the President could not suspend the writ in such areas, and a majority of five believed

---

[19] Fed. Case No. 9,487 (1861).
[20] 4 Wallace 2 (1866).

that not even Congress could do so. There has been no attempt since the Civil War by either Congress or the President to suspend the writ of habeas corpus in the United States. Immediately after the attack on Pearl Harbor in 1941, however, the governor of Hawaii, then a territory, with the approval of President Roosevelt, placed the islands under martial law. Not only was the writ of habeas corpus suspended but civil courts were also completely supplanted by military tribunals in which civilians were tried for crimes by summary procedures. This state of affairs persisted until 1944, long after the threat of invasion had ended. After the war was over the Supreme Court decided that this wholesale suppression of civil government in the islands had been invalid. But a majority of the justices based their decision on a finding that the Organic Act of 1900, under which the governor had acted, did not authorize the supplanting of courts by miliary tribunals. The majority, however, strongly intimated that such an extreme form of martial law did violate the Constitution.[21]

Congress has reinforced the right safeguarded by the habeas corpus guarantee by directing federal law-enforcement officials to take an arrested person before the nearest federal judicial officer for arraignment "without unnecessary delay" so that the accused may be advised of his rights and the issue of "probable cause" for his arrest promptly determined. The Supreme Court has vigorously enforced the requirement of prompt arraignment by refusing to allow in evidence statements obtained by federal officials from their prisoners during any but the shortest intervals between arrest and arraignment.[22]

The Right to Trial by Jury

The Constitution contains three separate provisions dealing with jury trial. Section 2 of Article III provides:

The trial of all crimes, except in cases of impeachment, shall be by jury; and such trial shall be held in the State where the said crimes shall have been committed; but when not committed within any State, the trial shall be at such place or places as the Congress may by law have directed.

This provision was further strengthened by the Sixth Amendment in the Bill of Rights:

In all criminal prosecutions the accused shall enjoy the right to a speedy and public trial, by an impartial jury of the State and district wherein the crime shall have been committed, which district shall have been previously ascertained by law. . . .

Finally, the Seventh Amendment states:

In suits at common law, where the value in controversy shall exceed twenty dollars, the right of trial by jury shall be preserved, and no fact tried by a jury shall be otherwise re-examined in any court of the United States, than according to the rules of the common law.

---

[21] *Duncan v. Kahanamoku,* 327 U.S. 304 (1946).
[22] See *McNabb v. United States,* 318 U.S. 332 (1943); and *Mallory v. United States,* 354 U.S. 449 (1957).

Although the Constitution says nothing about the common law tradition of a jury of twelve members or the requirement of a unanimous verdict, the Supreme Court has ruled that these are necessary features of the federal jury system. Moreover, the justices have held that the right of jury trial does not extend to equity or admiralty cases, since this was not traditional in 1789. The courts have also held that provision may be made for the trial of petty crimes without a jury.[23] The accused in a federal criminal case may waive the right to a jury trial and elect to be tried by a judge.

To date the Supreme Court has not held that the states are obliged to grant a jury trial in criminal cases but has taken the position that the Constitution demands only a fair trial, which is possible without a jury.[24] Where a state does grant the right to trial by jury—as most states do for serious crimes—the state may not systematically exclude from the jury panel members of the racial or ethnic group to which the defendant belongs.[25] Ironically, however, the Court has allowed states to exclude women from juries, even where the defendant is a woman.[26] The accused, of course, may not demand a jury wholly made up of Negroes or men or Irish-Americans, nor can he demand that the jury represent a cross section of the community.[27]

The Right of Defense

It is axiomatic in American law that the accused in a criminal case shall have a reasonable opportunity to defend himself in a court of law. Thus on several occasions the Supreme Court has reversed convictions where the justices felt that there had been so much adverse publicity that a truly unbiased jury verdict was improbable.[28] Trial by newspaper hardly fulfills the requirements of substantive or procedural due process of law.

To give additional weight to the right of defense, the Sixth Amendment provides:

In all criminal prosecutions the accused shall enjoy the right . . . to be informed of the nature and cause of the accusations; to be confronted with witnesses against him; to have compulsory process for obtaining witnesses in his favor, and to have the assistance of counsel for his defense.

There has been relatively little controversy about these guarantees in federal criminal procedure. In state courts, however, there has been much litigation concerning the right of an accused to counsel. In 1932, the Supreme Court ruled that states are compelled by the Fourteenth Amendment to provide a defendant in a

---

[23] *Springville v. Thomas,* 166 U.S. 707 (1897); *Thompson v. Utah,* 170 U.S. 343 (1898); *In re Debs,* 158 U.S. 564 (1895); *District of Columbia v. Clawans,* 300 U.S. 617 (1937).

[24] *Walker v. Sauvinet,* 92 U.S. 90 (1876); *Maxwell v. Dow,* 176 U.S. 581 (1900).

[25] *Norris v. Alabama,* 294 U.S. 587 (1935); *Hernandez v. Texas,* 347 U.S. 475 (1954).

[26] *Hoyt v. Florida,* 368 U.S. 57 (1961).

[27] *Fay v. New York,* 332 U.S. 261 (1947).

[28] *Marshall v. United States,* 360 U.S. 310 (1959); *Estes v. Texas,* 381 U.S. 532 (1965); *Irvin v. Dowd,* 366 U.S. 717 (1966); *Sheppard v. Maxwell,* 384 U.S. 333 (1966).

Clarence Gideon, convicted of robbery in a Florida court in 1963, appealed the case to the U. S. Supreme Court. The conviction was ruled invalid because Gideon had not been provided with legal counsel. The result of this decision is the provision that a state must now provide legal aid to its indigent defendants. (Flip Schulke from Black Star)

murder case, where the death penalty may be imposed, with counsel if he is unable to engage an attorney himself. Thereafter, however, the Court held that state courts had to appoint counsel for indigent defendants only under special circumstances, as, for example, where the offense was a capital one or the defendant was young, ignorant, or inexperienced. In 1963, Justice Black's long protests against the "special circumstances" rule bore fruit, and in *Gideon v. Wainwright* a unanimous Court laid down as a doctrine of constitutional law that states must provide lawyers for criminal defendants who cannot hire their own attorneys.[29]

Gideon left a series of questions unanswered, the most important of which was when this right to counsel became effective: Only at the trial? Immediately after arrest? Or at some point in between? The justices had been grappling with this question before *Gideon;* and at the very next term, in *Escobedo v. Illinois,*[30] they applied a new version of the special circumstances rule to hold that a young, inexperienced defendant who had engaged his own attorney had a right to consult with that counsel as soon as the proceedings shifted from a general investigation to an accusation of a specific person.

In 1966, the Court moved beyond *Escobedo* and once again abandoned a special circumstances rule for one of general application. In *Miranda v. Arizona*[31] five justices held that when a person is taken into custody "or otherwise deprived of his freedom of action in any way," police officers, whether state or federal, must warn him that anything he says may be used against him and that he has a constitutional right to remain silent, as well as to consult with a lawyer before answering any questions. Further, police must instruct the suspect that if he cannot afford a lawyer the government will provide him one free of charge. The Court also stated that a suspect's failure to ask for counsel did not in any way relieve the police of the duty of informing him of his right. Only, the Court said, if the suspect's lawyer is present, or if the police fully inform a suspect of his rights and he then knowingly

---

[29] 372 U.S. 335 (1963). Anthony Lewis has written a dramatic account of the case: *Gideon's Trumpet* (New York: Random House, Inc., 1964).
[30] 378 U.S. 478 (1964).
[31] 384 U.S. 436 (1966).

and freely waives those rights, can a statement made by a defendant in police custody be admitted in evidence. The majority justices also warned that the burden of proof that a defendant had intelligently and freely waived his constitutional rights would be on the government.

Freedom from Self-Incrimination

One of the most famous parts of the Bill of Rights is the provision of the Fifth Amendment that states: "No person . . . shall be compelled in any criminal case to be a witness against himself. . . ." In practical terms this means that the prosecutor in a criminal case cannot compel the accused to take the witness stand and answer questions. Instead, the government must prove its case against the defendant by evidence adduced against him. This is what is meant when it is said that Anglo-American criminal procedure is accusatorial rather than inquisitorial in character. Of course, if the defendant elects to take the witness stand in his own defense, he may be subjected to cross-examination by the prosecution.

Despite the apparent basic nature of this right, the Supreme Court twice held that it was not included in the protection of the Fourteenth Amendment.[32] In 1964, however, a majority of the Court reversed its older decisions and ruled that protection against self-incrimination was such an "essential mainstay" of the accusatorial system of justice that it must be respected by the states as well as by the federal government.[33] A year later the justices held[34] that the Fifth Amendment also forbade either the prosecutor or the trial judge to comment to the jury on the accused's failure to take the stand in his own defense.[35] "The constitutional foundation underlying the privilege [against self-incrimination]," the Court said in a later case, "is the respect a government—state or federal—must accord to the dignity and integrity of its citizens."

An integral part of protection against self-incrimination is a right to be free from police coercion. Fundamental fairness requires that any statement made by an accused and used against him should have been freely made without torture, fear of torture, promises of reward, or trickery. The Supreme Court has held that this right is protected against state or federal infringement. Earlier cases involved allegations of police brutality—"the third degree"—or long, extended periods of questioning in obtaining confessions.[36] More recent cases have tended to involve subtler kinds of pressure, such as interrogation of the accused by a psychiatrist hired by the police.[37] Here the justices have been willing to give the accused the benefit of the doubt and to refuse to allow the government to use any confession so obtained.

---

[32] *Twining v. New Jersey,* 211 U.S. 78 (1908); *Adamson v. California,* 332 U.S. 46 (1947).

[33] *Malloy v. Hogan,* 378 U.S. 1 (1964).

[34] *Griffin v. California,* 380 U.S. 609 (1965).

[35] *Miranda v. Arizona,* 384 U.S. 436, 460 (1966).

[36] For example, *Brown v. Mississippi,* 297 U.S. 278 (1936); *Chambers v. Florida,* 309 U.S. 227 (1940); *Ashcraft v. Tennessee,* 322 U.S. 143 (1944); *McNabb v. United States,* 318 U.S. 332 (1943).

[37] *Leyra v. Denno,* 347 U.S. 556 (1954). The Court still gets cases involving charges of police brutality.

The majority justices in the *Miranda* case explained that the principal reason for extending the right to counsel to the police station was to protect a suspect against all forms of police pressure, subtle or otherwise, and to insure that any confession would be voluntary in the full sense of the word. The minority justices were less sanguine about the effectiveness of the *Miranda* rule. As Justice Harlan noted for three members of the Court, police officers who would "use third-degree tactics and deny them in court are equally able and destined to lie as skillfully about warnings and waivers."

"What's the Supreme Court ruling on this?"

Drawing by Alan Dunn. © 1966 the *New Yorker Magazine*, Inc.

Freedom from Double Jeopardy

The Fifth Amendment also says: "nor shall any person be subject for the same offense to be twice put in jeopardy of life or limb. . . ." The idea behind this right, the Supreme Court has declared,[38]

is that the State with all its resources and power should not be allowed to make repeated attempts to convict an individual for an alleged offense, thereby subjecting him to embarrassment, expense and ordeal and compelling him to live in a continuing state of anxiety and insecurity, as well as enhancing the possibility that even though innocent he may be found guilty.

In accordance with this philosophy it has long been settled under the Fifth Amendment that a verdict of acquittal is final, ending a defendant's jeopardy, and even when "not followed by any judgment, is a bar to a subsequent prosecution for the same offense." Thus it is one of the elemental principles of our criminal law that the Government cannot secure a new trial by means of an appeal even though an acquittal may appear to be erroneous.

This guarantee, however, like the others in the Bill of Rights, is subject to certain exceptions. Under the federal plan of government an antisocial act may well violate federal and state laws, and the guarantee does not protect a person from prosecution by both governments for such an offense. Even where a person has violated only a federal or a state law, the possibility of a double prosecution is not completely ruled out, for a single act may violate two or more criminal statutes. In such circumstances the accused may be tried and convicted for each

---

[38] *Green v. United States,* 355 U.S. 184, 187–188 (1957).

separate offense. Again, freedom from double jeopardy does not prevent the prosecution from bringing a man to trial a second time when, following a first trial that resulted in a finding of guilt, the accused has persuaded a higher court to set aside the original verdict because of procedural errors. The Supreme Court has not yet squarely decided that this part of the Fifth Amendment binds states as well as the federal government, though it is probable that the Court will so rule in the future.[39] On the other hand, the justices have allowed the states, but never the federal government, to retry a man who was once acquitted when legal error had been committed during the trial.[40]

Freedom from Unusual Punishment

The Eighth Amendment protects accused persons from cruel and unusual punishments. This, of course, is a relative standard, since what is cruel and unusual depends on prevailing social mores. What is today acceptable—in some states, for instance, the death penalty—may tomorrow become repulsive. "The basic concept underlying the Eighth Amendment," Chief Justice Earl Warren has said,[41] "is nothing less than the dignity of man. . . . The Amendment must draw its meaning from the evolving standards of decency that mark the progress of a maturing society." Because of its fundamental nature, the Court has assumed that this restriction binds the states along with the federal government.[42]

EQUALITY OF OPPORTUNITY

In 1944, the Swedish scholar Gunnar Myrdal published a monumental study of race relations in the United States.[43] As Myrdal saw it, the American dilemma was caused by a white problem, not a Negro problem: the gap between principles and practices of whites with respect to equality of opportunity. He found the principles endorsed by white Americans from the time of Jefferson to be admirable statements of the doctrine of equality; but he also found that the practices of American whites left a good deal to be desired. Many states still required segregation in most phases of public life, denied Negroes the right to vote, provided unequal education, and thus doomed each new generation of nonwhites to second-class citizenship. Moreover, even when not commanded by law to do so, a large number of private citizens practiced similar discrimination in their social and economic activities. The creation of the North, Charles E. Silberman has said, was "*de facto* segregation."[44] This contrast

---

[39] See *Louisiana ex rel. Francis v. Resweber,* 329 U.S. 459 (1947).
[40] *Palko v. Connecticut,* 302 U.S. 319 (1937); *Brock v. North Carolina,* 344 U.S. 424 (1953); *Green v. United States,* 355 U.S. 184 (1957).
[41] *Trop v. Dulles,* 356 U.S. 86, 100 (1958).
[42] *Louisiana ex rel. Francis v. Resweber,* 329 U.S. 459 (1947).
[43] *An American Dilemma* (New York: Harper & Row, Publishers, 1944).
[44] *Crisis in Black and White* (New York: Random House, Inc., 1964).

between ideals and practice created a dilemma that has engendered the most serious problem in current domestic politics, and that in international affairs has handicapped American efforts to win the emerging nations of Africa and Asia from communism.

The Constitution and Equality

Equality of opportunity is not proclaimed in so many words in the Constitution. Only the Fourteenth Amendment approaches such a statement of principle in its equal protection clause. Yet the entire Constitution, like the era in which it was drafted, is permeated with the notion that all citizens should stand on an equal footing before the law. Indeed, when he was a member of the Supreme Court Arthur Goldberg argued that the doctrine of equality is not explicitly stated in the Constitution because the framers took it so much for granted it never occurred to them to include it.[45] Still, even in 1787 the dichotomy between principle and practice was sharp, for slavery was an established institution.

State governments in the United States have been following three different policies with regard to equality of opportunity. Some have enforced laws segregating and restricting minority group activities, in effect forcing private citizens as well as public officials to discriminate. At the other extreme some states have enacted laws that, at least on their face, endorse the principle of equal opportunity and forbid private citizens and government officials to discriminate on the basis of race, color, ancestry, or religion. Still other states have taken a neutral position, leaving problems of equality of opportunity to be worked out by private citizens. Since the Civil War the federal government has had laws that command a degree of equal treatment, but the effectiveness of many of these statutes has been small.

THE FATE OF SEGREGATION STATUTES

Segregation in Education

Beginning about 1890, some twenty states enacted segregation laws directed primarily at Negroes, but affecting in varying degrees persons of Oriental descent and Mexican origin and even American Indians. These laws varied greatly, but in the main they provided for compulsory segregation of people along racial lines in the enjoyment or use of both public and private facilities in such areas as education, transportation, recreation, housing, and eating in public places. The federal government was also responsible for some measure of compulsory segregation. The District of Columbia, which is

---

[45] "Equality and Governmental Action," *New York University Law Review,* 39 (April 1964), p. 205.

under the ultimate authority of Congress, until 1954 operated separate schools for Negroes. In varying degrees the armed services restricted the opportunities available to members of racial minorities, although largely successful efforts have been made since the close of World War II to eliminate these restrictions.

State laws requiring segregation of Negroes have been attacked on the ground that they violated the equal protection clause of the Fourteenth Amendment. In 1896, in *Plessy v. Ferguson,*[46] the Supreme Court, by a seven to one vote, upheld such statutes on the basis of the "separate but equal" doctrine. The majority rejected the idea that compulsory segregation in and of itself stamped segregated groups with "a badge of inferiority":

We consider the underlying fallacy of the plaintiff's argument to consist in the assumption that the enforced separation of the two races stamps the colored race with a badge of inferiority. If this be so, it is not by reason of anything found in the act, but solely because the colored race chooses to put that construction upon it.

In a ringing dissent, Justice John Marshall Harlan,[47] grandfather of the present justice, challenged the logic of the majority opinion:

Our Constitution is color-blind, and neither knows nor tolerates classes among citizens. . . . The arbitrary separation of citizens, on the basis of race, while they are on a public highway, is a badge of servitude wholly inconsistent with the civil freedom and the equality before the law established by the Constitution. It cannot be justified upon any legal grounds. . . .

We boast of the freedom enjoyed by our people above all other peoples. But it is difficult to reconcile that boast with a state of the law which, practically, puts the brand of servitude and degradation upon a large class of our fellow citizens, our equals before the law.

While rejecting the idea that compulsory segregation was inherently unconstitutional, the Court ruled that segregation could be enforced only when the accommodations provided for the "separated" persons were "equal" to those provided for other persons. This separate but equal rationalization provoked a vigorous reaction from Justice Harlan. His terse comment was, "The thin disguise of 'equal' accommodations . . . will not mislead anyone, nor atone for the wrong this day done."

At first history tended to bear out Justice Harlan's observations, for the Supreme Court made little effort to follow up its *Plessy* ruling by insisting upon proof that its requirement of equal accommodations was being met by the states with compulsory segregation laws. Indeed, the Court waited forty years before moving in such a direction in the field of education though in 1914 the justices had made a gesture toward equality in the field of interstate transportation.[48] Then, in 1938, the Court required Missouri to maintain within its own boundaries a separate school of law for Negroes or permit them to attend the regular law school at the state university. The justices declared inadequate an existing policy by which the state offered to pay a Negro's tuition at a law school of some other state having

---

[46] *Plessy v. Ferguson,* 163 U.S. 537, 551 (1896).
[47] Pp. 559, 562.
[48] *McCabe v. Atchison, Topeka & Sante Fe,* 235 U.S. 151 (1914).

no segregation policy.[49] Ten years later the Court reaffirmed this ruling in directing Oklahoma to provide a legal education for Negroes, and it added that the state must provide such an education "as soon as it does for applicants of any other group."[50]

In 1950, in cases concerning the University of Oklahoma and the University of Texas, the Court in effect declared that separate graduate schools for Negroes could not possibly meet the requirement of equality and that Negroes must be admitted to regular graduate schools and allowed freely to mingle with other students in these schools.[51]

In 1954, the Supreme Court finally ruled that the separate but equal doctrine, at least as applied to public schools, contradicted the Fourteenth Amendment. In a series of four cases involving segregated schools in Kansas, South Carolina, Virginia, and Delaware, the Court unanimously declared that the Constitution prohibits separate public schools for Negroes, even though buildings, curricula, teachers' salaries, and other tangible factors may have been brought up to a level of equality with white schools.[52] The Court concluded that:

In the field of public education the doctrine of "separate but equal" has no place. Separate educational facilities are inherently unequal. Therefore, we hold that the plaintiffs and others similarly situated for which the actions have been brought are, by reason of the segregation complained of, deprived of the equal protection of the laws guaranteed by the Fourteenth Amendment.

In a companion case the justices ruled that segregated public schools in the District of Columbia violated the due process of law clause of the Fifth Amendment.[53]

Implementation

A year later the Supreme Court dealt with the troublesome issue of the implementation of its 1954 rulings.[54] The justices recognized that desegregation "may require solution of varied local school problems," that local "school authorities have . . . primary responsibility for . . . solving these problems," and that federal district courts are the proper tribunals to decide in the first instance "whether the action of school authorities constitutes good faith implementation of the governing constitutional principles." The Court further recognized that "additional time" might be required to carry out the desegregation ruling in an effective manner, but it stated that good faith efforts

---

[49] *Missouri ex rel. Gaines v. Canada,* 305 U.S. 337 (1938).

[50] *Sipuel v. Board of Regents,* 332 U.S. 631 (1948); *Fisher v. Hurst,* 333 U.S. 147 (1948).

[51] *McLaurin v. Oklahoma State Regents,* 339 U.S. 637 (1950); *Sweatt v. Painter,* 339 U.S. 629 (1950).

[52] *Brown v. Board of Education of Topeka,* 347 U.S. 483 (1954).

[53] *Bolling v. Sharpe,* 347 U.S. 497 (1954).

[54] *Brown v. Board of Education,* 349 U.S. 294, 299–301 (1955). The two *Brown* cases and the *Bolling* case are now generally referred to as the *School Segregation Cases.*

should be made to reach the goal of racially nondiscriminatory public schools in every American community "with all deliberate speed."

The problems facing many school districts or cities in desegregating are fearfully complex. Because of the inferior education they have received in segregated schools, Negro school children have not always been ready for fully integrated school situations where they have to compete with white children of the same grade. Moreover, firmly established patterns of racial segregation in housing mean that in many cities Negroes are still more or less isolated in their neighborhood schools unless a carefully planned effort is made to mix white and Negro children in the same schools regardless of where they live. But such far-reaching efforts at integration by "busing" not only have to overcome deep-seated prejudices against racial mixing but also must contend with a tradition of "going to school near home."

At first there was encouraging progress. In many localities school boards, with some prodding from federal judges, set in motion plans for desegregation. In such cities as Washington, Baltimore, Louisville, and St. Louis substantial steps were taken. In the South, however, after a few token measures to comply with the Court's rulings, integration came to a virtual halt. Southern state legislatures vied with each other in passing cleverly worded statutes to maintain segregation. Most of these were clearly unconstitutional, but attacking them in the federal courts was a slow and costly process.

President Eisenhower made virtually no effort to support the Supreme Court rulings until 1957. Then, Governor Orval Faubus of Arkansas forced the President's hand by using the National Guard to prevent Negro school children from attending Central High School in accordance with a federal court order and later by failing to prevent a mob from using violence to keep them out. At that point Eisenhower federalized the Arkansas National Guard and called out regular units of the United States Army to enforce the court order and to protect the Negro children while they attended the school. But the President repeatedly refused to declare that he personally favored eliminating segregation from the schools of the nation, insisting that policy-making in this area is the province of the Supreme Court. In addition, on numerous occasions he stated his view that race relations cannot be satisfactorily controlled by law but depend primarily upon private, voluntary efforts.

Unlike his predecessor, President Kennedy publicly affirmed his support of the *School Segregation Cases.* Congress, however, still failed to take any step in support of school desegregation. Kennedy, too, soon seemed to have lost interest in the issue until September 1962, when Governor Ross Barnett of Mississippi resisted federal marshals seeking to enforce a court order to admit a Negro student, James Meredith, to the University of Mississippi. The President countered Barnett's attempted nullification by first sending in additional marshals and, when these proved insufficient to cope with white rioters, federal troops. Curiously, it has been a southern President, Lyndon B. Johnson, who has most effectively pushed the cause of integration. In the spring and summer of 1964, he patiently but firmly

National Guard troops protect Negro students at Little Rock Central High School, Little Rock, Arkansas. (Burt Glinn from Magnum)

negotiated with a bipartisan majority in Congress to secure passage of the most comprehensive civil rights law in American history. This statute included provisions allowing the Attorney General to initiate in the name of the United States school desegregation suits if requested to do so by a local citizen, established machinery for positive federal assistance to communities that are trying to desegregate, and required the U.S. Office of Education to make a comprehensive survey of school integration at all levels. The next year Johnson pushed another law through Congress, the Voting Act of 1965, which we analyzed in Chapter 8.

A little more than a dozen years after the decision in the *School Segregation Cases,* the President was actively promoting school integration, Congress had passed a strong law, more and more state officials and civic groups in southern and border states were conceding the inevitability of desegregation, and the Supreme Court was showing impatience at foot-dragging by recalcitrant officials.[55] The campaign, however, was far from over. During the 1967 school year only about 16 percent of Negro children in southern states were attending public schools with white children.

Even more significant is what was often overlooked in the years immediately after 1954: School desegregation is a national not a regional problem. More Negroes now live outside the South than in it, and Negroes, Puerto Ricans, and sometimes Mexican-Americans typically live in segregated ghettos like New York's Harlem, Los Angeles' Watts district, or Chicago's South Side. School segregation goes hand in hand with housing segregation, and in the North no less than in the South segregated schools are invariably inferior schools.

The ultimate solution, of course, is integrated housing; but because of the generally low economic condition of the Negro and other affected minority groups

---

[55] *Cooper v. Aaron,* 358 U.S. 1 (1958); *Goss v. Board of Education,* 373 U.S. 683 (1963); *Griffin v. Prince Edward County,* 377 U.S. 218 (1964); *Calhoun v. Latimer,* 377 U.S. 263 (1964). See also *Watson v. Memphis,* 373 U.S. 526 (1963).

—due in no small part to the inferior education they have received—and the ease with which apartment house owners, home builders, real estate agents, and even private citizens can evade state antidiscrimination statutes, integrated housing on a large scale is far in the future. To cope with the immediate problem, officials in several large cities have attempted to effect variations of the so-called Princeton plan, whereby the neighborhood school concept is modified and students attend centrally located institutions. What worked well in a small town, however, has not been a panacea for metropolitan woes. Modification of the neighborhood school arrangement has usually meant "busing" students across cities and has provoked cries of outrage from white parents whose children must attend predominantly Negro schools. These complaints have been accompanied by harassing lawsuits, and in the face of these difficulties there has been little progress. If, as has been predicted, white migration from the cities to the suburbs continues at current rates, in another decade the central city of most metropolitan areas will be solidly and exclusively nonwhite. Already Negro children outnumber white students by more than four to one in Washington, D.C., and make up about two thirds of the student body in Baltimore and St. Louis. In addition, Negroes are now in the majority in public schools in Chicago, Cleveland, Detroit, and Philadelphia.

Segregation in Other Public Areas

The rulings in the *School Segregation Cases* did not automatically outlaw the separate but equal doctrine in areas other than education, such as transportation, housing, or recreation. Long before its 1954 ruling, however, the Supreme Court had rejected some other forms of discrimination against minority groups. In particular, the Court had used the equal protection clause in cases of legal discrimination against Negroes involving the right to vote, the right to be tried by juries from which members of their own race had not been excluded, and the right to buy and hold real estate.[56] In recent years the Court has continued to invalidate other discriminatory laws. For example, on several occasions it has overturned state and local regulations ordering segregation in public recreational facilities,[57] in inter- or intrastate transportation,[58] in restaurants serving travelers in interstate commerce;[59] and it has time and again reversed convictions of "sit-in" demonstrators for trying to obtain service in local

[56] *Strauder v. West Virginia,* 100 U.S. 303 (1880); *Norris v. Alabama,* 294 U.S. 587 (1935); *Hill v. Texas,* 316 U.S. 400 (1942); *Nixon v. Herndon,* 273 U.S. 536 (1927); *Smith v. Allwright,* 321 U.S. 649 (1944); *Buchanan v. Warley,* 245 U.S. 60 (1917); *Shelley v. Kraemer,* 334 U.S. 1 (1948); *Hurd v. Hodge,* 334 U.S. 24 (1948). See John P. Frank and Robert F. Munro, "The Original Understanding of 'Equal Protection of the Laws,'" *Columbia Law Review,* 50 (February 1950), p. 131.

[57] For example, *Muir v. Louisville,* 347 U.S. 971 (1954); *Baltimore v. Dawson,* 350 U.S. 877 (1955); *Holmes v. Atlanta,* 350 U.S. 879 (1955); *New Orleans v. Detiege,* 358 U.S. 54 (1955).

[58] *Morgan v. Virginia,* 328 U.S. 373 (1946); *Gayle v. Browder,* 352 U.S. 903 (1956).

[59] *Boynton v. Virginia,* 364 U.S. 454 (1960); *Turner v. Memphis,* 369 U.S. 350 (1962).

RACIAL PROGRESS IN THE SOUTH

SCHOOL INTEGRATION

Percentage of Negro students attending integrated schools in 1966–67 school year

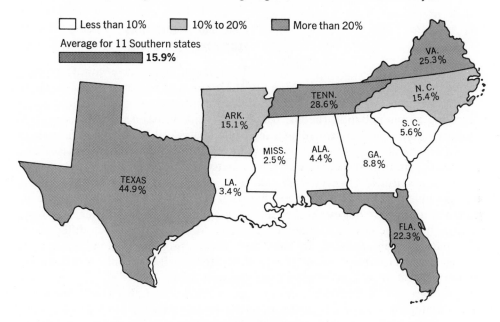

☐ Less than 10% ☐ 10% to 20% ■ More than 20%

Average for 11 Southern states
■ **15.9%**

VA. 25.3%

TENN. 28.6%

N. C. 15.4%

ARK. 15.1%

S. C. 5.6%

MISS. 2.5%

ALA. 4.4%

GA. 8.8%

TEXAS 44.9%

LA. 3.4%

FLA. 22.3%

VOTER REGISTRATION

Percentage of Negroes registered to vote as of late summer, 1966

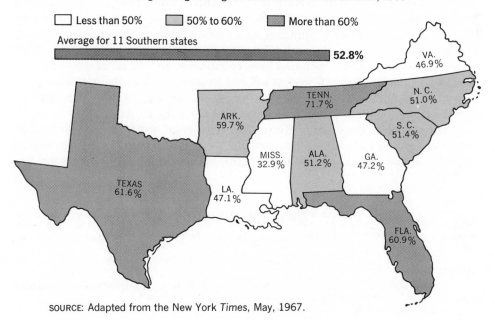

☐ Less than 50% ☐ 50% to 60% ■ More than 60%

Average for 11 Southern states
■ **52.8%**

VA. 46.9%

TENN. 71.7%

N. C. 51.0%

ARK. 59.7%

S. C. 51.4%

MISS. 32.9%

ALA. 51.2%

GA. 47.2%

TEXAS 61.6%

LA. 47.1%

FLA. 60.9%

SOURCE: Adapted from the New York *Times*, May, 1967.

restaurants.[60] Furthermore, the Court has also sustained the constitutionality of the 1964 Civil Rights Act's ban against discrimination or segregation in hotel or eating facilities connected in almost any way with interstate commerce.[61]

STATE AND FEDERAL LAWS
PROTECTING CIVIL RIGHTS

Thirty-eight states have laws forbidding segregation and discrimination. Many of these states at one time had segregation legislation. Now, virtually all of these states forbid operators of so-called places of public accommodation (hotels, restaurants, and theaters) to refuse service to minority groups or offer service on a segregated basis. All but a few of these states forbid private industry to discriminate in hiring. And about twenty of these states also have statutes that seem to go a long way toward open housing.[62]

These statutes, however, vary greatly in coverage and vigor of enforcement. For example, two out of every five states that forbid discrimination in public accommodations have not established any separate agency to administer these regulations; hence the laws are largely unenforced. Money also makes a difference in effectiveness of enforcement. In 1964, New York appropriated $2 million to carry out its antidiscrimination code, while New Mexico allotted only $2000 for the administration of its Fair Employment Practices Law.

Congress, too, has from time to time enacted civil rights laws designed to protect minority groups. In particular, in the decade after the Civil War Congress passed a series of seven laws to safeguard the position of the newly freed Negro. The last of these, the Civil Rights Act of 1875, protected Negroes against a wide range of discrimination by private citizens. This statute, however, was enacted under the authority of the Fourteenth Amendment, and in 1883 the Supreme Court declared the measure unconstitutional on the ground that this Amendment forbade discrimination only by *states* and did not empower Congress to outlaw discrimination by private citizens operating inns, restaurants, and places of amusement.[63] Profiting from this lesson, Congress utilized its control over interstate commerce as well as its authority under the Fourteenth Amendment when it adopted the public accommodations provisions of the 1964 Civil Rights Act.

Other federal laws of the Reconstruction period survived the test of constitutionality and have served through the years as the basis for a very limited federal program aimed at protecting equality of opportunity for all persons. En-

---

[60] The number of such cases is huge. Among the more interesting have been: *Garner v. Louisiana,* 368 U.S. 157 (1962); *Peterson v. Greenville,* 373 U.S. 244 (1963); *Robinson v. Florida,* 378 U.S. 153 (1964); *Bouie v. Columbia,* 378 U.S. 347 (1964); *Bell v. Maryland,* 378 U.S. 226 (1964); *Hamm v. Rock Hill,* 379 U.S. 306 (1964).

[61] *Heart of Atlanta Motel v. United States,* 379 U.S. 241 (1964); *Katzenbach v. McClung,* 379 U.S. 294 (1964).

[62] The provisions of these laws are analyzed in Duane Lockard, "The Politics of Antidiscrimination Legislation," *Harvard Journal on Legislation,* 3 (December 1965), p. 3.

[63] The *Civil Rights Cases,* 109 U.S. 3 (1883).

forcement of these surviving statutes was given a shot in the arm in 1939, when Attorney General Frank Murphy created a special civil rights section in the Department of Justice, with the duty of prosecuting public officials, and in some instances private citizens, for civil rights offenses. Ironically, the constitutional requirement of trial by jury has hampered the cause of federal protection of equality. For the victim in a civil rights case is usually an unpopular person in a community, whereas his oppressor often enjoys popular support. Under these circumstances it is difficult to secure a conviction because a unanimous jury verdict is required.[64]

It was not until 1957 that Congress passed the first federal civil rights law since Reconstruction.[65] This act raised the civil rights section of the Justice Department to the status of a full division headed by an Assistant Attorney General. The new statute also established a bipartisan Civil Rights Commission and authorized it to investigate interferences with the right to vote based on race, color, religion, or national origin; to study and collect information regarding denials of equal protection; and to evaluate relevant federal laws. The Commission could subpoena witnesses but it was given no law-enforcement powers.

In addition, the 1957 act authorized the Attorney General to seek injunctions from federal courts to restrain interferences with the right to vote. Earlier federal statutes had made it a crime to interfere with the exercise of the suffrage, but these laws had proved of limited value in the South because of the necessity of persuading juries to convict white defendants. The use of the injunction partly avoids this difficulty, since a court order directing an individual to desist from interfering with the right to vote can be enforced, as can all injunctions, through a contempt of court proceeding. And in this kind of proceeding the person who has refused to obey a court order is not customarily entitled to trial by jury. The 1957 act, however, distinguishes between civil and criminal contempt proceedings and provides that trial by jury shall be available in the latter case if a penalty of more than forty-five days in jail or a fine of more than $300 is to be imposed.

In its first report to the President and Congress in 1959, the Civil Rights Commission stated that the enforcement of the 1957 Civil Rights Act had produced results "hardly more encouraging than before," and recommended much more stringent legislation. This recommendation, and heavy political pressures from civil rights organizations, led to passage of the Civil Rights Act of 1960,[66] after ten weeks of bitter debate and filibustering in the Senate. The major provisions of this statute deal with voting rights and are summarized in Chapter 8.

The 1960 act gave the Department of Justice a fresh set of gums but few new teeth. It was clearly a piece of compromise legislation that could not work. But in 1962 and 1963, President Kennedy was unable to persuade Congress to adopt

---

[64] For examples of cases that have been prosecuted by the civil rights section, see *United States v. Classic,* 313 U.S. 299 (1941); *Screws v. United States,* 325 U.S. 91 (1945); *Crews v. United States,* 160 F. 2d 746 (1947); and *Williams v. United States,* 341 U.S. 70 and 97 (1951). See also Robert K. Carr, *Federal Protection of Civil Rights* (Ithaca, N.Y.: Cornell University Press, 1947).

[65] 71 *Stat.* 634.

[66] 74 *Stat.* 86.

a stronger law. After he took office President Johnson surprised many people by giving dynamic support to the bill, which, after eighty-three days of "debate" in the Senate, became the Civil Rights Act of 1964.[67] Chapter 8 describes in detail the parts of this act relating to voting rights, and earlier pages of this chapter discuss the act's provisions pertaining to school desegregation. In addition, the 1964 law:

1. Permits the Attorney General to bring suit to end discrimination because of race, color, religion or national origin in places of public accommodation, such as hotels, motels, restaurants, theaters, or sports arenas, that are operated by an agency of the state or federal government, or that serve patrons in interstate commerce, or that sell goods that move in interstate commerce. There are many specific exceptions to the statute's coverage, including private clubs, bars, neighborhood theaters, and small boarding houses.

2. Permits the Attorney General to bring suit to desegregate publicly owned facilities, such as parks and recreation areas.

3. Extends the life of the Commission on Civil Rights until January 31, 1968 and broadens the Commission's responsibilities.

4. Prohibits discrimination in any federally assisted program.

5. Forbids unions or management to discriminate in hiring, promoting, or classifying employees. This part of the statute did not go into effect until July 1965 and will gradually include more and more businesses until, by 1970, it covers all industries and unions with twenty-five or more workers.

6. Provides that except under the voting sections, in any criminal contempt of court proceeding growing out of the application of this statute defendants are entitled to trial by jury, and imposes a maximum punishment of six months in prison and a fine of $1000. For voting offenses the contempt provisions of the 1957 Civil Rights Act still apply.

In the long run one of the most effective sections of this statute may be the prohibition in Title VI against discrimination in federally assisted programs. This means that federal money now supporting a large number of local services, including public education, vocational training, hospitals, and welfare activities, would be withdrawn if segregation policies were followed. Accordingly, federal agencies have been requiring state and local officials to sign an assurance that they will not discriminate or segregate, and in some instances federal officers have formulated guidelines for integration that recipients of federal grants must follow.

"BLACK POWER" AND THE FUTURE OF EQUALITY

Favorable court decisions and antidiscrimination statutes have been the result of concerted political action. Negroes and whites in and out of government have worked long and hard for such victories.

[67] 78 *Stat.* 241.

For years the National Association for the Advancement of Colored People has financed lawsuits to strike down segregation statutes and has lobbied in Congress and state legislatures for positive action. The National Urban League has also been active, though it has focused its work on housing, welfare, and educational projects in an effort to obtain better general living conditions for Negroes.

Both the NAACP and the Urban League are biracial and until recently were by far the most important and influential civil rights organizations. But as the white South said "never" to the school segregation decisions and the white North appeared indifferent to the plight of masses of Negroes migrating to the cities, disillusionment with the gradualistic, legalistic methods of these two groups increased, and the power of more radical Negro groups also increased. At one extreme have been the Black Muslims, completely alienated from white society, with no faith in court decisions or legislation, favoring segregation but of a black supremacist kind, and teaching the eventual emergence of a Negro nation in the United States. The Muslims have trained a quasi-army, "the fruit of Islam," to police and protect their meetings, offices, and temples. Officially their leaders deny advocating violence against whites, but avow they will resist force with force. Muslim leaders have tried to educate their followers to achieve economic independence from whites and have integrated their social and political teachings with a theology borrowed in part from Mohammedanism but also in part the creation of Elijah Muhammad, the Muslims' founder.[68]

Much closer to the NAACP is Rev. Martin Luther King's Southern Christian Leadership Conference, a loosely organized group that, despite its name, operates in all parts of the country. In contrast to the NAACP's legalistic approach, however, the Leadership Conference has depended on mass action, such as demonstrations and marches. King is an avid student of Ghandi's political philosophy of passive resistance, and his group advocates nonviolence.

Left of the Leadership Conference are two other militant organizations, the Congress of Racial Equality (CORE) and the Student Nonviolent Coordinating Committee (SNCC). Both were initially biracial and have drawn their recruits largely from young people of college age. Both have arranged marches and demonstrations and have organized volunteers to live with poor Negroes, help educate them, and persuade them to register to vote. In 1966, CORE and SNCC (the latter more obviously), began squeezing out their white members and adopting a slogan of "black power." This vague phrase has had many different interpretations, ranging from a shrill cry for black racism to a reasoned call for Negroes to utilize fully their political resources to obtain their constitutional rights.

The NAACP and the Urban League tend to represent the Negro middle class and white intellectuals, while SNCC and CORE, like the Muslims, claim to speak for poorer Negroes. All three of the more recent groups evidence varying degrees of alienation from white society, and the leaders of each speak scornfully of white liberals, though SNCC and CORE have readily accepted, indeed courted, their assistance in the past and continue to request money from them. Occasional out-

---

[68] See E. U. Essien-Udom, *Black Nationalism* (Chicago: University of Chicago Press, 1962).

bursts of anti-semitism and the joy with which several spokesmen associated with SNCC greeted the rash of race riots in 1967 widened the divisions between the more radical Negro groups and white civil libertarians.

Chapter 1 pointed out that Negroes are apparently becoming more satisfied with the behavior of police officials toward them, but large numbers of colored citizens are obviously deeply disenchanted with this and other phases of American life. The alienation that Negroes feel is not confined to the leadership of a few organizations. The race riots that since 1964 have become an annual happening in northern cities offer glaring testimony of disillusionment and despair among large segments of the urban Negro population. The struggle for equality thus finds itself threatened by a vicious circle. Many Negroes listen to the idealistic principles of American society and see the tangible rewards that society offers—but only to others, not to them. They then often shout "black power" or riot, but in either case they further frighten many whites into opposing the cause of civil rights—the so-called white "backlash"—because of fear of Negro misconduct. Thus these Negroes are adding to their own isolation, alienation, and frustration; and so it goes around and around. The solution of each side's adhering to the principles it preaches is easier to advocate than to carry into operation, since members of both races vary in intelligence, information, social sophistication and sensitivity, dedication, and virtue. The need of Negroes is for equality now; the fear of many whites is that Negro equality means the corruption of accepted standards of behavior.

Frank recognition of several facts of life might help. On the one hand, some statistics seem to lend credence to white fears. Negroes account for about 11 percent of the general population but for 30 percent of the prison population. Furthermore, many thousands of Negroes immigrating from the rural South to the urban North are ignorant not only of the industrial skills needed to make a living but also of the standards of behavior expected by the white middle class. On the other hand, crime and poverty are closely correlated, and the wonder is that, given the average income of Negroes, their crime rate is not higher. Moreover, their ignorance is due not only to a lack of opportunity—unequal education over the years has resulted in unequal jobs, unequal pay, unequal housing, unequal education, and so on, for the next generation—but also to all too frequent punishment for taking full advantage of what opportunities were open, of being too "uppity." The remarkable success, by the highest of white middle class standards, of many Negroes who did not have an equal chance but still outdid their white competitors demonstrates that whatever disabilities they suffered were imposed by society and not by nature. Given this background, the principles of white society have often seemed to Negroes to be mere hypocrisy, a situation that cultivates contempt for established law and order.

There is no easy way out of the American dilemma. Certainly antidiscrimination statutes, even rigidly enforced regulations, offer no magic key. Caste, as experience in both India and America indicates, has a tendency to persist that is frustrating to progress. Yet laws can make a difference—small but not necessarily inconsequential. Knowledge that certain kinds of statutes are on the books, are being sincerely enforced, and are accepted as morally proper by most of the community can influence behavior patterns and also shape future attitudes.

This is the great problem of domestic politics in the United States during the second half of the twentieth century—elimination of the American dilemma and the achievement not only of a fair measure of equal opportunity but also the establishment of an American community to overcome differences of race as well as of religion, national origin, and social class.

Selected Bibliography

Broderick, Francis L., and August Meier, eds., *Negro Protest Thought in the Twentieth Century* (Indianapolis, Ind.: Bobbs-Merrill Company, Inc., 1965). An excellent collection of documents and essays that help put American civil rights problems in a sharp perspective.

Carr, Robert K., *Federal Protection of Civil Rights* (Ithaca, N.Y.: Cornell University Press, 1947). A study of the work of the civil rights section of the Department of Justice before the enactment of the Civil Rights Act of 1957.

Fellman, David, *The Defendant's Rights* (New York: Holt, Rinehart and Winston, Inc., 1958). A careful, systematic examination of all aspects of the civil rights of the defendant in criminal cases.

Greenberg, Jack, *Race Relations and American Law* (New York: Columbia University Press, 1959). An interesting summary of the development of American law and practice regarding racial matters, written by an NAACP counsel.

Hayden, Tom, *Rebellion in Newark: Official Violence and Ghetto Response* (New York: Random House, Inc., 1967). A graphic account of the 1967 race riots in Newark, N.J.

Lockard, Duane, *Toward Equality: A Study of State and Local Antidiscrimination Laws* (New York: Collier-Crowell and Macmillan Co., 1967). An analysis of the difficulties in enacting and administering civil rights legislation in the fields of housing, employment, and public accommodations.

Murphy, Walter F., *Wiretapping on Trial* (New York: Random House, 1965). An account of the *Olmstead* case and how public policy toward wiretapping has developed since then in the legislative, administrative, and judicial processes.

Myrdal, Gunnar, *An American Dilemma* (New York: Harper & Row, Publishers, 1944). This book has become a classic study of race relations. Written by a Swedish sociologist, it has had great influence in American thought and practice. The book is also available in a second edition, but this is the one that made such a deep impact.

Woodward, C. Vann, *The Strange Career of Jim Crow* 2d rev. ed. (New York: Oxford University Press, 1966). A revealing analysis of the origins of segregation statutes, done by a leading historian of the South.

Part 7 Providing for the Common Defense

Washington: Johnson's Foreign Policy Technique

By James Reston

WASHINGTON, June 14—President Johnson's technique for conducting foreign policy is highly personal and unpredictable, and even his principal aides in this field are not sure that they can define accurately what it is.

In some ways he relies more on the State Department and the Defense Department than President Kennedy, but in other ways he depends more on outsiders, special emissaries, *ad hoc* committees and personal friends.

It would be wrong to say that he uses or doesn't use the National Security Council as an informing guide—sometimes he does and sometimes he doesn't; that he counts on the State Department or doesn't—he counts on it and complains about it all the time; that he is advised by a kitchen Cabinet of private confidants—sometimes he is and sometimes he isn't.

Whims and Problems

The system changes with his problems and his whims. Former Secretary of State Dean G. Acheson headed a committee in the State Department that dealt with the French crisis in the North Atlantic Treaty Organization. It had the support of Secretary of State Rusk, and it worked very well.

Vietnam policy, however, which could use a little objective analysis by professionals uncommitted to past mistakes, is held closely within the State and Defense Departments. The President asks almost every visitor about it, but primarily his advisors in this field are Secretaries Rusk and McNamara.

On the other hand, the decisions to launch the dramatic peace offensive on Vietnam in over a dozen capitals, to summon Marshal Ky from Vietnam to the spetacular conference in Honolulu, to make a sudden trip to Mexico City and talk about a Latin-American summit meeting in the coming months—all of these were primarily personal initiatives of the President.

Intuition Unlimited

In the White House, as on Capitol Hill, he tends to rely on personal intervention and intuition. He carries on a large but intermittent correspondence with other world leaders. He telephones Prime Minister Wilson in London and Chancellor Erhard in Bonn as casually as he used to call up committee chairmen in the Congress.

Sometimes he will summon the members of the National Security Council to the Cabinet room and fill it up with so many staff aides that free discussion of critical questions is difficult if not embarrassing. Other times he will be elaborately secretive on less sensitive matters.

If there is any calculation to all this it is hard to be clear about what it is. Staff experts on a subject will be invited to sit in on their specialty one week but left out when the same subject comes up the next. Some days he will dominate foreign policy discussions with long monologues; others he will sit for an hour listening patiently and say nothing. Some days he will insist on careful agendas for its meetings; others there will be none.

Yet this is not because he is unaware of the need for more order. Recently he set up a new system of coordinating policy in a series of interdepartmental meetings under Secretaries Rusk and Ball and tried to turn his Tuesday lunch meetings into business sessions complete with topics for discussion and written reports on the agenda, but sometimes the meetings follow the plan and sometimes they do not.

The Contrasts

Some of this, of course, is inevitable, and much of it is not new. Franklin Roosevelt's Cabinet meetings were usually bull sessions. Harry Truman insisted on convening his Security Council and committing all decisions to writing. Eisenhower ran the Presidency like a military headquarters, complete with a Chief of Staff, and Kennedy bypassed the departments even more than President Johnson.

The main difference now, however, is that Mr. Johnson is in on everything. He is his own foreign secretary, press secretary, majority leader, bombing commander and campaign fund raiser, which is fine if it works, but does it?

Two of his best friends, Eugene Black and Under Secretary Thomas Mann, have recently been saying publicly that we need new ways of conducting foreign policy. Black wants us to do more through international agencies, Mann to give more authority to the Assistant Secretaries of State, and with both Mann and Under Secretary Ball leaving soon, there will be another chance to reappraise "the system."

22

American foreign policy

.

For the last two decades the central element in American foreign policy has been a belief that the Soviet Union and Communist China mortally threaten the security of the United States. American leaders have accordingly followed three basic and closely interrelated policies: containment, deterrence, and economic assistance to actual and potential allies as well as to uncommitted nations.

Containment

In the late summer of 1945, the United States, Great Britain, and the Soviet Union concluded a bloody war against Germany, Japan, and their allies. Within two years, however, the United States and Britain found themselves in a cold war with their erstwhile partner. After the Germans surrendered, Soviet troops, contrary to agreements with the United

451

States, continued to occupy northern Iran, and in 1945–1946, Russia began pressing Turkey for territorial concessions. At the end of the war Russian troops occupied most of eastern Europe, and the guerrilla leaders who had taken control of Albania and Yugoslavia were Communists. After some generally unsuccessful efforts to use free elections to legitimate their power, the Russians had by 1947 added Poland, Hungary, Rumania, Bulgaria, and Czechoslovakia to their satellite empire. Meanwhile, Communist guerrillas were pushing Greece into anarchy.

Confronted with these moves, the United States initially vacillated. But when Britain decided it could no longer defend the Mediterranean, President Truman reacted with a forthrightness that characterized his years in the White House. He protested to the Russians against their failure to leave Iran, implying that the United States was prepared to use force to free that country of foreign troops. Truman also sent American economic and military assistance to Turkey and Greece, enabling the Turks to withstand Soviet demands and the Greeks to crush the Communist guerrillas. In a speech before Congress in March 1947, the President made it clear that the United States was following a general policy, not making a series of unconnected decisions. Proclaiming what would come to be called the Truman Doctrine, he declared:

At the present moment in world history nearly every nation must choose between alternative ways of life. The choice is too often not a free one. . . . I believe that it must be the policy of the United States to support free peoples who are resisting attempted subjugation by armed minorities or outside pressures.

After mid-1947 the Truman Doctrine became the central tenet of containment, the policy of resisting Communist efforts to take over other nations. Occasionally and for widely differing reasons, as when Chinese Communists drove Chiang Kai-shek off the Asiatic mainland or when Fidel Castro took over Cuba, the United States has departed from a strict containment policy; but, despite criticisms that it is too timid or too aggressive, too rigid, or too grandiose, containment has remained a basic element in American foreign policy over the past twenty–odd years.

As another component of this policy the United States has entered into a series of regional military alliances providing for collective defense. In Europe it is a member of the North Atlantic Treaty Organization (NATO); in the Western Hemisphere, of the Organization of American States (OAS); in the Pacific, of the South East Asia Treaty Organization (SEATO) and the Australia-New Zealand-United States Treaty arrangement (ANZUS). In addition, the United States has bilateral alliances with a number of nations, including Korea, Japan, and the Philippines.

The first real test of the new containment policy came in the spring and summer of 1948. As part of an effort to squeeze Britain, France and the United States out of Berlin (a city completely surrounded by East German territory), the Russians refused to allow any traffic to use the highways and railroads leading into the western sectors of the city. The American response, an airlift of food, coal, medicine, and other supplies that kept the citizens of West Berlin existing for almost a year until the Russians lifted their blockade, demonstrated a successful application of the containment doctrine.

Truman Doctrine, 20 Years Old, Faces Reappraisal

By John W. Finney

SPECIAL TO THE NEW YORK TIMES

WASHINGTON, March 11 —Tomorrow is the 20th anniversary of the Truman Doctrine, the cornerstone of American postwar diplomatic strategy, but there is growing doubt in Congress about the doctrine's continued validity.

Taking note of the occasion, President Johnson acclaimed March 12 as "a proud anniversary" in letters today to former President Harry S. Truman, King Constantine of Greece and President Evdet Sunay of Turkey. He linked the Truman Doctrine with his own policies in Vietnam.

It was on March 12, 1947, that Mr. Truman went before a special joint session of Congress to announce a policy that was to prove a turning point in United States history in extending American military and political power around the world.

His purpose was to request $400-million in economic and military assistance to rescue Greece, which was on the edge of political and economic collapse and imperiled by a Communist guerrilla movement, and to bolster Turkey, which, with Greece, was losing her military and economic support from Britain.

But in its implications the policy went far beyond the immediate strategic considerations of preventing an extension of Communist power into the eastern Mediterranean.

The core of the Truman Doctrine, as it came to be called, was that "it must be the policy of the United States to support free peoples who are resisting attempted subjugation by armed minorities or by outside pressures."

Its premise was that "totalitarian regimes imposed on free peoples, by direct or indirect aggression, undermine the foundations of international peace and hence the security of the United States."

In a series of related steps, the doctrine led to the Marshall Plan, the North Atlantic Treaty Organization, the policy of containment against the Communist bloc, a network of military alliances stretching from Europe across Asia, and eventually to the American military involvement in South Vietnam.

It is the last step, more than anything else, that has prompted what is developing into a "great debate" in Congress over the continuing wisdom of the Truman Doctrine as a basic premise of American foreign policy.

Whether the Truman Doctrine originally envisioned the use of direct military power to "assist free peoples to work out their own destinies in their own ways" is a matter of historical debate. At least in the case of Greece and Turkey. Mr. Truman emphasized that "our help should be primarily through economic and financial aid," although the United States did supply military assistance and advice under the direction of Gen. James A. Van Fleet.

Furthermore, the Truman Doctrine was designed to deal with Communist insurgencies that were clearly a projection of Soviet power.

But to get the aid request approved by Congress—it would be necessary to "scare hell out of the country to get the measure through" was the advice of Senator Arthur H. Vandenberg at the time— the President framed his doctrine in rousing ideological terms that seemed to commit American power against all forms of Communist "coercion."

Ideological commitments of the Truman Doctrine now provide the main theme for the Administration's justification of the United States involvement in Vietnam. In any speech on "keeping the peace" or on Vietnam specifically, Secretary of State Dean Rusk is likely to cite the "lessons" of Greece and "the principles of the Truman Doctrine" as the historical precedents for confronting "Communist aggression" in Vietnam.

It is the ideological premise of the Truman Doctrine that is now being challenged on Capitol Hill, where in an uncoordinated way a re-examination of the world-wide commitments assumed by the United States since 1947 is under way in several committees.

The re-examination started with criticism of the Administration's policy in Vietnam. But it has been broadened in such disparate bodies as the Senate Foreign Relations Committee and the Joint Congressional Atomic Energy Committee into a critical study of the commitments versus the capabilities of the United States.

Even in normally pro-Administration ranks in Congress there is widespread concern that in extension of the Truman Doctrine the United States has cast itself in the role of "global policeman and protector," as Senator J. W. Fulbright put it in opening the recent hearings of the Senate Foreign Relations Committee into the world responsibilities of the United States.

To a certain extent, the Administration has contributed to this Congressional re-examination by its own attempts to mute the ideological stridency of the Truman Doctrine. The more the Administration emphasizes that the cold war has abated, in its attempt to win approval of such policies as East-West trade, the more the question arises in Congress whether the time has not come for the United States to begin reducing its wide commitments.

In his letter to Mr. Truman, President Johnson said:

"Today America is again engaged in helping to turn back armed terrorism. As in your day, there are those who believe that effort is too costly. . . . But our people have learned that freedom is not divisible; that order in the world is vital to our national interest; and that the highest costs are paid not by those who meet their responsibilities, but by those who ignore them."

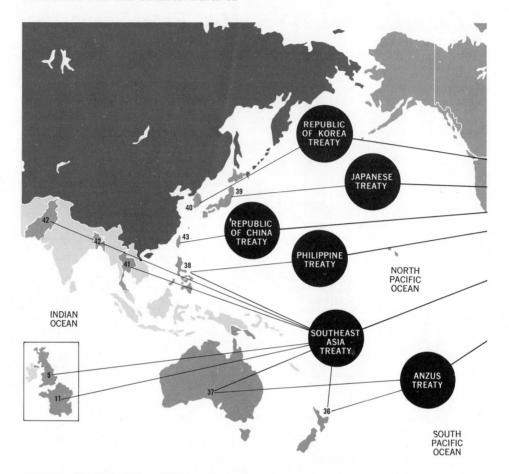

UNITED STATES COLLECTIVE DEFENSE ARRANGEMENTS

North Atlantic Treaty (15 Nations)

A treaty signed April 4, 1949, by which "the parties agree that an armed attack against one or more of them in Europe or North America shall be considered an attack against them all; and . . . each of them . . . will assist the . . . attacked by taking forthwith, individually and in concert with the other Parties, such action as it deems necessary including the use of armed force . . ."

1 UNITED STATES	9 LUXEMBOURG
2 CANADA	10 PORTUGAL
3 ICELAND	11 FRANCE
4 NORWAY	12 ITALY
5 UNITED KINGDOM	13 GREECE
6 NETHERLANDS	14 TURKEY
7 DENMARK	15 FEDERAL REPUBLIC
8 BELGIUM	OF GERMANY

Rio Treaty (22 Nations)

A treaty signed September 2, 1947, which provides that an armed attack against any American State "shall be considered as an attack against all the American States and . . . each one . . . undertakes to assist in meeting the attack . . ."

1 UNITED STATES	26 COLOMBIA
16 MEXICO	27 VENEZUELA
*17 CUBA	28 ECUADOR
18 HAITI	29 PERU
19 DOMINICAN	30 BRAZIL
REPUBLIC	31 BOLIVIA
20 HONDURAS	32 PARAGUAY
21 GUATEMALA	33 CHILE
22 EL SALVADOR	34 ARGENTINA
23 NICARAGUA	35 URUGUAY
24 COSTA RICA	44 TRINDAD
25 PANAMA	AND TOBAGO

*Has withdrawn.

Anzus (Australia–New Zealand–United States) **Treaty** (3 Nations)

A treaty signed September 1, 1951, whereby each of the parties "recognizes that an armed attack in the Pacific Area on any of the Parties would be dangerous to its own peace and safety and declares that it would act to meet the common danger in accordance with its constitutional processes."

    1 UNITED STATES
    36 NEW ZEALAND
    37 AUSTRALIA

Philippine Treaty (Bilateral)

A treaty signed August 30, 1951, by which the parties recognize "that an armed attack in the Pacific Area on either of the Parties would be dangerous to its own peace and safety" and each party agrees that it will act "to meet the common dangers in accordance with its constitutional processes."

1 UNITED STATES   38 PHILIPPINES

NORTH
ATLANTIC
TREATY

RIO
TREATY

WASHINGTON

NORTH
ATLANTIC
OCEAN

SOUTH
ATLANTIC
OCEAN

U.S. and countries with which it has mutual defense treaties

Communist bloc

Japanese Treaty (Bilateral)

A treaty signed September 8, 1951, whereby Japan on a provisional basis requests, and the United States agrees, to "maintain certain of its armed forces in and about Japan . . . so as to deter armed attack upon Japan."

   1 UNITED STATES   39 JAPAN

Republic of Korea (South Korea) **Treaty** (Bilateral)

A treaty signed October 1, 1953, whereby each party "recognizes that an armed attack in the Pacific area on either of the Parties . . . would be dangerous to its own peace and safety" and that each Party "would act to meet the common danger in accordance with its constitutional processes."

   1 UNITED STATES
   40 REPUBLIC OF KOREA

Southeast Asia Treaty (8 Nations)

A treaty signed September 8, 1954, whereby each Party "recognizes that aggression by means of armed attack in the treaty area against any of the Parties . . . would endanger its own peace and safety" and each will "in that event act to meet the common danger in accordance with its constitutional processes."

   1 UNITED STATES
   5 UNITED KINGDOM
  11 FRANCE
  36 NEW ZEALAND
  37 AUSTRALIA
  38 PHILIPPINES
  41 THAILAND
  42 PAKISTAN

   * Cuba has withdrawn.

Republic of China (Formosa) **Treaty** (Bilateral)

A treaty signed December 2, 1954, whereby each of the parties, "recognizes that an armed attack in the West Pacific Area directed against the territories of either of the Parties would be dangerous to its own peace and safety," and that each "would act to meet the common danger in accordance with its constitutional processes." The territory of the Republic of China is defined as "Taiwan (Formosa) and the Pescadores."

   1 UNITED STATES
  43 REPUBLIC OF CHINA
      (FORMOSA)

The Library of Congress, Legislative Reference Service, Robert L. Bostick 1-14-55, No. 1223, Revised 10-26-67.

The policy was severely tested a second time in June 1950, when North Korean armies, trained and equipped by the Russians, crossed the 38th parallel and invaded South Korea. Again Truman responded swiftly, though this invasion took place before Korea had been formally brought within the orbit of American protection. In a little more than a day after hostilities began the President ordered American air and naval units to support the South Koreans, and shortly thereafter he committed American ground troops to the war. In principle, the "Korean police action" was a United Nations operation. In fact, it was conducted by Americans and South Koreans, plus some assistance from nations allied with the United States, against North Korea and later China.

The war in Vietnam has presented a third crucial test, one that in the view of many critics shows that however effective the containment policy was in the 1940s and 1950s, it is now outmoded. In any event, the success of the Viet Cong and their North Vietnamese supporters in eroding the authority of South Vietnamese governments has brought about a gradually escalating American military response designed to halt the spread of Communist influence.

Deterrence

Following its traditional practice, the United States quickly demobilized most of its armed forces after World War II and relied on its monopoly of nuclear weapons for national defense. This monopoly, however, was short-lived. By 1949, the Russians had atomic bombs and soon developed aircraft capable of dropping those bombs on continental United States. In a few more years, perhaps earlier than America, the Soviets developed operational hydrogen bombs.

In response to this immediate threat to national survival the United States accepted the concept of deterrence. Although it can take a number of forms, including preventive war, as applied to date deterrence has meant maintenance of a military capacity to launch a devasting retaliation against any nation that attempts an attack against the United States or its major allies. For more than a decade the main instruments of deterrence were the bombers of the Strategic Air Command, but in the 1960s Polaris submarines and missiles based in the United States assumed the brunt of this responsibility.

Economic Assistance

Economic aid has been an integral part of containment. American money and material were important factors in enabling Greece and Turkey to resist Communist pressures. Later the United States adopted the Marshall Plan, an attempt to rebuild the economies of western European nations. So too in developing countries foreign aid has been an expensive and important aspect of American efforts to build up local capabilities to resist both external aggression and internal subversion.

Since neither the United States nor western Europe has yet been attacked, one can say that deterrence has so far succeeded in its purpose. Containment held

During June, 1962, as a part of President Kennedy's Food for Peace program, the U. S. Air Force provided emergency relief assistance to flood stricken natives of the Rufiji River Delta Area in Tanzania. Here, corn for flood victims is weighed and sacked in Dar es Salaam. (Monkmeyer Press Photo)

the line in Greece, Turkey, Iran, and Korea. Whether it will succeed in Southeast Asia remains to be seen. Economic aid restored prosperity to western Europe, to the extent that France, which after World War II was economically destitute, militarily impotent, and politically almost cannibalistic, felt strong enough in 1966 to withdraw most of its support from NATO and ask that American forces go home. In Southeast Asia, Latin America, the Middle East, and Africa, foreign aid began from a base of poverty and ignorance, in an atmosphere more medieval than modern. Not surprisingly, the results have been far less encouraging than in Europe. Japan has prospered, but few other nations have made much progress. Deterrence will be examined more fully in Chapter 23.

Cracks in the Iron Curtain

From the late 1940s through the 1950s, popular and often official discussions of foreign policy interpreted communism as a monolithic specter haunting the world. All Communists were pictured as equally dangerous. Loyalty to the cause of revolution and to the destruction of capitalism was held to transcend every national and ethnic difference. Some early evidence contradicted this simplistic view, and soon other events were to prove that it no longer provided, if it ever had, a true persective.

In 1948, Russia broke its alliance with Yugoslavia because of Tito's unorthodox politics, and in 1953, riots broke out in East Germany. In 1956, the Hungarians revolted against their Communist government and were beaten down only after a brutal, full-scale intervention by Russian troops. These were significant indications of unrest and discontent, yet still on a scale that the Soviets could control. But in a few more years the monolithic unity of the Communist bloc had splintered into a myth.

After the death of Stalin in 1953, new groups came to power in the U.S.S.R. First there were several coalitions, then Nikita Khrushchev commanded the government, though never with Stalin's iron hand. Khrushchev stayed in power for almost seven years before his ouster in 1964, when another coalition took over. What each of these regimes had in common was a desire to liberalize Soviet society, not in the sense of transforming it into a Western-style democracy but replacing terror with more efficient forms of social control and of meeting popular demands for increased production of consumer goods. The Russian people had twice built up their industry, the first time after the 1917 Revolution, the second after the devastation of World War II; and it was not unnatural that they wanted some immediate share of the material goods they had sweated and bled for.

During the early 1960s, the nations of eastern Europe pursued domestic and foreign policies that were gradually more independent, although all but Albania and Yugoslavia remained closely—and in times of international crisis probably intimately—associated with the Soviet Union. The real split in the Communist camp was between Russia and China. As the possibility of prosperity increased almost as fast as that of atomic destruction, Russian revolutionary ardor waned, while the Chinese grew more strident in their calls for militant action against the West.

The Russians, to be sure, were not averse to extending their influence by supporting Castro's Cuban revolution, and, far more seriously, in 1961, by placing intermediate-range missiles in Cuba. But the confrontation with the United States, in which President Kennedy coldly and firmly offered the Russians a choice between withdrawing the missiles and war, was sobering. The Soviets knew that if any of them survived a hydrogen war they would inherit a radioactive desert. On the other hand, Chinese leaders, with little experience with atomic weapons and a surfeit of several hundred million people, apparently found the prospect of nuclear war less terrifying.

From differences in emphasis on fine points of Marxist doctrine the Sino-Soviet dispute escalated to name-calling and open hostility. Whether the real cause was ideological or the more practical refusal of Soviet leaders to share atomic weapons with their allies, the split took on major proportions in 1966. The Russians angrily withdrew military and economic aid from the Chinese and began competing with them for leadership of Communist parties around the world. The Chinese readily joined in this competition, branding the Russians as lackeys of American imperialism.

The New Balance of Power

The split between Russia and China is bringing about far-reaching changes in the basic nature of contemporary international relations. For several centuries before World War I Europe was the center of world politics. Each large European nation could have a wide sphere of influence; but there were too many other contestants of comparable strength to allow free play of global ambitions. If one nation got so strong as to endanger the security or ambitions of others, those threatened were likely to join in an alliance against the upstart, as England, Russia, Austria, and Prussia did against Napoleon. This condition was known as a balance of power.

Nuclear weapons drastically altered the potential power of an individual nation. For several years after World War II, for example, it was possible for the United States to have used its atomic bombs to dominate the world and to utterly destroy any opposing country without risking significant danger to itself. Russian development of atomic and hydrogen bombs established a new and different kind of balance, known as a balance of terror. In the old balance of power there had been not only one or two strong nations (potential aggressors) and weak nations (potential victims) but also relatively strong balancers who could intervene in any dispute to prevent domination, at least to the extent of commanding a share of the spoils. But in the Soviet-American situation there was no set of strong nations whose physical power could deter either country from taking a particular course of action.

The break between China and Russia, accompanied by growing Chinese industrialization and development of nuclear weapons, has created a situation more analogous to the balance of power, though the character of nuclear weapons injects an element of destructiveness that the old system happily never knew. There are now three countries whose interests are apparently in conflict. Each also has interests in common; at a minimum, preventing the third from attaining dominance. War between any two may leave either or both so weakened that the third will be the real victor. This means that none can fully trust another to enter into an alliance to destroy the third, again because one of the winners may emerge much stronger than the other and complete the elimination of its rivals. Thus limited conflict or limited cooperation between any two of the three is more rational—though merely for that reason not inevitable—than a large-scale war or full-fledged alliance between any two.

The Neutrals

Each of the Big Three, the United States, the Soviet Union, and Red China, has a series of allies. In addition there is a mass of nonaligned nations, many of them newly independent. Americans have often been suspicious of these countries, at times with good reason, for some have flirted with communism and others have frankly tried to play Russia and the United States against each other to get increased aid. In many ways these nations are playing a game with the established powers much like the one that the United

States in its early years played with Europe. During the Revolutionary War Benjamin Franklin and other American diplomats cleverly exploited French ambitions to induce that country into a treaty of alliance with the colonies and to give the military aid that proved decisive in defeating the British. A dozen years later, when France faced a war against England and the monarchs of most of Europe, the United States looked to its own self-interest rather than to the spirit of its treaty with France and issued a proclamation of neutrality. As Samuel F. Bemis[1] points out, the theme that recurs through much of the early diplomatic history of the United States is that Europe's distresses were America's successes.

INSTRUMENTS OF FOREIGN POLICY

The ultimate purpose of foreign policy in modern diplomacy has been to persuade others to allow a nation to attain its objectives, usually by peaceful means if possible. Utter devastation of an opponent, such as Rome effected against Carthage, is less likely to be a primary goal than an act of desperation or despair. A nation's basic instruments of persuasion are military force, economic power, propaganda, and diplomacy.

Chapter 23 discusses in detail problems of national security as they relate to the military. Here it is sufficient to note that military force may vary from a lone saboteur to agents who stir up internal discord and plot revolution to guerrillas who fight a hit and run war to huge conventional armies and navies to missiles and hydrogen warheads and even to bacteriological warfare.

Propaganda

Propaganda is a second major instrument of foreign policy. While communications between governments must involve messages between public officials, propaganda is typically aimed at a wider public audience. Because of recent experience with "big lie" techniques of Nazi and Communist agencies, there is a tendency to think of propaganda as intrinsically a tool of deceit and deception. Propaganda may, however, be designed to tell the truth—sometimes a powerful weapon. Propaganda is an old and commonly used instrument of foreign policy that the United States has employed since the Revolutionary War. The fundamental purposes of propaganda in international relations are akin to those of public relations in the business world—to build up what Madison Avenue calls a desirable public image of a country and its aims and to help persuade others of the rightness or expediency of allowing that nation to attain its objectives. This image need not be a benevolent one. Machiavelli long ago claimed that in politics it was better to be feared than loved,[2] and propaganda is often used to instill dread. Nor need propaganda be restricted to such channels as radio, tele-

---

[1] Bemis uses this phrase frequently in *A Diplomatic History of the United States,* 5th ed. (New York: Holt, Rinehart, and Winston, Inc., 1965).

[2] Niccolo Machiavelli, *The Prince* (New York: Random House, Inc., 1940), Modern Library ed., Chap. 17.

vision, or newspapers. Mere detonation by the Russians in 1961 of hydrogen bombs of more than 50 million tons of TNT was convincing evidence to many neutralists and even to pro-Western government officials of the might of the Soviet Union.

The first highly organized, centrally administered efforts of the United States to utilize propaganda as an effective instrument of foreign policy occurred during World War I. In 1917, the United States established the Committee of Public Information under George Creel, a prodigiously energetic and imaginative man. Aiming at both foreign and domestic audiences, he organized artists, writers, professors, newspapermen, photographers, and actors to produce speeches, editorials, pictures, movies, and pamphlets (more than 100 million of the latter) demonstrating the depravity of the Germans and the wonderful virtues of Americans and their gallant allies. While Creel was unifying opinion at home and abroad against the barbarous "Hun," President Wilson was undermining German morale by distinguishing between evil governments and good people and appealing to a yearning for peace and a sense of justice. Wilson's technique was all the more successful because of his obvious sincerity.

In World War II the United States ran an Office of War Information on a scale similar to that of Creel's committee, and the armed forces devoted great attention to psychological warfare. After the war Congress established the U.S. Information Agency, whose primary function is to build up the American image abroad. The USIA represents an effort to put propaganda on a permanent and professional basis. Although the complaint has been made that the agency tends to "save the saved and convert the converted,"[3] USIA officials assert that they spend a large portion of their annual budget of about $150 million trying to save the fallen and to convert unbelievers through "targeting,"[4] that is, selecting specific means most likely to reach specific audiences. The agency employs over 10,000 people, stationed in almost every American embassy, and also operates such programs as the Voice of America radio network and libraries around the world.

Economic Power

Economic power constitutes a third instrument that has both a positive and a negative edge. Economic power may be used negatively as a set of sanctions against a nation, such as a boycott of goods, a discriminatory tariff, an embargo, or a refusal to give credit. Its most extreme form is a blockade, use of military force to cut off another nation's foreign trade.

Positively, economic aid may take the form of a program such as the Marshall Plan, designed to help allies or potential friends to build themselves up so that ultimately they can defend themselves. It may be given as money, credit to buy goods, goods themselves, or expert advisers or even workers to carry out projects.

---

[3] John F. Amory, *Around the Edge of War* (New York: Clarkson N. Potter, 1961), p. 890. Amory is a pseudonym for an author who the publisher says is an experienced diplomat.

[4] Carl T. Rowan, "The Policy of the USIA," in Harry H. Ransom, ed., *An American Foreign Policy Reader* (New York: Thomas Y. Crowell Company, 1965), pp. 283–285; and Joseph Kraft, "USIA: Uncle Sam's Interpreter Abroad," also in Ransom, pp. 272–283.

As an alternative or an addition to direct aid, one nation might offer economic inducements to a second nation so that it might in turn help out a third. While aid may create a favorable climate of opinion, both official and general, it is doubtful that economic assistance can buy national friendship. For most national leaders gratitude is a luxury, and they calculate cooperation with other countries in terms of current or anticipated benefits, rather than of past favors. Sophisticated leaders of the wealthier nations realize this, of course, and seek to support regimes whose interests are compatible with their own.

Since 1961, administration of American nonmilitary aid has been consolidated under the Agency for International Development (AID), which comes directly under the authority of the Secretary of State. AID annually disperses over $2 billion in outright grants or loans; it spends some for research into economic opportunities, some to guarantee private investments in developing countries. The agency also oversees U.S. contributions to international organizations and is responsible for administering several special operations, including the Alliance for Progress, designed to assist Latin America, and the Food for Peace program, under which American surplus farm products are sold or donated to needy countries.

Diplomacy

Military force, economic power, and propaganda give a nation the potential to achieve its aims; diplomacy can transform this potential into reality. Diplomacy is a magic word, conjuring up romantic visions of sophisticated parties and delightfully dark images of international intrigue, with liberal quantities of beautiful women and fine wine. The reality, however, is usually less glamorous. In its simplest form diplomacy is no more than an instrument of conveying official communications between governments.

In its broader meaning diplomacy is not itself an instrument of persuasion but a force that energizes and gives direction to foreign policy by skillful use of the other instruments. It may involve decisions of when to use blandishments or promises of economic assistance or threats of military action; it may involve bargaining to trade one advantage for another; it may involve frank statements that a certain course of action means war. In all phases of its operation diplomacy requires couching promises, demands, and threats in language calculated to achieve an objective while preserving the self-respect of other parties to the negotiations.

In international politics prestige and reputation are at least as important as in domestic affairs. Like a President who wishes to lead congressmen, a government that would persuade other governments must exhibit not only wisdom and prudence but also determination and, to an even greater degree than in internal politics, power. Folklore frequently places great hope on the efficacy of diplomacy. It may be the brain of policy instruments without whose coordination the most abundant economic, military, and propaganda resources are worth very little, but it needs a healthy body to command. Occasionally a shrewd diplomat, like the Frenchman Talleyrand at the Congress of Vienna in 1815, may capitalize on jealousy and suspicion to divide his opponents and so accomplish near miracles.

Far more often, however, the effectiveness of diplomacy is limited by the potential of the other instruments as well as by national determination to use any or all of them.

FORMATION OF FOREIGN POLICY

The formation of foreign policy is affected by numerous physical factors, such as a nation's geographical location, climate, and natural resources; and by such diverse human elements as the state of economic development, the status of scientific knowledge, the size and education of the population, and the personalities of particular public officials. Moreover, in any practical sense it is impossible to isolate foreign policy from domestic policy. One cannot, for instance, speak intelligently about problems of international trade without knowing about conditions of the national economy; about military power without knowing about allocations of resources for scientific research and development; or about foreign aid without knowing about the urgency and cost of domestic social welfare programs.

All of these elements have been influential in the making of American foreign policy. The distance of the United States from other strong nations, its temperate climate, its abundance of raw materials, its diffusion of scientific knowledge, and its large, well-educated population have all been important factors. In addition, the foreign policy of the United States has been affected by the character of the country's general political system—most significantly by federalism, presidential leadership, sharing of powers, decentralized political parties, and the spread of bureaucratic organization.

Federalism and Foreign Policy

In strict terms of constitutional law there can be few, if any, problems of federalism in the formulation of foreign policy. States can take little independent action toward foreign governments; Supreme Court decisions have unequivocally asserted federal supremacy in this field.[5] But, as in many phases of politics, actual practice does not always conform with judicial principles. Senators and representatives are elected from individual states and are sensitive to the wishes of their constituents and of state officials whose help they may need for reelection. It is no accident that in the past the Midwest, more rural and more cut off from the outside world than the Northeast, sent a number of isolationists to Congress, or that for years senators from the Northeast opposed joint Canadian-American development of the St. Lawrence seaway that has enabled ocean-going vessels to bypass eastern ports and go directly to Cleveland, Detroit, and Chicago.

A state can also affect foreign policy through its treatment of persons within its jurisdiction, whether foreign dignitaries or private citizens or even Americans.

---

[5] For instance, *Missouri v. Holland,* 252 U.S. 416 (1920); and *United States v. Curtiss-Wright,* 299 U.S. 304 (1936).

State efforts to maintain racial segregation have made it difficult for the United States to win the trust of African and Asian countries. A few years ago Maryland complicated American relations at the United Nations by allowing owners of restaurants and other public facilities along the main New York-to-Washington highway to refuse service to nonwhites, including many diplomats on their way between Washington and UN headquarters. Similarly, in the early 1900s, California helped increase Japanese hostility toward the United States by discriminating against immigrants from that country.

Presidential Leadership

His constitutional prerogative and access to secret information, together with the country's need for prompt action and for a strong single voice to speak for it in foreign affairs, combine to give the President opportunity for leadership. As in domestic politics, however, presidential power is hedged by formal constitutional limitations and by informal but no less significant practices of the American political system. The detailed discussions in Part 3 on Congress and Part 4 on the executive are relevant here.

The most important formal limitation results from the constitutional authority given to Congress in international relations. The Senate must consent to the appointment of a number of officials whose work centers on foreign policy, for instance, the Secretary of State, his chief assistants, and all ambassadors. In addition, the Senate must approve every treaty by a two thirds vote. The President can to some extent bypass the Senate by making executive agreements on his own authority. These have much the same force within the United States as treaties,[6] but there is serious question under international law whether such agreements bind succeeding Presidents.

In any event, almost all important treaties or agreements require legislation to carry them out, appropriations if nothing else. Moreover, the size of the armed forces, the equipment and bases available to them, the character of the foreign service, the amount and kinds of economic aid, the operations of the Central Intelligence Agency, the United States Information Agency, and every other government agency depend on the budget Congress adopts, just as tariff and immigration policies are largely set by statute.

As we have seen, Congress is too big and too busy to make decisions that require rapid evaluation of secret information. Thus the vital decisions of recent years, intervention in Korea, Vietnam, and the Dominican Republic, or the Cuban missile crisis, have all been made by the President and his advisers with little or only perfunctory consultation with Congress. On the other hand, the House and Senate make excellent forums for discussions of long-range policies. Hearings can be used to highlight possible alternatives, and testimony of expert witnesses can bring out the risks and rewards of each course. In 1966 and 1967, Senator Fulbright's Foreign Relations Committee held hearings on Vietnam that received

---

[6] *United States v. Belmont,* 301 U.S. 324 (1937); and *United States v. Pink,* 315 U.S. 203 (1942).

national attention. Similarly, floor debate can help clarify both problems and potential solutions.

The most important informal limitations on a President's power, in foreign as well as domestic affairs, result from his having to work through a weak, decentralized party system and through a diffuse series of administrative organizations. He may have to appoint men to important foreign posts whose views differ from his own; to get something in the domestic realm he may have to give up something he considers important in foreign policy.

Even when there is no deliberate effort to thwart or revise a President's objectives, he has to deal with the bureaucracy. The Department of State is only one of more than forty agencies concerned with making or implemeting foreign policy. The National Security Council, composed of the President, the Vice President, the Secretaries of State and Defense and the director of the Office of Emergency Planning, and anyone the President wishes to invite on an informal basis, is responsible for long-range planning. The work of the Department of Defense and the three armed services departments intimately involves foreign policy, both in deploying American forces abroad and in advising officials of other governments. The Central Intelligence Agency is by definition as well as inclination wrapped up in foreign affairs. Less well known are the roles played by many Cabinet-level departments such as Treasury, Agriculture, Labor, and Commerce, and many smaller agencies as well, such as the Atomic Energy Commission, the Export-Import Bank, the Civil Aeronautics Board, and the Tariff and Maritime Commissions.

The Secretary of State

The National Security Council is a super-planning board that meets at the pleasure of the President. Responsibility for day-to-day operations and coordination of foreign policy falls on the Secretary of State. He may from time to time negotiate directly with foreign officials, but most of his work involves four major functions: First, he must keep the President informed on all important developments in international politics and offer cogent advice on the best course of action. Second, he must run the Department of State, a far from easy task given its size and world-wide activities.

He is also responsible for coordinating the work of American ambassadors and special agents in their negotiations with foreign governments as well as the operations of all other federal agencies involved in international relations. To clarify this responsibility, President Johnson in March 1966 issued an executive order specifically delegating to the Secretary of State the President's authority to direct all American overseas operations, except those of tactical military forces. This order created two layers of interdepartmental committees to assist the Secretary. The lower level is composed of a series of six interdepartmental regional groups. Each is headed by an assistant secretary of state, with representatives from the Department of Defense, AID, the CIA, the Joint Chiefs of Staff, the USIA, and from the White House or the National Security Council. Above these regional groups is the senior interdepartmental group, established to handle more general problems or to reconsider ones that agency heads feel have been wrongly decided by regional committees. This senior group is headed by the Under Secretary of State as executive chairman. Like the heads of regional groups, the Under Secretary himself makes decisions after hearing the advice and views of the committee. The other members are the Deputy Secretary of Defense, the chairman of the Joint Chiefs, someone from the White House staff, and directors of the agencies represented on regional groups.

The Secretary of State must also perform a fourth function pertaining to public relations. To create a receptive mood for requests for appropriations and implementing legislation, he must periodically persuade congressmen of the wisdom of administration policies. To keep the President and his party in power, he also must help persuade American public opinion that the government is making sound and intelligent decisions. At the same time, the Secretary must maintain the prestige of the United States by persuading foreign officials of the good faith and firm resolve of the United States.

Many observers have noted a tendency in this century for Presidents to act as their own Secretaries of State. There are certain elements of truth in these observations. Before Woodrow Wilson went to the Paris Peace Conference in 1919, no American President had gone abroad to negotiate with a foreign government, and even at home negotiations had been almost completely carried on by the Secretary of State or his subordinates. From Franklin D. Roosevelt to the present, however, each President has engaged in personal diplomacy. Summit conferences have been taking place at frequent intervals. It is also true that Presidents Wilson, Roosevelt, Kennedy, and Johnson at times concentrated their energy on foreign policy, insisted on making most crucial—and many trivial—decisions themselves, and in making up their minds sometimes accepted advice of persons other than the Secretary of State.

Nevertheless, not all Presidents of earlier years listened to their Secretaries of State and not all recent Presidents have bypassed theirs. For instance, Lincoln certainly was selective in accepting advice from his Secretary of State, William Seward. At the other extreme, Harry Truman depended heavily on the advice of two of his Secretaries of State, General George C. Marshall and Dean Acheson; and Eisenhower gave John Foster Dulles a wide range of latitude in forming American policy.

Today a President has to be far more involved in foreign policy problems than his predecessor a few generations ago; but, as Dean Acheson[7] has said, the relationship between a President and his Secretary of State "is an intensely personal one." The Secretary's real power will depend in large part on the degree of confidence that the President has in his judgment, on the President's willingness to delegate authority, on the Secretary's readiness to accept full responsibility, and on how compatible the temperaments of the two men are. James Byrnes grated on Harry Truman and had to resign; John Foster Dulles complemented Eisenhower's personality and made full use of the President's confidence.

[7] "The President and the Secretary of State," in Don K. Price, ed., *The Secretary of State* (Englewood Cliffs, N.J.: Prentice Hall, Inc., 1960), p. 37.

The Department of State

Much of the information and advice on which the President and Secretary of State act are provided by the employees of the Department of State. Few of these people individually have a significant influence on policy-making; yet their combined impact is often decisive. State Department officials staff not only the department in Washington and liaison with the White House, Department of Defense, CIA, and other agencies but also man 112 embassies, 2 legations, 170 consulates, and 10 special missions. Through these offices much intelligence is generated and transmitted, a good share of international negotiations is carried on, and the basis is laid for most foreign policy decisions.

Abroad the functions of the State Department are divided between consular and diplomatic missions. The operations of the two overlap, but the primary objective of the first is to safeguard the interests of American citizens, that of the latter to represent and protect American political interests. Consular officers typically perform such mundane but necessary tasks as assisting American businessmen to find new markets, helping tourists who get into trouble with local police, issuing new passports to Americans who have lost theirs, obtaining visas for foreigners who wish to visit the United States, and administering American law, so far as it is applicable, to citizens abroad. In addition, consular officers are expected to keep their antennae tuned for hints of political developments that may concern the United States.

Diplomatic officers run the embassies and represent the United States to the government of the country in which they are stationed. As official representatives of a sovereign nation they have the privilege of immunity from most local laws. In return they have the burden of participating in many ceremonial observances. Diplomats present the views of the United States to foreign officials and in turn relay to Washington the views of the other government. Even more than their consular colleagues, diplomats are expected to collect political information relevant to the national interest. And as anyone can gather from frequent expulsions of diplomats (they cannot be arrested for espionage because of their immunity), the line between spying and obtaining information is at times a fine one.

At home the Department of State is organized to execute policy decisions and assist the Secretary of State in all his functions. Members must relay, collect, organize, and evaluate information that comes in from the field; instruct American ambassadors and other representatives about policy decisions; coordinate with other federal agencies; and even carry on actual negotiations with foreign emissaries. Moreover, the department must recruit and train personnel to maintain operational efficiency.

At the first working level of State Department organization are so-called country directors, relatively senior career officers who receive and transmit messages to and from the embassies. They may have contact with only a single country or with several in the same geographic area. The director and his assistants read the cables that literally pour in from the embassies, take action on them, refer them to the proper office, or send them up the chain of command for notation or decision.

The country directors are coordinated under five assistant secretaries of state, each one heading a regional bureau for Africa, Europe, the Western Hemisphere, the Far East, and the Middle East and Southeast Asia. A sixth bureau handles matters relating to the United Nations and its subordinate agencies. These six assistant secretaries also serve as executive chairmen of the regional interdepartmental groups that are responsible for coordinating the overseas operations of all government agencies.

The Secretary of State is also assisted by a number of high-level officials: two under secretaries, two deputy under secretaries, and seven assistant secretaries (not including the six who head the regional and UN bureaus). These people are in charge of such tasks as policy planning, inspection of department posts abroad, intelligence collection and research, loyalty-security programs, and protocol.

It came as no surprise when Secretary of State Dean Rusk[8] confessed to a Senate subcommittee that "inside of the Department our principal problem is layering." For between the country director and the Secretary of State stand six or seven layers of officials. Another problem of potentially equal seriousness is the communications torrent. Each day the department sends and receives about 3000 cables, containing over 400,000 words. On the one hand, the Secretary should not be isolated; he must know what is going on in the world to give prudent advice to the President and to coordinate the activities of all government agencies in foreign affairs. Furthermore, he must be accessible to ambassadors if he is to use them efficiently and to retain their confidence and cooperation. On the other hand, there must be some filtering system to protect the Secretary from the routine and trivial and allow him to concentrate on the really significant issues.

The State Department is staffed by over 25,000 persons. About 10,000 of these are "locals," citizens of the country in which an embassy or consulate is located. They act in such capacities as janitors, receptionists, typists, clerks, and translators. Locals provide a source of relatively cheap labor, facilitate communications with foreign citizens, and perhaps build up good will. They also present certain security risks.

American employees fall into three general categories: political appointees, usually found only at the highest levels; members of the civil service; and foreign service officers. The Rogers Act of 1924 unified the consulate and diplomatic corps into the foreign service. Thus an official may spend one tour of duty in a consulate, the next in an embassy. Nevertheless, through the middle 1950s and to a lesser extent today, another distinction has persisted between executives who are foreign service officers and executives who are civil service employees. The former typically spent most of their time abroad, while the civil service men usually stayed in Washington. Because of their higher admission standards, foreign service officers tended to look down on their civil service colleagues, but were themselves deficient in experience at home.

---

[8] U.S. Senate, Subcommittee on National Security Staffing and Operations, *The Administration of National Security,* 88th Cong., p. 398 (1965). Rusk testified on December 11, 1963.

Following the recommendations of a special committee headed by President Henry M. Wriston of Brown University, Congress and the President provided for the amalgamation of many civil services employees into the foreign service and in turn made it a policy for all foreign service officers to spend about a third of their careers in Washington. As a result of "Wristonization"—often scorned by career diplomats—about 75 percent of all executive positions in the department today are manned by foreign service officers, with the rest about equally divided between civil servants and political appointees.

The size of the foreign service has remained relatively small. As late as the end of World War II it comprised only 820 officers, though today it has grown to around 3800, plus several hundred foreign service reserve officers—persons with certain kinds of technical expertise who have foreign service status for a limited number of years. Almost every foreign service officer has a college degree and more than half have done graduate work. About three fourths have a working knowledge of a foreign language.[9]

Basically there are two means of joining the foreign service: by competitive examination and by lateral entry, or transfer from other departments. The first is the normal method. Each year the service offers a day-long written examination open to American citizens between the ages of twenty-one and thirty-one. This examination is designed to test a candidate's capacity to reason, to express himself in English, and to utilize his general knowledge. Those who pass take an oral examination, in which senior officers further probe their general knowledge and judge whether they are likely to become good diplomats. There are also careful security checks and personal interviews. Standards are high. About one out of five applicants passes the written examination, and only one out of every two or three of these survives the oral. Those accepted are usually appointed at the most junior level of the foreign service and typically undergo a period of additional training at the Foreign Service Institute in Washington before they are given overseas assignments.

In accordance with several acts of Congress, foreign service regulations also provide for transfer of middle-range executives from other government departments to the foreign service. These people have a high level of experience and expertise and are usually given a rank comparable to their previous one. Not including the approximately 1200 officers who entered the service at the time of Wristonization, relatively few people—perhaps 75 or 100 a year—join the Foreign Service through lateral entry.

The service prides itself on a system of discipline and promotion similar to that of the armed forces. Officers are expected to serve in all parts of the world and at a moment's notice. For promotional purposes senior officers must file detailed annual reports on the work of their juniors, and selection boards meet periodically to select officers for advancement. The rule is "up or out." That is, if after a certain time selection boards do not judge that an officer is fit for promotion, he is asked to resign or retire.

---

[9] John E. Harr, *The Anatomy of the Foreign Service* (New York: Carnegie Endowment for International Peace, 1965), presents a detailed analysis of the composition of the foreign service.

Ambassadors

An ambassador is the President's personal representative to a foreign government. Legally he is the senior American officer in a foreign country and has authority over all U.S. government officials serving there except for operational military forces under an area commander. As President Kennedy explained in a letter to all American ambassadors in 1961:[10]

In regard to your personal authority and responsibility, I shall count on you to oversee and coordinate all the activities of the United States Government in ———. You are in charge of the entire U.S. Diplomatic Mission, and I shall expect you to supervise all of its operations. The Mission includes not only the personnel of the Department of State and the Foreign Service, but also the representatives of all other U.S. agencies which have programs or activities in ———. . . . The U.S. Diplomatic Mission includes service attaches, military assistance advisory groups, and other military components attached to the Mission. It does not, however, include U.S. military forces operating in the field where such forces are under the command of a U.S. area military commander. The line of authority to these forces runs from me, to the Secretary of Defense, to the Joint Chiefs of Staff. . . . Although this means that the Chief of the American Diplomatic Mission is not in the line of military command, nevertheless, as Chief of Mission, you should work closely with the appropriate area military commander to assure full exchange of information. If it is your opinion that activities by the U.S. military forces may adversely affect our overall relations with the people or government of ———, you should promptly discuss the matter with the military commander and, if necessary, request a decision by higher authority.

An ambassador's real, as contrasted with his legal, authority may be somewhat different from his formal instructions. He must be able to control his own mission and at the same time win or retain support in the Department of State and Congress for his policy objectives. His problems with members of his mission are analogous to those of the President in dealing with the federal bureaucracy or to those of the Secretary of State in coordinating overlapping governmental activities. A large embassy may have officials from more than three dozen federal agencies. The ambassador has usually had no voice in selecting and perhaps little say in promoting these officials or in choosing the objectives toward which they are working.

Control is thus difficult—one would expect it to be when it includes such diverse officials as CIA agents, senior military officers, and psychologists from the USIA—but it is not impossible. After two and a half years as American Ambassador in Belgrade, George F. Kennan reported to a congressional committee:[11]

I encountered no difficulty whatever in exerting what seemed to me to be adequate authority over the entire American establishment in Yugoslavia. It may be that I was favored in being surrounded with a group of exceptionally able and loyal assistants. . . . But aside from this fortunate circumstance, I had the impression that the authority of an Ambassador over official American personnel . . . is just about whatever he wants to make it. So long as they are in his territory, they have to respect his authority, if he insists they do so.

---

[10] The letter is reprinted in *The Administration of National Security*, pp. 15–16.
[11] *The Administration of National Security*, p. 358. Kennan testified on November 3, 1963.

In dealing with Washington, however, Kennan found his problems were more serious. First, he complained that the State Department did not inform him about Yugoslav activities outside that country so that he might put his own negotiations in a sharper perspective. Second, he felt that he got little cooperation on any matter that was largely outside of the jurisdiction of the Department of State. Then recommendations were likely to be passed over or lost in an administrative maze.

It was partially in response to this second kind of criticism that President Johnson issued his 1966 executive order discussed earlier in this chapter. The model for the order and its interdepartmental groups was the "country team" headed by the ambassador.

Kennan felt most frustrated in his relations with Congress. He found his assessments of Yugoslav developments largely ignored on Capitol Hill and commented ruefully:[12]

If I had known how little value the Congress would assign to my own judgment, in the light of an experience of nearly 30 years in the affairs of Eastern Europe, I would never have accepted the appointment; for without the support of Congress it was impossible to carry out an effective policy there.

Institutional reforms are more difficult in the legislative branch, given congressional independence from executive control.

Some frustrations are inherent in the job of an ambassador. He sees at firsthand what the United States can do in its relations with a particular country, while officials in the State Department, thousands of miles away, are far less well informed. On the other hand, officials at home are receiving reports from embassies all over the world, and perhaps see that there are other problems that deserve priority. Furthermore, in recommending appropriations the President and his budget advisers—and congressmen evaluating those recommendations—have to allocate scarce resources to cover the spectrum of domestic and international needs. Even a nation as rich as the United States does not have enough wealth to carry out simultaneously, and at the rate that experts in each field would like, a war on poverty at home, a space program, a military defense program, foreign aid, and their thousands of concomitant subpolicies.

Furthermore, especially in many phases of negotiation, the importance of the ambassador has declined in recent years. Crucial negotiations are often carried on directly between the State Department and the foreign ministry of the other country, if not between the President and the head of the foreign government. If the matter is of lesser importance, the department is apt to use cables or jet trips by special envoys to give the ambassador minutely detailed instructions that leave little room for him to exercise discretion. The department may even send out a special representative to conduct the actual negotiations.

In other respects, however, the job of ambassador is more important than ever. He is in a position to see and know as a whole the country to which he is

---

[12] *The Administration of National Security,* p. 360.

accredited, something a Secretary of State, a President, or a special envoy can rarely do. Thus his information can help construct a framework within which officials in Washington will view specific foreign developments. Second, in his day-to-day contact with foreign officials an ambassador can build up—or destroy—international rapport. Third, and not least, is an ambassador's leadership and coordination of the numerous agencies represented in his mission.

This importance is reflected in the criteria by which ambassadors are chosen. Sometimes a President uses an ambassadorship as patronage to pay off past debts or to gain future advantages. On the whole, however, this practice has been declining, at least to the extent that few mediocre men are appointed to these posts. In the last few decades about 60 to 70 percent of ambassadors have been foreign service officers. Most of the nonprofessional appointees have had considerable governmental experience, and, not infrequently, like Adlai Stevenson or Henry Cabot Lodge, have been distinguished public servants.

THE UNITED NATIONS

After World War I Woodrow Wilson demanded establishment of a League of Nations to replace the instabilities and injustices of balance of power relationships with the order and the justice of a community of nations. The American Senate's rejection of the Treaty of Versailles dashed whatever prospect of success the League had to fulfill Wilson's dreams; but the United Nations, created after World War II by the victors, gave international organization a second chance. With headquarters in New York and offices spread all over the world, the UN has operated through more than twenty years of hot and cold war. It offers, President John F. Kennedy once remarked, a "hope and an instrument," though perhaps more often the former.

The principal political organs of the UN are the Secretariat, the Security Council, and the General Assembly. The Secretariat provides administrative direction for the various agencies of the organization. It is headed by a Secretary General, nominated by the Security Council and elected by the General Assembly, customarily for a term of five years. The power of the Secretary General depends mainly on his capacity for moral suasion, since the UN has at its disposal only whatever physical force member nations are willing to lend it.

The Security Council consists of representatives of fifteen nations. Five are permanent members: China (to date, Nationalist China on Formosa), France, Great Britain, the Soviet Union, and the United States; and ten are elected by the General Assembly for two-year terms. The UN charter gives the Security Council primary responsibility for maintaining peace; it may investigate any threatening dispute, either by its own decision or at the request of any nation. At the conclusion of its investigation the Council may recommend a solution to the parties involved or may call upon members of the UN to invoke sanctions, including military force, against a particular country or countries.

The great defect in the operation of the Security Council has been its voting system. Each of the fifteen members has one vote, and on procedural matters a majority of nine is all that is required for a decision. On substantive matters, however, there must be at least nine affirmative votes, and each of the five permanent members has an absolute veto. Time and again through the years the Russian "Nyet" has blocked affirmative UN action. United Nations participation in the Korean conflict was possible only because the Russians were temporarily boycotting the Council when the issue came to a vote.

The General Assembly is composed of representatives from all member nations. Each member nation has one vote, with a two thirds majority necessary to carry any motion. The charter authorizes the Assembly to investigate and make recommendations on any matter not actually before the Security Council, so long as the issue does not concern a problem of a nation's domestic politics. In 1950, the Assembly passed a "Uniting for Peace" resolution in an effort to overcome the veto barrier within the Security Council. This resolution asserted that if the Council could not take action on a dispute, the Assembly could assume jurisdiction if it wanted.

The judicial branch of the UN is the International Court of Justice, located at The Hague. This court is comprised of fifteen judges, elected by the General Assembly and the Security Council for nine-year terms. No two judges may be citizens of the same country. The Court's jurisdiction is basically limited to disputes between nations rather than between private citizens and a country or between two private citizens.

On the whole the United Nations has been most effective in dealing with disputes on the margins of the national interests of the great powers—various Arab-Israeli disputes, Cyprus, the Congo, or the India-Pakistan conflict—than in coping with problems central to the great powers—such as Berlin, Cuba, or Vietnam. Still, preventing small incidents from mushrooming into big wars is no mean accomplishment. After all, the assassination of the Austrian grand duke at Sarajevo in 1914 hardly seemed an occasion for war in itself, yet it triggered a series of re-

United States Ambassador to the UN Arthur Goldberg addresses a working committee on the financing of peace-keeping operations. On his left is Lord Caradon of the United Kingdom. (United Nations)

actions that led to World War I. Moreover, in building up a body of successful experience with international force rather than self-help, the UN may eventually establish processes that will enable it to cope more effectively with larger crises. Certainly it does at least provide an additional opportunity for peaceful solutions of disputes.

Selected Bibliography

Almond, Gabriel A., *The American People and Foreign Policy* (New York: Harcourt, Brace & World, Inc., 1950). A useful general study of the role of public opinion in American foreign policy.

Bartlett, Ruhl, *Policy and Power* (New York: Hill & Wang, Inc., 1965). A brief but solid account of the history of American foreign policy.

Bemis, Samuel F., *A Diplomatic History of the United States,* 5th ed. (New York: Holt, Rinehart and Winston, Inc., 1965). The latest edition of the standard diplomatic history of the United States.

Claude, Inis L., Jr., *Swords into Ploughshares* (New York: Random House, Inc., 1956). A study of the problems of international organizations.

Gordenker, Leon, *The UN Secretary-General and the Maintenance of Peace* (New York: Columbia University Press, 1967). A careful analysis of the influence of the UN in general and the Secretary General in particular.

Kennan, George F., *American Diplomacy, 1900–1950* (Chicago: University of Chicago Press, 1951). Historical treatment of American foreign policy, by a former leading participant in its formulation.

Price, Don K., ed., *The Secretary of State* (Englewood Cliffs, N.J.: Prentice-Hall, Inc., 1960). An examination of the role of the U.S. Secretary of State in the light of increasing American participation and leadership in foreign affairs; written by men who had major roles in the administration of foreign affairs.

Rostow, W. W., *View from the Seventh Floor* (New York: Harper & Row, Publishers, 1964). A summary rationalization of American foreign policy during the Kennedy-Johnson administration by an economic historian serving as chairman of the Policy Planning Council of the Department of State.

Stuart, Graham H., *The Department of State* (New York: Crowell-Collier & Macmillan Inc. 1949). A thorough historical survey of the State Department from its establishment to 1949.

23

National security

THE STRATEGIC PROBLEM

No aspect of American society today is immune to government activities designed to mobilize the resources of the United States for survival. In the 1960s, between 50 and 60 percent of all federal administrative budget expenditures were concerned with national security. Such immense military effort is necessary because of the changing conditions of modern warfare. On the one hand, all-out thermonuclear war has been a continual threat. On the other, the United States has in recent years fought in several brush-fire wars, and may have to involve itself in others. Korea was in part this kind of war, in that it was fought with limited forces for limited objectives; but that war was at least precipitated by a clear-cut act of aggression. The conflict in Southeast Asia, especially in Laos, Vietnam, and Thailand, began in a far more ambiguous way. In South Vietnam, for example, national insurgents who were supplied and equipped

475

from North Vietnam but who were nevertheless mostly South Vietnamese, fought against the government in Saigon for many years before American intervention. There is thus evidence to support the opinion of some that Communist wars of "national liberation" are civil wars and evidence to support others who consider them part of a global conflict.

Four aspects of military strategy today raise immensely difficult problems. First, security requires a growing industrial base to enable the country to maintain a long-term state of readiness, an adequate industrial plant to produce the constantly changing weapons required for defense, and an expanding pool of scientific talent to meet the challenge of basic research and changing technology. Second, translation of scientific development into operational weapons is difficult and time consuming. The time spread from drawing-board design to full-scale manufacture of working weapons has become increasingly important. Third, national capacity to survive may depend on the speed with which active military forces can be alerted and supplemented by reserves. Military planners can no longer count on an extended period of mobilization prior to the outbreak of hostilities. War comes too quickly—and perhaps too finally—for that. The fourth aspect of contemporary military strategy is the necessity for a versatile military establishment. The force that can deliver a crushing blow or deter a massive attack on the United States is not necessarily the most effective kind in limited warfare.

Faced with these problems, military planners must establish priorities of development among ground, sea, and air—and soon possibly space—forces. They must decide how much of limited defense funds should be spent for scientific research, basic and practical, satellite systems, improved missiles and anti-missiles, atomic-powered ships or planes, radar networks, and fallout shelters. The problems of choice are difficult. First of all, the cost of mistakes are awesome. If insufficient funds and lack of imagination go into weapons development and basic research, the country may suddenly find that other nations have available a totally new weapons system that makes American weapons obsolete. If the weapons of limited wars in contrast to those of massive wars are ignored or underrated, the nation's ability to aid its allies may be shattered.

Moreover, many decisions involve weighing intangibles. Information about Communist intentions and Communist progress along technological lines may be inaccurate or incomplete. The probability of error at best may be quite substantial. Fear of making a wrong decision may paralyze or slow down the ability to make any decision. Finally, long lead times in the development of weapons multiply the risks and uncertainties in military planning. For instance, it took more than six years to move the B-52 bomber from the drawing board to a position of combat readiness. Similar lead times may be required to find and train personnel and provide equipment needed for an airborne division, even longer for missile forces. The process requires both stability and strong motivating drive to shorten the time span as much as possible. Money and other scarce resources like laboratory facilities and scientific personnel have to be committed years before concrete results can be achieved.

THE TECHNOLOGICAL RACE

From 1919 to 1940 the equipment of American ground forces scarcely changed. Today, however, the hallmark of weapons systems is their astonishing rate of obsolescence. Almost before a weapon goes into production, it may become obsolete. The B-17 in several models was in operational use for eight years, but the B-36 intercontinental bomber became obsolete in less than five years, and the B-52 jet bomber was outdated before all wings of the Strategic Air Command were fully equipped with it. Liquid-oxygen missiles were soon outmoded by solid-fuel Minutemen.

One of the consequences of rapidly changing military technology is that the offense has many advantages. The speed and range of modern bombers and the perfection of missiles and rockets have drastically reduced the protection that the defensive side used to derive from being far away from a potential aggressor. Military defense now has to be geared to the possibility of an attack anytime, anywhere. Since the United States used the atomic bomb in 1945, weapons technology has become infinitely more complex. Missiles and rockets can probably be produced for almost any desired range today. Earth satellites and lunar probes will give way to space platforms and humans exploring outer space. Foreseeable new weapons are likely to be more sudden in action, more massive in their capacity for destruction, more difficult to protect against, and far more costly than weapons today.

The new military technology is also phenomenally destructive. The largest conventional bomb of World War II, the blockbuster, had an explosive force of under ten tons of TNT. The first atomic bomb had a power equivalent to 20,000 tons of TNT. Today a single hydrogen bomb in the lower-megaton range (a megaton equals a million tons) is equal to the total destructive power of all bombs dropped on all belligerents during World War II. The blast and thermal effects of a one-megaton thermonuclear bomb can destroy or damage the relatively soft structure of a city over an area about fifteen times as great as the twenty-kiloton bomb. Radioactive fall-out from a single bomb would kill people not in some form of shelter over an area of several hundred to a thousand or more square miles.

All weapons are becoming increasingly costly. In the 1960s, a nuclear submarine cost over ten times as much as a World War II submarine. The operating costs for an atomic-powered submarine are over three times as high as those for a conventional submarine. Although some increases in costs result from inflation and more limited production than that during World War II, the basic factor underlying increasing costs is the growing complexity of weapons systems. It has been estimated that each new weapons system probably costs more than double the one it replaces.

Soviet achievements have brought to light weaknesses in American education. The demand for talented trained persons not only for national security programs but also for industry and civil service already far outruns the available supply, and will for years to come. As a result, the federal government has been appropriating increasingly larger sums of money—about $2 billion in 1967—for education at the university level. Most of this money is directed toward the physical sciences, but more and more government officials are realizing that the social sciences and the humanities also have to be encouraged if man is to use intelligently his new-found control over nature.

MAJOR OBJECTIVES OF MILITARY POLICY

The major military objectives of the United States as they have evolved since 1950 include the following:

—to deter direct nuclear attack on the United States occurring either by design, accident, or miscalculation;

—if deterrence fails, to limit damage to the United States and secure the best possible outcome of the war;

—to deter aggression against allies and possibly even neutral nations, and if deterrence fails, to help defend them.

The principal objective of American security policy has come to be the deterrence of direct attack against the United States through the threat of thermonuclear retaliation. This objective requires, among other things, a strategic force prepared to survive a surprise assault and able to retaliate effectively. The problem is immense mainly because, as we have said, an aggressor has enormous advantages. Even without total surprise, the first thermonuclear blow against military bases, political centers, and large cities could be decisive. Consequently, the strength of a deterrent force is not to be measured in numbers of bombers and missiles. It is necessary to consider vehicles that can be readied on short notice; the numbers that can be launched if they survive the initial attack; the proportion that could operate without a failure and get through enemy defenses to hit assigned targets are all factors in deterrence.

The problem is delicate. The deterring force must be sufficiently large to punish severely any nation that launches an attack, and foreign policy decisions must reflect determination so that the threat of its use will be credible. Yet the deterring force must not be so awesome, nor its power so suddenly escalating that an opponent will be panicked into making a surprise attack out of fear that tomorrow he will be overwhelmed. Nor must foreign policy decisions reflect such belligerence.

Deterring attack by threat of retaliation is the primary mission of missile and long-range bomber forces. Major units in the arsenal of deterrence include the intercontinental ballistic missiles of the Strategic Air Command, the Navy's Polaris submarines, and, at least for a few more years, B-52 bombers. In addition, the continental air defense system protects these retaliatory forces by giving early warning of attack and by being capable of shooting down some part of any attacking force.

Defense planners must allow for the possibility that deterrence may fail. The task would then become one of limiting damage from thermonuclear attack. Shooting down enemy bombers is the major, though largely outmoded, function of the

These Hercules surface-to-air missiles are part of the North American Air Defense Command. NORAD maintains an inner ring of defenses around more than thirty target areas, encompassing over one hundred cities and military bases. (PIX, Inc.)

air defense system. A second principal method of limiting damage is attacking enemy offensive forces on the ground—missile sites, bomber bases, and similar targets. Even though the enemy makes the first strike, American forces might be able to hamper further attack by damaging uncommitted enemy forces. Civilian defense—bomb shelters, radiation decontamination, and so forth—can be an important way to limit damage, but American efforts along this line have been timid and halting.

In his work under the Kennedy and Johnson administrations, Secretary of Defense Robert S. McNamara changed the basic American deterrence strategy from one of massive retaliation to "controlled response." That is, any enemy attack on the United States or one of its close allies would not necessarily be met immediately with all-out hydrogen bomb reprisal on population centers, but first by counterattacks against military concentrations. If these limited counterattacks failed to persuade the enemy to desist from his aggression, then the blows would become increasingly more powerful. Only as a last resort would America deliberately obliterate large cities.

Containment in the 1960s

As we saw in Chapter 22, containment has been the handmaiden of deterrence in American foreign policy. To counter the Soviet threat, NATO nations initially relied on nuclear retaliation by the United

States plus a large enough army to slow invasion. The emphasis in NATO strategy has shifted in recent years. No longer is there any real fear of a large-scale invasion in the World War II sense, although the West has maintained an army of sufficient size to discourage limited wars. Allied leaders view thermonuclear war or, more likely, thermonuclear blackmail, as the principal danger. One of the reasons for General Charles De Gaulle's opposition to American leadership of NATO and his construction of atomic weapons for France has been his fear that if faced with nuclear destruction, the United States would save itself at the cost of abandoning Europe or even allowing that continent to be destroyed.

Outside of Europe, containment poses more difficult problems, both political and military. Along the arc of countries running from Iran through Asia to Japan, Communists have proved to be adept at guerrilla warfare. The United States is far away, while the Soviet Union and, more important, China are close. Whatever the political situation, there are few targets that would make use of atomic weapons economical. Furthermore, the nations along this arc are militarily weak and politically divided, with little experience in self-government, much less in coping with the problems of power politics at the international level. Throughout much of the period since 1950, the United States has relied heavily on threats of nuclear retaliation to counter Chinese aggression. But the Chinese have begun to test their own atomic devices, and within a decade they will certainly have missiles and aircraft capable of delivering these bombs to any target in Asia, if not in the world. Thus the United States is destined soon to lose its advantage of being able to obliterate any Chinese target without triggering retaliation in kind. (The Russians, of course, have for some years been able to retaliate for the Chinese, but it has become far less than certain that they would in fact do so.) American air and naval power have been effective in checking the Chinese in the Formosan Straits and, combined with a heavy ground commitment, in Korea as well. How effective this latter combination will be in the Indochina peninsula remains to be seen. Through 1967 the propects were at best only mildly encouraging.

The Problem of Roles and Missions

Much of the uncertainty that has pervaded the area of national security policy reflects a lack of agreement regarding the best strategy for the United States to follow. In addition, the familiar boundaries between the military services have been outmoded by modern military technology, with the result that traditional missions and roles assigned to individual services have become competitive rather than complementary. Each service now duplicates certain functions of the others. The Army, Navy, and Marine Corps, for instance, all have air arms separate from the Air Force; and, while the Air Force is responsible for coordinating air defense in general, the Army is responsible for coordinating air defense of specific targets. Part of this problem was resolved by Congress in 1958 when it created the post of director of research and engineering in the Department of Defense and clarified the authority of the Secretary of Defense to direct and supervise the service departments and to decide which service shall be assigned particular weapons programs. It was not until McNamara became Secretary of Defense in 1961 that this authorization to proceed toward centralization was fully taken advantage of. His principal influences on the defense establishment were, first, his emphasis on flexibility, building up a military capacity to cope with any crisis, from counterinsurgency to all-out hydrogen bomb war, and, second, his insistence on moving toward unified methods of procuring equipment for the services.

ORGANIZATION FOR NATIONAL SECURITY

The National Security Act of 1947

The National Security Act of 1947, as amended and altered by later statutes and presidential reorganization plans, provides the basic organizational structure for managing the program of national security. The 1947 act declared that its purposes were:[1]

to provide for the establishment of integrated policies and procedures for the departments, agencies, and functions of the Government relating to the national security; to provide three military departments for the operation and administration of the Army, the Navy (including Naval Aviation and the Marine Corps) and the Air Force . . . ; to provide for their authoritative coordination and unified direction under civilian control but not to merge them; to provide for the effective strategic direction of the armed forces and for their operation under unified control and for their integration into an efficient team of land, naval, and air forces.

The Department of Defense

The National Security Act created a Department of Defense to supervise and coordinate all military activities. The military departments—Army, Navy, and Air Force—were included as statutory agencies. The Defense Department was designed to establish integrated policies and procedures for the three military departments, even though each one was separately organized under its own Secretary. Only the Secretary of Defense is a member of the President's Cabinet. In addition to the military departments and the military services within those departments, the Department of Defense has under it the Joint Chiefs of Staff, the unified and specified commands, and a group of Defense Staff Officers. The latter includes defense research and engineering, the comptroller's staff, civil defense operations, and logistics planning and management.

In addition to the central departmental organization and the military departments, the defense complex includes five agencies. The National Security Agency oversees highly specialized and top secret intelligence and security funtions; its headquarters are at Fort Meade, Maryland. The Defense Atomic Support Agency performs various technical operations. The Defense Communica-

---

[1] 61 *Stat.* 495.

The underground command post at the Strategic Air Command's headquarters near Omaha, Nebraska, contains special telephone consoles that provide split-second communications with a world-wide strike force of planes and missiles. (UPI)

tions Agency manages the intricate, world-wide network of Defense Communications Systems. The Defense Intelligence Agency carries out various centralized intelligence functions and coordinates those retained by the military departments. Finally, the Defense Supply Agency is responsible for providing common supplies and services to the military departments and defense agencies. Specialized supply centers, located in various cities, provide a centralized procurement service, including inventory control and distribution. The directors of these five agencies are responsible to the Secretary of Defense, either directly or through the Joint Chiefs of Staff.

The Secretary of Defense carries an enormously heavy managerial burden. He is the President's principal assistant on defense matters. He serves as a member of the National Security Council, the Civil and Defense Mobilization Board, the North Atlantic Council, and the National Aeronautics and Space Council. He rates next to the Secretary of State in Cabinet prestige. He has charge, under the commander in chief, of the military power of the United States. He supervises a world-wide organization of thousands of installations, more than a million civilian employees, and 3 million service men and women.

In the Defense Reorganization Act of 1958, Congress authorized a direct line of command from the Secretary of Defense to operational commands in the field, and clarified the general authority of the Secretary to supervise the service departments. Congress, however, preserved its surveillance of the services in three ways: It retained the right of individual service chiefs and secretaries to bring complaints to Congress "on their own initiative"; it provided for a legislative veto over decisions of the Secretary to transfer, merge, or abolish traditional service functions; and it specifically protected the National Guard, the Marine Corps, and naval aviation against alteration by executive order of the President.

The Joint Chiefs of Staff

The Joint Chiefs of Staff are the top military planners in the Defense Department. Their major task is the formulation of strategic war plans. Its members are the chief of naval operations, the chiefs of staff of the Army and of the Air Force, and, where matters involve the Marine Corps, the commandant of the Marine Corps. In addition, the President designates a fifth officer to serve as chairman. Since 1958, the chairman has had power to vote in sessions of the Joint Chiefs and authority to select the director of the Joint Staff to supervise an enlarged roster of military officers. The Joint Staff was enlarged in order to permit the Joint Chiefs to deal with operational problems as well as strategic planning. Congress, however, specifically prohibited a single chief of staff system and an over-all armed forces general staff. Interservice rivalries and clashes of personality have often hampered the effectiveness of the Joint Chiefs. Such clashes make more difficult the task of reconciling and compromising divergent strategic views of the various services. It is difficult for the members to avoid being advocates of a service point of view. Each is dedicated to his own service and its concepts of proper strategy and tactics, indeed is responsible for its status and morale. When money is scarce each battles vigorously to protect his own branch; and more than one member of the Joint Chiefs has resigned in anger and taken his fight with his colleagues or with the administration to the public. General Maxwell D. Taylor, for instance, bitterly opposed the military policies of the Eisenhower Administration, which, Taylor thought, were destroying the capacity of the United States to fight any conflict except a total thermonuclear war.[2] Taylor's advocacy of a "flexible response" found a receptive audience in the next two administrations, and he served for some time as a special adviser to President Kennedy, then as chairman of the Joint Chiefs, and later, under President Johnson, as ambassador to South Vietnam and again as a special adviser to the President.

The inability of the Joint Chiefs of Staff to eliminate interservice rivalries has also helped shape the role of the Secretary of Defense. In order to resolve disputes among the Joint Chiefs, the Secretary increasingly has acted as referee and arbitrator. Moreover, because they have not been able to rise above interservice rivalry, the Joint Chiefs have not been able to play fully their projected role in framing security policy, and responsibility for strategic planning has been assumed by the National Security Council or the Secretary of Defense. The primary function of the Joint Chiefs today seems to lie in providing basic facts and expert military advice upon which policies are based.

The National Security Council

The National Security Council, located within the executive office of the President, is really a five-man super Cabinet whose function is to advise the President on the integration of domestic, foreign,

---

[2] General Taylor summed up his opposition in his book *The Uncertain Trumpet* (New York: Harper & Row, Publishers, 1959).

and military policies relating to national security. Its establishment was perhaps the outstanding feature of the 1947 act, next to the grouping of the separate armed services under a single secretary. The statutory members of the council are the President, the Vice President, the Secretary of State, the Secretary of Defense, and the director of the Office of Emergency Planning. In addition, the Secretary of the Treasury, the Budget director, the chairman of the Joint Chiefs, and the director of the Central Intelligence Agency usually attend the Council's weekly meetings. The President may also invite others to sit in when he deems it appropriate. During the Cuban missile crisis in 1962, President Kennedy brought in ten or twenty additional people, including his brother, then Attorney General, several Soviet and Latin American specialists, two or three close White House aides, and occasionally a few others such as the American ambassador to the United Nations or Dean Acheson, who had been Secretary of State under President Truman.[3] The Council is assisted by a staff headed by a civilian executive secretary, appointed by the President, and consisting of specialists from the State Department, the Central Intelligence Agency, the Army, Navy, and Air Force, as well as other agencies. Personnel must be trained and widely experienced in the complexities of political-military strategy. One of the Council's chief problems is to develop civilian officials who are as well grounded in broad security affairs as are the best military officers. Charged with responsibility for assessing and appraising American objectives, commitments, and risks in the light of an actual and potential military power, the National Security Council may lay the foundation for decisions in the form of "policy papers." It may anticipate security problems and initiate studies of its own. It may define long-term objectives of foreign policy. When its work is done, however, the Council acts as adviser; the President alone makes the decisions.

The Central Intelligence Agency, an extremely important part of the national security organization, functions under the National Security Council, planning, developing, and coordinating all foreign intelligence activity. Its work centers on discovering how strong a possible enemy is and what he is up to. In recent years the CIA has employed about 20,000 American citizens plus thousands of foreign-born personnel. The most vital function the CIA performs is the production of "national estimates." These should be reasoned appraisals of such matters as a country's potential for war, its strategic capabilities, and its vulnerability to attack or pressure. The soundness of national estimates depends upon the data and judgment that go into them. Intelligence information is gathered from such open sources as technical journals and other published documents, but it is also gathered by secret agents and by the intelligence services of the Army, the Navy, the Air Force, the CIA, and by similar agencies of friendly governments.

In order to protect the CIA's cloak and dagger operations from publicity that would undermine its effectiveness, Congress exempted it from normal legisla-

---

[3] Theodore C. Sorensen, *Kennedy* (New York: Harper & Row, Publishers, Inc., 1965), Chap. 24; Arthur M. Schlesinger, Jr., *A Thousand Days: John F. Kennedy in the White House* (Boston: Houghton Mifflin Company, 1965), Chap. 30.

tive surveillance and from the General Accounting Office. But many politicians regard the CIA as an inviting target of investigation. Its files would reveal tales of mystery, intrigue, espionage, and critical decisions affecting national security. The CIA's bungling of the Cuban refugees' effort at the Bay of Pigs in 1961 to overthrow the Castro regime and its manipulation of student organizations, revealed in 1967, make it particularly vulnerable to criticism, but so far the CIA's friends on Capitol Hill have protected it against attempts to subject its operations to closer scrutiny.

Congress and the Pentagon

Growing centralization of power in the office of the Secretary of Defense since 1950 has resulted in clashes between the executive and legislative branches. In 1962, a Senate subcommittee investigating censorship of speeches of military officers refused to accept a plea of executive responsibility for withholding the names of censors. The subcommittee feared that such a policy would further erode the ability of Congress to get the facts on controversial matters and to exercise its constitutional right to raise and maintain armies. Secretary of Defense McNamara argued that executive responsibility for editorial censorship or any other administrative act meant that top executives were accountable for actions of their subordinates. But the subcommittee accepted only the argument of executive privilege—the right of a President and, on his order, his official family, to withhold from Congress information pertaining to the operations of the executive branch, a practice initiated by President Washington and followed by succeeding Presidents.

Congressmen often view such changes in Defense Department organization and procedures with alarm because they seem to reduce legislative supervision of the armed services. Veterans organizations normally give Congress strong support, and the military services have had long experience in developing alliances with congressional committees to dilute, delay, or prohibit concentration of authority, whether in a Secretary of Defense or in a single super Chief of Staff. In addition, some legislators consider centralization of Defense Department activities an issue involving the separation of powers. Since Congress has constitutional authority to raise and support armies and naval forces, it cannot carry out its duties and maintain civilian supremacy in military matters, some people assert, unless it preserves strong authority over the military. On the other hand, the President, as commander in chief, needs to have effective control over the military. If generals or admirals can execute an end run around the President and his Secretary of Defense and appeal to Congress or to public opinion, presidential control is substantially weakened. This clash—between the rights of the President and those of Congress—is built into the system of shared and separated powers. Short of a constitutional amendment, neither side can find a legal solution; it is inevitably a political problem involving negotiation and compromise and probably only temporary agreements.

NATIONAL DEFENSE AND THE ECONOMY

Economic Impact of the High Cost of Defense

Expenditures for national defense include the cost of maintaining the Defense Department, the atomic energy program, and defense-related activities such as stockpiling and the Selective Service System. The largest single items are military equipment and personnel salaries. Close behind are costs of building, maintaining, and operating bases and equipment for Army and Marine divisions, Air Force planes and missiles, and Navy ships and shore installations. Only about one eighth of the military budget goes into research and weapons development.

Expenditures for national defense have varied considerably in the postwar period. For four years following the end of World War II national security expenditures were about $11 to $14 billion. Beginning in 1951, however, expenditures jumped rapidly as the result of the Korean conflict and sharply revised security policies and programs. Again in 1957, the Russian achievement in placing a rocket in orbit around the earth stimulated a substantial increase in defense spending. The Vietnamese war brought a further increase, with the Department of Defense admitting in 1966 and 1967 to "special" war costs of over $15 billion; and the 1968 military budget ran to more than $77 billion.

In recent years direct military expenditures have consumed over half the federal budget, and if indirect expenditures were counted—for example, the cost of veterans' benefits and much of the work of the Atomic Energy Commission and various space agencies—the proportion would be more than two thirds. Even more significant, direct national security costs now consume about 15 percent of the total national income. The magnitude of defense spending has raised fears that the economy of the country may be undermined.

Economists sharply disagree in their analyses of the impact of defense spending. Two important factors are the government's ability to pay for defense without further borrowing and how much defense production and military recruitment drain other resources. If taxes are sufficient to pay for defense costs and enough other resources are available for civilian needs, the danger to the economy is minimized. The possibility of inflation, however, becomes great when the federal government has to borrow large sums and/or when there is already full employment of the labor force and relatively full utilization of other resources, such as steel and copper.

The economic significance of national security programs can also be measured in terms of the importance of government procurement contracts to American business. Many large industrial and manufacturing firms do a big share of their total business with the government. In recent years small businesses have received only one sixth to one fifth of all military procurement business. Small-business experts have criticized the concentration of defense contracts in large corporations, but generally only these giants can handle prime contracts requiring complex and specialized types of equipment. While no one questions the need for industrial activity for national security purposes, it may strengthen the trend toward concentration of productive facilities in a few huge corporations.

Changing Patterns of Defense Procurement

Since World War II, and particularly since the Korean war, significant changes have occurred in the nature of military hard goods purchased by the Department of Defense, not only in the types of weapons but also in the kinds of industry stimulated by government purchases and in the geographical areas affected. Changes in weapons are reflected in manufacturing processes. A large part of military purchases during the Korean conflict were mass production items: tanks, vehicles, small weapons. In the 1960s, these dwindled in importance. Much traditional hardware, such as rifles, continued to be produced and their designs continued to be improved; but the emphasis was shifting to procurement of fewer and far more costly weapons. Older metal-fabricating processes were giving way to more intricate and sophisticated techniques. Blue collar workers were being replaced by scientists, engineers, and technicians.

Geographically, the north central states and the middle Atlantic areas have apparently lost defense business, as have mid-western states such as Michigan.[4] The gainers have been the west coast and mountain states. New York, New Jersey, and Pennsylvania lost business in the more traditional lines, but they regained some of it in electronics and missiles. Gains made by California, which does about one fourth of all prime-contract hard-goods business (more than twice as much as New York, the second leading state), and Massachusetts, Texas, Colorado, and Florida are almost entirely in missiles and electronics. There has been a strong tendency toward concentration of such contracts in California and the coastal strip from Boston to Washington, D.C.

Funds devoted to basic research amount to only a piddling percentage of all defense research and development, test, and evaluation work; however, the long-range importance is great. Most contracts for basic research are awarded to universities and nonprofit organizations, particularly in Massachusetts, California, Maryland, New York, and Illinois. About half of these dollars have gone to Massachusetts and California because of the complex of research organizations clustered around the Massachusetts Institute of Technology and the institutions in the San Francisco Bay and Los Angeles areas, including the California Institute of Technology, UCLA, and the University of California at Berkeley.

---

[4] Department of Defense data on geographical shifting must be taken as suggestive rather than definitive because half of all prime contract funds for hard goods are subcontracted to other suppliers.

INDUSTRIAL MOBILIZATION

One of the most important aspects of national defense is the mobilization of economic resources to meet both military and civilian requirements. The primary objective of industrial mobilization is adequate production at stable prices. The first ingredient is a system of facilities able to produce the goods and services for military requirements and to keep the economy functioning in high gear. This system must provide physical facilities of production, such as manufacturing plants, tools and mechanical equipment, electric energy and fuels needed for industrial production, and facilities of transportation by rail, water, and highway.

The second ingredient of industrial mobilization is adequate materials to make the equipment required for defense purposes. The government may have to ration scarce resources and cut down or suspend production of less essential items. The government has also established stockpiles of more than seventy critical and strategic materials that can be used as reserves for war and defense production in case the normal supply of such materials is cut off.

The third ingredient is man power to meet civil and military requirements. It may become necessary to encourage work in plants producing essential goods for defense and to reduce employment in dispensable or less essential occupations and to allocate man power to essential civilian occupations as well as to the military services. The government may also have to organize vocational training schools.

Finally, in order to prevent runaway inflation, the government must develop ways and means of preventing upward spiraling of prices, wages, and rents and hoarding of commodities by consumers. Development of long-run stabilization measures may also include rationing of essential goods in short supply to consumers.

The Office of Emergency Planning

The military departments are responsible for mobilizing the fighting strength of the nation for national security. The Office of Emergency Planning in the executive office of the President has the task of planning mobilization of civilian resources. It must develop plans to organize industrial and economic facilities and resources in order to meet both the needs of the armed forces for man power, supplies, and equipment and the needs of the civilian economy. Its director, a member of the National Security Council, is the principal civilian adviser to the President on matters relating to economic mobilization.

CIVIL DEFENSE

A crucial element in a program of mobilization for national security is defense of the civilian community against armed attack. Responsibility for planning such a program is assigned to the Office of

Emergency Planning, while responsibility for operating civil defense programs is vested in the Department of Defense. Three complex factors are involved: development of a military defense capable of keeping civil defense within manageable bounds; preparation of plans to reduce the vulnerability of urban communities to atomic and other types of attack; and organization of a *civilian* civil defense in which important tasks of defense and protection are assigned beforehand to agencies or groups that have been trained to carry them out.

Little has been done to minimize the effects of an attack. Civil defense appropriations have been small. Although several public and private groups have studied civil defense problems, not much has been done to alert civilian populations to existing danger or to organize civil defense forces effectively.

Since the United States has in the past been almost invulnerable to military attack, Americans have found it hard to concentrate attention and resources on problems of civil defense. Part of the inattention can be traced to the difficulty of protecting against massively destructive weapons. The consequences of a twenty-megaton thermonuclear bomb will inevitably be catastrophic. On the other hand, it may be less difficult to protect the population against the effects of an atomic explosion or radioactive fall-out. Lack of understanding and information about the dimension of the damage that can be inflicted by a sudden attack have probably contributed to failure to come to grips with a problem of civil defense.

Selected Bibliography

Bock, C. P., and Morton Berkowitz, eds., *American National Security* (New York: The Free Press, 1965). A useful collection of essays on national security problems.

Gilpin, Robert, *American Scientists and Nuclear Weapons Policy* (Princeton, N.J.: Princeton University Press, 1962). A stimulating study of scientists as active participants in the formulation of national security policy.

Huntington, Samuel P., *The Soldier and the State* (Cambridge, Mass.: Harvard University Press, 1957). A detailed examination of the theory and politics of civil-military relations in the United States.

Janowitz, Morris, *The Professional Soldier: A Social and Political Portrait* (New York: The Free Press, 1960). A rewarding study of the power position of the military in the United States, with emphasis on the social origins of American military leaders and the changing character of military life.

Kahn, Herman, *On Thermonuclear War* (Princeton, N.J.: Princeton University Press, 1960). A controversial and provocative analysis of the likely consequences of the use of hydrogen weapons.

Ries, John C., *The Management of Defense* (Baltimore, Md.: The Johns Hopkins Press, 1964). An examination of the three major reorganizations of the United States armed services since 1947 and an analysis of centralized control in the Pentagon.

Schilling, Warner R., Paul Y. Hammond, and Glenn H. Snyder, *Strategy, Politics, and Defense Budgets* (New York: Columbia University Press, 1962). A study of American security policy and defense spending between 1948 and 1955.

For Further Research:

The student's attention should be called to certain general sources of information on political subjects. The *Encyclopaedia of the Social Sciences* (New York: The Macmillan Company, 1930–1935) is an excellent collection of signed articles by leading authorities on almost all topics within the field of political science. Almost ready for publication in 1968 is a revised edition of this massive work, *The International Encyclopedia of the Social Sciences*. There are a number of learned journals in the political science field to which the student may profitably turn in a search for articles on subjects of interest to him. The *American Political Science Review* (1527 New Hampshire Ave., N.W., Washington, D.C.) is published by the American Political Science Association, which is the national association of the political science profession. Several regional political science associations also publish journals: Academy of Political Science (sponsored by Columbia University)—*Political Science Quarterly* (Fayerweather Hall, Columbia University, New York City); The American Academy of Political and Social Science (sponsored by the University of Pennsylvania)—*The Annals* (University of Pennsylvania, Philadelphia); Southern Political Science Association—*Journal of Politics* (University of Florida, Gainesville); Southwestern Social Science Association—*Southwestern Social Science Quarterly* (University of Texas Press, Austin); Midwest Conference of Political Scientists—*Midwest Journal of Political Science* (Wayne State University Press, Detroit); Western Political Science Association and Pacific Northwest Political Science Association—*Western Political Quarterly* (Institute of Government, University of Utah, Salt Lake City).

Many government publications provide an excellent record of the work of Congress. The work of the congressional committees is recorded in documents known as *Hearings,* which contain the verbatim testimony given by witnesses at the public hearings of each committee, and as *Reports,* which give the complete formal reports of each committee to the House or the Senate.

The official record of the work of the two houses themselves is found in the *House* and *Senate Journals,* which the Constitution directs shall be kept. These publications provide only the bare record as to the putting of formal motions, the vote on bills, and similar matters. They are far less widely known or used than is the *Congressional Record,* which provides a nearly verbatim reporting of everything that is said or done on the floor of each house. The *Record* dates back only to 1873. The record of congressional debate for the years before 1873 is to be found in three privately printed publications: the *Annals of Congress,* for the period 1789–1824; the *Register of Debates,* for the period 1824–1837; and the *Congressional Globe,* covering the period 1833–1873. The present-day *Record* is published in two editions: a daily issue, which appears within twenty-four hours of a meeting of Congress, and a permanent edition, consisting of a dozen or more bound volumes appearing at the close of a year's session.

The statutes enacted by Congress are available in three forms. Immediately following its enactment, a statute is published in the *Slip Law* format, a pamphlet providing the text of the single law. The *Slip Law* citation of a statute is given in this form: Public Law 637–83d Congress; Chapter 886–2d Session. The *United States Statutes at Large* are bound volumes containing in chronological order the text of all laws passed by each Congress. The *Statutes at Large* citation of a law is given in this form: 60 *Stat.* 812 (the sixtieth volume of the *Statutes at Large* at page 812). Third, the laws of the United States are found in various codified collections. A "code" represents an attempt to do two things: (1) to weed out

491

statutes that have been repealed or superseded and to present only the law that is actually in effect at the time the code is published; and (2) to arrange the laws topically, rather than chronologically, so that all statutory provisions dealing with a single subject, such as immigration, agriculture, or internal revenue, may be found in one place. The federal government revises and republishes the *United States Code* at frequent but irregular intervals, but the government does put out annual supplements to keep the *Code* up to date. The latest full revision was in 1964. Two private publishers also put out a 100-odd volume set entitled the *United States Code Annotated*. These books, also kept current by annual supplements, contain summaries of legislative history and judicial interpretations as well as the actual statutes. The *Code* citation of a provision of law is given as follows: 18 U.S.C. 241 (the 18th title of the *United States Code*, section 51).

A private organization, the Congressional Quarterly Inc. (1735 K Street, N.W., Washington, D.C.), issues a weekly publication known as the *Congressional Quarterly Weekly Report*. The *Quarterly* is designed primarily for use by newspapers and contains a remarkably detailed and accurate summary of congressional activities. Roll-call votes on important issues are reproduced, substantive analyses of pending bills are provided, and the work of interest groups is examined. At the end of the year this material is presented systematically in a single volume called *The Congressional Quarterly Almanac*.

Biographical information about the current members of Congress is found in the *Congressional Directory* (Washington, D.C.: Government Printing Office), published in several editions each year. *The Biographical Directory of the American Congress* (Washington, D.C.: Government Printing Office, 1950) contains a brief biography of every person who served in the Congress (and its predecessor bodies) between 1774 and 1949.

Publication of court decisions has always been an important characteristic of the American and British judicial systems. The reporting system now in use in the federal courts is a remarkably complete one. All of the opinions of the Supreme Court—majority, concurring, and dissenting—are published each year in a series of volumes known as the *United States Reports*. Until shortly after the Civil War the volumes bore the name of the Court reporter and were privately published. Thus the citation of the *Dred Scott* case is 19 Howard 393 (the 19th volume edited by Howard, beginning at page 393). Since 1875, the volumes have been cited simply as *United States;* the Wagner Act cases are found in 301 U.S. 1 (the 301st volume of the *United States Reports* beginning at page 1). In addition to the *United States Reports*, which is an official publication of the federal government, two commercial editions of Supreme Court decisions are published by private concerns. One of these is known as the *Supreme Court* reporter (the citation of the Wagner Act cases is 57 Sup. Ct. 615), and the other as the *Lawyers' Edition* (the citation of the Wagner Act cases is 81 L. Ed. 893). These private series are annotated and carry additional aids that make them somewhat more useful to students than the official edition.

Most of the important rulings of the lower federal courts are published by the West Publishing Company of St Paul. There are five separate series. The rulings of the lower federal courts from "the earliest times" to 1880 are contained in thirty volumes known as the *Federal Cases*. The cases are numbered (1 to 18,313) and arranged alphabetically rather than chronologically, since lower-court decisions were not published contemporaneously until 1880. From 1880 to 1924 lower-court cases were reported year by year in chronological fashion in 300 volumes known as the *Federal Reporter*. In 1924, the *Federal Reporter* (2d series) was started. In 1932, this series was limited to the decisions of the courts of appeals, and beginning in that year the miscellaneous rulings of the district courts were reported in a series known as the *Federal Supplement*. Federal decisions relating to rules of procedure are now published in the *Federal Rules Decisions*. The work of lower federal courts is so vast that the West Company publishes only a fraction of the total number of decisions.

The Constitution of the United States of America

(LITERAL PRINT)

[PREAMBLE]

We the People of the United States, in Order to form a more perfect Union, establish Justice, insure domestic Tranquility, provide for the common defence, promote the general Welfare, and secure the Blessings of Liberty to ourselves and our Posterity, do ordain and establish this Constitution for the United States of America.

ARTICLE I

Section 1

[LEGISLATIVE POWERS]

All legislative Powers herein granted shall be vested in a Congress of the United States, which shall consist of a Senate and House of Representatives.

Section 2

[HOUSE OF REPRESENTATIVES, HOW CONSTITUTED, POWER OF IMPEACHMENT]

The House of Representatives shall be composed of Members chosen every second Year by the People of the several States, and the Electors in each State shall have the Qualifications requisite for Electors of the most numerous Branch of the State Legislature.

No Person shall be a Representative who shall not have attained to the Age of twenty-five Years, and been seven Years a Citizen of the United States, and who shall not, when elected, be an Inhabitant of that State in which he shall be chosen.

Representatives and *direct Taxes*[1] shall be apportioned among the several States which may be included within this Union, according to their respective Numbers, *which shall be determined by adding to the whole Number of free Persons, including those bound to Service for a Term of Years,* and excluding Indians not taxed, *three fifths of all other Persons.*[2] The actual Enumeration shall be made within three Years after the first Meeting of the Congress of the United States, and within every subsequent Term of ten Years, in such Manner as they shall by Law direct. The Number of Representatives shall not exceed one for every thirty Thousand, but each State shall have at Least one Representative; *and until such enumeration shall be made, the State of New Hampshire shall be entitled to chuse three, Massachusetts eight, Rhode-Island and Providence Plantations one, Connecticut five, New-York six, New Jersey four, Pennsylvania eight, Delaware one, Maryland six, Virginia ten, North Carolina five, South Carolina five, and Georgia three.*[3]

When vacancies happen in the Representation from any State, the Executive Authority thereof shall issue Writs of Election to fill such Vacancies.

The House of Representatives shall chuse their Speaker and other Officers; and shall have the sole Power of Impeachment.

Section 3

[THE SENATE, HOW CONSTITUTED, IMPEACHMENT TRIALS]

The Senate of the United States shall be composed of two Senators from each State, *chosen by the Legislature thereof,*[4] for six Years; and each Senator shall have one Vote.

Immediately after they shall be assembled in Consequence of the first Election, they shall be divided as equally as may be into three Classes. The Seats of the Senators of the first Class shall be vacated at the Expiration of the second Year, of the second Class at the Expiration of the fourth Year, and of the third Class at the Expiration of the sixth Year, so that one third may be chosen every second Year; *and if Vacancies happen by Resignation, or otherwise, during the Recess of the Legislature of any State, the Executive thereof may make temporary Appointments until the next Meeting of the Legislature, which shall then fill such Vacancies.*[5]

No person shall be a Senator who shall not have attained to the Age of thirty Years, and been nine Years a Citizen of the United States, and who shall not, when elected, be an Inhabitant of that State for which he shall be chosen.

The Vice President of the United States shall be President of the Senate, but shall have no Vote, unless they be equally divided.

The Senate shall chuse their other Officers, and also a President pro tempore, in the Absence of the Vice President, or when he shall exercise the Office of President of the United States.

The Senate shall have the sole Power to try all Impeachments. When sitting for that Purpose, they shall be on Oath or Affirmation. When the President of the United States is tried, the Chief Justice shall preside: And no Person shall be convicted without the Concurrence of two thirds of the Members present.

Judgment in Cases of Impeachment shall not extend further than to removal from Office, and disqualification to hold and enjoy any Office of honor, Trust or Profit under the United States: but the Party convicted shall nevertheless be liable and subject to Indictment, Trial, Judgment and Punishment, according to Law.

---

[1] Modified by Sixteenth Amendment.
[2] Modified by Fourteenth Amendment.
[3] Temporary provision.
[4] Modified by Seventeenth Amendment.
[5] *Ibid.*

Section 4

[ELECTION OF SENATORS AND REPRESENTATIVES]

The Times, Places and Manner of holding Elections for Senators and Representatives, shall be prescribed in each State by the Legislature thereof; but the Congress may at any time by Law make or alter such Regulations, except as to the Places of chusing Senators.

The Congress shall assemble at least once in every Year, and such Meeting shall be on the first Monday in December, unless they shall by Law appoint a different Day.[6]

Section 5

[QUORUM, JOURNALS, MEETINGS, ADJOURNMENTS]

Each House shall be the Judge of the Elections, Returns and Qualifications of its own Members, and a Majority of each shall constitute a Quorum to do Business; but a smaller Number may adjourn from day to day, and may be authorized to compel the Attendance of absent Members, in such Manner, and under such Penalties as each House may provide.

Each House may determine the Rules of its Proceedings, punish its Members for disorderly Behavior, and, with the Concurrence of two thirds, expel a Member.

Each House shall keep a Journal of its Proceedings, and from time to time publish the same, excepting such Parts as may in their Judgment require Secrecy; and the Yeas and Nays of the Members of either House on any question shall, at the Desire of one fifth of the present, be entered on the Journal.

Neither House, during the Session of Congress, shall, without the Consent of the other, adjourn for more than three days, nor to any other Place than that in which the two Houses shall be sitting.

Section 6

[COMPENSATION, PRIVILEGES, DISABILITIES]

The Senators and Representatives shall receive a Compensation for their Services, to be ascertained by Law, and paid out of the Treasury of the United States. They shall in all Cases, except Treason, Felony and Breach of the Peace, be privileged from Arrest during their Attendance at the Session of their respective Houses, and in going to and returning from the same; and for any Speech or Debate in either House, they shall not be questioned in any other Place.

No Senator or Representative shall, during the time for which he was elected, be appointed to any civil Office under the authority of the United States, which shall have been created, or the Emoluments whereof shall have been encreased during such time; and no Person holding any Office under the United States, shall be a Member of either House during his Continuance in Office.

Section 7

[PROCEDURE IN PASSING BILLS AND RESOLUTIONS]

All Bills for raising Revenue shall originate in the House of Representatives; but the Senate may propose or concur with Amendments as on other Bills.

Every Bill which shall have passed the House of Representatives and the Senate, shall, before it become a Law, be presented to the President of the United States; if he approve he shall sign it, but if not he shall return it, with his Objections to that House in which it shall have originated, who shall enter the Objections at large on their Journal, and proceed to reconsider it. If after such Reconsideration two thirds of that House shall agree to pass the

---

[6] Modified by Twentieth Amendment.

Bill, it shall be sent, together with the Objections, to the other House, by which it shall likewise be reconsidered, and if approved by two thirds of that House, it shall become a Law. But in all such Cases the Votes of both Houses shall be determined by Yeas and Nays, and the Names of the Persons voting for and against the Bill shall be entered on the Journal of each House respectively. If any Bill shall not be returned by the President within ten Days (Sundays excepted) after it shall have been presented to him, the Same shall be a Law, in like Manner as if he had signed it, unless the Congress by their Adjournment prevent its Return, in which Case it shall not be a Law.

Every Order, Resolution, or Vote to which the Concurrence of the Senate and House of Representatives may be necessary (except on a question of Adjournment) shall be presented to the President of the United States; and before the Same shall take Effect, shall be approved by him, or being disapproved by him, shall be repassed by two thirds of the Senate and House of Representatives, according to the Rules and Limitations prescribed in the Case of a Bill.

Section 8

[POWERS OF CONGRESS]

The Congress shall have Power

To lay and collect Taxes, Duties, Imposts and Excises, to pay the Debts and provide for the common Defence and general Welfare of the United States; but all Duties, Imposts and excises shall be uniform throughout the United States;

To borrow Money on the Credit of the United States;

To regulate Commerce with foreign Nations, and among the several States, and with the Indian Tribes;

To establish an uniform Rule of Naturalization, and uniform Laws on the subject of Bankruptcies throughout the United States;

To coin Money, regulate the Value thereof, and of foreign Coin, and fix the Standard of Weights and Measures;

To provide for the Punishment of counterfeiting the Securities and current Coin of the United States;

To establish Post Offices and post Roads;

To promote the Progress of Science and useful Arts, be securing for limited Times to Authors and Inventors the exclusive Right to their respective Writings and Discoveries;

To constitute Tribunals inferior to the supreme Court;

To define and Punish Piracies and Felonies committed on the high Seas, and Offences against the Law of Nations;

To declare War, grant Letters of Marque and Reprisal, and make Rules concerning Captures on Land and Water;

To raise and support Armies, but no Appropriation of Money to that Use shall be for a longer Term than two Years;

To provide and maintain a Navy;

To make Rules for the Government and Regulation of the land and naval forces;

To provide for calling for the Militia to execute the Laws of the Union, suppress Insurrections and repel Invasions;

To provide for organizing, arming, and disciplining, the Militia, and for governing such Part of them as may be employed in the Service of the United States, reserving to the States respectively, the Appointment of the Officers, and the Authority of training the Militia according to the discipline prescribed by Congress;

To exercise exclusive Legislation in all Cases whatsoever, over such District (not exceeding ten Miles square) as may, by Cession of particular States, and the Acceptance of Congress, become the Seat of the Government of the United States, and to exercise like Authority over all Places purchased by the Consent of the Legislature of the State in which the Same shall be, for the Erection of Forts, Magazines, Arsenals, dock-Yards, and other needful Buildings;—

And

To make all Laws which shall be necessary and proper for carrying into Execution the foregoing Powers, and all other Powers vested by this Constitution in the Government of the United States, or in any Department or Officer thereof.

Section 9

The Migration of Importation of such Persons as any of the States now existing shall think proper to admit, shall not be prohibited by the Congress prior to the Year one thousand eight hundred and eight, but a Tax or Duty may be imposed on such Importation, not exceeding ten dollars for each Person.[7]

The privilege of the Writ of Habeas Corpus shall not be suspended, unless when in Cases of Rebellion or Invasion the public Safety may require it.

No Bill of Attainder or ex post facto Law shall be passed.

No Capitation, or other direct, Tax shall be laid, unless in Proportion to the Census or Enumeration herein before directed to be taken.[8]

No Tax or Duty shall be laid on Articles exported from any State.

No Preference shall be given by any Regulation of Commerce or Revenue to the Ports of one State over those of another: nor shall Vessels bound to, or from, one State, be obliged to enter, clear, or pay Duties in another.

No Money shall be drawn from the Treasury, but in Consequence of Appropriations made by Law; and a regular Statement and Account of the Receipts and Expenditures of all public Money shall be published from time to time.

No Title of Nobility shall be granted by the United States: And no Person holding any Office of Profit or Trust under them, shall, without the Consent of the Congress, accept of any present, Emolument, Office, or Title, of any kind whatever, from any King, Prince, or foreign State.

Section 10

[RESTRICTIONS UPON POWERS OF STATES]

No State shall enter into any Treaty, Alliance, or Confederation; grant Letters of Marque and Reprisal; coin Money; emit Bills of Credit; make any Thing but gold and silver Coin a Tender in Payment of Debts; pass any Bill of Attainder, ex post facto Law, or Law impairing the Obligation of Contracts, or grant any Title of Nobility.

No State shall, without the Consent of the Congress, lay any Imposts or Duties on Imports or Exports, except what may be absolutely necessary for executing its inspection Laws: and the net Produce of all Duties and Imposts, laid by any State on Imports or Exports, shall be for the Use of the Treasury of the United States; and all such Laws shall be subject to the Revision and Control of the Congress.

No State shall, without the Consent of Congress, lay any Duty of Tonnage, keep Troops, or Ships of War in time of Peace, enter into any Agreement or Compact with another State, or with a foreign Power, or engage in War, unless actually invaded, or in such imminent Danger as will not admit of Delay.

ARTICLE II

Section I

[EXECUTIVE POWER, ELECTION, QUALIFICATIONS OF THE PRESIDENT]

The executive Power shall be vested in a President of the United States of America. *He*

---

[7] Temporary provision.
[8] Modified by Sixteenth Amendment.

shall hold his Office during the Term of four Years and, together with the Vice President, chosen for the same Term, be elected, as follows:[9]

Each State shall appoint, in such Manner as the Legislature thereof may direct, a Number of Electors, equal to the whole Number of Senators and Representatives to which the State may be entitled in the Congress: but no Senator or Representative, or Person holding an Office of Trust or Profit under the United States, shall be appointed an Elector.

The electors shall meet in their respective States, and vote by ballot for two Persons, of whom one at least shall not be an Inhabitant of the same State with themselves. And they shall make a List of all the Persons voted for, and of the Number of Votes for each; which List they shall sign and certify, and transmit sealed to the Seat of the Government of the United States, directed to the President of the Senate. The President of the Senate shall, in the Presence of the Senate and House of Representatives, open all the Certificates, and the Votes shall then be counted. The Person having the greatest Number of Votes shall be the President, if such Number be a Majority of the whole Number of Electors appointed; and if there be more than one who have such Majority and have an equal Number of Votes, then the House of Representatives shall immediately chuse by Ballot one of them for President; and if no person have a Majority, then from the five highest on the List the said House shall in like Manner chuse the President. But in chusing the President, the Votes shall be taken by States, the Representation from each State having one Vote; A quorum for this Purpose shall consist of a Member or Members from two-thirds of the States, and a Majority of all the States shall be necessary to a Choice. In every Case, after the Choice of the President, the person having the greatest Number of Votes of the Electors shall be the Vice President. But if there should remain two or more who have equal vote, the Senate shall chuse from them by Ballot the Vice President.[10]

The Congress may determine the Time of chusing the Electors, and the Day on which they shall give their Votes; which Day shall be the same throughout the United States.

No Person except a natural born Citizen, or a Citizen of the United States, at the time of the Adoption of this Constitution, shall be eligible to the Office of President; neither shall any Person be eligible to that Office who shall not have attained to the Age of thirty-five Years, and been fourteen Years a Resident within the United States.

In Case of the Removal of the President from Office, or of his Death, Resignation, or Inability to discharge the Powers and Duties of the said Office, the same shall devolve on the Vice President, and the Congress may by Law provide for the Case of Removal, Death, Resignation, or Inability, both of the President and Vice President, declaring what Officer shall then act as President, and such Officer shall act accordingly, until the Disability be removed, or a President shall be elected.

The President shall, at stated Times, receive for his Services, a Compensation, which shall neither be encreased nor diminished during the Period of which he shall have been elected, and he shall not receive within that Period any other Emolument from the United States, or any of them.

Before he enter on the Execution of his Office, he shall take the following oath or Affirmation:—"I do solemnly swear (or affirm) that I will faithfully execute the Office of President of the United States, and will to the best of my Ability, preserve, protect and defend the Constitution of the United States."

Section 2

[POWERS OF THE PRESIDENT]

The President shall be Commander in Chief of the Army and Navy of the United States, and of the Militia of the several States, when called into the actual Service of the United States; he may require the Opinion, in writing, of the principal Officer in each of the executive

---

[9] Number of terms limited to two by Twenty-second Amendment.
[10] Modified by Twelfth and Twentieth Amendments.

Departments, upon any Subject relating to the Duties of their respective Offices, and he shall have Power to grant Reprieves and Pardons for Offences against the United States, except in Cases of Impeachment.

He shall have Power, by and with the Advice and Consent of the Senate to make Treaties, provided two thirds of the Senators present concur; and he shall nominate, and by and with the Advice and Consent of the Senate, shall appoint Ambassadors, other public Ministers and Consuls, Judges of the supreme Court, and all other Officers of the United States, whose Appointments are not herein otherwise provided for, and which shall be established by Law: but the Congress may by Law vest the Appointment of such inferior Officers, as they think proper, in the President alone, in the Courts of Law, or in the Heads of Departments.

The President shall have Power to fill up all Vacancies that may happen during the Recess of the Senate, by granting Commissions which shall expire at the End of their next Session.

Section 3

[POWERS AND DUTIES OF THE PRESIDENT]

He shall from time to time give to the Congress Information of the State of the Union, and recommend to their Consideration such Measures as he shall judge necessary and expedient; he may, on extraordinary Occasions, convene both Houses, or either of them, and in Case of Disagreement between them, with Respect to the Time of Adjournment, he may adjourn them to such Time as he shall think proper; he shall receive Ambassadors and other public Ministers; he shall take Care that the Laws be faithfully executed, and shall Commission all the Officers of the United States.

Section 4

[IMPEACHMENT]

The President, Vice President and all civil Officers of the United States shall be removed from Office on Impeachment for, and Conviction of, Treason, Bribery, or other high Crimes and Misdemeanors.

ARTICLE III

Section 1

[JUDICIAL POWER, TENURE OF OFFICE]

The judicial Power of the United States, shall be vested in one supreme Court, and in such inferior Courts as the Congress may from time to time ordain and establish. The Judges, both of the supreme and inferior Courts, shall hold their Offices during good Behavior, and shall, at stated Times, receive for their Services, a Compensation, which shall not be diminished during their Continuance in Office.

Section 2

[JURISDICTION]

The judicial Power shall extend to all Cases, in Law and Equity, arising under this Constitution, the Laws of the United States, and Treaties made, or which shall be made, under their Authority;—to all Cases affecting Ambassadors, other public Ministers and Consuls;—to all Cases of admiralty and maritime Jurisdiction;—to Controversies to which the United States shall be a party;—to Controversies between two or more States;—*between a State and Citizens of another State;*—between Citizens of different States,—between Citizens of the same

State claiming Lands under Grants of different States, *and between a State,* or the Citizens thereof, *and foreign States, Citizens or Subjects.*[11]

In all Cases affecting Ambassadors, other public Ministers and Consuls, and those in which a State shall be Party, the supreme Court shall have original Jurisdiction. In all the other Cases before mentioned, the supreme Court shall have appellate Jurisdiction, both as to Law and Fact, with such Exceptions, and under such Regulations as Congress shall make.

The Trial of all Crimes, except in Cases of Impeachment, shall be by Jury; and such Trial shall be held in the State where the said Crimes shall have been committed; but when not committed within any State, the Trial shall be at such Place or Places as the Congress may by Law have directed.

Section 3

[TREASON, PROOF AND PUNISHMENT]

Treason against the United States, shall consist only in levying War against them, or in adhering to their Enemies, giving them Aid and Comfort. No Person shall be convicted of Treason unless on the Testimony of two Witnesses to the same overt Act, or on Confession in open Court.

The Congress shall have Power to declare the Punishment of Treason, but no Attainder of Treason shall work Corruption of Blood, or Forfeiture except during the Life of the Person attained.

ARTICLE IV

Section I

[FAITH AND CREDIT AMONG STATES]

Full Faith and Credit shall be given in each State to the public Acts, Records, and judicial Proceedings of every other State. And the Congress may by general Laws prescribe the Manner in which such Acts, Records and Proceedings shall be proved, and the Effect thereof.

Section 2

[PRIVILEGES AND IMMUNITIES, FUGITIVES]

The Citizens of each State shall be entitled to all Privileges and Immunities of Citizens in the several States.

A person charged in any State with Treason, Felony or other Crime, who shall flee from Justice, and be found in another State, shall on Demand of the executive Authority of the State from which he fled, be delivered up to be removed to the State having Jurisdiction of the Crime.

No person held to Service or Labour in one State, under the Laws thereof, escaping into another, shall, in Consequence of any Law or Regulation therein, be discharged from such Service or Labour, but shall be delivered up on Claim of the Party to whom such Service or Labour may be due.[12]

Section 3

[ADMISSION OF NEW STATES]

New States may be admitted by the Congress into this Union; but no new State shall be formed or erected within the Jurisdiction of any other State; nor any State be formed by the

---

[11] Modified by Eleventh Amendment.
[12] Repealed by the Thirteenth Amendment.

Junction of two or more States, or Parts of States, without the Consent of the Legislatures of the States concerned as well of the Congress.

The Congress shall have Power to dispose of and make all needful Rules and Regulations respecting the Territory or other Property belonging to the United States; and nothing in this Constitution shall be so construed as to Prejudice any Claims of the United States, or of any particular State.

Section 4

[GUARANTEE OF REPUBLICAN GOVERNMENT]

The United States shall guarantee to every State in this Union a Republican Form of Government, and shall protect each of them against Invasion; and on Application of the Legislature, or of the Executive (when the Legislature cannot be convened) against domestic Violence.

ARTICLE V

[AMENDMENT OF THE CONSTITUTION]

The Congress, whenever two thirds of both Houses shall deem it necessary, shall propose Amendments to this Constitution, or, on the Application of the Legislatures of two thirds of the several States, shall call a Convention for proposing Amendments, which, in either Case, shall be valid to all Intents and Purposes, as Part of this Constitution, when ratified by the Legislatures of three fourths of the several States, or by Conventions in three fourths thereof, as the one or the other Mode of Ratification may be proposed by the Congress; *Provided that no Amendment which may be made prior to the Year One thousand eight hundred and eight shall in any Manner affect the first and fourth Clauses in the Ninth Section of the first Article;*[13] and that no State, without its Consent, shall be deprived of its equal Suffrage in the Senate.

ARTICLE VI

[DEBTS, SUPREMACY, OATH]

All Debts contracted and Engagements entered into, before the Adoption of this Constitution, shall be as valid against the United States under this Constitution, as under the Confederation.

This Constitution, and the Laws of the United States which shall be made in Pursuance thereof; and all Treaties made, or which shall be made, under the Authority of the United States, shall be the supreme Law of the Land; and the Judges in every State shall be bound thereby, any Thing in the Constitution or Laws of any State to the Contrary notwithstanding.

The Senators and Representatives before mentioned, and the Members of the several State Legislatures, and all executive and judicial Officers, both of the United States and of the several States, shall be bound by Oath or Affirmation, to support this Constitution; but no religious Test shall ever be required as a Qualification to any Office or public Trust under the United States.

ARTICLE VII

[RATIFICATION & ESTABLISHMENT]

The Ratification of the Conventions of nine States, shall be sufficient for the Establishment of this Constitution between the States so ratifying the Same.[14]

---

[13] Temporary provision.

[14] The Constitution was submitted on September 17, 1787, by the Constitutional Conventions, was ratified by the conventions of several states at various dates up to May 29, 1790, and became effective on March 4, 1789.

done in Convention by the Unanimous Consent of the States present the Seventeenth Day of September in the Year of our Lord one thousand seven hundred and Eighty seven and of the Independence of the United States of America the Twelfth. *In Witness whereof* We have hereunto subscribed our Names,

G:⁰ WASHINGTON—
*Presidt, and Deputy
from Virginia*

New Hampshire	JOHN LANGDON NICHOLAS GILMAN
Massachusets	NATHANIEL GORHAM RUFUS KING
Connecticut	WM SAML JOHNSON ROGER SHERMAN
New York	ALEXANDER HAMILTON
New Jersey	WIL: LIVINGSTON DAVID BREARLEY WM PATERSON JONA: DAYTON
Pennsylvania	B FRANKLIN THOMAS MIFFLIN ROBT MORRIS GEO. CLYMER THOS. FITZSIMONS JARED INGERSOLL JAMES WILSON GOUV MORRIS
Delaware	GEO READ GUNNING BEDFOR JUN JOHN DICKINSON RICHARD BASSETT JACO: BROOM
Maryland	JAMES MCHENRY DAN OF ST THOS. JENIFER DANL CARROLL
Virginia	JOHN BLAIR — JAMES MADISON JR.
North Carolina	WM BLOUNT RICHD DOBBS SPAIGHT HU WILLIAMSON
South Carolina	J. RUTLEDGE CHARLES COTESWORTH PINCKNEY CHARLES PINCKNEY PIERCE BUTLER
Georgia	WILLIAM FEW ABR BALDWIN

Amendments
to the Constitution

The first ten amendments were proposed by Congress on September 25, 1789; ratified and adoption certified on December 15, 1791.

AMENDMENT I

[FREEDOM OF RELIGION, OF SPEECH, AND OF THE PRESS]

Congress shall make no law respecting an establishment of religion, or prohibiting the free exercise thereof; or abridging the freedom of speech, or of the press; or the right of the people peaceably to assemble, and to petition the Government for a redress of grievances.

AMENDMENT II

[RIGHT TO KEEP AND BEAR ARMS]

A well regulated Militia, being necessary to the security of a free State, the right of the people to keep and bear Arms, shall not be infringed.

AMENDMENT III

[QUARTERING OF SOLDIERS]

No Soldier shall, in time of peace be quartered in any house, without the consent of the Owner, nor in time of war, but in a manner to be prescribed by law.

AMENDMENT IV

[SECURITY FROM UNWARRANTABLE SEARCH AND SEIZURE]

The right of the people to be secure in their persons, houses, papers, and effects, against unreasonable searches and seizures, shall not be violated, and no Warrants shall issue, but upon probable cause, supported by Oath or affirmation, and particularly describing the place to be searched, and the persons or things to be seized.

AMENDMENT V

[RIGHTS OF ACCUSED PERSONS IN CRIMINAL PROCEEDINGS]

No person shall be held to answer for a capital, or otherwise infamous crime, unless on a presentment or indictment of a Grand Jury, except in cases arising in the land or naval forces, or in the Militia, when in actual service in time of War or in public danger; nor shall any person be subject for the same offence to be twice put in jeopardy of life or limb; nor shall be compelled in any Criminal Case to be a witness against himself, nor be deprived of life, liberty, or property, without due process of law; nor shall private property be taken for public use, without just compensation.

AMENDMENT VI

[RIGHT TO SPEEDY TRIAL, WITNESSES, ETC.]

In all criminal prosecutions, the accused shall enjoy the right to a speedy and public trial, by an impartial jury of the State and district wherein the crime shall have been committed, which district shall have been previously ascertained by law, and to be informed of the nature and cause of the accusation; to be confronted with the witnesses against him; to have compulsory process for obtaining Witnesses in his favor, and to have the Assistance of Counsel for his defence.

AMENDMENT VII

[TRIAL BY JURY IN CIVIL CASES]

In suits at common law, where the value in controversy shall exceed twenty dollars, the right of trial by jury shall be preserved, and no fact tried by a jury shall be otherwise re-examined in any Court of the United States, than according to the rules of the common law.

AMENDMENT VIII

[BAILS, FINES, PUNISHMENTS]

Excessive bail shall not be required, nor excessive fines imposed, nor cruel and unusual punishments inflicted.

AMENDMENT IX

[RESERVATION OF RIGHTS OF PEOPLE]

The enumeration in the Constitution, of certain rights, shall not be construed to deny or disparage others retained by the people.

AMENDMENT X

[POWERS RESERVED TO STATES OR PEOPLE]

The powers not delegated to the United States by the Constitution, nor prohibited by it to the States, are reserved to the States respectively, or to the people.

AMENDMENT XI

[Proposed by Congress on March 4, 1794; declared ratified on January 8, 1798.]

[RESTRICTION OF JUDICIAL POWER]

The Judicial power of the United States shall not be construed to extend to any suit in law or equity, commenced or prosecuted against one of the United States by Citizens of another State, or by Citizens or Subjects of any Foreign State.

AMENDMENT XII

[Proposed by Congress on December 9, 1803; declared ratified on September 25, 1804.]

[ELECTION OF PRESIDENT AND VICE-PRESIDENT]

The Electors shall meet in their respective states, and vote by ballot for President and Vice-President, one of whom, at least, shall not be an inhabitant of the same state with themselves; they shall name in their ballots the person voted for as President, and in distinct ballots the person voted for as Vice-President, and they shall make distinct lists of all persons voted for as President, and of all persons voted for as Vice-President, and of the number of votes for each, which lists they shall sign and certify, and transmit sealed to the seat of the government of the United States, directed to the President of the Senate;—The President of the Senate shall, in presence of the Senate and House of Representatives, open all the certificates and the votes shall then be counted;—The person having the greatest number of votes for President, shall be the President, if such number be a majority of the whole number of Electors appointed; and if no person have such majority, then from the persons having the highest numbers not exceeding three on the list of those voted for as President, the House of Representatives shall choose immediately, by ballot, the President. But in choosing the President, the votes shall be taken by states, the representation from each state having one vote; a quorum for this purpose shall consist of a member or members from two-thirds of the states, and a majority of all states shall be necessary to a choice. And if the House of Representatives shall not choose a President whenever the right of choice shall devolve upon them, before the fourth day of March next following, then the Vice-President, shall act as President, as in the case of the death or other constitutional disability of the President. The person having the greatest number of votes as Vice-President, shall be the Vice-President, if such a number be a majority of the whole numbers of Electors appointed, and if no person have a majority, then from the two highest numbers on the list, the Senate shall choose the Vice-President; a quorum for the purpose shall consist of two-thirds of the whole number of Senators, and a majority of the whole number shall be necessary to a choice. But no person constitutionally ineligible to the office of President shall be eligible to that of Vice-President of the United States.

AMENDMENT XIII

[*Proposed by Congress on January 31, 1865; declared ratified on December 18, 1865.*]

Section 1

[ABOLITION OF SLAVERY]

Neither slavery nor involuntary servitude, except as a punishment for crime whereof the party shall have been duly convicted, shall exist within the United States, or any place subject to their jurisdiction.

Section 2

[POWER TO ENFORCE THIS ARTICLE]

Congress shall have power to enforce this article by appropriate legislation.

AMENDMENT XIV

[*Proposed by Congress on June 13, 1866; declared ratified on July 28, 1868.*]

Section 1

[CITIZENSHIP RIGHTS NOT TO BE ABRIDGED BY STATES]

All persons born or naturalized in the United States, and subject to the jurisdiction thereof, are citizens of the United States and of the State wherein they reside. No State shall make or enforce any law which shall abridge the privileges or immunities of citizens of the United States; nor shall any State deprive any person of life, liberty, or property, without due process of law; nor deny to any person within its jurisdiction the equal protection of the laws.

Section 2

[APPORTIONMENT OF REPRESENTATIVES IN CONGRESS]

Representatives shall be apportioned among the several States according to their respective numbers, counting the whole number of persons in each State, excluding Indians not taxed. But when the right to vote at any election for the choice of electors for President and Vice-President of the United States, Representatives in Congress, the Executive and Judicial officers of a State, or the members of the Legislature thereof, is denied to any of the male inhabitants of such State, being twenty-one years of age, and citizens of the United States, or in any way abridged, except for participation in rebellion, or other crime, the basis of representation therein shall be reduced in the proportion which the number of such male citizens shall bear to the whole number of male citizens twenty-one years of age in such State.

Section 3

[PERSONS DISQUALIFIED FROM HOLDING OFFICE]

No person shall be a Senator or Representative in Congress, or elector of President and Vice-President, or hold any office, civil or military, under the United States, or under any State, who, having previously taken an oath, as a member of Congress, or as an officer of the United States, or as a member of any State legislature, or as an executive or judicial officer of any State, to support the Constitution of the United States, shall have engaged in insurrection or rebellion against the same, or given aid or comfort to the enemies thereof. But Congress may by a vote of two-thirds of each House, remove such disability.

Section 4

[WHAT PUBLIC DEBTS ARE VALID]

The validity of the public debt of the United States, authorized by law, including debts incurred for payment of pensions and bounties for services in suppressing insurrection or rebellion, shall not be questioned. But neither the United States nor any State shall assume or pay any debt or obligation incurred in aid of insurrection or rebellion against the United States, or any claim for the loss or emancipation of any slave; but all such debts, obligations and claims shall be held illegal and void.

Section 5

[POWER TO ENFORCE THIS ARTICLE]

The Congress shall have power to enforce, by appropriate legislation, the provisions of this article.

AMENDMENT XV

[*Proposed by Congress on February 26, 1869; declared ratified on March 30, 1870.*]

Section 1

[NEGRO SUFFRAGE]

The right of citizens of the United States to vote shall not be denied or abridged by the United States or by any State on account of race, color, or previous condition of servitude.

Section 2

[POWER TO ENFORCE THIS ARTICLE]

The Congress shall have power to enforce this article by appropriate legislation.

AMENDMENT XVI

[*Proposed by Congress on July 12, 1909; declared ratified on February 25, 1913.*]

[AUTHORIZING INCOME TAXES]

The Congress shall have power to lay and collect taxes on incomes, from whatever source derived, without apportionment among the several States, and without regard to any census or enumeration.

AMENDMENT XVII

[Proposed by Congress on May 13, 1912; declared ratified on May 31, 1913.]

[POPULAR ELECTION OF SENATORS]

The Senate of the United States shall be composed of two Senators from each State, elected by the people thereof, for six years; and each Senator shall have one vote. The electors in each State shall have the qualifications requisite for electors of the most numerous branch of the State Legislature.

When vacancies happen in the representation of any State in the Senate, the executive authority of such State shall issue writs of election to fill such vacancies: Provided, That the Legislature of any State may empower the executive thereof to make temporary appointment until the people fill the vacancies by election as the Legislature may direct.

This amendment shall not be so construed as to affect the election or term of any Senator chosen before it becomes valid as part of the Constitution.

AMENDMENT XVIII

[Proposed by Congress December 18, 1917; declared ratified on January 29, 1919.]

Section 1

[NATIONAL LIQUOR PROHIBITION]

After one year from the ratification of this article the manufacture, sale, or transportation of intoxicating liquors within, the importation thereof into, or the exportation thereof from the United States and all territory subject to the jurisdiction thereof for beverage purposes is hereby prohibited.

Section 2

[POWER TO ENFORCE THIS ARTICLE]

The Congress and the several states shall have concurrent power to enforce this article by appropriate legislation.

Section 3

[RATIFICATION WITHIN SEVEN YEARS]

This article shall be inoperative unless it shall have been ratified as an amendment to the Constitution by the legislatures of the several states, as provided in the Constitution, within seven years from the date of the submission hereof to the states by the Congress.

AMENDMENT XIX

[Proposed by Congress on June 4, 1919; declared ratified on August 26, 1920.]

[WOMAN SUFFRAGE]

The right of the citizens of the United States to vote shall not be denied or abridged by the United States or by any state on account of sex.

Congress shall have power, by appropriate legislation, to enforce the provision of this article.

AMENDMENT XX

[Proposed by Congress on March 2, 1932; declared ratified on February 6, 1933.]

Section 1

[TERMS OF OFFICE]

The terms of the President and Vice-President shall end at noon on the 20th day of January, and the terms of the Senators and Representatives at noon on the 3rd day of January, of the years in which such terms would have ended if this article had not been ratified; and the terms of their successors shall then begin.

Section 2

[TIME OF CONVENING CONGRESS]

The Congress shall assemble at least once in every year, and such meeting shall begin at noon on the 3rd day of January, unless they shall by law appoint a different day.

Section 3

[DEATH OF PRESIDENT-ELECT]

If, at the time fixed for the beginning of the term of the President, the President elect shall have died, the Vice-President elect shall become President. If a President shall not have been chosen before the time fixed for the beginning of his term, or if the President elect shall have failed to qualify, then the Vice-President elect shall act as President until a President shall have qualified; and the Congress may by law provide for the case wherein neither a President elect nor a Vice-President elect shall have qualified, declaring who shall then act as President, or the manner in which one who is to act shall be selected, and such person shall act accordingly until a President or Vice-President shall have qualified.

Section 4

[ELECTION OF THE PRESIDENT]

The Congress may by law provide for the case of the death of any of the persons from whom the House of Representatives may choose a President whenever the right of choice shall have devolved upon them, and for the case of the death of any of the persons from whom the Senate may choose a Vice-President whenever the right of choice shall have devolved upon them.

Section 5

Sections 1 and 2 shall take effect on the 15th day of October following the ratification of this article.

Section 6

This article shall be inoperative unless it shall have been ratified as an amendment to the Constitution by the legislatures of three-fourths of the several States within seven years from the date of its submission.

AMENDMENT XXI

[Proposed by Congress on February 20, 1933; declared ratified on December 5, 1933.]

Section 1

[NATIONAL LIQUOR PROHIBITION REPEALED]

The eighteenth article of amendment to the Constitution of the United States is hereby repealed.

Section 2

[TRANSPORTATION OF LIQUOR INTO "DRY" STATES]

The transportation or importation into any State, Territory, or Possession of the United States for delivery or use therein of intoxicating liquors, in violation of the laws thereof, is hereby prohibited.

Section 3

This article shall be inoperative unless it shall have been ratified as an amendment to the Constitution by conventions in the several States, as provided in the Constitution, within seven years from the date of the submission hereof to the States by the Congress.

AMENDMENT XXII

[*Proposed by Congress on March 21, 1947; declared ratified on February 26, 1951.*]

Section 1

[TENURE OF PRESIDENT LIMITED]

No person shall be elected to the office of the President more than twice, and no person who has held the office of President, or acted as President, for more than two years of a term to which some other person was elected President shall be elected to the Office of the President more than once. But this Article shall not apply to any person holding the office of President when this Article was proposed by the Congress, and shall not prevent any person who may be holding the office of President, or acting as President, during the term within which this Article becomes operative from holding the office of President or acting as President during the remainder of such term.

Section 2

This Article shall be inoperative unless it shall have been ratified as an amendment to the Constitution by the legislatures of three-fourths of the several states within seven years from the date of its submission to the States by the Congress.

AMENDMENT XXIII

[*Proposed by Congress on June 21, 1960; declared ratified on March 29, 1961.*]

Section 1

[ELECTORAL COLLEGE VOTES FOR THE DISTRICT OF COLUMBIA]

The District constituting the seat of Government of the United States shall appoint in such manner as the Congress may direct:

A number of electors of President and Vice President equal to the whole number of Senators and Representatives in Congress to which the District would be entitled if it were a State, but in no event more than the least populous State; they shall be in addition to those appointed by the States, but they shall be considered, for the purposes of the election of President and Vice President, to be electors appointed by a State; and they shall meet in the District and perform such duties as provided by the twelfth article of amendment.

Section 2

The Congress shall have power to enforce this article by appropriate legislation.

AMENDMENT XXIV

[Proposed by Congress on August 27, 1963; declared ratified on January 23, 1964.]

Section 1

[ANTI-POLL TAX]

The right of citizens of the United States to vote in any primary or other election for President or Vice President, for electors for President or Vice President, or for Senator or Representative in Congress, shall not be denied or abridged by the United States or any State by reasons of failure to pay any poll tax or other tax.

Section 2

The Congress shall have power to enforce this article by apropriate legislation.

AMENDMENT XXV

[Proposed by Congress on July 7, 1965; declared ratified on February 10, 1967.]

Section 1

[VICE PRESIDENT TO BECOME PRESIDENT]

In case of the removal of the President from office or his death or resignation, the Vice President shall become President.

Section 2

[CHOICE OF A NEW VICE PRESIDENT]

Whenever there is a vacancy in the office of the Vice President, the President shall nominate a Vice President who shall take the office upon confirmation by a majority vote of both houses of Congress.

Section 3

[PRESIDENT MAY DECLARE OWN DISABILITY]

Whenever the President transmits to the President pro tempore of the Senate and the Speaker of the House of Representatives his written declaration that he is unable to discharge the powers and duties of his office, and until he transmits to them a written declaration to the contrary, such powers and duties shall be discharged by the Vice President as Acting President.

Section 4

[ALTERNATIVE PROCEDURES TO DECLARE AND TO END PRESIDENTIAL DISABILITY]

Whenever the Vice President and a majority of either the principal officers of the executive departments, or of such other body as Congress may by law provide, transmit to the President pro tempore of the Senate and the Speaker of the House of Representatives their written declaration that the President is unable to discharge the powers and duties of his office, the Vice President shall immediately assume the powers and duties of the office as Acting President.

Thereafter, when the President transmits to the President pro tempore of the Senate and the Speaker of the House of Representatives his written declaration that no inability exists, he shall resume the powers and duties of his office unless the Vice President and a majority of either the principal officer of the executive department, or of such other body as Congress may by law provide, transmit within four days to the President pro tempore of the Senate and the Speaker of the House of Representatives their written declaration that the President is unable to discharge the powers and duties of his office. Thereupon Congress shall decide the issue, assembling within 48 hours for that purpose if not in session. If the Congress, within 21 days after receipt of the latter written declaration, or, if Congress is not in session, within 21 days after Congress is required to assemble, determines by two-thirds vote of both houses that the President is unable to discharge the powers and duties of his office, the Vice President shall continue to discharge the same as Acting President; otherwise, the President shall resume the powers and duties of his office.

Index